Incon ⌐ux

2021-22

Juliet Connolly • Megan Saksida
Karen Speight • Lucy Webb

www.carbonbalancedpaper.com
UPM FINE

WORLD LAND TRUST™

The carbon emissions of the paper used to produce this book have been offset via the World Land Trust's Carbon Balanced Paper scheme.

This product is made of material from well-managed, FSC®-certified forests and other controlled sources.

Income Tax

2021-22

Juliet Connolly • Megan Saksida
Karen Speight • Lucy Webb

Published by:

Claritax Books Ltd
6 Grosvenor Park Road
Chester, CH1 1QQ

www.claritaxbooks.com

ISBN: 978-1-912386-39-0

Main titles from Claritax Books

General tax annuals

- Capital Gains Tax
- Income Tax
- Inheritance Tax *
- Stamp Duty Land Tax

* First published October 2020, this will be part of the general tax annuals series from its second (2022-23) edition.

Specialist tax annuals

- Advising British Expats
- A-Z of Plant & Machinery
- Capital Allowances
- Financial Planning with Trusts
- Pension Tax Guide
- Property Investment

Other specialist titles

- Construction Industry Scheme
- Discovery Assessments
- Disguised Remuneration
- Employee Share Schemes
- Employment Status
- Enterprise Investment Scheme
- Furnished Holiday Lettings
- Living and Working Abroad
- Main Residence Relief
- Personal Representatives
- Research and Development
- Residence: The Definition in Practice
- Schedule 36 notices
- Tax Appeals
- Tax Losses
- Taxation of Partnerships
- Taxpayer Safeguards and the Rule of Law

See claritaxbooks.com for details of all our titles.

About the authors

Ray Chidell MA (Cantab), CTA (Fellow) has worked as a tax specialist for more than 30 years and is one of the UK's leading authorities on capital allowances. Ray originally qualified as a tax inspector but switched to the accounting profession in 1989, working for Baker Tilly and later Mazars, the latter role including six years as a tax partner.

Ray has written about capital allowances matters for more than two decades. He launched Claritax Books in 2011, and continues to have a fully hands-on role with the growing publishing business.

Juliet Connolly BA (Hons), ACA, CTA is also an expat herself, having lived in Melbourne, Australia for over ten years. Juliet has worked in the accounting profession for over 30 years. She trained with small firms and then for a number of years worked at a Big 4 firm, where in 1996 she started advising on expatriate taxation. Juliet left in 2002 to set up her own business, UK Expat, advising and assisting expatriates – from all walks of life and located all over the world – on their UK tax affairs.

Juliet can be contacted by email at jgc@ukexpat.net or by phone on +44 (0)20 3239 4140 (UK) or +61 (0)3 9017 0179 (Australia). Visit www.ukexpat.net.

Megan Saksida is a qualified Chartered Accountant, Chartered Tax Adviser, and Trust and Estate Practitioner.

Megan has her own business lecturing both for exam training and post-qualification CPD courses, and guest speaking at taxation conferences throughout the country. Alongside this, Megan is a regular contributor to the professional tax press and is a technical editor for CTA manuals.

Megan is also a tax examiner for two UK tax papers, and is on the CIOT technical committee for successions.

Karen Speight LL.B has worked for more than 25 years in professional services, including 11 years as a tax partner with Ernst & Young. Her area of expertise is employer services and, over the course of her career, she has collaborated with a large number of different organisations to address the challenges that stem from motivating, rewarding and dealing with diverse employee populations.

Karen currently has her own business providing education services for tax professionals. This includes lecturing on CTA and ATT exam training courses as well as creating and delivering post-qualification CPD courses. She is also responsible for preparing study manuals and support material for one of the UK's main providers of CTA Human Capital exam training.

Lucy Webb ACA, CTA is a freelance tax writer. Lucy specialises in writing about recent cases in income tax and capital gains tax, and is a regular contributor to AccountingWEB.

Lucy also contributes to other tax publications, writing both short-form articles on the latest trends in tax as well as in-depth guides and CPD courses.

Prior to writing, Lucy worked in the asset management tax team at Deloitte.

Abbreviations

A&M	Accumulation and maintenance
ADR	Alternative dispute resolution
AIA	Annual investment allowance
AQE	Available qualifying expenditure
ATED	Annual tax on enveloped dwellings
AUT	Authorised unit trust
AWE	Average weekly earnings
BADR	Business asset disposal relief
BIM	Business Income Manual
BPA	Blind person's allowance
CA	Capital Allowances Manual
CAA 2001	Capital Allowances Act 2001
CEST	Check Employment Status for Tax
CG	Capital Gains Manual
CGT	Capital gains tax
CH	Compliance Handbook
Ch.	Chapter
CIR	Commissioners of Inland Revenue
CIS	Construction Industry Scheme
CISR	Construction Industry Scheme Reform Manual
COLA	Cost of living allowance
COP	Code of practice
CPI	Consumer prices index
CPSE	Commercial property standard enquiry
CSOP	Company share option plan
CT	Corporation tax
CTA	Corporation Tax Act
CTC	Child tax credit
CTF	Child trust fund
CTM	Company Taxation Manual
DOTAS	Disclosure of tax avoidance schemes
DT	Double Taxation Relief Manual
DVLA	Driver and Vehicle Licensing Agency
DWP	Department for Work and Pensions
EEA	European Economic Area
EFRBS	Employer-financed retirement benefits scheme
EIM	Employment Income Manual
EIS	Enterprise investment scheme
EME	Estate management expenses
EMI	Enterprise management incentive
EPS	Employer payment summary
ERSM	Employment Related Securities Manual

ESA	Employment and Support Allowance
ESC	Extra-statutory concession
ESM	Employment Status Manual
ETASSUM	Employee Tax Advantaged Share Scheme User Manual
EU	European Union
EYU	Earlier year update
FA	Finance Act
FHL	Furnished holiday letting
FIFO	First in, first out
FOTRA	Free of tax to residents abroad
FPS	Full payment submission
FSR	Foreign service relief
FTC	Foreign tax credit
FTCR	Foreign tax credit relief
FTT	First-tier Tribunal
FY	Financial year
FYA	First-year allowance
GAAP	Generally accepted accounting practice
GAAR	General anti-abuse rule
HICBC	High income child benefit charge
HMRC	Her Majesty's Revenue and Customs
HP	Hire purchase
IAS	International Accounting Standards
ICTA 1988	Income and Corporation Taxes Act 1988
IEIM	International Exchange of Information Manual
IF	Integral feature
IHT	Inheritance tax
IHTM	Inheritance Tax Manual
IIDB	Industrial injuries disablement benefit
IiP	Interest in possession
IME	Internationally mobile employee
INTM	International Manual
IPTM	Insurance Policyholder Taxation Manual
IRC	Inland Revenue Commissioners
ISA	Individual savings account
ITA 2007	Income Tax Act 2007
ITEPA 2003	Income Tax (Earnings and Pensions) Act 2003
ITSA	Income tax self-assessment
ITTOIA 2005	Income Tax (Trading and Other Income) Act 2005
JSA	Jobseeker's Allowance
JSA 1995	Jobseekers Act 1995
LBTT	Land and Buildings Transaction Tax
LBTT(S)A	Land and Buildings Transaction Tax (Scotland) Act 2013
LIFO	Last in, first out
LLA	Long-life asset
LLM	Lloyd's Manual

LLP	Limited liability partnership
LLPA 2000	Limited Liability Partnerships Act 2000
LP	Limited partnership
LPA 1907	Limited Partnership Act 1907
LTT	Land transaction tax
MCA	Married couple's allowance
MPAA	Money purchase annual allowance
MSC	Managed service company
MTD	Making Tax Digital
NI	National Insurance
NIC	National Insurance contributions
NICA 2014	National Insurance Contributions Act 2014
NIM	National Insurance Manual
NMWA 1998	National Minimum Wage Act 1998
NMWM	National Minimum Wage Manual
NRLS	Non-resident landlord scheme
NS&I	National Savings and Investments
NT	No tax (PAYE code)
OECD	Organisation for Economic Co-operation and Development
OEIC	Open-ended investment company
ONS	Office for National Statistics
OpRA	Optional remuneration arrangements
ORI	Official rate of interest
OWR	Overseas workday relief
PA 1890	Partnership Act 1890
PAYE	Pay As You Earn
PE	Permanent establishment
PENP	Post-employment notice pay
PGA	Payroll giving agency
PILON	Payment in lieu of notice
PIM	Property Income Manual
PIP	Personal independence payment
PM	Partnership Manual
PMA	Plant and machinery allowances
PPB	Personal portfolio bond
PR	Personal representative
PSA	PAYE settlement agreement
Pt.	Part
PTM	Pensions Tax Manual
QROPS	Qualifying recognised overseas pension scheme
QW	Qualifying week
R&C	Revenue and Customs
R&D	Research and development
RAS	Relief at source
RAT	Rate applicable to trusts
RBC	Remittance basis charge

RDRM	Residence, Domicile and Remittance Basis Manual
Reg.	Regulation
REIT	Real estate investment trust
ROPS	Recognised overseas pension scheme
RPI	Retail prices index
RTI	Real time information
SACM	Self Assessment Claims Manual
SAIM	Savings and Investment Manual
SALF	Self Assessment: the Legal Framework
SAM	Self Assessment Manual
SAP	Statutory adoption pay
SAYE	Save As You Earn
SBA	Structures and buildings allowances
Sch.	Schedule
SDC	Supervision, direction or control
SDLT	Stamp duty land tax
SDLTM	Stamp Duty Land Tax Manual
SDS	Status determination statement
SEIS	Seed enterprise investment scheme
SEISS	(Covid-19) Self-Employment Income Support Scheme
ShPP	Shared parental pay
SI	Statutory instrument
SIP	Share incentive plan
SLA	Short-life asset
SMP	Statutory maternity pay
Sp C	Special Commissioners
SP	Statement of Practice
SPBP	Statutory parental bereavement pay
SPP	Statutory paternity pay
SRIT	Scottish rate of income tax
SRT	Statutory residence test
SSCBA 1992	Social Security Contributions and Benefits Act 1992
SSP	Statutory sick pay
SS(S)A 2018	Social Security (Scotland) Act 2018
STBV	Short-term business visitor
STEP	Society of Trust and Estate Practitioners
STTG	Scottish Taxpayer Technical Guidance
SWT	Special withholding tax
TA	Trustee Act
TAS	Taxed award scheme
TC	Tax Chamber
TCGA 1992	Taxation of Chargeable Gains Act 1992
TIOPA 2010	Taxation (International and Other Provisions) Act 2010
TMA 1970	Taxes Management Act 1970
TME	Trust management expenses
TRS	Trust Registration Service

TSEM	Trusts, Settlements and Estates Manual
TUPE	Transfer of Undertakings (Protection of Employment)
UKFTT	United Kingdom First-tier Tribunal
UKHL	United Kingdom House of Lords
UKSC	United Kingdom Supreme Court
UKUT	United Kingdom Upper Tribunal
UN	United Nations
UT	Upper Tribunal
UTR	Unique taxpayer reference
VAT	Value added tax
VATA 1994	Value Added Tax Act 1994
VCT	Venture capital trust
WDA	Writing-down allowance
WLR	Weekly Law Report
WRA 2012	Welfare Reform Act 2012
WRIT	Welsh rate of income tax
WTC	Working tax credit
WTTG	Welsh Taxpayer Technical Guidance

Publisher's preface

Income tax is a fact of life for most adults, most businesses and nearly all accountants and tax advisers.

Despite acknowledgements from many quarters of the need for simplicity, tax law moves inexorably in the opposite direction. A higher priority is in practice given to promoting – or discouraging – certain behaviours, and to the goal of fairness (however that may be defined or perceived), as well as the need to raise as much money as possible within the bounds of what is politically expedient.

As complexity increases, so too does the need for clear guidance for the professional adviser, who must have at least a working familiarity with an array of different statutory and other provisions. Income tax, though a huge topic in itself, is usually just one of numerous areas of law that the practitioner must grasp.

This volume, first published in May 2021 (as Claritax Books marks its tenth anniversary) is part of a new series of general tax annuals designed to help professionals find reliable answers fast. The books are written for three main categories of reader: accountants and others who work as general practitioners and who need an appropriate level of commentary across a wide range of issues; more specialised tax advisers requiring clear and accurate guidance on other tax topics that inevitably interact with their specialist fields; and in-house professionals seeking a practical day-to-day reference work for issues arising.

In addition to the obvious requirement for technical accuracy, this book aims to be the clearest single-volume guide to income tax. The concept of clarity is at the heart of our publishing business, and applies most obviously to the writing style, but also to the layout on the page and to the detailed indexing.

Producing a high quality tome of this nature is a big task for a smaller publisher (as we still are), especially in an area such as income tax where the goalposts are being moved almost daily. Any feedback from our readers will be welcome, including in particular any views on how we can build on this first edition in future years.

I am sincerely grateful to all those who have made this volume possible.

Writing commentary that is clear, practical and helpful requires precision and dedication, so my thanks go first and foremost to the four main authors (as it happens, an all-female team), who have busy professional lives but who have somehow managed to find the time to make their valuable contributions in their respective specialist areas.

Particular thanks go also to Jane Moore who, with eagle eyes and a wealth of experience as a tax editor, has conducted a final review and made innumerable helpful suggestions.

Jacqui Allen has supported me consistently and loyally since the inception of Claritax Books back in 2011, working patiently and systematically to ensure that the text of our books is laid out clearly and attractively. As always, Jacqui has tackled the challenges of this book methodically and with calm good humour.

Finally, Claritax Books still operates very much as a family business, even though our content is now used by nearly all the largest UK accountants and by thousands of others. My wife and fellow director Maryla convinced me to launch this series of general tax annuals, and has been supportive and encouraging throughout the process, as indeed she has been since we posted out our first book order in 2011. Two of our sons, Mike and Philip, have also been involved with the business from the outset; Mike designs all of our book covers and marketing materials, and Philip is my right-hand man on a day-to-day basis, dealing with orders, customer queries, phone calls, etc. Our oldest son, Adam, lends moral support from a safe distance!

Ray Chidell MA (Cantab), CTA (Fellow)
Director, Claritax Books
May 2021

Table of contents

INTRODUCTION AND COMPLIANCE

1.   Introduction

1.1   Brief overview

Income tax is one of the largest sources of revenue for the UK government, generating £193.6 billion for 2019-20, 23.4% of all receipts. The reason for this is that personal income, upon which income tax is charged, is the nation's main source of income. It includes income from employment and self-employment, unincorporated business profits, investment and savings income, rental and pension income and some social security benefits such as the state pension and jobseeker's allowance. Around 83% of income tax is collected via the Pay As You Earn (PAYE) system, with the remaining 17% via self-assessment.

According to the latest OECD figures for 2018, the average percentage of GDP that countries raise by taxes on personal income is 8.30%. The UK was slightly above this at 9.12%, the highest being Denmark at 24.42%, and the lowest being Chile at 1.41%. In comparison, the percentage of GDP for the UK in respect of corporation tax was 2.88% and for property taxes was 4.14%, so income tax is well above these taxes, though below VAT which was 10.72%. These figures highlight the importance income tax plays in generating income for the government.

Some more statistics (although the following do not take into account the possible effects of the Covid-19 pandemic) illustrate the progressive nature of the UK's income tax system. Of the estimated 32.3 million income tax payers in 2020-21, approximately 85% are basic rate taxpayers, with 58% being male. The top 50% of taxpayers receive approximately 75% of the total income, but pay around 90% of the total income tax (the top 1% receive between 12% and 13% of the total income and pay around 30% of the total income tax). London and the South East account for the highest number of taxpayers, Northern Ireland and the North East the lowest.

Guidance: https://tinyurl.com/rbwx2znc (Office for Budget Responsibility); https://tinyurl.com/yrvcd4wb (HMRC income tax liabilities statistics); https://tinyurl.com/e74ujz8x (OECD Revenue Statistics)

1.2   History

William Pitt the Younger famously introduced income tax as a temporary tax in his 1798 Budget to pay for the Napoleonic Wars and it came into effect from 1799. At the time it was the modest sum of two old pence in the pound for incomes over £60, increasing to a maximum of two shillings on incomes over £200. It initially taxed a person's income, regardless of who was actually beneficially entitled to it, unlike today where an individual has to be beneficially entitled to the income to be taxed on it.

Since Pitt's introduction of the tax, it has been abolished on a number of occasions only to be reintroduced, and by the 20th century it became entrenched in the British way of life, even though it has always remained a temporary tax that expires each year on 5 April. The annual Finance Act renews it every year, although legislation enables the government to continue collecting taxes until the Finance Bill becomes law. The concept of income tax is little questioned now, if at all – save by certain fringe political parties. However, the rates of tax – and what is taxed under the regime – often cause high-profile controversies.

The collection of tax under the PAYE system was introduced in 1944 and self-assessment from 1996. Independent taxation of husbands and wives was introduced in 1990, when they started being taxed as separate individuals. Prior to this, a married woman's income was included in her husband's income, and was taxed as such.

Companies were subject to income tax until 1965, when corporation tax was introduced. The highest rate income tax has reached was a whopping 99.25% during the Second World War, falling to 90% during the 1950s and 1960s.

From the 1970s, the rates of income tax have generally fallen, in particular under Margaret Thatcher's government when all rates of income tax were reduced significantly. Rates were then reduced further under subsequent governments (including Labour governments) to the levels we see today. Only once in recent times has there been an increase in rates, with the introduction of the additional rate of 50% in 2010 following the global financial crisis, though this has subsequently fallen to the current level of 45%.

All tax cuts and increases are very much a swings and roundabouts situation – giving with one hand, but taking with the other – so even though income tax has fallen in the last few decades, other less obvious increases have occurred in taxes like VAT and National Insurance contributions (NIC) to compensate, along with new taxes – the so-called "stealth taxes". Income tax is very much a high-profile tax and it could be argued that it has become a political football, with other taxes being raised rather than income tax for fear of upsetting the voting public. It remains to be seen whether the Covid-19 pandemic will change this.

In 2016, the devolution of tax powers within the UK started, with the Scottish Parliament given control over the income tax rates and bands in Scotland, as was Wales in 2019. The latter's rates are still in line with England and Northern Ireland, but Scottish rates and bands do now differ significantly with the introduction of starter and intermediate tax bands and five tax rates varying between 19% and 46% for 2021-22. This complicates the UK income tax system even further, as one of the first steps now is to establish whether an individual is a Scottish or Welsh taxpayer (see **Chapter 4**).

Indeed, the income tax system, despite the government's aim of simplification, has become more and more complex over the years and hefty penalties can arise for errors (see **Chapter 2**).

1.3 Structure

Income tax is covered by various tax laws, but the main primary legislation is found in the:

- Income Tax (Earnings and Pensions) Act 2003;
- Income Tax (Trading and Other Income) Act 2005;
- Income Tax Act 2007; and
- Finance Acts (usually annual).

The basic rule is to assume that all personal income is liable to income tax, unless there is a specific exemption in the legislation (such as income from National Savings Certificates and ISAs) or under an agreement such as a double tax treaty. In addition, some income may be in the nature of capital gains, but is actually taxed under income tax and not CGT rules, for example gains from some investments (see **25.3.2**).

A multitude of factors may affect what income, and how much of it, is subject to UK income tax, along with how much tax is actually due. A person's tax residence status (see **Chapter 34**) is fundamental, and if there is a foreign element, such as dual residence, then this further complicates the matter with double tax treaties becoming involved (**Chapter 35**).

Various tax reliefs and deductions may be available in establishing the taxable amount (for example, relief for pension contributions made – see **Chapter 30**), along with allowances, the main one being the personal allowance (see **Chapter 3**).

Once this taxable amount has been established, then there are various tax bands with specific tax rates (which, as mentioned above, vary depending on where in the UK the taxpayer is resident) to calculate the tax due.

The above is a simplified overview and there are many and varied issues that need to be considered and that complicate the above process. Many of these are covered in the following chapters.

1.4 Collection of tax

The collection of income tax is largely covered by the *Income Tax (Pay As You Earn) Regulations* 2003 (see **Chapter 14**) and the *Taxes Management Act* 1970.

For many taxpayers in employment, whose only source of income is their salary, all their tax is collected at source via the PAYE system. Individuals whose situation is more complicated – for example, an individual with sources of income other than salary or an employee who exercised share options or who was terminated from his or her employment – may well be required to file a tax return under the self-assessment system.

Retirees also receive their pension net of tax via the PAYE system, other than the state pension.

Individuals receiving income other than earnings or pensions are also likely to be required to file a tax return and to pay any tax due under the self-assessment system.

As an alternative to self-assessment, HMRC have introduced simple assessment, a more straightforward way for certain individuals whose tax situation is less complex to declare and pay tax.

1.5 The future of income tax?

It is difficult, if not impossible, to predict how income tax might be affected in the medium term following the Covid-19 pandemic and the UK's withdrawal from the EU. HMRC have indicated that they will continue to drive forward the digitalisation of the tax system, particularly in respect of administration and the collection of tax, and the Covid-19 pandemic has only emphasised the need for this. There is likely to be more real-time reporting, and more usage of data from third-party sources, and there will be the introduction of Making Tax Digital beyond VAT to income tax in 2023. This in turn means that taxpayers and their agents will also need to digitise.

With regard to the pandemic, some are suggesting that any tax rises may be delayed as the government tries to stimulate the economy by encouraging spending. Generally, the public probably realise that the cost of the pandemic has to be met somehow, so are perhaps expecting a possible rise in taxes, which may well occur at some future point. Only time will tell if and when this is to happen, and how.

1.6   Scope of this book

The following chapters explain the main areas of income tax as it relates to 2021-22. The text highlights issues that need special attention, along with potential planning points, and is illustrated with plenty of examples. Some reference is also made to NIC, though this is largely outside the scope of this book.

2. Tax administration and compliance

2.1 Self-assessment

2.1.1 Introduction

Most taxpayers in the UK pay their tax via the PAYE system (see **Chapter 14**). For individuals who just have earnings, perhaps with minor amounts of investment income, there is usually no reason to file a tax return under self-assessment. Instead, HMRC may issue a P800 tax calculation after the tax year, or use simple assessment (see **2.5**), to adjust for any PAYE overpayments or shortfalls.

An individual who is self-employed, or who is receiving income that is not taxed, may be required to file a self-assessment return. HMRC state that a tax return must be filed if, in a tax year, an individual was:

- self-employed as a sole trader and earned more than £1,000 gross before the deduction of expenses and tax reliefs; or
- a partner in a business partnership.

A tax return must also be filed for a tax year if an individual:

- is a company director, unless all of the individual's income is taxed at source (e.g. under PAYE) and there is no tax liability;
- has annual income over £100,000;
- has income over £50,000 if the individual or his or her partner receives child benefit payments;
- has any other untaxed income such as:
  - income from land and property in the UK;
  - income from savings and investments, including dividends;
  - taxable foreign income;
  - taxable income from a trust or settlement;
  - commission or cash-in-hand payments; or
  - certain pension payments/charges; or
- has sold shares, property or other assets liable to CGT.

HMRC have a specific tool to enable an individual to check if he or she is required to file a tax return for a particular tax year – see below.

Any individual may choose to file a tax return if he or she wishes to do so. This may be the case, for example, if the individual wishes to claim tax relief for pension contributions or for donations made under gift aid, or to claim the seafarers' deduction (see **38.6.4**).

Income tax self-assessment (ITSA) is also relevant for partnerships (see **Chapter 16**) and for trusts (see **Chapter 41**).

Under self-assessment, the individual is responsible for creating his or her correct tax charge each tax year.

Law: TMA 1970

Guidance: https://www.gov.uk/check-if-you-need-tax-return; HMRC manuals: *Self assessment: The legal framework* (SALF); *Self assessment manual* (SAM); *Self assessment claims manual* (SACM)

2.1.2   Registration

Once it is established that an individual has to file a tax return, the first step is to register for self-assessment by completing form SA1. There are separate registration processes for self-employed individuals (see **Chapter 15**) and for partners (see **Chapter 16**).

If an individual has not received a notice to file a tax return, and starts receiving untaxed income or has a capital gain during a tax year, he or she should inform HMRC of this by 5 October following the end of the relevant tax year.

Once registered, there is no need for the individual to re-register every year, unless there has been a tax year for which the individual was not required to file a tax return.

After registering, the individual will receive a UTR (unique taxpayer reference – a 10-digit reference), which is needed to file a tax return.

A notice to file a return will usually be sent to the individual immediately after the end of the tax year. If no such notice is issued, the individual is free to file a voluntary return, in which case notice will be deemed to have been issued when HMRC receive the return. This means that such a return can never be late, so no late filing penalties arise in respect of a voluntary return.

Guidance: https://tinyurl.com/s4xyyvck (HMRC documents re registering for self-assessment); https://www.gov.uk/register-for-self-assessment

2.1.3   Filing

Once an individual has been issued with a notice to file a return for a tax year, there is a legal duty to do so by 31 January (or 31 October if submitting a paper tax return) following the relevant tax year.

However, if the notice is issued after 31 July following the tax year, the filing deadline may differ depending on when the notice is issued and whether the return is being filed online or in hard copy. The deadline will then be the later of:

- the usual 31 January/31 October deadline; or
- three months after the notice is issued (see **Appendix 1**).

An individual who believes that a tax return is not required for a tax year, but who has been issued with a notice to file a return, can ask HMRC to cancel this notice, which HMRC will do if they agree that no tax return is required (TMA 1970, s. 8B). This can be done after the filing deadline and, if cancelled, any late filing penalties charged will also be cancelled.

Components of the return

A self-assessment tax return is made up of a core tax return (SA100), to which various supplementary pages are added. These cover, for example:

- income from employment (SA102);
- income from self-employment (SA 103);
- income from UK property (SA105);
- additional information (SA101);
- foreign income (SA106);
- residence, remittance basis, etc. pages (SA109); and
- the tax calculation summary pages (SA110).

It is the individual's responsibility to complete and file the relevant pages depending on his or her circumstances.

Any claims or elections that an individual needs to make, can be done via the tax return.

HMRC guidance and online filing

There is HMRC guidance (SA150) on how to complete the core return, with separate guidance for each set of supplementary pages, and various helpsheets – see guidance note below.

Most taxpayers now file online. HMRC's website provides a basic tax return filing service, though certain individuals (e.g. non-residents) are unable to use this service as it does not include all the supplementary pages. In this situation, the individual will either need to engage an accountant/tax adviser to file the return or purchase commercial tax return software that has all the relevant supplementary pages.

Guidance: https://www.gov.uk/government/collections/self-assessment-helpsheets-main-self-assessment-tax-return

Short returns

A short tax return (SA200) can be filed by an individual who:

- was a paid employee or had taxable benefits or expense payments;
- was self-employed with an annual turnover of less than £85,000;
- was repaying a student loan and/or a postgraduate loan;
- received a UK pension (state, occupational or private) or a retirement annuity;
- received income from a purchased life annuity;
- received taxable state benefits such as jobseeker's allowance (see **Chapter 33**);
- had property income of less than £85,000 from rents or letting a room in the individual's home;
- received income from UK savings, such as interest from a bank or building society;
- received company dividends (including foreign dividends of up to £300); or
- wants to claim relief for gift aid payments.

In all other situations a full tax return has to be filed. Non-residents and individuals with a foreign domicile cannot file a short return.

Calculation of tax liability

Under self-assessment, the individual is responsible for calculating his or her tax liability for a tax year, as part of the return. If a paper return is filed before 31 October following the relevant tax year, HMRC will calculate the tax due if required. For those filing online, most tax return software packages automatically calculate the tax due.

Self-assessment statements are issued by HMRC on a regular basis, detailing transactions on an individual's self-assessment account.

2.1.4   Errors and overpayments

Once filed, a tax return can be amended by the taxpayer up to 12 months after the filing deadline if an error is found in the return. After this, HMRC should be contacted in respect of any error causing a tax liability to arise. If an error has led to an overpayment of tax, an overpayment relief claim can be made under TMA 1970, Sch. 1AB within four years of the end of the relevant tax year. HMRC are very strict with regard to this time limit and do not allow a claim beyond it.

There are certain situations in which an overpayment relief claim cannot be made – see SACM 12065. A claim must be made in the correct format and must state how much the individual believes he or she has overpaid. SACM 12150 provides details of what needs to be included in a claim.

Generally, HMRC have a "process now, check later" approach to tax returns and when processing returns will amend any obvious mistakes such as arithmetical errors. This needs to be done within nine months of the return having been filed (or amended) and the individual can appeal against such changes within 30 days of the issue of the notice of correction.

Law: TMA 1970, s. 9ZA, 9ZB, Sch. 1AB
Guidance: SACM 12000-12215

2.1.5   Payment of tax

The due date for the payment of any outstanding tax for a tax year (the balancing payment) is 31 January following the relevant tax year.

In addition to the balancing payment, two payments on account need to be made for the following tax year, if the tax due for the current tax year (less tax that has been deducted at source) is either:

- £1,000 or more; or
- at least 20% or more of the tax collected at source.

These payments on account will be the tax liability less any tax deducted at source for the current year. 50% is due for payment by 31 January in the tax year to which the liability relates and 50% by 31 July after that tax year.

Example 1

Jane's total tax liability for 2021-22 is £19,200, before deducting £10,000 tax that was withheld at source.

Jane's outstanding tax liability for 2021-22, after the deduction of tax withheld at source, is above £1,000. Also, less than 80% of the tax liability for 2021-22 was collected at source. Therefore, she falls under the payments on account regime.

Jane has to make a balancing payment of £9,200 for 2021-22, plus the first payment on account for 2022-23 of £4,600, by 31 January 2023, so a total of £13,800.

The second payment on account for 2022-23 will be another £4,600, which must be paid by 31 July 2023.

An individual who believes that his or her tax liability will be lower for the following tax year can make a claim to reduce the payments on account under TMA 1970, s. 59A. If these are reduced too far, interest on the late payment of tax will arise from the due dates of the payments on account.

The claim to reduce payments on account can be made on form SA303, on page TC1 of the self-assessment tax return or in a letter to HMRC. The grounds for making the claim must be given.

There are penalties for making an incorrect statement on a fraudulent or negligent basis, the maximum penalty being the amount of tax that should have been paid had the incorrect statement not been made.

Individuals need to be aware of the cash-flow consequences of falling within the payments on account regime, as significant amounts of tax may need to be paid by the 31 January deadline, especially in the first year of having to make payments on account.

Example 2

In the above example, Jane has to pay £13,800 by 31 January 2023 and then a further £4,600 by 31 July 2023, so a total of £18,400 in a six-month period.

If, say, Jane's balancing payment for 2022-23 was £10,000, then her payments on account for 2023-24 will be £5,000 each. A total of £15,000 will be due for payment by 31 January 2024. However, from this she can deduct the payments on account she made for 2022-23 of £9,200, leaving £800 to pay for 2022-23, and so a total of £5,800 to be paid by 31 January

2024. Her second payment on account for 2023-24 of £5,000 will have to be paid by 31 July 2024.

If Jane believed her balancing payment for 2023-24 would be £5,000, she could make a claim to reduce her payments on account for this year to this amount and so reduce the two payments to £2,500 each.

If a taxpayer is unable to pay his or her tax, and the liability is less than £30,000, he or she may be able to arrange an online self-assessment payment plan to pay the outstanding tax (including penalties) by instalments over 12 months. Further conditions are that:

- the individual must have no other payment plans or debts with HMRC;
- his or her tax returns must be up to date; and
- the arrangement must be set up within 60 days after the payment deadline.

If the above conditions do not apply, the individual should call the self-assessment payment helpline on 0300 200 3822 to discuss further options.

For other taxes outside self-assessment, a "time to pay" arrangement may be possible, again allowing the tax to be paid by instalments. Again, HMRC should be contacted to discuss this.

If an individual's balancing payment is less than £3,000, and the tax return is filed by 30 December following the relevant tax year, then HMRC will include the outstanding tax in the individual's PAYE tax code if requested on the tax return.

Law: TMA 1970, s. 59A-59C

Guidance: SALF 300; https://www.tax.service.gov.uk/pay-what-you-owe-in-instalments; *Debt Management and Banking Manual* at DMBM 800040; https://taxaid.org.uk/guides/taxpayers/tax-debt

2.1.6 Records

Records should be kept to support a complete and correct tax return under self-assessment. All records supporting a return must be retained and HMRC have a right to request these. Penalties are in place for not keeping records or if they are not accurate, complete or readable (see **Appendix 1**). There is no prescribed way of keeping these records.

If the individual files the tax return on time, records need to be kept for at least a year after the 31 January filing deadline, so 2021-22 records must be kept until 31 January 2024. If the return was issued after 31 October following the relevant tax year, records need to be kept for 12 months after the deadline for that return.

If the return is filed late, the records need to be kept for 12 months after the quarter in which it was filed.

If an individual is self-employed or rents out property, the records need to be kept longer – for five years after the filing deadline. If the return is filed four years or more after the filing deadline, records need to be kept for at least 15 months after the return is filed.

The above time limits may change if an enquiry is under way into a tax return. Records should be kept until the date of the final closure notice if this is later than the standard time limit.

Law: TMA 1970, s. 12B
Guidance: SALF 211; *Compliance Handbook* CH 10000

2.1.7   Penalties and interest

Penalties

Numerous (often hefty) penalties exist for non-compliance such as:

- not informing HMRC of chargeability to tax;
- failing to file a self-assessment tax return on time;
- late payment of any tax due;
- not keeping accurate records; or
- filing an inaccurate tax return.

See **Appendix 1** for more details.

Some of these penalties are based on a person's behaviour, so an individual who deliberately evades tax will be penalised far more heavily than one who made an error but comes forward on a voluntary basis.

Appeals can be made against these penalties on various grounds.

Reasonable excuse

One important basis for an appeal is if there is a "reasonable excuse". Note that:

- Insufficiency of funds cannot be a reasonable excuse, unless the insufficiency can be attributed to events that are outside the person's control.

13

- Reliance on another person (e.g. an accountant) can only be a reasonable excuse if the taxpayer took reasonable care to avoid any default.

Common examples of reasonable excuse would include:

- health-related events (death, serious illness, an unexpected hospital stay, delays caused by disability); and
- one-off events (e.g. fire, flood, theft, unpredictable postal delays, sudden computer failure).

HMRC will in certain circumstances accept delay due to Covid-19 as a reasonable excuse (see **Appendix 11**).

If a person has a reasonable excuse, but the excuse comes to an end, the person must remedy the failure without unreasonable delay once the excuse has finished.

There is extensive case law on what constitutes a reasonable excuse. In *The Clean Car Company Ltd* (a VAT case), Judge Medd QC set out two tests, both of which must be taken into consideration:

- an objective test: the standard of reasonableness expected of someone with "a responsible attitude to his duties as a taxpayer"; and
- a subjective test: particular factors the tribunal might consider relevant, including age, experience, health or "the incidence of some particular difficulty or misfortune".

In *Pokorowski*, the taxpayer's homelessness was readily accepted by the tribunal as an example of this "particular difficulty or misfortune", even though the delay had gone on for 17 months.

HMRC acknowledge that:

> "What is a reasonable excuse for one person's circumstances and abilities may not be a reasonable excuse for another person."

Cases: *The Clean Car Company Ltd v C&E Commrs* (1991) VATTR 234; *Pokorowski v HMRC* [2019] UKFTT 86 (TC)

Guidance: https://www.gov.uk/tax-appeals/reasonable-excuses (HMRC view of "what may count as a reasonable excuse"); CH 61540*ff*.

Late filing penalties

In *Jackson*, a non-resident CGT return case (which has the same late filing penalties as self-assessment tax returns), the judge cancelled the late-filing penalties for being six and 12 months late, on the grounds that the taxpayer's liability had to be referred to in order to establish the penalty due. HMRC had overlooked the provisions of FA 2009, Sch. 55, para. 1(3) and 17(3), stating that where an individual is liable for a penalty under more than one paragraph of Sch. 55 which is determined by reference to a liability to tax, those penalties must not in aggregate exceed 100% of the liability to tax (or a higher percentage if information has been deliberately withheld).

In Mr Jackson's case, there was no liability to tax. Therefore the total penalties due for being six and 12 months late, which refer to the tax liability of nil, must be nil. It followed that HMRC should not have raised these penalties and so the tribunal quashed them.

A similar decision was reached in *Jagger.*

In reality, HMRC often raise a penalty of £300 when a tax return is six months late and another £300 when it is 12 months late, even though no tax is due. Advisers should therefore be ready to challenge these.

Law: FA 2009, Sch. 55, para. 1(3), 17(3)
Cases: *Jackson v HMRC* [2018] UKFTT 64 (TC); *Jagger v HMRC* [2018] UKFTT 623 (TC)

Suspension of penalties

Penalties for careless inaccuracies can be suspended by HMRC for a period (less than two years) if certain conditions are set and if the taxpayer meets these during the suspension period. The conditions are designed to help the individual not to repeat the behaviour/actions that led to the inaccuracy. If the taxpayer meets these conditions to HMRC's satisfaction, the penalties will not become due. If he or she fails to do so, the penalties will become due for payment. Penalties for deliberate behaviour cannot be suspended. See HMRC compliance checklist CC/FS10 and CH 83100.

Special reduction

On rare occasions, HMRC may make a "special reduction" (reducing or staying a penalty) in "special circumstances":

- which are uncommon or exceptional; or
- where the strict application of the penalty law produces a result that is contrary to the clear compliance intention of that law.

Once more, a shortage of funds cannot constitute special circumstances.

Law: FA 2009, Sch. 55, 56
Guidance: CH 170000

Special relief

Once a determination of tax has become final and conclusive, and the tax is due and payable, that is normally the end of the matter. However, the principle of "special relief" (formerly "equitable liability") may offer one further chance in exceptional circumstances, for example in relation to:

- vulnerable taxpayers (see, for example, *Clark*); or
- individuals who did not receive notices or other communications from HMRC for reasons beyond the individual's control.

The relief may operate where it would be "unconscionable" to seek to recover the tax due (or to deny a tax repayment). "Unconscionable" means "completely unreasonable or unreasonably excessive" (*Maxwell*).

The taxpayer's tax affairs must otherwise be up to date, or there must be satisfactory arrangements in place to bring them up to date.

A taxpayer may not normally claim special relief more than once.

Law: TMA 1970, Sch. 1AB, para. 3A
Cases: *Maxwell v HMRC* [2013] UKFTT 459 (TC); *Clark v HMRC* [2015] UKFTT 324 (TC)
Guidance: SACM 12240

New penalty regime

From 6 April 2023, a points-based system will be introduced for penalties for the late submission of self-assessment tax returns by individuals falling under ITSA, who have income from businesses and/or properties of over £10,000 per year. For all other individuals under ITSA the new system will apply from 6 April 2024.

Interest on tax paid late

In addition to penalties, interest arises on a daily basis on the late payment of tax until the tax due is paid. There is no right of appeal against interest being charged.

Repayment supplement may be due on any repayment of overpaid tax from the later of:

- the date it was paid; and
- the date the tax was due to be paid.

Law: FA 2007, Sch. 24, para. 14; FA 2009, s. 101-102, Sch. 53-55

Guidance: CH 60000-84500, 140000, 150000, 170000, 400000; https:// tinyurl.com/vf8d4vxr (compliance checks factsheets); https://tinyurl. com/48f8s82w (guidance re late submission penalties); https://tinyurl. com/yt7ksusc (interest rates on late and early tax payments)

2.2   Enquiries, checks and deterrents

2.2.1   Overview

Over the years, HMRC have been putting more resources into investigation work to try and reduce the "tax gap". They have a number of options when checking an individual's tax liability, including:

- compliance checks;
- enquiries into a self-assessment tax return;
- inspections; and
- record reviews.

Tax law governing HMRC powers – and underpinning taxpayer safeguards against those powers – is an extensive and complex area, and specialist advice will often be required, especially if a client is at risk of criminal prosecution.

HMRC guidance is available in various forms, referred to in this chapter.

These topics are also something of a specialist area for Claritax Books, and readers may like to refer to the following publications in particular, where the topics are dealt with in depth:

- *Tax Appeals*, by Keith Gordon;
- *Discovery Assessments*, again by Keith Gordon; and
- *Taxpayer Safeguards and the Rule of Law*, by Robin Williamson.

Taxpayers with an international dimension to their affairs are subject to an additional layer of compliance burdens, and these are referred to as appropriate in **Chapters 34-40** below. Readers may also be interested in the more detailed coverage in *Advising British Expats*, again from Claritax Books.

2.2.2   Compliance checks

HMRC can raise a compliance check into a person's self-assessment tax return, business accounts etc. if the HMRC officer believes these are wrong. This will often be an "informal" enquiry, but HMRC may use more formal powers if the individual is uncooperative or if there is an unreasonable delay in supplying information requested.

HMRC have powers to obtain the necessary information and documents to carry out this check.

HMRC offer a number of factsheets in respect of compliance checks.

Guidance: https://tinyurl.com/vf8d4vxr (compliance checks factsheets)

2.2.3   Enquiries

An enquiry is a formal statutory process into a self-assessment tax return or an amended return. HMRC may open an enquiry within 12 months after the self-assessment tax return has been delivered if filed on time.

These enquiries are conducted under the information powers given to HMRC under FA 2008, Sch. 36.

HMRC must send a written notice to the individual stating their intention to enquire into the tax return. Once the enquiry has finished, a closure notice will be issued to the individual under TMA 1970, s. 28A.

HMRC may amend a self-assessment tax return during an enquiry under TMA 1970, s. 9C if they believe that there will be a loss of tax if they do not do this immediately. HMRC may use this power if, for example, the individual refuses to make a payment on account of the tax that is due or if HMRC believe that assets may be transferred abroad.

An individual can apply to the tax tribunal under TMA 1970, s. 28A for the enquiry to be closed, if he or she believes that there are no reasonable grounds for the enquiry to continue. An individual has the right to appeal in writing against HMRC conclusions or amendments made under s. 28A within 30 days.

The taxpayer can also appeal against an amendment made under s. 9C, but the appeal will not be heard and determined until HMRC have finished their enquiries.

TMA 1970, s. 43C allows certain out-of-time claims if HMRC have amended an individual's tax return as a result of an enquiry.

Law: TMA 1970, s. 9A-9C, 28A-31A, 43C; FA 2008, Sch. 36; FA 2016, s. 162, Sch. 20

Guidance: SALF 400

2.2.4 *Discovery assessments*

HMRC can raise a discovery assessment outside normal time limits if they discover that, through careless or deliberate behaviour:

- not enough tax has been paid;
- a tax relief claim has been excessive; or
- not all income has been declared.

This may arise, for example, because of a tip-off (e.g. from a disgruntled former spouse), or because an error in one year gives grounds to believe that similar errors may have occurred in the past.

There is some evidence that HMRC will use the discovery process to review tax liabilities for earlier years simply because HMRC failed to open an enquiry on time, but this is (in principle) not permitted by the legislation so such cases are open to particular challenge.

Law: TMA 1970, s. 29

2.2.5 *Codes of Practice*

HMRC may investigate under a code of practice in more serious cases.

Code of Practice 8 (COP8) is used when HMRC suspect there is deliberate and significant loss of tax, including where the taxpayer has taken advantage of a scheme to reduce tax liabilities. HMRC will conduct an in-depth investigation, though under COP8 there is no intention of a criminal prosecution.

If HMRC suspect or find evidence of fraud the investigation will proceed under Code of Practice 9 (COP9). Under COP9, the individual is given the opportunity to make a complete and accurate disclosure of all deliberate and non-deliberate acts that have led to irregularities in his or her tax affairs. To use COP9, the individual must admit to fraudulent behaviour, but the benefit is that COP9 provides protection from prosecution.

However, if HMRC suspect that not all irregularities have been disclosed, a criminal investigation may be started with a view to prosecution.

Guidance: CH 180000-191400, 200000, 880000; https://tinyurl.com/n5z3995h (COP8); https://tinyurl.com/9rrn5265 (COP9)

2.2.6   Deterrents

A number of deterrents have been introduced, such as:

- naming and shaming individuals whose behaviour was deliberate if the loss of tax was over £25,000;
- HMRC powers to take action against tax agents they believe have engaged in dishonest conduct;
- managing serious defaulters who have deliberately evaded tax and whom HMRC consider to be high risk; and
- tackling enablers of offshore tax evasion or non-compliance.

Guidance: CH 500000

2.2.7   Promoters of avoidance schemes

There are specific rules for those who persistently promote aggressive tax avoidance arrangements and whom HMRC regard as exhibiting high risk behaviour.

Promoters of tax avoidance schemes are required to disclose these to HMRC within five days of the scheme being made available or implemented. The user of a scheme is also required to make a disclosure under the Disclosure of Tax Avoidance Schemes (DOTAS) regime.

Law: FA 2004, Pt. 7; FA 2009, s. 94, Sch. 48; FA 2012, s. 223, Sch. 38; FA 2014, Pt. 5, Sch. 34-36

Guidance: https://tinyurl.com/2a2bmzma (Promoters of tax avoidance schemes); https://tinyurl.com/9pw4v5cz (Marketed tax avoidance schemes in the UK); https://tinyurl.com/63pu7789 and https://tinyurl.com/3w5bwj5s (Disclosure of avoidance schemes)

2.3   Appeal process

In most cases there is a right of appeal against an HMRC decision, normally with a time limit of 30 days from the notice of HMRC's decision.

HMRC will consider the appeal and amend their decision if they agree with the appeal, or confirm their decision if they do not agree. If HMRC do not accept it, the taxpayer can forward the appeal to the tribunal within 30 days.

In addition, there is the option of an "internal review" whereby another officer of HMRC, independent of the case (usually from their Solicitors' Office or Legal Services Team), will carry out a review of the decision.

Internal review can be requested by the taxpayer, or HMRC may offer it if agreement cannot be reached, in which case the individual has 30 days from being offered the review to accept it.

The individual is not obliged to have a review and instead can appeal directly to the First-tier Tribunal (FTT). If a review has been requested but the individual changes his or her mind, it is not possible to appeal to the tribunal until the review has finished.

If a review is performed, a decision should be sent to the individual within 45 days (or 90 days if an extension has been agreed). The review will either agree with the appeal wholly or partly and cancel or amend HMRC's decision accordingly, or agree with HMRC's decision and turn down the appeal. In the latter situation, the individual has 30 days to appeal to the FTT.

An individual can request (or HMRC may offer) alternative dispute resolution (ADR) to be carried out to try to end disputes. This is a mediation process between the individual and HMRC with a facilitator from within HMRC who is independent of the case and who acts impartially. HMRC's guidance on ADR lists when this process can or cannot be used. ADR is entirely optional but it can be useful in a wide range of situations, including enquiries and compliance checks. It is important to lodge any necessary appeals within the statutory time limits, even if ADR is in progress.

If the individual decides to appeal to the tribunal, a form needs to be submitted – see https://www.gov.uk/tax-tribunal/appeal-to-tribunal. Each party normally pays for its own costs at the FTT, though costs can be awarded if one party is regarded as having acted unreasonably.

See *Tax Appeals – Law and Practice at the FTT* by Keith Gordon, available from Claritax Books, for detailed guidance on the processes and practicalities of appealing to the FTT.

A case may be heard in the Upper Tribunal (UT) if an appeal is made on a point of law by either the individual or HMRC against the FTT decision. Complex cases may bypass the FTT altogether. Both parties' costs at the UT are paid by the losing party, unless the individual has opted out of this cost regime, in which case the same cost regime applies as for the FTT, i.e. each party is responsible for its own costs.

If the individual consistently fails to follow the tribunal's directions, the case may be struck out, in which case HMRC will automatically win.

The UT may give permission for the case to go before a relevant appellate court if either party wishes to appeal against its decision.

During an appeal, the individual may apply under TMA 1970, s. 55 for the disputed tax to be postponed until the appeal is settled.

Law: TMA 1970, s. 31, 31A, 47C-50, 54, 55, 56, 57

Guidance: *Appeals, Reviews and Tribunals Manual;* https://tinyurl.com/jh26dn9y (HMRC guidance on appealing to the FTT); https://tinyurl.com/vjpkn4jv (guidance on alternative dispute resolution)

2.4 Voluntary disclosures

One of HMRC's aims is to make compliance easier for taxpayers and to encourage voluntary disclosure when errors have occurred.

In respect of the former, HMRC have developed a number of toolkits, including those specifically for agents, though anyone can use these. They are updated every year and although their use is not compulsory, it may demonstrate that reasonable care has been taken. The toolkits highlight common errors in certain areas.

HMRC have run a number of voluntary disclosure campaigns in the past, often targeting specific groups of taxpayers, e.g. medical professionals and internet traders. Currently there are two ongoing campaigns:

- The let property campaign is for landlords (in the UK or overseas) who have been receiving rental income that has not been declared (for whatever reason) or who have underpaid tax on rental income, e.g. where an error has occurred on the individual's self-assessment tax return.
- The worldwide disclosure facility is available for individuals who owe UK tax as a result of an offshore matter.

Both of these campaigns provide an opportunity for the individual to declare the income, pay the correct tax (plus interest and penalties) and "wipe the slate clean". The advantage of these schemes is that penalties will be lower than if HMRC had discovered the non-declaration/underpayment. Both campaigns use HMRC's digital disclosure service.

In all other situations, a voluntary disclosure can be made directly to HMRC.

Guidance: https://www.gov.uk/government/collections/tax-agents-toolkits; https://tinyurl.com/266av7cs (re let property campaign); https://tinyurl.com/p3uyvvxv (worldwide disclosure facility); https://tinyurl.com/64m2y4fy (disclosure service); https://tinyurl.com/spvs9y32 (how to make a voluntary disclosure)

2.5   Simple assessment

HMRC are removing some taxpayers from self-assessment, meaning that those individuals are no longer required to file self-assessment tax returns, but will instead pay their tax via simple assessment.

HMRC will send a tax calculation to the individual which will be based on information HMRC already hold on the individual. The tax must be paid before 31 January following the relevant tax year or, if the simple assessment is raised after 31 October following the year of assessment, three months after this.

If the taxpayer does not agree to this simple assessment tax liability, he or she will have 60 days to query it. HMRC must give a response to this query.

HMRC can postpone all or part of the simple assessment, if they require further time or details, and the taxpayer is then not required to pay the amount postponed at the time. Any amended simple assessment raised as part of HMRC's final response cannot be queried, but an appeal against it can be made within the normal 30-day period.

Taxpayers will still be able to file self-assessment tax returns if they prefer, in which case HMRC will cancel any simple assessments. If HMRC incorrectly remove an individual from self-assessment, and a self-assessment tax return is required to be filed, it is the taxpayer's responsibility to inform HMRC of this. The 5 October deadline for notifying HMRC of chargeability to tax will still apply.

At the time of writing, simple assessment is limited to individuals who are:

- in receipt of the state pension only, and where this exceeds the personal allowance (quite a rare occurrence); or

- under PAYE and who have an underpayment of tax which cannot be collected via the PAYE tax code.

Law: TMA 1970, s. 28H-28J, 31-31AA, 59BA

Guidance: https://tinyurl.com/y87mh7c6 (simple assessment)

2.6 Digitalisation

HMRC's drive over the next years is to continue to digitalise the UK tax system, the core of which will be real-time information and the vision that each taxpayer will have just one digital account. The aim is for there to be parallel services for agents, allowing them to see and do what their clients can and allowing the agent access from the start. HMRC's report *Building a trusted, modern tax administration system* (July 2020) sets out their vision for the future over the next ten years.

Many forms and services are already online, including personal tax accounts, which enable individuals to access their tax accounts in real time and to perform various functions. However, agents do not (at the time of writing) have access to these. The accounts show various tax and NIC details, including a person's self-assessment and PAYE details, including PAYE codes.

Services that can be performed via a person's personal tax account include:

- checking tax estimates and tax codes;
- filing and viewing a tax return;
- claiming a tax refund;
- tracking tax forms that have been submitted online;
- checking or updating the marriage allowance;
- telling HMRC about a change of address; and
- checking or updating benefits in kind.

Agents (as well as using existing online services such as for self-assessment) will need to set up an agent services account to perform certain services for clients.

Making Tax Digital (MTD) is planned to come into effect for ITSA purposes from 6 April 2023 for individuals (both resident and non-resident) who:

- have business and/or rental income of over £10,000 per annum; and
- are liable to income tax.

The individual will be required to file a summary of his or her income and expenses on a quarterly basis using MTD-compatible software.

Although this may seem some way off, advisers need to start preparing themselves and their clients for the introduction of MTD for income tax.

Guidance: https://www.gov.uk/personal-tax-account (personal tax accounts); https://tinyurl.com/yntfkn8r (building a modern tax system); https://tinyurl.com/yk8xkvy9 (HMRC services for tax agents); https://tinyurl.com/ccv8e7ts (draft MTD ITSA regulations)

2.7   Pitfalls and planning points

Deadlines and penalties

For any compliance task, check what deadlines and penalties apply and perform the task in a timely manner – the longer the time by which a deadline is missed, the higher the penalty is likely to be.

Cash-flow

Always consider the cash-flow implications early and plan accordingly, e.g. for the first year under the payments on account regime.

Making Tax Digital

Start preparing for MTD ITSA.

Documentation

Make sure that all relevant documentation is kept to back up any claims, actions, returns, payments, etc. HMRC may request these or make an enquiry, or the individual may wish to query a matter with HMRC.

COMPUTATIONAL ASPECTS

3.   The computation of income tax

3.1   Introduction

3.1.1   Overview

Income tax is charged on income earned by individuals in the UK. The sources of this income are varied and may include employment, pension and trading income from sole trading or partnership businesses, property income, income from investments such as interest or dividends, and other miscellaneous income such as royalties, other receipts from intellectual property, or income from trusts and estates.

Income is normally taxed on the amount that arises or is received (depending on the source of the income) in the tax year, which runs from 6 April to 5 April. A system of basis periods operates for trades, etc. (see **15.4**).

To calculate the tax due on the income assessable in the tax year, the legislation lists out seven steps (*Income Tax Act* 2007, s. 23).

3.1.2   The steps of the calculation

Step	Details
1	Identify the amounts of income on which the taxpayer is charged to income tax for the tax year. The sum of those amounts is "total income". Each of those amounts is a "component" of total income. See *pro forma* for this step at **3.2.6**.
2	Deduct from the components the amount of any relief under a provision listed in s. 24 to which the taxpayer is entitled for the tax year (see deductible payments at **3.3**). The sum left after this step is "net income".
3	Deduct from the net income any allowances to which the taxpayer is entitled for the tax year, such as the personal allowance and blind person's allowance (see **3.4.1**).
4	Calculate the tax at each applicable rate on the amounts of the components left taxable after applying step three. See **3.5.1** for the tax rates and **3.5.4** for the *pro forma* for this step. If the taxpayer is a trustee, see **Chapter 41** for the applicable rates and techniques.
5	Add together the amounts of tax calculated at step four.

Step	Details (cont.)
6	Deduct from the amount of tax calculated at step five any "tax reducers" to which the taxpayer is entitled for the tax year (e.g. the married couple's allowance). See **3.6** for details.
7	*Add* to the amount of tax left after step six any amounts of tax for which the taxpayer is liable for the tax year, such as pension charges – e.g. annual allowance and lifetime allowance charges (see **Chapter 30**) – and the high income child benefit charge (see **33.5.6**).
	Deduct any amounts for which a deduction is due, such as amounts already paid by trustees or through PAYE. (Note that the reduction of the tax already paid at source is not an "official" step in the legislation but is essential in order to establish the correct tax payable figure.)

The result is the taxpayer's liability to income tax for the tax year.

These steps can be summarised as two stages:

- First, all the income must be accumulated, any deductible reliefs and personal allowances subtracted and the "taxable income" found. This is an important figure and is also used in other taxes such as capital gains tax as a reference for calculating tax due.

- Once the taxable income is known, the second stage is to apply the appropriate tax rates to each component of the taxable income. This stage may also encompass allowances, such as the savings and dividend allowances outlined in **Chapters 23** and **24**.

Once calculated, this income tax will be collected either through the PAYE system, if the individual is employed or in receipt of a pension, and/or through the self-assessment tax return submitted by the taxpayer annually, or through simple assessment (see **2.5**).

Law: ITA 2007, s. 23

3.2 Step one – calculating the taxable income

3.2.1 Introduction

Calculating the income is the first step outlined by ITA 2007, s. 23.

Essentially this step is to establish the amounts of income on which the individual is to be charged income tax. The sum of these amounts is the "total income". To determine what is taxable it is essential first to know what is exempt.

3.2.2 Exempt income

Many sources of income are exempt from income tax. The following sources of income do not need to be included in a taxpayer's self-assessment tax return as they are exempt:

- certain types of income from National Savings and Investments (NS&I), such as winnings on the premium bonds, and interest from NS&I certificates;
- income from specified investment plans, such as individual savings accounts (ISAs);
- income from savings-related share option (SAYE) schemes;
- dividends paid on the first £200,000 purchased of venture capital trust (VCT) shares;
- income from "free of tax to residents abroad" (FOTRA) securities;
- the exempt capital element of purchased life annuities;
- certain annual payments;
- certain types of other income, such as income from winnings and betting, gaming or lotteries;
- some social security benefits, for example universal credit, housing benefit, and winter fuel allowance for pensioners (although jobseeker's allowances are taxable);
- child benefit (but there may be a high income child benefit charge – see **3.7.1**); and
- certain scholarship awards.

Income arising on money and investments in a child trust fund account is also exempt from tax.

Law: ITEPA 2003, s. 677; ITTOIA 2005, s. 692, 709, 776; SI 1998/1870
Guidance: SAIM 11120

3.2.3 Chargeable income

To establish the total chargeable income to be taxed, the first stage is to separate the various items of income into their appropriate category, according to the source of the income. It will not matter if the individual's income is from a UK or a non-UK source, as the worldwide income of a

UK tax resident will be taxable. See **Chapters 34-40** for more information on the taxation of foreign income.

All income is generally from one of three sources: non-savings, savings or dividend income. The need to split the income into the different sources arises from the fact that each source has different tax rules associated with it; either different tax rates (in the case of dividends) or different rules and methods are applied to each source to calculate the tax due.

3.2.4   Non-savings income

The first category of income is non-savings and non-dividend income, shortened to "non-savings income". Examples are employment income, trading income, property income, pension income, royalties, and income from discretionary trusts and estates.

Employment income covers both basic salary received and any extras such as benefits in kind and annual bonuses (see **Chapters 5-14**).

Trading income covers income from a profession or vocation as well as income from a merchandising or manufacturing business. Trading income could be from a sole trader or a partnership share. More information on such sources can be found in **Chapters 15-19**.

Property income is taxed net of any deductible expenses (see **Chapters 26-28**).

More information on pension income, and on state and other benefits, can be found at **Chapters 29-33**.

3.2.5   Savings income

The second source is savings income, mostly interest from banks and building societies (see **Chapter 23**).

3.2.6   Dividend income and other sources

The third source is dividend income (see **Chapter 24**).

Sometimes there might be a fourth source. This is for income that must be taxed at the individual's highest rate of income, such as the charge for pension contributions above the annual allowance (see **Chapter 30**).

Law: ITEPA 2003, s. 677; ITTOIA 2005, s. 692, 709, 776; SI 1998/1870
Guidance: SAIM 11120

3.2.7   The pro forma

It is a good idea to complete the income tax calculation in the same way every time. A standard *pro forma* separates the main three categories and allows an opportunity to deduct any amounts deductible from the total income in a logical and organised way.

	Non-savings income	Savings income	Dividend income
	£	£	£
Employment income	X		
Property income	X		
Pension income	X		
Income from interest		X	
Income from dividends			X
Income from interest-in-possession trusts	X	X	X
Income from estates	X		X
Income from discretionary trusts	X		
Taxable foreign income (for those not on the remittance basis)	X	X	X
Income remitted from overseas (for those on the remittance basis)	X		
Total income	X	X	X

3.3   Step two – deductible payments

3.3.1   Overview

Once the total income has been calculated, the next step is to find if there are any deductible amounts to reduce the income down to net income (ITA 2007, s. 23).

	Non-savings income	Savings income	Dividend income
	£	£	£
Total income	X	X	X
Less: deductible payments	(X)	(X)	(X)
Net income	X	X	X

Some payments made by the taxpayer reduce the amount of income liable to income tax. Those that come off the total amount of taxable income are called "deductible payments" and are taken from non-savings income in priority to savings, and then from dividend income. A non-exhaustive list of such deductible payments includes the following, (though many of these are subject to a cap on the amounts that may be deducted – see **3.3.2** below):

- trade losses made in the first four years of trade (see **17.2.1**);
- trade losses offset against general income (see **17.2.2**);
- terminal trade losses (see **17.2.5**);
- post-cessation loss relief (see **17.3**);
- share loss relief (but not EIS, SEIS or social investment shares);
- property loss relief against general income and post-cessation property loss relief (see **17.7**);
- employment loss relief against general income;
- loss relief against miscellaneous income, where the profits would be taxable (see **17.4**);
- gifts of shares or real property to charities;
- payments to trade unions or police organisations (if conditions met);
- trade losses carried forward from previous periods (see **17.2.4**);
- qualifying interest payments;
- irrecoverable peer-to-peer loans;
- liabilities relating to former employment;
- pension contributions to an employer scheme that could not be fully deducted under net pay arrangements;
- annual payments;

- losses of strips of government securities; and
- losses on listed securities held since 26 March 2003.

Trade losses, for example, should be offset in accordance with the particular rules (see **Chapter 17**). Where no such rules exist, the taxpayer can offset deductions so as to give the lowest tax bill – normally non-savings income first, then savings and finally dividend income, but this will depend on the facts of the specific taxpayer.

Law: ITA 2007, s. 24, 25, 27, 457, 458
Guidance: SAIM 7120

3.3.2   Limit on deductibility

There is a limit on the deductibility (technically, a "cap on income tax reliefs") for an individual taxpayer, in relation to the following deductions:

a) trade losses offset against general income (see **17.2.2**);

b) trade losses made in the first four years of trade (see **17.2.1**);

c) post-cessation loss relief (see **17.3**);

d) property loss relief against general income;

e) post-cessation property loss relief (see **17.7**);

f) employment loss relief against general income;

g) share loss relief (but not EIS, SEIS or social investment shares);

h) qualifying interest payments;

i) liabilities relating to former employment;

j) losses of strips of government securities; and

k) losses on listed securities held since 26 March 2003.

The cap is set at £50,000 or, if greater, 25% of the individual's "adjusted total income".

This cap will not apply to reliefs that can be deducted directly from a source of the "component" income. For example, opening trade losses when deducted are simply deducted against total income, rather than a specific component, so they will be subject to the cap.

Trade losses brought forward from previous years, on the other hand, are set against a specific element, i.e. future profits of the same trade, rather than total income. This means that there will only be a restriction if there are not enough profits from the same trade against which to offset them.

By way of a further example, qualifying interest payments are set against total income (and are therefore subject to the cap) whereas irrecoverable peer-to-peer loans are deducted from income from peer-to-peer loans, so the maximum offset depends only on the amount of income from such loans.

The calculation of relief subject to the cap

Three stages are required to establish the amount of such reliefs that can be offset.

The first stage is to identify all the amounts that are subject to the restriction, i.e. those listed at (a) to (k) above.

The second stage is to subtract the following from those reliefs just identified in the first stage:

- trade or property losses (within categories (a) to (e)) that are deducted from profits of the same trade or property business;
- trade losses or opening year relief where it is attributed to overlap profits in the final tax year or on change of accounting date; and/or
- share loss relief relating to EIS, SEIS or social enterprise investments.

This will leave the amount of deduction subject to the cap.

The third stage is to compare this figure with the taxpayer's adjusted total income. If the deduction subject to the cap is less than £50,000, or 25% of adjusted total income if higher, no restriction is necessary.

Example 1

Randall has several trading and property businesses which together made £80,000 net profit in 2021-22.

He made no charitable or pension contributions. Randall paid interest on a qualifying loan of £70,000. The maximum amount that can be applied to his profit is £50,000 or 25% of his adjusted income, whichever is higher.

25% of his adjusted total income is £20,000.

£50,000 is greater, so £50,000 is the maximum of the qualifying loan interest that can be offset. The balance of the loan interest is wasted.

Adjusted total income

Adjusted total income will only need to be calculated if the taxpayer's income is over £200,000 (as the maximum will otherwise always be £50,000). The legislation (s. 24A) calculates this in four steps:

- Take the amount of the taxpayer's total income.
- Add back the amounts of any (gross) deductions allowed under payroll giving in calculating the taxpayer's income which is charged to tax for the tax year.
- If the taxpayer is given relief at source for any pension contributions paid in the tax year, deduct the gross amount of the contributions.
- If the taxpayer is entitled to a deduction for pension excess relief under net payment arrangements or relief on making a claim, deduct the amount of the excess or contribution.

Example 2

Roy had total income from let property and employment of £350,000 in 2021-22. His relief limit is therefore 25% of £350,000 which is £87,500.

He has the following available deductions in 2021-22:

Qualifying loan interest £75,000

Property losses £36,000

As the total claim for relief will exceed Roy's limit, he can choose how to use the reliefs. He decides to use the qualifying loan interest first and £12,500 of the property losses. He does this as he is unable to use the qualifying loan interest in another year, but he can use the property losses in 2022-23.

Law: ITA 2007, s. 24, 24A, 25
Guidance: SAIM 7120

3.4   Step three – deduct personal allowances

3.4.1   Overview

Deducting the personal allowance, and where appropriate the blind person's allowance, is the third step outlined by ITA 2007, s. 23.

3.4.2   The personal allowance

The personal allowance is £12,570 in 2021-22. This is available to all UK resident taxpayers and to certain taxpayers not resident in the UK, specifically:

- nationals of the UK (see note below);
- nationals of countries in the EEA (again, see below);
- employed in the service of the British Crown – or a widow, widower or surviving civil partner whose late spouse or civil partner was employed in the service of the Crown;
- employed in the service of any UK missionary society;
- employed in the service of any state under the protection of Her Majesty;
- resident in the Isle of Man or the Channel Islands;
- formerly resident in the UK and now resident abroad for the sake of the individual's health or the health of a member of his family living with him; and
- a national or resident of a long list of other countries, listed at section 3 of form R43, available online.

Note: the UK national category was recently added (effective from 31 December 2020) to ensure that UK nationals who are not UK resident still qualify for the personal allowance (and the marriage, blind person's and married couple's allowance) post-Brexit. In addition, HMRC have confirmed that those claiming a UK personal allowance on the basis of being an EEA national will continue to be able to do so post-Brexit.

The personal allowance is available in full in the year a baby is born and in the year of a person's death. No pro-rating is required.

Restriction of the personal allowance

The personal allowance is restricted if an individual's adjusted net income is more than £100,000. In such cases, £1 of personal allowance is lost for every £2 of adjusted net income the individual has over £100,000 up until £125,140, when the allowance is fully abated.

"Adjusted net income" is the individual's net income (as calculated in step two) less any trading or property losses and less gross payments, gift aid and pension payments (those that are either paid gross or where tax relief is given at source). The provisions (ITA 2007, s. 59) once again give a step-by-step guide to arrive at the adjusted net income:

- Take the individual's net income.
- If the individual has made a qualifying gift aid donation, subtract the gross amount of this donation.
- If the individual has made pension contributions and received a deduction of tax at source, subtract the gross amount.
- Add back any payments to trade unions that were deducted under deductible payments above.

Example 1

Rafi earned £75,000 from his employment, £25,000 from property income and £10,000 in dividends in 2021-22. He gifted £4,000 under gift aid.

His personal allowance will be reduced by £1 for every £2 by which his adjusted net income exceeds £100,000.

Rafi's adjusted net income is:

	£
Employment	75,000
Property income	25,000
Dividends	10,000
Net income	110,000
Gift aid payments (£4,000 x 100/80)	(5,000)
Adjusted net income	105,000

As Rafi's adjusted net income is £5,000 more than £100,000 the personal allowance will be reduced by half of the excess. Half of the excess is £5,000 x 50% = £2,500.

The final personal allowance will therefore be £10,070 (£12,570 – £2,500).

Example 2

Raheel was employed as a firefighter on a salary of £55,000 a year.

As he had several days off when not on his firefighting shifts, he formed a business with his brother as a window cleaner, earning £40,000 in

2021-22. He took out a loan to purchase his share of the partnership and paid £800 in interest during the tax year.

Raheel also had investment income through his bank deposits totalling £8,000 and dividends of £13,500. He contributed £2,000 out of his income to a private pension scheme during 2021-22.

Show Raheel's taxable income in 2021-22

Step one is to establish Raheel's total income. As he has two sources of non-savings income, employment and trading, both will need to be included in the non-savings income column. He also has savings income (interest) and dividend income. The total of all these sources is "total income".

	Total income £	Non-savings income £	Savings income £	Dividend income £
Employment income	55,000	55,000		
Trading income	40,000	40,000		
Bank interest	8,000		8,000	
Dividend income	13,500			13,500
Total income	116,500	95,000	8,000	13,500

Step two is establishing whether Raheel has any deductible payments. He does. Interest paid by an individual on a loan taken out to buy into a partnership is as a "qualifying payment" that can be deducted from total income. This reduces the total income to the net income as follows:

	Total income £	Non-savings income £	Savings income £	Dividend income £
Total income as above	116,500	95,000	8,000	13,500
Qualifying loan interest	(800)	(800)		
Net income	115,700	94,200	8,000	13,500

Step three is reducing the net income by any applicable personal allowances. Raheel is entitled to the personal allowance of £12,570. However, as it appears that his adjusted net income may be over £100,000, an additional calculation is needed to see if his personal allowance must be reduced.

Raheel's adjusted net income was:

Adjusted net income	£
Net income	115,700
Gross personal pension payments (£2,000 x 100/80)	(2,500)
	113,200

As Raheel's adjusted net income is £13,200 more than £100,000, the personal allowance will be reduced by half of the excess (£6,600).

The final personal allowance will therefore be £5,970 (£12,570 - £6,600).

	Total income	Non-savings income	Savings income	Dividend income
	£	£	£	£
Net income	115,700	94,200	8,000	13,500
Personal allowance	(5,970)	(5,970)		
Taxable income	109,730	88,230	8,000	13,500

Raheel's taxable income is thus a total of £109,730.

Law: ITA 2007, s. 34, 35, 41, 56, 58
Guidance: INTM 334580

3.4.3   Blind person's allowance

The blind person's allowance (BPA) is combined with the personal allowance to make a larger allowance available for deducting against total income. In 2021-22 the BPA is £2,520, making a total allowance, including the personal allowance, of £15,090. Unlike the personal allowance, the BPA must be claimed.

Eligibility criteria

To be eligible for the BPA the taxpayer must meet the same residence or other requirements as set out above in **3.4.2** for the personal allowance. In addition, he or she must be:

- registered in England or Wales as a severely sight-impaired adult; or
- ordinarily resident in Scotland or Northern Ireland, and because of the individual's blindness, unable to do any work for which eyesight is essential.

The individual can have the BPA for the previous year as well as the year of registration if the blindness or severe sight-impairment which formed the basis of the registration was evident in the preceding tax year.

Transferable to spouse or civil partner

The BPA is fully transferable to a spouse or civil partner if they are living together in a year and the blind taxpayer does not have enough total income to use it. It is also transferable in certain other circumstances.

Law: ITA 2007, s. 38, 39, 40

3.5   Steps four and five – taxing the taxable income

3.5.1   Overview

The calculation of the tax and adding together all the income tax calculated on the various sources of income are steps four and five at ITA 2007, s. 23.

3.5.2   The tax bands

Income tax rates depend on the "band" into which the individual taxpayer's income falls.

For 2021-22, the first £12,570 will be covered by the personal allowance, so no tax is payable. The following £37,700 will be in the basic rate band. Once the basic rate band has been exhausted, the following £112,300 will be in the higher rate band, and finally any income over £150,000 (by which time the personal allowance will have been withdrawn) will be taxed at the additional rates.

	£
Personal allowance	12,570
Basic rate band	The next 37,700
Higher rate band	The next 112,300
Additional rate band	>150,000

These tax bands can be extended to reflect gift aid payments and payments to pension schemes that are given tax relief at source.

3.5.3 The tax rates

For a complete listing of income tax rates see **Appendices 3** and **4**. The main rates are as follows:

	Non-savings income	Savings income	Dividend income
Starting rate band for savings income where non-savings taxable income is under £5,000		0%	
Personal savings allowance		0%	
Basic rate (ordinary rate for dividends)	20%	20%	7.5%
Higher rate (upper rate for dividends)	40%	40%	32.5%
Additional rate	45%	45%	38.1%
Dividend allowance			0%

3.5.4 The pro forma

The *pro forma* for the taxation of the income will always start with the taxable income as calculated in steps one to three. The taxable income is already split into non-savings, savings and dividend income and the tax should be calculated in that order.

Running down the left-hand side of the *pro forma* for the tax calculation is the total amount that is being taxed. Even amounts taxed at 0% – such as those covered by the personal savings or dividend allowances – will take up some of the band, so these should be included in the total income column. Having this column also acts as a double-check to make sure all the income has been taxed.

Taxable income	Total income £	Total tax due £
Non-savings income Tax on non-savings income at basic rate £X x 20%/40%/45%	X	X
Savings income Starting rate band £X x 0%	X	X
Personal savings allowance £1,000 or £500 x 0%	X	X
Other savings income x 20%/40%/45%	X	X
Dividend income Dividend allowance £2,000 x 0%	X	X
Other dividend income £X x 7.5%/32.5%/38.1%	X	X
Total income tax liability	X	X

3.5.5   The order of taxing

The order of taxing is from left to right. In other words, non-savings income is the first calculation to make, then savings income and finally dividend income, all at their appropriate rates.

Example

Continuing with our example of Raheel. From **3.4.2** above we can see that Raheel had £109, 730 in taxable income, as below:

	Total income £	Non-savings income £	Savings income £	Dividend income £
Taxable income	109,730	88,230	8,000	13,500

Taxation of his income will commence with the non-savings, move to the savings and end with the dividend income.

	Total income	Total tax due
	£	£
Tax on non-savings income at basic rate £37,700 x 20%	37,700	7,540
Tax on non-savings income at higher rate £50,530 x 40%	50,530	20,212
Savings income Personal savings allowance £500 x 0%	500	0
Other savings income £7,500 (£8,000 - £500) x 40%	7,500	3,000
Dividend income Dividend allowance £2,000 x 0%	2,000	0
Other dividend income £11,500 (£13,500 – £2,000) x 32.5%	11,500	3,737
Total income tax liability	109,730	34,489

Law: ITA 2007, s. 16

3.5.6　Gift aid

The gift aid scheme encourages individuals to give to charity by allowing tax relief for the gift. Both the individual and the charity can benefit.

Without the scheme, an individual wanting a charity to receive £100 would need to give the charity £100. With the scheme, the individual only needs to give the charity £80 and HMRC will top it up to £100. The gift to the charity is therefore received from two sources: the donor taxpayer and HMRC. The part received from HMRC will be the basic rate tax associated with the donation, i.e. £20 (£80 x 20/80).

Gift aid declaration

HMRC would, however, be out of pocket if the donor to the charity was not a tax-paying individual, as no tax would then have been paid by the donor to HMRC. To counteract this, individuals who give to charity and who wish the charity to obtain the tax relief from HMRC must complete a "gift aid declaration" to confirm that they have paid at least as much tax in the tax year as HMRC will be paying over to the charity at basic rates. If the donor uses the gift aid scheme incorrectly, because he or she has not paid sufficient tax to HMRC in the tax year to cover the tax on the gift, the liability for the tax will need to be met by that taxpayer.

Charities cannot generally claim gift aid from HMRC without the declaration (though they can if they use the small donations scheme).

Carry-back of relief

A taxpayer making a gift aid claim may elect to carry the donation back for one tax year, i.e. treating the gift as donated in the previous tax year. This may be required if the taxpayer did not pay enough tax in the current year, but did in the previous year. It may also be a good idea if the taxpayer was paying a higher rate of tax in the earlier year.

The claim to backdate the gift has to be made on the *original* self-assessment tax return of the earlier year; the legislation is clear that the claim to carry back cannot be made in an amended tax return. In *Cameron* (where the taxpayer had included it on an amended return), Judge Hellier commented that "common sense and fairness appear to be on the taxpayer's side", but it was still held that the legislation was "unambiguous", and that an amended self-assessment tax return could not be valid to backdate the gift aid donation.

Law: ITA 2007, s. 426
Case: *Cameron v HMRC* [2010] UKFTT 104 (TC)

Requirements of the individual

The taxpayers making the gift aid donations must simply complete the gift aid declaration confirming they have paid enough income or capital gains tax in the appropriate tax year. Since 2011, there is no longer any restriction on their tax residence status.

Requirements of the gift

A gift will qualify for gift aid as long as seven conditions are satisfied. These are that the gift is:

- a payment of a sum of money;
- not subject to any conditions (as to repayment);
- not a "payroll giving donation" (see **8.5.2**), as such donations are subject to different rules);
- not deductible from income for tax purposes;

- not associated with any arrangement for the charity to acquire property from the individual or a connected person;
- not in substance a waiver of entitlement to sums due to the individual from the charity in respect of an amount advanced to the charity (irrespective of social investment relief); and
- not associated with any benefits, other than those within specified statutory limits.

Law: ITA 2007, s. 16

Requirements of the charity

The charity must retain a gift aid declaration from the donor, having explained to the donor its significance, with a proper audit trail.

Higher or additional rate taxpayers

As seen above, gift aid ensures that basic rate tax relief is given, but individuals paying tax at a higher rate are entitled to further relief. To achieve this, the basic tax rate band of the taxpayer (see **3.5.3**) is increased by the gross amount of the gift. This has the effect that more of the donor's taxable income falls into the basic rate band, saving tax automatically at the amount of the gross donation multiplied by the differential between the higher and basic rate bands, which is 20%. This will leave the donor with a 20% tax saving at source (through paying 80% rather than a 100% of the donation) and a further 20% saving as more income is taxed at 20% rather than 40%.

This works just as neatly for an additional rate tax payer, giving the additional tax relief of 25%.

Example

Reagan and her sister Reilly are both committed to giving to charity. They are both taxpayers and so make the gift aid declarations for their donations every year. Reagan is a 40% taxpayer, earning £70,000. Reilly pays tax at the additional rate as she earns £165,000.

In 2021-22 they make donations to charity of £8,000 each.

20% of their tax relief is obtained at source, as they each pay £8,000 but the charity receives £10,000 in respect of each sister (£8,000 directly from each sister and a further £2,000 for each from HMRC).

Further relief will be obtained by increasing their basic tax rate bands by the gross amount of their donations.

Without the increase their taxable income would be as follows:

	Total income	Non-savings income	Total income	Non-savings income
	Reagan		Reilly	
	£	£	£	£
Taxable income	70,000	70,000	165,000	165,000
Personal allowance	(12,570)	(12,570)	Abated	Abated
Taxable income	57,430	57,430	165,000	165,000

Their tax liabilities would then be calculated as follows (assuming, for simplicity, that all income is taxed as non-savings income):

	Total income	Total tax due	Total income	Total tax due
	Reagan		Reilly	
	£	£	£	£
Tax at basic rate £37,700 x 20%	37,700	7,540	37,700	7,540
Tax at higher rate **Reagan** (£57,430-£37,700) x 40%	19,730	7,892		
Reilly (£150,000-37,700) x 40%			112,300	44,920
Tax at additional rate £15,000 x 45%			15,000	6,750
Total income tax liability	57,430	15,432	165,000	59,210

However, as they have paid £8,000 to charity each and are higher and additional rate taxpayers respectively, they have received 20% tax relief at source by signing the gift aid declaration and can now extend the basic rate band by the gross amount of the gift (£8,000 x 100/80 = £10,000), in order to obtain the additional 20% and 25% tax relief respectively. With the gift relief band extension the tax payable will be as follows:

	Total income	Total tax due	Total income	Total tax due
	Reagan		**Reilly**	
	£	£	£	£
Tax at basic rate (£37,700 + £10,000) x 20%	47,700	9,540	47,700	9,540
Tax at higher rate **Reagan** (£57,430-£47,700) x 40%	9,730	3,892		
Reilly (£150,000 + £10,000)-£47,700 = £112,300 x 40%			112,300	44,920
Tax at additional rate (£165,000- £112,300- £47,700)			5,000	2,250
Total income tax liability	57,430	13,432	165,000	56,710

Reagan's tax payable has reduced from £15,432 to £13,432, a saving of £2,000 representing the other 20% of the gross gift of £10,000. The first 20% she received from being able to pay the donation net of 20% and the second 20% through the extension of the tax bands.

Reilly receives 20% relief by paying the donation net of 20% and a further 25% through the extension of the basic rate tax bands.

3.5.7   Pension contributions

The system of tax relief for personal pension contributions also works by extension of the basic rate band. These are contributions that are said to have received tax relief at source as the system again gives tax relief at the point of the contribution.

A taxpayer wishing to pay £100 into a pension pot only needs to pay 80% (i.e. £80). The other £20 is added by HMRC.

As with gift aid, further relief is given to higher and additional rate taxpayers by extending the basic rate tax band (see the example at **3.5.6** immediately above). See also **30.2.5** for further examples.

Law: ITA 2007, s. 413, 414, 416

3.6 Step six – deducting the tax reducers

3.6.1 Overview

Deducting the tax reducers is the sixth step outlined by ITA 2007, s. 23.

3.6.2 Marriage allowance

The marriage allowance (not to be confused with the married couple's allowance available where at least one party to a marriage was born before 6 April 1935 – see **3.6.3**) gives the facility to transfer 10% of the personal allowance between spouses and civil partners. To qualify, neither spouse should be liable to tax at a rate higher than the basic rate or the dividend ordinary rate and this must still be the case even if the dividend allowance is ignored. Given that the amount of the transfer is a percentage and not an absolute number, this will increase with increases of the personal allowance.

To be eligible for the marriage allowance, the residence condition is the same as for the personal allowance (see **3.4.2**) but the couple do not need to be living together during the tax year. In the year of the marriage, or forming the civil partnership, the allowance is available in full, as it is for the year in which one of the couple dies.

The transferor

The partner who gives up part of the personal allowance is known as the transferor or the "relinquishing spouse or civil partner" per the legislation. The transferor then retains 90% of his or her personal allowance, rather than 100%, so in 2021-22, this will be £11,310 (actually £11,313 rounded – see below) rather than £12,570.

The recipient

The recipient is the partner who receives the benefit of the extra personal allowance (the "gaining party" per the legislation). This party receives the benefit as a "tax reducer" rather than an extra personal allowance as such.

The recipient will therefore receive a direct £252 deduction to his or her tax liability. This is calculated by taking 10% of the personal allowance received, so £1,257 (£12,570 x 10%), rounding this up to the closest multiple of £10, and multiplying it by the basic rate of 20%. So the actual reduction is £252, calculated as £1,260, at 20%. A negative figure cannot lead to a repayment of tax for the recipient.

The election

The transferor must make the application for the transfer online, via HMRC's marriage allowance digital service on the government website. This process amends the tax codes of both the transferor and the recipient.

A claim must be made within four years from the end of the tax year to which it relates, so in 2021-22 claims can be backdated to the 2017-18 tax year (if the couple were eligible for the allowance in the intervening years but had not yet claimed). The amount to be claimed will be based on the personal allowance in the tax year(s) for which the claim is made.

Once a claim has been made for the marriage allowance, and the couple continue to satisfy the conditions, the transfer will happen automatically every year until the conditions for the allowance cease or the transfer is cancelled by the transferor. The election will cease where one or both of the couple are no longer paying tax at the basic rate, one of the couple is deceased, or the couple are no longer in a relationship.

The marriage allowance is not available to those claiming the married couple's allowance. Usually, it will be more beneficial to claim the married couple's allowance if both are an option.

Law: ITA 2007, s. 55B, 55C, 55D

3.6.3   Married couple's allowance

The married couple's allowance (MCA) is only available for elderly taxpayers, where one of the couple was born before 6 April 1935, so aged at least 86 in 2021-22. Claimants need to satisfy the residence requirements seen at **3.4.1**.

The term "married" is now a misnomer, as civil partners have also been able to claim since 5 December 2005. For marriages and civil partnerships since that date, the allowance is given to the partner with the higher net income, even if he or she is not at least 86 in 2021-22.

Before this date, the allowance was, by default, given to the husband of the couple (irrespective of whether his birthday was prior to 6 April 1935). If the spouses party to a marriage entered into prior to 5 December 2005 wish to move to the newer rules they must make an irrevocable joint election before the tax year from which they wish the new rules to apply.

The MCA must be apportioned in the year of marriage but is given in full in the year of a separation. In years after the separation, the MCA may not be claimed. If the separation is not permanent or is due to other factors rather than a wish to conclude the relationship – such as sickness, working away, being in care due to old age, problems with immigration, or being incarcerated – the MCA will still be available. The full MCA is available in the year in which the claimant dies.

The amount

The total amount of the MCA in 2021-22 is £9,125. It is not, however, added to the personal allowance like the blind person's allowance, but is given as a "tax reducer", meaning that the deduction comes directly from the calculated amount of tax payable. The deduction is a flat rate of 10% of the total allowance, so the tax reduction is £913.

The restriction

In the same way that the personal allowance is restricted for those whose adjusted net income is over £100,000, so the MCA is restricted for those whose adjusted net income is over £30,400 (for 2021-22). For every £2 by which adjusted net income is above £30,400, £1 will be deducted from the MCA available to the taxpayer. However, the MCA can never be reduced below a specified minimum amount (£3,530 in 2021-22). The minimum tax saving for any eligible taxpayer will therefore be £353.

Transfer of the MCA

If the primary claimant does not have enough income to use all or part of the MCA reduction, or if the couple prefer to share the allowance, the MCA may be transferred wholly or partly to the other partner.

Law: ITA 2007, s. 44-47

Claiming

For those needing to complete a self-assessment return, there is space on the return for claiming the MCA. Others can claim by contacting HMRC, and will need to provide details of the marriage or civil partner ceremony and also of the spouse or civil partner (including date of birth).

3.6.4   Maintenance relief

When a couple divorces, or a civil partnership ends, "maintenance" may be payable to a former spouse or civil partner, for the recipient personally and/or for any children. Usually this is paid by the ex-spouse with the higher income to the ex-spouse with the lower income. It can be awarded for a defined period only, or indefinitely, and can be paid in one lump sum or by regular payments.

Maintenance payments are paid out of taxed income but are then tax-free in the hands of the recipient. If made regularly (rather than as a lump sum), and in accordance with a court order (or similar written agreement in the EU), such payments can in certain cases obtain a small form of relief from income tax.

As for the MCA, such relief is only available for elderly taxpayers, born before 6 April 1935, and is similarly received by way of a tax reducer. The couple must be divorced, or have had their civil partnership annulled, and they cannot be still living together. The relief is given to the payer on the amount of payments due and paid during the year, but capped at £3,530. Tax relief is a reduction of 10% of this figure, so the maximum tax relief in 2021-22 is £353.

Example

Rana married Mauve in 1973 but they divorced in 1986. The court ordered Rana to pay maintenance payments of £4,000 annually, which he has paid every year since. Rana is now 88 years old, is single, and has an annual income from a private pension of £27,000. Mauve is 85.

Rana will be eligible for a tax reducer of £353 (10% of the lower of £3,350 and £4,000).

Law: ITA 2007, s. 453-455

3.7 Step seven – additional tax and the deduction of tax paid at source

3.7.1 Introduction and overview

Calculating any additional tax due is the final step (step seven) outlined by ITA 2007, s. 23.

Although not an official step in the legislation, it is also necessary to deduct any income tax that has already been paid for the tax year, either by the taxpayer or on the taxpayer's behalf, by another party. So, deduction of tax paid at source is incorporated into this final step. Common examples of this are tax payments made to HMRC through PAYE or by a trustee or executor.

3.7.2 Additional tax

There are several examples of situations where additional tax needs to be calculated.

Gift aid payments – various circumstances

Where an individual makes a donation net under basic rate tax to a charity, the gift is deemed to be net of tax at 20%. If the taxpayer was a Scottish or Welsh taxpayer, his or her tax rate may well have been less than 20%. Any difference would be charged at this stage.

Again, because donations to charity under gift aid are treated as being net of 20% basic rate tax, if the tax liability after the deduction of any tax reducers is less than the relief given at source, the balance may be charged as an extra liability here.

Where there is a "tainted" gift aid donation, the relief at source is re-charged to the donor. A gift is tainted if there are "arrangements" that secure a direct or indirect financial advantage to the donor or anyone connected to the donor from the charity or a connected charity.

Law: ITA 2007, s. 414, 809ZJ, 809ZN, 813A

Pension payments – various circumstances

If pension contributions generate relief at source (such as personal or group pension contributions), the relief is given the appropriate basic rate (English, Scottish or Welsh). If the wrong rate was applied, any adjustments or amendments will be made at this stage (except where a Scottish taxpayer has not paid enough income tax to cover the relief given at source because he or she pays tax at the Scottish starter rate).

A short-service lump sum charge is levied if a member's payment to a pension scheme is refunded when the employment ends. If the amount received by the member is more than the contributions made by the member, the fund must have grown and a tax charge is payable.

An unauthorised payments surcharge occurs when there are unauthorised pension payments to a member or sponsoring employer. The surcharge is incurred if the value of the unauthorised payment made to a member of a pension scheme (or to a sponsoring employer) is 25% or more of the fund value, or where more than one unauthorised payment is made to one of the members or sponsoring employers in a given period. The surcharge is payable as well as the charge.

The lifetime allowance charge (see **Chapter 30**) is incurred when benefits are payable from a pension scheme in which payments into the pension scheme, which have been tax relieved, exceed the lifetime limit (£1,073,100 for 2020-21 to 2025-26). The government has now legislated to remove the link that the lifetime allowance currently has to the consumer price index, and the £1,073,100 level will be maintained for the tax years 2021-22 to 2025-26.

The annual allowance charge is applied to excess pension input amounts over and above the annual allowance available for that taxpayer (see **Chapter 30**).

Law: FA 2004, s. 192B, 205, 208, 209, 214, 227

State pension lump sum

Prior to 6 April 2016, if the state pension age was reached, part of the state pension could be deferred and rolled up into a lump sum. If, after a period of deferral of the pension income, the individual started claiming the state pension, income tax on the lump sum was charged only at the individual's marginal income tax rate, even if the lump sum straddled another tax band.

This is because the receipt of the lump sum does not count as a part of "total income", as that might affect the availability or calculation of the married couple's allowance or other age-related allowances. It therefore has no impact on the tax rates charged on other income but, instead, tax at the marginal rate on the lump sum is added here.

High income child benefit charge

If the taxpayer receives child benefit, but the adjusted net income of the taxpayer or of his or her partner is between £50,000 and £60,000, the child benefit will be abated through a tax charge on the higher-earning partner.

A person liable to the charge is required to declare the child benefit on his or her self-assessment return, and to register for self-assessment if not already required to complete a return. See **33.5.6**.

The Low Incomes Tax Reform Group (LITRG) also offers useful commentary on this charge.

Law: ITEPA 2003, s. 681B

Guidance: www.gov.uk/child-benefit-tax-charge/pay-the-charge; https://tinyurl.com/9k7m8m56 (LITRG guidance)

3.7.3 Deductions of tax paid at source

PAYE

Earnings from employment, and pension income, are received by the individual taxpayer net of tax already deducted through the Pay As You Earn (PAYE) system. Although the amounts earned in the tax year must be entered gross into the tax computation, any income tax already paid can be offset. Sometimes further income tax is due if the employer has not deducted enough income tax, or there could be an overpayment, for example if the employee's tax code was incorrect or not up to date.

Payments on account

It may also be necessary to deduct payments on account. Taxpayers must make these unless their self-assessment tax payable was under £1,000, or they already paid at least 80% of the total tax liability at source. Payments on account must be paid by 31 January in the tax year, and by 31 July after the end of the tax year. Each is calculated as 50% of the previous year's tax due, excluding any CGT.

For example, if the tax liability for 2021-22, after deducting amounts paid at source, is £5,000, this amount will be used as an estimate of the tax liability for the following tax year, 2022-23. Half of this figure, £2,500, has to be paid on 31 January 2023 and the other half on 31 July 2023.

Tax for 2022-23 is due to be paid on 31 January 2024. If the liability is, say, £7,000, the £5,000 paid on account is deducted to leave £2,000 as the balancing tax payment for 2022-23. A payment on account for 2023-24 of £3,500 will be added to this amount, and so the system continues.

A taxpayer whose income reduces, or whose tax reliefs increase, may apply to reduce payments on account, at any time up to 31 January following the end of the tax year in question. Interest will always be charged on amounts underpaid, and penalties may also be imposed if the claim was fraudulent or negligent.

Law: TMA 1970, s. 59A

Investment income

Since 5 April 2016, all banks and building societies have paid interest gross. Dividends are also paid gross without a tax credit (unless the taxpayer is non-UK resident).

However, if an individual receives interest from a company, basic rate tax will have been deducted and paid to HMRC by the company, so the taxpayer will receive the interest net of income tax.

Law: ITA 2007, s. 874

Non-resident landlord scheme

Income tax may have been deducted at source if the taxpayer's "usual place of abode" is outside the UK and if he or she is earning income from property in the UK. If this is the case the obligation is on the tenant or the agent to pay the rent to the landlord net of basic rate income tax. If tax has been deducted at source in this way, it can be subtracted at this point in the calculation.

A landlord who prefers to receive the rent in full, and to pay income tax on it through self-assessment, will need to apply to do so by completing a form NRL1 (see **38.7**).

Law: ITA 2007, s. 971

Trustee or personal representative payments

Tax may also be deducted at source where trustees or personal representatives pass income payments to the taxpayer with a tax credit (see **Chapters 41** and **42**). The taxpayer can reduce the income tax accordingly.

3.8   Comprehensive example

Renée is 62 years old. She is the managing director of a company making fitness watches, Runsfit Ltd, and she holds 100% of the shares. She set the company up in 2016 and took out a personal loan to buy the share capital, on which she pays £900 interest every year. For 2021-22, she has other income from various sources, including her salary and dividends from Runsfit Ltd, as listed below.

	£
HSBC interest	13,678
Barclays interest	272
Dividends from broker	24,670
Dividends from Runsfit Ltd	65,500
Salary and benefits from Runsfit Ltd	15,500
PAYE deducted	586

In addition, she loaned her brother's company £40,000 in 2020 and the loan document agreed a 2.5% interest payment annually which the company always pays on time, a gross amount of £1,000 (on which the company will deduct tax of £200 and pay it over to HMRC).

In March 2021, Renée's father died and named her as the residuary beneficiary of the estate. The period of administration was ongoing at 5 April 2022 and the executors sent Renée the following form R185 summarising the income she had been assigned during the tax year.

	Gross £	Tax £
Non-savings income	3,000	600
Dividends	1,800	135

Renée paid £8,000 into a personal pension plan during the year and gifted £2,400 to the Red Cross. She completed a gift aid declaration on the donation.

Step one – identify the amounts of income on which Renée is charged to income tax for the tax year.

	Total income £	Non-savings income £	Savings income £	Dividend income £
Employment income – Runsfit Ltd	15,500	15,500		
Bank interest	13,950		13,950	
Interest from brother's company	1,000		1,000	
Income from deceased estate	4,800	3,000		1,800
Dividend income	90,170			90,170
Total income	125,420	18,500	14,950	91,970

Step two – deduct any reliefs to which Renée is entitled.

Renée has paid qualifying interest on the loan she took out to purchase the shares in her close company. This can be deducted from the total income to find the net income for the year.

	Total income £	Non-savings income £	Savings income £	Dividend income £
Total income as above	125,420	18,500	14,950	91,970
Qualifying loan interest	(900)	(900)		
Net income	124,520	17,600	14,950	91,970

Step three – deduct any allowances to which Renée is entitled for the tax year.

As Renée is not blind, she will only be entitled to the personal allowance. However, because she has net income above £100,000, her adjusted net income must be considered. If it is above £100,000, the personal allowance available to Renée will be reduced accordingly.

Renée's adjusted net income was:

	£
Net income	124,520
Less: Gross gift aid payments (£2,400 x 100/80)	(3,000)
Gross personal pension payments (£8,000 x 100/80)	(10,000)
	111,520

As Renée's adjusted net income is £11,520 more than £100,000 the personal allowance will be reduced by half of the excess. Half of the excess is 11,520 x 50% = £5,760.

The final personal allowance will therefore be £6,810 (£12,570 - £5,760):

	Total income	Non-savings income	Savings income	Dividend income
	£	£	£	£
Net income	124,520	17,600	14,950	91,970
Personal allowance	(6,810)	(6,810)		
Taxable income	117,710	10,790	14,950	91,970

Steps four and five – calculate the tax at each applicable rate on the different components of Renée's income.

First, it is necessary to establish what the amended basic rate band is, as Renée has contributed to a personal pension scheme as a higher rate taxpayer and she has made a donation and signed a gift aid declaration. The band will thus be increased by the gross amount of both transfers which are £ 10,000 and £3,000 respectively, so the bands are now:

	£
Basic rate band – first (£37,700 + £13,000)	50,700
Higher rate band – next ((£150,000 + £13,000) – £50,700)	112,300

	Total income £	Total tax due £
Tax on non-savings income at basic rate £10,790 x 20%	10,790	2,158
Personal savings allowance £500 as a higher rate taxpayer x 0%	500	0
Tax on savings income at basic rate (£14,950 – £500) x 20%	14,450	2,890
Dividend allowance	2,000	0
Dividend income at dividend ordinary rates Balance of basic rate band (£50,700-£10,790 -£500-£14,450-£2,000) = £22,960 x 7.5%	22,960	1,722
Dividend income at upper rates (£91,970 - 2,000 - 22,960) = £67,010 x 32.5%	67,010	21,778
Total income tax liability	117,710	28,548

Step six – Deduct any tax reducers to which Renée is entitled.

As Renée was not born before 1935, she will not be entitled to either the married couple's allowance or the maintenance payments tax reducers, even if she was married or divorced and paying spousal support. As she is not a basic rate taxpayer, even if she was married or in a civil partnership, she could not claim a percentage of her partner's personal allowance. None of the tax reducers will thus apply to Renée.

Step seven – Add any additional liabilities and/or make any allowable deductions.

As Renée received taxed income from the executors of her father's estate, she can offset this amount as a tax credit. In addition, as her brother's company deducted the tax on the interest she received, she can offset the tax paid on that interest. Finally, she has paid PAYE in the year which can reduce the amounts she is due to pay.

	Total tax due £
Total income tax liability – as above	28,548
Tax reducers	–
Net income tax liability	28,548
Deduction for tax credit on income from estate (£600 + £135)	(735)
Deduction for tax credit on income from brother's company (£1,000 x 20%)	(200)
Deduction for tax paid through PAYE	(586)
Total income tax payable	27,027

As Renée's income tax liability is over £1,000, and has not been 80% collected at source, she will need to pay both this year's income tax of £27,027 and two payments on account in advance for 2022-23. The first payment on account is of £13,513 on 31 January 2023, making a total payment of £40,540 on that day, and the second is of £13,514, due on 31 July 2023.

3.9   Pitfalls and planning points

One spouse incurring the higher rate band and one with the basic rate band

If one spouse is a basic rate payer, or a non-taxpayer, and one is a higher rate taxpayer, the marriage allowance is not available. Consideration should be made to transferring income-generating assets to the other spouse enough to maximise the personal allowance, the starting rate band, the personal savings allowance or the dividend allowance of the basic rate or non-tax paying spouse. This may also help to avoid the high income child benefit charge.

The married couple's allowance

It is the income received by the partner with the higher level of income that is relevant for the MCA restriction, not the income of the spouse who is old enough to obtain eligibility. Transferring assets may again be helpful, and it may also be worth reviewing which partner is making gift aid payments.

Law: ITTOIA 2005, s. 626

Non-residents landlord scheme

The scheme applies to individuals who spend more than six months a year living abroad; it does not matter if they are considered UK or non-UK resident under the statutory residence test. If abroad for more than six months, deductions of tax must be made from the tenants or agents unless an application is made to HMRC for the landlord to receive the income gross.

Family distribution of the personal allowance

Income up to the level of the personal allowance is free from income tax completely. It has always been good planning therefore to ensure that a taxpayer does have income up to this amount, and distributions of income within families often occur to allow this to be realised (within the anti-avoidance parameters). For example, a spouse or child could be employed on a part-time basis in the family business in order to earn up to the personal allowance. As the personal allowance has increased over the years, regular reviews should be undertaken to try to use the whole of each personal allowance.

However, remuneration must always be at a fair and acceptable level. If it is too high, an adjustment will need to be made to the business profits.

If too low, the requirements of the national living/minimum wage may be breached. There is an exception for a family business, in the case of an employee who is participating in the running of the business and who lives in the family home of the employer. However, this does not apply to limited companies, as these are a separate legal entity.

Law: SI 2015/621, reg. 58
Guidance: NMWM 05160

Filing of tax returns

Penalties are charged for late returns and late payments of tax (see **Chapter 2**). The penalties are chargeable even if the return shows a repayment, so taxpayers should ensure that returns are made in good time to avoid such penalties. Various relaxations have been applied in connection with Covid-19, and reference should be made to online sources (see **Appendix 11**) to check the current position.

Law: FA 2009 s. 106, Sch. 55

Notification of new sources of income

Any new source of income must be notified to HMRC by 5 October in the year after the new source is due to be taxed, unless the individual is already within self-assessment. This gives HMRC an opportunity to send a notice to file a tax return. Again, there are penalties for non-compliance based on the amount of tax outstanding. A taxpayer who does not need to submit a tax return, or notify a new source, must still notify HMRC if subject to a high income child benefit charge.

Tax underpayments

If the tax calculation shows an additional income tax liability of £3,000 or less, and the taxpayer is an employee, he or she can arrange to have the underpayment collected through PAYE. A further advantage of this is that payments on account may no longer fall due as at least 80% of the individual's tax may end up being collected at source.

Reductions of payments on account

Taxpayers need to be careful if applying to reduce payments on account, as any reduction not reflected in the final amount of tax liability will attract interest from the date of the due date for the payment on account to the date of the eventual payment. If the application was made fraudulently or negligently, penalties may also be incurred.

Changing levels of income

Individuals may have more income in some years than in others. Examples of this may be fluctuating employment bonuses or the impact of external economic factors such as the Covid-19 pandemic on business profits. Years with lower income may be a good time to receive savings income and dividend income, or to realise income by surrendering single premium bonds or by selling units in non-reporting offshore funds.

Personal allowance abatement

The personal allowance is abated by £1 for every £2 the taxpayer's income is over £100,000 (see **3.4.2** above). This makes the point between £100,000 and £125,140 a very expensive marginal income level with earnings being taxed at the marginal tax rate of 60% plus NIC. This can be relieved by contributing to personal pensions, donating to charity, or paying qualifying loan interest. Consideration could also be given to investing in capital-producing investment products, rather than income producing ones, to reduce income to below £100,000.

4. Devolution of taxes

4.1 Introduction

4.1.1 History

Prior to 1999, all parts of the United Kingdom were accountable to a central UK government. However, as a result of referenda in Scotland and Wales in 1997, and in Northern Ireland in 1998, decentralisation in 1999 formed three separate administrations: one in Scotland, one in Wales and one in Northern Ireland. These administrations were formed by, respectively, the *Scotland Act* 1998, the *Government of Wales Act* 1998 and the *Northern Ireland Act* 1998.

The process of the formation of these administrations was called "devolution", and it allowed each administration a measure of self-government. Powers were given to the Scottish and Welsh governments and to the Northern Ireland Executive.

Despite this devolution, all UK tax legislation continued to be enacted in Westminster by the central government. The then Inland Revenue collected the taxes on behalf of the Treasury. The Treasury then decided how these taxes would be spent. This created a gap between the devolved administrations' ability to generate taxes and their spending; the responsibility and legislative powers for *generating* the taxes having remained with central UK government.

However, Scotland and Wales do now have certain tax raising powers.

Scottish income tax was implemented following the Calman commission with the *Scotland Act* 2012, taking effect from 6 April 2016, for the 2016-17 tax year. Welsh income tax was implemented following the Silk commission and the *Wales Act* 2014. Income tax rates were implemented from April 2019, for the 2019-20 tax year.

Although the UK parliament still retains the power to legislate on all matters throughout the UK, and so remains sovereign, the UK government has made it clear that it will not do so in respect of devolved matters without the permission of the administration in question.

Law: *Northern Ireland Act* 1998; *Scotland Acts* 1998, 2012 and 2016; *Wales Acts* 1998 (superseded by the *Government of Wales Act* 2006), 2014 and 2017

Guidance: https://tinyurl.com/The-Calman-commission; https://tinyurl.com/The-Silk-commission

4.1.2   Which taxes are devolved?

Scotland

Taxes devolved to Scotland are:

- stamp duty land tax ("land and buildings transaction tax");
- landfill tax ("Scottish landfill tax");
- income tax for non-savings and non-dividend income (except for the personal allowance);
- some VAT collected in Scotland (may be assigned to Scotland, but temporarily on hold); and
- some local taxes (such as council tax and business rates).

Revenue Scotland are responsible for the collection of these taxes (and local councils for local taxes). In 2020-21, 31% of revenue from taxes in Scotland was derived from devolved taxes.

Wales

Taxes devolved to Wales are:

- stamp duty land tax ("land transaction tax");
- landfill tax (Welsh landfills disposals tax);
- income tax for non-savings and non-dividend income (partially only: UK income tax rates have been reduced by 10p in each band, then the Welsh government applies its own rate of income tax); and
- local taxes (such as business rates).

The Welsh Revenue Authority are responsible for the collection of these taxes (and local councils for local taxes).

In 2020-21, 20% of revenue from taxes in Wales was derived from devolved taxes.

Northern Ireland

Taxes devolved to Northern Ireland are:

- corporation tax (subject to commencement regulations);
- landfill tax; and
- local taxes, including domestic and business rates.

Guidance: https://tinyurl.com/Devolved-taxes-statistics

4.1.3   Tax codes

The tax code issued by HMRC to a Scottish taxpayer will be prefixed with an S, and to a Welsh taxpayer with a C.

4.2   The Scottish rate of income tax

4.2.1   A Scottish taxpayer

The headline definition of a Scottish taxpayer from the government site states that:

"You pay Scottish income tax if you live in Scotland."

However, this is not the full definition of a Scottish taxpayer in the *Scotland Act* 1998 (as amended). In fact, the Scottish rate of income tax (SRIT) is charged on any taxpayer under s. 80D of that Act who is resident in the UK per the statutory residence test (including one who is able to use the split year – see **Chapter 34**), and:

- has a close connection with Scotland;
- has no close connection with England, Wales or Northern Ireland, but spends more days in Scotland than in any other part of the UK; or
- is a Scottish Parliamentarian.

For most taxpayers the question will be determined by the place of residence, so it is usually fair to say that an individual will be liable to pay the SRIT if he or she "lives in Scotland".

Furthermore, if a taxpayer does *not* live in Scotland, he would not be considered to have a close connection to Scotland (and thus wouldn't be classified as a Scottish taxpayer). This is true even if he regards himself as Scottish, for example because he grew up in Scotland or had Scottish ancestry. Similarly, even if he works in Scotland, receives a pension from

Scotland or visits often, a liability to SRIT will not arise unless he lives there.

Close connection

A close connection is a concept stemming from the *Scotland Act* 1998 and defines a close connection with other parts of the UK as well as to Scotland. A close connection can be established by considering two scenarios: a taxpayer with only one place of residence in the UK and a taxpayer with more than one.

If the taxpayer has only one residence in the UK, a close connection (with either England or Scotland, for example) is evident when the taxpayer lives in that residence for at least a part of the year. For example, if a taxpayer had only one residence and this was in Scotland, a close connection to Scotland would be evident – even if that taxpayer lived in his residence for only part of the year, and even if he had visited England several other times in the year.

If the taxpayer has more than one residence in the UK, a close connection to a certain part of the UK is evident when the taxpayer's *main* residence is in that part of the UK and he or she actually lives in it for at least a part of the year. If the individual changes his main residence during the year from one part of the UK to another (say from England to Scotland or *vice versa*), or concurrently has two residences, one in each part, he will have a close connection to the part in which he spends the longest time in that main residence.

Place of residence

Although reference is made several times in the legislation to the "place of residence", the term is not defined therein. HMRC state in their guidance that it should be given its ordinary meaning and confirm that this has been supported by much case law. The ordinary meaning given to one's place of residence has been given as:

> "the dwelling in which that person habitually lives; in other words his or her home"

or

> "a place that a reasonable onlooker, with knowledge of the material facts, would regard as the dwelling in which that person habitually lives".

The question of whether the property is rented or owned is not of consequence to the definition of place of residence. Nor does the property need to be occupied continuously to be classified as a main residence. However, a holiday home or such other "temporary retreat" would not be classed as a place of residence.

Example

Ramsay is UK resident under the statutory residence test (SRT) in 2021-22. He works as a teacher in Glasgow, and lives with his parents in a small cottage in Kirk of Shotts.

Ramsay's two sisters Rhona and Rodina are also UK resident under the SRT. Rhona lived in an apartment in Edinburgh which she sold on 13 May 2021 and moved to London renting a flat there from 14 May. Rodina works full time 37.5 hours a week in a café in Gretna (Scotland) but lives in Penrith (England) a short half an hour's drive away.

Are Ramsay, Rhona and Rodina Scottish taxpayers in 2021-22?

Ramsay

Ramsay does not own the residence that he lives in, but this is not fatal to having a place of residence in any part of the UK. It is his only residence in the UK and because it is in Scotland, Ramsay's place of residence is in Scotland. As such, he will have a close connection to Scotland and be a Scottish taxpayer.

Rhona

Rhona has had two places of residence during 2021-22. Between 6 April and 12 May 2021, her main place of residence was Scotland, and from 13 May it was in England. As Rhona has spent more time in her main residence in England than in her main home in Scotland during the tax year, she will not be classified a Scottish taxpayer for 2021-22.

Rodina

Rodina, like Ramsay, only has one residence. This residence is in England, so despite her working full time in Scotland, and commuting there every day, she has a close connection with England not Scotland and will not be a Scottish taxpayer.

Law: *Scotland Act* 1998, s. 80D
Guidance: STTG 2000, 3000, 3400, 3600

4.2.2   Scottish income tax

Scottish tax is only charged on income that is non-savings and non-dividend income. Examples of income that fall into this category would be:

- employment income (including salary, wages, benefits in kind and bonuses);
- trading income from self-employment and partnership income;
- property income;
- pension income (including state, personal and occupational);
- some state benefits and grants (such as the Self-Employment Income Support Scheme (SEISS));
- income from trusts; and
- royalty income.

Income from banks and building societies, other income classified as savings income, and dividend income is not affected by Scottish rates and the normal UK rates will be applied to these sources of income. These will also be calculated the same way for Scottish taxpayers as non-Scottish taxpayers (see **Chapters 23** and **24)**.

The rates of Scottish income tax for 2021-22 are as follows:

Bands of taxable income	Cumulative income £	Absolute income £	Scottish tax rate
Starter	0-2,097	2,097	19%
Basic	2,098-12,726	10,629	20%
Intermediate	12,727-31,092	18,366	21%
Higher	31,093-150,000	118,908	41%
Top	Over 150,000	Excess	46%

The mechanics for the calculation of non-savings income are the same using the Scottish rates as they are using the normal UK rates, using steps one to seven as outlined at **3.1.2**.

Example

Roidsear is a Scottish taxpayer living and working in Aberdeen. He is a company director and his only source of income is his salary. He is paid £160,000 in basic salary and earned a £20,000 bonus in 2021-22.

His income tax is calculated as follows:

	Total income £	Non-savings income £
Employment income	180,000	180,000
Total income	180,000	180,000
Personal allowance	Fully abated	(–)
Taxable income	180,000	180,000

His taxable income will be taxed as follows:

	Total income £	Total tax due £
Tax on non-savings income at starter rate: £2,097 x 19%	2,097	398
Tax on non-savings income at basic rate: £10,629 x 20%	10,629	2,125
Tax on non-savings income at intermediate rate: £18,366 x 21%	18,366	3,856
Tax on non-savings income at higher rate: £118,908 x 41%	118,908	48,752
Tax on non-savings income at top rate: £30,000 x 46%	30,000	13,800
Total income tax liability	180,000	68,931

4.3 The Welsh rate of income tax

As in Scotland, the devolution of taxes has allowed the Senedd (formerly the Welsh Assembly until May 2020) to alter the income tax of Welsh taxpayers. There has been a Welsh rate of income tax (WRIT) rate since 6 April 2019.

4.3.1   A Welsh taxpayer

The headline definition of a Welsh taxpayer from the government site states that:

"You pay Welsh income tax if you live in Wales."

Again, as with Scottish taxpayers, this is not the precise definition of a Welsh taxpayer in the *Wales Act* 2014. In fact, s. 116E of the Act shows that the WRIT is charged on all taxpayers who:

- are resident in the UK according to the statutory residence test (including those where split-year treatment applies); and

- satisfy exactly the same criteria as the Scottish taxpayers above (see **4.2.1**), but obviously with Welsh and Wales being substituted for Scottish and Scotland.

In summary, therefore, the individual needs to have a close connection with Wales, be a Welsh Parliamentarian, or not have a close connection with any other part of the UK and spend more days in Wales than any other parts of the UK in the tax year.

Law: *The Wales Act* 2014, s. 116E
Guidance: WTTG 2000, 3000, 3400, 3600

4.3.2   Welsh rates of income tax

The power to amend the income tax rates is only available for non-savings and non-dividend income. The Welsh Assembly has agreed with the central UK government that the Welsh government will pay 10 pence less for every band of tax – basic, higher and additional rate – per £1 earned, to the central Treasury. Instead, the Welsh government sets its own amount on top of this lower rate.

For example, the UK government has a basic rate of 20%, meaning that £20 is paid in income tax per £100 earned. The Welsh government is obliged to charge at least 10% and will give £10 to the central government. It then has the option to charge more, and any additional amounts charged can be kept by the Welsh government.

So far, in 2019-20 and 2020-21, the additional rate the Welsh government added to the tax rate has been 10%, meaning that the overall rates are the same as the standard UK rates. The current administration has pledged not to raise this until after the next Senedd elections, scheduled for May 2021.

For every £1 a Welsh taxpayer earns, he or she therefore pays:

To which government	Basic Rate p	Higher Rate p	Additional Rate p
To the UK government (UK income tax)	10	30	35
To the Welsh government (Welsh income tax)	10	10	10
Total income tax	20	40	45

These rates will not affect a Welsh taxpayer's savings and dividend income, which are taxed according to the UK rates.

4.4 Complications

4.4.1 The basic rate band for establishing the personal savings allowance

A basic rate taxpayer is eligible for a personal savings allowance of £1,000, which is in practice a 0% band. If the taxpayer is a higher rate taxpayer this falls to £500, and for an additional taxpayer it is £0. See **Chapter 23** for further information.

Because the Welsh tax rates are currently identical to the main UK rates there is no complication with Welsh taxpayers.

However, in order to apply this to a Scottish rate taxpayer, it is necessary to establish which tax bands put them into the basic rate band or the higher rate band in the other parts of the UK. To do this, the Scottish tax bands are ignored and the total taxable income will be compared to the basic, higher and additional rate bands for the rest of the UK. The Scottish taxpayer's position within these bands (basic, higher or additional) will determine how much of the personal savings allowance he or she is entitled to.

Example

Ròidh is a Scottish taxpayer living and working in Inverness. He is a hospital nurse and his only sources of income are his salary of £35,000 and £10,000 of interest from a bank deposit. His taxable income is £32,430, being his total income of £45,000 less the personal allowance of £12,570.

Although he will be a higher rate taxpayer under Scottish income tax rules, as he earns taxable income over £31,092, under non-Scottish tax rules he will be a basic rate taxpayer with taxable income of £32,430 falling under £37,700. He will therefore be eligible for the personal savings allowance at £1,000, not £500.

4.4.2   The marriage allowance

As set out in detail in **Chapter 3,** the marriage allowance is only available for those couples where neither is paying tax at a rate higher than the basic rate.

Welsh taxpayers must not pay income tax at any other rate than the Welsh basic rate. Given that this is the same as the UK income tax basic rate, Welsh taxpayers not paying the higher or additional rates will still be able to use the marriage allowance if they satisfy the other conditions.

Scottish taxpayers are able to use the marriage allowance if they pay tax at the starter, basic or intermediate income tax rates. If eligible, the tax reducer given for the recipient spouse will still be at 20% (the basic rate of tax in the UK) and not 21% (the Scottish basic rate).

Law: ITA 2007, s. 55B

4.4.3   Gift aid

As set out in detail at **3.5.6**, gift aid payments are deemed to be made to the charity net of basic rate tax. HMRC pay the charity the other 20% out of taxed money as long as the donor has signed a gift aid declaration.

This system operates in the same way for Scottish and Welsh taxpayers as they too pay basic rate tax at 20%. If the Scottish taxpayer is a starter rate payer, however (i.e. paying at a rate of 19%), HMRC may well be out of pocket, and the taxpayer may have to pay additional tax (see **3.7.1**).

If the donor is paying tax at an intermediate or higher rate, bands are increased by the gross amount of the gift for a Scottish taxpayer as they are for others. The starter rate is not extended.

Example

Rothach is a Scottish taxpayer living in Elgin. He is a designer of cashmere articles and earns £85,000 annually. In 2021-22 he made a £2,000 charitable donation to the Elgin Samaritans, a registered charity.

	Total income £	Non-savings income £
Employment income	85,000	85,000
Total income	85,000	85,000
Personal allowance	(12,570)	(12,570)
Taxable income	72,430	72,430

His taxable income will be calculated as:

	Total income £	Total tax due £
Tax on non-savings income at starter rate: £2,097 x 19%	2,097	398
Tax on non-savings income at basic rate: (£10,629 + (£2,000 x 100/80 = £2,500)) = £13,129 x 20%	13,129	2,625
Tax on non-savings income at intermediate rate: £18,366 x 21%	18,366	3,856
Tax on non-savings income at higher rate: £38,838 x 41%	38,838	15,923
Total income tax liability	72,430	22,802

4.5 Miscellaneous issues

4.5.1 Trusts and estates

Trustees and PRs administering death estates cannot be Scottish or Welsh taxpayers in their capacity as trustees and PRs. They will instead use the appropriate UK tax rates.

A beneficiary who receives income from a trust or an estate, and who is a Scottish or Welsh taxpayer, will be charged Scottish or Welsh tax rates on the receipt, but the tax charged in the trust and in the death estate will be UK rates.

If the trust is a discretionary trust, there will always be a tax credit on the non-savings income to be applied, irrespective of the rate incurred by the beneficiary, of 45%.

If the trust is an interest-in-possession trust, amounts will have a tax credit attached at either the UK basic or ordinary dividend rate. If the trust is settlor-interested, and the settlor is a Scottish or Welsh taxpayer, Scottish rates will be used for non-savings income. See **Chapters 23** and **24** for more information.

4.5.2   Armed forces

Members of the UK armed forces who are Scottish taxpayers will initially need to pay income tax at the Scottish rates. However, if this causes them to incur more tax than they would have had to pay as non-Scottish taxpayers, a retrospective repayment will be made to them, bringing their take-home pay to the equivalent amount of a non-Scottish taxpayer. The UK government has committed to continuing this measure indefinitely.

4.6   Pitfalls and planning points

Main residence

A main residence, for the definition of a close connection to a part of the UK, is not restricted to the property that is treated as the main residence for CGT principal private residence relief.

Record-keeping

To establish and prove a status of residence other than one of a UK resident, records may need to be kept of both evidence of residence and days spent in Scotland and elsewhere. These should be retained for at least 22 months. Self-employed taxpayers completing a self-assessment return should keep the records for at least five years after the submission deadline.

EMPLOYMENT INCOME

EMPLOYMENT LAW

5. Identifying employment income

5.1 Introduction

According to the Office for National Statistics, nearly £164 billion was deducted in PAYE in 2019-20, representing almost 26% of total annual fiscal revenues. Indeed, for most people, the income tax paid on their employment income represents the main, if not only, direct taxation they incur.

The rules relating to what constitutes employment income, how that employment income is valued and what can be disregarded as exempt have been debated, developed, amended and expanded since they were first introduced in the *Income Tax Act* 1803. Today, however, most of the relevant rules can be found in one consolidating statute, the *Income Tax (Earnings and Pensions Act)* 2003 (ITEPA 2003). Statutory references in this chapter are to ITEPA 2003 unless indicated otherwise.

ITEPA 2003 imposes a charge on "employment income". In the first instance, therefore, it is necessary to consider whether the income arises from employment or from some other source.

Guidance: ONS Tax and NIC Receipts: Statistics Table (Sept 2020)

5.2 Assessing employment status

5.2.1 Meaning of employment

Section 4 defines "employment" as any employment under a "contract of service", a "contract of apprenticeship" or "in the service of the Crown".

The statute does not go on to define what is meant by a "contract of service". However, case law indicates that there is no single satisfactory test governing the answer to this question (see *Ready Mixed Concrete*). Indeed, HMRC take the approach that employment status is a question of fact dependent on all the circumstances of the case, and in determining which circumstances are relevant, regard must be had to the debate and rulings set down in the many cases dealing with this point.

Relevant factors in determining whether someone is an employee or is self-employed are set out in the following paragraphs.

Mutuality of obligation

A key factor in determining employment status is the presence of an obligation on the engager to provide and pay for work, coupled with an obligation on the individual to accept and perform the work. Self-employed persons have no guarantee of work and typically can refuse work if it is offered to them. In contrast, employees do not have this freedom.

The existence of mutual obligation is usually obvious from the contract between the two parties. While the existence of mutual obligation is a strong indicator of employment, HMRC will not accept lack of mutual obligation on its own as conclusive to establish that there is no employment.

Right of control

In a typical employer/employee relationship, the employer tells the employee what to do, and how and by when to do it. By contrast, a self-employed person can refuse to undertake tasks and can set his or her own method of working and timescales.

Care has to be taken where specialist experts are involved. Here the individual may appear to have control over his or her own workload, e.g. a cardiac surgeon. However, where this control comes solely from the nature of the individual's expertise, it will not be an indicator of self-employment.

Multiple paymasters

A typical employee has one paymaster. By contrast, a person who typically performs services for various different businesses is more likely to be regarded as self-employed.

Right of substitution

An employee will have no freedom to send a substitute in his place if, for whatever reason, he is unable to perform his duties. Similarly, an employee will rarely be allowed to engage the services of a helper or assistant.

By contrast, if a self-employed person has contracted to do a job and is either sick or double-booked, that self-employed person will usually have the freedom to provide a substitute to complete the job in his place.

The presence of a clause in the contract giving the individual the right to provide a substitute is not usually enough. There must be clear evidence of occasions when a substitute has actually been used.

Financial risk

Employees are not usually expected to risk their own capital, so individuals who take the risk of profit or loss are highly likely to be regarded as self-employed.

Financial risk could take the form of quoting a fixed price for a job, with the consequent opportunity of additional profit if organised effectively and the risk of making a loss if there are unexpected issues.

Other examples of financial risk are:

- investment in infrastructure, overheads or training where costs are not directly recoverable from a client;
- the requirement to pay for overheads and materials in order to undertake the work; and
- the requirement to rectify unsatisfactory work at the individual's own expense.

Provision of own equipment

An employee is rarely responsible for providing his or her own equipment.

A self-employed person, on the other hand, will customarily be responsible for providing the necessary equipment to enable him or her to undertake the work offered.

Integration into the organisation

An employee will be integrated into the employer's business. Having a dedicated office space, an email address, a landline phone number, bespoke stationery, access to employee facilities such as a staff restaurant, invitations to staff functions, and access to the employer's premises (often by means of a security pass) are all indicators of an employment relationship.

Example

Jason is contracted by We Love Sweets to design and set up the window displays in its stores across the UK.

We Love Sweets guarantees to offer at least one window a month and expects Jason to accept these. Additional windows may be offered but Jason is not obliged to accept.

On receipt of a window display request, Jason must indicate a time to completion which must be within four weeks of the request. He cannot substitute another window dresser without prior approval of We Love Sweets, which has indicated that it would rather rearrange the timeframe than provide consent.

The contract can be terminated on two months' notice by either party.

Jason will be paid a set fee for each window of £3,000 plus materials which can be invoiced on completion of the window display. Jason must arrange his own transport to the relevant store at his own expense. He has free creative control but it is expected that his window displays will reflect the seasons as well as any new products We Love Sweets is offering. Pre-approval of the costs and the design must be obtained before installation commences.

Jason has no access to any premises without prior arrangement and, apart from the performance of the agreed tasks, has no other contact with We Love Sweets.

In determining Jason's employment status, the economic reality of his situation must be considered. He is guaranteed an amount of work and there is an element of control in terms of the need for pre-approval of his costs and designs. Furthermore, there is no practical right to provide a substitute. All these indicate that he is an employee.

However, the financial risk is clearly his. He must arrange his own workload and fund his own transport and equipment to complete the work. Although the costs of materials are reimbursed, he must fund the purchase up front. The fixed cost means there is an opportunity to profit if he is efficient. These factors, as well as the fact that he is not integrated into the organisation in any way, would seem to indicate he is self-employed.

Responsibility for determining whether an individual is employed or self-employed rests with the person engaging the services. It is possible to obtain the HMRC view by using the online tool, Check Employment Status for Tax (CEST). Provided the answers given to the CEST questions accurately reflect the terms and conditions under which the services are provided, HMRC will be bound by the outcome. However, the CEST tool is based on direct questions requiring yes/no answers and therefore may not be appropriate in more complex situations.

For a full discussion of employment status matters, see *Employment Status* from Claritax Books.

Law: ITEPA 2003, s. 1-4

Case: *Ready Mixed Concrete (South East) Ltd v Minister of Pensions and National Insurance* [1968] 1 All ER 433

Guidance: https://www.gov.uk/guidance/check-employment-status-for-tax (HMRC's CEST tool); *Employment Status Manual*

5.2.2   Other office-holders

Unless specifically stated otherwise, the rules on employment income also apply to income from offices such as:

- company directors, company secretaries and board members of statutory bodies;
- Crown appointments;
- appointments under the internal constitution of an organisation, such as club treasurers or trade union secretaries;
- appointments under a trust deed, such as trustees; and
- ecclesiastical appointments, such as members of the clergy.

It is possible to be both an office-holder and an employee in respect of the same position if the terms and conditions are such that the criteria for employment referred to in **5.2.1** above are satisfied.

5.3   Scope of charge

5.3.1   Meaning of general earnings

Once it is established that there is an employment or office to which ITEPA 2003 applies, the next step is to consider what income will be caught by the charging provisions.

The charge to tax is limited to general earnings and specific employment income (s. 6).

"General earnings" are defined in s. 7 as:

- earnings within s. 62;
- any amount treated as earnings where agencies or employment intermediaries are involved (see **Chapter 13**);
- any amount treated as earnings under Pt. 3, Ch. 2-10 (the benefits code – see **Chapter 6**);

- any amount treated as earnings under Pt. 3, Ch. 12 (including sick pay, sporting testimonials, payment of non-deductible expenses and payments for restrictive covenants – see **5.3.3** below); and
- balancing charges treated as earnings under CAA 2001, s. 262 (see **20.4.7**).

Section 62 states that earnings in relation to employment include:

- any salary, wages or fees;
- any gratuity or other profit or incidental benefit in kind obtained by the employee if it is money or money's worth; and
- anything else that constitutes an emolument of employment.

This definition is extremely wide. Most money payments are covered, and the definition extends beyond this to encompass benefits or profits that can be said to be "money's worth". Section 62(3) assists by defining "money's worth" as something that is "capable of being converted into money or something of direct monetary value to the employee".

Clearly, any asset that is capable of being sold is capable of being converted into money. However, the case of *Heaton v Bell* emphasises that the definition goes further than that. The employee was provided with the use of a car by his employer in return for a deduction from his wages. The car could be surrendered at any time and the wages increased to their original level. Today, the car would be taxed under the benefits code (see **6.2**), and probably be treated as being part of an optional remuneration arrangement (see **6.10**). However, at that time neither of these provisions existed. The House of Lords held that the provision of the car was an emolument because it could be turned into money by surrendering it back to the employer.

Even if an asset is not involved, the definition of money's worth extends to something that is of direct monetary value to the employee. This includes payments by the employer to discharge a debt or other pecuniary liability of the employee. The idea is that by paying money owed by the employee, money is effectively freed up for the employee to spend on something else. See *Nicoll v Austin* which involved the employer paying for the employee's heating and lighting, and *Hartland v*

Diggines where the employee's income tax was discharged by the employer on his behalf.

Law: ITEPA 2003, s. 7, 62

Cases: *Hartland v Diggines* (1926) 10 TC 247; *Nicoll v Austin* (1935) 19 TC 531; *Heaton v Bell* (1969) 46 TC 211

5.3.2 "Relating to the employment"

In order to be taxable, the earnings must relate to the employment.

Where earnings are provided in return for the performance of services, the position is clear enough. However, consideration has also to be given to other payments made by an employer.

In *Shilton v Wilmhurst,* a signing-on bonus paid to the former England goalkeeper, Peter Shilton, was regarded as an emolument from the employment he was about to enter into. It was held that payments for services about to be performed, or performed in the past, will be taxable as arising directly from the employment. (See **Chapter 9** for more detail on payments after employment ceases.)

Other lump sum payments, such as payments made to employees in recognition of changes made in their conditions of service or loss of rights, are also regarded as relating to the employment. This was demonstrated in *Hamblett v Godfrey*, where the employee received a payment of £1,000 in return for loss of employment protection, principally the right to join a trade union. Neill LJ took the view that the payment was referable to the employment and nothing else and, as such, was taxable as earnings.

Payments that are not from the employer, or are not lump sums, can also be regarded as earnings. In *Calvert v Wainwright*, a taxi driver employed by a taxi hire company was held to be chargeable in respect of tips he received on the basis that the sums were an ordinary and accepted way of rewarding the service received and, as such, must be received by reason of the employment.

However, there are limitations. It is not enough that the person who receives it happens to be an employee. Nor is it enough that it is paid by or on behalf of an employer. The earnings must come to the employee *because* he or she is an employee and for no other reason.

In *Laidler v Perry*, Lord Reid put succinctly the question that has to be answered in all cases:

"Did this profit arise from the employment? The answer will be no if it arose from something else."

In *Hochstrasser v Mayes*, Lord Radcliffe said:

"It is not sufficient to render a payment assessable that an employee would not have received it unless he had been an employee; it is assessable if it has been paid to him in return for acting as or being an employee."

Example

An independent coffee shop situated on the bottom floor of an office building decides to offer a 10% discount to all workers in the building. Janice works in the building and qualifies for the discount. Although she would not have received the benefit if she was not an employee, she is not receiving it in return for acting as or being an employee but rather because the coffee shop wants to attract custom. The discount is not taxable as employment income.

Law: ITEPA 2003, s. 7, 62

Cases: *Calvert v Wainwright* (1947) 27 TC 475; *Hochstrasser v Mayes* (1959) 38 TC 673; *Laidler v Perry* (1965) 42 TC 351; *Hamblett v Godfrey* [1987] BTC 83; *Shilton v Wilmhurst* [1991] BTC 66

5.3.3   Payments treated as "general earnings"

As mentioned above, "general earnings" also include a number of specific payments set out in ITEPA 2003.

These include payments of tax on the employee's behalf and payments while absent from work due to sickness. Details of these can be found in **Chapters 6** and **12** respectively.

Part 3, Ch. 12 also covers payments for restrictive covenants. Typical examples of restrictive covenants include employees agreeing not to approach or solicit existing customers of the employer after they leave (non-solicitation covenant) or agreeing not to work in the same industry for a period after they leave (non-competition covenant).

Payments in connection with these types of covenant are treated as general earnings if the conditions in s. 225 apply:

- a restrictive undertaking is given in connection with a current, future or past office or employment;
- the undertaking involves restrictions on conduct or activities; and

- a payment is made in respect of the giving of the undertaking or its partial or total fulfilment.

Section 225 only applies where the payment is not otherwise treated as general earnings. Therefore, a restrictive covenant contained in an employment contract would not trigger a charge under s. 225, as any payments under that employment contract are likely to be taxable already as general earnings. However, a payment made to an employee to enter into new restrictive covenants as part of a compromise agreement after termination of employment would be caught by s. 225.

It does not matter if the undertaking is absolute or qualified or whether it is legally binding or not. Furthermore, it does not matter who receives or makes the payment.

Where the payment is in the form of an asset or other valuable consideration, rather than money, the tax charge will arise on the cash value.

Law: ITEPA 2003, s. 221-226E

5.3.4 Meaning of "specific employment income"

As mentioned above, ITEPA 2003 brings specific employment income into charge as well as any general earnings. This is defined as:

- amounts charged under Pt. 6 (non-approved pension payments and payments under EFRBS – see **Chapter 31**);
- amounts charged under Pt. 7 (employment-related securities – see **Chapter 10**);
- payments treated as termination payments within s. 401, above the exemption threshold (see **Chapter 9**);
- amounts under Pt. 7A (employment income provided through third parties – see **Chapter 13**); and
- amounts which count as employment income through any other enactment.

In other words, specific employment income is income taxable under ITEPA 2003 other than general earnings. The distinction is important. Certain rules in relation to the taxation of non-UK residents and non-UK domiciles apply only to general earnings (see **Chapter 34**). Furthermore, deductible expenses relating to specific employment income can only be set off against specific employment income and deductible expenses relating to general earnings can only be set off against general earnings (see **Chapter 8**).

Law: ITEPA 2003, s. 6-7

5.4 When does the charge to income tax arise?

5.4.1 The receipts basis

Employment income is typically taxed on the "receipts" basis, as defined at s. 18. Essentially, an amount of income will be treated as received on the earliest of:

- the time when payment is made of, or on account of, the earnings (rule one);
- the time when a person becomes entitled to payment of, or on account of, the earnings (rule two); and
- if the person is a director (rule three) the earliest of:
  - o the time when sums are credited in the company's accounts or records;
  - o if the amount of earnings for a period is determined by the end of the period, the time when the period ends; and
  - o if the amount of earnings for a period is not determined until after the period ends, the time when the amount is determined.

Example

Archie (who is not a director) is paid a bonus on 31 May 2021 in relation to a work project he carried out in November 2020. Under the receipts basis, the bonus will be taxed on 31 May 2021.

Non-UK domiciled employees may be taxed on the remittance basis in relation to certain overseas employment duties (see **Chapter 37**).

Law: ITEPA 2003, s. 18

5.4.2 Meaning of the "date of payment" in rule one

The date of payment is the date the employee is first able to access the money for his or her own use and benefit.

There are various ways in which money can be "paid" to employees. The most straightforward is the handing over of cash. However, other common scenarios include:

- a cheque (the date of payment arises when the employer posts the cheque or hands it over to the employee; the date the cheque is cashed or put into the bank does not matter);
- a credit transfer to a bank or building society account;
- crediting an account in the employer's books on which the employee is free to draw at will (*Newsmith Stainless Ltd*); and
- paying the income to a third party or using it in some way at the employee's discretion or with his consent to a purpose of his choosing.

Earnings are also treated as received when a payment is made "on account of earnings", i.e. when the employer agrees to pay the employee money the employee has earned, but which is not yet due for payment.

Example

Suzanne is paid at the end of each month. In June 2021, she runs into financial difficulties and the employer agrees to pay her June salary on 15 June 2021, two weeks before it is normally paid. This is a payment on account of earnings and the date of receipt is 15 June 2021.

Care has to be taken not to confuse a payment on account with a loan. A payment to an employee where there is an expectation of repayment (even if that repayment is out of future salary payments) is not a payment on account of earnings. There may be a taxable benefit if the interest payable is at a low rate (see **Chapter 6**) but there will be no payment on account of earnings at the time the amount is advanced.

It is vital to look at the reality of the arrangement – just because something is described as a payment on account or a loan does not make it so. This was reinforced by Gibson J in *Williams v Todd* when he refused to regard an interest-free advance from an employer to his employee to purchase a new residence as a payment on account of earnings. He ruled that the existence of a right to repay on demand is enough to categorise the advance as a loan, regardless of what the parties called it.

A non-cash benefit is "paid" on the date it is first made available to the employee.

Law: ITEPA 2003, s. 18(1)

Cases: *Garforth v Newsmith Stainless Ltd* (1978) 52 TC 522; *Williams v Todd* [1988] BTC 315

5.4.3   Meaning of "date of entitlement" in rule two

If an employee becomes entitled to the payment of earnings earlier than the date of payment, the earnings will be treated as received on the date of entitlement. Here the "date of entitlement" means the date on which the employee has a legal right to the payment of the earnings and beyond which those earnings cannot be removed or withdrawn.

In practical terms, the contract of employment and/or terms of service agreed by the employer and employee will assist in identifying when an employee is entitled to be paid earnings.

It is important to note that the date of entitlement to payment of earnings is not necessarily the same as the date on which an employee acquires a right to be paid.

Example

Raquel's employer operates a bonus plan under which a bonus for the year ending 31 December 2020 is payable on 30 June 2021, if she is still an employee on 31 March 2021. Assuming she stays in employment, she becomes eligible for the payment on 31 March 2021 but is not actually entitled to receive the payment until 30 June 2021. She will be treated as receiving the earnings for tax purposes on 30 June 2021.

More clarity on what is meant by "entitlement" is given in *White*, concerning a number of police officers who did not receive an additional housing allowance despite details being included in recruitment literature. The Police Federation, which represented the officers, selected a test case but a negotiated settlement was reached before it could be held. The Police Authority agreed to make *ex gratia* payments of housing allowance from 1 September 1994 as if the constables had first been employed on 31 August 1994.

One officer, Mr White, received payment in August/September 1997 including sums attributable to 1995-96 and 1996-97. He accepted that the award was taxable as earnings, but debate arose as to the timing of the charge to income tax. Did entitlement arise in 1995-96 and 1996-97 or in 1997-98?

The Special Commissioner decided that although the aggregated award was calculated in terms of amounts due for earlier years, Mr White was not entitled to receive payment until 1997 when the Police Authority agreed to pay a negotiated settlement. Tax therefore arose in 1997-98.

Case: *White v IRC* (2003) Sp C 357

5.4.4   Directors and rule three

Rule three applies only to directors. This includes any person who:

- manages the affairs of a company alone, or is a member of a board of directors or similar body that does so;
- is a member of a company whose affairs are managed by its members; or
- is a person in accordance with whose direction or instructions the directors of a company are accustomed to act (otherwise known as a "shadow director").

The effect of rule three is that a charge to tax can arise before the director has received an amount or even become entitled to it if, at an earlier date, sums are credited in the company's accounts or are otherwise determined.

Example

Jade Green is a company director earning £120,000 per annum. She normally receives a discretionary annual bonus based on the company's results for each year ending on 31 December. At a board meeting on 31 March 2021, the board agree the draft accounts for the year ended 31 December 2020. The board agree that Jade Green will be paid a bonus of £40,000 and she duly receives this on 31 May 2021.

Both the date of payment and the date of entitlement to the payment are 31 May 2021. (In terms of the latter, the fact that the board agree and determine the bonus before 31 May 2021 does not give Jade Green an earlier legal entitlement to payment as the board could change their mind – see **5.4.2** above.)

However, as Jade Green is a director, rule three also needs to be considered. Nothing has been credited in the company's accounts before the payment date of 31 May 2021. However, it can be said that her bonus was determined by the board on 31 March 2021. This is after the end of the accounting period on 31 December 2020, so the relevant date is 31 March 2021 under the third part of rule three. This is earlier than the date of payment and entitlement to payment and so the date of receipt for employment income purposes is 31 March 2021.

Although determination of directors' fees is typically made by board meeting, it can also arise automatically where the director's service agreement provides for a bonus or commission if certain targets are met.

In this case, determination will occur when the sales or profit figures are known.

Crediting in the company's accounts will also give rise to a tax point if earlier than the determination. What exactly constitutes a company's accounts is thought to be extremely wide, so that a note in board minutes or a general remuneration account is sufficient. However, for a tax point to arise under part (a) of rule three, the director needs to be identified and an amount of earnings credited.

HMRC identify examples where the entries in company books do not amount to a credit of earnings:

- draft entries in accounts and records;
- provisions for contingent earnings; and
- reserves or provisions for earnings that may be payable in the future, but which have not yet been agreed.

Where rule three applies, *all* earnings the individual receives from the company of which he is a director are covered – whether the amounts are paid to him as a director or as an employee.

Furthermore, rule three applies to an individual who is a director at any point in the same tax year in which earnings are credited or determined, even if the crediting or determination occurs prior, or subsequent, to the director's appointment.

Example

Liam is both a director and an employee of ANT plc and under his contract of service receives an annual salary of £240,000, paid monthly in arrears. At the company's year-end on 31 December 2021, he steps down from his director role but continues with his other employment duties. On 12 January 2022, the shareholders approve a non-contractual bonus of £50,000 to be paid to Liam in recognition of his contribution in 2021. He is paid this on 31 March 2022.

Although the £20,000 paid to Liam each month is in his capacity as an employee, rule three will still apply. However, in most cases, rule three is unlikely to bring forward the tax point from the end of each month.

The bonus payment is more problematic. At the point the shareholders agree it, Liam is no longer a director. However, the determination is in the same tax year as Liam ceased to be a director and so rule three is still relevant. Here the determination occurs after the end of the financial period and so the relevant date under rule three is the date of determination, which is 12 January 2022. This is earlier than the date of payment, which is 31 March 2022, and so 12 January 2022 becomes the tax point.

Law: ITEPA 2003, s. 18(1)
Guidance: EIM 42320

5.4.5   Waivers of earnings

Once an entitlement has arisen, the earnings will be taxable, even if the employee subsequently refuses them.

However, if employees have effectively waived their rights to receive earnings before the date when entitlement arises, they are not treated as having "received" earnings.

Case: *Parker v Chapman* (1928) 13 TC 677

5.4.6   Payments before employment starts or after employment ends

As mentioned in **5.3.2** above, sums paid by reason of employment are capable of being earnings, even if paid before the employment starts or after it has ended.

Where payments are identified as employment-related, the general rules under s. 18 apply unaffected so that the charge arises on the earlier of the date of payment or entitlement to payment (or the date under rule three if the individual is a director).

5.4.7   Statutory entitlements

Both the *Equal Pay Act* 1970 and the *National Minimum Wage Act* 1998 insert a clause into the employment agreement, if it does not already exist, giving the worker the right to equal pay and/or the appropriate national minimum wage rate. Entitlement to equal or higher pay, and hence the tax point on such payments, arises from the time when the lower or discriminatory wages were paid.

Any sum paid under these statutes is therefore not assessable in the year paid, but rather in the year(s) to which the arrears are attributable. The practical consequence is that the tax is calculated at the rates applicable to the earlier years (if different).

The employee is therefore always assessable upon the gross arrears for each year, although he or she is entitled to a credit for the PAYE referable to each year so that no liability arises. See **Chapter 14** for more details on the operation of PAYE.

Law: *Equal Pay Act* 1970, s. 1; NMWA 1998, s. 17

5.4.8   Clawback or forfeiture of earnings

It is not uncommon for provision to be made for bonuses or payments to be recoverable by the employer in certain circumstances, for example, where the performance of the business is worse than expected or an employee leaves earlier than anticipated.

These circumstances were considered in *Martin*, in which it was held that tax should not be re-assessed for the year in which the original payment was made. Instead, the amount of clawback should be treated as "negative earnings" in the year the clawback is made. These negative earnings reduce any employment income arising in the same year when calculating the amount of taxable employment income.

If the clawback amount exceeds employment income in the year so as to give a negative amount, this can be set off against general income of the same or preceding tax year under ITA 2007, s. 128. There is no statutory equivalent to enable set-off against NIC liability.

Example

Jordan works for DDDD Ltd at a salary of £60,000 a year. In December 2021, she receives a bonus of £120,000 for her contribution to a project designed to save costs. The bonus is subject to a *malus* clause which requires part-repayment of the bonus by December 2023 if the savings prove to be significantly less than expected. At the end of December 2023, it is clear the project has not had the desired effect and Jordan has to repay £80,000.

Jordan's employment income for 2021-22 is unaffected. Instead, in 2023-24, she is treated as having negative earnings of £80,000. This reduces her taxable employment income to nil in 2023-24 (and any amount already paid under PAYE can be recovered). The excess £20,000 can be set against general income she may have in 2023-24 and/or 2022-23.

For more details on PAYE and NIC, see **Chapter 14**.

Law: ITEPA 2003, s. 11(3); ITA 2007, s. 128
Case: *HMRC v Martin* [2014] UKUT 429 (TCC)

5.5   Pitfalls and planning points

Determining the correct employment status

In determining employment status, the starting point is the contract and any other documentation such as letters and minutes. Care should be taken to ensure that these documents properly reflect the intention of the parties.

However, the documentation in itself is not enough. Whether a person is treated as employed or self-employed depends on what happens on a day-to-day basis. Regular reviews should take place and regard should be had to the factors HMRC take into account when determining the correct tax position. See **5.2.1** above.

If unclear, agreement should be sought from HMRC.

Payments to directors

The tax point in relation to payments to directors is complex and can easily be misaligned with actual receipt, resulting in potential cash-flow issues in discharging PAYE. Care should be taken, particularly at board meetings and in drafting contracts, to ensure that liabilities do not arise earlier than intended. See **5.4.4**.

Effective waivers

Occasionally, employees or directors may wish to waive earnings or bonuses, for example to give effect to salary sacrifice or to participate in an alternative incentive or pension scheme. Any waiver should be in writing, and signed by the employee, before the entitlement to the earnings/bonus arises, as it will otherwise be ineffective. See **5.4.5**.

6. Taxable employment benefits

6.1 Introduction

Whenever an employee receives non-cash items and benefits, there are challenges in determining:

- whether the benefit constitutes employment income;
- if so, the amount to be treated as taxable employment income in relation to the benefit; and
- when such employment income arises.

Although, as might be expected, there is a large volume of case law exploring these issues, at the current time the position is comprehensively legislated for in ITEPA 2003, Pt. 3, Ch. 2-10 (the "benefits code"). Statutory references in this chapter are to ITEPA 2003 unless otherwise stated.

The benefits code contains a number of specific rules in relation to:

- expenses payments;
- vouchers and credit tokens;
- living accommodation;
- company cars, vans, and fuel; and
- loans.

In addition, there are generic provisions covering all other employment-related benefits (see **6.9** below).

It is possible that a benefit could already be taxed as employment income by virtue of the rules on general earnings. Where this happens, Pt. 3 will only operate to the extent that the amount calculated exceeds the amount already included in general earnings. The exception is living accommodation where the calculation under Pt. 3 takes priority (s. 64 and 109).

Similarly, where a third party provides the benefit, a charge under Pt. 7A (disguised remuneration) may arise. See **Chapter 13** for more details. In this case, the Pt. 7A charge will take priority over the benefits code charge.

Any amount calculated under the benefits code may also be affected by any connected salary sacrifice or optional remuneration arrangement (see **6.10** below).

Law: ITEPA 2003, Pt. 3, Ch. 2-10; Pt. 7A; s. 64, 109, 554Z2

6.2   The benefits code – some common principles

There are some common rules that apply to benefits regardless of whether they are covered by specific legislation or the general charging provisions:

- The benefits code does not apply to any benefit that is exempt under the legislation (see **Chapter 7**).
- The benefit must be provided by reason of the employment.
- The benefit can be provided for an employee even if it is provided for a member of his family or household (defined by s. 721 as the employee's spouse or civil partner, children and their spouses or civil partners, parents, servants, dependants and guests).
- The benefit can be provided by the employer or a third party.
- Where the benefit is provided by an employer, there is an assumption that it is provided by reason of employment unless the employer is an individual and the benefit is provided in the normal course of the employer's domestic, family or personal relationships.

Example 1

Andy is a sole trader operating a business which manufactures artisan pet toys. His son and his daughter are both employed in the business. For his daughter's birthday, he gives her a voucher to spend at a local electronics store.

Although this voucher is provided by an employer to an employee and, as such, falls within the assumption that it is received by reason of employment, Andy should be able to rely on the "family relationships" exemption to exclude the voucher (which is a personal gift rather than relating to the business) from the benefits code.

- The person providing the benefit is the person who ultimately bears the cost of the benefit, whether this person physically hands over or makes the benefit available to the employee or not (see *Wicks v Firth*).

- In each case, the amount subject to tax (referred to as the "cash equivalent") is reduced by the amount "made good" by the employee. This simply means giving money, or something that can be measured in money, to the employer or third party providing the benefit, so as to reduce the element of "bounty" or value of the benefit involved. HMRC at EIM 21120 identify the typical examples of when an employee will make good. These include the making of a direct payment, a deduction from salary, or a suitable debit to the employee's current account in the employer's books and records. The giving of services by the employee, or anything that is not measured in money terms, is not making good (see *Stones v Hall*). Where specific benefits are dealt with, there may be rules on how the amount made good is applied (see, for example, capital contributions towards the use of a car in **6.5** below).

- Payments made or benefits provided where the employee is entitled to a matching deduction (see **Chapter 7**), effectively reducing the earnings element to nil, will be treated as exempt under s. 289A or s. 289D respectively, as long as there is no tax avoidance motive. Where s. 289A or s. 289D applies, the practical impact is that the payment or benefit is not taxable and so the corresponding deduction is not needed. This reduces administration time for the employer, the employee and HMRC.

Example 2

Max ordinarily works in London but is required by his employer to attend a work-related meeting for two days in Manchester. The employer books overnight accommodation for Max at a cost of £170.

Theoretically the accommodation constitutes a benefit within the benefits code (see **6.9** below). However, Max would be entitled to a deduction of the same amount and so ITEPA 2003, s. 289A can be relied on to exempt the provision (and ignore the corresponding deduction).

Law: ITEPA 2003, s. 64, 70-72, 289A, 289D, 289E, 721
Cases: *Wicks v Firth* (1983) 56 TC 318; *Stones v Hall* (1988) 60 TC 737
Guidance: EIM 21120

6.3   Vouchers and credit tokens

The provision of vouchers and credit tokens is taxable under ITEPA 2003, Pt. 3, Ch. 4.

There are different types of voucher, each with its own treatment for tax purposes.

6.3.1   Cash vouchers

These are vouchers, stamps, or other documents capable of being exchanged for a sum of money that is not substantially less than the expense incurred by the provider in providing it. "Not substantially less" is not defined, but in EIM 16110, HMRC consider that cash vouchers have limited application; they give the example of premium bonds.

Cash vouchers give rise to an amount of taxable earnings equal to the full value for which the voucher can be exchanged at the time the employee receives it.

Law: ITEPA 2003, s. 73-81
Guidance: EIM 16110

6.3.2   Non-cash vouchers

A non-cash voucher is any voucher, stamp, document or token capable of being exchanged for goods or services. It is important to note that the voucher must be given up for the goods or services and so would not include a membership card or a pass (although childcare vouchers and travel vouchers are specified exceptions).

A non-cash voucher gives rise to an amount of taxable earnings equal to the cost to the employer of providing it at the time the employee receives the voucher.

There are, however, a number of exemptions, so the following vouchers are exempt:

- a non-cash voucher provided to be exchanged for goods or services that would have entitled the employee to a deduction from earnings, had he paid for them himself (s. 267);
- vouchers for fuel for a company car (s. 269);
- vouchers for car parking at or near the employee's workplace (s. 266(1)(a));
- vouchers for incidental overnight expenses (s. 268); and

- vouchers for mobile phone top-ups if there is no chargeable benefit in respect of the phone itself (s. 266(2)(d)).

Law: ITEPA 2003, s. 82-87, 265-269

6.3.3 Transport vouchers

A transport voucher is a ticket, pass, document or token enabling a person to obtain passenger transport services.

Typically, the employee is taxable on the cost to the employer of providing the transport voucher, at the time it is first received by the employee.

Where the transport voucher covers multiple journeys, such as a season pass or an Oyster card, the tax position depends on the nature of the journeys:

- wholly private use – the full cost to the employer is taxable on the employee;
- wholly business use – exempt (see **8.2**); and
- mixed use – on a strict reading of the travel expenses legislation at s. 337-338, the full amount would be taxable, on the basis of mixed private and business use. However, HMRC will accept there is only a taxable amount to the extent that the cost of the travel card exceeds the total cost of all the qualifying business journeys if paid for separately.

Law: ITEPA 2003, s. 84, 337-338
Guidance: EIM 16066

6.3.4 Credit tokens

The definition of a credit token is wide enough to cover any type of card, document or token that can be used to obtain money, goods or services upon production. However, the most common example is a company credit card provided for use by the employee or by a member of his or her family or household.

The cash equivalent of the benefit of the credit card is tied to its use. There is no chargeable benefit if the card is used to obtain exempt goods or services, or goods or services for which the employee could claim a deduction if he or she paid for them personally.

If the employee uses the card to obtain other goods or services, or to obtain money, a chargeable benefit arises at the point of use equal to the cost incurred by the employer or third party in discharging the credit card bill.

Law: ITEPA 2003, s. 90-94

6.4 Living accommodation

6.4.1 Liability to tax

A taxable benefit arises if an employee is provided with living accommodation by reason of his or her employment.

The legislation does not provide any definition of "living accommodation", although it is commonly accepted that living accommodation is a place where the occupant has the necessary facilities to live domestic life independently without reliance on others to supply basic needs. In practice, HMRC expect that an individual would have at least the use of a refrigerator and full cooking facilities, even if such facilities are shared.

In any event, it is important to differentiate between the provision of living accommodation and the provision of board and lodging. The cash equivalent of the latter is calculated in accordance with the generic rules based on the cost to the employer (see **6.9** below).

It does not matter if the employee or his or her family actually lives in the accommodation or not; the fact it is made available is enough to trigger a benefit charge.

Law: ITEPA 2003, s. 97
Guidance: EIM 11321

6.4.2 Exemptions from charge

There are a number of exemptions from the charge to tax on provided living accommodation:

Provision of local authority accommodation

There is no taxable benefit arising if the employer is a local authority making living accommodation available to an employee on terms that are no more favourable than those for other local authority tenants.

Provision in connection with the performance of duties

There is no taxable benefit where:

- the provided accommodation is necessary to enable the employee to perform the employment duties properly; or
- the accommodation is provided to enable the employee to perform those duties better *and* it is customary for employers to provide living accommodation to such employees.

Note, however, that these exemptions are not available to a director unless he is either a full-time working director or the company is non-profit-making or established for charitable purposes and, in either case, the director does not have a "material interest" (essentially more than 5% of the company – see ITEPA 2003, s. 68 for more details).

Accommodation will be "necessary" for the proper performance of the job where it can be demonstrated that the occupation of the property is *essential* (not merely convenient) for the proper performance of the duties. Typically, this applies to employees who are required by their employers to live on site in order to do their job. HMRC at EIM 11342 mention the following as being acceptable:

- agricultural workers who live on farms or agricultural estates;
- lock-gate and level-crossing gate keepers; and
- stewards and greenkeepers living on the premises.

The second exemption relates to the situation where accommodation is provided for the "better performance" of the employee's duties. This is an objective test and the employee must demonstrate that, by occupying the accommodation provided, he or she really can perform the duties better than if living elsewhere. In practice, HMRC will accept this test is satisfied if the employee is required to be on call outside normal hours, the employee is in fact frequently called out and the accommodation is provided so that the employee may have quick access to the place to which the employee is called.

Even if occupation is regarded as being for the better performance of duties, the exemption is only available if it is also customary for living accommodation to be provided. There is no statutory definition, but if given its usual meaning, "customary" is recognisable as the normal practice.

It is not, however, enough that a custom exists in a particular employment with a particular employer. It must be shown that the provision of accommodation is customary in that type of employment generally. HMRC believe that the onus is on the employee to produce evidence to support a claim, although in their guidance at EIM 11351, they set out occupations accepted as satisfying both the "better performance" and "customary" tests. These include, among others, prison governors, officers and chaplains, clergymen and ministers of religion unless engaged on purely administrative duties, members of HM Forces or the Diplomatic Service and managers of public houses living on the premises.

Provision as a result of a security threat

Living accommodation will be exempt if it is provided for the employee because there is a special threat to the employee's physical security (though this provision is interpreted strictly). An example of this exemption is the provision of living accommodation on Downing Street for the prime minister.

Overseas holiday home owned through company

Individuals may acquire overseas property through a limited company (rather than directly) – usually to comply with local laws. To avoid an inadvertent taxable benefit arising when the individuals use the property, there is an exemption where overseas living accommodation is provided by a limited company to directors. Essentially, the company must be wholly owned by the director (alone or with other individuals), the overseas property must be the company's only or main asset and the company can have no activities other than those incidental to the ownership of the property.

Law: ITEPA 2003, s. 98-100B
Guidance: EIM 11342, 11351

6.4.3   Determining the cash equivalent

The amount to be included in employment income each year will depend on whether the living accommodation is rented or owned by the provider.

Living accommodation rented by the provider

Where the living accommodation is rented by the provider, the amount to be included in employment income is the higher of:

- the rents paid by the provider for the use of the property; and
- the property's annual value.

The "annual value" of living accommodation is defined in s. 110 as the rent which might reasonably be expected to be obtained on letting the property if the tenant paid all the usual household bills and the landlord met all repair and maintenance costs.

In practice, HMRC will normally use the gross rateable value of the property under the old rating system as the annual value. This will be much lower than the annual value as defined in ITEPA 2003. If the property has no rateable value (for example, because it was built recently), an estimate must be made. Any disputes as to the amount of the annual value will be dealt with by the First-tier Tribunal.

Where the accommodation is not available for the whole year, the annual value will be reduced on a *pro rata* basis.

Where the lease is for ten years or less, s. 105A provides for any lease premium to be treated as rent allocated over the life of the lease. This eliminates any potential advantage of having a small rent coupled with an up-front lease premium, rather than regular rent payments. Further anti-avoidance rules exist to prevent the rule on lease premiums being circumvented by the use of longer-length leases with break clauses which can terminate the lease before its tenth anniversary.

Example 1

Davinia is provided with a house by her employer on 1 August 2021. Her employer leased the property for a period of six years commencing 1 August 2021 and paid a premium of £30,000. The rent is £300 per month and the annual value of the property is £2,000. No exemption is available.

The yearly rent paid by the employer is:

	£
£300 x 12 months	3,600
£30,000 premium/length of lease of six years	5,000
	8,600
Pro-rated to reflect lease started on 1 August (8/12)	5,733
Annual value is 8/12 x £2,000	1,333
The taxable benefit for 2021-22 is therefore the higher of the rent and the annual value	5,733

Law: ITEPA 2003, s. 105-105B, 110

Living accommodation owned by the provider

Where the living accommodation is owned by the provider, the amount to be included in employment income for any tax year depends on the "cost" of the accommodation.

If the cost is £75,000 or less, the annual benefit is the annual value (see **6.4.2** above).

If the accommodation cost the employer more than £75,000, there will be an additional benefit, referred to as the "additional yearly rent" (s. 106).

The additional yearly rent is determined by the following formula:

(Cost of accommodation - £75,000) x ORI

where ORI is HMRC's official interest rate at the start of the tax year (2% for 2021-22).

Much depends, therefore, on how the cost of the accommodation is determined. There are two different approaches depending on whether the property was acquired more or less than six years before it was first made available to the employee.

If the acquisition was less than six years before it is first made available to the employee then the cost will be the price paid for the accommodation plus the cost of any improvements carried out before the beginning of the tax year (s. 104).

The legislation refers to costs incurred by a person "involved in providing the accommodation". This is not just the employer but covers the provider of the accommodation (where not the employer) and any person connected with either the employer or the provider other than the employee himself. "Connected" in this context has the meaning given to it in ITA 2007, s. 993 (see **Appendix 2**).

What constitutes "improvements" is not defined. However, at EIM 11430, HMRC confirm that the term would include structural alterations such as additions and extensions, but not repairs and maintenance.

Once the costs have been identified, the amount is reduced by any amount paid by the employee to reimburse the costs of acquiring the property or of the improvements, or as consideration given for the grant to the employee of a tenancy or sub-tenancy.

Example 2

Leah is provided with living accommodation by her employer in January 2021. The employer bought the property early in 2020 for £180,000. It was in bad repair, so a further £20,000 was spent on redecorating the whole property. An extension was added at the cost of £50,000 to create additional living space. In September 2021, a garage is built in the garden of the property at a cost of £15,000. The annual value is £1,000.

For 2021-22, the accommodation benefit will be the annual value plus additional rent. The cost will be based on the acquisition price plus any structural improvements made before the start of the year. This will include the cost of the extension but will exclude the cost of redecorating (not structural improvements) and the garage (during the tax year in question). The benefit is therefore:

£1,000 + ((£180,000 + £50,000 − £75,000) x 2%) = £4,100

If the property was acquired more than six years before it was first made available to the employee, the cost is determined under s. 107. Here the cost is the sum of:

- the market value of the property at the point it is made available to the employee (being the value the property might reasonably be expected to fetch when sold with vacant possession on the open market); and
- the cost of any improvements between the valuation date and the start of the tax year in question.

Any amount paid by the employee towards the cost or improvements, or in the form of consideration for a tenancy, should be deducted.

Example 3

Sandsea Ltd acquired a property in 2010 for £200,000. In 2022, Sandsea Ltd agrees to let its employee, Hei, occupy it rent free. At the time the value of the property is £240,000.

In calculating the accommodation benefit, the additional rent will be based on a cost of £240,000.

However, it is important to remember that the additional yearly rent only applies to properties where the original cost was more than £75,000. Where the six-year rule applies and the original cost, plus improvements, does not exceed this amount, the benefit is limited to the annual value (s. 107(1)(b)).

Example 4

Sandsea Ltd also has another property that it acquired in 1990 at a cost of £45,000. In 2010, an extension was added at the cost of £26,000. In April 2021, Zach, an employee of Sandsea Ltd, occupies it rent free. At the time Zach starts to use the property, it is worth £140,000, with an annual value of £800.

Although the property was acquired more than six years before Zach occupies it, the original cost plus improvements is less than £75,000. Therefore, although the current market value is more than £75,000, the taxable benefit is limited to the annual value of £800.

If property prices fall, such that when the employee moves in more than six years later the market value is less than original cost, the market value of the property should still be used to calculate the benefit even though it is less than original cost.

Law: ITEPA 2003, s. 105-107, 112; ITA 2007, s. 993
Guidance: EIM 11430

Scaling down for partial availability

As might be expected, if the accommodation is only made available to the employee for part of the tax year, the benefit has to be apportioned.

Where the same living accommodation is provided for more than one employee at the same time, the cash equivalent of the benefit (as calculated above) is apportioned between the employees on a "just and reasonable" basis.

Law: ITEPA 2003, s. 108

6.4.4   Household expenses

If the employer pays any household or utility bills on behalf of the employee, this will give rise to an additional and separate benefit based on the cost to the employer under the general rule in s. 201 (see **6.9** below). The cost of repairs or structural alterations is excluded as these are regarded as the responsibility of the employer (although where the structural alterations amount to improvements, these will affect the calculation of the main living accommodation charge – see **6.4.2** above).

The provision of furniture and domestic appliances by the employer will also give rise to an additional taxable benefit. If the items are given to the employee, then the cash equivalent will be the cost to the employer. If, however, the items are merely for the use of the employee while in the living accommodation, a benefit will arise based on the use of the asset. See **6.9.2** below for details of how this is calculated.

Sections 314 and 315 modify the rules on household expenses where the accommodation itself is exempt because it is provided in connection with the performance of duties or as a result of a security threat. In such cases, the payment of council tax or water charges by the employer is an exempt benefit. Where the employer discharges other household expenses, the amount that can be included as taxable employment income is capped at 10% of other earnings from the same employment for the year.

Law: ITEPA 2003, s. 201, 314-315

6.5 Company cars

6.5.1 Definition of "car"

If a car is made available by reason of the employment for private use by the employee (or by a member of his or her family), a taxable benefit will arise.

It is important to ensure that the vehicle is a "car" within the definition, as there are different rules for vehicles that are not cars (such as vans). A car is defined at s. 115 as a "mechanically propelled vehicle" that is not a goods vehicle, a motorcycle, an invalid carriage, or "a vehicle of a type not commonly used as a private vehicle and unsuitable to be so used".

A goods vehicle is a vehicle that is "of a construction primarily suited for the conveyance of goods or burden". The Upper Tribunal decision in the *Coca-Cola* case highlighted the importance of "primarily suited" and emphasised that actual usage was not relevant when determining whether a vehicle is primarily suited to transport goods or passengers. If the vehicle is not constructed primarily for carrying goods, and there is nothing that renders it unsuitable for carrying people, then it is a car.

Estate cars, luxury 4x4s, motor homes and multipurpose vehicles are all regarded as "cars" for the purposes of the benefits code. Double cab pick-ups are more problematic as they are clearly designed for carrying goods, although they also have additional passenger capacity compared to a normal pick-up truck. Rather than take a blanket approach, HMRC consider the facts and the specification; a payload of 1,000 kg or more is accepted as being designed primarily for the carrying of goods and therefore is more likely to be classed as a van.

Where a car does falls within the legislation, the fact it is provided to the employee on terms that represent a "fair bargain" – for example, in return for the payment of the going rate for leasing or hiring the car – does not prevent a taxable benefit arising. The provision of the car in these circumstances will still constitute a taxable benefit with the annual cash equivalent being computed in accordance with the legislation, with credit given for the employee's contribution as permitted. The only exception is where the employer runs a vehicle hire business and provides a vehicle to the employee on the same terms as are available to the public generally.

Law: ITEPA 2003, s. 115, 117(3), 121

Case: *HMRC v Payne, Garbett and Coca-Cola European Partners Great Britain Ltd* [2019] UKUT 90 (TCC)

Guidance: EIM 23100, 23115, 23145, 23150

6.5.2   Calculating the cash equivalent

The cash equivalent of a company car – i.e. the taxable benefit on which the employee pays income tax and the employer pays NIC – is based on its list price multiplied by the "relevant percentage".

Looking at each of these steps in turn:

Price of the car

The cost to the employer is irrelevant in determining the price. Instead, the starting point is the manufacturer's list price when new, including delivery charges and any applicable taxes (s. 122).

The list price of any accessories (including taxes and any fitting costs) provided with the car is then added. Accessories include any optional extras provided with the car, for example, satellite navigation, leather seats and in-car entertainment systems. However, the following are specifically excluded:

- any item necessarily provided for use in the employee's duties;
- equipment to allow the car to run on road fuel gas;
- hands-free apparatus to allow use of a mobile phone while driving the car;
- equipment to enable a disabled employee to use the car; and
- where the nature of the employment creates a special threat to the employee's personal security, accessories designed to

enhance the security of the car, such as bulletproof glass and armour plating.

Additional accessories added to the car after it is first made available to the employee are ignored unless they cost £100 or more.

The replacement of accessories is ignored if it is simply a replacement like-for-like for an accessory already included in the calculation. However, where the replacement involves an upgrade, the old accessory will be ignored and the cost of the new accessory will be included.

Example 1

Niamh's company car has a list price, including taxes and delivery, of £40,000. To this was added a satellite navigation and entertainment system costing £2,000, equipment to enable her to use her phone hands-free at a cost of £500 and a tow bar to enable her to transport the material she needs for attending trade shows as part of her role at a cost of £400. The employer negotiates a 5% discount on the total price.

After delivery, Niamh's employer pays for parking sensors to be fitted at a cost of £250 and a boot protection mat at a cost of £60.

Her "cost" for the purposes of calculating the cash equivalent of the benefit is:

	£
List price	40,000
Satnav	2,000
Parking sensors	250
	42,250

The discount procured by the employer is irrelevant and both the phone equipment and the tow bar necessary for work fall within specified exceptions. The boot protection mat is also ignored as it is below £100.

The final step in calculating the price of the car is to deduct any capital contributions made by the employee. A capital contribution is a one-off payment made by the employee for the car or for any accessory taken into account in calculating the price. The maximum deduction is £5,000.

Law: ITEPA 2003, s. 122-126, 131

The relevant percentage

The relevant percentage can be found in tables published by HMRC (set out in **Appendix 5**). These change every tax year, so it is important to use the most up-to-date version.

To determine which figure to use, the following information is needed:

- whether the car was first registered on or after 6 April 2020;
- the carbon dioxide (CO_2) emitted by the car measured in grams per kilometre (g/km);
- where the car is electric, the distance it can travel on a single electric charge; and
- where the car has a diesel engine, whether or not it complies with Real Driving Emissions 2 (RDE2). RDE2 is a test applied by the manufacturer to all cars registered since April 2018. Essentially, if a car emits less than 0.08g/km of nitrogen oxide, it is considered RDE2 compliant.

The registration date can be found on the registration certificate (V5C) published by DVLA. The other details can be found in the manufacturer's specification for the car.

Essentially the higher the CO_2 emissions, the higher the percentage. Long-range electric cars are cheaper than older, diesel cars.

In any event, there is a maximum percentage of 37%.

Doing the calculation

Having determined the price and the relevant percentage, the next step is to multiply the two to give an annual cash equivalent.

Example 2

Stanley has use of a company car with a list price of £36,000 including taxes and delivery. The employer buys multiple cars for a number of employees and secures a 10% discount. Before Stanley gets the car, a state-of-the-art navigation and entertainment system is installed at an extra cost of £3,000. Stanley makes a contribution of £2,000 towards this. The car is first registered in August 2020. It has a petrol engine and recorded CO_2 emissions of 160g/km.

Here the amount paid by the employer is irrelevant. The price of the car will be the sum of the list price of £36,000 and the cost of the accessory of £3,000 (assuming none of the exclusions applies) less the £2,000 paid by Stanley, that is £37,000.

Looking at the table in **Appendix 5**, the relevant percentage is 36%.

The cash equivalent is therefore £37,000 x 36% = £13,320.

The benefit is reduced in a number of circumstances:

- If the employee does not have use of the car throughout the whole of the tax year. Apportionment is available not only when the benefit of having a car starts or stops at some point in the tax year, but also if the car is off the road (e.g. for repairs) for a continuous period of a least 30 days (s. 143).

- If the car is available for private use by more than one employee. Where this is the case, the cash equivalent is calculated separately for each employee but reduced on a just and reasonable basis (s. 148).

- If payments are made by the employee for the use of the car in the tax year in question. The payments must be specifically for the private use of the car. If they are paid towards a specific aspect of the car's running costs, such as servicing or insurance, or to enable an employee to have use of a more expensive car, then they will not be deductible (s. 144).

Law: ITEPA 2003, s. 122-126, 131, 143-144, 148

6.5.3   Classic cars

If an employee is provided with a classic car, the cash equivalent is calculated using the greater of:

- the price of the car as calculated in accordance with the normal rules; and

- the market value of the car on the last day in the tax year that the car is available to the employee.

To qualify as a classic car, the car must be at least 15 years old and the market value figure must be at least £15,000.

If the car is worth less than £15,000, the cash equivalent will be based on the original list price, which will be low compared to modern cars. For example, a Triumph Spitfire Mk II from 1965 has a list price of £550.

However, the market value needs to be considered in each tax year, so the treatment will change if the value rises to at least £15,000.

Law: ITEPA 2003, s. 147

6.5.4   Pool cars and emergency vehicles

No taxable benefit will arise if the employee merely has use of a pool car, namely a car:

- made available to, and actually used by, more than one employee;
- made available, in the case of each employee, by reason of employment;
- not ordinarily used by one of those employees to the exclusion of others;
- where any private use by the employee is incidental to the employee's other use of the car in the same tax year; and
- not ordinarily kept overnight on or in the vicinity of where the employee lives.

Whether all the conditions are satisfied is a question of fact. If a pool car is made available to everyone, but in reality only one employee uses it, it will not be a pool car. Incidental private use is permissible, but HMRC regard this as a qualitative test not a quantitative one. For example, someone who takes the pool car to visit a client and stops to pick up a parcel on the way is only making incidental use of the car for a private purpose. However, taking the car out on a lunchtime specifically to do supermarket shopping is clearly private use.

Furthermore, the car should not ordinarily be kept overnight at the employee's home. At EIM 23465, HMRC suggest that "ordinarily" might be construed as 60% or more of the total number of nights the car is available. However, if the number of nights approaches this level, there is a good chance that one of the other tests is not satisfied. For example, taking a car home to make an early start the next day will have the incidental private use of the work-to-home journey in the context of a clear business purpose of the next day's journey. However, if this happens regularly, it brings the "incidental" nature into question.

115

There is also no taxable benefit when emergency service vehicles used by fire, police or ambulance workers are taken home when on call.

Law: ITEPA 2003, s. 167, 248A
Guidance: EIM 23465

6.5.5   Impact of car benefit charge on other benefits

Where there is a car benefit charge under s. 120, all residual liability under the general principles, except for the provision of a driver or fuel for private use, is excluded. This underpins the idea that the car benefit charge is for "making a car available". Therefore, there is no extra benefit charge where the employer incurs associated car costs such as insurance, servicing, and vehicle excise duty.

Where a driver is provided, the cash equivalent will be calculated on general principles (see **6.9** below). The provision of private fuel is discussed in **6.7** below.

Law: ITEPA 2003, s. 239

6.5.6   Cars provided for disabled employees

No liability to tax will arise in relation to specially adapted cars (including automatic transmission cars where this is necessary to facilitate driving) provided for the use of a disabled employee. This is on the basis that the car can be used for business purposes and ordinary commuting only and is so used.

Law: ITEPA 2003, s. 247

6.6   Company vans

Where an employer allows an employee unrestricted private use of an employer-owned van, a taxable benefit may arise. A "van" for these purposes is a mechanically propelled road vehicle which is a goods vehicle weighing not more than 3.5 tonnes. Where a heavy goods vehicle weighing more than 3.5 tonnes is made available to an employee, it is regarded as exempt under ITEPA 2003, s. 238 provided that ownership is not transferred, and it is not used wholly or mainly for private use.

However, a taxable benefit will not arise if the van is made available to the employee for business travel in the course of employment and private use is prohibited except for the purposes of ordinary commuting (see **8.2.6** for the meaning of ordinary commuting). "Insignificant" private use is disregarded, although this is not defined. HMRC will regard private use as insignificant if it is:

- limited in quantity, for example an employee who uses the van to take rubbish to the tip once or twice a year;
- limited in quality, for example a slight detour regularly made by the employee to pick up a spouse from work on the way home;
- very much the exception in terms of the pattern of use of that van by the employee or his household in the tax year in question; and
- small in absolute terms, not merely as a proportion of other use.

Where a van is made available to an employee and the private use is not restricted or insignificant, a taxable benefit arises. The cash equivalent is a flat rate:

- nil for zero emission vans; and
- £3,500 otherwise.

In other respects – for example, where the employee makes a payment for private use, the van is not available for the whole of the year, the van is a pool van or is shared with other employees, or related benefits such as insurance and servicing are provided – there are very similar provisions to those outlined in **6.5.2** above (in relation to cars) to reduce the benefit proportionately.

A similar exemption for vans provided to disabled employees exists as for cars (see **6.5.6** above).

Law: ITEPA 2003, s. 115, 154-159, 168, 202, 238
Guidance: EIM 22745

6.7   Private fuel

The provision of fuel for a company car or van, or the reimbursement of the cost of fuel where the fuel is used for private motoring, will amount to a taxable benefit, distinct from the car or van benefit charge.

No private fuel benefit charge arises in relation to the provision of electricity (as HMRC do not regard electricity as a fuel).

6.7.1   Provision of private fuel for cars

The cash equivalent of private fuel is a fixed amount regardless of the number of private miles driven or the proportion of private miles to business miles. For 2021-22, the cash equivalent is £24,600 multiplied by the appropriate percentage. The appropriate percentage is the same percentage as used to calculate the amount of the car benefit.

The fuel benefit is reduced to nil if the employee is required to reimburse the whole of the expense incurred by the employer in providing private fuel and actually does so. If the employee only makes a partial reimbursement, this will have no effect and the benefit will be calculated as above. Therefore, an employee contribution towards the costs of private fuel will not result in a "pound-for-pound" reduction in the taxable amount as it does for other benefits.

The fuel benefit will be reduced proportionately if private use fuel is not provided to the employee for the whole of the tax year. However, if private fuel is withdrawn but then reinstated in the same tax year, the benefit charge will apply for the whole tax year. This prevents employees opting in and out of the car fuel benefit during holidays or other periods where no private mileage is done.

Example

Foley is provided with a new car by his employer on 1 January 2022. The car has a list price of £25,000, a petrol engine and CO_2 emissions of 126g/km. All fuel costs are met by the employer. In 2021-22, the costs of private fuel amounted to £1,000 of which Foley reimbursed £400.

Two benefits will arise in 2021-22 – the car benefit and the fuel benefit.

Using the principles set out in **6.5** above, the car benefit is £25,000 x 29% (taken from the table in **Appendix 5**) = £7,250, scaled down to £1,812 to reflect the fact he only has it for three months of the year.

The fuel benefit is £24,600 x 29% = £7,134, again scaled down to £1,783 as the benefit is only received from the beginning of January. There is no reduction for partial reimbursement of private fuel.

To ensure the employee is only provided with fuel for business purposes (and so avoids the fuel benefit charge), one of two processes can be adopted:

- the employer pays for all fuel and the employee reimburses the employer for all private mileage before 6 July following the end of the tax year in question; or

- the employee pays for all fuel and the employer reimburses him or her for business mileage.

HMRC publish advisory fuel rates each quarter (see **Appendix 5**) and these can be used to calculate the level of reimbursement due. Where these rates are used, no taxable benefit will arise. The level of reimbursement can be actual cost, although this will need to be agreed with HMRC and evidence provided where this differs from the published rates.

Electricity is not regarded as a fuel for the purposes of calculating private fuel benefits and therefore where it is provided (or reimbursed) for private use, no fuel benefit will arise.

Law: ITEPA 2003, s. 149-153

6.7.2   Provision of private fuel for vans.

Where fuel is used for private journeys in a van, and the fuel is provided or the costs reimbursed by the employer, a chargeable benefit arises.

The annual cash equivalent is a flat rate of £669 for 2021-22.

Similar rules to cars apply for reducing the benefit where private mileage is reimbursed, where the van is shared or where private fuel is not provided for the whole year (see **6.7.1** above).

Law: ITEPA 2003, s. 154-164

6.7.3   Provision of private fuel for disabled employees

Where an adapted car or van is provided for the use of disabled employees on terms that mean that no taxable benefit arises under ITEPA 2003, s. 247 (see **6.5.6** above), any fuel provided for permitted non-business use will also be exempt.

Law: ITEPA 2003, s. 247

6.8   Employment-related loans

When an employee receives a "taxable cheap loan" (often referred to in practice as a "beneficial loan") by reason of his or her employment, a taxable benefit may arise.

6.8.1   Meaning of "taxable cheap loan"

To fall within the legislation, the loan must meet all of the following conditions:

- It must be a cheap loan, in that the interest charged (or the alternative finance return) must be less than interest at HMRC's official rate of interest (ORI), 2% since 6 April 2021.
- It must be provided to an employee or a relative of the employee (unless the relative is also an employee). "Relative" here is different from the usual family or household definition used in relation to benefits. ITEPA 2003, s. 174(6) defines relative as including:
  - ○ a spouse or civil partner;
  - ○ a parent or child or a remoter relative in the direct line;
  - ○ a sibling of the employee or of the employee's spouse or civil partner; and
  - ○ the spouse or civil partner of anyone mentioned above.
- It must be received from the employer, or a company in the same group as the employer, or a person with a material interest in either a close company which is the employer or a company in the same group as the employer or a company or partnership which controls the said close company. The employer in this context also includes a prospective or former employer.
- The loan must be in the form of a cash loan, credit, or alternative finance arrangement.
- It must be provided by reason of employment. This will not be the case if the loan is made in the course of the employee's domestic, family, or personal relationships or if the loan is made to a relative and the employee derives no benefit from it.

Law: ITEPA 2003, s. 173-174; SI 2021/249

6.8.2 Exceptions

Even if the loan is potentially within the legislation, it will not be classed as a taxable cheap loan if any of the exceptions applies:

- The aggregate of all loans to or for the benefit of the employee outstanding throughout the tax year is £10,000 or less (s. 180).
- Loans made by banks or financial institutions to their employees on ordinary commercial terms (s. 176).
- Loans for fixed terms with a fixed rate of interest that is not lower than the ORI at the outset (s. 177).

- Loans made by an employer to an employee by way of an advance to cover either necessary expenses or incidental overnight expenses provided that (s. 179):
  - the outstanding advance does not exceed £1,000 at any time;
  - the advance is spent by the employee within six months of receiving it; and
  - the employee accounts to the employer at regular intervals in relation to the expenditure covered by the advance.
- Loans used for a purpose that attracts income tax relief under ITA 2007, s. 383. It is important to note the exception only applies where all of the loan attracts income tax relief. Where only part of the loan interest qualifies for tax relief, the cash equivalent of the benefit will be based on the whole amount of the loan. It is then up to the employee to claim tax relief on the qualifying part of the loan, treating the cash equivalent amount of the benefit as if it were interest paid on the loan, in addition to any interest actually paid (s. 178).

Law: ITEPA 2003, s. 176-180; ITA 2007, s. 383

6.8.3   Calculating the cash equivalent

Essentially, the cash equivalent of the benefit of a taxable cheap loan is the difference between the interest that would have been payable at the ORI and any interest that is actually paid. There are two methods set out in the legislation for doing the calculation:

- the average method; and
- the precise, or strict, method.

The average method should be used as a starting point. It is then up to HMRC or the taxpayer to impose or elect for the precise method to apply, should either wish to do so, on or before 31 January following the filing deadline for self-assessment relating to the relevant tax year.

Average method

The purpose of the average method is to find the average amount of the loan over the tax year and apply average ORI to that amount.

This is achieved by adding together:

- the amount of the loan outstanding at the start of the tax year or, if nil, the amount outstanding at the point the loan was made during the tax year; and
- the amount of the loan outstanding at the end of the tax year or, if nil, the amount of the loan at the point it was repaid during the tax year.

The resulting sum must be divided by two to come to a simple average and this is then multiplied by the average ORI for the year.

Example 1

Alice is provided with an interest free loan of £30,000 by her employer on 1 February 2021. She repays £5,000 on 30 November 2021. None of the exceptions in ITEPA 2003 apply.

For the 2021-22 tax year, using the average method:

	£
Amount outstanding at 6 April 2021	30,000
Amount outstanding at 5 April 2022	25,000
(£30,000 + £25,000)/2 x 2%	550
The cash equivalent of the beneficial loan is	550

Precise method

Under the precise method, interest is calculated on a daily basis on the exact amounts of the loan outstanding over the course of the tax year.

Example 2

Using the same example as above but applying the strict method for 2021-22:

	£
239 days (6 Apr 2021 - 30 Nov 2021) x £30,000 x 2%) / 365 =	393
126 days (1 Dec 2021 - 5 Apr 2022) x £25,000 x 2%) / 365 =	173
Total taxable benefit	566

Alice is slightly better off with the average method, rather than the precise method. HMRC are unlikely to elect for the precise method either, as their approach is only to opt for the precise method where a large amount of tax is at stake.

If the employee is required to make some sort of contribution, or pays some interest to the employer on the loan, the cash equivalent will be reduced accordingly.

Law: ITEPA 2003, s. 181-182

6.8.4 Specific situations

Jointly held loans

Where a loan is made to two or more employees jointly (for example where a husband and wife are both employed by the same company) the cash equivalent of the loan should be split between them in a just and reasonable way.

Multiple outstanding loans

Where more than one employment-related loan is held by or in relation to the same employee, the taxable benefit on each loan should be calculated separately.

There is an exception in the case of chargeable beneficial loans made to directors of close companies, where the lender can choose to aggregate the loans and treat them as if there were a single loan, provided they are in the same currency and are not part of a salary sacrifice arrangement.

The election must be made to HMRC no later than 6 July following the end of the tax year in question.

Death of the employee

Any loans outstanding at the date of an employee's death will be treated as no longer being due, with the effect that no tax charge will arise from that point on.

Replacement loans

Where an employee receives an employment-related loan as a replacement for a previous such loan, both are treated as a single loan for the purpose of calculating the taxable benefit using the average method.

To prevent avoidance, this treatment also applies where:

- the employee changes employment, provided the new employment is still with the same employer or with another person connected with the original employer; or

- an employment-related loan is replaced with a non-employment-related loan which is in turn replaced by a new employment-related loan from the same employer (or connected party) either within the same tax year or within 40 days following the end of the tax year.

If, however, there is a salary sacrifice in relation to the loan or its replacement, the loans must be treated separately.

Loans released or written off

When an employment-related loan is released or written off, wholly or in part, the amount released or written off is treated as earnings of the employee.

There are two exceptions to this:

- where the loan is deemed to be written off or released following the death of the employee, in which case there is no tax charge; or

- where the employer is a close company and has had to pay tax in respect of the loan under CTA 2010, s. 455 (see **24.7** – Loans to participators).

Law: ITEPA 2003, s. 185-190

6.9   General benefits

6.9.1   Introduction

ITEPA 2003, s. 201 covers all employment-related benefits that do not fall within the specific rules and are not otherwise subject to tax. It is a form of "sweeping up" charge.

The cash equivalent of these benefits will, unless exempt (see **Chapter 7** below), be treated as earnings for the tax year in which they are provided.

The cash equivalent is defined as:

> "the cost of the benefit less any part of that cost made good by the employee to the persons providing that benefit".

Law: ITEPA 2003, s. 201, 203(2)

6.9.2   Assessing the cost of providing the benefit

The cost of providing the benefit is relatively straightforward where the employer (or the other provider if the benefit is provided by a third party) procures the benefit from an external source.

Example 1

Daryl receives a jet ski from his employer. The jet ski normally sells at £9,000 from Easyski Inc. but the employer negotiates a discount and buys it for £8,100.

The taxable benefit is the cost to the employer, that is £8,100.

The position is more complicated where the benefit does not have an external source. In *Pepper v Hart,* a schoolmaster's child attended the school where the father worked, for substantially discounted fees. HMRC and Mr Hart both agreed that a benefit had arisen, but a dispute arose over how this benefit should be valued. HMRC contended that the cost to the employer was the average cost per child of running the school. Mr Hart argued that the cost to the school was the additional costs arising as a result of his child attending the school, which in practice would be negligible. The House of Lords agreed with Mr Hart that a marginal cost method is the correct one.

It is for this reason that employees of the London Underground can travel on the trains, and employees of airlines can enjoy cheap flights, without a taxable benefit arising. This is on the basis that the trains and planes would be operating anyway and the cost of an additional passenger filling an otherwise empty seat is negligible.

Transfers of assets previously used in the business

Where the employee receives a benefit in the form of an asset that has previously been used or written down in value by the employer (or other person providing the asset), the cash equivalent is usually the market value of the asset at the time it is transferred to the employee. Market value for this purpose is defined at s. 208 as the price which the asset might reasonably be expected to fetch on a sale in the open market.

Where the asset has been made available to an employee (not necessarily the one now receiving it) before being transferred, the cash equivalent is different. It is the greater of:

- the market value of the asset at the time of the transfer; and
- the market value of the asset at the time it was first made available to employees giving rise to a taxable benefit, reduced by subsequent taxable amounts.

Example 2

JDH Pets Ltd operates a pet store and allows its employees to take home and use its spare fish tanks. In 2019-20, Ginny is given use of one of the fish tanks. At that time, the market value of the fish tank is £600, and she has it for two years, giving rise to a taxable benefit of £120 in each year. She leaves in April 2021 and JDH Pets Ltd decide to give the fish tank to her replacement, Steve. At the time it is worth £250.

Because the asset has been used to provide taxable benefits, the cost of providing the benefit will be the greater of:

- £250; and
- £600 – (£120 x 2) = £360.

The cash equivalent of the benefit to Steve is £360.

This rule does not apply to cycles and cycling equipment falling within s. 244 (see **7.4.1** below) and cars. Where these assets are involved, the cash equivalent will be the market value at the date of transfer, regardless of previous taxable benefits.

Use of an asset

On occasion, assets are loaned to an employee, or made available for his or her use, as opposed to giving outright ownership. In this situation, the cash equivalent is the higher of:

- the annual value of the asset; and
- the annual amount of rent or hire charge paid by the provider.

The annual value of any asset other than land is 20% of the market value of the asset when it is first made available as an employee benefit. Again, market value is the price which the asset might reasonably be expected to fetch on a sale in the open market.

If the asset is land (including buildings), the cost of the benefit is taken to be the annual rental value of the land (s. 205(3)). The annual rental value is the amount of rent that could reasonably be expected to be obtained from letting the land from year to year.

Section 205B applies where an employee does not have use of the asset for the entire year, or shares use with another person.

The starting point is that the asset is fully available for the whole year for private use unless private use is forbidden. This is the case even if the asset is not actually used for private reasons. However, the cash equivalent is reduced where:

- the asset is not available for private use before or after the employee receives it; or
- the asset is in the hands of the employee but, for more than 12 hours in a day, is broken, being maintained, cannot lawfully be used, is used for the performance of his duties or is used other than at the direction of the employee or his family/household.

The deduction is a proportion of annual cost depending on the days unavailable.

Example 3

Ethan has the use of his employer's villa for the months of January and August. A gas leak occurs at the villa near the end of July 2021 and Ethan cannot access it until 4 August. In January 2022, Ethan decides to use the villa for only one week. The annual benefit would have been £60,000 had he been able to use the villa all year.

Ethan is entitled to a reduction of the cash equivalent for:

- the three days the property is unavailable in August; and
- the days in the ten months Ethan has no access to the villa.

The cash equivalent is therefore £60,000 – (306/365 x 60,000) = £9,699.

Ethan does not get a reduction for the days in January when he does not use the villa, because it was available to him.

Law: ITEPA 2003, s. 203-208
Case: *Pepper v Hart* (1992) UKHL 3

6.9.3 When is a benefit provided?

A benefit is taxable in the year it is provided. In *Templeton v Jacobs* it was made clear that this means when it is available to be enjoyed by the employee. Therefore, it is irrelevant when the employer acquires or pays for the benefit.

Law: ITEPA 2003, s. 203(1)
Case: *Templeton v Jacobs* (1996) 68 TC 735

6.10 Optional remuneration arrangements

6.10.1 Introduction

The cash equivalent of a benefit determined in accordance with the rules set out in this chapter can be affected if there is in place an optional remuneration agreement (OpRA) – i.e. a benefit is provided in exchange for a "salary sacrifice".

An OpRA is a formal arrangement between an employer and an employee under which the employee agrees to a lower taxable salary, or gives up a right (or future right) to earnings in return for a non-cash benefit or package of benefits.

In the past, tax savings were achieved by swapping taxable salary for tax-free benefits. The OpRA rules nullify any such tax advantage.

Law: ITEPA 2003, s. 69A-69B

6.10.2 Assessing the impact of OpRA

Where there is an OpRA in place, the cash equivalent of the affected benefit (referred to in the legislation as the "relevant amount") is the greater of:

- the cash equivalent of the benefit as calculated under the benefits code; and
- the amount of earnings given up (referred to as the "amount forgone").

Example

EJR Systems Ltd is willing to provide health insurance to its employees in return for the surrender of £80 of salary per month. The policy costs EJR Systems Ltd £800 per year.

Under the benefits code, the cash equivalent of the health insurance is the cost to the employer, in this case £800. However, employees who take up the insurance will forgo salary of £960. As this amount is higher than the usual cash equivalent, the cash equivalent will be modified from £800 to £960.

The impact of the OpRA rules is to change the taxable amount – the nature of the benefit is not changed. In the example above, the employees are still provided with a non-cash benefit in the form of health insurance. This is important for determining whether PAYE and National Insurance are due (see **Chapter 14**).

Contributions by employees and amounts "made good"

The cash equivalent of benefits is ordinarily reduced to the extent the employee contributes towards the benefit, or otherwise makes good the element of bounty he or she is receiving.

Where an OpRA is in place, the amount of any contribution is ignored in calculating the cash equivalent under the benefits code for the purposes of comparison with the amount of salary forgone. Once it has been determined whether the relevant amount is the cash equivalent under the benefits code or the amount forgone, credit can be given for the contributions to determine the actual taxable amount.

This avoids any risk of the employee being over-compensated for contributions where there are also OpRAs in place.

Where the benefit is a car, the position is further complicated, as capital contributions are ordinarily taken into account in determining the list price of the car. Therefore, when giving credit after comparison with the amount forgone, the capital contribution needs to be scaled back to the appropriate percentage.

Example

Jack has a company car under the terms of an OpRA in which he gives up £600 salary per month (£7,200 per year). Jack also makes a capital contribution of £2,000 towards the car so that he can have a sports model. The car has a list price of £30,000 and an appropriate percentage of 23%.

Under the benefits code, the cash equivalent (in the absence of an OpRA) would be £6,440 ((£30,000 less capital contribution £2,000) x 23%). However, because there is an OpRA in relation to the car, the capital contribution is ignored, giving a cash equivalent of (£30,000 x 23%), so £6,900.

The amount of salary given up is £7,200. This is greater than the modified cash equivalent of £6,900 and is therefore used to determine the taxable amount.

It is at this stage that the capital contribution is brought into the calculation, reducing the taxable amount by a proportion of the capital contribution equivalent to the appropriate percentage of 23%. Accordingly, the taxable amount will be:

£7,200 less £460 (£2,000 x 23%) = £6,740.

Law: ITEPA 2003, s. 69A-69B

6.10.3   Circumstances when OpRA does not apply

The OpRA rules do not apply to all benefits. The following are excluded:

- cars with CO_2 emissions of 75g/km or less;
- counselling, outplacement and re-training in connection with redundancy;
- cycle-to-work schemes;
- pension savings under registered and qualifying overseas plans (including related pension advice);
- tax-exempt childcare (including qualifying nursery provision and childcare vouchers); and
- purchase of annual leave.

These benefits will be taxed on their usual cash equivalent as calculated under the benefits code regardless of whether there is a related salary sacrifice arrangement.

Example

EJR Systems Ltd offers bicycles and safety equipment to its employees for use in commuting to and from work. The scheme is open to all employees provided they agree to give up £250 of their gross salary each year for three years. In return, the employee will receive the use of a bicycle and safety equipment package over that period. The retail price of this package is £800 but EJR Systems Ltd has been able to secure a discount so the cost to it is £720. Expectations are that the bicycle will last in the region of three years before it needs to be replaced.

Although there is a salary sacrifice arrangement, the OpRA rules do not apply. Therefore, provided the conditions are satisfied, the provision of cycles and safety equipment is exempt from tax. A basic rate taxpayer who participates in the scheme will lose £170 in net pay each year (£250 gross salary less 20% tax and 12% employee NIC), which equates to £510 over three years. However, in return, the employee receives the use of a cycle package worth £800.

Law: ITEPA 2003, s. 69A

6.10.4   Special case exemptions

Some exemptions (see **Chapter 7**) have their own rules as to the impact of salary sacrifice arrangements. For example, the exemption for subsidised meals does not apply if there is a salary sacrifice arrangement in relation to them.

The rules on OpRA do not affect these "special case exemptions" which can be summarised as:

- exemption for paid or reimbursed expenses or benefits where there is a corresponding deduction (s. 289A and s. 289D);
- exemption for independent advice in respect of conversions and transfers of pension schemes (s. 308B);
- limited exemption for qualifying bonus payments by an employee share trust (s. 312A);
- exemption for subsidised meals (s. 317);
- exemption for recommended medical treatment (s. 320C); and
- exemption for trivial benefits provided by employers (s. 323A).

Law: ITEPA 2003, s. 69A

6.10.5   Creating a valid OpRA

As seen in **Chapter 5**, a tax point will arise as soon as an employee becomes entitled to an amount of salary. Therefore, care needs to be taken in structuring a salary sacrifice or OpRA to ensure that the employee does not have an unexpected tax liability.

From HMRC's perspective, a valid OpRA has all of the following features:

- The entitlement to future remuneration must be given up before it is treated as received for tax or NIC purposes.
- The construction of the revised contract between the employer and the employee must be that the employee is entitled to lower cash remuneration and a benefit.

- The employee's participation in the OpRA must be entirely voluntary. At the end of the agreement period, which should be at least 12 months long, the employee should be able to opt out such that pay reverts to its original level.
- The arrangement should only be capable of being changed at the end of the agreement period or if there is a lifestyle change such as marriage, divorce or becoming a parent.

Once an OpRA is in place, employers can ask the HMRC clearances team to confirm the tax and NIC implications.

Guidance: EIM 42760

6.11   Pitfalls and planning points

Employee contributions to company cars

Where the employee is making payments towards a company car, care should be taken to structure the agreement properly. Only capital contributions or payments for private use will reduce the taxable amount. See **6.5.2** above.

Private fuel

The cash equivalent of providing private fuel is based on the amount of CO_2 emissions and not the actual private mileage done. In most cases, the tax arising on the employee will exceed the cost of paying for fuel for private use, so steps should be taken to ensure that the fuel benefit is avoided. See **6.7.1** above.

Contributions to private fuel

Contributions towards private fuel do not reduce the fuel benefit unless *all* private miles are reimbursed to the employer. See **6.7** above.

Using OpRAs

Although the OpRA rules have nullified the tax advantages of some salary sacrifice planning, there are some exceptions such as pension contributions and cycle-to-work schemes. Furthermore, other benefits might still be attractive where the buying power of the employer is such that the benefit on offer would still cost the employee more if purchased out of net pay.

Impact of OpRAs on pay levels

Optional remuneration arrangements can help keep pay below the thresholds where student loans become repayable and where personal allowances start to be scaled back. However, salary is also reduced for the purposes of the national minimum wage/national living wage, holiday pay, overtime rates, pension contributions and certain statutory payments such as sick pay and maternity pay. This should be borne in mind when designing a scheme.

7. Exempt employment benefits

7.1 Introduction

The legislation in ITEPA 2003, Pt. 4 sets out a number of employee benefits which do not give rise to a tax liability. All statutory references in this chapter are to ITEPA 2003 unless otherwise stated.

7.2 Removal benefits and expenses

There is an exemption for the provision of qualifying removal benefits, or the reimbursement of qualifying removal expenses, up to a maximum amount of £8,000.

For the exemption to apply, all of these conditions must be met:

- The employee must change his or her main residence.
- The employee must have changed employment or duties or the place where duties are performed.
- The old residence must not be within reasonable daily travelling distance of the employee's normal workplace.
- The new residence must be within reasonable daily travelling distance of the employee's normal workplace.
- The expenses must have been reasonably incurred in connection with the change of residence.

"Reasonable daily travelling distance" is not defined in the legislation. HMRC at EIM 03104 indicate that what is reasonable depends on common sense and should take into account local conditions as well as the time needed to travel to and from work.

Section 272 sets out the removal benefits/expenses which potentially qualify:

- acquisition and disposal costs (including any abortive costs) such as:
  - legal fees (including Land Registry fees and stamp duty land tax);
  - costs in connection with early redemption of a mortgage;

- o any maintenance, insurance or security costs or rent paid while the old residence is empty;
  - o advertising and estate agents' or auctioneers' fees;
  - o survey costs; and
  - o disconnection/reconnection of utilities;
- removal and transportation costs;
- travelling and subsistence associated with looking for the new residence;
- replacement domestic goods for the new residence;
- cost of temporary accommodation where the new residence is not ready. Here the "cost" is calculated on the same basis as employer-provided living accommodation (see **6.4**); and
- bridging loan interest to the extent the loan does not exceed the value of the interest in the old residence.

If the bridging loan is a taxable cheap loan that might otherwise produce a benefits charge, and is taken out before the "limitation day" (see below), the interest can be exempted from being a taxable benefit for a limited number of days. These are calculated by the formula:

$$\frac{\text{Unused exemption}}{(\text{amount of loan} \times \text{official rate of interest})} \times 365$$

The qualifying benefits and expenses must be incurred by the "limitation day", which is 5 April following the end of the tax year in which the employee relocated.

Any excess paid over the £8,000 will be taxable on the employee in the normal way under s. 287

Law: ITEPA 2003, s. 271-289
Guidance: EIM 03104

7.3   Childcare

7.3.1   Introduction

There are a number of exempt benefits designed to encourage the employer to facilitate childcare provision. Where applicable, they cover children up to 1 September following their 15th birthday (or 16th birthday in the case of a disabled child).

7.3.2   On-site crèche or nursery

The provision by an employer of a crèche or nursery for employees' children is a tax-exempt benefit. A key requirement for this is that the employer must provide the premises in which the crèche or nursery operates (although employers can join together to share in providing a nursery on a site occupied by one of those employers).

Law: ITEPA 2003, s. 318

7.3.3   Off-site crèche or nursery

A partial exemption applies where other childcare for employees' children is provided by the employer – whether by way of childcare vouchers, or under a contract with an approved childcare provider such as a commercial nursery. However, this partial exemption only applies to employees who:

- were already in an employer-supported or voucher scheme before 5 October 2018;
- stay with the same employer who continues to run the scheme; and
- do not take an unpaid career break of longer than a year.

The amount of the exemption is dependent on the relevant earnings from the employment in question (as opposed to earnings from all sources). In 2021-22, the amount of exemption is:

- £55 per week where relevant earnings are equal to or below the basic rate limit;
- £28 per week where relevant earnings are between the basic rate and higher rate limits; and
- £25 per week where relevant earnings are above the higher rate limit.

These income-based limits do not apply to employees who joined their employer's childcare voucher scheme before 6 April 2011 (and have remained in the same employment since). For such employees, the previous flat-rate limit of £55 continues to apply. This is obviously of diminishing relevance but may still be seen in practice.

Example

Alison joined her employer's scheme to provide childcare vouchers on 6 April 2017. In 2021-22, she is expected to receive relevant earnings of

£58,000, which is above the higher rate threshold of £50,270. Therefore the first £25 per week of childcare vouchers will be exempt, but any excess above this amount will be taxable.

The employer must determine the level of the exemption available at the beginning of each tax year, by estimating the employee's relevant earnings for the tax year in which the childcare or vouchers are to be provided. (In practice, this means any subsequent drop or increase in earnings during the tax year is irrelevant, although it will impact on the following year's estimate.)

Relevant earnings are essentially taxable contractual earnings after deduction of certain pension contributions, payroll giving and personal allowances. For more details on what constitutes relevant earnings for these purposes, and details of how to do the calculation, see s. 270B and SI 2011/1798, and also EIM 16055.

Law: ITEPA 2003, s. 270A-270B, 318-318D; SI 2001/1798
Guidance: EIM 16055

7.4   Exemptions related to transport

7.4.1   Cycles and cycle safety equipment

Cycles and cycle safety equipment are exempt if they are generally made available to all employees, there is no transfer of ownership to the employee and the cycles/equipment are used mainly for qualifying journeys (which has the same definition as for work transport services – see **7.4.7** below).

For the period from 16 March 2020 to 5 April 2022, the condition relating to use for qualifying journeys is deemed to have been met.

Law: ITEPA 2003, s. 244; *Finance Bill* 2021, cl. 25

7.4.2   Late-night taxis

The provision of a taxi or private road transport up to a maximum of 60 journeys in a tax year is exempt where:

- the employee has to work until at least 9 pm;
- it is not the employee's usual working hours; and
- public transport has ceased by the time the employee finishes work or it is unreasonable to expect the employee to use it.

Provision will also be exempt where the employee usually car-shares, but unforeseen and exceptional circumstances arise, such as the driver being taken ill, leaving the employee without transport.

Law: ITEPA 2003, s. 248

7.4.3   Transport for disabled employees

The provision of transport, or reimbursement of the costs of transport for ordinary commuting (or between two places that would be regarded as substantially ordinary commuting), is exempt where the employee is disabled.

A disabled employee for these purposes is a person with a physical or mental impairment which has a substantial and long-term adverse effect on the ability to carry out normal day-to-day activities.

Where the employee is provided with a car, see **6.5**.

Law: ITEPA 2003, s. 246

7.4.4   Travel and subsistence during public transport strikes

There is an exemption for the provision of (or the reimbursement of the costs of) transport to and from a permanent workplace, or the provision of accommodation at or near the employee's permanent workplace, where industrial action disrupts a public transport service normally used by the employee.

Law: ITEPA 2003, s. 245

7.4.5   Vehicle-charging facilities

The provision of facilities to recharge all-electric or plug-in hybrid vehicles at or near the workplace (including the cost of the electricity) is exempt provided that the facilities are made available generally to the employer's employees.

Law: ITEPA 2003, s. 237A

7.4.6   Workplace parking

The provision of a parking space (including spaces for motorcycles and bicycles) at or near the employee's place of work is a tax-exempt benefit.

Law: ITEPA 2003, s. 237

7.4.7   *Works transport services*

The provision of a works bus is an exempt benefit if:

- it is generally available to employees of the employer concerned;
- it is substantially used only by employees or their children/stepchildren under the age of 18;
- it is used for qualifying journeys; and
- it is either a bus seating 12 or more, or a minibus seating nine or more.

SI 2002/205 identifies qualifying journeys as including a journey on a workday between work and shops or other local amenities no more than ten miles away (covering situations where the workplace does not have easy access to facilities). However, little other help as to what constitutes a "qualifying journey" is provided in the legislation. HMRC take it to mean – in addition to journeys within SI 2002/205 – journeys between home and work and from one workplace to another.

The support or subsidising of a public transport road service is also exempt provided it is generally available to employees for qualifying journeys and, where it is a local bus service within the *Transport Act* 1985, s. 2, is provided on terms that are no more favourable than for non-employees.

Example

JKY plc has a factory on the outskirts of town. A local bus service passes by, which employees often use to get to work, but it stops at 10.30 pm before the last shift at JKY plc finishes. JKY plc agrees to subsidise the bus company so that it can operate bus services until 11.30 pm.

This would be an exempt benefit, provided that the terms on which the employees use the bus are no more favourable than for other customers.

Law: *Transport Act* 1985, s. 2; ITEPA 2003, s. 243; SI 2002/205
Guidance: EIM 21850

7.5 Exemptions related to the work environment

7.5.1 Facilitating disabled employees to work

Equipment provided to disabled employees to allow them to perform their duties is exempt – even if there is significant private use.

Law: SI 2002/1596

7.5.2 Fees for DBS certificates

Fees paid or reimbursed by the employer for Disclosure and Barring Service (DBS) certificates, or other criminal record checks where the employee concerned works with vulnerable people, are exempt.

Law: ITEPA 2003, s. 326A

7.5.3 Incidental overnight expenses

Employees who are required to stay away from home overnight may incur incidental expenses. These are expenses that would not have been incurred had the employees not been away but that are not incurred necessarily in performing duties and so are not deductible. An example would be laundry costs.

Employer payments (but not reimbursement of employee costs) are exempt for incidental expenses up to £5 per night (or £10 per night if working abroad). The employee must be away from home for at least one night and the travelling expenses must be deductible under the normal rules.

Law: ITEPA 2003, s. 240

7.5.4 Mobile phones

The provision of a single mobile phone, and the payment of associated charges (or reimbursement to the employee of the costs), is exempt.

However, the exemption does not extend to phones provided to persons other than the employee, for example a spouse. Nor does it cover any private calls or standing charges in relation to the employee's own mobile phone.

Law: ITEPA 2003, s. 319

7.5.5   Personal physical security

There is an exemption for the provision of assets or services to protect the employee from special threats to his or her personal physical security arising as a result of work. The exemption also covers the reimbursement of the costs of such assets or services.

The rules for exemption are interpreted very strictly, however.

Law: ITEPA 2003, s. 377
Guidance: EIM 21810

7.5.6   Suggestion awards

Awards by an employer to an employee under a staff suggestion scheme will be exempt provided:

- the scheme is open to all employees generally, or to a defined group of them;
- the suggestion relates to activities carried on by the employer;
- the suggestion is not one that the employee could reasonably be expected to make in the course of his duties, having regard to his experience; and
- the suggestion is not made at a meeting held for the purpose of proposing suggestions.

Where the exemption applies, awards that generate a financial benefit will be exempt up to £5,000, although more can be given if the savings generated are significant. Non-financial suggestions are exempt to a maximum of £25.

Law: ITEPA 2003, s. 321-322

7.5.7   Working from home

An exemption is given for payments made by employers in respect of the reasonable additional costs incurred by an employee working from home. There must be a formal arrangement where the employee is required to work regularly from home, rather than choosing to do so.

Some relaxation of the rules (allowing more employees who are not reimbursed to claim a deduction) has been given during the Covid-19 pandemic. It is important to note, however, that where an employee has taken advantage of this relaxation in 2020-21, a new claim will need to be made for the 2021-22 tax year.

HMRC do not require records to be kept for payments up to £6 per week or £312 per year. However, evidence needs to be retained if payments exceed these limits.

See also **8.4.5** for further commentary on working from home.

Law: ITEPA 2003, s. 316A

Guidance: https://tinyurl.com/y25zr89v

7.5.8   Work-related training

The provision of (or the reimbursement of costs of) work-related training – and the associated travel, accommodation and expenditure – is exempt.

The course or other activity must relate to developing or improving knowledge, skills or personal qualities that are useful or necessary to the employee in performing the duties of the employment or in participating in charitable or voluntary activities arising through the employment.

Example

Prolly Ltd contracts with a language school to provide language courses in Spanish to its employees.

The provision of language lessons is not in itself work-related training. Much depends on whether it is useful to the employees in their employment, for example, if the employees deal with Spanish-speaking clients or suppliers.

Law: ITEPA 2003, s. 250-260

7.6   Exemptions relating to lifestyle benefits

7.6.1   Annual staff celebrations

The provision of a party or other similar annual function for the employees is exempt provided the costs of the party do not exceed £150 per head, including VAT.

If the costs exceed £150 then the whole of the benefit is taxable, not just the excess.

If the employer provides two or more functions, all the functions will be exempt provided the total cost per head does not exceed the £150 limit.

Law: ITEPA 2003, s. 264

7.6.2   Gifts etc. from third parties

Hospitality, entertainment, and gifts from third parties will be exempt provided:

- the employer is not connected with the third party or involved in procurement of the hospitality, entertainment or gift in any way;
- the total cost to the donor of gifts received by the employee in any one tax year does not exceed £250; and
- the hospitality, entertainment or gift is not in recognition of services performed or to be performed by the employee.

There are additional limitations on gifts. They must not exceed £250 in total in any one year from one donor and must not be in the form of cash, cash vouchers or shares.

Law: ITEPA 2003, s. 265, 324

7.6.3   Insurance

Payments are exempt if made for life or critical illness assurance for the benefit of the employee, or of his or her spouse or civil partner.

Law: ITEPA 2003, s. 325C

7.6.4   Long-service awards

Awards made to the employee in recognition of long service are exempt provided:

- the employee has accrued at least 20 years of service with the employer;
- the value of the award does not exceed £50 per year of service;
- the award is not in the form of cash, cash vouchers or shares; and
- it is at least ten years since the employee received a long-service award from the same employer.

Law: ITEPA 2003, s. 323

7.6.5   Medical check-ups

The provision of medical check-ups, and the costs of health screening, are exempt provided there is no more than one per tax year.

Eye tests (and the consequential provision of corrective glasses or lenses) are also exempt where an employee is required to use a visual display unit in the employment.

Law: ITEPA 2003, s. 320A-320B

7.6.6   Medical treatment

Medical treatment provided to an employee, including the payment or reimbursement of the cost of such treatment, is exempt where:

- the treatment has been recommended to assist an employee to return to work after an absence due to injury or ill health up to a maximum amount of £500 (any excess is taxable); or
- the treatment is overseas and is provided to an employee outside the UK to enable him to perform employment duties.

Providing insurance to cover overseas medical treatment is also exempt.

Law: ITEPA 2003, s. 320C, 325

7.6.7   Sports or recreational facilities

There is an exemption for the provision of recreational facilities such as sports grounds. The facilities must be available to all employees, and not available to the public generally, and must be used wholly or mainly by reason of the employment.

The legislation has certain specific exclusions, including holiday or overnight accommodation, mechanically-propelled vehicles such as ships, and facilities provided on domestic premises.

Law: ITEPA 2003, s. 261-262

7.6.8   Staff canteens

Subsidised staff canteens are exempt provided the facilities are available to all employees. This exemption is not available, however, if the provision is part of a salary sacrifice or other flexible benefit arrangement.

Law: ITEPA 2003, s. 317

7.6.9 Trivial benefits

Trivial benefits are exempt provided that they:

- cost less than £50;
- are not in the form of cash or cash vouchers; and
- are not in recognition of particular services carried out by an employee.

Example 1

Orsay Developments Ltd provides all its employees with a store voucher on their birthday at a cost of £30 per voucher. This would be exempt as a trivial benefit.

However, if the voucher was awarded for excellent customer service or was in the form of cash, it would be outside the rule on trivial benefits and would be taxable.

Care needs to be taken where a series of items/events could together be regarded as constituting a single benefit and exceed the £50 threshold. This would have the impact of making the whole benefit taxable.

Example 2

Really Reilly Ltd has a baseball season ticket which averages out at a cost of £30 per match. If an employee is able to use the ticket for one match, this would be a trivial benefit. However, if the same employee uses it more than once, HMRC could take the view that access to the ticket is a single benefit valued at £60 (or more) and therefore is fully taxable.

There is no limit on the number of trivial benefits that can be provided in the tax year to any particular employee, except where the individual is a director in a close company. In this case, the total value of trivial benefits cannot exceed an annual cap of £300.

Law: ITEPA 2003, s. 323A

7.7   Exempt benefits for specific employees

7.7.1   Introduction

Part 4, Ch. 8 sets out a number of exemptions in relation to specific types of employment:

Occupation	Relevant benefits	ITEPA 2003 reference
Members of UK parliaments/ assemblies	Certain payments on ceasing to be an MP, accommodation, travel and subsistence expenses	s. 290-294
Government ministers	Transport and subsistence	s. 295
Members of local authorities	Travel expenses	s. 295A
Members of UK armed forces	Travel in relation to leave; food and drink allowances; operational allowances; council tax relief payments; continuity of education allowances	s. 296-297D
Members of reserves and auxiliary armed forces	Training allowances; bounties for undertaking training	s. 298
Members of visiting armed forces	Payments made by own employer	s. 303
Diplomatic staff	Payments made by own employer	s. 300-302
Crown employees on foreign service	Accommodation; cost of living allowances	s. 299
Offshore oil and gas workers	Travel between mainland and offshore installation	s. 305
Voluntary office-holders	Expenses; compensation for lost employment income	s. 299A-299B
Carers	Board and lodging	s. 306A
Colliery workers	Coal or coal allowance	s. 306

Occupation (cont.)	Relevant benefits	ITEPA 2003 reference
Ministers of religion	Council tax and water rates; certain other benefits and expenses where earnings less than £8,500	s. 290-290G
Sports players	Certain sporting testimonial payments	s. 306B

Law: ITEPA 2003, s. 290-306B

7.8   Pitfalls and planning points

Exemptions generally

Making the most of exemptions is a non-aggressive way of building a remuneration package that appeals to employees in a tax-efficient way. However, the rules around exemptions are complex and it is easy to fall outside them. For example, an annual party costing £151 per head is fully taxable, whereas a party costing £150 is tax free. Understanding the detail is essential (see **7.6.1** above).

Removal expenses

The exemption only relates to reimbursed expenses. It is therefore essential that the employee keeps all receipts and records necessary to substantiate the amounts paid (see **7.2** above).

Closure of childcare voucher schemes to new entrants

Childcare voucher schemes (and equivalent) have been closed to new entrants from 5 October 2018 (see **7.3.3** above).

Interaction of childcare voucher schemes with tax-free childcare

Following the closure of childcare voucher schemes to new entrants, a replacement system has been put in place to assist with childcare funding (known as tax-free childcare).

Tax-free childcare operates directly between the employee and the government through an online childcare account. It is not, however, possible to benefit under both a childcare voucher scheme and tax-free childcare. As soon as the employee notifies the employer of an intention to operate a tax-free childcare account, the tax and NIC savings associated with the childcare voucher scheme cease. Furthermore, if the claimant subsequently leaves tax-free childcare, the childcare voucher tax benefits cannot be reinstated.

Interaction of childcare voucher schemes with tax credits and universal credit

The value of any childcare vouchers must ordinarily be deducted when calculating childcare costs for the purposes of entitlement to tax credits and universal credit. The exact position depends on personal circumstances but where childcare vouchers are taken in return for a salary sacrifice or OpRA, the tax and NIC savings may amount to less than the corresponding reduction in tax credits or universal credit.

Impact of salary sacrifice arrangements

The availability of some exemptions, such as subsidised canteen meals, is affected if there is a related salary sacrifice or optional remuneration arrangement (see **6.10.4**).

8.   Employment expenses

8.1   Introduction

8.1.1   Overview

Although ITEPA 2003 brings employment income within the charge to income tax, the amount on which tax will be calculated is limited to net taxable earnings (in relation to general earnings – see **5.3.1 to 5.3.3**) and net taxable specific income (in relation to specific employment income – see **5.3.4**).

This chapter discusses the deductions that can be made from employment income to arrive at the net taxable figure. Statutory references are to ITEPA 2003 unless otherwise stated.

Law: ITEPA 2003, s. 11, 12

8.1.2   General principles

Before examining the permitted deductions in detail, it is worth considering some general principles.

Three scenarios can arise in the way deductible expenses are incurred:

- the employee can bear the expenses personally;
- the employee can incur the expenses directly and be reimbursed by the employer or on the employer's behalf; or
- the employer can pay for the expense directly.

Payroll giving and pension contributions operate slightly differently. Here, the employment income is reduced by the employee's contributions to either scheme.

Where the employee incurs the expenses, a claim for the deduction is typically made through his or her self-assessment and either a repayment may be made or an adjustment to the individual's tax code (see **Chapter 14**). However, if the employer reimburses or incurs the expense, theoretically the employee receives additional earnings (the amount incurred by the employer) and a corresponding right to a deduction under s. 334. To avoid unnecessary administration, the two offset each other so that the earnings are ignored, and no further reporting/claim is required per s. 289A.

Deductions can usually only be made from the earnings of the employment in connection with which they arise (s. 328(1)). The most notable exception is ministers of religion, where permitted expenses can be set off against any employment as a minister of religion (see **8.4.7** below).

No double deduction is allowed in respect of the same cost, for example where an individual incurs an expense which is allowed as a deduction under general rules and has a fixed allowance. In these circumstances, unless statutory provisions state otherwise (as in the case of seafarers (see **38.6.4**)), the deduction taken first is the one which gives the greatest reduction of liability to income tax (s. 330-331).

Example

Damian pays £120 per year to clean his work uniform. He qualifies for a £60 fixed allowance in respect of these expenses under s. 367 (see **8.4.6** below). However, he is also entitled to a deduction of £120 based on the actual cost. Damian cannot claim for both, but he is entitled to claim for the larger amount to reduce his tax liability as much as possible.

If deductions exceed the amount of earnings, the earnings will be reduced to nil. There is no provision for claiming a loss or repayment.

Law: ITEPA 2003, s. 327-334

8.1.3   Deductions from general earnings – basic rules

To calculate net taxable earnings in any tax year, taxable earnings must be reduced by the following deductions allowed under s. 327(3)-(5):

- employee expenses permitted under Pt. 5 (see **8.2** below);
- mileage allowance relief under s. 232 (see **8.3** below);
- certain capital allowances on qualifying expenditure incurred by the employee under CAA 2001, s. 262 (see **8.4.8** below);
- charitable contributions made under payroll giving in ITEPA 2003, Pt. 12 (see **8.6** below); and
- contributions made to registered pension schemes under FA 2004, s. 188-194 (see **Chapter 30**).

Law: ITEPA 2003, s. 11, 327

8.2 Expenses

8.2.1 General employee expenses

Section 336 sets out the general principles relating to deductions against general earnings. Essentially, a deduction against earnings is allowed if the employee is obliged to incur and pay the expense as holder of the employment and the amount is incurred wholly, exclusively and necessarily in the performance of his or her duties.

This is a complex test, which is difficult to satisfy in practice. It can be broken into a number of elements:

- there must be an obligation to incur the cost;
- the obligation must arise as a result of holding the employment; and
- the expense must have been wholly, exclusively and necessarily incurred in the performance of duties.

Each element must be satisfied in order for the expense to be deductible. Whether this is the case is a question of fact which must be looked at objectively based on the exact nature of the job and the duties involved (see *Taylor v Provan*).

Law: ITEPA 2003, s. 336
Case: *Taylor v Provan* (1975) 49 TC 579

8.2.2 Employee is obliged to pay

Not only must the expense arise on the employee in his capacity as employee, rather than in any other capacity, but it must be something he has to pay, rather than something he merely chooses to pay.

Example

Andrew has a job working from home as a market researcher. He is obliged to provide his own stationery for printing out and posting surveys. He buys standard paper and envelopes used solely for the role. He likes to listen to music as he works so he also subscribes for a music streaming service to use while working.

Here the obligation to buy the stationery is falling on Andrew in his capacity as an employee. He has an obligation to make the purchase and if it wasn't Andrew doing the job then his replacement would also have the same obligation. On this basis it cannot be said to be something he chooses to pay on a personal level.

By contrast, the cost of the music streaming service would not be deductible. Andrew has spent the money but there is no employment-related obligation on him to do so. It is a purely personal and voluntary purchase.

The position must be viewed objectively, taking account of all the facts of the case and ignoring the personal choices of the particular employee.

8.2.3 Wholly and exclusively

There is no statutory definition of the phrase "wholly and exclusively", although there is sufficient case law to suggest that it should be interpreted very narrowly.

In *Williams*, the First-tier Tribunal found that the cost of professional hair styling and colouring incurred by a TV newsreader was not deductible. There was no contractual requirement for the expenditure, and it was found that she required the services as a person, not just in her capacity as a newsreader. Therefore, there was a duality of purpose preventing relief.

In practice, HMRC will allow a deduction for the part of the expense relating to the employment if it is possible to apportion the costs between private and work use. Furthermore, HMRC will not disallow an expense which would otherwise be deductible if the private use element is so small as to be merely incidental to the expense as a whole.

Example

Stacey works as a telemarketer from home and has a landline which she uses for making mainly work telephone calls. She also makes some personal calls, although she does not get an itemised bill which would enable her to identify the cost or time attributable to these.

On the face of it, an apportionment between personal and work calls is not possible and therefore the whole bill will be disallowed unless the personal calls can be shown in some other way to be merely incidental.

Case: *Williams v HMRC* [2010] UKFTT 86 (TC)

8.2.4 Necessarily

It is not enough that the expense is incurred wholly in connection with employment. It also has to be "necessary". If the job can be done without the expense being incurred then, arguably, the expense is not necessary and is therefore not deductible.

8.2.5   In the performance of the duties

Even if it can be established that the employee meets the wholly, exclusively and necessary test, a deduction is only available if the expense is incurred in the actual performance of duties.

Examples of expenses that are not deductible under this principle include:

- expenses that only facilitate the performance of duties, such as payments for childcare;
- expenses related to the purpose of preparing for the employee's future duties, such as the costs of gaining the necessary qualifications; and
- expenses related to improving or maintaining the performance of the employee while in the job.

The narrow interpretation of the concept of "performance of the duties" is illustrated in *Abbott*. In this case, the employee was a journalist and received an allowance from his employer to purchase newspapers. This allowance was treated as an emolument and the taxpayer sought a corresponding deduction as an allowable expense. The House of Lords considered that reading newspapers was not a journalist's job but rather was done to help a journalist do his job. As such the deduction was not allowable.

Case: *Smith v Abbott and Ors* [1994] BTC 66

8.2.6   Treatment of travel expenses

The general principles relating to travel expenses have been developed over a number of years and are now codified and consolidated in s. 337-338. These provide for a deduction of an employee's travel costs where they are:

- "necessarily incurred on travelling in the performance of the duties of the employment" (s. 337(1)); or
- "attributable to the employee's necessary attendance at any place in the performance of the duties of the employment" (s. 338(1)).

Example 1

Randolph works at an office in Sheffield five days a week. Usually, clients visit him, but occasionally he will travel to meet with them at their premises. Any travel costs incurred are paid for by his employer.

153

Randolph is clearly travelling to a place where attendance is necessary for the performance of his duties and, as such, the reimbursed travel expenses will not be taxable.

The definition of work-related travel costs is potentially very wide but s. 338 goes on to exclude the expenses of private travel and ordinary commuting. Ordinary commuting in this context means travel between a permanent workplace and the employee's home or a place that is not a workplace.

Example 2

Randolph lives in Rotherham and normally catches a bus to his office in Sheffield. One night a month, he tends to stay over at a friend's house to the south of Sheffield and catches the tram into work.

Although the bus and tram fares are incurred by Randolph and are necessary to attend the office to carry out his employment duties, a deduction from earnings is not allowable as he is simply travelling from his home (or its equivalent in the case of the friend's home) to his usual place of work.

Section 338(7) also prevents a deduction for travel between any two places where there is no substantial impact on the journey or on the expenses incurred. In other words, the journey is for all practical purposes the same as ordinary commuting.

Example 3

One day, Randolph attends a training day at a venue half a mile from his office. He takes the same bus as he usually does when he goes to the office but gets off at the next stop.

Here, the journey to the training venue is substantially the same as the journey to the office and will be a similar expense. Accordingly, no deduction will be allowed for travel costs to the college.

The examples above are very straightforward, but this is not always the case in reality. What if the employee travels directly from his home to a client's premises and does not go into the office first? What if the employee works across multiple sites? What is the employee is based at home and works at different client sites consecutively?

To determine the correct tax treatment, it is necessary to consider the definition of a "permanent workplace" on the basis that it is travel to a permanent workplace that is disallowed.

Essentially, a permanent workplace is a place an employee regularly attends in the performance of employment duties which does not amount to a temporary workplace. Section 339 defines a temporary workplace as a place which the employee attends in the performance of his duties in order to perform a task of limited duration or for some other temporary purpose.

Drawing together the key statutory provisions, HMRC guidance and available case law, a workplace will be temporary if:

- the employee attends for a period of less than 24 months, unless the period comprises of all or almost all of the period of employment; or
- the employee does not spend a significant amount of his or her working time (taken by HMRC to mean less than 40%) at that place.

Therefore, if an employee is visiting a client for a day, or a few days or even a few months, the client's premises will be a temporary workplace and costs of travel to and from that workplace will be a deductible expense.

Example 4

Randolph's employer asks him to spend one day a week at a new office in Doncaster. He will continue working at the Sheffield office for his remaining four days a week.

Because Randolph will spend only 20% of his working time at the Doncaster office, it will be a temporary workplace and the associated travel costs will be deductible.

In practice, an employee could have two or more permanent workplaces, or none. It is important to look at each workplace in the context of both the overall contract and the "temporary workplace" criteria.

Care should be taken in three particular circumstances:

- If the employment duties are defined by reference to a geographical area, and the employee attends different places in the area in the course of his job, he will be treated as an area-based employee and the area will be treated as the permanent workplace. As such, travel costs to and from that area will not be deductible (s. 339(8)).
- A workplace can start as being temporary but may subsequently become permanent. For example, if it is

155

anticipated at the outset that the employee will be at the workplace for a period of less than 24 months, but it later becomes apparent that this time limit will be exceeded. In these circumstances, travel costs up to the point the period is expected to be less than 24 months are deductible, but costs after that point are not.

- Special rules exist for employment intermediaries which, in certain circumstances, treat the workplace attended by the individual providing the services as a permanent workplace. See **Chapter 13** for more details.

For oil and gas workers, there is a statutory exemption relating to the cost of commuting to an offshore installation. The employer must meet the cost and the exemption is restricted to:

- travel between the mainland port or airport which the employer normally uses for transfers to and from the offshore installation, and the location of the installation itself; and

- any local travel, accommodation and subsistence provided by the employer for employees who have to wait at or near the mainland port or airport before or after the transfer because of a gap before the next leg of their journey.

Law: ITEPA 2003, s. 337-339
Guidance: EIM 32080

8.2.7   *Treatment of subsistence expenses*

The decision in *Nolder v Walters* established that travel costs within s. 337-339 include not only actual costs of travel but also accommodation and subsistence costs associated with the travel.

There are some limitations:

- The cost of accommodation is only deductible where an overnight stay is needed because, for example, the temporary workplace is too far or does not have the transport connections to get to and from home the same day. Someone choosing, therefore, to stay in a hotel near the office because he or she would prefer not to go home in the same city cannot be said to "need accommodation" to perform the duties.

- The subsistence costs must be attributable to the business travel. For example, an employee might buy a magazine to read on the train, or travel-sized toiletries. These are definitely being bought because the employee is travelling but are not expenditure directly attributable to business travel and are therefore not deductible (but see the exemption for personal incidental expenses in **7.5.3**).

- Costs the employee would ordinarily incur if he or she were not travelling on business are not deductible. For example, if the employee brings a packed lunch from home, the cost is not deductible, but the cost of a sandwich from a café at the temporary workplace is.

- Costs arising as a result of the business travel that are a consequence of the employee's personal circumstances are not deductible. For example, the cost of a house-sitter or dog walker while away from home.

Where the employee has incurred allowable subsistence expenses, it is not necessary to reduce these by savings the employee has made as a result of not being at home. Equally, the cost of business travel is not usually relevant in determining whether a deduction is due. There is no obligation to choose the cheapest hotel, meal or transport option, although if the expenditure is extremely lavish, HMRC may query whether there is an element of reward in the amount expended.

Law: ITEPA 2003, s. 337-339
Case: *Nolder v Walters* (1931) 15 TC 380
Guidance: EIM 31835

8.2.8 Overseas travel and subsistence – additional statutory provisions – introduction

In addition to the general rules on travel and subsistence, there are a number of statutory provisions which allow for a deduction for overseas travel, accommodation and subsistence expenses where otherwise the expenditure would be excluded.

8.2.9 Travel at start and finish of overseas employment

Section 341 allows a deduction in respect of the first and last journeys to and from the UK where an employee works wholly abroad, provided all three conditions are met:

- The duties of the employment are performed wholly outside the UK (although UK duties that are merely incidental to the overseas employment can be disregarded).

- The employee is UK resident in the tax year in which the travel takes place.

- Where the employer is a foreign employer, the employee is domiciled in the UK.

See **Chapter 34** for details on residence, domicile and incidental duties.

The deduction extends to expenses incurred in relation to the journey; in other words, the cost of travel and subsistence *en route*. It would not, however, cover accommodation or meals at the destination (although this may be available under other provisions – see below).

If the travel is partly for a private purpose, the deduction is limited to the amount attributable to the taking up of the employment.

Example

Owen is a UK resident and is due to start a new job in San Francisco on a fixed-term contract for 12 months. He decides that he will go travelling in the US for three months before the contract starts and for three months afterwards.

A deduction would be allowed under ITEPA 2003, s. 341 but it would be limited to the amount attributable to the work; in this case, two thirds.

There is no statutory formula for working out the amount of the deduction in this scenario. It is a question of fact that may need to be agreed between the taxpayer and HMRC.

Law: ITEPA 2003, s. 341

8.2.10 *Subsistence costs where duties performed wholly abroad*

Section 376 does provide some relief in relation to accommodation and subsistence expenses where the employee works wholly overseas. However, it only applies where an employee's earnings include an amount in relation to such costs; in other words, they are paid for or provided by the employer.

For the relief to be available, all of the following conditions must be satisfied:

- The duties of the employment are performed wholly outside the UK.

- The employee is UK resident.

- If the employer is a foreign employer, the employee is
domiciled in the UK.

Relief extends to the reimbursement of expenses or the provision of
accommodation or subsistence outside the UK for the employee for the
purpose of enabling the employee to perform the duties of the
employment.

Example

Nathan normally lives and works in the UK. However, in July 2021, he
accepts a contract to teach windsurfing at a hotel in Barbados for four
months. He remains UK resident for tax purposes throughout.

The employer pays for his flights to and from Barbados and provides
accommodation and all meals while he is there.

In these circumstances, the contract consists of the whole of the
appointment, so no deduction would be available under general
principles. However, s. 376 would provide relief for the meals and
accommodation and s. 341 (see **8.2.9** above) would provide relief for the
cost of the flights.

Law: ITEPA 2003, s. 376

8.2.11 *Travel costs and expenses where duties performed partly abroad*

Most costs for overseas business travel as part of a wider UK-based role
are covered by the general rules relating to temporary workplaces.
However, there are some occasions when these rules do not provide
relief, for example if an employee works permanently across two or
more locations and both represent 40% or more of his time. Section 370
gives relief where the employee is UK resident for tax purposes and the
employer pays for, reimburses or provides:

- the costs of interim visits back to the UK during the course of
the employment (for instance, to visit family and friends)
where the duties of the employment are performed wholly
outside the UK (Case A);

- the costs of travel from and back to the UK where the
employment duties are carried out partly overseas, cannot be
carried out elsewhere and are not performed on a vessel (Case
B); or

- the costs of travel from and back to the UK in a case where the employment duties are performed partly outside the UK and are performed on a vessel (Case C). In determining whether duties carried out on a vessel are overseas or in the UK, regard is had to the actual location of the vessel; s. 40(2) (which deems certain duties on a vessel or aircraft to be performed in the UK) should be disregarded (s. 372).

There is no limit to the number of journeys that can qualify under s. 370, provided that, in each case, the journey is made wholly and exclusively for the purpose of performing the non-UK duties.

The relief is limited to the costs of travel. Accommodation and subsistence overseas are not covered.

Example

Jamie lives in London. He is a marketing executive and works for three days in the London office and two days in the Paris office each week. His employer pays for his Eurostar tickets to and from Paris, as well as his accommodation while there. Jamie buys his own meals.

Jamie spends at least 40% of his working time in Paris and therefore it is not a temporary workplace and so the general rules for deductible travel and subsistence expenses do not apply. The cost of the train fare will be relieved under s. 370, Case B. The accommodation will be a taxable benefit. No deduction is available for the cost of meals in Paris.

Law: ITEPA 2003, s. 370

8.2.12 *Travel costs and expenses of visiting spouses and children*

Section 371 ensures that no taxable benefit arises in respect of the provision, reimbursement or payment by an employer of the travel costs of visiting family. All of the following conditions must be satisfied:

- The employee is UK resident.
- The employee is absent from the UK for a continuous period of at least 60 days for the purpose of performing the employment duties.
- The journey is between a place in the UK and a place outside the UK where such duties are performed.
- The employee's spouse, civil partner or minor child is either accompanying the employee at the beginning of the period,

visiting the employee during that period or returning to the UK after accompanying or visiting the employee.

There are some important limitations:

- The journey must be to where the employee works. For example, working in Madrid but meeting up with the family for a week in Lanzarote is not covered.
- The family must be a spouse, a civil partner or a child of 18 or less on the outward journey from the UK. Adult children and co-habitees are not covered.
- Costs are limited to travel. Accommodation and subsistence costs of visiting family are not covered.
- Relief is limited to a maximum of two trips a year (although there is no maximum on the amount of expenses and no obligation to go by the cheapest route).

Law: ITEPA 2003, s. 371

8.2.13 *Travel costs and expenses of non-domiciled employees where duties performed in the UK*

Section 373 permits a deduction against earnings for the travel expenses of non-domiciled employees working in the UK, where all of the following conditions are met:

- The employee is non-UK domiciled (see **Chapter 36**).
- The employee has earnings relating to UK duties which are taxed on a receipts basis.
- The employer has paid for or reimbursed the expenses of travelling to and from the country where the employee usually lives to the UK in order to carry out the duties of his or her employment.
- The expense is incurred within five years of a qualifying arrival date.

A "qualifying arrival date" will be the date on which the employee arrives in the UK to perform UK duties, provided:

- he has not been in the UK for any purpose during the period of two years before coming to work in the UK; or
- he was not resident in the UK in either of the two preceding tax years.

161

If the employee fails either of these conditions, there will be no qualifying arrival date, so no relief will be available.

Where an employee makes repeated UK work visits of less than five years without becoming UK resident, the travel deduction can be claimed indefinitely. This is because the start of the five-year period will be re-set upon each arrival.

In addition to the costs of flights, transfers and subsistence costs, HMRC accept that the above expenses of travelling can include the costs of vaccinations and visas needed.

Where a non-domiciled employee is working in the UK for 60 or more continuous days, s. 374 provides relief for the travel costs of the employee's spouse and minor children (restricted to two return journeys per person per tax year). These family journeys must take place within five years of the employee's qualifying arrival date and the deduction is only available where the travel costs in question form part of the employee's UK earnings and are taxed on a receipts basis.

Law: ITEPA 2003, s. 373-374

8.3 Business mileage in own vehicle

Not all business travel is on public transport. Where an employee uses his own transport, an amount can be deducted from earnings to represent the cost of owning and running the vehicle, including the fuel used. To simplify matters, HMRC publish approved mileage rates for cars, motorcycles and bicycles (see **Appendix 8**). Where the employer reimburses amounts not exceeding the approved rates for business mileage, there will be no taxable benefit. If the reimbursement is less than the rates, then the employee is entitled to claim the shortfall as a deduction.

Example

Ivan does 14,000 business miles in his own car during the 2021-22 tax year. His employer pays him 30p per mile, i.e. £4,200.

To calculate the tax position, a comparison needs to be made between the total amount paid and the total amount of approved mileage allowance.

	£
Payment to Ivan: 14,000 miles x 30p	4,200
Total mileage allowance	
10,000 x 45p	4,500
4,000 x 25p	1,000
Total	5,500

Ivan can claim an additional deduction equal to the unused allowance, i.e. £1,300 (£5,500 - £4,200).

Different rates apply where the employee uses a motorcycle or bicycle, or a company-owned car or van (see **Appendix 8**).

Law: ITEPA 2003, s. 231

8.4 Other expenses

8.4.1 Annual subscriptions

Annual subscriptions paid to certain approved bodies (published by HMRC and referred to as List 3) are also deductible from earnings.

The activities of the approved body must be of direct benefit to the performance of the duties of the particular employment, or concern the profession practised in.

The deduction does not extend to entrance fees or life membership subscriptions.

Law: ITEPA 2003, s. 344
Case: *Brown v Bullock* (1961) 3 All ER 129
Guidance: *Approved Professional Organisations and Learned Societies* (List 3)

8.4.2 Professional fees

A deduction from taxable earnings is allowed for certain professional fees where the fees must be paid to enable the duties of the employment to be performed.

ITEPA 2003, s. 343 lists the deductible professional fees. These include, for example, payments by medical professionals, legal professionals, security workers and architects.

Law: ITEPA 2003, s. 343

8.4.3   Employee liabilities and indemnity insurance

A deduction is available for costs and expenses incurred:

- in or towards the discharge of a liability related to the employment;

- in connection with a claim, or proceedings arising out of a claim, that the employee is subject to a liability related to the employment;

- in connection with giving evidence in, or for the purposes of, proceedings (or some other process or an investigation) about a matter related to the employment; and

- in discharging premiums on an insurance policy taken out solely to cover the above costs and expenses.

However, no deduction is allowed if the liability relates to a matter which it is unlawful to insure against – for example, fines and penalties for criminal actions – or which relates to arrangements for which tax avoidance is one of the main purposes.

Law: ITEPA 2003, s. 346

8.4.4   Entertainment expenses

A deduction for expenses incurred in connection with entertainment is only available if the expense has been paid or reimbursed by the employer and has been disallowed in arriving at the employer's taxable profit. Client entertaining (and employee entertaining incidental to client entertaining) is not an allowable deduction for the employer, so a deduction will be permitted where an employee is required for genuine business reasons to entertain clients in the course of performing the duties of the employment; in other words, where the expense meets the usual "wholly, exclusively and necessarily in the performance of duties" test (see **8.3** above).

Law: ITEPA 2003, s. 336, 356

8.4.5   Working from home

A deduction is available for additional household costs incurred as a result of working from home (including having to work from home as a result of Covid-19) under general principles.

The deduction is limited to those costs that are incurred wholly, exclusively and necessarily in the performance of the duties and as such will not apply if the duties are incidental or if the employee has a suitable place of work but chooses to work from home.

Example

Sophie is a schoolteacher in a local secondary school. She often takes marking home to do at the weekend and so has an office set up in her spare room. Here a deduction for the additional costs would not be available as she could do the marking at school and is merely choosing to do it at home. However, if she has to teach from home due to the Covid-19 pandemic, then a deduction for additional costs is available.

In all cases, the deduction is limited to costs incurred which actually increase as a result of working from home, such as heating, business calls, enhanced broadband connection and metered water bills.

A deduction for significant equipment expenses (such as laptop computers) is also available in the form of a capital allowance if necessary for the job. The allowances must be reduced to reflect any private use.

See also **7.5.7** above.

Law: CAA 2001, s. 15, 205; ITEPA 2003, s. 336

Guidance: https://tinyurl.com/2tefantp (HMRC guidance re working from home)

8.4.6   Fixed allowances for uniforms, work clothing and tools

Buying tools or clothing for work is not deductible as it is capital expenditure. However, a deduction is available under general principles for:

- repairing or replacing small tools needed for the job, such as scissors or an electric drill;
- repairing or replacing specialist clothing, such as a uniform or safety boots; and
- cleaning specialist clothing, unless the employer provides a laundering service and the employee chooses not to use it.

No deduction is permitted for personal protective equipment, as the employer is responsible for providing it or reimbursing the cost to employees. Furthermore, everyday clothing does not count as a uniform, even if it is only worn for work and is a specified colour and/or style, for example, a restaurant that wants its bar staff to wear black t-shirts and jeans. Clothing will only amount to a uniform if it is a set of specialised

165

clothing that is recognisable as identifying someone as having a particular occupation, for example nurse or police uniforms. Only nurses and midwives can claim for the cost of replacing shoes, socks and underwear.

The amount deductible is the cost incurred. However, to ease administration, flat rate deductions have been agreed for certain industries. HMRC's published List of Industries and Occupations sets out the agreed amounts, which vary from £60 (e.g. for workers in the food industry) to £1,022 (for airline cabin crew). If an industry is not on the list a £60 deduction is available. No receipts are needed for flat rate deductions made in line with HMRC rates.

Law: ITEPA 2003, s. 336

Guidance: https://tinyurl.com/2xd7ufz8 (List of Industries and Occupations)

8.4.7   Ministers of religion

In addition to expenses incurred wholly, exclusively and necessarily in the performance of the duties of their employment, ministers of religion are entitled to some additional deductions which may not be allowed under the general rules. These are:

- a proportion, not exceeding one-quarter, of the rent paid for a dwelling-house, any part of which is used mainly and substantially for the purposes of the minister's duties; and

- one-quarter of the expenditure on the maintenance, repair, insurance or management of any accommodation that is made available to the minister.

The expenses are only allowable if an ecclesiastical corporation or charity owns an interest in the accommodation and the minister performs the duties of the employment from the accommodation. As noted at **8.1.2** above, permitted expenses incurred by a minister of religion can be offset against *any* employment as such a minister.

Law: ITEPA 2003, s. 351

8.4.8   Capital allowances

The general rules for deducting employees' expenses do not specifically prevent a deduction for capital expenditure. However, substantial expenditure on capital items such as machinery or equipment will not usually qualify as a deductible expense because it tends to put employees in a position to perform the duties rather than being incurred in the actual performance of duties.

It is, however, possible to claim capital allowances for expenditure on plant and machinery under the *Capital Allowances Act* (CAA) 2001, Pt. 2 (see, generally, **Chapter 20**). There is no statutory definition of what constitutes "plant", although, generally speaking, an item must have an expected working life of at least two years to qualify. Employees are not entitled to claim capital allowances for cars, vans, motorcycles or bicycles.

The general rule is that employees and office-holders are entitled to capital allowances for expenditure that they incur on acquiring machinery or plant which is "necessarily provided for use in the performance of their duties". This phrase imposes the same objective test as the general rule for employees' expenses in ITEPA 2003, s. 336 (see **8.2** above). It follows that capital allowances are not available for expenditure on items which employees provide simply for their own convenience or for other reasons personal to themselves, even if those items are used to carry out work.

HMRC take the view that to qualify for capital allowances, the duties of an employee must objectively require the use of the machinery or plant in question. HMRC state it is important to establish what the employees' duties require and whether it is necessary for the employees to provide the items themselves. In HMRC's view, an item will not have been "necessarily provided" by the employee if the employer is willing to provide or pay for it. Equally, a refusal by the employer to pay for or provide the item on the basis that it is not necessary is damaging to the claim.

By contrast, a specific reference in the contract of employment to the requirement to incur expenditure on plant or machinery is helpful, as is evidence that other workers with similar duties have also incurred the same sort of expense.

The machinery or plant does not have to be "wholly and exclusively" used for the performance of the duties. If there is private use the allowances can be apportioned.

In calculating the capital allowances available, the legislation applies to offices and employments in the same way it applies to trades. In practice, nearly all claims by employees will be by way of annual investment allowances (AIAs) (see **Chapter 20**). A balancing charge will normally be made where capital allowances have been claimed and the employee subsequently:

- sells or otherwise disposes of the plant or machinery;
- ceases to use it in the employment because the employment ends; or
- permanently ceases to use it in the performance of the duties of the employment.

Example

Iain works for a cosmetics company, focusing on door-to-door retail sales, and incurs qualifying expenditure on work equipment at a cost of £8,000.

He uses the equipment solely for work until he leaves the job after four years and sells it for £1,000.

The expenditure of £8,000 will be deductible, by way of AIAs, in the year the expense is incurred. When Iain sells the equipment, the £1,000 received will be treated as a balancing charge and added to his earnings for the year of sale.

Both allowances and balancing charges have to be adjusted to take private use into account.

Law: CAA 2001, s. 15, 36, 57, 65, 262
Guidance: EIM 36540, 36560

8.5   Deductions against specific employment income

The deductions mentioned in this chapter so far are only available against general earnings.

Where specific employment income arises, only the following deductions operate to reduce the taxable amount:

- charitable contributions made under payroll giving in ITEPA 2003, Pt. 12 (**see 8.6 below**);
- contributions made to registered pension schemes under FA 2004, s. 188-194 (see **Chapter 30**); and
- expenses directly attributable to the specific employment income in question, as permitted by ITEPA 2003.

For more details on the deductions permitted in relation to different types of specific employment income, please refer to the relevant individual chapters: **Chapter 9** (termination payments), **Chapter 10** (employment-related securities), **Chapter 13** (disguised remuneration) and **Chapter 31** (payment from EFRBS).

Law: ITEPA 2003, s. 12

8.6   Payroll giving

Donations made to charity through a formal payroll giving scheme are deductible from employment income (whether general earnings or specific employment income). Such schemes are operated by the employer and tax relief is effectively given at source by deducting the donations from gross pay before calculating any tax due.

To set up a payroll giving scheme, the employer must sign up with an HMRC-approved payroll giving agency (PGA). The PGA receives the deductions from the employer and distributes them to the chosen charities.

There is no limit on the amount of pay that an employee can choose to donate under payroll giving and an employee can leave the scheme at any time by giving reasonable notice to the employer or to the PGA.

Law: ITEPA 2003, s. 713-715

Guidance: https://tinyurl.com/6ee5wvbd (approved agencies for payroll giving)

8.7   Pitfalls and planning points

Aligning expense policy with deductible expenses

Where the employer only pays for or reimburses expenses that are wholly deductible by the employee, there is no consequential withholding or reporting. This saving in administration and cash-flow is extensive, so formal expense policies that directly reflect deductible expense rules are advised.

It is not, however, enough that policies are created; they should be followed. It is also worth reviewing on a regular basis as rates and small details do change.

Making the most of expenses

Certain expenses – such as business mileage reimbursement, cost of home-working, provision of uniforms and payment of professional subscription fees – can, if not paid for by employers, be cumbersome for employees to track and claim an appropriate deduction. Often, employees do not bother. Consider restructuring remuneration packages so that the cost of these is borne by the employer, thereby potentially generating savings for both employer and employee.

Monitoring changes in circumstances

Not only do the rules change, but an employee's circumstances can too. What starts as a deductible expense can inadvertently become a taxable benefit. Common examples of these are where a work pattern changes and a temporary workplace becomes a permanent workplace or where family visit flights continue to be provided to children who reach the age of 18. Again, the best way to avoid compliance issues is to conduct a regular review of the expense and benefits policy.

9. Termination payments

9.1 Introduction

As mentioned in **Chapter 5**, employment income includes not only earnings and employment-related benefits, but also specific employment income. This in turn includes a payment on or in connection with the termination of employment within ITEPA 2003, s. 401. All statutory references in this chapter are to ITEPA 2003 except where indicated to the contrary.

One of the key advantages of an amount being taxed under s. 401 is that the first £30,000 is exempt from tax and NIC. However, s. 401(3) makes it clear that this only applies if the payment or benefit is not otherwise chargeable to income tax under any other provision. It follows that if an amount could be treated as earnings then it will be taxed under s. 62 (in full) instead of under s. 401 (with the advantage of a £30,000 exemption).

In reality, a payment received on the termination of an employment is likely to consist of a number of elements, such as accrued holiday pay, redundancy payments, payments in lieu of notice and compensation for loss of office. Each of these elements could be taxed differently and therefore it is vital to consider each one separately.

Law: ITEPA 2003, s. 6-7, 401

9.2 Contractual payments

The starting point when looking at any element of a termination payment is to determine whether it can be classified (and taxed) as earnings of the employment.

HMRC take the approach that a payment will be taxable as earnings if either of the following applies:

- There is a contractual right to the payment, either as a result of a clause contained in the employment contract or any other documentation such as a side letter, union agreement or staff handbook, or as a result of an informal agreement between the parties.
- There is a reasonable expectation that the payment would be made. Although quite difficult to prove in practice, HMRC take

the view that this could arise if, for example, there has been an informal agreement or, more commonly, if the employer has taken a similar approach in the same situation in such a regular and consistent manner that the employer is effectively implying that the employee will also receive the payment.

Example

Books R Us Ltd does not have any formal or written contractual provisions on what happens on a termination of employment. However, it typically allows every employee who is made redundant, or who leaves due to ill health, to choose and keep books up to the value of £1,000. Here the receipt of books has become such common practice that it takes on the nature of a right. In this case, the provision of the books would be treated as fully taxable under the general rules.

In reaching their opinion, HMRC will look first at the employment contract. If the contract is silent, the approach is to look at other documents including notes of meetings, and if necessary to interview the parties involved.

Examples of typical payments that are treated as contractual include:

- pay or benefits provided in relation to the employee working out his or her notice period;
- bonuses relating to performance of past services;
- termination bonuses included in the contract of employment;
- payments in lieu of notice where the right to make this payment is included in the contract of employment; and
- accrued holiday pay.

A statutory redundancy payment (or a payment from an employer's formal redundancy scheme) will not be taxable as general earnings, even if it is contractual (see **9.5** below).

Guidance: EIM 12850, 12977

9.3 Payments for restrictive covenants

Agreements between the employer and the employee in relation to the termination of employment often incorporate some form of covenant by the employee, restricting where and/or for whom the individual can work for a set period of time after leaving his or her current employment.

Section 225 provides that any consideration or payment for entering into a restrictive covenant is taxable in full. See also **5.3.3**.

Law: ITEPA 2003, s. 225

9.4 Retirement payments

If an employer makes a payment to an employee "on or in anticipation of the retirement", s. 394 applies to treat the sum as being paid from a non-registered pension scheme (often referred to as an employer-financed retirement benefits scheme or EFRBS). The consequence is that the payment will be fully taxable and outside the scope of s. 401.

Where an EFRBS involves a third party, any benefits provided will be charged under Pt. 7A (see **Chapter 13**) as opposed to s. 394, but the effect is the same – the amount is fully taxable.

Care must be taken to ensure that any payment on termination is not classified as a taxable retirement payment. There is no statutory definition of the word "retirement" and therefore its ordinary and natural meaning applies. HMRC do interpret it very widely and therefore if dealing with a termination of employment of an employee over the age of 45, it is important to consider whether any payments amount to a retirement payment.

However, age in itself is not a deciding factor. A man aged 50 who gives up work to travel is more likely to be regarded as retiring than a woman of 65 who moves to another employer. Equally, just because a termination of employment is called an "early retirement" does not mean that it is so (even if the employee is entitled to benefits from a registered pension scheme following termination). Each case must be decided on its own facts.

Law: ITEPA 2003, s. 394

9.5 Redundancy payments

9.5.1 Tax treatment

Where a payment on the termination of employment is properly classed as a redundancy payment, it will automatically fall within s. 401, even if it is contractual.

9.5.2 Meaning of redundancy

To qualify as a redundancy payment, the related termination of employment must be as a result of a genuine redundancy. The

Employment Rights Act 1996, s. 139 defines this as a dismissal attributable wholly or mainly to:

> "(a)   the fact that the employer has ceased, or intends to cease:
>
> - to carry on the business for the purposes of which the employee was employed by him; or
>
> - to carry on that business in the place where the employee was so employed; or
>
> (b)   the fact that the requirements of that business:
>
> - for employees to carry out work of a particular kind; or
>
> - for employees to carry out work of a particular kind in the place where the employee was employed by the employer
>
> have ceased or diminished or are expected to cease or diminish."

9.5.3   Statutory redundancy payments

Where the dismissal falls within the definition of redundancy, the employee is entitled to a statutory redundancy payment. This is calculated as the sum of:

- half a week's pay for each complete year of service where the employee's age during the year is less than 22;

- a week's pay for each complete year of service where the employee's age during the year is between 22 and 40; and

- a week and a half's pay for each complete year of service where the employee's age during the year is 41 or more.

The maximum number of years of service that can be taken into account is 20.

A week's pay is the lower of:

- £544 (for 2021-22); and

- the contractual amount due at the date the minimum notice of termination was or should have been given (essentially one week prior to the termination of employment for each year of service up to a maximum of 12 weeks).

Example

Lee is 28 years old and has worked for PIF Ltd for seven years. He earns £24,960 per year (£480 per week). In July 2021, PIF Ltd makes Lee redundant as part of the closure of a number of its sites. Lee's statutory redundancy payment is:

	£
0.5 x £480 (£24,960/52) x 1	240
1 x £480 x 6	2,880
Total	3,120

It is possible for an employer to establish an alternative enhanced redundancy scheme. Where this is in place, an order will be made under the *Employment Rights Act* 1996, s. 157 (or the *Employment Rights (Northern Ireland) Order* 1996, art. 92) to exempt the employer from paying statutory redundancy calculated as above. Payments under such an alternative scheme are referred to as "approved contractual payments" for the purpose of ITEPA 2003.

Statutory redundancy payments and approved contractual payments (as defined at s. 309(4)-(6)) are treated as taxable under s. 401 and, as such, benefit from the £30,000 exemption.

Furthermore, s. 402C makes it clear that statutory redundancy payments and approved contractual payments up to the level of a statutory redundancy payment cannot be re-classified as post-employment notice pay (see **9.6.4** below).

Law: *Employment Rights Acts* 1996; ITEPA 2003, s. 309, 401, 402C; *Employment Rights (Northern Ireland) Order* 1996 (SI 1996/1919)

9.5.4   Non-statutory redundancy payments

HMRC will, as a matter of practice, treat genuine redundancy payments as falling within s. 401, even if contractual. However, genuine redundancy payments must be distinguished from other payments that would be taxable as earnings. For example, a payment that is really a terminal bonus for doing additional work during the redundancy consultation period is not compensation for redundancy.

Guidance: EIM 13775

9.6 *Ex gratia* payments within s. 401

9.6.1 Introduction

Once all contractual and other payments mentioned above are identified, any residual *ex gratia* amount received in connection with the termination of an office or employment, or with a change in the duties or earnings from an office or employment, has the potential to fall within s. 401.

Where this is the case, the first £30,000 of the *ex gratia* payment will be free of tax and NIC (see s. 403(1)).

In applying the exemption, the following points should be noted:

- If more than one termination payment is made to the same employee in respect of the same employment or by associated employers, the £30,000 exemption applies to the aggregate of all payments (s. 404(1)-(3)).

- If termination payments are staggered so that the employee receives them in different tax years, the £30,000 exemption applies to the earlier payment first (s. 404(4)).

- A termination payment can comprise of assets as well as cash. Where assets are transferred to employees as part of the termination agreement, the employees will be treated as if they received cash of an amount equal to the market value of the asset at the date of transfer (s. 415).

- Employees may continue to receive certain benefits from the employer after the employment has terminated (e.g. health insurance). If the benefits would ordinarily be taxable during employment, they will be taxable in the year of receipt on the greater of the value (or money's worth) and the cash equivalent calculated under the benefits code (see **Chapter 6**). This is of course subject to the £30,000 exemption, although it is set against cash payments in a tax year in priority to non-cash benefits (s. 404(5) and s. 415).

- Payments taxable under s. 401 are taxed in the year of receipt. When the payment is "received" is determined under the usual rules (see **5.4**).

9.6.2 Exclusions from s. 401

Of course, some payments that are not taxable elsewhere may also fall outside s. 401. In this situation, the payment will be outside the charge to income tax altogether.

Payments on death

Section 406 exempts termination payments made on the death of an employee from charges under s. 401.

However, as s. 401 only applies if the payment is not already taxable, very few payments on death benefit from the exemption. More likely, payments on death will be either:

- taxable as earnings, if contractual; or
- chargeable under s. 394 as a payment from a non-registered pension scheme.

Payments for injury or disability

Payments made to an employee on termination of employment on account of injury or disability are exempt from the scope of s. 401.

The exemption extends to mental health issues such as stress, anxiety or depression affecting the employee's ability to work, as well as physical injuries. It does not, however, extend to injury to feelings.

The case of *Hasted v Horner* established that to qualify for the exemption:

- there must be an identified medical condition that disables or prevents the employee from carrying out the duties of the particular employment; and
- the payment must be made on account of that disability and on account of nothing else.

At EIM 13610, HMRC state that medical evidence and documentation must be produced to confirm both tests are complied with.

Payments relating to registered pension schemes

Contributions to a registered pension scheme are exempt from s. 401.

Section 407 also exempts a lump sum or other benefit paid from a registered pension scheme if:

- the lump sum or other benefit is paid as compensation for either loss of employment or loss/diminution of earnings due to ill-health; or

- the lump sum or other benefit is properly regarded as earned by past service (essentially it is part of the individual's retirement benefits).

A pension will, however, continue to be taxable as income under general rules.

Compensation not connected with the employment

Section 401 only applies to compensation for loss of office and other payments connected with the termination of employment. This extends to damages paid as a result of a successful claim by an employee for unfair or wrongful dismissal. HMRC will, however, accept that any element of the compensation which relates solely to discrimination occurring before the employment was terminated, is not connected with the employment and, as such, will be outside the scope of s. 401.

Legal costs

Legal costs recovered by the employee from the employer will not be charged under s. 401 if the costs are paid direct to the employee's solicitor under the terms of a compromise agreement or a court order. See s. 413A for more details.

Outplacement counselling

Payments by the employer for outplacement counselling – on coping with job loss and finding new work – are exempt under s. 310.

Legal indemnities

If the employee has incurred legal liabilities as a result of action against him in connection with his duties of employment, a payment or benefit made to meet those costs or liabilities may be exempt from s. 401 if:

- the employee pays the liability (or the employer pays on his behalf);

- the amount of the payment or benefit would have been deductible under s. 346 (see **8.4.3**) had the employee still been in employment when the amount was paid; and

- the amount is paid between the day the employment terminated and the 5 April which is the last day of the sixth tax year following the end of the tax year in which the employment terminated.

Law: ITEPA 2003, s. 310, 406-410, 413A
Case: *Hasted v Horner* (1995) 67 TC 439
Guidance: EIM 12965, 13610

9.6.3   Post-employment notice pay

In the absence of a serious breach of contract, such as gross misconduct, contracts of employment will only come to an end after appropriate notice has been given by one of the parties to the other and the notice period has duly expired. There is a statutory minimum amount of notice, depending on which party is giving it:

- The employer must give the employee at least one week's notice but, after two years, this increases to one week's notice for each complete year worked, up to a maximum of 12 weeks.
- The employee must give the employer at least one week's notice.

Notice periods are normally specified in the employment contract and may exceed the statutory minimum notice period if desired.

Occasionally, employers do not wish employees to work during the notice period, for example because they believe it may be disruptive to the business. In these circumstances, the employee may agree to leave early in return for compensation for lost pay during the notice period (often referred to as a payment in lieu of notice or PILON).

Where the right for the employer to make a PILON is set out in the contract of employment, the sum will be taxable under general earnings (see **9.2** above).

Where there is no such right in the contract of employment, with the consequence that s. 401 may be relevant, consideration has to be given to s. 402A-402E. These sections apply to a termination payment (other than a statutory redundancy payment or an approved contractual payment replacing a statutory redundancy payment) made before what would have been the expiration of the contractual notice period.

Where this occurs, the termination payment has to be divided into:

- post-employment notice pay (PENP); and
- other amounts.

The PENP is taxable as earnings and the other amounts are taxed under the usual rules for termination payments.

PENP is calculated using the formula set out in s. 402D:

$$((BP \times D)/P) - T$$

where:

BP is the employee's basic pay for the pay period (week or month) immediately before the "trigger date" (usually the date on which notice is given, but see s. 402E). Basic pay excludes taxable benefits and any extraordinary payments such as bonuses, commissions, overtime payments and share-option gains.

D is the number of calendar days from the last day of employment to the date when the notice period would have expired if given in full (the "post-employment notice period").

P is one of the following:

- 30.42, where the last pay period is a month, the employee is paid in equal monthly instalments and the payment is made on or after 6 April 2021 in connection with a termination of employment that takes place on or after that date;

- in other cases, the number of calendar days in the pay period immediately preceding the trigger date.

T is the amount paid on termination that is already taxable as earnings (excluding holiday pay and termination bonuses). For example, contractual payments, restrictive covenant payments or the writing-off of an employment-related loan.

Where there is no pay period prior to the trigger date, BP and P are calculated by reference to the days between the start of the employment and the trigger date (s. 402D(5)).

To simplify matters, it is acceptable to work in months where the last pay period is a month, the employee is paid in equal monthly instalments, the contractual notice period is specified in months and the post-employment notice period is in whole months. See s. 402D for details on how to modify the formula where this is the case.

The impact of identifying and taxing PENP is to ensure that non-contractual PILONs are taxable in the same way as contractual PILONs.

Example

Xavier works for Uffi Art Ltd. He has a basic salary of £84,000 per annum and is paid monthly. His employment contract specifies a 14-week notice period.

Uffi Art Ltd terminates Xavier's employment contract on 10 May 2021 without notice and pays him a termination payment of £45,000 in full and final settlement of all claims. HMRC confirm that the whole of the payment falls within s. 401.

Because the payment is made before the expiry of the contractual notice period (16 August 2021), s. 402A-402E apply.

BP (basic pay for April 2021)	£7,000
D (days in the post-employment period)	98
P (30.42 as Xavier paid in monthly instalments)	30.42
Amount of termination period already taxed as earnings	£nil
PENP = ((£7,000 x 98)/30.42) – 0	£22,551

This will be fully taxable as earnings. The remaining £22,449 (£45,000 – £22,551) is subject to the usual s. 401 rules. As this is within the £30,000 exemption, no further tax will be due.

This exercise needs to be carried out for every termination payment which is made to an employee before the contractual notice period would have expired.

Law: *Employment Rights Act* 1996, s. 86; ITEPA 2003, s. 309, 401, 402A-404

9.6.4 Foreign service relief

Termination payments made to employees at a time when they are non-UK resident for tax purposes (see **Chapter 34**) are still potentially subject to UK tax. This is because specific employment income is taxed by reference to its source rather than the residence status of the employee at the time of receipt (see *Nichols v Gibson*).

Section 413 does, however, provide for foreign service relief (FSR) where a termination payment is made to a non-UK resident individual or a seafarer (defined in s. 414B(8)).

FSR applies to service carried out overseas. The whole of the termination payment will be exempt if any of the following applies:

- at least three quarters of the total service comprises of overseas service;

- where the total service exceeds ten years, the last ten years comprises wholly of overseas service; or

- where total service exceeds 20 years, at least half of the total service, including ten of the last 20 years, comprises of overseas service.

Where there is overseas service, but the amount falls short of the limits, proportionate relief is still available to exempt the part of the termination payment which is attributable to overseas service. The reduction in taxable income is calculated by first reducing the income by the £30,000 exemption, if relevant, and then calculating the partial relief reduction by taking the length of foreign service as a proportion of the total service and multiplying this by the taxable income. For example, if the total service was 15 years and three of those years were foreign service, the partial relief reduction would be 20% of the taxable termination package.

Example

Orla commenced work for Groveland plc on 1 May 2006. She was initially based in the head office in the UK but moved to work at Groveland plc's office in Belgium on 1 May 2012. Her employment is terminated, and on 31 July 2021 she finishes work after expiry of her notice period. She is paid an *ex gratia* payment of £100,000 as compensation for loss of office.

Although Orla is non-UK resident at the date of the termination payment, the payment is still subject to UK tax as it relates to a UK employment of which some of the duties were carried out in the UK. Her foreign service amounts to nine years and nine months out of a total 15 years and three months, which is insufficient for full FSR. However, proportional relief is available under s. 414.

The £30,000 exemption is applied to the termination payment before any proportionate reduction in the charge by FSR. Therefore:

	£
Termination payment	100,000
Less: exemption	(30,000)
	70,000
Less: FSR £70,000 x 117/183 months	(44,754)
Amount subject to UK tax	25,246

FSR is a personal claim and so, strictly speaking, Groveland plc should apply PAYE to the amount of the termination payment ignoring FSR and the overpayment should be claimed back by the employee through her income tax return. See **Chapter 14** for more details on PAYE obligations.

See also Example 1 at EIM 13985.

Where a termination payment is made to an employee who has been working outside the UK, it may be that the UK does not have sole taxing rights. In such cases the provisions of any double taxation agreement between the UK and the other country need to be considered.

See also **38.8.6** and see **Chapter 35** for more details on double tax agreements.

Law: ITEPA 2003, s. 413, 414-414C
Case: *Nichols v Gibson* (1996) BTC 439
Guidance: EIM 13680-13705, 13970-13985

9.6.5   Interaction of FSR and PENP

Prior to 6 April 2021, HMRC took the view that PENP was not taxable in the UK where it was paid to an individual who is non-UK resident in the year of receipt. There was an exception where the employment terminated in one tax year and the termination payment was not made until the subsequent tax year; in this situation, s. 30 applied, with the effect that PENP was treated as earnings for the year of termination. If the employee was UK resident in that earlier year, PENP would be treated as taxable earnings.

For termination payments made in relation to employments ending on or after 6 April 2021, the tax position is different. Any PENP element will be subject to UK tax in the hands of a non-UK resident if and to the extent that it represents pay that would have incurred UK tax had the employee worked out his or her notice – in other words, where there are taxable UK work days during the notice period.

Law: ITEPA 2003, s. 27, 30, 402B
Guidance: EIM 13877

9.7 Reporting requirements

Any PAYE or NIC due on termination payments will be reportable through real time information and payable to HMRC in the usual way (see **Chapter 14**).

Provided the termination payment is wholly in cash, no further reporting is required. Where the termination payment consists of non-cash assets or benefits and will exceed the £30,000 threshold (so that there is tax to pay), the employer must provide details to HMRC by 6 July following the end of the tax year.

Law: SI 2003/2682

9.8 Pitfalls and planning points

Drafting the contract of employment

As all contractual payments are taxable in full (see **9.2** above), inclusion of payments on termination in the contract of employment (or other supporting documentation which forms part of the contract) should only occur where there is a compelling commercial reason.

Tracking custom and practice

Care should be taken to minimise the risk of payments on termination becoming so regular and consistent as to create a reasonable expectation that they will be paid (and as such being incorporated by implication into the contract). See **9.2** above.

Enhanced redundancy schemes

Where an employer plans to provide enhanced redundancy payments, agreement can be sought in advance from HMRC that the payments are genuine redundancy payments and as such are taxable under s. 401. See **9.5** above.

Make the most of exempt payments

Where appropriate, consider the use of exempt payments on termination. For example, the provision of outplacement counselling, payments of the employee's legal costs direct to his or her legal representative, and contributions to registered pension schemes within the annual allowance are free of income tax and are in addition to the £30,000 exemption under s. 401. See **9.6.2** above and **Chapter 30**.

Foreign service relief

Foreign service relief is only available to non-UK residents and seafarers. Where there is a choice as to when termination of employment takes place in relation to a globally mobile employee, consideration should be given to the impact of foreign service relief. For example, terminating employment prior to repatriation rather than after return to the UK may give rise to a more beneficial tax treatment (subject, of course, to any overseas liabilities). See **9.6.4** above.

Compromise agreements

Any payments on termination are usually bound up with settlement of any potential claim by the employee as against the employer. It is recommended that legal advice is sought to ensure that the terms of the agreement are appropriately reflected in writing.

10. Employment-related securities

10.1 Introduction

In 1935, the case of *Weight v Salmon* established the general principle that the purchase or acquisition of securities by an employee can amount to an emolument of the employment even if the securities are not sold for a profit. Essentially, the court viewed the difference between the market value of the securities and the amount paid for them as money's worth and taxable as earnings under what is now ITEPA 2003, s. 62 (see **Chapter 5**).

This general principle is still valid today. However, it must be considered in conjunction with ITEPA 2003, Pt. 7, which modifies and supplements the rules in a number of areas:

- tax-advantaged plans (see **Chapter 11**);
- convertible securities (see **10.4**);
- securities options (see **10.5**); and
- restricted securities (see **10.6**).

ITEPA 2003, Pt. 7 also includes a number of anti-avoidance provisions designed to bring into charge arrangements that do not fall into any other part of the legislation. This is discussed further at **10.8**.

Statutory references in this chapter are to ITEPA 2003 unless otherwise stated.

The main HMRC guidance is in the *Employment Related Securities Manual* (ERSM).

Law: ITEPA 2003, s. 6-7, 401
Case: *Weight v Salmon* (1935) 19 TC 174

10.2 The scope of Part 7

10.2.1 Overview

To fall within the scope of Pt. 7, securities or an interest in securities must amount to "employment-related securities". These are defined as:

> "securities, or an interest in securities, acquired by a person where the right or opportunity to acquire the securities or interest is

available by reason of employment of that person or any other person".

Law: ITEPA 2003, s. 421B

10.2.2   The meaning of securities

The definition of a security is extremely wide, so it not only covers shares in a body corporate (wherever situated) but also any other types of securities such as debentures, warrants, loan stock, bonds, certificates of deposit, units in a collective investment scheme, insurance contracts, contracts for differences, futures and options.

Section 420(5) does, however, specifically exclude the following from the definition of securities:

- cheques, other bills of exchange (unless accepted by a banker), bankers' drafts and letters of credit;
- money and statements showing balances on a current, deposit or savings account;
- leases and other dispositions of property and, in respect of Scotland, heritable securities; and
- certain securities options (see **10.5** for the consequences of this).

Reference to shares "in a body corporate" does give rise to some uncertainty around a limited liability partnership (LLP), which is a body corporate for tax purposes. However, HMRC confirm at ERSM 20120 that they will not regard an employee being promoted to partner in an LLP as the acquisition of an employment-related security, unless the partnership is a collective investment scheme.

Law: ITEPA 2003, s. 420
Guidance: ERSM 20120

10.2.3   Interest in securities

Part 7 does not only relate to securities but extends to an "interest" in securities. This is essentially anything less than full beneficial ownership, including an interest in proceeds of sale.

However, to avoid any confusion over the treatment of options (see **10.5**), s. 420(8) makes it clear that a right to acquire a security is not an interest in a security.

Law: ITEPA 2003, s. 420(8)

10.2.4   Available by reason of employment

Generally, securities (or interests in securities) will be treated as employment-related securities if they are acquired by reason of employment.

This is a very similar test to that used in the benefits code (see **Chapter 6**). If the opportunity for an employee to acquire securities or an interest in securities is made available by the employer or someone connected with the employer, the securities are deemed to be acquired by reason of employment. The only exception to this is where the person who makes the opportunity available is an individual and the opportunity is being made available in the normal course of domestic, family or personal relationships of that person.

Law: ITEPA 2003, s. 421B, 471

10.2.5   Exclusions from Part 7

There are certain instances where employment-related securities are involved but no income tax charge arises:

- Where there is a fair bargain. If, for example, the employee has paid the full market value for securities in the employer company, there is no element of reward and so no employment income will arise on the acquisition of the securities.

- Where an employee has either paid in full for his or her securities or has been duly taxed on the full value received. Any subsequent normal commercial return (such as dividends or profit on transfer where there are no employment-related preferential terms) will be subject to tax on the basis that the employee is a shareholder, rather than an employee.

- Where the chargeable event occurs immediately on or after the death of the employee. This exemption does not extend to chargeable events which occur before the death of the employee but the tax has not yet become due; in this case the tax will be the responsibility of the personal representatives (s. 421B(6)).

- Where the chargeable event is not the exercise of an option and occurs seven years or more after the cessation of the relevant employment (s. 421B(7)).

- Where securities are offered to employees in priority to the public as part of an initial public offering of the employer (s. 542-548).

Law: ITEPA 2003, s. 225

10.2.6   Basis of assessment

Where Pt. 7 applies, the value accruing to the employee will be taxed as specific employment income (see **5.3.4**). Typically, the charge arises at the point the employee acquires a beneficial interest in the securities or the interest in securities, although much depends on the nature of the securities and the conditions surrounding their acquisition (see, for example, securities options (**10.5** below) and restricted securities (**10.6** below)).

In determining the taxable amount, regard is had to the market value at the point of the tax charge. "Market value" has the same definition as given in TCGA 1992, Pt. VIII, which is based on the price the assets might be expected to bring on a sale in the open market.

For quoted securities, the market value is the closing price on the day (unless there are two prices, in which case it is the lower of the two prices plus one-half of the difference between those prices). If the stock exchange is closed on the day in question, the value on the latest preceding day it was open can be taken. In each case, a different value can be used if to do otherwise would give rise to an incorrect value (for example, if the securities are actually acquired at arm's length at a different price).

For unquoted securities, regard is had to the open market price assuming the purchaser has access to all the information a prudent purchaser might reasonably require if buying by private treaty and at arm's length.

In calculating the tax due, deductions can be made from the market value for any consideration or payment made, either for the security or interest itself or for any related dealing or acquisition costs.

Any tax due will be accountable under self-assessment, unless the shares or securities are "readily convertible assets", in which case, the tax and Class 1 NIC will need to be accounted for through the PAYE system.

For a wider discussion as to what amounts to a readily convertible asset and the operation of the PAYE system, see **Chapter 14**. However, in the context of securities, there will be a readily convertible asset if:

- the securities are listed on a recognised stock exchange;

- there is an arrangement in place for the securities to be sold at the time of acquisition, for example because a buyer has been identified and is negotiating for the acquisition of the securities; or

- the statutory corporation tax deduction under CTA 2009, s. 1008 is not available. (This deduction is permitted where securities are issued pursuant to a tax-advantaged scheme (see **Chapter 11**) or the securities are ordinary shares with no special rights in a listed company, a subsidiary of a listed company or a company which is not under the control of another company.)

Law: TCGA 1992, s. 272-273; ITEPA 2003, s. 421-421B, 702(5A); CTA 2009, s. 1008; SI 2015/616

10.2.7 *Associated persons*

References are made throughout Pt. 7 to "associated persons". The specific legislation has to be considered in each case but, essentially, the intention is to ensure that:

- a tax charge is not avoided by making securities available to associated persons of the employee, instead of the employee; and

- a tax charge is not inadvertently triggered by a transfer to an associated person where there is no employment benefit or anti-avoidance.

An "associated person" is defined in s. 421C as:

- the person who acquired the employment-related securities on the acquisition;

- (if different) the employee; and

- any relevant linked person.

A "relevant linked person" is:

- a person "connected" (as defined in ITA 2007, s. 993 – see **Appendix 2**) with the employee or the person acquiring the security; and

- a person who is or has been a member of the same household as the employee or the person acquiring the security (defined by s. 721 as a spouse or civil partner, children and their spouses or civil partners, parents, servants, dependants and guests).

However, the employer company or, if different, the company which has made the securities or options available is not a "relevant linked person".

Law: ITEPA 2003, s. 421C, 472, 721

10.3   Acquisition of securities

As mentioned above, where an employee receives or acquires securities and pays less than full market value for them, employment income will usually arise on the basis of the general earnings charge under s. 62.

The s. 62 charge takes priority. Theoretically, however, the value calculated as money's worth could be lower than the value calculated under Pt. 7, as the s. 62 charge is based on the arm's length price with the knowledge the employee has, as opposed to the prudent arm's length purchaser. Where this is the case (or if s. 62 does not apply), any uncharged amount would fall within the remit of Pt. 7, Ch. 3C (see **10.8.4**).

Special valuation rules apply where employment-related securities are acquired in relation to research institution spin-out companies (s. 451-460).

Of course, where the securities fall within the provisions for restricted securities, convertible securities or securities options, the rules in Pt. 7 will prevail (see **10.5-10.7** below).

Law: ITEPA 2003, s. 394

10.4   Contingent awards

As the tax point only arises when the employee acquires a beneficial interest in securities, awards made contingent on certain conditions being satisfied will not give rise to a tax charge until such time as the conditions are satisfied.

When the conditions are met, the amount charged to tax is the market value of the securities at that time. Any amount paid for the securities will reduce the taxable amount.

Care should be taken to ensure there is a genuine contingent award. Where there is a right to a security, this will be treated as a securities option (see **10.5**). Alternatively, if the securities are given at the outset but can be lost if certain events occur, for example if the employee leaves employment, these will be forfeitable securities and will be taxed as restricted securities (see **10.6**).

Guidance: EIM 13775

10.5 Securities options

A securities option is essentially a right to acquire securities in the future at a set price. It is an extremely popular way of incentivising employees, as the exercise of the option can be made subject to performance conditions. It can also be structured so that it bears no inherent risk for either the employer or the employee – if the employee leaves, the option can lapse, and if the employee stays, but the share price goes down, the employee can decide not to exercise it.

Where the option is employment-related, the tax treatment is governed by Pt. 7, Ch. 5 instead of the general rules on earnings and benefits.

There is no tax on the grant of an option. Instead, when the option is exercised, a charge will arise on the difference between the market value at the point of exercise and the price paid (including acquisition-related expenses, if any).

Example

Juliet is granted an option to acquire 1,000 shares in her employer at a price of £1.50 each. The option is exercisable in three years provided she is still in employment at that time.

After three years, Juliet exercises the option, paying £1,500, and receives the shares. At that time the market value is £3.50 per share.

Juliet will pay no tax when the option is granted. On exercise, taxable specific employment income of £2,000 will arise (being the difference between the market value of £3,500 and the exercise price of £1,500).

Her base cost for capital gains tax (CGT) purposes on future disposals will be the sum of the price paid and the taxable amount, i.e. £3,500.

The charge on exercise will also arise if the option is granted or the securities are delivered to an associated person of the employee.

If the option is not exercised, but is assigned to a third party other than an associated person (see **10.2.7** above), or it is given up, any amount received over and above any consideration given will constitute taxable specific employment income.

Law: ITEPA 2003, s. 471-484

10.6   Restricted securities

10.6.1   Introduction

Prior to 2003, it was not unusual for restrictions to be placed on securities to reduce their value (and therefore the tax charge) on acquisition. Later expiry of these restrictions would not give rise to a further income tax charge.

To counter this, Pt. 7, Ch. 2 was introduced and applies whenever an employee acquires "restricted securities".

Section 423 recognises two main restrictions:

- Securities where the employee is required to transfer them on the occurrence of certain events or circumstances and could receive less than market value ("forfeiture restriction").
- Securities which have restrictions on when (or to whom) they may be sold ("transfer restriction").

Example 1 – forfeiture restriction

Nicola subscribes for shares in her employer at a discounted price of £1. It is a term of the subscription agreement that if she leaves within three years, she must sell the shares back to her employer for £1.

Example 2 – transfer restriction

Nicholas is awarded shares in his employer, but it is a term of the award that he cannot sell or transfer the shares for at least two years.

In each case, the restriction must have the effect of reducing the market value of the securities.

It is important to identify whether a restriction is a forfeiture restriction or a transfer restriction, as different tax treatments apply to each.

Law: ITEPA 2003, s. 422-444

10.6.2   Forfeiture restrictions lapsing within five years

If the securities in question are subject to a forfeiture restriction which lapses within five years of the date on which the securities are acquired, there is no tax charge on the date of acquisition. Instead, a charge will arise on a chargeable event. "Chargeable events" are:

- the employment-related securities ceasing to be restricted securities (that is, the lifting of the restriction) at a time when owned by an associated person;
- the variation of the restrictions over the employment-related securities without them ceasing to be restricted securities or an interest in restricted securities; and
- the disposal for consideration of employment-related securities by an associated person to someone other than an associated person at a time when they are still restricted securities.

See **10.2.7** above for the definition of "associated person" (which includes the person who acquired the employment-related securities in the first place).

Section 428 sets out the formula for working out the taxable amount on a chargeable event:

$$UMV \times (IUP - PCP - OP) - CE$$

where:

- **UMV** is the market value of the employment-related securities immediately after the chargeable event;
- **IUP** is the proportion of the initial value which has not been charged to tax/paid for (see below);
- **PCP** is the proportion charged to tax on a previous chargeable event;
- **OP** is the proportion of share value still subject to restrictions; and
- **CE** is any expenses of the employee in relation to the chargeable event.

IUP can in turn be worked out using the formula:

$$IUP = (IUMV - DA)/IUMV$$

where:

- **IUMV** is the initial unrestricted market value of the securities (i.e. market value at the time of acquisition ignoring any reduction in value because of restrictions); and

- **DA** is the deductible amounts (any amount paid by the employee for the securities and any amount taxed as employment income on acquisition).

Example

Akeyo purchases 1,000 shares in his employer company for £1 per share when the market value is £5 per share. These shares are subject to a restriction that if he leaves the company within three years, he must sell them back to the company for the price paid. HMRC agree that the restriction reduces the value to £2 per share.

Akeyo stays with the company and three years later the restriction lifts. The market value of unrestricted shares at that time is £9 per share.

The shares are employment-related restricted securities. Because the restriction is in the nature of a forfeiture restriction, and lasts for less than five years, there will be no tax on the acquisition of the shares. Instead, there will be a charge, when the restriction lifts, based on the proportion of the current market value that has not previously been paid for or subject to tax.

Here it is relatively straightforward. At the outset, Akeyo paid £1 against a value (ignoring restrictions) of £5, i.e. 20%. Therefore, 80% remains untaxed or unpaid.

The charge will therefore be on 80% x £9 = £7.20.

To check, apply the formula:

$$9 \text{ (UMV)} \times \text{IUP}$$

where:

$$\text{IUP} = \frac{5 \text{ (IUMV)} - 1 \text{ (DA)}}{5 \text{ (IUMV)}}$$

9 x 0.80 = £7.20 per share.

There are no remaining restrictions, no previous amounts taxed and no expenses, so the PCP, OP and CE values are nil.

So for 1,000 shares, there is a total of £7,200 employment income, taxable at the point the restrictions lift.

HMRC regard the five-year period as running from midnight at the end of the day of acquisition to midnight on the fifth anniversary of the day of acquisition. So, if the shares are acquired on 1 July 2021, the period ends at midnight on 1 July 2026 (and not 30 June 2026).

Law: ITEPA 2003, s. 425-428

10.6.3 Forfeiture restrictions lapsing five years or more after award

Securities subject to a forfeiture restriction which lasts five years or more after the date of acquisition are taxed as follows:

- a charge on the date the securities are acquired, based on the difference between the price paid for the securities and the market value on that date taking into account the impact of the restrictions (referred to as "actual market value" (AMV)); and
- a further charge on a chargeable event (see **10.6.2**).

Example

Gizi purchases 1,000 shares in her employer company for £1 per share when the market value is £6 per share. These shares are subject to a restriction that if she leaves the company within six years, she must transfer them back to the company for the price paid. HMRC agree that the restriction reduces the value to £1.50 per share.

Gizi stays with the company and six years later the restriction lifts. The market value of unrestricted shares at that time is £12 per share.

The shares are employment-related restricted securities. Because the restriction is in the nature of a forfeiture restriction and lasts for more than five years, there is a charge on acquisition based on the difference between the restricted market value of £1.50 (AMV) and the price paid:

£1.50 – £1 = £0.50 per share x 1,000 shares = £500 taxable income

When the restrictions lift, there will be a further income tax charge, based on the proportion not yet taxed or paid. Gizi has paid £1 and tax on £0.50 per share already. This is 25% of the unrestricted market value at the time of acquisition of £6, leaving 75% still to be charged.

Apply the formula:

$$12\ (UMV) \times IUP$$

where:

$$IUP = \frac{6\ (IUMV) - (1 + 0.50\ (DA))}{6\ (IUMV)}$$

12 x 0.75 = £9 per share.

There are no remaining restrictions or previous amounts taxed or expenses and so the PCP, OP and CE values are nil.

So taxable income on the lifting of the restriction is £9,000.

Law: ITEPA 2003, s. 425-428

10.6.4   Transfer restrictions

As noted above, a transfer restriction is a restriction on when (or to whom) securities may be sold. The tax treatment is the same as for forfeiture restrictions lasting more than five years, i.e. a charge both on the acquisition of the securities and on a subsequent chargeable event. This is regardless of the length of time the transfer restriction is in force.

Law: ITEPA 2003, s. 425-428

10.6.5   Exemption from charges on chargeable events

No tax charge will arise under s. 428 where:

- a whole class of securities is affected by the same restriction;
- all the securities within that class are affected in the same way by a chargeable event; and
- either the company is employee-controlled by virtue of holdings of the same class, or the majority of the company's securities of the class are held by persons unrelated to the company.

Example

In 2019, the employees of Red and Blue Ltd join together and buy the shares from the owners. There is a single class of shares and a provision in the articles of association requires a sale at cost of an employee's shares if that employee leaves within four years. In 2022, Green and Yellow Ltd offers to buy the whole of Red and Blue Ltd's share capital.

The disposal to Green and Yellow Ltd is of restricted securities and therefore is potentially a chargeable event. However, because all the shares have the same restriction, all are being sold and Red and Blue Ltd is employee-controlled, s. 429 will apply and no income tax charge will arise (although CGT will).

However, the exception in s. 429 will not apply if there is tax or NIC avoidance.

Law: ITEPA 2003, s. 429

10.6.6   Two or more restrictions

It is possible for securities to have two or more restrictions that lift at different times. In these circumstances, there will be a chargeable event each time a restriction lifts. When calculating the amount to be treated as employment income, the proportion will be adjusted to take into account any previous chargeable events (PCP in the formula) and the proportion of value still subject to restrictions (OP in the formula).

Example

Annette is given 1,000 shares in her employer company when the market value is £3 per share. These shares are subject to a restriction that if she leaves the company within three years, she will forfeit them back to the company. For a further two years, she cannot transfer the shares to anybody. HMRC agree that the restrictions reduce the value to £1 per share.

Annette stays with the company and three years later the forfeiture restriction lifts. The market value of unrestricted shares at that time is £8 per share. HMRC agree that the existence of a transfer restriction reduces the value to £6 per share.

Two years later, the transfer restriction lifts. The shares are worth £12 per share.

The employment income is as follows:

On acquisition

No employment income (as one of the restrictions is a forfeiture condition lasting less than five years).

On lifting of forfeiture restriction

$$UMV \times (IUP - PCP - OP)$$

where

$$IUP = \frac{3\,(IUMV) - 0(DA)}{3\,(IUMV)} = 1$$

PCP (proportion charged to tax on a previous chargeable event) = 0

OP (proportion of share value still subject to restrictions) $= \dfrac{8\,(UMV) - 6(AMV)}{8\,(UMV)}$

$= 0.25$

$8 \times (1 - 0 - 0.25) = 8 \times 0.75 = £6$ per share

£6,000 total employment income.

On lifting of transfer restriction

$$UMV \times (IUP - PCP - OP)$$

where

$$IUP = \frac{3\,(IUMV) - 0(DA)}{3\,(IUMV)} = 1$$

PCP (proportion charged to tax on a previous chargeable event) = 0.75

OP (proportion of share value still subject to restrictions) = 0

$12 \times (1 - 0.75 - 0) = 12 \times 0.25 = £3$ per share

£3,000 total employment income.

Without any restrictions, Annette would have paid tax on £3,000 when she first received the shares. However, the existence of restrictions has ensured that the charge is postponed, bringing some of the growth into the charge to income tax and resulting in a total of £9,000 of employment income.

Law: ITEPA 2003, s. 425-428

10.6.7   Elections to disapply the rules

Part 7, Ch. 2 identifies two elections that can be made to change the tax treatment of restricted securities.

Section 425(3)

An election under s. 425(3) can be made where the securities are subject to a forfeiture restriction for up to five years from the date of acquisition. If made, the securities will be taxed as if the forfeiture restriction lasted for longer than five years. In other words, there will be a tax charge on acquisition based on the difference between the actual market value of the securities (taking into account the restrictions) and the price paid.

When the restriction lifts, or there is some other chargeable event, a lower proportion will be subject to income tax (see **10.6.2**).

Section 431

An election under s. 431 can be made in relation to any restricted securities regardless of the nature and length of the restrictions. The effect of a s. 431 election is to disregard the impact of all the restrictions attaching to the securities. Income tax will be charged on the acquisition of the securities based on the market value at the time, ignoring the impact of any restrictions. Any consideration paid will reduce the taxable amount.

When the restrictions lift or another chargeable event occurs, there are no further charges to income tax under this part of the legislation.

Making the election

In both cases the election:

- must be made jointly between the employer and the employee;
- must be made within 14 days following the award of the securities; and
- is irrevocable.

There is no requirement to send the election to HMRC, but it must be kept on file by the company in case of an enquiry.

The advantage of creating a charge on acquisition is that the percentage of the later value subject to income tax on a subsequent chargeable event is reduced. This can, in certain circumstances, lead to a lower income tax burden.

Example 1

Mira is awarded 1,000 shares in her employer at no cost to her. At the time of acquisition, the market value of the shares is £4 per share. However, there is a restriction that if she leaves within four years, the shares must be transferred back to the employer. HMRC agree that the value with the restriction is £2. Mira stays with the employer and when the restriction lifts, the market value is £10 per share.

Without an election, the securities would be treated as restricted securities with a forfeiture restriction lasting less than five years. In other words, there would be no tax on the date of acquisition, but when the restriction lifts, because nothing has been previously paid or taxed, the full £10 per share (so £10,000 in total) will be subject to income tax.

If, however, a s. 431 election is made, the restrictions are disregarded. Mira will be taxed on acquisition on the unrestricted market value of £4 per share, that is, on £4,000. When the restriction lifts, there is no further tax charge.

Her CGT base cost will be lower: £4,000 instead of £10,000. However, CGT only arises on a subsequent disposal and reliefs may be available.

Elections will be advantageous where the employee remains in employment (thereby not triggering any forfeiture restriction) and the securities increase in value between the date of the award and the date on which the restrictions are lifted.

However, an election can have the effect of increasing the tax liability where:

- the securities are forfeited (as the tax paid on the initial award will not be refunded); or
- the securities fall in value between the date of the award and the date the restrictions are lifted.

Example 2

Using the example above, if Mira leaves employment within four years, she will lose her shares.

Without an election, she will have paid no tax on acquisition. On leaving, the tax charge is based on the amount she receives, in this case nothing.

If she and her employer had made the joint s. 431 election, she would have paid income tax on £4,000 on acquisition. On the forfeiture of the shares, there is no income tax to pay. However, the income tax she has paid is not refunded. Instead, she will have a capital loss of £4,000 to take forward against future gains (but she may not have any).

Bearing in mind that an election must be made within 14 days of the acquisition if it is to take effect, careful consideration needs to be given as to the likelihood of the future outcome.

Law: ITEPA 2003, s. 425(3), 431

10.6.8 Roll-over relief on exchange of restricted securities

Where employment-related restricted securities are exchanged for new restricted securities, the disposal is not treated as a chargeable event if:

- the restricted securities are wholly exchanged for new restricted securities;
- the value of the consideration received in exchange is not more than the unrestricted market value of the old securities; and
- avoidance of tax or NIC is not a main purpose of the transaction.

Instead, the rules in Pt. 7, Ch. 2 apply to the new securities in the same way as they applied to the original securities, i.e. an income tax charge will arise when either the restriction on the new securities is lifted or the new securities are disposed of while the restriction remains in place.

If the employee receives anything other than new restricted securities in exchange for his or her original securities, such as cash or unrestricted securities, only the proportion relating to the new restricted securities will be rolled over. There will be a chargeable event in relation to the remainder and income tax will be payable as appropriate.

If a s. 431 or s. 425 election had been made in relation to the original restricted securities, it will still be valid in relation to the new restricted securities.

Law: ITEPA 2003, s. 430A

10.7 Convertible securities

Sections 436-444 deal with convertible securities.

Securities will be convertible if:

- they carry an entitlement for the holder to convert them into securities of a different description;
- there is an agreement in force which requires or authorises the grant of such an entitlement if certain circumstances do or do not occur; or
- there is provision for the securities to be converted into securities of a different description, otherwise than by the holder.

With convertible securities, there are two potential tax charges:

- when the securities are acquired, an income tax charge will arise on the difference between the market value of the securities, ignoring the right to convert, and any price paid; and
- when a chargeable event occurs, there will be a further charge on the increase in value relating to the right to convert.

The exact calculation of the second charge depends on the nature of the chargeable event.

"Chargeable events" include:

- the conversion of the securities into securities of a different description where the beneficial interest of the new securities is owned by an associated person;
- the disposal of convertible securities by an associated person to someone who is not an associated person in return for consideration;
- the release of the entitlement to convert; and
- any other receipt by an associated person of money or money's worth in relation to the right to convert.

For the meaning of "associated person", see **10.2.7** above.

Where the chargeable event is the conversion of the securities, the amount of the gain (referred to as "AG" in the legislation) is calculated as:

CMVCS − (CMVERS + CC)

where:

- **CMVCS** is the market value of the securities immediately after the conversion;

- **CMVERS** is the market value of the securities immediately before the conversion, assessed on the basis that the right to convert is disregarded; and
- **CC** is any consideration given by the employee for the conversion of the securities (often nil).

Essentially this is the increase in value accruing to the employee as the result of the conversion.

Example

In September 2021, Owen is given 5,000 non-voting preference shares in his employer's company. These shares do not carry rights to share in surplus assets on a winding-up of the company but do carry a right to a fixed dividend.

The shares can be converted to full ordinary voting shares at Owen's request in two years provided he is still employed by the company.

The preference shares are worth £15,000 in September 2021. Without the conversion rights, the shares would be worth £7,000.

Two years later, Owen requests that the shares be converted. At the time the preference shares are worth £14,000 ignoring the conversion rights and 5,000 ordinary shares are worth £50,000.

On acquisition, taxable income arises based on the value of the preference shares without the conversion rights, that is, £7,000.

On conversion, the taxable amount will be £36,000, being the difference between the market value at the time of the "new" ordinary shares (£50,000) and the "old" preference shares ignoring the right to convert (£14,000).

Where the chargeable event is the disposal of the securities before conversion, the amount of the gain will be the difference between the consideration received and the market value of the original securities immediately before the chargeable event, calculated as if they were not convertible.

Where the chargeable event is the release of the entitlement to convert, the taxable amount is simply the amount of the consideration received in exchange for that release.

It is also potentially possible for convertible securities to come within the rules for restricted securities. An example of this would be where the conversion is from one class of securities to another class which carries restrictions.

Law: ITEPA 2003, s. 436-444

10.8   Tackling tax avoidance

10.8.1   Introduction

The flexibility that exists when structuring the securities of a company potentially gives rise to schemes designed to put securities into the hands of employees with minimal taxable employment income. The rules on restricted securities (see **10.6** above) and convertible securities (see **10.7** above) will prevent many of these arrangements from creating a tax advantage. Part 7 also contains a number of rules designed specifically to tackle tax avoidance in this area.

10.8.2   Securities with artificially depressed market value

Part. 7, Ch. 3A imposes a tax charge where the market value of employment-related securities falls as a result of anything done other than for a genuine commercial purpose.

Where Pt. 7, Ch. 3A applies, the taxable amount is the difference between the actual market value of the securities and the market value assuming the non-commercial action had not taken place.

A charge will not, however, arise if the difference is less than 10% or if the action takes place more than seven years before the chargeable event.

Where restricted securities are involved, the charge is based on the value ignoring all restrictions and the restricted securities rules (see **10.6** above) are disapplied.

However, the charge is not limited to situations where employment-related securities are acquired. Where there is any chargeable event under Pt. 7, the charge needs to be considered.

Law: ITEPA 2003, s. 446A-446J

10.8.3   Securities with artificially enhanced market value

Taxable employment income will arise if the market value of employment-related securities is increased by anything done other than for a genuine commercial purpose over the relevant period.

The relevant period is:

- in the year the securities are acquired, the period from the date of acquisition to the following 5 April;
- in the year the securities are disposed of, or otherwise cease to be employment-related securities, the period from the preceding 6 April to the date of disposal or cessation; and
- in any other case, the 6 April to the following 5 April.

A non-commercial action is interpreted in the same way as for **10.8.2** above.

The amount that is taxable is the difference between the market value of the securities on the last day of the relevant period and the amount that would have been the market value on that date if the non-commercial increase is disregarded.

No charge will arise if the increase is less than 10%.

Section 446N ensures there is no double taxation where the securities subject to a charge for artificially enhanced market value are also restricted securities.

Law: ITEPA 2003, s. 446K-446P

10.8.4   Securities acquired for less than market value

When securities are acquired by reason of employment at a discount to their full value, a charge to income tax will usually arise on the basis of the general earnings charge under s. 62 (see **10.3** above).

However, there may be circumstances where the "discount" is not caught by the general rules. HMRC in their guidance at ERSM 70100 identify two examples:

- where there is no discount, but the obligation to pay is deferred; and
- where the valuation of the benefit under the general rules is less than the charge under Pt. 7 (see **10.3** above for a summary of the different valuation rules).

In these circumstances, the difference between the market value of the securities and any amount paid and/or already subject to tax will be treated as if it were an employment-related loan (see **Chapter 6**).

An income tax charge will arise if:

- the securities are transferred to a person other than an associated person (see **10.2.7**) without being paid up;
- the obligation to pay for the securities by an associated person is removed; or
- something is done affecting the securities as part of a tax or NIC avoidance scheme.

In these circumstances, the notional loan is treated as if it has been written off and the outstanding amount at that point becomes employment income of the employee. There is no refund of this tax charge if the employee subsequently pays any outstanding amount.

If the securities in question are restricted securities due to a forfeiture restriction that lasts less than five years (see **10.6** above), the notional loan provisions do not apply until there is a chargeable event under Pt. 7, Ch. 2, such as restrictions being lifted or varied.

Law: ITEPA 2003, s. 446Q-446W
Guidance: ERSM 70100

10.8.5   Securities disposed of for more than market value

Where the employment-related securities are disposed of by an associated person (see **10.2.7**) to someone other than an associated person for more than market value, the excess is treated as employment income as opposed to a capital gain.

Law: ITEPA 2003, s. 446X-446Z

10.8.6   Post-acquisition benefits

ITEPA 2003, Pt 7. Ch. 4 provides a "sweeping-up" charge which ensures that the market value of any benefit provided in connection with employment-related securities is taxed as employment income if it is not taxed under any other provision.

It is extremely wide, but does not apply if:

- the benefit applies to all holders of securities of the same class;
- tax or NIC avoidance is not involved; and
- immediately before the benefit is received, the company is either employee-controlled by virtue of the holdings of the class of securities in question, or the majority of the securities of the class are not employment-related securities

Law: ITEPA 2003, s. 310, 406-410, 413A

10.9 Internationally mobile employees

Part 2, Ch. 5B applies where an employee acquires employment-related securities and is either non-UK resident or is UK resident but on the remittance basis of taxation over the "relevant period". The relevant period will vary according to the nature of rights accruing to the employee; for example, a securities option has a relevant period commencing on the date of grant and ending on the date the option first becomes capable of being exercised (see s. 41G for more details).

Where Pt. 2, Ch. 5B applies, any foreign securities income (calculated on a fair and reasonable basis) is excluded from the immediate charge to UK tax.

Foreign securities income comprises of two elements:

- non-chargeable foreign securities income (non-UK work days where the employee is non-UK resident); and
- chargeable foreign securities income (overseas work days taxed on the remittance basis where the employee is UK resident, but the remittance basis applies).

The first is never chargeable to tax and the second will only be charged as and when the proceeds are remitted to the UK (although if the employment-related securities are in a UK company, they will be deemed to have been remitted).

See **Chapter 37** for more details of the remittance basis.

To allocate the income to each category, HMRC will assume that the taxable amount is spread equally over the relevant period and will then apportion the gain on a just and reasonable basis (typically by reference to periods of residence and non-residence as well as location of work days).

Example

Maria has never previously lived or worked in the UK.

On 6 April 2021, she receives an option to acquire shares in her employer. The option is exercisable in three years.

On 6 April 2022, she goes on assignment to the UK and spends all her working days from that point in the UK. She is classed as UK resident from her date of arrival.

On 6 July 2024, she exercises her option, at which time the market value is £30,000 above her exercise price.

Ordinarily, the £30,000 would be taxable specific employment income. However, as she was non-UK resident at some point during the relevant period (which runs from 6 April 2021 to 6 April 2024), she is an internationally mobile employee and Pt. 2, Ch. 5B applies.

The foreign securities income must be deducted. As Maria was non-UK resident for one year of the relevant period and UK resident for two years of the relevant period, with no overseas work days, one third (£10,000) will be treated as non-chargeable foreign securities income. Only £20,000 will be subject to UK tax.

Consideration has to be given as to whether there is liability in any other jurisdiction and/or whether the position is affected by a double tax agreement. For details on UK residence, the remittance basis of taxation and double tax agreements, see **Chapters 34-40**.

Law: ITEPA 2003, s. 41F-41L

10.10 PAYE and National Insurance

PAYE and NIC will only be due if the securities are readily convertible assets. If the securities are not a readily convertible asset, then income tax is accountable by the individual through self-assessment.

Where NIC is payable, this will be Class 1 NIC.

Securities will be regarded as readily convertible assets if any of the following applies:

- They are listed on a recognised stock exchange (which includes the London Stock Exchange but not the Alternative Investment Market).

- There is an arrangement in place for them to be sold at the time of acquisition. This means that if an employer gives unquoted securities to one of its employees, and is already in negotiations for a sale of its securities, or if there is a potential buyer identified such as an employee benefit trust, the securities will be readily convertible.

- The issuing company is not entitled to a corporation tax deduction in respect of the securities awarded. A corporation tax deduction is available if either the securities are awarded under a tax-advantaged scheme or the securities are ordinary shares with no special rights in a listed company, a subsidiary of a listed company or a company which is not under the control of another company.

Law: ITEPA 2003, s. 702; CTA 2009, s. 1008; SI 2001/1004

10.11 Registration and annual returns

Any scheme or arrangement providing employment-related securities must be registered with HMRC no later than the 6 July following the tax year in which the first reportable event is made (i.e. typically providing an employee with securities, making some form of award or granting an option – full details are set out in s. 421K).

An annual return must then be sent to HMRC detailing all reportable events arising in the tax year (even if there are none). The deadline is 6 July following the end of the tax year in question. Returns are submitted online, and enough information has to be provided to determine any tax charge.

If the employer fails to file a return by the 6 July deadline, an automatic penalty of £100 will be charged. Additional penalties may be charged depending on how long the return is outstanding:

- an additional £300 penalty if the return is outstanding for more than three months;
- a further £300 if the return is outstanding for more than six months; and
- £10 per day if the return is outstanding for more than nine months.

Penalties do not apply if there is a reasonable excuse for the failure.

If a return is negligent or fraudulent, the penalty can be up to £5,000.

Law: ITEPA 2003, s. 421J-421L

10.12 Pitfalls and planning points

Failure to identify restricted securities

Failing to identify restricted securities, with the consequential impact and the loss of an opportunity to make an election, can have catastrophic consequences, creating an income tax charge (with potential PAYE and NIC consequences) when the employee is expecting to be within the CGT regime (see **10.6**).

Failure to make an annual return

The definition of reportable events is very wide, and it is easy to overlook the fact that an annual return is due (see **10.11**).

Failing to identify that the securities are a readily convertible asset

If the securities are not a readily convertible asset, any tax charge arising on the employment income will be accounted for by the employee through his or her self-assessment tax return. If, however, the securities are readily convertible assets, PAYE and Class 1 NIC are due. Failure to recognise this can lead to compliance failures and any PAYE not recovered from the employee can itself become a taxable benefit (see **Chapter 14**).

Employer's National Insurance

It is possible for the employer and the employee to agree that the employee will pay the employer's NIC on the employment-related securities. The agreement must be in advance, in writing, signed by both parties and approved by HMRC.

Any amount of employer's NIC paid by the employee is deductible in calculating the taxable employment income.

Sourcing the securities

On a practical level, a decision has to be made as to where the securities will be sourced from. An employer will essentially have a choice of issuing new securities, obtaining them from an existing shareholder or using any securities it may have previously designated as treasury stock (typically shares it has bought back from shareholders but has decided not to cancel).

If the employer wishes to issue new securities, it will need to be clear that it has sufficient authorised but unissued securities available, and the authority to issue new securities, as well as ensuring that any pre-emption rights are disapplied.

Another key issue is that securities cannot be issued for less than the nominal value. Therefore, if the intention is that the employee will pay nothing for the securities, a routing mechanism will be needed, such as issuing them to an employee benefit trust which can then award them to an employee.

It can be more straightforward to use existing securities. However, funding will be needed to acquire these. There may also be stamp duty to pay on the transfer (usually 0.5% of the consideration).

Stakeholders

Companies will need to comply with any applicable listing rules, disclosure regulations and institutional investor guidelines. In practice, these do affect what share plans are used, how many securities are given to employees and the conditions which attach to these.

Funding the tax

Unless there is a market for the securities (for example, if the securities are listed on a stock exchange or there are trading arrangements in place), the employee will not be able to sell sufficient securities to fund any acquisition price and/or tax. Consideration has to be given as to how this will be managed. Some employers feel this is a matter for the employee, while others seek to assist the employee with loans or bonuses. If the employer does provide loans or bonuses, the usual rules on taxation of these benefits must be considered.

11. Tax-advantaged share schemes

11.1 Introduction

Although there is comprehensive legislation designed to ensure that benefits accruing to employees linked to employment-related securities are properly taxed as employment income, the UK government also recognises the need to support and encourage employee share ownership.

Accordingly, there are a number of tax-advantaged share schemes, which, if structured within the parameters set down in ITEPA 2003, deliver shares to employees in a tax-efficient way. These are:

- company share option plans (see **11.3**);
- enterprise management incentives (see **11.4**);
- savings-related share option schemes (see **11.5**); and
- share incentive plans (see **11.6**).

Tax-advantaged share schemes can be a useful constituent of a remuneration package. According to the Office for National Statistics, there were 14,420 tax-advantaged schemes registered as at June 2020, and over the 2018-19 tax year, these generated savings in the region of £540 million in income tax and £330 million in National Insurance.

Statutory references in this chapter are to ITEPA 2003 unless otherwise stated.

Law: ITEPA 2003, Pt. 7, Ch. 6-9; Sch. 2-5

Guidance: ONS table: *Companies with tax-advantaged employee share schemes* (June 2020)

11.2 Market value

Throughout the legislation dealing with tax-advantaged plans, there is reference to the market value of the shares. "Market value" has the same definition as in TCGA 1992, Pt. VIII, which is based on the price the assets might be expected to bring on a sale in the open market. See **10.2.6**.

HMRC Shares and Assets Valuation team will agree in advance the market value of shares for the purpose of an award under a tax-advantaged plan.

Law: TCGA 1992, s. 272-273; ITEPA 2003, Sch. 2, para. 92; Sch. 3, para. 48; Sch. 4, para. 36; Sch. 5, para. 54; SI 2015/616 (*The Market Value of Shares, Securities and Strips Regulations* 2015)

11.3 Company share option plans

11.3.1 Introduction

Under a company share option plan (CSOP), the employee is granted a right to buy shares at a fixed price within a specified period of time.

For employees to benefit from the tax advantages, the plan must be registered with HMRC (see **11.7**) and must only provide benefits in the form of share options that comply with the conditions set out in Sch. 4.

Law: ITEPA 2003, s. 521-526, Sch. 4

11.3.2 Key features

The key features of a CSOP are:

- It is discretionary, in that the company can choose which of its eligible employees can participate.

- An employee or director is eligible to participate in a CSOP if he or she does not have a material interest in the company (owning 30% or more). A director must also work at least 25 hours per week.

- The options must be granted over ordinary, non-redeemable fully paid-up shares in either the employer company or a holding company or parent company of the employer company.

- The shares must be listed on a recognised stock exchange, in a company which is not controlled by another company or in a company which is subject to an employee-ownership trust.

- The price at which shares can be acquired cannot be less than the market value at the date the option is granted.

- The option can only be exercised in accordance with its terms. (Although there are no specific requirements as to when the option can be exercised, or when it will lapse, plans are often drafted to reflect the circumstances in which beneficial tax treatment will be available.)

- The value of shares held under CSOP options by any one person at any time (market value at the date of grant) must not exceed £30,000.

- On certain changes of control, provision can be made for options to be exchanged for options in the acquiring company. Where the new options qualify as equivalent, there will be no tax charge on the exchange. Instead the new options are treated as if they had been granted on the date(s) that the original options were granted.

Law: ITEPA 2003, Sch. 4

11.3.3   Tax implications

There is no charge to income tax or NIC when a CSOP option is granted.

There is also no charge to income tax or NIC when a CSOP option is exercised, in accordance with its terms, between three and ten years from the date the option is granted.

Where the CSOP option is exercised within three years from the date of grant (assuming exercise is allowed under the terms of the CSOP option), there will be no charge to income tax or NIC if the option is exercised:

- within 12 months of the death of the option holder;
- within six months of the option holder ceasing to be a full-time director or qualifying employee for a "good leaver" reason (see below); or
- following a change of control of the company as a result of a general offer, a reorganisation within Companies Act 2006, s. 425, or a voluntary winding up. The timing of the exercise of options varies, although it is typically within six months of the event occurring.

"Good leaver" reasons are set out in s. 524(2B) and include:

- injury or disability;
- redundancy within the *Employment Rights Act* 1996;
- retirement;
- being transferred under TUPE *(Transfer of Undertakings (Protection of Employment) Regulations* 2006); and

- the employing company ceasing to be controlled by the scheme organiser company.

On the subsequent sale of the shares acquired under option, the base cost for calculating any capital gains tax (CGT) will be calculated by reference to the option exercise price.

Example

Elliot is granted a CSOP option to acquire 1,000 shares at an exercise price of £2 on 1 October 2021.

In June 2023, the business he works in is sold to another company and he transfers employment to the acquiring company in accordance with TUPE.

Under the terms of the scheme, his option has become capable of exercise. He duly exercises the option at a time when the shares are worth £3.50 per share.

There is no tax on grant. Although he exercises his option within three years of the date of grant, his reason for leaving is within s. 524(2B) and so is free of income tax.

On a subsequent sale, his CGT base cost will be equal to the exercise price of £2 per share.

If the exercise takes place in circumstances other than those outlined above, a charge to income tax will arise. The rules applying to the exercise of non-tax-advantaged securities options will apply to calculate the amount of the income tax payable (see **10.5**).

The tax will only be accountable through PAYE, and attract NIC, if the shares are readily convertible assets (see **10.10**).

Law: ITEPA 2003, Sch. 4

11.4 Enterprise management incentives

11.4.1 Introduction

The enterprise management incentive (EMI) is another type of tax-advantaged discretionary share option scheme. However, it is much more flexible and potentially more valuable than the CSOP and, as a result, is by far the most popular type of tax-advantaged plan (representing over 85% of all tax-advantaged plans in operation).

For employees to benefit from the tax advantages offered to an EMI, the plan must be registered with HMRC (see **11.7** below) and must only provide benefits in the form of share options which comply with the conditions set out in Sch. 5. The terms of the option must be in writing and the option must be notified to HMRC within 92 days of grant.

The EMI is aimed at encouraging entrepreneurs. Accordingly, there are strict criteria that limit the number of companies that qualify:

- The company must be a trading company with a permanent establishment in the UK.
- The company must not carry on excluded activities – such as financial and legal services, farming, property development and certain other trades (see Sch. 5, para. 15-16) – unless these are only incidental to its qualifying trade.
- The total gross assets of the company cannot exceed £30 million.
- The company must have fewer than 250 full-time equivalent employees.
- The company must not be controlled by another company.
- If the company has any subsidiaries, it must own more than 50% of the share capital and no other person can be capable of exercising control. If the subsidiary is a property management company, the shareholding requirement increases to 90%.

Where the company is part of a group, the tests for gross assets and number of employees must be met by the group as a whole. The requirement for a permanent establishment in the UK can be met by the parent company or by a qualifying subsidiary which carries out a qualifying trade.

Law: ITEPA 2003, s. 527-540, Sch. 5

11.4.2   Key features

The key features of the EMI are:

- It is discretionary, in that the company can choose which of its eligible employees can participate.
- An employee or director is eligible to participate in an EMI if he or she does not have a material interest in the company (owning 30% or more) and works at least 25 hours per week (or, if less, at least 75% of his or her working time). For the

period from 19 March 2020 to 5 April 2022, absence for a reason related to Covid-19 will not reduce an employee's working time for the purpose of calculating eligibility.

- The options must be granted over ordinary, non-redeemable, fully paid-up shares.

- There is no restriction on the price at which shares can be acquired.

- The option can only be exercised in accordance with its terms. (Although there are no specific requirements as to when an EMI option can be exercised and when it will lapse, plans are often drafted to reflect the circumstances in which beneficial tax treatment will be available.)

- The value of shares held under an EMI option (when taken together with any CSOP option) by any one person at any time must not exceed £250,000. (The value is calculated by reference to the market value of the shares at the date of grant.) Once this limit has been reached, no further EMI qualifying options may be granted until three years after the grant of the last EMI option that came within the limit. This is the case even if during that period some of the existing options are exercised or released.

- The total value of shares in a company over which EMI options are held cannot exceed £3 million.

- On certain changes of control, provision can be made for options to be exchanged for options in the acquiring company. Where the new options qualify as equivalent, there will be no tax charge on the exchange. Instead the new options are treated as if they had been granted on the date(s) on which the original options were granted.

Law: ITEPA 2003, Sch. 5

11.4.3 Tax implications

There is no charge to income tax on the grant of a valid EMI option.

The income tax on exercise will depend on when the EMI option is exercised, and on the exercise price.

If an EMI option is exercised within ten years of the date of grant, and the exercise price is not less than the market value on the date of grant, there is no income tax on exercise.

If an EMI option is exercised within ten years from the date of grant, and the exercise price is less than the market value at the date of grant, an income tax charge will arise on the level of the "discount". This is the difference between the exercise price and the lower of the market value on the date of grant and the market value on the date of exercise.

Example

Katie receives an EMI option to buy 30,000 shares in her employer company at a price of £2 per share. At the date of grant the market value of each share is £2.50. Three years later, when the shares are worth £6 each, she exercises the EMI option.

There is no income tax charge on grant of the EMI option. When she exercises her option, there is a tax charge on £0.50 per share. This is the difference between the exercise price of £2 and the lower of the market value on the date of grant, £2.50, and the market value on the date of exercise, £4.50.

When an EMI option is exercised more than ten years from grant, it is treated as a non-tax-advantaged option and any difference between market value on the date of exercise and the price paid will be subject to income tax (see **10.5**).

Any tax will only be accountable through PAYE and attract National Insurance if the shares are readily convertible assets (see **10.10**).

The CGT base cost is the exercise price plus any value on which income tax is paid. For the purposes of calculating entitlement to business asset disposal relief (BADR), the period of holding is calculated from the date of grant of an EMI option rather than the date of exercise.

Law: ITEPA 2003, s. 527-532

11.4.4   Disqualifying events

A number of changes or developments can disqualify an EMI option. These "disqualifying events" include:

- the company ceasing to qualify for EMI as a result of the loss of independence, or because it starts carrying on excluded activities;

- the employee ceasing to be eligible because he or she has left employment or no longer works the required number of hours (but for the period from 19 March 2020 to 5 April 2022, any reduction in hours as a result of a reason related to Covid-19 is disregarded);

- the terms of the option or the underlying shares being altered, so increasing the value of the shares under option or resulting in the shares no longer meeting the requirements of the legislation; and

- the grant of a CSOP option resulting in the employee having more than £250,000 in value of unexercised options.

Where a disqualifying event occurs, any exercise of the option within the subsequent 90 days will be treated for tax purposes in accordance with the normal EMI rules.

If the EMI option is not exercised within 90 days of a disqualifying event, there will be a tax charge, on exercise, on the increase in value of the shares since the date of the disqualifying event. This is in addition to any charge already accruing where the exercise price is less than the market value on the date of grant.

Example

In September 2021, Theo is granted EMI options over 20,000 shares in his employer company. The exercise price is £1 per share and the market value on the date of grant is £3 per share. Under the terms of the option, Theo can exercise the option at any time after September 2023.

In July 2022, Theo is made redundant. The terms of his option are that he may exercise his option within six months of leaving. He exercises his option in December 2022. Immediately before the termination of his employment, the shares are worth £4 per share. When he exercises his option, the shares are worth £8 each.

The exercise has taken place more than 90 days after the disqualifying event. The income tax charge will be calculated on:

	£
Lower of market value at date of grant (£3) and date of exercise (£8)	3
less exercise price	(1)
	2
plus Value at exercise	8
Less value at disqualifying event	(4)
	4
Total employment income is (£2 + £4) x 20,000 shares =	120,000

Essentially the amount that is tax-free is the growth in value between grant of the option and the disqualifying event.

Law: ITEPA 2003, s. 533-539

11.5 Savings-related share option schemes

11.5.1 Introduction

Under a savings-related share option scheme (often referred to as a Save As You Earn or SAYE scheme), an employee is granted an option to acquire shares. At the same time, the employee starts a linked savings arrangement with a bank or building society and deductions are made from net pay and paid into this account. When the option is exercised, the employee uses the money saved in the account to pay the exercise price.

For employees to benefit from the tax advantages, the plan must be registered with HMRC (see **11.7** below) and must only provide benefits in the form of share options which comply with the conditions set out in Sch. 3.

Law: ITEPA 2003, s. 516-520, Sch. 3

11.5.2 Key features

The key features of a qualifying SAYE scheme are:

- All employees and full-time directors must be offered the opportunity to participate on equal terms. (HMRC allow extension to part-time directors if desired but there is no compulsion to do so (see ETASSUM 32110)). The scheme organiser can also set a minimum period of employment and can exclude non-resident employees.

- The options must be granted over ordinary, non-redeemable, fully paid-up shares in either the employer company or a holding company or parent company of the employer company.

- The shares must be listed on a recognised stock exchange, in a company that is not controlled by another company or in a company that is subject to an employee-ownership trust.

- The price at which the shares can be acquired is fixed at the point the option is granted and must be a minimum of 80% of the market value of the shares at that time.

- Deductions are made from net pay for three or five years (depending on what the company offers). At the end of this savings period, the option matures and can be exercised within six months.

- There is provision for early exercise in the event of termination of employment by reason of death, injury, redundancy, retirement, a business transfer or the employer leaving a group. If the employee leaves for any other reason, the option will lapse and the savings will be returned.

- There is also provision for early exercise on certain corporate events such as a change of control.

- On exercise, the monies in the savings account are used to pay the exercise price. The number of shares the employee will acquire depends on the amount of money available.

- The maximum amount an employee can contribute to SAYE schemes is £500 per month.

- On certain changes of control, provision can be made for options to be exchanged for options in the acquiring company. Where the new options qualify as equivalent, there will be no tax charge on the exchange. Instead the new options are treated as if they had been granted on the date(s) on which the original options were granted.

Law: ITEPA 2003, Sch. 3
Guidance: ETASSUM 32110

11.5.3   Tax implications

There is no charge to income tax or NIC when the SAYE option is granted.

There is no charge to income tax or NIC when the option is exercised within six months after the end of the savings contract (after 36 or 60 monthly contributions depending on the length of the option period offered).

Where the SAYE option can be exercised before the maturity of the option, there will be no charge to income tax or NIC if the option is exercised:

- within 12 months of the death of the option holder;
- within six months of the option holder ceasing to be a qualifying employee for a "good leaver" reason (defined as for CSOPs – see **11.3.3** above); or
- following a change of control of the company as a result of a general offer, a reorganisation within *Companies Act* 2006, s. 425, or a voluntary winding-up. The timing of the exercise of options varies, although it is typically within six months of the event occurring.

On the subsequent sale of the shares acquired under option, the CGT base cost will be calculated by reference to the option exercise price.

Example

Saria is granted an SAYE option on 1 May 2021 with a three-year contract. The exercise price is £1.60 per share, which is a 20% discount to the market value of £2.00.

Saria saves £20 per month, which is deducted by her employer from her net pay and paid into a linked savings account.

In May 2024, Saria has £720 in her account. She exercises her option within the six-month window from 1 May 2024 to 1 November 2024 at a time when the market value of the shares is £4 per share. She is able to acquire 450 shares (£720 savings divided by the exercise price of £1.60). Although the shares are worth £1,800 in total, there is no income tax to pay on the exercise.

Any capital gain when Saria sells the shares will be based on an acquisition cost of £1.60 per share.

Law: ITEPA 2003, s. 516-520

11.6   Share incentive plans

11.6.1   Introduction

The share incentive plan (SIP) enables employees to receive shares in any one or more of the following ways:

- free shares, given to participating employees;
- partnership shares, purchased by employees out of gross salary;
- matching shares, given free to employees who acquire partnership shares; and
- dividend shares, purchased using dividends paid (if any) on shares while in the SIP.

For employees to benefit from the tax advantages, the plan must be registered with HMRC (see **11.7** below) and must only provide benefits in the form of share options that comply with the conditions set out in Sch. 2.

Law: ITEPA 2003, s. 488-515, Sch. 2

11.6.2   Key features

The key features of a qualifying SIP are:

- All employees must be offered the opportunity to participate on equal terms. The scheme organiser can, however, set a minimum period of employment and can exclude non-resident employees.
- The shares used in the SIP must be ordinary, non-redeemable fully paid-up shares in either the employer company or a holding company or parent company of the employer company.
- The shares must be listed on a recognised stock exchange, in a company which is not controlled by another company or in a company which is subject to an employee-ownership trust.
- When awards are made, the legal title is held by a trust set up to operate the SIP. Free, matching and dividend shares must be kept in the trust for a minimum of three years, unless the employee leaves or there is a "corporate event" (see **11.6.4** below).

- When an employee leaves employment, the shares must be removed from the trust. Provision can be made for shares awarded as free or matching shares to be forfeited if the reason for leaving is not a "good leaver" reason (see below).

- The right to vote and the right to receive dividends can be suspended while the shares are in the trust.

- A maximum of £3,600 of free shares can be awarded to any one employee in any one year. For partnership shares, the maximum gross deduction that can be made is £1,800 per year (or, if less, 10% of salary). Matching shares can be awarded at a maximum ratio of two matching shares for every one partnership share acquired.

Law: ITEPA 2003, Sch. 2

11.6.3   Tax implications

The tax treatment depends on the nature of the awards.

If income tax does arise, it will only be accountable through PAYE and attract NIC if the shares are readily convertible assets (see **10.10**).

Free and matching shares

There is no charge to income tax or NIC when the shares are originally awarded to the employee.

When shares are withdrawn from the trust, the tax treatment will depend on how long the shares have been held within the plan, and the reason for the shares having been withdrawn:

- If withdrawn five years or more after the date of the award, there is no tax to pay. In addition, the employee receives an uplift in the CGT base cost to the market value at the date the shares are withdrawn.

- If withdrawn from the plan between three and five years from the date of the award, an income tax charge will arise based on the lower of the market value of the shares at the date of the award and the market value of the shares at the date of withdrawal. However, there will be no tax charge on the withdrawal if the reason for leaving is either:

    o a "good leaver" reason within s. 498(2) (see **11.3.3** – essentially a change of control of the company or the employee leaving due to injury, retirement, redundancy, death or TUPE transfer); or

-   o a corporate event (see **11.6.4** below) where the employee has no choice but to sell the SIP shares in return for cash.

- If the shares are withdrawn within three years of the date of award and are not forfeited, there will be an income tax charge on the market value of the shares at the date they are withdrawn from the plan. Again, there is an exception where a "good leaver" reason exists or if there is a corporate event where the SIP shares must be sold in return for cash.

Example

Manaus is awarded 1,000 free shares in his employer's company in January 2021. At the time, the shares are worth £2 per share.

In April 2024, Manaus leaves to work for another company. The value of the shares on the day he leaves is £3.60 per share.

The free shares must be withdrawn from the trust when Manaus leaves.

As this is between three and five years from the date of the award, and he does not have a "good leaver" reason for leaving, income tax will arise on £2 x 1,000 shares = £2,000 (£2 being the lower of the market value at the date of award (£2) and the market value at the date of withdrawal (£3.60)).

Partnership shares

Purchasing the partnership shares out of gross pay effectively gives the employee tax and NIC relief at source. The employer also saves the secondary Class 1 NIC of 13.8%.

The tax treatment on withdrawal is the same as for free and matching shares.

Dividend shares

The dividends used to purchase dividend shares are free of income tax. If the employee wishes to keep the dividends, and not use the cash to purchase more shares, the dividends not reinvested are taxable in the normal way.

If dividend shares are left in the trust for at least three years, they can be withdrawn free of tax.

If the dividend shares are withdrawn from the trust within three years (due to the employee leaving or a corporate event), the dividends originally used to purchase the shares become taxable in the tax year in which the shares are withdrawn. However, there will no tax charge on the withdrawal if the reason for leaving is a change of control of the company or the employee leaving due to injury, retirement, redundancy, death or TUPE transfer.

Law: ITEPA 2003, s. 488-515

11.6.4   Corporate events

In contrast to the other tax-advantaged plans, a SIP involves shares as opposed to rights to acquire shares. Accordingly, if a company takeover or re-organisation occurs, the SIP plan shares are treated in the same way as those of an ordinary shareholder.

Trustees can only dispose of shares in accordance with directions given by or on behalf of the employee. If the company takeover or re-organisation falls within s. 498(3), and alternative shares are offered, all SIP shares are converted to the alternative shares and all holding, forfeiture and tax conditions will remain the same.

If a cash offer is made, the trustees will sell the shares and pay the cash out to the employee. No income tax will arise if the participant has no choice but to accept cash.

Law: ITEPA 2003, s. 498

11.7   Registration and annual returns

Any tax-advantaged scheme must be registered online with HMRC and certification must be provided showing that the relevant schedule is complied with. This must be done no later than 6 July following the tax year in which the first award or grant is made.

An annual return must then be filed online detailing all grants, awards, lapses, maturities, cancellations and other events affecting the awards or options in the tax year. If there are no reportable events, a nil return must be filed. The deadline is 6 July following the end of the tax year in question.

If the employer fails to file a return by the 6 July deadline, an automatic penalty of £100 will be charged. Additional penalties may be charged depending on how long the return is outstanding:

- an additional £300 penalty if the return is outstanding for more than three months;
- a further £300 if the return is outstanding for more than six months; and
- £10 per day if the return is outstanding for more than nine months.

Penalties do not apply if there is a reasonable excuse for the failure.

If a return is negligent or fraudulent, a penalty of up to £5,000 can be levied.

There is an additional filing requirement where EMI options are concerned. Details of any EMI option must be notified to HMRC within 92 days of grant. Failure to do so leads to the EMI option being treated as a non-tax-advantaged option.

Law: ITEPA 2003, Sch. 2, para. 81A-81K; Sch. 3, para. 40A-40K; Sch. 4, para. 28A-28K; Sch. 5, para. 44-53, 57A-57E
Guidance: ETASSUM 11300, 11400

11.8   Pitfalls and planning points

Going outside the rules

Awards and options under tax-advantaged plans can only be dealt with in the way set out in the rules (and the rules cannot contain anything that contradicts the legislation or provides other benefits not anticipated in the legislation). The practical consequence is that any variation of the rights set out in the rules is treated as a cancellation of the existing award and a deemed grant of a new one. This can undermine the tax benefits.

Corporate takeovers and changes of control

Although permitted early exercises of options/vesting of awards do not attract a tax charge if there is a corporate event within the legislation, there are a number of potential pitfalls to be aware of:

- The definition of a corporate event for CSOPs and SAYEs only covers takeovers by general offer. A change of control achieved by a different route – for example, a series of one-off deals with individual shareholders at different times – may not trigger a permitted early exercise.
- If a right to early exercise arises, the employee cannot be prevented from exercising his options if he chooses to do so.

Conversely, if he chooses not to, the options will lapse (which may not be the desired effect). To minimise disruption, careful consideration should be given to the particular situation both when setting up the plan and when a potential corporate event approaches.

- Under a SAYE scheme, shares can only be acquired with the funds in the linked savings account. Therefore, on an early exercise, the number of shares may be less than the employee is expecting.

Tax-advantaged plans and restricted shares

It is possible that an award under a tax-advantaged plan relates to shares that amount to restricted securities (see **10.6**). In most cases, a s. 431 election is deemed to be given (with the consequence that there is no further income tax on any subsequent chargeable events). If, however, there is an EMI option and the exercise price is at a discount, the restricted securities election is not automatic. If one is not entered into within 14 days of the exercise of the option, there is potential for an income tax charge when restrictions are lifted or varied, or if the shares are sold (see s. 431A).

Failure to notify EMI options to HMRC

Forgetting to notify HMRC of the details of the grant within 92 days will lead to the option being treated as non-tax-advantaged. See **11.7** above for more details.

12. Statutory payments

12.1 Introduction

An employee may be entitled to statutory payments if he or she is absent from work due to:

- sickness;
- having to self-isolate as a result of contact with Covid-19;
- having or adopting a child; or
- the death of his or her child.

These payments are made by the employer (although in some circumstances can be recovered from HMRC – see individual sections below) and represent the minimum that an employee is entitled to. Employers can, and often do, pay more.

All statutory payments, and any enhanced amount paid by the employer, form part of an employee's earnings for tax and NIC purposes.

Statutory references in this chapter are to the *Social Security Contributions and Benefits Act* (SSCBA) 1992 unless otherwise stated.

Law: SSCBA 1992

12.2 Statutory sick pay

12.2.1 Eligibility for SSP

Qualifying employees are entitled to an amount of statutory sick pay (SSP) when they are absent from work due to illness or if forced to self-isolate due to Covid-19.

Employees will qualify for statutory sick pay provided:

- they have not received employment support allowance within 12 weeks of starting the current employment;
- they are not currently receiving statutory maternity pay or similar statutory payments (see **12.3 to 12.6** below);
- the employee has notified the employer in writing that he or she is unfit for work within seven days of the first qualifying day of absence; and

- the employee's average weekly earnings subject to Class 1 NIC (typically cash excluding pension and payroll giving contributions) equal or exceed the weekly lower earnings limit for NIC purposes (£120 for 2021-22).

In calculating average weekly earnings, the pay received from the employment over the eight-week period before the illness is taken into account (or, if not in employment for eight weeks, the amount the individual should have received under the employment contract).

Where employees are paid monthly, the total earnings in the eight-week period must be converted to weekly earnings.

Example

Bronagh earns £12,000 per year paid monthly in arrears. With effect from 1 July 2021, her salary increases to £13,200. She becomes ill and is absent from work on 1 August 2021.

To calculate her weekly average earnings:

	£
Pay received in previous eight weeks	2,200
Average pay per month (£2,200/2)	1,100
Average weekly earnings = £1,100 x 12/52	253.85

Bronagh's average weekly earnings exceed the weekly lower earnings limit.

An employee who is not entitled to SSP, but who has been off sick for four or more consecutive days, may be entitled to state employment and support allowance (see **Chapter 33**).

The employer must give an employee who is not entitled to SSP a completed form SSP1, typically no later than seven days after the later of:

- the day on which the employer is notified that the employee is sick; or
- the fourth day of the period of incapacity for work.

Law: SSCBA 1992, s. 151-156, Sch. 11-13; SI 1982/894

12.2.2 Calculating SSP

The actual amount of SSP depends on there being a period of incapacity for work (PIW).

A PIW is simply a period of four or more consecutive days – including weekends, bank holidays and other non-working days – when an employee is incapable of carrying out his or her normal duties due to illness or because the individual is having to self-isolate due to Covid-19.

SSP is only paid in respect of normal work days within a PIW (referred to as qualifying days). Except where the reason for absence is related to Covid-19, the first three qualifying days in a PIW are disregarded.

In 2021-22, SSP is paid daily at a flat rate of £96.35 per week. The actual daily amount paid therefore depends on the number of qualifying days an individual has in a week.

Example

Tariq usually works Monday to Friday each week. On Monday 13 October, he is absent from work due to a knee injury. He returns to work on Friday 24 October.

The PIW is eleven days. During the PIW, there are nine qualifying days (Saturday and Sunday are ignored as they are not Tariq's normal working days). The first three qualifying days are disregarded and so Tariq is entitled to SSP for six days.

Tariq ordinarily works five days a week. His daily rate of SSP is therefore £96.35/5 = £19.27. Therefore for this absence, he will receive £115.62.

If an employee has already received 28 weeks of SSP and the current period of illness is linked to the last period, then no further SSP is due. PIWs are linked if there are fewer than 56 days between them.

Law: SSCBA 1992, s. 151-156; SI 1982/894; SI 2020/374

12.2.3 Ending SSP

An employee's entitlement to receive SSP ends for a number of reasons, such as if:

- the employee returns to work or no longer produces evidence of incapacity;
- the employee has exhausted his or her entitlement (total 28 weeks);

- the contract of employment ends (unless this has been done by the employer to avoid SSP liability); or
- the start of the maternity pay period (see **12.3** below) or maternity allowance period (see **Chapter 33**).

Law: SSCBA 1992, s. 151-156, Sch. 11; SI 1982/894

12.3   Statutory maternity pay

12.3.1   Eligibility

When an employee is on maternity leave, she will be entitled to receive statutory maternity pay (SMP) from her employer for up to 39 weeks (the "maternity pay period") while not working if she meets all of the following conditions:

- She has an employer in the UK and earnings that attract a liability for Class 1 NIC.
- She has been continuously employed by the same employer for at least 26 weeks continuing into the qualifying week (QW) – which is the 15th week before the week the baby is due – or would have worked for that employer into the QW, had her baby not been born early.
- She is not in legal custody.
- She has average weekly earnings (AWE) in the eight weeks ending with the last pay day on or before the Saturday of the qualifying week of at least £120 (calculated in the same way as for SSP (see **12.2.1** above)).
- She is still pregnant at the 11th week before the week the baby is due, or has had her baby by that time.
- She has provided medical evidence of the date the baby is due, or was born, ordinarily within three weeks of the start of the maternity pay period, typically using form MAT1B.
- She has given the employer 28 days' notice of when she expects the employer to start paying her SMP (although the employer can accept late notice if there is a good reason for the delay).

If an employee satisfies the conditions above she qualifies for SMP, even if she does not intend to return to work for the employer in question after her baby is born.

There are special rules for calculating length of employment and AWE for agency, contract and casual workers to ensure that they are not disadvantaged. See the *Statutory Maternity Pay (General) Regulations* 1986 for more details.

If the relevant conditions are not met the employer must inform the employee that she is not entitled to any payment, using form SMP1, within seven days of the decision not to make a payment.

Law: SSCBA 1992, s. 164-171; SI 1986/1960

12.3.2 Calculating SMP

Where SMP is due:

- the employee receives 90% of AWE for the first six weeks of the maternity pay period (with no upper limit); and
- she receives the lower of 90% of AWE and £151.97 per week for the remainder of the period.

Example

Lana is entitled to SMP and has average weekly earnings of £245.

For the first six weeks she will receive £220.50 (90% of £245) per week.

For each of the remaining 33 weeks she will receive £151.97.

Law: SSCBA 1992, s. 164-171; SI 1986/1960

12.4 Statutory adoption pay

When an employee adopts a child, he or she will be entitled to statutory adoption pay ("SAP") for up to 39 weeks while on adoption leave provided that all of the following conditions are satisfied:

- The employer is in the UK and the employee has earnings that attract a liability for Class 1 NIC.
- The employee has been continuously employed by the same employer for at least 26 weeks continuing into the qualifying week, which is the week in which the employee is notified that he or she has been matched with a child for adoption.
- The employee is not in legal custody.
- He or she has average weekly earnings (AWE) in the eight weeks ending with the last pay day on or before the Saturday of the qualifying week of at least £120 (calculated in the same way as for SSP (see **12.2.1** above)).
- The employee has provided evidence of the adoption.

- He or she has given the employer 28 days' notice of when the employer is expected to start paying the SAP (although the employer can accept late notice if there is a good reason for the delay). Where the child is adopted from the UK, the employee can choose to start being paid and/or start leave from the date the child is placed, or up to 14 days before the child is expected to be placed. Where the child is adopted from overseas, the SAP/leave can start on the date the child enters the UK within the following 28 days.

Where a couple is involved in the adoption, only one person (known as the "primary adopter") can obtain SAP and leave. The other partner may be eligible for statutory paternity pay (see **12.5** below).

The amount of SAP is exactly the same as SMP, i.e. 90% of AWE for the first six weeks then the lower of 90% of AWE and £151.97 per week for the remaining weeks.

Law: SSCBA 1992, s. 171ZL-171ZT; SI 2002/2822

12.5   Statutory paternity pay

An employee will generally be eligible for statutory paternity pay (SPP) while on paternity leave if all of the following conditions are met:

- The employee's spouse/civil partner is having a baby or adopting a child.
- The same tests regarding length of employment and minimum AWE are met as for SMP (see **12.3.1** above) or SAP (see **12.4** above) as appropriate.
- The employee continues to work for the employer until the baby is born (or placed, in the case of adoption).
- The leave is being taken to look after the child or partner.
- The employee is responsible for the child's upbringing.
- Application is made in writing for SPP at least 15 weeks before the week the baby is due or, in the case of adoption, at least 28 days before the employee wants the SPP to start.
- In the case of adoption, proof is provided to the employer of both the adoption and the fact that the employee's partner is receiving statutory adoption pay.

The amount of SPP payable during paternity leave is the lower of 90% of AWE and £151.97 per week. This will be for one or two weeks depending on the length of the paternity leave.

Law: SSCBA 1992, s. 171ZA-171ZK; SI 2002/2822

12.6   Statutory shared parental pay

Parents have an option to stop statutory maternity or adoption leave (after at least two weeks) and take shared parental leave instead. This effectively allows the leave ordinarily available to the mother or primary adopter to be taken by the other partner, or by both parents, either consecutively or concurrently. Provided it is taken within one year of the birth or adoption of the child, there is flexibility around whether it is taken as a continuous period or in a maximum of three "blocks" of complete weeks.

Where shared parental leave is taken, shared parental pay (ShPP) replaces the SMP/SAP. ShPP is paid at the rate of £151.97 per week or 90% of AWE (defined as for SSP – see **12.2.1**) if lower. The usual pay period of 39 weeks is reduced by the number of weeks that SMP or SAP has been paid.

The eligibility criteria are complex and depend on whether both parents are taking the leave or just one. More details can be found in the *Statutory Shared Parental Leave (General) Regulations* 2020 and the *Statutory Shared Parental Pay (General) Regulations* 2020.

If an employee wants to start shared parental leave and ShPP, at least eight weeks' written notice must be given to the employer.

Law: SI 2014/3050, 2014/3051

12.7   Statutory parental bereavement pay

An employee may be eligible for statutory parental bereavement pay (SPBP) if he or she, or his or her partner, is taking parental bereavement leave.

Employees will be eligible if all of the following conditions are met:

- There is a stillbirth after 24 weeks of pregnancy, or a child who has died under 18 years of age.

- At the time of the child's death or stillbirth, the employee is the child's parent – whether biological, adoptive or the parent of a child born to a surrogate. (A partner of the child's parent or a person with day-to-day responsibility for the child will also be eligible provided no-one with parental responsibility for the child is also living in the household.)
- The employee is employed on the day the child dies or is stillborn.
- The employee's average weekly earnings (calculated as for SSP) are at least £120.
- The employee asks the employer for SPBP within 28 days starting with the first day of leave.

SPBP is paid at the rate of £151.97 a week or, if lower, 90% of the employee's AWE, for a maximum of two weeks.

Law: SI 2020/233

12.8   Administration

Generally, an employer is only able to recover SSP where it has fewer than 250 employees as at 28 February 2020 and the reason for paying SSP is because the employee has contracted Covid-19 or is required to self-isolate (for a reason other than coming to the UK from overseas). The amount recovered is restricted to two weeks per employee.

In addition, an employer can recover 92% of the gross amount of SMP, SAP, SPP, ShPP and SPBP paid. This increases to 103% of the amount paid where the total annual employer and employee Class 1 NIC contributions do not exceed £45,000. (The supplement of 3% is to compensate for the fact that employer's Class 1 NIC is paid in respect of the payments.)

The £45,000 limit is compared to the total contributions for the tax year prior to that in which the qualifying or matching week starts.

The employer must keep records of amounts paid or refused, including any supporting documentation, for at least three years after the end of the relevant tax year. There is an exception for statutory sick pay that is not recoverable by the employer. However, it is still recommended that records are maintained in case there is a dispute over eligibility.

Statutory payments are made through payroll in the same way as salary, with any claims for repayment recorded on the employer payment summary and off-set against PAYE/NIC due to HMRC. For more details on the process for recovery of statutory payments and reporting requirements, see **Chapter 14**.

Law: SI 1994/1230, 2002/2820, 2014/2929, 2020/246, 2020/512

12.9 Pitfalls and planning points

Statutory sick pay procedures

An employer can draw up its own procedures for notifying sickness to fit its business arrangements better, for example by asking the employee to tell the employer that he or she is ill on the first day of absence. The employees must be notified of what the procedures are and the procedures must not be unreasonable.

See **12.2.1** and SI 1982/894, reg. 7.

Interaction between maternity or adoption pay and shared parental pay

Shared parental leave is available to replace maternity and adoption leave after two weeks. However, all ShPP is capped at £151.97 per week, whereas the first six weeks of maternity and adoption pay are set at 90% of AWE. It therefore makes sense, if practical, for parents to stop maternity and adoption leave only after this period has elapsed.

See **12.6** above for more details.

13. Other income treated as employment income

13.1 Introduction

As mentioned at **5.3.4**, employment income encompasses not only general earnings but also income brought into charge by virtue of ITEPA 2003. This includes, for example, termination payments (see **Chapter 9**), income arising from employment-related securities (see **Chapter 10**), and unregistered pension payments (see **Chapter 31**).

In this chapter, consideration is given to three other key areas which, by virtue of ITEPA 2003, give rise to taxable employment income:

- deemed employment payments where employment intermediaries are used (see **13.2**);
- disguised remuneration (see **13.3**); and
- salaried partner income (see **13.4**).

Statutory references in this chapter are to ITEPA 2003 unless otherwise stated.

Law: ITEPA 2003, Pt. 2, Ch. 7-10, Pt. 7A; ITTOIA 2005, s. 863A-863G

13.2 Employment intermediaries

13.2.1 Introduction

An individual may choose to provide services to a client through a third party rather than contracting directly with the client. There are many reasons for this, including:

- the third party may provide contacts or assistance with finding work and/or providing administrative support;
- a company cannot, by definition, be an employee and therefore the client potentially avoids the risk associated with determining employment status when the contract is with an intermediary rather than with an individual; and
- if the individual performing the services owns all or part of the third party, he or she can take the profits as dividends or trading income, instead of salary, which can be more tax-efficient.

From a fiscal perspective, however, the use of an intermediary can lead to an inequality of treatment (and potentially lost revenue).

Example

ZZZ Ltd wishes to engage Vinnie as an IT consultant to work with it on a six-month project. It is agreed that the terms of the engagement are such that if taken on directly he would be an employee. Any salary therefore would be subject to PAYE and NIC (see **Chapter 14**).

Instead Vinnie sets up V's Ltd, which enters into a contract with ZZZ Ltd for the provision of Vinnie's services. V's Ltd invoices ZZZ Ltd for the cost of Vinnie's services.

In the absence of any counter-legislation, the payment to V's Ltd is not employment income and is therefore free of PAYE and NIC. V's Ltd would be subject to corporation tax on any profits and could pay these out to Vinnie as dividends.

To nullify this financial advantage, there are a number of statutory provisions:

- Under certain circumstances, agencies must treat payments made to the individuals they have placed at clients as payments of employment income ("agency rules" – see Pt. 2, Ch. 7, covered at **13.2.2** below).

- Where the agency rules do not apply, then unless the client is a small or overseas business, payments to a qualifying intermediary will be deemed employment income if services have been provided by an individual who would have been an employee or office holder if engaged directly ("off-payroll working rules" – see Pt. 2, Ch. 10, and see **13.2.3** below).

- Where neither the agency rules nor the off-payroll working rules apply, consideration must be given to the rules on managed service companies (in Pt 2, Ch 9 – see **13.2.4**) and personal service companies (in Pt 2, Ch 8 – see **13.2.5**). If either of these apply, the intermediary is deemed to make an employment payment to the individual.

Law: ITEPA 2003, Pt. 2, Ch. 7-10

13.2.2   Agencies

The rules in Pt. 2, Ch. 7 apply if an individual personally provides services to a client, and there is a contract in place between the client (or a person connected with the client) and a third party (the agency), under which the third person receives payment for the services the individual provides.

In such cases, the third party must deduct PAYE and NIC from payments it makes to the individual as if the individual were an employee of the third party and as if the payment were employment income. The exception to this is where the agency's client pays the individual direct. In this case, it is the client who must operate PAYE in respect of the payments made to the individual. For more details on the operation of PAYE and NIC, see **Chapter 14**.

The rules will not, however, apply if:

- the third party contracts with the individual's intermediary, rather than the individual direct (in which case see **13.2.3, 13.2.4** and **13.2.5** below);
- the individual is an actor, entertainer or model, or the work is carried out in the individual's home or a place not controlled or managed by the client (see s. 47); or
- when providing the services in question, the individual is not subject to supervision, direction or control by any person (see s. 44).

The concept of supervision, direction or control (SDC) is not defined. HMRC's view is that there will be SDC unless it can be shown otherwise. A detailed discussion is contained in ESM 2037 and ESM 2055-2068. In summary, though, where there are procedures, methods and instructions which must be followed (other than health and safety instructions), this points to SDC in the manner in which services are provided.

In most cases, the agency is treated as the employer for the purposes of PAYE in respect of income earned by the individuals that it supplies to end clients. This means that the agency must deduct income tax and NIC from payments made to the individual and is also liable for secondary Class 1 NIC.

Law: ITEPA 2003, s. 44-47
Guidance: ESM 2037, 2055-2068

13.2.3   Off-payroll working rules

The off-payroll working rules in Pt. 2, Ch. 10 apply where all of the following apply:

- The client is either a public authority or (since 1 April 2021) is a medium or large business with a UK connection.
- There is an individual who personally performs, or is under an obligation to perform, services for a client.
- The services are not provided under a contract directly between the client and the individual but are instead provided under arrangements involving a qualifying intermediary.
- The circumstances are such that if the services had been provided under a contract directly between the client and the individual, the individual would have been regarded for tax purposes as being an employee or office-holder of the client.

If an agency is already accounting for PAYE and NICs in respect of payments to the individual under Pt. 2, Ch. 7, the off-payroll working rules do not apply.

There is also an exclusion where the client is an individual and receives services other than in the course of his or her business (see s. 61M(1A)).

There are a number of definitions to consider:

Phrase	Meaning
Public authority	Defined in the *Freedom of Information Act* 2000 and includes government departments and their executive agencies, universities, local authorities, parish councils, the NHS and primary healthcare providers such as GPs, dental surgeries, opticians and pharmacies (s. 61L).
Medium or large business	A business that is not within the small companies regime in the *Companies Act* 2006, s. 382-383 for the financial year "relevant" to the tax year in question, usually the financial year ending immediately before the beginning of the tax year. Note that where there is a group of companies, the test applies to the group as a whole. Furthermore, where the business is not a corporate, the financial measures in the small companies regime are still used to ascertain size (s. 60A-60G).
UK connection	Immediately before the beginning of the tax year the client is not resident in the UK for tax purposes and does not have a permanent establishment in the UK (s. 60I).

Phrase (cont.)	Meaning
Qualifying intermediary	**Either:** the intermediary is a company, it is not an associate of the client and the individual has an interest of more than 5% in the intermediary;
	Or: the intermediary is a company, it is not an associate of the client and the individual has an interest of 5% or less in the intermediary, and has an entitlement to or expectation of receiving a payment or other benefit for services to the client which will not constitute employment income (if it were not for Pt. 2, Ch. 10);
	Or: the intermediary is a partnership and
	(a) the individual, together with associates, is entitled to 60% or more of the profits of the partnership; or
	(b) most of the profits covered by the personal service company rules or the off-payroll working rules relate to a single client (and its associates); or
	(c) the profits of any of the partners are based on the types of services covered by the personal service company rules or the off-payroll working rules;
	Or: the intermediary is an individual.
	See s. 61N(9)-(11).

If the client falls within the scope of Pt. 2, Ch. 10, a number of obligations arise.

The individual or the intermediary must advise the client whether the intermediary fulfils one of the conditions or not. Failure to provide information will result in the client assuming that the conditions are met and that the off-payroll working rules apply.

The client needs to consider each and every engagement where personal services are provided to it through an intermediary and make a determination as to whether the individual would be an employee if contracted with directly. This needs to be done on or before the contract for services is entered into or, if later, when the services start to be performed.

In making the determination, the client will have regard to the usual factors around employment status, e.g. mutuality of obligation, financial risk, control, right to use a substitute and integration into the organisation (see **Chapter 5**).

The client will issue a status determination statement (SDS) to the individual and any other party to the contract setting out the conclusion reached. To be valid, the SDS must set out the decision and the reasons for coming to the decision. The client must also take reasonable care in coming to its conclusion. HMRC set out in detail at ESM 10014 what they regard as reasonable care; essentially, they expect clients to "act in a way that would be expected of a prudent and reasonable person in the client's position".

The recipients of the SDS can query the reasons for reaching the conclusion set out in the SDS and, if they do so, the client must respond in writing within 31 days.

Where the client concludes that the rules apply, the client must also determine the "deemed employer". In a chain of the contracting parties with the client at the top and the intermediary at the bottom, the party responsible for operating PAYE/NIC (known as the "fee-payer") will be the lowest qualifying person above the intermediary. To be a qualifying person, the entity must have received an SDS, be UK resident and not be controlled by the individual or associates or be a company in which the individual or associates has a 5% or more material interest.

Where the lowest party above the intermediary fails these tests, the fee-payer will be the next highest in the chain which does qualify. This could be the client itself if it is contracting directly with the intermediary or is dealing with an offshore entity or has failed to provide the SDS.

The deemed employer must add the individual to the payroll and deduct PAYE and NIC, as well as account for employer's NIC and apprenticeship levy on the "deemed direct payment". This is the VAT-exclusive amount due to be paid by the deemed employer less any direct costs of materials and expenses met by the intermediary that would have been deductible from taxable earnings if the individual was an employee and expenses had been met out of those earnings.

The rules are structured so that failure to discharge obligations – for example, providing fraudulent information, not responding to a request or not taking reasonable care in reaching a conclusion – results in the defaulting party having responsibility for PAYE, NIC and apprenticeship levy in relation to any payments to the individual for that engagement. Furthermore, anti-avoidance provisions apply to arrangements that seek to ensure that the intermediary is not a qualifying intermediary within Pt. 2, Ch 10. Where these apply, the participating person is treated as the deemed employer. If there is more than one participating person, the deemed employer will be the highest person in the chain that HMRC regard as being able to recover the tax involved.

To avoid double taxation on any payment covered by the rules:

- the net amount received by the intermediary is not taxable (CTA 2009, s. 141A; ITTOIA 2005, s. 164B); and
- the intermediary does not have to operate PAYE or NIC on a salary payment to the extent that it is covered by a deemed payment, although the payment still needs reporting on the FPS as non-taxable income (s. 61W).

The VAT liabilities of the intermediary remain unchanged by the rules.

Law: ITEPA 2003, s. 60A-60I, 61K-61X; ITTOIA 2005, s. 164B; CTA 2009, s. 141A
Guidance: ESM 10014

13.2.4   *Managed service companies*

The off-payroll working rules will not apply if the individual owns an insufficient proportion of the intermediary (see **13.2.3** above). However, in these circumstances, the use of an intermediary may still be caught by the managed service company (MSC) rules in Pt. 2, Ch. 9.

An intermediary is within Pt. 2, Ch. 9 if all of the following conditions are met:

- Its business consists wholly or mainly of providing (directly or indirectly) the services of an individual to other persons.
- A person who carries on a business of promoting or facilitating the use of companies to provide the services of individuals (an "MSC provider") is involved with the intermediary. In this context, "involved" means giving or promoting an undertaking to make good any tax loss, benefitting financially on an ongoing basis from the provision of the services of the individual, or influencing or controlling the provision of those services, the way payments to the individual are made, the company's finances or any of its activities. A person is not, however, involved with the company merely by virtue of providing legal or accountancy services in a professional capacity. There is also a partial carve-out for certain recruitment businesses. See s. 61B (2)-(4) for the full definition.

- Payments are made to the individual performing the services that are equal to the greater part or all of the consideration for the provision of the services (the "size of payments" test).
- The individual has received more than he would have done had he been employed directly by the client (the "receipts" test).

The MSC rules must be applied each time a payment is made to ensure the size of payments and receipts tests are met. Where the MSC rules are met, deemed employment income will arise based on the value of the payments or benefits that can reasonably be said to relate to the services and which have not previously been charged as employment income. Certain expenses can be deducted, as can an amount representing employer's NIC on the deemed payment (s. 61E).

To avoid double taxation, relief is available to reduce the amount of dividends received by the individual where a charge has arisen under Pt. 2, Ch. 9 in respect of the same income (s. 61H).

Law: ITEPA 2003, s. 61A-61J

13.2.5   Personal service companies

The legislation contained in Pt. 2, Ch. 8 applies where:

- there is a qualifying intermediary who contracts with the client for the individual's services;
- the individual would be treated as an employee or office holder of the client if engaged by the client direct; and
- the agency rules in Pt. 2, Ch. 7, the off-payroll working rules in Pt. 2, Ch. 10 and the MSC rules in Pt. 2, Ch. 9 do not apply.

A qualifying intermediary has the same definition as for the off-payroll working rules (see **13.2.3** above).

The effect of the personal service company rules is that the intermediary must treat any income from "relevant engagements" over the tax year, that has not been paid to the individual as salary, as if it is an additional payment of employment income paid on 5 April.

An engagement is a relevant engagement if the individual would be an employee or office-holder of the client if the individual were engaged directly. The usual employment status criteria (see **Chapter 5**) are used to determine the correct approach.

In calculating the amount of deemed employment income, the following deductions can be made from relevant engagement income:

- 5% of the income to cover administrative expenses;
- any expenses paid for or reimbursed by the intermediary which would be deductible from taxable earnings if met by the individual (see **Chapter 8**). Note that s. 339A provides that each engagement should be treated as a separate employment, so that travel to and from the client site is ordinary commuting (and, as such, not an allowable expense);
- any contributions made by the intermediary to a registered pension scheme on behalf of the individual;
- the amount of earnings already paid to the individual in the year, including the cash equivalents of any benefits provided; and
- employer's secondary Class 1 and Class 1A NIC paid/payable by the intermediary in respect of earnings/benefits provided to the individual during the tax year.

The resulting sum is regarded as a gross amount including the associated employer's Class 1 NIC. This must therefore be excluded to obtain the final amount of the deemed employment payment.

Example

Love Leoni Ltd provides training services to various employers on an *ad hoc* basis. The training is provided by Leoni, the sole employee and shareholder of Love Leoni Ltd.

In 2021-22, there are three contracts. The first is with Extra Large plc and the fees of £20,000 have PAYE and NIC deducted at source under the off-payroll working rules. The second is with Medium Ltd and the fees of £10,000 are paid gross on the basis that Leoni would not have been an employee had Medium Ltd appointed her directly. The final contract is with Small Ltd, which confirms that the off-payroll working rules do not apply to it as it is within the small companies regime. The fees from Small Ltd amount to £30,000 gross and it is determined that these are a relevant engagement.

Leoni is paid a salary of £1,500 per month by Love Leoni Ltd. Her travel to Small Ltd's premises of £800 is reimbursed.

In 2021-22, there will be a deemed employment payment in relation to the fees from Small Ltd.

	£
Income from relevant engagements	30,000
Less: 5% deduction	(1,500)
Less: allowable expenses	Nil
Less: employer's NIC on pay ((£18,000 – £8,840) @ 13.8%)	(1,264)
Less: individual's pay	(18,000)
Gross deemed payment	9,236
Less: employer's NIC included (£9,236 x 13.8/113.8)	(1,120)
Net deemed employment payment	8,116

The sum of £8,116 will be treated as a payment of salary to Leoni on 5 April 2022.

To avoid double taxation, dividends paid to the individual are only taxed to the extent they exceed the deemed salary payment (s. 58).

Law: ITEPA 2003, s. 48-60

13.3 Disguised remuneration

13.3.1 Introduction

The charge to tax on earnings only arises at the point a payment is actually made or, if earlier, the point at which legal entitlement arises. (See **5.4** for more details, including additional rules where a director is involved.)

During the late 1990s and early 2000s, a number of tax planning arrangements were implemented using third parties, typically trusts, to provide value to employees, often in the form of loans, without triggering a tax point. After various legal challenges and piecemeal legislation designed to bring the use of these schemes to an end, Pt. 7A was implemented in 2011 to ensure that taxable employment income will be deemed to arise in relation to disguised remuneration.

Pt. 7A is extremely widely drafted and while it has effectively achieved the goal of stopping the tax avoidance schemes, it can also catch other, more legitimate, arrangements.

13.3.2   Scope of Pt. 7A – the main case

Section 554A sets out the situations where Pt. 7A will potentially apply (known as the "main case"). This is when:

- there is an existing, former or prospective employee, non-executive director or office holder or a relevant person "linked to the employee";
- there is an "arrangement" in relation to that person;
- the arrangement is, in essence, wholly or partly a means of providing rewards, recognition or loans in connection with employment;
- a "relevant third person" takes a "relevant step"; and
- it is reasonable to suppose that, in essence, the step is taken pursuant to the arrangement or there is some other connection (direct or indirect) between them.

There are a number of definitions to consider:

Phrase	Meaning
Person linked to the employee	Spouse/civil partner, relatives and spouses/civil partners of those relatives, plus relatives of their spouse/civil partner, as well as close companies in which any of them are or have been a participator or 51% subsidiaries of such close companies (s. 554Z1).
Arrangement	An agreement, scheme, settlement, transaction, trust or understanding, whether formal or informal, and whether the employee knows of it or not (s. 554Z(3)).
Relevant third person	The employer or the employee acting as trustees or any other person, although there is an exception for group companies if they are not trustees and no tax avoidance is involved (s. 554A(7)-(9)).
Relevant step	Actions listed in s. 554B-554D, including (for example) paying sums, making loans or credit available, earmarking assets with a view to taking another relevant step in the future, making assets, writing off or transferring debts, granting leases, and taking steps to enable employees to acquire securities or interests in securities (see s. 554Z(9)).

Essentially, whenever a third party does anything that provides or potentially provides, or is part of an attempt to provide, some form of benefit to someone by reason of employment, Pt. 7A potentially applies.

Sections 554E-554XA do, however, go on to set out a number of exceptions which disapply Pt. 7A. These are focused on legitimate arrangements which would otherwise fall within Pt. 7 and include, for example, tax-advantaged share schemes, earmarking securities to deliver on previously granted share awards or options, loans on commercial terms and arm's length transactions in the ordinary course of a third party's business.

Law: ITEPA 2003, s. 554A, 554B-554XA, 554Z-554Z1

13.3.3 Scope of Pt. 7A – the close company gateway

In addition to the main case (see **13.3.1** above), s. 554AA applies Pt. 7A to close companies where all of the following apply:

- A close company (defined in s. 554AA(2)) enters into a "relevant transaction", either pursuant to a "relevant arrangement" or in circumstances where there is some other connection between the relevant transaction and the relevant arrangement.
- The employee is a director or employee at the time of the relevant transaction or at any time within the three previous years.
- The employee has a material interest of 5% or more at the time of the relevant transaction or at any time within the three previous years.
- A relevant step is taken by a third party and the relevant step relates to money or assets subject to the relevant transaction or to money or assets derived therefrom.
- The main purpose, or one of the main purposes, is to gain a tax advantage.

This is known as the "close company gateway". The definitions of "relevant step" and "third party" are the same as for the main case.

"Relevant transaction" is extremely widely drawn, so that it will catch most sales, purchases, transfers, loans and write-offs (s. 554AB). However, certain transactions are excluded (s. 554AC):

- distributions to shareholders;
- transactions on an arm's length basis in the ordinary course of the company's business; and
- disposals of shares in the close company on an arm's length basis.

Law: ITEPA 2003, s. 554AA-554AF

13.3.4   *The amount of employment income under Pt. 7A*

Where Pt. 7A applies, the amount of taxable employment income equates to the value of the relevant step.

Where the relevant step involves a payment or loan of a sum of money, the value of the relevant step is the amount of that sum.

In all other cases, the value of the relevant step is the higher of:

- the market value of the asset which is the subject of the step; and
- the cost of the relevant step.

The value of any payment or other consideration made by the employee is deducted in arriving at the amount that counts as employment income under Pt. 7A.

If a Pt. 7A charge arises, it takes precedence over a charge to tax under the benefits code and can result in a higher amount of taxable income than would have otherwise been the case.

Example

DDD Ltd sets up an employee benefit trust to provide benefits to its employees. The trust decides to provide Colin, an employee of DDD Ltd, with an interest-free loan of £100,000.

In the absence of Pt. 7A, Colin would have a taxable benefit based on the official rate of interest (2% from 6 April 2021) for the period the loan is outstanding. However, Pt. 7A applies and so Colin will be deemed to have employment income of £100,000 at the point the loan is made.

Provision is made for relief against double taxation.

For in-depth coverage of this topic, see *Disguised Remuneration and the Loan Charge* from Claritax Books.

Law: ITEPA 2003, s. 554Z2-554Z14

13.4 Salaried partner income

Ordinarily, income from partnerships is taxable as trading income (see **Chapter 16**). However, in certain circumstances, ITTOIA 2005, s. 863A-G treats the income of certain members of limited liability partnerships (LLPs) as taxable employment income.

The following conditions must all be met:

- It is reasonable to expect that 80% of the member's share of the profits of the LLP is "disguised salary", i.e. a fixed amount or an amount which can be varied but only by factors other than profits or losses of the partnership and, in each case, is not affected by the overall amount of those profits or losses (Condition A).

- The individual does not have significant influence over the affairs of the LLP (Condition B).

- The individual's capital contribution to the LLP must be less than 25% of the disguised salary (Condition C).

The rules are aimed at individuals who are called partners but are effectively employees – see also **16.10.2**. Where the rules apply, any deemed employment income will be subject to PAYE and NIC (see **Chapter 14**).

Law: ITTOIA 2005, s. 863A-863G; SI 2014/3159

13.5 Pitfalls and planning points

Realignment of risk where employment intermediaries are used

The expansion of the off-payroll working rules to the private sector (other than for small businesses) transferred the risk of PAYE and NIC liability from the intermediary to the client. Businesses that use individuals other than employees to provide services need to determine whether, in their capacity as a client, the off-payroll rules apply to them. If so, processes must be put in place to deal with their obligations in respect of each engagement (see **13.2.2** above).

Relationship between client and individual worker

As many of the tests rely on the employment status of the individual providing services, it is important to ensure that this is recorded properly. HMRC will look at the contract documentation first, but will also take into account the reality of the relationship. See **Chapter 5** for more details.

Relevance of the salaried partner income rules to professional partnerships

Salaried partners with little involvement in management are extremely common in professional partnerships. Where they are treated as employees, there is a significant additional cost in terms of compliance and NIC. Consideration should be given to constructing their share of the profits to take them outside the ambit of ITTOIA 2005, s. 863A-863G (see **13.4** above).

14. PAYE and other employer reporting obligations

14.1 Introduction

Most tax payable by an employee on employment income is collected directly by the employer and accounted for to HMRC on the employee's behalf. This collection mechanism is referred to as Pay As You Earn (PAYE).

In addition, most employment income attracts National Insurance contributions (NIC), which (depending on the Class of NIC) are payable by both the employer and the employee (see **14.5** below).

Employers also have a number of other withholding and reporting obligations, including:

- deducting and accounting for student loan repayments (see **14.8**);
- deducting and accounting for tax deducted through the Construction Industry Scheme (CIS – see **Chapter 19**);
- paying the apprenticeship levy (see **14.9**);
- registering and making annual returns in relation to employment-related securities and tax-advantaged share schemes (see **10.11** and **11.7** respectively);
- deducting and accounting for PAYE and NIC where there is a deemed direct payment under the off-payroll working or other employment intermediary rules (see **13.2**); and
- where the agency rules apply, reporting any employment income that is paid but not covered by PAYE (see **13.2.2**).

Unless otherwise stated, references in this chapter to primary legislation are to ITEPA 2003. References to regulations are to the *Income Tax (Pay As You Earn) Regulations* 2003, SI 2003/2682.

The main HMRC guidance is in the *PAYE Manual*.

14.2 Operating PAYE

14.2.1 Responsibility for operating PAYE

A PAYE scheme must be registered with HMRC if the business has at least one employee who is paid at least £120 (the lower earnings limit for

Class 1 NIC purposes for 2021-22), who has another job, or who receives pension income.

An employer will not, however, have obligations to operate PAYE unless it has a tax presence in the UK. This principle was established in the case of *Oceanic* and HMRC confirm at PAYE 81610 that it means more than simply having employees in the UK. There must be a branch, agency or UK office that gives the employer a UK address for HMRC to correspond with.

Where registration and reporting are required, these must be carried out online and the employer will need to decide on an appropriate software package (although HMRC's Basic PAYE Tool is suitable for businesses with fewer than ten employees).

An exemption from the requirement for online filing is, however, available in any of the following limited circumstances:

- The employer is a member of a religious society or order with beliefs incompatible with the use of electronic methods of communication.
- All of the following conditions are met:
  o The employment relates to care and support services provided to the employer or a family member.
  o The recipient of the services is elderly, infirm or has a physical or mental disability.
  o The employer has not received a tax-free payment in respect of online filing in the last three years.
  o The employer (rather than an agent) is filing the return.
- It is not "reasonably practicable" for the employer to file online (reg. 67D(11)). This could be, for example, because the employer lives in an area with poor broadband connection, or is unable to use a computer due to age or disability. HMRC (at PAYE 21095) take a narrow view of when this exemption applies, saying that if broadband is the problem, the employer must prove that no-one else can file on their behalf, and giving elderly people as the only other relevant exempt category – but these limitations are not in the legislation.

Law: SI 2003/2682, reg. 2A, 67B, 67D
Case: *Clark v Oceanic Contractors Inc.* (1983) 56 TC 183
Guidance: PAYE 81610

14.2.2   Scope of PAYE

PAYE must be operated on "PAYE income". This is defined in s. 683 to include:

- PAYE employment income;
- PAYE pension income; and
- PAYE social security income and statutory payments.

In most cases, pension income will have PAYE deducted from it by the pension administrators.

PAYE employment income is employment income calculated under s. 10(2)-(3) (s. 693-700A, and see **Chapter 5**). In summary, it comprises:

- salary, bonuses and other cash earnings, except for payments to suppliers discharging an employee's private expense and mileage payments in excess of the authorised amounts (see **8.3.1** for the meaning of authorised amounts);

- payments in kind which can be surrendered for cash, such as premium bonds or cash vouchers;

- payments to employees in the form of "readily convertible assets" (s. 696 and s. 702) or vouchers to acquire readily convertible assets. These include an asset which is tradeable on a recognised stock or commodities exchange (e.g. gold bullion or listed shares). They also include assets for which trading arrangements exist so that the employee is able to obtain cash if required;

- the value of any enhancements made to an asset where the asset with the enhancement is a readily convertible asset (s. 697);

- tips received or distributed by the employer. Note that if the tips are pooled, and then distributed to employees by someone other than the employer, the person responsible for distributing the tips to employees (the "troncmaster") is responsible for administering PAYE on those tips, as if he or she were an employer (reg. 100);

- termination payments taxable under s. 401 (see **Chapter 9**);

- deemed employment payments under the rules on employment intermediaries (see **13.2**);

- the value of any relevant steps taxable under Pt. 7A (s. 695A, and see **13.3**); and

- amounts taxable in relation to employment-related securities under Pt. 7 where the underlying securities are readily convertible assets (s. 698-700, and see **10.10**).

Law: ITEPA 2003, s. 689-702; SI 2003/2682, reg. 100

14.2.3   PAYE reporting obligations

PAYE reporting is based on the principle of real time information (RTI). In other words, HMRC are notified of payments made to employees throughout the tax year, on or before the payments are made. These ongoing notifications are supplemented, in certain cases, by other annual or quarterly reports.

Full payment submission

A full payment submission (FPS) is filed electronically with HMRC every time a payment of PAYE income is made to employees.

Generally, the deadline for filing is the day on which an employee is paid. However, there are some exceptions:

Event	Revised deadline
Payment day is a non-banking day	Next banking day
Ad hoc payments outside normal payroll cycle	At time of next regular payroll run
Payment based on work done on day (and cannot be known in advance)	Seven days after payment day
Readily convertible assets	14 days after end of tax month in which payment made
P11D expenses/benefits subject to Class 1 NIC	14 days after end of tax month in which payment made
Payment from third parties or overseas employers	End of pay period, by 19th of following month or as soon as practicable.
Employer has reasonable excuse for delay	As soon as possible after the reasonable excuse ends.

The FPS contains details of employees, of payments made to date and in the current period, and of PAYE/NIC paid and payable. It is automatically generated by the payroll software being used and, once submitted, enables HMRC to work out what payments to expect from the employer.

Law: SI 2003/2682, reg. 67B-67C

Employer payment summary

Although the FPS sets out all PAYE and Class 1 NIC arising in relation to payments made to employees, this may not be the same as the amount actually due to be paid to HMRC by the employer. For example, the employer may be entitled to recover tax deducted from payments made to the employer under the CIS, or statutory payments made to employees, such as maternity pay.

In these circumstances, an employer payment summary (EPS) must be submitted to report the amounts set off against the payments of PAYE/NIC due, enabling HMRC to reconcile the FPS with the amount paid to them.

If an employer does not pay any employees in a tax month, an EPS will have to be submitted rather than an FPS, indicating that no payments have been made.

If the employer has no amounts to offset, and has submitted an FPS in relation to the pay period, no EPS is required. Where an EPS does have to be submitted, the deadline is the 19th following the end of the tax month to which it relates.

New employees

Details of a new employee have to be recorded on the FPS submitted on the first occasion a payment is made to that employee.

HMRC have a "starter checklist" which can be used to collect the information needed. The employer will obtain the required information from the P45 given to the employee by his or her previous employer or, if there is no P45, from the employee direct.

Law: SI 2003/2682, Sch. A1, para. 35
Guidance: https://tinyurl.com/fwbkt8y4 (HMRC starter checklist)

Leavers

The employer must show the date an employee leaves on the FPS that includes the final payment made to the employee. In addition, the employer must give the employee a form P45, containing details of pay and tax in the current tax year and other information such as student loan deductions and the employee's tax code.

The employee keeps Part 1A of the form and gives the rest to the new employer. No part of the form is submitted to HMRC.

Law: SI 2003/2682, reg. 36

End-of-year procedures

The last report in relation to a tax year (which could be an FPS or EPS depending on the circumstances) must indicate that it is the final report. Additional information must be included, such as whether forms P11D (see **14.3**) and P11D(b) (see **14.5.2**) are due.

In addition, every employee above the NIC lower earnings limit must be provided with form P60 no later than 31 May following the end of the tax year. This details the taxable pay, together with the deductions made, during the tax year.

Law: SI 2003/2682, reg. 67

14.2.4   Paying PAYE

PAYE must be applied at the time payment is made. The calculation of income tax due under PAYE is usually carried out on a cumulative basis, with the total payable for the year to date being compared with the total already paid.

The payment dates for PAYE depend on the size of the employer:

- If the total tax and Class 1 NIC payable by the employer is less than £1,500 per month on average, the employer has the option to make payments on a quarterly basis. For this purpose, the four tax quarters end on 5 July, 5 October, 5 January and 5 April, so PAYE payments in respect of these quarters are due by 19 or 22 July, October, January and April respectively, depending on whether payment is made by cheque or electronically (reg. 70).

- For all other employers (including small employers who do not take the quarterly option), PAYE is due monthly. Where payment is electronic (which is mandatory for employers with 250 or more employees), the due date is the 22nd after the end of each tax month (or the last working day prior to this unless paying by faster payment). If not paying electronically, the due date is the 19th of each month (reg. 69, 198A, 199).

Law: SI 2003/2682, reg. 198A, 199

14.2.5 Correcting errors

If an employer has made a payroll reporting error in the current year, the error can be corrected by using revised year-to-date figures on the next FPS. Alternatively, the adjustment can be shown by submitting an additional FPS for the same pay period.

Where the error relates to a previous tax year, corrections can be made by submitting an additional FPS with the correct figures or submitting an earlier year update (EYU). The correct form depends on the tax year being corrected:

Tax year	Form used to make corrections to prior year FPS
2017-18 or earlier	EYU
2018-19 and 2019-20	EYU or an additional FPS
2020-21 onwards	Additional FPS

If an error has been made in an EPS in the current tax year, another EPS should be submitted to show the correct year-to-date figures. If the EPS relates to a previous tax year, an EPS should be submitted to show the correct total figures for that year.

14.2.6 Recovering PAYE from employees and employers

The employer will deduct the due amount of PAYE from cash payments (typically salary) made to the employee. However, to prevent financial hardship, the amount of tax deducted is limited to a maximum of 50% of the payment being made to the employee. The exception is where PAYE needs to be accounted for in respect of a readily convertible asset; in these circumstances, the tax deducted may reduce an employee's cash pay to nil.

Any surplus PAYE that cannot be deducted from cash pay must be recovered from the employee subsequently. If this is not done within 90 days of the end of the tax year in which the PAYE arose, the unrecovered amount will itself be treated as an employment benefit (s. 222).

Where an employer fails to operate PAYE correctly, HMRC can seek to recover any underpayment of tax from the employer or from the employee. If HMRC are satisfied that the employee has full knowledge that the employer has under-deducted tax or, alternatively, that the employer has taken reasonable care and any underpayment of tax has arisen due to an error made in good faith, HMRC may seek recovery of the tax from the employee (reg. 72).

In the majority of cases, however, HMRC will choose to recover the tax from the employer. A formal determination to this effect can be issued (reg. 80). The employer has a right to appeal this determination if he thinks it is incorrect but if no appeal is lodged, the determination becomes final and conclusive after 30 days.

Law: ITEPA 2003, s. 222; SI 2003/2682, reg. 2(1), 23(5), 28(5), 72, 80

14.2.7   Compliance failures

When operating PAYE, there are four potential areas where a compliance failure can arise:

- late filing of submissions and reports (or not filing at all);
- making an error on a submission or return;
- paying PAYE late; and
- paying the incorrect amount of PAYE.

Each of these is considered in turn below.

Late or missing submissions and reports

Where an FPS or an EPS is submitted late during a tax month, a penalty may be charged. The amount charged will depend on the number of employees covered by the PAYE scheme.

Number of employees	Amount of penalty
	£
9 or fewer	100
10 to 49	200
50 to 249	300
250 or more	400

Where a submission is three months late, a further penalty of 5% of the tax and NIC which would have been shown in the submission may be charged. This will not apply if the information has been included in a later submission (FA 2009, Sch. 55, para. 6D).

A penalty will not, however, be charged if:

- it is the first month in the tax year for which a return has been late;
- the employer is new and it is the first FPS (provided it is not more than 30 days late);
- there is a reasonable excuse for the late filing, for example such unforeseen events as fire, flood, prolonged industrial action or systems failure; or
- HMRC decide not to impose a penalty. Generally HMRC take a risk-based approach focused on persistent and deliberate or careless offenders.

Where HMRC decide to impose a penalty, assessment notices are issued quarterly in July, October, January and April. Any penalties will be due for payment within 30 days of the date of the penalty notice. Interest will be charged where a penalty is paid late.

The decision to issue a penalty or the amount of the penalty can be appealed against (FA 2009, Sch. 55, para. 20).

Law: FA 2009, Sch. 55, para. 6C(3), 6C(4), 6D, 20

Incorrect returns

Penalties can be charged for an inaccurate FPS or EPS. The level of penalty is based on a percentage of the additional tax due as a result of correcting the error and depends on:

- the behaviour in connection with the error;
- the time that has elapsed between the error occurring and coming to light; and
- whether the disclosure is prompted or unprompted.

The maximum and minimum percentages that can apply are:

Behaviour	Maximum penalty	Minimum penalty – unprompted disclosure	Minimum penalty – prompted disclosure
Deliberate and concealed	100%	30%	50%
Deliberate but not concealed	70%	20%	35%
Careless	30%	0%	15%

The minimum penalty thresholds are increased by 10% where the employer has taken a "significant period" of time in correcting or disclosing the inaccuracy (regarded by HMRC as being three years unless the overall disclosure covers a longer period).

Disclosure takes place when HMRC are notified of the error and are given reasonable assistance in calculating any unpaid tax or NIC, including allowing HMRC access to records. Disclosure will be regarded as unprompted if the employer has no reason to believe that HMRC have discovered or are about to discover the error.

A penalty for a careless error may be suspended by HMRC for a period of up to two years. If the conditions set by HMRC are met over the suspension period, the penalty will be cancelled. See also **Chapter 2**.

Law: FA 2007, Sch. 24

Late payment of PAYE

If an employer makes payments late, HMRC will charge the employer interest (2.6% from 7 April 2020) on the late paid tax, from the due date to the date of payment.

In addition, HMRC may charge a penalty based on the number of late payments or "defaults" and the amount of tax paid late in the tax year:

No. of defaults	Level of penalty
1	nil
2 to 3	1%
4 to 6	2%
7 to 9	3%
10 or more	4%

An additional penalty of 5% can be levied if payment is six months late, rising to 10% where the tax is still outstanding 12 months from the due date. These additional penalties will apply to the first late payment of tax even though the first late payment does not count as a default.

In deciding whether to levy penalties, HMRC take a risk-based approach, focusing on persistent late payers. Penalties will not be charged where there is a reasonable excuse.

Where an assessment notice is issued, interest will be charged unless late payment penalties are paid within 30 days of the date of such notice. The decision to issue a penalty, or the amount of the penalty payable, can be appealed against by the taxpayer (FA 2009, Sch. 56, para. 13).

Taxpayers who cannot afford to make payments of tax by the due date may request a "time to pay arrangement". If agreed by HMRC, payment is deferred, and no late payment penalties will be charged provided that the terms of the agreement are complied with.

Law: FA 2009, Sch. 56

14.3 Employment income outside the PAYE regime

A form P11D must be completed and submitted to HMRC in respect of every employee who receives benefits in the tax year (apart from those that are voluntarily payrolled – see **14.4**). A copy must also be provided to the employee concerned. The deadline in both cases is 6 July following the end of the tax year.

If these forms are late, HMRC can charge an initial penalty of up to £300 per late form, plus a further penalty of up to £60 per day for each day that the failure continues.

If an incorrect form P11D is filed fraudulently or negligently, a penalty of up to £3,000 can be levied in respect of each form.

Law: TMA 1970, s. 98

14.4 Voluntary payrolling

The voluntary payroll system allows employers to put employees' benefits in kind through the payroll. This negates the need for the employee to pay the tax through self-assessment.

The employer must register online with HMRC before the start of the tax year in which the benefits are payrolled. Once set up, the registration will roll forward automatically to subsequent tax years.

All benefits can be payrolled with the exception of taxable employment-related loans (see **6.8**) and living accommodation (see **6.4**). The employer can choose which benefits are payrolled for which employees. However, it should be borne in mind the tax deducted on each payday cannot be more than 50% of the employee's actual pay (excluding the value of the payrolled benefit). Furthermore, once the tax year has started, the benefit must be payrolled for the whole year.

The effects of payrolling a benefit are as follows:

- The tax is deducted from pay in equal instalments over the tax year, rather than the employee having to submit a self-assessment return and/or agreeing a tax code adjustment with HMRC.

- Employers will not need to include the payrolled benefits on form P11D at the end of the tax year.

- If car and fuel benefits are being payrolled, form P46 is not needed.

When first registering for voluntarily payrolling, the employer must write to the affected employees to explain what is happening. After the end of each tax year (and before 1 June), the employer must provide each affected employee with a summary of all benefits that have been payrolled and the amount that has been included in the payroll for each such benefit for that tax year.

Payrolled benefits still attract Class 1A NIC, and the employer still needs to complete form P11D(b) (see **14.5.2**).

Law: ITEPA 2003, s. 684(2); SI 2003/2682, reg. 61A-61L

14.5   Dealing with NIC

14.5.1   Overview

NIC is collected via the PAYE system. Employers are concerned with three classes of NIC:

- Class 1 – paid by both employees (primary contributions) and employers (secondary contributions), on earnings from employment (see **14.5.2**);

- Class 1A – paid by employers only, on benefits awarded to certain employees (see **14.5.3**); and

- Class 1B – paid by employers only, on PAYE settlement agreements (see **14.5.4**).

14.5.2   Class 1 NIC

Class 1 NIC is paid on earnings from the employment. Generally, the definition of earnings for Class 1 NIC purposes is the same as for PAYE income (see **14.2.2**). However, Class 1 NIC is also due on:

- excess mileage payments above the approved mileage rates;
- the amounts paid by the employer directly to a supplier to discharge an employee's personal liability;
- the value of cash or non-cash vouchers; and
- private fuel provided for use in an employee's own car, unless the fuel is provided from the employer's own fuel pump or using a company credit card or garage account and the garage is told that the fuel is being bought on behalf of the employer.

Primary contributions are paid by employees on earnings above the primary threshold (£797 per month for 2021-22) and below the upper earnings limit (£4,189 per month), at a rate of 12%. Above the upper earnings limit, that rate is 2%.

Secondary contributions are paid by employers above the secondary threshold (£737 per month for 2021-22) at a rate of 13.8%. There is a reduced rate of 0% on earnings between the secondary threshold and the upper secondary threshold (£4,189 per month) where the employee or director is under the age of 21 or is an apprentice under the age of 25.

NIC is calculated by reference to earnings periods, which for most employees will be a month.

Example

Jared has a salary of £24,000 per annum which is paid monthly. He also has the use of a company car, which gives rise to a taxable benefit of £5,000 per year and is voluntarily included in payroll. At the end of July, he receives a cash bonus of £6,000.

The salary and the bonus constitute earnings for Class 1 NIC, but the company car benefit does not. (The fact the car benefit is payrolled is irrelevant for NIC purposes.)

For 11 months of the year, Jared's earnings are £2,000 (£24,000/12). Primary contributions are (£2,000 – £797) x 12% = £144 per month and secondary contributions are (£2,000 – £737) x 13.8% = £174 per month.

In July, his earnings are £8,000 (£2,000 + £6,000) and exceed the upper earnings limit. Therefore primary contributions are:

	£
(£4,189 – £797) x 12%	407
(£8,000 – £4,189) x 2%	76
Total	483

Secondary contributions are (£8,000 – £737) x 13.8% = £1,002.

All directors have an annual earnings period, whether paid on a weekly, monthly or other basis. This is to prevent a company director from manipulating the NIC rules by being paid a salary in such a way as to minimise his or her NIC for the year (SI 2001/1004, reg. 8).

Both primary and secondary contributions are accounted for under the PAYE system using the RTI system. Details are included in the FPS and NIC is paid over to HMRC at the same time as the PAYE (see **14.2.3** and **14.2.4**).

An employer's total Class 1 NIC liability may be reduced by up to £4,000 by the employment allowance (see NICA 2014, s. 1-8).

The interest and penalty provisions for compliance failures are the same as for PAYE (see **14.2.7**).

Law: SSCBA 1992, s. 5-9B; ITEPA 2003, s. 702; NICA 2014, s. 1-8; SI 2001/1004, reg. 8, 67A, 67B

14.5.3   Class 1A NIC

Class 1A NIC is paid, by employers only, generally on the cash equivalent of non-cash employment benefits. However, there are some exceptions:

- Class 1A NIC is paid on certain cash payments such as the excess over £30,000 of an *ex gratia* termination payment (see **Chapter 9**) and any qualifying relocation expenses and benefits paid for by the employer in excess of the £8,000 limit (see **7.2**).
- Any non-cash payment categorised as earnings is charged to Class 1 NIC (see **14.5.2**), and is not subject to Class 1A.
- If the benefit is charged to Class 1B (see **14.5.4**), Class 1A is not payable.

The amount of Class 1A NIC payable is notified to HMRC on form P11D(b) no later than 6 July following the end of the tax year. If filed late, a late filing penalty can apply. The amount of the penalty is £100 per month (or part month) that the return is late, for each group of up to 50 employees provided with benefits.

Where Class 1A NIC is due, payment is to be made in one sum by 22 July following the end of the tax year (but by 19 July if payment is not made electronically).

Interest is charged on the late payment of Class 1A from the due date.

Where the payment of Class 1A is outstanding more than 30 days after the payment due date, a penalty of 5% of the unpaid NIC may be charged. This can rise to 10% where the NIC is still outstanding six months after the due date and to 15% 12 months after the due date (FA 2009, Sch. 56, para. 3).

If the form P11D(b) is incorrect, the penalty charged will be a percentage of the extra tax due as a result of the discovery of the error. The level of the penalty will be based on the behaviour giving rise to the error. This is the same penalty regime as applies to incorrect full payment submissions (see **14.2.7**).

Law: SSCBA 1992, s. 10; FA 2007, Sch. 24; FA 2009, Sch. 56, para. 3

14.5.4   *Class 1B NIC*

Class 1B contributions are employer-only contributions due in respect of items included in a PAYE settlement agreement (PSA) (see **14.6**).

Class 1B NIC is charged at a rate of 13.8% on the total of the cash value of benefits included within the PSA plus the income tax due in respect of those benefits.

Class 1B NIC is collected annually on 22 October following the end of the tax year (19 October if payment is not made electronically).

Late payments are subject to the same penalty regime as Class 1A NIC (see **14.5.3**).

Law: SSCBA 1992, s. 10A

14.6   PAYE settlement agreements

The PSA is an optional arrangement which allows an employer to settle an employee's tax liability on minor or irregular benefits, rather than following the normal process of reporting them on form P11D and accounting for Class 1 or Class 1A NIC.

The PSA passes the tax liability on these benefits to the employer, so the employee can feel that he or she is receiving a tax-free benefit.

Example

BBBB Ltd intends to hold a staff party to celebrate 25 years in business. The total cost of the function is £260 per head and a PSA is obtained in advance as it is the intention of BBBB Ltd to pay any tax liability on behalf of the attendees. 60 employees attend and records show that 40 of them pay tax at the rate of 20% and 20 at 40%.

The cost of the function, i.e. £260 per head, is regarded as the net benefit received by each employee after all tax has been deducted. For basic rate taxpayers, this gives a gross benefit of £325 (£260 x 100/80). For higher rate taxpayers, this gives a gross benefit of £433 (£260 x 100/60).

The total tax payable by BBBB Ltd under the PSA would be:

	£
40 employees x (£325 – £260)	2,600
20 employees x (£433 – £260)	3,460
Total tax	6,060

Class 1B NIC of £2,989 would also be due. This is calculated at 13.8% on the earnings of £15,600 (£260 x 60) and the tax of £6,060.

For an item to be suitable for inclusion in a PSA, it must be minor, irregular and hard to quantify for PAYE purposes. A common example of an irregular benefit which potentially falls within a PSA is a staff party costing more than the tax-free threshold of £150 per person.

HMRC make it clear at PSA 1050 that PSAs should not be used as a vehicle for settling tax liabilities on cash payments or on major benefits such as company cars or taxable cheap loans.

A PSA can be entered into at any time before 6 July following the end of the relevant tax year. The PSA must, however, be arranged before a PAYE (and any Class 1 NIC) liability arises, as it cannot apply retrospectively.

Once agreed with HMRC, a PSA continues until the employer or HMRC cancel it. It is possible to vary a PSA, subject to HMRC's agreement.

The due date for payment of the tax and Class 1B NIC under a PSA is 22 October (19 October if payment is not made electronically) following the end of the tax year. There is no formal deadline for sending HMRC the calculation of amounts due, but if it is not submitted by 31 October following the end of the tax year, HMRC treat the PSA as invalid, with consequential liabilities for failing to include the relevant benefits on forms P11D (FA 2007, Sch. 24).

Interest (at 2.6% since 7 April 2020) is charged from the due date to the date of payment.

Where the payment is outstanding more than 30 days after the due date, a penalty of 5% of the unpaid liabilities may be charged. This can increase to 10% where the tax and NIC is still outstanding six months after the due payment date and to 15% if still outstanding after 12 months (FA 2009, Sch. 56, para. 3).

Penalties may be waived if the employer has a reasonable excuse for the delay in payment.

Penalties can also be charged on incorrect PSA calculations, or if the employer does not provide necessary supporting information to HMRC within 30 days of it being requested. These are levied in accordance with the general penalty regime in FA 2007, Sch. 24, and so are based on a percentage of the potentially understated liabilities and depend on the behaviour of the employer (see **14.2.7**).

Law: SSCBA 1992, s. 10A; ITEPA 2003, s. 703-707; FA 2007, Sch. 24; SI 2003/2682, reg. 105-117

14.7   Third party benefits

14.7.1   *Liability for PAYE and NIC*

As discussed in **Chapter 5**, employment income can consist of cash or benefits provided by parties other than the employer. The liability to account for PAYE and NIC depends on the nature of the benefit and on the level of the employer's involvement:

- Where the award comprises cash or benefits ordinarily subject to Class 1 NIC, the third party must deduct income tax from the award and pay it to HMRC. In addition, the employer must deduct Class 1 NIC on the combined value of the award and the PAYE tax paid on it by the third party.

- Where the award comprises benefits ordinarily subject to Class 1A NIC, and the employer has not arranged or facilitated these, the third party must account for the tax due on the award and pay any Class 1A NIC due on the value of the award and on the tax paid on it.

- Where the award comprises benefits ordinarily subject to Class 1A NIC and the employer arranges the award with the third party, the third party must still account for the tax. However, it is the employer's responsibility to deal with the Class 1A NIC.

14.7.2   Taxed award schemes

If the third party does not wish to deduct PAYE, or if it wants to ensure that the employee receives the benefit "free of tax", it can enter into a taxed award scheme (TAS) with HMRC. A TAS is similar to a PSA in that the provider of a non-cash benefit will account for the tax on a grossed-up basis to HMRC on the employee's behalf.

The process for applying for a TAS and associated obligations are set out in PAYE 27040. The operator of a TAS can choose whether tax should be calculated at basic or higher rate.

Any income tax and NIC due under a TAS must be paid to HMRC by 22 July (19 July if not paying electronically) following the end of the tax year for which the award is assessable.

Unlike awards covered by PSAs, awards accounted for through a TAS remain assessable on the employee. The employee must therefore enter the grossed-up value of the award and the tax paid on it on his or her self-assessment tax return, if required to complete one. However, no further tax will be due unless the employee pays tax at a higher rate than paid under the TAS.

Guidance: PAYE 27040

14.8   Student and postgraduate loans

Where an employee has previously received a student or postgraduate loan, the employer is responsible for deducting repayments from pay and accounting for them to HMRC as part of the PAYE process.

The employer has no direct contact with the Student Loans Company and does not know anything about the amount of the student loan nor any balance of the loan outstanding. Deductions must be made when either:

- a start notice (form SL1 for student loans and form PGL1 for postgraduate loans) is received in relation to a particular employee; or

- a new employee provides a form P45 showing that he or she is making repayments for a student or postgraduate loan (or otherwise indicates this to the employer).

In the latter case, deductions should be made from the first pay date, but HMRC will issue form SL1 to confirm the position as soon as the first FPS with the new starter information has been received.

The amount of the deduction will depend on the type of loan:

Student loan plan 1 (taken out before 30 August 2012)	9% of earnings above £19,895
Student loan plan 2 (taken out on or after 1 September 2012)	9% of earnings above £27,295
Scottish student loan plan 4	9% of earnings above £25,000
Postgraduate loan	6% of earnings above £21,000

For the weekly and monthly thresholds, see **Appendix 6**.

Earnings for this purpose are the same as earnings for Class 1 NIC purposes (see **14.5.1**).

Only one deduction is made if the employee has more than one student loan. However, where the employee has both a student loan and a postgraduate loan outstanding, deductions are due on both loans (assuming the appropriate thresholds have been reached).

The total student and postgraduate loan repayments recovered in the current period and in the tax year to date must be recorded on the FPS (see **14.2.3**). The total amount deducted is also recorded on the employee's form P60 (see **14.2.3**).

The loan deductions are paid over to HMRC at the same time as the PAYE tax and NIC for the same period.

Deductions continue until HMRC issue a stop notice (form SL2 or PGL2). If the employee leaves prior to such a notice being issued, the employer will indicate on form P45 given to the departing employee that student or postgraduate loan deductions should continue.

Law: SI 2009/470, Pt. 4

14.9 Apprenticeship levy

The apprenticeship levy is payable by employers who are secondary contributors for Class 1 NIC purposes.

The levy is 0.5% of the amount of total payments to employees that are subject to Class 1 NIC (see **14.5.1**), including amounts below earnings thresholds or which attract the 0% rate.

The levy is offset by an annual levy allowance of £15,000 (meaning that only employers whose annual pay bill is £3 million or more will actually have any levy to pay). However, where there are connected companies (under common control or one having control over the other using the definition of "control" in CTA 2010, Pt. 10), only one levy allowance is available and must be split between them. This will be in equal shares unless the connected companies elect otherwise before the start of the tax year.

The apprenticeship levy is reported on the employer payment summary (see **14.2.3**) and paid at the same time as PAYE. Any failure to make returns, as well as inaccuracies and late payments of the levy, will be subject to the same penalty regime as PAYE returns and payments (see **14.2.7**).

Employers who make apprenticeship levy payments can access funding for apprenticeship training by creating an account under the digital apprenticeship service on the government website. The account will show the amount of levy paid by the provider plus the 10% government top-up. Funds held in the digital apprenticeship account are only available for the levy-payer's use for 18 months. After that they go into a central fund. Funds used to provide training are taken from the account on a first-in, first-out basis.

Law: FA 2016, s. 99-121
Guidance: https://www.gov.uk/employing-an-apprentice/get-funding

14.10 Pitfalls and planning points

Late FPS

The FPS includes a special field to identify the reason for the late reporting, using letters as provided by HMRC. This avoids HMRC seeking to apply penalties in respect of the late FPS where there is a reasonable excuse.

No P45

If no P45 is available, the employer can only operate tax on a cumulative basis if the employee can certify that this is his or her first job since 6 April, and that the employee has not been receiving taxable jobseeker's allowance, employment and support allowance, incapacity benefit or a pension. If the employee has another job, or receives a pension, the employer will need to deduct PAYE at basic rate without any personal allowances being given. In all other circumstances, the employer will need to operate an "emergency code" which operates on a Month 1/Week 1 basis, giving the employee one week/month's worth of personal allowance against one week/month's worth of pay.

Student and postgraduate loans

Loan deductions are calculated on a non-cumulative basis by reference to the earnings in each pay period. This can sometimes mean that the employer correctly makes a deduction from earnings during the year, but the employee's earnings may be less than the annual threshold at the tax year end. If this occurs, the employer must not make any refund to the employee. The employee can, however, make a refund application to the Student Loans Company at the end of the tax year.

INCOME FROM SELF-EMPLOYMENT

15. Business profits

15.1 Introduction

An individual can choose between a number of structures through which to operate his or her business.

Typically, an individual may decide to operate as a sole trader, provide services or goods through a limited company, or work with others through a partnership.

The question of which vehicle is best for an individual to use is dependent on a number of factors, including the importance of limited liability for the trader, administrative and compliance considerations, and cost.

This chapter outlines the income tax treatment of individuals who carry on business as sole traders or as individual partners in partnership. Broadly speaking, professions and vocations are taxed in the same way as trades, but see **15.2.14** for discussion of this point.

15.2 The existence of a trade

15.2.1 Is there a trade?

Section 5 of the *Income Tax (Trading and Other Income) Act* 2005 (ITTOIA 2005) states that "income tax is charged on the profits of a trade, profession or vocation".

Although the question of whether an individual is trading is critical when determining any income tax liability, there is no statutory definition of "trade", aside from a brief mention in s. 989 of the *Income Tax Act* 2007 (ITA 2007) that trade "includes any venture in the nature of trade".

HMRC's *Business Income Manual* sheds some further light on what may be considered a trade, stating that:

> "Broadly, 'trade' can be taken to refer to operations of a commercial kind by which the trader provides to customers for reward some kind of goods or services. The extension of the definition to 'ventures in the nature of trade' allows for the inclusion of isolated or speculative transactions, although not all such transactions will be within the definition."

As the statute provides little assistance, we must turn to the considerable body of case law that exists for guidance as to when a trade may exist.

In particular, the "badges of trade" – considered below – are a helpful indicator of whether there is a trade.

Law: ITTOIA 2005, s. 5; ITA 2007, s. 989
Guidance: BIM 20060

15.2.2   The badges of trade – overview

HMRC list nine badges of trade, developed through case law over the years:

- profit-seeking motive;
- number of transactions;
- nature of the asset;
- existence of similar trading transactions or interests;
- changes to the asset;
- the way the sale was carried out;
- the source of finance;
- time between purchase and sale; and
- method of acquisition.

Each badge is considered in detail below. A summary table can be found at BIM 20205.

An activity does not need to have every badge in order for it to be a trade. Some activities may have only a few badges of trade, but those badges may be sufficient to conclude that a trade exists. In other cases, there may be a few badges that point to trading activity and some that point away from that conclusion.

Whether a trade exists is very much a question of fact based on the particular circumstances of each case, with the weight attached to each badge dependent on the exact circumstances.

Guidance: BIM 20205

15.2.3   Profit-seeking motive

An intention to make a profit supports the notion that a trade is being carried on. A simple example would be acquiring goods in order to resell them at a profit.

However, certain assets may be more likely to be held for investment purposes. Shares, for instance, may be purchased with the intention of realising a profit. However, given the inherent investment nature of shares, if there is an absence of other badges of trade, the individual will simply be making and realising capital investments.

Whether there is a profit-seeking motive is a question of fact and does not automatically correlate to an individual's stated intentions. This is well summarised in *Hyndland Investment Co Ltd*:

> "The question is not what business does the taxpayer profess to carry on, but what business does he actually carry on."

Case: *CIR v Hyndland Investment Co Ltd* (1929) 14 TC 694
Guidance: BIM 20210

15.2.4   Number of transactions

Systematic and repeated transactions are an indication of trading.

Conversely, a single isolated transaction is less likely to indicate the presence of a trade, although it is not impossible.

For an isolated transaction to be trading for tax purposes, the operations involved in the transaction should have the same kind or character, or be carried on in the same way, as those that are characteristic of ordinary trading in that line of business.

It is also possible for one isolated transaction to turn into a trade where the transaction is systematically repeated over time. Whether this is the case depends on the number of transactions carried out, as well as the frequency with which they are repeated.

This is summarised in *Pickford v Quirke*:

> "It is very well known that one transaction of buying and selling a thing does not make a man a trader, but if it is repeated and becomes systematic, then he becomes a trader and the profits of the transactions, not taxable so long as they remain isolated, become taxable as items in a trade as a whole."

Case: *Pickford v Quirke* (1927) 13 TC 251

15.2.5   Nature of the asset

The nature of an asset can be highly instructive in determining whether there is a trade.

Certain assets are generally realised by way of trade, and in such cases it is highly likely that there is, indeed, a trade. However, other assets may not give rise to an initial presumption of trade, examples being shares, or assets acquired for personal use (e.g. classic cars).

Where an asset yields a regular income (e.g. dividends from shares, or rental income from property) the initial presumption is that the asset is more likely held as an investment.

However, this presumption can be overturned. Land, for instance, may be held either as an investment or as trading stock.

15.2.6   Existence of similar trading transactions or interests

If a trade is already carried on, then any similar transaction undertaken by the trader is also likely to have a trading character.

For example, an antiques dealer making a one-off purchase of an antique is more likely to indicate trading than if a baker purchases the same item.

15.2.7   Changes to the asset

An asset that is repaired, modified, or improved in order to sell it more easily (or to realise a greater profit) is another indication of trade.

This also applies in cases where an asset is broken down into smaller components to facilitate a sale.

Expenditure on an asset between purchase and sale is not always a pointer to trading activity, however. For example, normal maintenance and repair of an asset to keep it in working order is expenditure that any owner would incur, and so does not indicate trading on its own.

15.2.8   The way the sale was carried out

An asset that is sold in a way typical of that used by trading organisations is, unsurprisingly, likely to indicate a trade.

However, it is equally possible for an asset to be sold in a way that does not indicate trade (for example, an asset sold to raise funds for an emergency situation).

15.2.9   The source of finance

The source of finance used to purchase an asset can be an indicator of trade, particularly where an asset was purchased with finance that could only be repaid by selling the asset in question.

15.2.10 Time between purchase and sale

The length of time between the purchase and sale of an asset may, or may not, point to trading.

Generally, where an asset is purchased and sold, or intended to be sold, within a relatively short period, it is more likely to be indicative of trading activity.

As an extreme example, if a contract for the resale of an asset is already in place before the asset is even purchased, it is a very strong indication that the activity is trading.

Conversely, assets that are held for a number of years before sale, or that are held indefinitely, are more likely to be investments.

15.2.11 Method of acquisition

Assets that were acquired by gift or inheritance are less likely to be the subject of a trade, although it is not impossible.

15.2.12 Case law

The question of whether an activity amounts to a trade is a complex one and has been the subject of a number of court cases over the years.

The following are summaries from a few prominent cases, which serve to highlight how the question of whether there is a trade very much depends on the facts and circumstances of each case.

CIR v Fraser

Fraser, a woodcutter, purchased a consignment of whisky in bond and sold it through an agent at a profit.

Fraser was held to be trading, with the court commenting that:

> "The purchaser of a large quantity of a commodity like whisky, greatly in excess of what could be used by himself, his family and friends, a commodity which yields no pride of possession, which cannot be turned to account except by a process of realisation, I can scarcely consider to be other than an adventurer in a transaction in the nature of a trade [...] Most important of all, the actual dealings of the respondent with the whisky were exactly of the kind that take place in ordinary trade."

Case: *CIR v Fraser* (1942) 24 TC 498

Marson v Morton

The taxpayers carried on business as wholesale potato merchants and purchased land as an investment. The land had planning permission and was later resold.

The court found that the transaction was far removed from the taxpayers' normal trading activity and that they intended to make an investment. Accordingly, the transaction was not in the nature of a trade.

Case: *Marson v Morton and Ors* (1986) 59 TC 381

Salt v Chamberlain

The taxpayer was a mathematics graduate who used his knowledge of computers to forecast the movements in share prices.

Over a number of years, the taxpayer entered into approximately 200 transactions for the purchase and sale of securities. He used his own funds as well as borrowings from the bank and against life assurance policies.

The court found that the taxpayer was not trading and that the transactions were capital in nature.

HMRC take the view that transactions in shares by individuals normally amount to investment activity, or speculation falling short of trading. Accordingly, such transactions are within the remit of capital gains tax. This is a position that continues to hold, even in more recent cases (see *Manzur*).

For completeness, while it is possible for an individual buying and selling shares or other financial instruments to be considered to be trading, there must be factors that are "out of the norm" for this to be the case.

Cases: *Salt v Chamberlain* (1979) 53 TC 143; *Manzur v HMRC* [2010] UKFTT 580 (TC)

Graham v Green

The taxpayer's sole means of livelihood came from betting on horses at starting prices. The taxpayer was not found to be trading; having expertise or being systematic is not enough to create a trade of being a professional gambler.

The more recent case of *McMillan* also confirms the principles outlined in HMRC's guidance: the fact that a taxpayer has a system by which to place bets, or that he or she is sufficiently successful to earn a living by gambling, does not make the activities a trade.

While a gambler is not normally carrying on a trade, however, those carrying on an organised activity to make profits out of the gambling public (e.g. bookmakers) will usually be considered to be trading.

Cases: *Graham v Green* (1925) 9 TC 309; *McMillan v HMRC* [2020] UKFTT 82 (TC)

15.2.13 Illegal activities

Illegal activities, if deemed to be trading in nature, are still subject to tax – the fact that they are illegal does not provide any shelter from tax.

15.2.14 Trade or profession?

There is no comprehensive statutory definition of trade, and no statutory definition of "profession" or "vocation".

Accordingly, trade, profession and vocation take their ordinary meanings. This means that a profession usually involves some substantial exercise of intellectual skill (e.g. doctors and lawyers), while a vocation indicates a calling (e.g. authors and dramatists).

The distinction matters because there are some specific statutory provisions which only apply to a trade, or to a profession or vocation, such as research and development expenses (ITTOIA 2005, s. 87), and expenses for patents, designs and trademarks (s. 89 and 90).

These are exceptions, however, so unless stated otherwise, references to a "trade" in the remainder of this chapter also include reference to a profession or vocation.

Guidance: BIM 14010

15.3   Transactions in land

Anti-avoidance provisions, known as the "transactions in UK land" rules, apply to all persons (i.e. individuals as well as corporates).

Broadly, the provisions prevent a taxpayer avoiding tax on land transactions that are effectively trading transactions but where the profit emerges in a capital or non-taxable form.

Where the rules are in scope, the capital gain from the land transaction is treated as if it were income, and a free-standing charge to tax as income applies on the full amount of the gain realised in the tax year.

The transactions in UK land provisions are contained within ITA 2007, Pt. 9A.

The legislation is detailed, but in brief, a disposal of UK land may be within the scope of, and treated as, a profit of a trade of dealing in or developing UK land, if one of the following conditions is met:

- Condition A is that a main purpose of acquiring the land was to realise a profit or gain from disposing of the land.

- Condition B is that a main purpose of acquiring any property deriving its value from the land was to realise a profit or gain from disposing of the land.

- Condition C is that the land is held as trading stock.

- Condition D is that (in a case where the land has been developed) a main purpose of developing the land was to realise a profit or gain from disposing of it when developed.

To the extent that profits or gains from a land disposal would be brought into account as income by other sections of legislation, it will not be taxed again by these rules.

Law: ITA 2007, s. 517A-517U

15.4 Basis periods

15.4.1 Overview

Where an individual carries on a trade, profession or vocation, the resulting profits are chargeable to income tax. Those profits are taxed as they arise in a "basis period" for a given tax year.

The general rule is that the basis period for a tax year is the period of 12 months ending with the accounting date in that tax year (i.e. the date in the tax year to which accounts are drawn up, or if there are two or more such dates, the latest of them). This is also known as the current year basis (see **15.4.3**).

However, there are times when a different basis period may apply, examples being when a taxpayer commences trading (see **15.4.2**), ceases to trade (see **15.4.4**), or changes accounting date (see **15.6**).

Law: ITTOIA 2005, s. 196-198

15.4.2   Commencement (years one and two)

When a taxpayer starts to carry on a trade, basis periods for the first and second tax years will generally be different from those for year three onwards (when most businesses move to the current year basis – see **15.4.3**).

Year one

Year one is straightforward – the basis period for the tax year in which a person starts to carry on a trade begins with the date on which the trade commences, and ends with 5 April in the tax year.

Example 1

Miranda starts to trade on 1 October 2021. Her basis period for the first tax year (2021-22) will be from the date of commencement to 5 April 2022.

Law: ITTOIA 2005, s. 199

Year two

Year two is more involved. The basis period for the second tax year is determined by whether the taxpayer has an accounting date falling within the second tax year, and if so, how long after commencement of trade that accounting date is.

Where there has been no permanent cessation of trade, or change in accounting date, the rules are as follows:

- If the accounting date falls in year two, and is less than 12 months after commencing the trade, the basis period is 12 months beginning with the date on which the person starts to carry on the trade.
- If the accounting date falls in year two, and is 12 months or more after commencing the trade, the basis period is the period of 12 months ending with the accounting date in year two.
- If there is no accounting date in year two the basis period is the same as the tax year (6 April to 5 April).

Example 2 – accounting date less than 12 months after commencement

Mia starts to trade on 6 March 2022 and decides to prepare accounts to 31 December each year. Mia's basis periods would be as follows:

Year one (2021-22)

Mia's basis period would be 6 March 2022 to 5 April 2022.

This is the date she started to trade to the end of the tax year.

Year two (2022-23)

To determine Mia's basis period in year two, we need to ask a few questions:

- Does the accounting date fall within the tax year (2022-23)? Yes, 31 December 2022 is within the tax year.
- Is the accounting date more or less than 12 months after commencement? It is less than 12 months after commencement.

This means that Mia's basis period is 12 months beginning with the date of commencement. Her basis period for 2022-23 is therefore 6 March 2022 to 5 March 2023.

This would give rise to one month of overlap profit, discussed in further detail at **15.5** below.

Example 3 – accounting date 12 months or more after commencement

Omar starts to trade on 6 January 2022 and draws up his first set of accounts to 31 March 2023, and annually to 31 March thereafter. Omar's basis periods would be as follows:

Year one (2021-22)

Omar's basis period would be 6 January 2022 to 5 April 2022.

This is the date he started to trade to the end of the tax year.

Year two (2022-23)

To determine Omar's basis period in year two, we need to ask a few questions:

- Does the accounting date fall within the tax year (2022-23)? Yes, 31 March 2023 is within the tax year.
- Is the accounting date more or less than 12 months after commencement? It is more than 12 months after commencement.

This means that Omar's basis period is the 12 months ending with the accounting date.

Omar's basis period for 2022-23 is therefore 1 April 2022 to 31 March 2023.

Example 4 – no accounting date in year two

Michelle starts to trade on 1 February 2022 and decides to draw up her first set of accounts to 30 June 2023, and annually to 30 June thereafter. Michelle's basis periods would be as follows:

Year one (2021-22)

Michelle's basis period would be 1 February 2022 to 5 April 2022. This is the date she started to trade to the end of the tax year.

Year two (2022-23)

To determine Michelle's basis period in year two, we need to ask:

- Does the accounting date fall within the tax year (2022-23)? No, 30 June 2023 does not fall in the 2022-23 tax year.

This means that her basis period in year two is the same as the tax year (6 April 2022 to 5 April 2023).

Year three (2023-24)

Michelle's basis period in year three will be the 12 months from 1 July 2022 to 30 June 2023.

This will give rise to nine months of overlap profit, discussed in further detail at **15.5** below.

Apportionment

In the opening (and closing) years of a trade, it is quite likely that the basis period for a tax year will not coincide with the accounting period for the business.

In such cases, it may be necessary to add or apportion the profits/losses of one or more accounting periods to determine the profits/losses for the basis period.

The legislation specifies that the apportionment should be made by reference to the number of days in the periods concerned.

However, apportioning by reference to weeks or months is acceptable, provided it is reasonable to do so, and the approach is used consistently.

Law: ITTOIA 2005, s. 199-201, 203

15.4.3   Current year basis

By year three, most businesses will use the current year basis (i.e. the results of the 12-month accounting period that ends in the tax year).

Example

A sole trader prepares accounts to 30 June each year.

Using the current year basis, the results for the year to 30 June 2021 would be taxed in 2021-22.

15.4.4   Closing year basis

The basis period for the tax year in which a person permanently ceases to carry on a trade begins immediately after the end of the basis period for the previous tax year, and ends with the date on which the person permanently ceases to carry on the trade.

This means that it is important to identify the tax year in which the trade ceases, as this is the tax year subject to the closing year basis. The penultimate tax year is taxed as usual (typically on the current year basis).

Example 1

Cynthia commenced trading on 1 December 2015. She prepares accounts to 31 December. On 30 June 2021, Cynthia ceases trading.

Her basis periods for her final years of trading are as follows:

2019-20 – 12 months to 31 December 2019 (current year basis)

2020-21 – 12 months to 31 December 2020 (current year basis)

2021-22 – 6 months to 30 June 2021 (closing year basis)

Example 2

Adapting the above example, suppose that Cynthia ceases trading on 31 March 2022 (instead of 30 June 2021).

Her basis periods for her final years of trading would be:

2019-20 – 12 months to 31 December 2019 (current year basis)

> 2020-21 – 12 months to 31 December 2020 (current year basis)
>
> 2021-22 – 12 months to 31 December 2021, *plus* three months to 31 March 2022 (closing year basis)
>
> As Cynthia ceased trading in the 2021-22 tax year, the profits of both the usual 12-month accounting period and the three-month period to cessation are brought into account.

In both examples, overlap relief is also available in the final tax year of trading –see **15.5**.

Commencement and cessation in the same tax year

Where a person starts and permanently ceases to trade in the same tax year, the basis period is simply the date of commencement to the date of cessation.

Law: ITTOIA 2005, s. 202

15.5   Overlap profits and overlap relief

The nature of the basis period rules means that, depending on the accounting date of the business, overlap profit may arise.

Specifically, overlap profits can arise when there are overlap periods (i.e. periods that fall within two basis periods).

This typically happens either in years two or three, as a result of the opening year rules, or following a change of accounting date.

Example 1 – commencement

Ann commences trading on 1 July 2021 and prepares accounts to 30 June.

Ann's basis periods for the first two years of trading will be:

> Year one (2021-22) – 1 July 2021 to 5 April 2022
>
> Year two (2022-23) – 1 July 2021 to 30 June 2022

This means there are nine months of overlap profit, as the profits between 1 July 2021 and 5 April 2022 have been brought into account in two basis periods. If the profits for the year to 30 June 2022 are £12,000, Ann's overlap profit will therefore be £9,000.

In practice, the only time a business will *not* have overlap profit is where that business continually uses 5 April as its annual accounting date.

Overlap relief

To counteract the fact that overlap profits are charged to income tax in two basis periods, a deduction is allowed for overlap profit when calculating the profits of the trade in the tax year of cessation, or in certain circumstances where there is a change of accounting date (see **15.6**). This is known as overlap relief.

Example 2 – cessation

A business has traded for many years and has always prepared its accounts to 30 June. It has overlap profit available for overlap relief of £15,000.

The business ceases to trade on 31 May 2021. The final two basis periods will be:

> 2020-21 – 12 months to 30 June 2020

> 2021-22 – 11 months from 1 July 2020 to 31 May 2021

The business has profits for the 11 months to 31 May 2021 of £30,000. Overlap relief is given against these profits, leaving taxable profits in the final year (2021-22) of £15,000 (being £30,000 less £15,000 overlap relief).

A business may also have overlap periods where a loss arises.

Where there is an "overlap loss", the amount of loss is brought into account in calculating the profits of the first basis period, but it is not brought into account in calculating the profits of the second basis period (i.e. the loss cannot be relieved twice).

Example 3 – overlap loss

Chelsea commences trading on 1 July 2021 and prepares accounts to 30 June 2022, making a loss in the year of £12,000.

Chelsea's basis periods for the first two years of trading will be:

> Year one (2021-22) – 1 July 2021 to 5 April 2022

> Year two (2022-23) – 1 July 2021 to 30 June 2022

This means that Chelsea's results in year one are a loss of £9,000 (being the loss of £12,000 x 9/12). However, this loss is not brought into account in calculating the results of year two. Instead, the results in year two are a loss of £3,000 (being the remaining three months of loss).

Law: ITTOIA 2005, s. 204-206

15.6   Change in accounting date

If a business changes its accounting date, different rules apply depending on whether the change happens in the opening years of trade, or if the trade is established and the current year basis is being used.

15.6.1   General principles

The legislation states that where there is a change from one accounting date to another, the change of accounting date occurs at the earlier of:

- the first tax year in which accounts are drawn up to the new accounting date; or
- the first tax year in which accounts are not drawn up to the old accounting date.

In relation to a tax year, the accounting date means the date in the tax year to which accounts are drawn up, or if there are two or more such dates, the latest of them.

If, as a result of the above principles, a change of accounting date occurs in a tax year in which there is no actual accounting date, the date corresponding to the new accounting date is treated as the accounting date in that tax year for the purpose of determining the basis period for that year.

Example – change of accounting date

Billy has prepared accounts to 31 December for many years, most recently to 31 December 2021. He then decides to prepare accounts to 30 April 2023.

To determine the tax year in which there is the change of accounting date, we find the earlier of:

- the first tax year in which accounts are drawn up to the new accounting date (2023-24); or
- the first tax year in which accounts are not drawn up to the old accounting date (2022-23).

The change in accounting date therefore takes place in 2022-23.

However, as the change of accounting date occurs in a tax year in which there is no actual accounting date, for the purpose of determining the basis period in 2022-23, the accounting date is taken to be 30 April 2022.

Law: ITTOIA 2005, s. 197, 214

15.6.2   Change of accounting date in opening years of trade (years one to three)

Where there is a change in accounting date within the opening years of trading, the basis periods are as follows:

Year one

The same rule applies as per **15.4.2** – the basis period is the date the trade commenced to the end of the tax year (5 April).

Year two

Generally, the same approach is taken as per **15.4.2**, where the basis period depends on whether the new accounting date is in year two, and whether that date is more or less than 12 months after commencement.

However, if no accounts end in year two, and the accounting dates in years one and three are different, the change in accounting date is taken to be in year two. The accounting date for year two becomes the corresponding accounting date in year three, and the basis period that applies in year two depends on whether this new accounting date is more or less than 12 months after commencement.

Example 1 – change of accounting date in year two – new date less than 12 months after commencement

Garry starts to trade on 1 October 2021 and prepares his first accounts to 31 December 2021.

His second accounts are prepared to a different date – 30 June 2022 – and his accounts are prepared to 30 June thereafter.

Garry's basis periods would be as follows:

   Year one (2021-22) – 1 October 2021 to 5 April 2022

   Year two (2022-23) – 1 October 2021 to 30 September 2022

Although there was a change in accounting date in year two, the new date (30 June 2022) is less than 12 months after the trade commenced. Therefore, the basis period runs for 12 months from the start of the trade.

   Year three (2023-24) – 1 July 2022 to 30 June 2023

The basis period for year three is 12 months to the accounting date in 2023-2024, as this is 12 months or less after the end of the basis period for year two (see "Year three" below).

In total, this leads to nine months of overlap profits (six months for the period 1 October 2021 to 5 April 2022, and three months for the period 1 July 2022 to 30 September 2022).

Guidance: BIM 81040

Year three

There are two possibilities:

- If the new accounting date in year three is 12 months or less after the end of the basis period for year two, the basis period for year three is 12 months to the accounting date in year three.

- Where the new accounting date falls more than 12 months after the end of the basis period for year two, the basis period for year three begins immediately after the end of the basis period for year two and ends with the new accounting date in year three.

Law: ITTOIA 2005, s. 215

Example 2 – change of accounting date in year three – new date more than 12 months after end of year two basis period

Barry starts to trade on 1 July 2021 and prepares his first accounts to 31 May 2022. He decides to prepare his second set of accounts to 30 September 2023, and annually to September thereafter.

Barry's basis periods would be as follows:

Year one (2021-22) – 1 July 2021 to 5 April 2022

Year two (2022-23) – 1 July 2021 to 30 June 2022

As the accounting date in year two is less than 12 months after commencement, the basis period is 12 months, beginning with the date on which Barry starts to carry on the trade. See **15.4.2**.

Year three (2023-24) – 1 July 2022 to 30 September 2023 (15 months)

As the new accounting date (30 September 2023) is more than 12 months after the end of the basis period for year two, year three's basis period begins immediately after year two's basis period and ends with the new accounting date in year three.

Year four (2024-25) – 1 October 2023 to 30 September 2024

There are nine months of initial overlap profits (for the period 1 July 2021 to 5 April 2022). However, as the basis period in 2023-24 is longer than 12 months, three months' worth of overlap relief is available in 2023-24. See **15.5** above for more information on overlap profits and overlap relief.

Guidance: BIM 81040

15.6.3   Change of accounting date for established trades (year four onwards)

A business may change its accounting date whenever it wishes, but from year four onwards, there are certain conditions that must be met if the change is to be recognised for tax purposes:

- The person carrying on the trade should give appropriate notice of the change of accounting date. Notification should be given in a self-assessment tax return for the year of change that applies to the person carrying on the trade and must be given on or before the date that the return is required to be made.

- The first accounts to the new date must not exceed 18 months.

- There should have been no change of accounting date (resulting in a change of basis period) in the five tax years immediately before the tax year in which the change of accounting date occurs. If there has been such a change, the latest change of accounting date must be for commercial reasons, and the reasons for the change must be set out in the self-assessment tax return.

Where all conditions are met, the basis period for the year of change is as follows:

- Where the new accounting date is less than 12 months after the end of the basis period for the previous tax year, the basis period for the year of change is 12 months ending with the new accounting date.

- Where the new accounting date is more than 12 months after the end of the basis period for the previous year, the basis period for the year of change begins immediately after the end of the basis period for the previous tax year and ends with the new accounting date.

If the conditions to change the accounting date are not met, the basis period is the period of 12 months ending with the old accounting date ending in the tax year.

Note that these conditions do not need to be met for a change of accounting date during commencement (i.e. years one to three).

Example – adapted from BIM 81060

A business commences trade on 1 July 2014 and prepares accounts to 5 April each year. In 2021-22, the business (meeting all conditions to do so) changes its accounting date and prepares accounts for a short period of three months from 6 April 2021 to 30 June 2021.

The basis periods for the business are as follows:

Tax year 2020-21 – 6 April 2020 to 5 April 2021

Tax year 2021-22 – 1 July 2020 to 30 June 2021

Tax year 2022-23 – 1 July 2021 to 30 June 2022

As the new accounting date in 2021-22 is less than 12 months after the basis period for the previous year, the basis period for 2021-22 is 12 months ending with the new accounting date of 30 June 2021.

This means there are nine months of overlap profit (1 July 2020 to 5 April 2021). This overlap profit will be available for overlap relief in a later year (see **15.5**).

Law: ITTOIA 2005, s. 216-219
Guidance: BIM 81035, 81060

15.7   Adjustments to profit

15.7.1   Introduction

The basic rule is that the profits of a trade must be calculated in accordance with generally accepted accounting practice (GAAP), subject to any adjustment required or authorised by law in calculating profits for income tax.

Instead of using GAAP, an eligible business may decide to calculate profits using the cash basis (see **15.9**).

Regardless of whether a business adopts GAAP or the cash basis to compute profits, the profit reported in the accounts will not always equal its taxable profit for income tax purposes. This is because certain items of income and expenditure must be adjusted for income tax purposes when calculating the taxable profit of a period.

The most common adjustments, and underlying principles for these, are discussed below. For a discussion of the treatment of lease premiums for tenants, see **27.4.5**.

Law: ITTOIA 2005, s. 25

15.7.2   Pre-trading expenses and post-cessation receipts

Pre-trading expenses

If a person incurs expenses for the purposes of a trade within the seven years before he or she starts to carry on the trade, those expenses can be treated as if they were incurred on the date of commencement (and so a deduction is allowed for them).

This is provided that no deduction would otherwise be allowed for the expenses, but a deduction would have been allowed had they been incurred post-commencement.

For capital allowances purposes, pre-trading expenditure is treated as incurred on the first day on which the activity is carried on (see **20.1.1**).

Law: CAA 2001, s. 12; ITTOIA 2005, s. 57

Post-cessation receipts

A post-cessation receipt is a sum received after a person permanently ceases to carry on a trade, profession or vocation, and which arises from the carrying on of the trade before the cessation.

A post-cessation receipt is charged to income tax under ITTOIA 2005, s. 242, but only so far as it is not otherwise chargeable to tax. Certain receipts are specifically included or excluded (see ITTOIA 2005, Ch. 18).

If, immediately before a person permanently ceases to carry on a trade, a cash basis election is in effect for the trade, a sum is to be treated as a post-cessation receipt only if it would have been brought into account in calculating the profits of the trade on the cash basis had it been received at that time.

For information on post-cessation expenses, see **17.3**.

Law: ITTOIA 2005, s. 241-257

15.7.3   Capital versus revenue

For tax purposes, when calculating the profits of a trade, no deduction is allowed for items of a capital nature. Similarly, items that are capital in nature are not brought into account as receipts when disposed of, unless there is express provision to do so.

However, see **15.9** for the treatment of capital receipts/expenses under the cash basis.

When it comes to expenses, it is important to determine whether expenditure is revenue in nature (and so in principle deductible) or capital in nature (and so non-deductible). The question of whether an expense is revenue or capital is one of law and is dependent on the specific facts of the case. An item's treatment is not necessarily determined by how it is classified in the business accounts.

Generally, in line with the oft-quoted definition from Viscount Cave, an expense is likely to be capital where it is made "with a view to bringing into existence an asset or an advantage for the enduring benefit of a trade" *(Atherton v British Insulated and Helsby Cables Ltd).*

Where an income tax deduction is not allowed, relief may still be available through capital allowances (see **Chapters 20-22**). A CGT deduction may also be available when the asset is ultimately sold or otherwise disposed of.

Case: *Atherton v British Insulated and Helsby Cables Ltd* (1925) 10 TC 155

Repairs and renewals

When "repairs" are said to be made to an asset, it is important to determine whether the expenditure is truly a repair (and so revenue in nature) or whether it is really capital. Generally, repairs are allowable as a deduction when computing trading profits, whereas capital expenditure is not.

Improvements

Expenditure that restores an asset to its original condition is considered to be a repair, and so is normally allowable as a deduction when calculating trade profits.

By contrast, expenditure that alters or improves an asset is capital and not a repair, and no deduction is permitted. An improvement or alteration means that the asset has not merely been restored to what it was before; it has in some way been changed.

Where the work undertaken amounts to an alteration or improvement, there is no revenue deduction for any part of the expenditure.

Repair or improvement – Auckland Gas Co Ltd

In this New Zealand case, the company supplied its customers through a network of mainly low-pressure underground cast iron or steel pipes.

However, the joints holding the pipes together would fracture due to ground subsidence, traffic vibration, or corrosion, which led to leakage.

The company then adopted the technique of inserting polyethylene pipes into the existing cast iron and steel pipes.

The new pipes were able to take higher pressure/capacity and were suited for natural gas. The old pipes, by contrast, were not.

The Privy Council found that, far from restoring the gas distribution system to its original state, the work changed the character of the existing gas distribution system, as a significant portion of it had been upgraded. The work on replacing a pipe network was capital expenditure and not allowable as a deduction.

Case: *Auckland Gas Co Ltd v CIR* (2000) 73 TC 266

Repair or improvement – Transco Plc

This case, like *Auckland Gas Co*, involved the insertion of polyethylene pipes into existing cast iron and steel pipes.

However, there were a number of key differences: there was no plan to replace the whole network, and less than 1% of the whole pipeline was replaced with polyethylene each year. Further, the pipes were only replaced when necessary for safety reasons.

It was also relevant that the replacement pipes did the same job as the old pipes; there was no increase in capacity or pressure, and the old pipes had been successfully carrying natural gas for years.

The Special Commissioners found that the work was a repair to a part of the network, as the pipeline was simply restored to its previous efficiency. The works were therefore allowable.

Case: *Transco Plc v Dyall* (2002) Sp C 310

Initial repairs

Two cases provide instructive guidance on this matter: *Law Shipping* and *Odeon Associated Theatres*.

Initial repairs – Law Shipping

The company acquired a ship in poor condition that needed to be repaired before it could be used as a profit-earning asset.

As a result of its poor condition, the purchase price of the ship was substantially less than if it had been in a fit state of repair.

There was also no evidence that on sound commercial accountancy principles the deferred repairs could be charged as revenue expenditure.

Accordingly, the works were deemed to be capital expenditure on acquiring a working asset, and so were not allowable as a revenue deduction.

Case: *The Law Shipping Co Ltd v CIR* (1923) 12 TC 621

Initial repairs – Odeon Associated Theatres

In contrast to *Law Shipping*, in the *Odeon Associated Theatres* case the company operated its cinemas for a number of years before carrying out the repairs. The price paid on acquisition was also not reduced to reflect the state of repair.

The expenditure was found to be on repairs and so was an allowable revenue expense.

Case: *Odeon Associated Theatres Ltd v Jones* (1971) 48 TC 257

Replacement of the entirety

The cost of replacing the whole or the "entirety" of an asset is not a repair; it is capital expenditure and not an allowable expense.

Again, what forms the asset or entirety is a question of fact. HMRC's guidance at BIM 46910 suggests the following:

> "With buildings and structures, the question is whether the item replaced appears to be a free-standing asset. The fact that it is connected to another structure, for example by a flue, does not make it part of that larger asset.
>
> Another question is whether something has become part of something else. If something is a "fixture" then it has become part of the building and not an entirety in its own right. Except where an "integral feature" is being replaced [...] replacing a fixture is a repair to the building."

For further information on fixtures and integral features, see the content on capital allowances in **Chapter 21**.

Modern materials

In some cases, it may no longer be possible to carry out a repair using the same materials or equipment as originally used. Generally, provided the asset just does the same job following the works as previously, the expenditure is considered to be a repair.

A continuing question

In summary, when works are carried out to an asset, the question should be asked whether those works are revenue or capital in nature.

The divide is one that continues to find its way to the courts today, as the recent example of *Steadfast Manufacturing & Storage Ltd* shows. This case before the First-tier Tribunal (FTT) considered whether expenditure incurred in respect of resurfacing a yard used by vehicles was a replacement of the yard, and so a capital expense, or a repair of the yard.

Some of the key findings of fact were as follows:

- The cost of the works was approximately £74,000. The cost to replace the entire site would have been approximately £6.5 million.
- Before and after the relevant expenditure, the whole of the yard was used to unload articulated lorries, to move those lorries, and to provide trailer storage. There was no increase in size of the useable area and no increase in the load-bearing capacity of the yard.

One of HMRC's arguments was that, as a result of the works, there would be no need for further repairs for potentially 20 years, and therefore the taxpayer gained an enduring advantage.

The FTT found the works to be repairs, and so allowable, noting that the reduced need for repairs did not of itself make the expenditure capital. The works carried out simply restored the yard to its original state and did not bring something new into existence.

Law: ITTOIA 2005, s. 33

Case: *Steadfast Manufacturing & Storage Ltd v HMRC* [2020] UKFTT 286 (TC)

Guidance: BIM 46900, 46910

15.7.4   Grants and compensation payments

Grants

A grant is typically taxed according to ordinary principles of taxation. In other words, the tax treatment of a grant depends on whether it is capital or revenue in nature.

Grants that meet revenue expenditure are normally taxed as trading receipts, while grants that meet capital expenditure (e.g. a grant paid to acquire a capital asset) are not usually treated as trading receipts.

Grants that cannot be pinned down for a specific purpose are known as undifferentiated receipts. Undifferentiated receipts should be treated as revenue, with the exception of Highlands and Islands Enterprise grants, which may be treated as non-revenue receipts.

Compensation payments

Other compensation receipts should similarly be taxed according to the underlying nature of the receipt.

Usually, compensation receipts referable to the taxpayer's trading operations are treated as trade receipts and are taxable as such. Payments received in respect of the permanent loss, deprivation or sterilisation of a fixed capital asset are capital receipts.

The taxation of compensation payments may differ where the trader is using the cash basis and the receipt is capital in nature (see **15.9**).

Covid-19 support payments

The tax treatment of Covid-19 (coronavirus) support payments, including the Self-Employment Income Support Scheme (SEISS), is provided for in FA 2020, s. 106 and Sch. 16. See also **Appendix 11**.

All Covid-19 support payments are considered revenue in nature, and should be brought into account in calculating the profits of the trade, profession, or vocation where the business is still trading.

Where such a payment is received after the trade has ceased, and the receipt was not recognised in the period the trade was carried on, the payment is treated as a post-cessation receipt.

If an amount of Covid-19 support payment is referable to more than one business, the payment should be allocated between those businesses on a just and reasonable basis.

Covid-19 support payments, as a general rule, should be recognised in accordance with GAAP or the cash basis (as applicable). In respect of SEISS payments, the whole payment is taxed in the tax year in which it is received. This means that payments of the fourth and fifth SEISS grants should be recognised in the 2021-22 tax year.

Where a partner in a trading partnership receives a SEISS payment, it is added to the partner's trading profit share unless the partner pays the amount into the partnership and it is not retained by the partner. Where the payment is transferred to the partnership it is treated as the partnership's trading income in the same way as any other trading income received by the partnership, and the amount will be taxable income of the accounting period of the partnership.

Where there is an assessment to recover overclaimed SEISS, the amount of taxable payment is reduced accordingly.

Further HMRC guidance regarding the SEISS, including eligibility criteria, can be found by following the link below.

Law: FA 2020, s. 106, Sch. 16

Guidance: BIM 40456, 40457, 40458; https://tinyurl.com/59sd45un (SEISS official guidance)

15.7.5 Non-trade income

A business may derive income from non-trading sources. Such income is taxed according to its nature.

Example

A business receives rental income from a sub-let premises. This income is non-trade income and is instead assessable as property income (see **Chapter 26**). However, if the income arises from trading accommodation that is temporarily surplus to requirements, HMRC may allow the income to be treated as a trading receipt (see PIM 4300).

15.7.6 Wholly and exclusively

When calculating the profits of a trade, no deduction is allowed for expenses that are not incurred wholly and exclusively for the purposes of the trade, or for losses not connected with or arising out of the trade.

Where an expense is incurred for more than one purpose, a deduction may still be claimed for any identifiable part or proportion of the expense which is incurred wholly and exclusively for the purposes of the trade.

HMRC provide extensive guidance on the topic of "wholly and exclusively" in the *Business Income Manual*, beginning at BIM 37000. Further guidance relating to two common areas of difficulty (clothing, and costs of working from home) is outlined below.

Clothing

Ordinary clothing (i.e. clothing that forms part of an everyday wardrobe) worn by a trader while carrying on his or her trade is not a deductible expense. This was considered in the case of *Mallalieu v Drummond.*

In this case, the taxpayer (a barrister) claimed a deduction on the replacement and laundering of her professional clothes, which were consistent with Bar requirements on court dress, and which she only wore in the course of carrying on her profession. The costs were held to be non-deductible: there was a duality of purpose as the clothes also served a private purpose.

Deductions for clothing may, however, be claimed in some situations: costs of uniforms (for example, a nurse's uniform) and protective clothing are typically allowable.

Use of home

It is not uncommon, particularly in light of recent Covid-19 restrictions, for a trader to carry on some or all of his or her trade from home.

Where part of a trader's property is used solely for trade purposes, a deduction may be claimed for that part of household expenses.

The types of expenses that may be deductible are dependent on the exact facts and working arrangements of each trader. However, home working costs can generally be divided into:

- fixed costs, such as council tax, mortgage interest/rent, and insurance;
- running costs, such as heating and lighting; and
- other costs, such as internet and phone expenses.

Generally, such expenses are only deductible to the extent that they are attributable to trade use. An apportionment of qualifying relevant expenditure is often acceptable.

HMRC at BIM 47815 summarise the factors to be taken into account when apportioning an expense:

- Area: what proportion in terms of area of the home is used for trade purposes?
- Usage: how much is consumed? This is appropriate where there is a metered or measurable supply such as electricity, gas or water.
- Time: how long is it used for trade purposes, as compared to any other use?

The method of apportioning an expense depends on the relative importance of each of these factors. HMRC provide examples at BIM 47825.

Where there is only minor use of the home, then HMRC accept a reasonable estimate of costs. An example of minor use would be writing up business records at home.

Note that a trader may choose instead to use the simplified method to calculate working from home costs – see **15.10.3**.

Law: ITTOIA 2005, s. 34
Guidance: BIM 37000, 47815-47825
Case: *Mallalieu v Drummond* (1983) 57 TC 330

15.7.7 Common non-deductible expenses

There are a number of statutory provisions that dictate when an expense is non-deductible in calculating the profits of a business for income tax purposes.

Some of the most common ones are discussed below.

Bad and doubtful debts

When calculating the profits of a trade, no deduction is allowed for a debt owed to the person carrying on the trade, unless:

- the debt is bad;
- the debt is estimated to be bad; or
- the debt is released wholly and exclusively for the purposes of the trade as part of a statutory insolvency arrangement.

Law: ITTOIA 2005, s. 35

Depreciation

As depreciation relates to capital expenditure, it is not permitted as a deduction when calculating business profits. Instead, a deduction for capital expenditure may be available under the capital allowances regime (see **Chapter 20**).

The exception to this is where a trader holds an asset under certain types of finance lease. Broadly, the depreciation and interest elements charged to the profit and loss account may then be allowable for tax purposes. For further information on lease accounting and taxation see BLM 13000 and BLM 00525.

Drawings

A sole trader or partner in partnership may take drawings from the business.

Drawings should not be confused with wages or salaries – drawings are non-deductible expenses, as the individual is subject to tax on the tax-adjusted profits of the business (or on his or her allocation of partnership profits in the case of a partnership – see **Chapter 16**).

If a trader has included a deduction for drawings in the profit and loss account, it should be added back.

Entertainment

Generally, no deduction is allowed for expenses incurred in providing entertainment (including hospitality of any kind) in connection with the trade. This includes expenses incurred in providing anything incidental to the provision of entertainment.

There are limited exceptions to this. For example, where the entertainment is of a nature that it is the trader's trade to provide (e.g. a restaurant providing food and drink), and the entertainment is provided in the ordinary course of the trade, either for payment or free of charge in order to advertise to the public generally, a deduction is permitted.

Another exception to the general rule is staff entertaining. This is allowable, except where the staff entertainment is incidental to client entertainment. For example, a staff Christmas party that only staff members can attend would normally be allowable, but an event put on for clients, that a few employees also attend, would not be allowable.

Staff entertainment may give rise to PAYE/NIC implications – see **Chapter 6** and **7.6.1**.

Law: ITTOIA 2005, s. 45, 46

Gifts

Gifts, in general, are treated in the same way as entertainment (i.e. expenses incurred in providing gifts are non-deductible).

There are some exceptions to this, for example gifts to charity.

A deduction is also typically permitted for a gift that incorporates a conspicuous advertisement for the trader. However, gifts of this nature are not allowable where:

- the gift is food, drink, tobacco or a token or voucher exchangeable for goods; or
- the cost of the gift to the trader, together with any other gifts (except food, drink, tobacco or a token or voucher exchangeable for goods) given to the same person in the same basis period, exceeds £50.

The full list of exceptions for gifts is provided in ITTOIA 2005, s. 47.

Law: ITTOIA 2005, s. 45, 47

Fines and penalties

The tax treatment of fines and penalties depends on whether they meet the "wholly and exclusively" test.

In general, where a penalty is intended as punishment, it is not allowable as a deduction. Similarly, a penalty incurred for breaching the law is not a deductible expense.

Example

A common example in this category is a parking fine.

A parking fine is, in itself, non-deductible. However, if an employer pays or reimburses a parking fine that is the liability of an employee, the cost to the employer of paying the fine is allowable in computing trading profits. This is because the employee will be taxable on the payment as employment income.

High-emission cars

Where a trader uses a hire car in the business, and that car is a high-emissions vehicle (above 50g/km from April 2021, or above 110g/km from April 2018), the amount of deduction that would otherwise be allowed for its leasing costs should be reduced by 15%.

This restriction applies to most types of cars, but not motorcycles.

Law: ITTOIA 2005, s. 48-50B

Interest

Interest is allowable as a deduction in computing business profits or losses to the extent that it is incurred wholly and exclusively for the purposes of the business. Where only part of the interest meets the wholly and exclusively test, only that part is allowable as a deduction.

Interest is always considered to be an item of revenue when calculating the profits of a trade, whatever the nature of the loan.

Interest on late paid income tax is not deductible.

Law: ITTOIA 2005, s. 29, 54

Legal fees

Legal or professional fees that are capital (e.g. legal fees associated with the purchase or sale of a capital item), or that do not meet the "wholly and exclusively" test, are non-deductible.

However, HMRC concede that professional fees incurred on the renewal of a short lease, although capital in nature, are likely to be small, and so can be allowed on *de minimis* grounds. A short lease is a lease with a remaining term of 50 years or less. For further information on the taxation of property leases, see **Chapter 27**.

Guidance: BIM 46420

Private expenses

Expenses relating to private (i.e. non-trade-related) matters should be adjusted to exclude the private use element where the expense relates to the business owner.

Where a business has employees and pays an expense for an employee that is private in nature (e.g. a gym membership), that expense is an allowable deduction (i.e. there is no corresponding adjustment for the private use element). Instead, the employee will usually end up with a taxable benefit related to the expense. Further information on the taxation of employee benefits is provided at **Chapters 6** and **7**.

15.7.8   Salaries

Wages or salary costs for employees are deductible trading expenses of the business. Tax relief will, however, be delayed if the payment is not made within nine months from the end of the period of account.

Law: ITTOIA 2005, s. 36(2)

15.7.9   Trading stock

Goods for own use

Where a trader takes stock from the business for his or her private use, the transfer should be treated as though it were a sale at market value, with the sale deemed to take place on the date of appropriation. The value of anything that was, in fact, received for the stock is not brought into account.

Example 1 – Shelly

Shelly runs a lighting shop. In the 2021-22 tax year, she takes a lamp from her business to use in her own home. The cost price of the light is £50, and she normally sells it for £75.

When calculating Shelly's taxable trading profit for the 2021-22 tax year, £75 should be added back, being the market value of the pendant light.

The costs of any services rendered by the business to the trader personally (or to his or her household) are not deductible as they do not meet the "wholly and exclusively" test. Such costs should be disallowed.

Example 2 – Shelly (cont.)

Later in the tax year, Shelly asks one of her employees to install a different, privately purchased, light in her home. The employee was paid £30 for the installation. Usually the charge for a customer is £50.

Such costs are not allowable. The £30 paid for the installation should be added back when calculating Shelly's 2021-22 trading profits.

See **15.9.4** below for different treatment if the cash basis applies.

Trading stock supplied by trader

A trader may have an item that is not trading stock, but that later becomes so – for example, a property developer who holds an investment property that is later developed as part of the trade. For income tax purposes, the cost of the stock is taken to be its market value, with the cost deemed to be incurred on the date the item became trading stock. The value of anything that may have been given for it is left out of account.

Law: ITTOIA 2005, s. 172A-172F

15.7.10 Trading stock at cessation of trade

When an individual ceases to carry on his or her trade, profession or vocation, or all persons in partnership cease to carry on a business in partnership, the trading stock belonging to the trade at the time of the cessation must be valued when calculating the profits of the trade.

The provisions are outlined at ITTOIA 2005, Pt. 2, Ch. 12 but the general rule is that the value of the stock or work in progress is taken to be its arm's length value at the time of cessation.

There are, however, specific rules, including for the following three instances where the stock is transferred to another trader who will deduct the cost of that stock in computing his or her own trading profits:

- where the two parties are not connected;
- where the two parties are connected; or
- where the two parties are connected but an election for substituted value has been made.

HMRC have a flowchart that summarises how trading stock should be valued at BIM 33475.

See **15.9.4** for the rules that apply if a cash basis election has been made.

Law: ITTOIA 2005, s. 97A-97B, 173-186
Guidance: BIM 33475

15.7.11 Travel and subsistence

As a general principle, the costs of accommodation and food and drink consumed by a trader are not expenses incurred wholly and exclusively for the purposes of the trade, as such costs are, in whole or part, normal costs of living.

However, there are some instances where such expenses may be allowable.

Accommodation

Hotel accommodation and reasonable costs of overnight subsistence are deductible where a business trip necessitates one or more nights away from home.

However, this does not extend to overnight accommodation and subsistence at the base of trade operations, even if there is a contractual requirement for the trader to reside there.

Food and drink

A deduction may be allowed for reasonable expenses on food and drink for consumption by the trader, either at a place to which the trader travels in the course of the trade or while travelling in the course of the trade.

For such a deduction to be allowable, both of the following conditions should be met:

- Condition A – a deduction for the expenses incurred by the trader in travelling to the place is allowed, or would be if the trader incurred any such costs.
- Condition B – the trade is itinerant at the time the expense is incurred, or the trader does not travel to the place more than occasionally in the course of the trade, and either:
  - o the travel concerned is not part of the trader's normal pattern of travel in the course of the trade, or
  - o the trader does not have such a normal pattern of travel.

Travel

The costs of ordinary commuting are not allowable. This includes where a trader has several permanent places of work.

The costs of travelling for an "itinerant" trader may be allowable. An itinerant trader is one who travels from his home to a number of different locations for the purely temporary purpose at each such place of completing a job of work, at the conclusion of which he attends a different location. Builders are a typical example. In certain cases, the costs of travelling between their residence and the sites where they work may be allowable as a deduction. The deductibility of such expenses should be considered on a case-by-case basis.

Law: ITTOIA 2005, s. 57A

15.7.12 Adjustments to trading profits – worked examples

To recap, the basic rule is that the profits of a trade must be calculated in accordance with GAAP, subject to any adjustment required or authorised by law in calculating profits for income tax purposes.

In practice, this means a two-step process in determining the taxable profits of the trade:

- calculate trading profits for the relevant period under GAAP; then
- adjust those profits in accordance with income tax rules.

Businesses using the cash basis should also refer to section **15.9**.

Tax adjustments are not always necessary. In some cases, there may not be any relevant tax rules or principles that dictate an adjustment to profit. In such instances, the taxable trading profit will equal the profit per the business accounts.

Example 1

Katy has been trading for several years.

For the year ended 31 December 2021 she has the following results:

	£
Sales	25,000
Cost of sales	(5,000)
Gross profit	20,000
Administrative expenses	(2,500)
Subscriptions	(100)
Profit before tax	17,400

All Katy's subscription costs are trade related.

In the above example, Katy's profits for accounting purposes of £17,400 would equal her taxable trading profits, as no adjustments to profit for tax purposes are needed.

More usually, however, some adjustments are required.

Example 2

Constance has been trading for several years.

For the year ended 31 December 2021 she has the following results:

	£
Sales	75,000
Cost of sales	(20,000)
Gross profit	55,000
Administrative expenses	(5,500)
Client entertainment	(1,000)
Depreciation	(1,750)
Fines	(100)
High-emission car lease	(800)
Legal and professional fees	(750)
Office costs	(6,500)
Salaries	(5,000)
Subscriptions	(300)
Profit before tax	33,300

Capital allowances for the year to 31 December 2021 totalled £5,000.

Constance took an item of trading stock for her private use. The cost of the item was £50 and it has a mark-up of 20%.

£250 of legal fees relate to the renewal of a long-term lease.

The fine relates to a late filing penalty for the late submission of Constance's 2019-20 self-assessment tax return.

The high-emission car is used by Constance 60% of the time for business purposes.

Salaries were all paid within nine months following the year-end (see **15.7.8**).

All subscriptions were trade related, with the exception of £30 relating to Constance's subscription to *Total Carp*, a fishing magazine.

Constance's tax-adjusted trading profits are as follows:

	£
Profit per accounts	33,300
Adjustments:	
Add back	
Client entertainment	1,000
Depreciation	1,750
Fines	100
High-emission car lease (see below)	392
Legal and professional fees	250
Trading stock adjustment (goods for own use)	60
Subscriptions (not trade-related)	30
Deduct	
Capital allowances	(5,000)
Taxable trading profits	31,882

The high-emission car lease adjustment is calculated as follows:

	£
Allowable portion of lease (pre-private use adjustment) (£800 x 85%)	680
Allowable portion taking private use into account (£680 x 60%)	408
Amount to be disallowed (£800 - £408)	392

Law: ITTOIA 2005, s. 25

15.8   The trading allowance

From 6 April 2017, there has been a trading allowance and a separate property allowance. Further information on the property allowance is available at **26.8**.

The trading allowance provides relief of up to £1,000 in a tax year against trading income and/or miscellaneous income, where certain conditions are met.

Where the individual qualifies for full relief, the individual's "relevant income" is not charged to income tax.

Where an individual's relevant income exceeds the trading allowance for the tax year, partial relief is available.

Full relief

Where the total of an individual's relevant income does not exceed £1,000, full relief is available under the trading allowance.

An individual's relevant income for a tax year is the sum of the receipts from the individual's "relevant trades" for that tax year, plus his or her miscellaneous income for the tax year.

A trade is a relevant trade if it is not carried on in partnership, and it is not a "rent-a-room trade" (as defined).

Miscellaneous income is all of an individual's income that would be taxable for the year under ITTOIA 2005, Pt. 5, Ch. 8 (income not otherwise charged), but excluding certain rent-a-room receipts.

Where an individual has more than one relevant trade and qualifies for full relief, then the profits/losses of each relevant trade are deemed to be nil for the tax year. The same is true where the taxpayer qualifies for full relief and his or her relevant income includes miscellaneous income (i.e. income is deemed to be nil).

The trading allowance cannot be used to create a loss.

Example 1 – trading allowance – full relief

Susan babysits on weekends and earns £800 during the 2021-22 tax year. Her allowable expenses for the year for advertising her services are £100, meaning a net profit of £700.

Susan qualifies for full relief using the trading allowance, as her £800 gross income is less than the £1,000 trading allowance. The profits of her trade are deemed to be nil. Susan does not have to make an election to claim full relief.

Partial relief

Where an individual's relevant income (i.e. trading and/or miscellaneous income) exceeds the amount of trading allowance, the trading allowance can be used to provide partial relief.

Where an individual qualifies for partial relief, and his or her relevant income comprises receipts of one or more relevant trades, the profits/losses for the tax year are calculated as follows:

Step 1. Calculate the total of all the amounts which would ordinarily be brought into account as a receipt in calculating the profits of the trade for the tax year.

Step 2. Subtract the individual's trading allowance for the tax year.

Step 3. Subtract from the amount given by step 2 any deduction for overlap profit allowed in the tax year (i.e. due to a change in accounting date, or where it is the final year of trade – see **15.5**).

Where an individual qualifies for partial relief and his or her relevant income consists only of miscellaneous income, the amount of miscellaneous income chargeable to income tax for the tax year is the amount of that income for the tax year, less the trading allowance.

An individual who has income from more than one trade (and/or has income from a trade and miscellaneous income), can choose how best to allocate the trading allowance.

An election for partial relief is made in the individual's self-assessment tax return.

Example 2 – trading allowance – partial relief – single trade

Johnny has carried on a trade for several years. In 2021-22, he has total receipts of £3,200 and expenses of £800.

As his receipts exceed the amount of the trading allowance, only partial relief is available.

If Johnny claims the trading allowance, £1,000 is deducted from total receipts of £3,200, leaving taxable profits for the trade of £2,200. As the trading allowance is claimed, no deduction is permitted for any expenses that would have otherwise been allowable (i.e. the £800).

Restrictions

The trading allowance is for individuals; it does not apply to trading income from a partnership. Further, the allowance cannot be claimed on trading/miscellaneous income from:

- a company owned or controlled by the individual or by a connected person;

- a partnership in which the individual or a connected person is a partner; or
- the individual's employer or the employer of his or her spouse or civil partner.

The trading allowance is also not available on receipts arising from the rent-a-room scheme, nor can it be claimed against Covid-19 SEISS receipts.

When to claim

Use of the trading allowance is voluntary. There are certain circumstances in which it may be better not to use it, e.g. where actual expenses are greater than £1,000.

Reporting

HMRC's guidance states that where a trader's annual gross income is £1,000 or less, HMRC do not need to be notified (unless the trader cannot use the trading allowance, or the trader must otherwise register for self-assessment with HMRC).

- Where gross trading income exceeds £1,000, the individual should register for self-assessment.
- Where other gross income exceeds £1,000 up to £2,500 the individual should contact HMRC.
- Where other income exceeds £2,500, the individual should register for self-assessment.

Law: ITTOIA 2005, s. 783A-783AR

Guidance: tinyurl.com/4vf8jprm (tax-free allowances); BIM 86000

15.9   Cash basis

15.9.1   Introduction

Smaller businesses may opt to calculate the profits of their trade using the cash basis, instead of in accordance with GAAP.

Under the cash basis, the income and expenses of a business are accounted for when the cash is received/paid respectively.

This makes reporting and record-keeping simpler, as a business need only show the cash movements in an accounting period, as opposed to preparing a full profit and loss account and balance sheet.

As income and expenses are recognised in line with the underlying cash movements, there are also no balance sheet items such as debtors and creditors to consider when using the cash basis.

Similarly, there is no need to account for stock when using the cash basis, except where there is a permanent cessation of trade – see **15.9.4** below.

Law: ITTOIA 2005, s. 25A

15.9.2   Eligibility

Broadly, in order to be eligible to calculate profits on the cash basis, the aggregate of the cash basis receipts of each trade, profession or vocation carried on by the person during a tax year should not exceed the "relevant maximum". Since 2017-18 the "relevant maximum" has been £150,000, or £300,000 for universal credit claimants.

Where the basis period for the tax year is less than 12 months, the relevant maximum is proportionately reduced.

In the case of individuals who control a partnership, or partnerships controlled by an individual, the total cash basis receipts for all trades carried on by the individual or partnership in a tax year must not exceed the relevant maximum amount. Further, the individual or partnership must use the cash basis for all those trades.

The cash basis is optional. Once an election is made, it has effect for the tax year for which it is made and for all subsequent years, and applies to every trade carried on during those years.

Certain persons are excluded from using the cash basis, including companies, LLPs, and taxpayers who have made a herd basis election or who have claimed income averaging (see **Chapters 16** (partnerships) and **18** (farmers and creative artists).

Law: ITTOIA 2005, s. 31A-31D

15.9.3   Calculation of profits – general principles

The profits of a trade for a tax year on the cash basis are determined as follows:

- Calculate the total receipts of the trade received during the basis period for the tax year.
- Deduct from that amount the total expenses of the trade paid during that basis period.

The above is subject to any adjustment as required or authorised by law in calculating the profits for income tax purposes. So, tests such as "wholly and exclusively" should continue to be applied, even where a business uses the cash basis.

BIM 70005 states that a business can choose when to treat income as received and expenses as paid, provided the treatment is consistent. For example, an expense may be treated as paid when a card payment is made, or on the date that entry is shown on the bank statement.

Law: ITTOIA 2005, s. 31E-31F
Guidance: BIM 70005

15.9.4 Calculation of profits – effects of cash basis election

Where a cash basis election has been made, certain tax adjustments must be considered when calculating the profits of the trade.

When using the cash basis, certain capital receipts *can* be included in the calculation of trading income. This goes against the general principle that capital items are excluded when calculating trading profits.

The rules around how much of a capital receipt should be included as a trade receipt depend on whether the receipt arises while a business is using the cash basis, or after it has left that basis. See BIM 70020.

When determining the deductibility of expenses, general principles still apply (e.g. the "wholly and exclusively" principle). However, various specific rules apply, as below.

Capital expenditure

In general, capital expenditure under the cash basis is treated as an allowable business expense, subject to some exceptions. Broadly, these exceptions relate to expenditure on or in connection with:

- the acquisition or disposal of a business (or part thereof);
- education or training; and
- the provision, alteration or disposal of assets including:
  - assets that are not depreciating assets;
  - assets not acquired or created for continuing use in the trade;
  - land; and
  - cars.

The full provisions can be found in ITTOIA 2005, s. 33A.

Capital allowances may be claimed for cars, provided the business mileage rate (see **15.10.2**) has not been claimed.

Goods for own use

Where a trader has elected to compute trade profits on the cash basis, the cost of any goods taken by the trader for personal use is disallowed. This differs from the treatment outlined in **15.7.9**, which applies where trading profits are computed on the accruals basis.

However, if a person who has made a cash basis election for a tax year permanently ceases carrying on a trade in that year, the value of any trading stock at cessation should be brought into account as a receipt. That value should be determined on a just and reasonable basis.

Law: ITTOIA 2005, s. 172AA

Hire cars

Under the cash basis, high-emission hire cars are not subject to the 15% restriction (see **15.7.7**).

Interest payments on loans

Where the profits of a trade are calculated on the cash basis, the general rule is that no deduction is allowed for the interest paid on a loan (ITTOIA 2005, s. 51A).

However, a further provision in s. 57B permits a deduction for interest payments on loans – and the incidental costs of obtaining finance – up to a maximum of £500 in cases where a deduction for the interest would otherwise be disallowed by virtue of s. 51A, or because it was not an expense incurred wholly and exclusively for the purposes of the trade.

Where interest is charged on a purchase that is itself an allowable expense (e.g. interest on the leasing of plant and machinery), the £500 cap does not apply and the interest may be allowed in full. However, if there is any private use, only the portion of interest related to the business use is allowable.

Capital gains tax

Where an asset is disposed of and has been relieved at any time under the cash basis, it is not chargeable to CGT. Instead, proceeds are brought

319

into account as a trading receipt, or brought into account as disposal proceeds for capital allowances purposes where applicable.

Post-cessation expenses

Expenses paid after the cessation of a trade using the cash basis are treated as post-cessation expenses.

Law: CAA 2001, s. 1A; ITTOIA 2005, s. 33A, 51A, 57B

15.9.5 The cash basis and VAT

The cash basis does not affect the way a business should account for VAT.

For VAT-registered businesses using the cash basis, business receipts and payments may be recorded either excluding or including VAT.

If VAT is included, the net VAT payments to HMRC should be recorded as expenses and the net repayments from HMRC as receipts.

Guidance: BIM 70005

15.9.6 Leaving the cash basis

Once a person starts to use the cash basis, he or she will remain in the scheme until such time as the conditions to use it are no longer met, or an election is made to compute profits by reference to GAAP.

Since 2017-18, a person must leave the cash basis in the tax year following the year in which total cash basis receipts of all trades carried on by that person exceed £300,000.

The exception to this is where total cash basis receipts in the later year do not exceed the relevant maximum for that year (i.e. £150,000 or £300,000 for universal credit claimants).

Transitional adjustments when joining/leaving the cash basis

To ensure that income/expenses are not taxed/relieved twice, transitional adjustments may be required where a business joins or leaves the cash basis.

The transitional adjustment calculation is set out in s. 231. In essence, a business will bring into account either adjustment income or an adjustment expense.

Where a business switches from the cash basis to GAAP, and has adjustment income, the income is spread evenly over six tax years, with the first sixth of income charged to tax in the first period after leaving the cash basis. A person may, however, elect to accelerate the tax charge on the adjustment income (s. 239B).

An adjustment expense is deducted in full in the first period after leaving the cash basis (i.e. the expense is not similarly spread).

The provisions relating to cash basis adjustments for capital allowances can be found at ITTOIA 2005, Pt. 2, Ch. 17A.

See also **26.4.4** for a discussion of the adjustments in the context of a rental business.

Law: ITTOIA 2005, Pt. 2, Ch. 17, 17A
Guidance: BIM 70000

15.10 Simplified expenses

15.10.1 Introduction

The simplified expenses rules were introduced in FA 2013, and are designed to simplify business expenses for unincorporated businesses (including professions and vocations), regardless of whether or not they use the cash basis.

As with the cash basis election, the decision to use simplified expenses is optional.

There is no business income limit when it comes to using simplified expenses. However, certain entities are prohibited from using simplified expenses, including limited companies and mixed-member partnerships (see **Chapter 16**).

The rules cover three categories of expense:

- motor vehicles;
- use of home for business purposes; and
- private use of business premises.

All other expenses should be calculated on an actual basis.

Law: ITTOIA 2005, s. 94B-94I

15.10.2 Motor vehicles

If simplified expenses are used for a motor vehicle, this means that a flat rate is claimed for mileage, as opposed to claiming for the actual costs of maintaining the vehicle and claiming capital allowances.

Eligible motor vehicles include cars, motorcycles or goods vehicles used in the trade.

The mileage rate is applied on a vehicle-by-vehicle basis. Once a business starts using the mileage rate for a vehicle it must continue to do so while the vehicle remains in the business. Further, no actual expenditure or capital allowances can be claimed in relation to that vehicle.

The mileage rate does not include incidental expenses of travel, such as tolls and parking fees. These costs are still allowable as a deduction where they are incurred solely for business purposes.

The mileage rate can only be claimed for journeys (or an identifiable portion thereof) that are wholly and exclusively for business purposes. Records should therefore be kept to substantiate the number of miles claimed.

A business cannot use the mileage rate:

- for a vehicle on which capital allowances have already been claimed; or
- where a business using the cash basis has claimed a deduction on acquiring a vehicle (other than a car).

Instead, the actual costs of running and maintaining the vehicle can be claimed, alongside any capital allowances that may be available.

A summary of the business mileage rates is provided at **Appendix 8**.

Law: ITTOIA 2005, s. 94D-94G
Guidance: BIM 75005

15.10.3 Use of home for business purposes

A person using his or her home partly for business purposes may claim a flat rate deduction in respect of household running costs, rather than claim a deduction for actual expenditure.

The flat rate deduction is based on the number of hours spent wholly and exclusively on qualifying work. Qualifying work is work done by the person, or any employee of the person, in the person's home wholly and exclusively for the purposes of the trade.

An individual must work from home for at least 25 hours per month before the deduction can be claimed.

The deduction allowable for a period is the sum of the applicable flat rate amounts for each month (or part month) falling within the period. A summary of the flat rates is provided at **Appendix 8**.

Using the flat rate does not prohibit a separate deduction for the business portion of telephone and broadband/internet expenses.

Similarly, it does not prohibit a separate deduction for fixed costs such as council tax, insurance and mortgage interest, where an identifiable proportion can be attributed to business use.

See **15.7.6** for details of how use-of-home expenses are deducted.

Law: ITTOIA 2005, s. 94H
Guidance: BIM 75010

15.10.4 Living at business premises

If a person uses a property mainly for the purposes of the trade, but also as a home (e.g. a bed and breakfast), a flat rate can be used to calculate the non-business portion of expenditure.

This removes the need to work out the actual split between the private and business use of expenses related to use of the premises. Instead, a business can claim a deduction for actual expenses for the premises, less the flat rate adjustment for non-business use.

The non-business use amount for a period is the sum of the flat rates for each month (or part month) falling within that period, and is also based on the number of occupants using the premises in each month otherwise than in the course of the trade, including non-paying guests and children. A summary of the flat rates is provided at **Appendix 8**.

Law: ITTOIA 2005, s. 94I
Guidance: BIM 75015

15.10.5 HMRC checker

HMRC offer a simplified expenses checker, which can help sole traders and eligible partnerships determine whether they would be better off using simplified expenses or calculating expenses on an actual basis.

Guidance: https://www.gov.uk/simplified-expenses-checker

15.11   National Insurance contributions

15.11.1 *Class 2*

Subject to some exceptions (see below), Class 2 NIC is payable by self-employed earners aged between 16 and the state pension age.

Class 2 NIC becomes payable once an individual's trading profits exceed the small profits threshold (£6,515 for 2021-22).

Class 2 NIC is applied at a flat rate of £3.05 (2021-22) for each contribution week or part of a week that a person was self-employed.

There are some exceptions as to when a self-employed earner is liable to Class 2 NIC. For example, an individual who receives sickness benefit for the whole of a contribution week is excepted from Class 2 liability for that contribution week. A full list is available at SI 2001/1004, reg. 43.

Law: SSCBA 1992, s. 11; SI 2001/1004

Registration and payment

When a self-employed individual registers for self-assessment with HMRC (see **15.12**), the registration process covers both income tax and NIC (both Class 2 and Class 4).

Typically, an individual will pay Class 2 NIC through the self-assessment system. The liability is not paid on account but should instead be paid in full by 31 January following the tax year end. (The alternative is to set up an arrangement with HMRC to pay through the year.)

An individual with earnings below the Class 2 small profits threshold may still pay voluntary Class 2 contributions in order to preserve entitlement to certain benefits, including the state pension.

15.11.2 *Class 4*

Class 4 NIC is generally payable by self-employed earners carrying on a trade, profession or vocation who are aged between 16 and the state pension age.

Class 4 NIC becomes payable once an individual's trading profits exceed the lower profits limit (£9,568 for 2021-22). See **Appendix 7** for rates and thresholds.

Law: SSCBA 1992, s. 15-18

Payment

An individual making payments on account of income tax (see **Chapter 3**) will pay Class 4 NIC in the same way (i.e. on account).

Where an individual does not make payments on account, the Class 4 NIC liability is payable in full by 31 January following the end of the relevant tax year.

Trading losses

Sometimes, an income tax loss may be set against income that is not liable for Class 4 NIC (for example, employment income). Where this occurs, relief has not been given for Class 4 NIC purposes.

That portion of unused loss (for Class 4 NIC purposes) can be carried forward against Class 4 NIC profits of the same trade. An example is available at **17.2.8**.

Law: SSCBA 1992, Sch. 2, para. 3

15.11.3 Annual maximum

A person who is both employed and self-employed may be liable for Class 1 NIC, as well as Class 2 and Class 4 NIC. There is an annual maximum to which an individual is liable in a tax year.

Law: SI 2001/1004, reg. 21, 100

15.11.4 Class 3

Individuals who have gaps in their contributions record may decide to pay Class 3 voluntary contributions, in order to qualify for certain benefits such as the state pension.

For 2021-22, there is a flat rate of £15.40 a week. See HMRC tables at https://tinyurl.com/ptbzeg8 and https://tinyurl.com/yyjab62j for guidance on choosing between Class 2 or Class 3 voluntary contributions in appropriate cases.

15.12 Registration and administration

A sole trader who needs to file a self-assessment tax return but did not submit one for the previous tax year (for example, a sole trader who has commenced trading) should register for self-assessment and NIC with HMRC.

The deadline for registration is the 5 October following the end of the tax year in which the trade begins.

Example

Brenda commences trading on 30 January 2022. She should register for self-assessment by 5 October 2022.

Sole traders can register for self-assessment through form CWF1. The form is filled in on screen and can then be printed and posted to HMRC.

Form CWF1 should not be used, however, where a partner or partnership needs to register for self-assessment, nor should it be used to register a director. Information on how to register a partner or partnership for self-assessment is provided at **16.11**.

There are penalties for failure to notify. For details, and for other matters relating to administration and compliance, see **Chapter 2**.

15.13 Pitfalls and planning points

Choice of business structure

A taxpayer generally chooses to operate as a sole trader, a partner in partnership, or through a limited company. The decision is dependent on a number of factors, including the importance of limited liability, and administration and compliance considerations, as well as tax differences. See **Chapter 16** for further information on the taxation of partnerships.

Is there a trade?

Income tax is charged on the profits of a trade, profession or vocation. Although in many cases it is obvious when an activity amounts to a trade, it is not always so clear cut. The badges of trade can be used to determine whether a trade is being carried on (see **15.2.1**).

Adjustment to profits – general

As a guiding principle, capital receipts and expenses are not taxable/deductible when calculating trading profits (see **15.7.3**). Similarly, business expenses are not deductible unless they meet the "wholly and exclusively" test (see **15.7.6**). See **15.7** generally for other statutory provisions.

Adjustment to profits – private use

If an expense has a private use element, remember that a business owner's private use of an expense/asset should be adjusted for when calculating taxable profits. However, expenses paid by a business relating to an employee's private use are not adjusted (i.e. they are allowable as a deduction in full). This is because the employee usually ends up with a taxable benefit on the expense. See **15.7.7** and **Chapters 6-8** for further information on the taxation of employees.

Basis periods

The profits of a trade, profession, or vocation are taxed as they arise in a basis period for a given tax year. How a basis period is determined depends on whether the business is in its opening years of trade (see **15.4.2**), is established (see **15.4.3**) or is in its closing year (**15.4.4**). Adjustments to basis periods may also be required where there is a change in accounting date (see **15.6**).

Overlap profits

Unless a business has always prepared its accounts to 5 April, there will be some form of overlap profit. Overlap relief is available in the final tax year of a business, or may be available on a change in accounting date. See **15.5** for further information.

Cash basis

Smaller businesses may wish to calculate their taxable profits using the cash basis (i.e. by reference to when income is received and expenses paid). Businesses using the cash basis are subject to slightly different rules when it comes to bringing capital receipts and expenses into account – see **15.9** for further information.

National Insurance contributions

Where an individual is both employed and self-employed, or has more than one employment, the amount of NIC to be paid may be capped (see **15.11**).

16. Partnerships

16.1   Introduction

The *Partnership Act* 1890 defines a partnership as:

> "the relation which subsists between persons carrying on a business in common with a view of profit."

A business, for the purposes of determining if a partnership exists, is widely defined, and includes "every trade, occupation or profession".

As the definition of "business" is so broad, it also includes the business of making investments, provided there is sufficient organisation and continuity.

There are few restrictions on who can be a partner, meaning that in practice partners in a partnership include individuals, bodies corporate, and even limited liability partnerships (LLPs) (see **16.10**). There is no maximum limit on the number of partners there can be in a partnership.

Law: PA 1890, s. 1(1), 45
Guidance: PM 120100

16.1.1   *When is there a partnership?*

The question of whether a partnership exists is one of fact, based on all available evidence. No single factor is likely to be conclusive on its own.

The mere existence of a partnership deed, or the assertion that there is a partnership, is not sufficient in itself to give rise to a partnership, unless there is other supporting evidence.

Case law

In *Williamson*, a father and his sons worked a farm. There was no partnership deed, no evidence that profits were shared, and the father conducted all financial arrangements. The court decided there was not a partnership.

In *Fenston v Johnstone*, an agreement for the joint purchase and development of land stated that it did not constitute a partnership.

Despite this, it was held to be one on a proper construction of the agreement between the parties.

Cases: *CIR v Williamson* (1928) 14 TC 335; *Fenston v Johnstone* (1940) 23 TC 29

16.1.2   When does a partnership start to exist?

HMRC's *Partnership Manual* at PM 134100 states that:

> "A partnership may exist without a written agreement, on the basis that a later written agreement gives formal expression to an oral agreement already existing. The date of the formation of the partnership remains the date on which the terms of the oral agreement were implemented.
>
> Where, however, a written agreement creates a partnership where none exists already, it is effective only from the date of execution and implementation of the written agreement. It has no retrospective effect."

Law: PA 1890, s. 2
Guidance: PM 133000, 134100

16.2   Types of partnership

There are several types of partnership, including general partnerships, limited partnerships, and limited liability partnerships (LLPs). A brief overview is provided below.

16.2.1   General partnerships

In a general partnership, all partners are general partners (see **16.3.1**) and have unlimited liability for the debts of the partnership.

General partnerships are governed by PA 1890.

16.2.2   Husband and wife partnerships

Sometimes, spouses (or civil partners) may set up in partnership.

There are many reasons why a couple may choose to do this: they may be in business together, or a partnership may have been created as a tax-effective vehicle for profit sharing. In certain situations, HMRC consider that the settlements legislation (see **41.7**) applies to such partnerships, with the result that the profits transferred to one partner continue to be assessed on the other.

In particular, regard should be had to the settlements legislation where there is an arrangement under which the property received by one spouse or civil partner is wholly or mainly a right to income.

HMRC provide an example, in the *Trusts, Settlements and Estates Manual* at TSEM 4215, of when they believe the settlements legislation applies:

HMRC example

Mr Y, an architect, commences business as a sole trader. The business is successful and a few years later annual profits are in the region of £80,000. The business is transferred to a new partnership of Mr and Mrs Y. A deed is executed under which income profits are to be shared equally but the rights to share in capital profits belong solely to Mr Y.

Mrs Y subscribes no new capital and carries out no work whatsoever for the partnership, that is to say she is a sleeping partner. Profits for the year are £80,000 and £40,000 belongs to Mrs Y. This is a bounteous arrangement transferring income from one spouse to another. The settlements legislation will apply, and Mrs Y's share of the profits will continue to be assessed on Mr Y.

Guidance: BIM 82065; TSEM 4215

16.2.3 Limited partnerships

In a limited partnership, at least one partner is a limited partner (see **16.3.3**) and has limited liability for the debts and obligations of the partnership.

A limited partnership must also have at least one general partner who manages the partnership business (see **16.3.1**) and who has no limited liability.

Limited partnerships are governed by the *Limited Partnership Act* (LPA) 1907 and are also subject to the *Partnership Act* 1890 and general partnership law (except where LPA 1907 takes precedence).

Limited partnerships must be registered at Companies House.

Guidance: PM 131200, 131310

16.2.4 Limited liability partnership

A member of an LLP has his liability for the partnership's debts limited to the extent of his capital contribution.

However, a member of an LLP is able to take part in the management of the partnership business (in contrast to limited partners in a limited partnership).

LLPs are governed by the *Limited Liability Partnerships Act* 2000. An LLP must be registered at Companies House and must have at least two designated members.

LLPs are discussed in greater detail at **16.10**.

Guidance: PM 131200

16.2.5   Mixed-member partnerships

A mixed-member partnership is a partnership (including an LLP) that has both:

- individual partners or members; and
- persons that are not individuals (e.g. a company) as partners or members.

There are specific anti-avoidance provisions in place for mixed-member partnerships to prevent allocations of profits or losses that reduce the tax liabilities of individual partners/members.

Broadly summarised, the excess profit allocation rules prevent profits from being diverted by an individual member to a non-individual member, e.g. to a company, in order to reduce tax on the individual's profit share. The excess loss allocation rules prevent losses being claimed by an individual member instead of a non-individual.

The specific legislative provisions are detailed in FA 2014, Sch. 17.

For a recent case concerning profit-sharing arrangements involving a mixed-member partnership, see *HFFX LLP & Ors*, in which individual members of an LLP were held to be liable to income tax on amounts reallocated to them by a corporate partner.

Law: FA 2014, Sch. 17, Pt. 2
Case: *HFFX LLP & Ors* [2021] UKFTT 36 (TC)

16.2.6   Scottish partnerships

A Scottish partnership is considered a legal person (PA 1890, s. 4(2)). This stands in contrast to English, Welsh or Northern Irish general or limited partnerships.

In practice, this has very few consequences for tax purposes. For income tax purposes, ITTOIA 2005, s. 848 directs that, unless otherwise indicated, a partnership is not regarded as an entity separate and distinct from the partners (see **16.4**). This principle applies even where the partnership is a Scottish partnership.

Law: PA 1890, s. 4(2); ITTOIA 2005, s. 848
Guidance: PM 131700

16.3   Types of partner

An overview of different types of partner is provided below.

16.3.1   General partner

A general partner is liable jointly with the other partners (and in Scotland, also severally liable), for all debts and obligations of the partnership incurred while a partner.

Law: PA 1890, s. 9

16.3.2   Indirect partner

Where a partnership has its own legal identity (e.g. an LLP or Scottish partnership) it is possible for that partnership to be a partner in another partnership.

A partner in a partnership that is itself a partner in another partnership is an indirect partner.

A person can also be an indirect partner in a partnership if the person is a partner in:

- a partnership that is a partner in the underlying partnership; or
- any partnership that is an indirect partner in the underlying partnership.

HMRC provide an example of an indirect partner at PM 132100:

HMRC example

Partnership A allocates profits to partnership B, and partnership B then allocates profits to Person C.

Partnership B is a partner in partnership A. Person C is a partner in partnership B. Person C is therefore also an indirect partner in partnership A.

Guidance: PM 132100

16.3.3   Limited partner

A limited partner is a limited member of a limited partnership (see **16.2.3**). A limited partner's liability is typically limited to his or her capital contribution. This contrasts with the position of a general partner, whose liability is unlimited.

To preserve his or her limited liability, a limited partner must not take part in the management of the partnership's business, nor may he or she bind the partnership, e.g. by entering into contracts on its behalf.

Limited partners are also subject to further restrictions when it comes to loss relief – see **Chapter 17**.

Law: LPA 1907, s. 4
Guidance: PM 131310

16.3.4   Nominated partner

A nominated partner is the partner responsible for managing the partnership's tax return, i.e. submitting the return to HMRC and dealing with matters that may arise from an HMRC enquiry into the return. The nominated partner is also responsible for the partnership's record-keeping.

16.3.5   Salaried partner

A salaried partner can either be a genuine partner, who has entitlement to the first share of partnership profits, or (depending on the facts) an employee to whom the title of partner is conferred for prestige and in name only.

There are specific anti-avoidance provisions for LLPs (the salaried member rules – see **16.10.2**) to determine whether a member of an LLP is a genuine partner or a partner in name only.

16.3.6   Sleeping partner

Although not a legal concept, a sleeping partner is one who plays no active part in the partnership, but who has contributed capital and who shares in the partnership's profits and losses.

16.4 Transparency

Generally, a partnership (including an LLP) is considered "transparent" for income tax purposes.

In other words, the vast majority of partnerships are not regarded as a separate entity for income tax purposes but are instead "looked through" to the partners in the partnership.

This means that the partnership itself has no tax liability. Instead, the partnership's profits (or losses) are computed at the partnership level and then allocated to the partners. Each partner then pays tax on his or her own allocation of partnership profits.

Sometimes the transparency of partnerships is exploited in a bid to obtain a tax advantage. In *First De Sales*, three LLPs and one LP made significant payments for millions of pounds for which deductions were claimed under ITTOIA 2005, s. 69 and CTA 2009, s. 69 (in each case, payments for restrictive undertakings). This generated losses that could be allocated to the partnerships' members. HMRC determined that the payments were not deductible – a conclusion also reached by the FTT in striking out the appeals.

Law: ITTOIA 2005, s. 69, 848; CTA 2009, s. 69
Case: *The First De Sales Limited Partnership & Ors* [2018] UKFTT 106 (TC)
Guidance: PM 136000

16.5 Partnership computations

16.5.1 Profit-sharing ratios

A partnership's profit-sharing arrangements are relevant when computing the liability to tax of each of the partners on their share of partnership profit.

The default position is that profits and losses of a partnership are shared between partners equally. PA 1890, s. 24 states that "all the partners are entitled to share equally in the capital and profits of the business, and must contribute equally towards the losses [...] sustained by the firm".

However, and more commonly, profits and losses are shared between the partners as they mutually agree. Furthermore, the agreed-upon profit-sharing ratio does not need to be in proportion to the partners' contributions of effort or capital.

Law: PA 1890, s. 19, 24
Guidance: PM 137000

16.5.2   *Computing partnership profits*

A partnership itself has no tax liability. Instead, profits are allocated to and paid by the partnership's partners in accordance with the partnership's profit-sharing arrangements.

To determine how much profit or loss to allocate to a partner for an accounting period, it is first necessary to compute the profit or loss of the partnership at the partnership level.

Basis of computation

Broadly, there are three steps to be taken when allocating taxable trading profits or losses of a partnership to a partner.

HMRC summarises these steps at PM 163070 as:

- Ascertain the profit of the trade computed in accordance with generally accepted accounting practice (GAAP).
- Adjust the accounting profit in accordance with any specific tax rules applicable, under income tax provisions for individuals and company tax provisions for companies, giving effect to any claims or elections made.
- Allocate a share of the adjusted profits to the partners in accordance with the profit-sharing arrangements during the accounting period.

These three steps are considered in detail below.

Step 1 – Ascertain the profit of the trade in accordance with GAAP

ITA 2007, s. 997 defines "generally accepted accounting practice" as UK generally accepted accounting practice or, in the case of entities that prepare IAS (International Accounting Standards) accounts, generally accepted accounting practice in relation to IAS accounts.

Step 2 – Adjust accounting profits for tax purposes

Where a partner within a trading partnership is chargeable to income tax, the profits or losses of the partnership's trade are calculated under income tax principles, i.e. adjustments as needed are made to trading income and expenses, including any adjustments for capital allowances.

These adjustments are discussed in **Chapter 15** and broadly apply to partnerships as they do to sole traders.

Any "salary" drawn by a partner is not treated as a deduction when computing the overall profit or loss of the partnership. Instead, such amounts are treated as allocations of profits to the partners, and are considered in Step 3 below.

Resident and non-resident partners

When preparing the partnership tax computation, regard needs to be had to the tax residence of the partners.

ITTOIA 2005, s. 849 provides that where the partner is a UK resident individual, the profits or losses of the trade should be calculated as if the partnership were a UK resident individual.

However, not all partners in a partnership may be UK resident individuals; there may be corporate partners, and/or non-UK resident partners. In such cases, additional partnership computations are required.

A partnership with a corporate partner (such as a mixed-member partnership) should also prepare a partnership computation under corporation tax principles, while partnerships with partners who are non-UK resident individuals/companies should prepare additional computations as if the partnership were a non-UK resident individual/company as applicable.

A brief example is provided in PM 163030, and is re-created below.

HMRC example (adapted)

Mr Armstrong, a UK resident, and Mrs Beeton, a non-resident, are in partnership. The partnership's worldwide trade profits amount to £10,000 and included in that sum is its UK profit of £7,500. Partnership profits are shared equally. Two tax computations are required, as follows:

Computation for resident partner

			£
Step 1	Trade profits		10,000
Step 2	Allocation	Mr Armstrong	5,000
		Mrs Beeton	5,000
Step 3	Profit taxable on	Mr Armstrong	5,000

Computation for non-resident partner

			£
Step 1	Trade profits		7,500
Step 2	Allocation	Mr Armstrong	3,750
		Mrs Beeton	3,750
Step 3	Profit taxable on	Mrs Beeton	3,750

Step 3 – Allocate the tax adjusted profits to the partners

Once the trading profits/losses of the partnership have been computed for tax purposes, they should be allocated to each partner in the partnership.

How profits are allocated can vary, depending on factors such as changes in profit-sharing ratios, and the existence of notional profit or loss allocations.

Further detail on partnership allocations is provided at **16.6**.

Law: ITTOIA 2005, s. 849, 850; ITA 2007, s. 997
Guidance: PM 163030, 163070

16.6   Allocation of partnership profit to partners

16.6.1   Allocations – general principles

Once the relevant partnership computation has been prepared, the tax-adjusted profit or loss of the partnership is allocated to the partners in accordance with the partnership's profit-sharing arrangements during that period.

It is also possible that a partner will receive a fixed "salary" from a partnership, or interest on a capital account. Such payments are treated as an initial allocation of profit.

A basic example is provided below:

Example

Abigail, Bianca and Claire carry on a business in partnership.

Bianca and Claire are each allocated a salary of £5,000. The remaining profits of the partnership are to be shared equally among the partners.

The partnership makes a profit of £17,500.

The partnership profit allocation is as follows:

	Total £	Abigail £	Bianca £	Claire £
Salary	10,000	Nil	5,000	5,000
Balance	7,500	2,500	2,500	2,500
Total allocation	17,500	2,500	7,500	7,500

Law: ITTOIA 2005, s. 850

16.6.2 Notional trade

For each tax year in which a partnership carries on a trade, each partner's allocation of partnership profit or loss is treated for basis period purposes as though it is a profit or loss of a "notional trade" that is carried on by the partner alone.

For more on basis periods, see **15.4**.

When does a notional trade commence?

A partner is considered to start to carry on a notional trade at the later of:

- becoming a partner in the partnership; and
- when the partnership starts to carry on the actual trade.

If a partner carried on the actual trade alone prior to the partnership commencing the trade, the partner is considered to have commenced the notional trade at the time he or she started to carry on the actual trade.

When does a notional trade cease?

A partner is considered to cease permanently to carry on a notional trade at the earlier of:

- the partner ceasing to be a partner in the partnership; and
- when the partnership permanently ceases to carry on the actual trade.

Where a partner continues to carry on the actual trade alone after the partnership permanently ceases to carry it on, the partner is considered to have permanently ceased to carry on the notional trade at the time he or she permanently ceases to carry on the actual trade.

Law: ITTOIA 2005, s. 852

16.6.3   Basis periods

The usual basis period rules for calculating trading profits and losses (see **15.4**) apply to each partner's notional trade.

In other words, a partner's profits are computed on a current year basis for existing partners, and opening or closing year rules are applied to partners joining or leaving the partnership.

Additionally, a partner's basis period is in line with the accounting period of the partnership, subject to other events changing a basis period (e.g. commencing or ceasing to be a partner).

Law: ITTOIA 2005, s. 853

Change in accounting date

When a partnership changes its accounting date, the underlying principle is that the change of accounting date rules are applied to the partnership as if it were an individual.

See **15.6** for how a change in accounting date affects basis periods.

Law: ITTOIA 2005, s. 214-220
Guidance: PM 163110

16.6.4   Notional losses

In certain circumstances, a partnership may have a trading profit but, due to the nature of the partnership's profit-sharing arrangements, a partner is allocated a loss.

This loss, known as a notional loss, is not recognised for tax purposes. Instead, the loss is reallocated to the other partners in proportion to their own initial allocation of partnership profit.

Example

Amelie, Bertie and Charlie carry on a business in partnership.

Under the partnership agreement, Amelie is entitled to a salary of £5,000, while Bertie is entitled to a salary of £2,500. The remaining profits of the partnership are to be shared equally among the partners.

The partnership makes a profit of £6,750.

The initial profit allocation would look as follows:

| | Total | Amelie | Bertie | Charlie |
	£	£	£	£
Salary	7,500	5,000	2,500	Nil
Balance	(750)	(250)	(250)	(250)
Allocation	6,750	4,750	2,250	(250)

In the above table, Charlie initially has a net loss, despite the fact that the partnership made an overall profit. This notional loss must be reallocated to the other partners who were allocated a profit.

The reallocation is made in proportion to the other partners' initial allocation of partnership profit.

For Amelie, this proportion is: £4,750/(£4,750 + £2,250) = 68%

For Bertie, this proportion is: £2,250/(£4,750 + £2,250) = 32%

The reallocation of the notional loss (and the final allocation to the partners) therefore looks as follows:

| | Total | Amelie | Bertie | Charlie |
	£	£	£	£
Initial allocation	6,750	4,750	2,250	(250)
Reallocation of notional loss		(170)	(80)	250
Revised allocation	6,750	4,580	2,170	Nil

16.6.5   *Notional profits*

In a similar vein to the notional losses discussed at **16.6.4**, it is possible for a partnership to have an overall trading loss but for an individual partner to be allocated a profit because of the nature of the firm's profit-sharing arrangements.

A profit such as this is known as a notional profit, and it is not recognised for tax purposes. Instead, the profit is reallocated to the other partners in proportion to their own initial allocation of partnership loss.

Example

Ava, Billy and Catherine carry on a business in partnership.

Under the partnership agreement, Ava is entitled to a salary of £20,000. The remaining profits/losses of the partnership are to be shared equally among the partners.

The partnership makes a loss of £4,000.

The initial profit allocation would look as follows:

	Total	Ava	Billy	Catherine
	£	£	£	£
Salary	20,000	20,000	Nil	Nil
Balance	(24,000)	(8,000)	(8,000)	(8,000)
Allocation	(4,000)	12,000	(8,000)	(8,000)

In the above table, Ava has an initial profit allocation, despite the fact that the partnership made an overall loss. This notional profit must be reallocated to the other partners who were allocated a loss.

The reallocation is made in proportion to the other partners' initial allocation of partnership loss.

For Billy, this proportion is: £8,000/(£8,000 + £8,000) = 50%

Catherine's proportion is the same (i.e. 50%).

The reallocation of the notional profit (and the final allocation to the partners) therefore looks as follows:

| | Total | Ava | Billy | Catherine |
	£	£	£	£
Initial allocation	(4,000)	12,000	(8,000)	(8,000)
Reallocation of notional loss		(12,000)	6,000	6,000
Revised allocation	(4,000)	Nil	(2,000)	(2,000)

Law: ITTOIA 2005, s. 850A-850B

16.6.6   Excessive allocations

Anti-avoidance legislation is in place to combat excessive partnership profit allocations where a partnership has mixed (i.e. individual and non-individual) members (see **16.2.5** above).

16.7   Types of partnership income

A partnership can derive profits from trading activities, but may also have other sources of income, such as dividends, interest or rental income.

16.7.1   Trading income

Trading income for an accounting period is allocated to partners in accordance with the partnership's profit-sharing arrangements (see **16.6** above).

16.7.2   Non-trading income

Where a trading partnership has other (i.e. non-trading) sources of income, it is necessary to establish whether the income is "taxed" or "untaxed" as this determines the basis period into which the income falls.

Untaxed income

Untaxed income means any income that is *not*:

- income from which income tax has been deducted;
- income from or on which income tax is treated as having been deducted or paid;
- dividends or other distributions of a company chargeable to income tax under ITTOIA 2005, Pt. 4, Ch. 3;

- stock dividends from UK resident companies; or
- income related to the release of a loan to a participator in a close company.

Where a partnership receives untaxed income, each partner's share of the untaxed income is effectively treated as income from a notional business, carried on in parallel to the partner's notional trade.

A partner starts to carry on a notional business at the later of becoming a partner in the partnership, and when the partnership starts to carry on a trade.

This notional business is deemed to continue, even if separate sources of income that comprise the business start and cease, and/or if no income arises during a particular tax year.

However, this does not apply if a partner ceases to be a partner in the partnership, or (if earlier) the partnership permanently ceases to carry on a trade. In such cases, the notional business is also deemed to cease.

The effect of these provisions is that, in most instances, a partner's share of untaxed income is charged to tax using the same basis period as the partner's trading income.

Law: ITTOIA 2005, s. 854

Taxed income

Taxed income is computed and allocated to partners in accordance with the partnership's profit-sharing arrangements (as with ordinary trading income).

However, taxed income is not assessed by reference to basis periods. Instead, it is assessed on an actual tax year basis (i.e. 6 April to 5 April), effectively treating the income as though it arose to the partner from a personal source and not from the partnership.

HMRC's *Partnership Manual* states:

> "This rule only applies to taxed income other than trading income. It does not apply to any form of trading receipt that may have tax deducted at source (for example, income which has suffered tax under the Construction Industry Scheme). Credit for the tax deducted from such a trading receipt is given for the tax year in which it is deducted."

Guidance: PM 163520

16.7.3 Partnerships with investment business

Where a partnership does not carry on a trade or profession, the income generated from an investment business is first calculated as if the partnership were an individual, before being allocated to the partners in accordance with the partnership's profit-sharing arrangements.

However, there are no special basis period rules for any such shares of income. Instead, a tax-year (6 April to 5 April) basis of assessment applies.

Law: ITTOIA 2005, s. 847, 849, 850
Guidance: PM 163130

16.8 Capital gains

The CGT position of partnerships is outlined in TCGA 1992, s. 59, with provisions relating to LLPs provided at s. 59A.

Broadly, chargeable gains arising on the disposal of a partnership asset are assessed and charged on each partner separately. This upholds the transparency principle of partnerships, as the partnership itself does not pay CGT.

For further details, see *Capital Gains Tax* or *Taxation of Partnerships*, both available from Claritax Books.

Law: TCGA 1992, s. 59, 59A

16.9 Partnership changes

16.9.1 Changes to profit-sharing ratio

A partnership may decide to change its profit-sharing ratio. This may be as a result of a partner leaving or joining the partnership, or simply because the partners feel that a change in profit-sharing arrangements is needed.

For tax purposes, a change in partnership profit-sharing arrangements has an impact on how the profits of the partnership are allocated, particularly where the change takes place during an accounting period.

Where a change occurs part way through an accounting period, the computation of partnership profits should be split into two parts, with the break at the date of change. If there are several changes, the period will need to be split into further component parts.

In each of these "split" periods, the profits of the partnership are calculated in accordance with the profit-sharing arrangements in force at the relevant time.

Example

Bernie and Bobby are carrying on a business in partnership.

For the year ended 31 July 2021, profits are shared equally to 31 December 2020. Thereafter, profits are agreed to be shared 70/30 between Bernie and Bobby.

Adjusted profits for the year ended 31 July 2021 are £120,000.

When determining how much profit to allocate to each partner, the year should first be broken down into two periods:

- 1 August 2020 to 31 December 2020 (when profits are allocated 50/50); and
- 1 January 2021 to 31 July 2021 (when profits are allocated 70/30).

Period one (1 August 2020 – 31 December 2020)

	Total	Bernie	Bobby
	£	£	£
Profit (£120k x 5/12)	50,000		
Allocation (50/50)	50,000	25,000	25,000

Period two (1 January 2021 – 31 July 2021)

	Total	Bernie	Bobby
	£	£	£
Profit (£120k x 7/12)	70,000		
Allocation (70/30)	70,000	49,000	21,000

Bernie's allocation for the year is £74,000 (£25,000 + £49,000).

Bobby's allocation for the year is £46,000 (£25,000 + £21,000).

16.9.2 Joining a partnership

When a partner joins a partnership, the partner's notional trade is considered to commence from that time (see **16.6.2**).

When allocating partnership profits or losses to a partner who joined during an accounting period, the joining partner should use the opening year rules for basis period purposes to determine his or her taxable profits (and any overlap profit or loss).

See **Chapter 15** for further information on basis periods.

Existing partners in the partnership continue to be allocated profits or losses from the partnership on a current year basis.

An example of how profits would be allocated to partners where the partnership has joiners and/or leavers is provided at **16.9.3**.

Guidance: PM 163160

16.9.3 Leaving a partnership

When a partner leaves a partnership, the partner's notional trade is considered to cease (see **16.6.2**).

When allocating partnership profits or losses to a partner who left during an accounting period, the leaving partner should use the closing year rules for basis period purposes to determine his or her taxable profits (and any overlap relief).

Example – joiners and leavers in a partnership

Alesha and Ben are carrying on a business in partnership and prepare accounts to 31 December. They agree to share profits equally.

On 1 July 2021, Clara is admitted to the partnership, and the profit-sharing ratio is changed to 40% for Alesha, 40% for Ben, and 20% for Clara.

On 1 October 2021, Ben leaves the partnership. Alesha and Clara agree to share profits, with 60% to Alesha and 40% to Clara.

The adjusted profit for the year to 31 December 2021 is £100,000.

When determining how much profit to allocate to each partner, the year should first be broken down into three periods:

- 1 January 2021 to 30 June 2021 (before Clara's admission to the partnership);
- 1 July 2021 to 30 September 2021 (between Clara's admission and Ben leaving); and
- 1 October 2021 to 31 December 2021 (after Ben's departure).

Period one (1 January 2021 – 30 June 2021)

	Total £	Alesha £	Ben £
Profit (£100k x 6/12)	50,000		
Allocation (50/50)	50,000	25,000	25,000

Period two (1 July 2021 – 30 September 2021)

	Total £	Alesha £	Ben £	Clara £
Profit (£100k x 3/12)	25,000			
Allocation (40/40/20)	25,000	10,000	10,000	5,000

Period three (1 October 2021 – 31 December 2021)

	Total £	Alesha £	Clara £
Profit (£100k x 3/12)	25,000		
Allocation (60/40)	25,000	15,000	10,000

Allocate profits

For the year ended 31 December 2021:

Alesha is allocated profits of £50,000 (£25,000 + £10,000 + £15,000).

Ben is allocated profits of £35,000 (£25,000 + £10,000).

Clara is allocated profits of £15,000 (£5,000 + £10,000).

Basis periods

Alesha was a partner in the partnership for the full year and is taxed on a current year basis.

Ben left the partnership during the year. He is subject to the closing year rules, and his final tax year will be 2021-22. Overlap relief is available if Ben has any overlap profit brought forward.

Clara joined the partnership during the year. She is subject to the opening year rules.

Guidance: PM 163160

16.9.4   *Effect of changing partners on partnership*

Typically, when a partner joins or leave a partnership, but there is at least one continuing partner, the partnership business is deemed to continue (i.e. the business itself does not commence or cease every time there is a change in partner). This is provided that the partnership carries on the same business before and after the change.

However, when there is a complete change in the ownership of the partnership's business, the business is deemed to have ceased and then recommenced.

16.10   Limited liability partnerships

16.10.1 *Basic principles*

An LLP is effectively an entity subject to a mix of corporation tax and income tax principles.

Under general law, an LLP is considered a body corporate, meaning that it has a legal personality that is distinct from its members. LLPs are governed by the *Limited Liability Partnerships Act* (LLPA) 2000.

However, for tax purposes, an LLP is usually treated as a transparent partnership, meaning that the members are subject to income tax/corporation tax (as appropriate) on their allocations from the LLP, as they would be if they were partners in a general partnership.

When an LLP is opaque

There are some exceptions to the general principle that an LLP is treated as transparent for tax purposes.

If an LLP is being wound up and the period of the winding-up is not unreasonably prolonged, and does not involve the avoidance of tax, the LLP can continue to be regarded as transparent (i.e. as a partnership). This is also the case where an LLP only temporarily ceases to trade.

However, where an LLP does not carry on a business with a view to profit, or is in liquidation or is being wound up by the order of the court, the LLP is not treated as transparent. Instead, it is considered a body corporate and so subject to corporation tax, which is payable by the LLP rather than by the partners.

Law: ITTOIA 2005, s. 863; CTA 2009, s. 1273

16.10.2 Salaried member rules

FA 2014 introduced anti-avoidance legislation, the "salaried member rules", that applies only to LLPs formed under LLPA 2000.

The legislation is designed to combat members of LLPs, if effectively engaged on similar terms to an employee, from being taxed as a partner.

For the salaried member rules to apply, an individual member must meet all three conditions stipulated by the legislation. In other words, if an individual LLP member fails at least one of the conditions, the salaried member rules will not apply.

The conditions are broadly as follows:

Condition A (disguised salary)

Condition A is met where it is reasonable to expect that at least 80% of the total amount payable by the LLP for the member's services in his or her capacity as a member of the LLP will be "disguised salary".

An amount is "disguised salary" if it:

- is fixed;
- is variable, but is varied without reference to the overall amount of the profits or losses of the LLP; or
- is not, in practice, affected by the overall amount of those profits or losses.

Condition B (significant influence)

Condition B is met where the mutual rights and duties of the members and the LLP do not give the member significant influence over the affairs of the LLP.

Condition C (capital contribution)

Condition C is met where, at the relevant time, the member's contribution to the LLP is less than 25% of the disguised salary that it is reasonable to expect will be payable by the LLP in respect of the member's performance during the relevant tax year.

Where the legislation applies, an individual member of an LLP will be treated as an employee for tax purposes, instead of being taxed as a member of the partnership. The LLP will have to account for PAYE and Class 1 NIC on amounts paid or credited to the member.

The salaried member rules only apply to the taxation of LLP members – they are separate from employment law, and so falling foul of them does not confer the associated benefits of genuine employment.

Law: FA 2014, Sch. 17, Pt. 1
Guidance: PM 250000*ff.*

16.10.3 General partnership becomes an LLP

There are tax implications if a general partnership converts to an LLP.

For income tax purposes, where an LLP succeeds to the business carried on by the old partnership, and a partner becomes a member of the LLP, his or her notional trade is deemed to continue. This means that losses can be carried forward by the partner for offset against future allocations of profits from the LLP, and terminal loss relief may also be available for a member of the LLP in respect of profits accrued to the member while still a member of the old partnership. Entitlement to overlap relief is also retained by each partner.

For CGT purposes, the transfer of a business from a general partnership to an LLP does not amount to a disposal by the partners of their interests in the original partnership's assets, unless their fractional interests in partnership assets are changed as a result of the transfer.

A few further practical points:

- **Self-assessment.** The LLP will be issued its own self-assessment record, with a new unique taxpayer reference

(UTR) number. The nominated partner of the LLP should contact HMRC to advise whether the LLP intends to use the new UTR, or whether it will continue to use the UTR assigned to the old partnership.

- **PAYE.** The PAYE succession rules may apply where the old partnership and new LLP agree that the PAYE scheme can continue, with the new LLP taking responsibility for the operation of the scheme. In the alternative, the new LLP is considered to commence a new PAYE scheme, meaning the old partnership ceases its PAYE scheme and issues forms P45 to all employees.

Note that there are also VAT implications on the transfer of a business from a general partnership to an LLP.

Guidance: PAYE 30045; PM 131430, 131530

16.11   Partnership self-assessment

16.11.1   Registration

Registering a general partnership

The individual partners of a general partnership, and also the general partnership itself, should register for self-assessment. Each partner must register for self-assessment and NIC separately.

The nominated partner must register a new general partnership for self-assessment by 5 October in the partnership's second tax year. This is achieved by completing form SA400.

Example

A partnership commenced during the 2021-22 tax year. The partnership should register for self-assessment on or before 5 October 2022.

Registering a limited partnership or LLP

The process for registering a limited partnership or an LLP is slightly different.

A new limited partnership or LLP will be automatically registered for self-assessment with HMRC from the information already provided as part of its registration with Companies House.

Registering individual partners

When an individual becomes a partner in a partnership, form SA401 is used to register that individual partner for self-assessment and Class 2 NIC. Form SA402 is available for non-individuals (e.g. a company that is a partner in a partnership).

Each partner (including partners in a limited partnership or LLP) must complete a separate form SA401 or SA402, as applicable. This applies even if a partner already sends in tax returns and is registered for self-assessment in his or her own right.

Failure to register on time can attract penalties under the "failure to notify" regime (see **Chapter 2**).

16.11.2 Reporting obligations

The profits or losses of a partnership are reported to HMRC in two ways: through a partnership tax return and through each partner's own tax return. Each is considered in turn below.

Partnership tax return (SA800)

Although a partnership is transparent (i.e. it has no tax liability itself), it is still required to file a partnership tax return (SA800) along with any supplementary pages, as required.

The partnership tax return should contain a partnership statement that shows the total profits or losses for each period of account ending in the return period, as well as each partner's share of that profit or loss.

Generally, the filing deadline for the partnership tax return is 31 October following the tax year end (for paper returns) and 31 January following the tax year end (for online returns).

Different deadlines are in place for partnerships with corporate or mixed membership: a summary can be found in *Self Assessment: the legal framework* at SALF 503.

The partnership tax return should be filled in and signed by either:

- a specific partner (where the partnership tax return has been issued with that partner's name); or
- the nominated partner.

If the partners cannot decide who should be the nominated partner, a request can be made for HMRC to nominate a partner.

Penalties

Where a partnership tax return is not submitted to HMRC by the filing deadline, late filing penalties may apply:

- An initial fixed £100 penalty is charged to each relevant partner.
- Three months after the filing deadline, daily penalties of £10 are charged to each relevant partner for a period of up to 90 days (or until the return is filed).
- Six months after the filing deadline, each relevant partner is subject to a £300 penalty.
- Where the failure continues 12 months after the filing deadline, a further £300 penalty is charged to each relevant partner.

A relevant partner is "a person who was a partner at any time during the period for which the return was made or is required, or the personal representatives of such a person".

For the avoidance of doubt, note that *all* partners are charged a late filing penalty, not just the nominated partner. Furthermore, additional penalties may arise if the partners' individual returns are made late as a result of a delay at the partnership level.

Enquiries

An enquiry into a partnership statement automatically extends to the partners' own tax returns. However, this does not mean that the non-partnership aspects of a partner's tax return are automatically under enquiry.

Equally, an enquiry into an individual partner's tax return does not automatically open the partnership return for enquiry.

Further information relating to administrative matters, including record-keeping requirements, can be found at **Chapter 2**.

Law: TMA 1970, s. 12AA, 12AC; FA 2009, Sch. 55
Guidance: SALF 503

Partner's tax return

In addition to the partnership tax return, partners should each report their allocation from the partnership in their own self-assessment tax return (SA100), or corporation tax return (CT600), as applicable.

Within the SA100, an individual partner should report his or her partnership allocation in either supplementary pages SA104S or SA104F.

Supplementary pages SA104S report a short version of a partner's partnership income and can be used where a partner only needs to declare partnership trading income, and interest or alternative finance receipts received after tax was deducted from banks or building societies.

Supplementary pages SA104F report full partnership income and should be used in instances where a partner does not qualify to use the short version (SA104S).

The filing deadline for an SA100 is generally 31 October following the tax year end (for paper returns) and 31 January following the tax year end (for online returns).

Where a partner submits a return to HMRC after the filing deadline, the usual self-assessment late filing penalties may apply (see **Chapter 2**).

Guidance: PM 138000

When a partnership return is not required

There may be some circumstances in which HMRC will agree that a partnership return is not required. This may be the case where, for example, the partnership has no UK resident partners, has no UK source income and gains, and is managed and controlled outside the UK.

Details on how a partnership can request that a partnership return not be filed can be found at PM 287000.

16.12   Transfers of assets or income streams through partnerships

Anti-avoidance legislation counters the use of partnerships to dispose of income streams or assets without triggering a charge to tax on income. The rules apply to both partnerships and LLPs.

Broadly, the legislation applies if the main purpose, or one of the main purposes, of the disposal, or any of the steps by which the disposal is effected, is to secure a tax advantage in relation to the charge to income tax (or corporation tax) on income.

Where the rules apply, the legislation imposes a charge to tax on income on the person making the disposal.

The rules do not apply where a disposal by or through a partnership is from a member to the member's relative.

Law: ITA 2007, Pt. 13, Ch. 5AA, 5D

16.13   Recent changes to partnership taxation

In recent years, legislation has been added to provide greater clarity around how partnerships are taxed. A brief summary is provided below.

Finance Act 2018

The following provisions were added in FA 2018, and apply from the 2018-19 tax year except where indicated to the contrary:

- **Bare trusts.** Where a beneficiary in a bare trust arrangement is entitled absolutely to any income of that bare trust but is not himself a partner in the partnership, he will be subject to the same rules for calculating profits etc. and reporting as actual partners.

- **Indirect partners.** Provisions were introduced to clarify when an indirect partner is considered to carry on or cease a notional trade.

- **Partnership returns including indirect partners.** The provisions ensure that partnerships that are partners in other partnerships have access to the appropriate profit calculations and can complete their own partnership statement correctly.

- **Overseas partners in investment partnerships.** A partner's tax reference number does not need to be included in the partnership return provided that certain specified conditions are met. The provisions apply to returns made after 15 March 2018.

- **Shares of partnership profits.** The amounts allocated to partners in a partnership tax return are now considered final for tax purposes, although there is a mechanism in place for a partner to dispute his or her reported allocation to the tribunal. Note that there is no process in place where a partner wishes to dispute the amount of overall partnership profit/loss for a period.

Law: FA 2018, Sch. 6

Finance Act 2020

FA 2020 included an anti-avoidance provision designed to combat a small minority of LLPs that are used as tax avoidance vehicles to share certain losses among the members who seek to offset them against their personal income in their own tax returns.

The provisions have retrospective and prospective effect, but do not introduce any new obligations or liabilities for taxpayers.

Law: FA 2020, s. 104

16.14 Pitfalls and planning points

Types of partnerships

An LLP is considered a body corporate under general law but is commonly treated as a partnership for tax purposes. A summary of partnership types is provided at **16.2**. For further information on the taxation of LLPs see **16.10**.

Transparency of partnerships

Almost all partnerships, including LLPs, are treated as transparent for tax purposes, with no tax liability for the partnership itself. Instead, the profits or losses of the partnership are taxed at the level of each partner/member (see **16.4**).

Partners' basis periods

For basis period purposes, an individual partner's profits or losses are computed on a current year basis for existing partners, while partners joining or leaving a partnership are subject to opening/closing year rules respectively. See **16.6.3** and **Chapter 15**.

Notional profits and losses

A notional profit or loss is not recognised for tax purposes. Instead, it is reallocated to the other partners in proportion to their own initial allocations from the partnership. See **16.6.4** and **16.6.5**.

17. Losses

17.1 Introduction

In an ideal world, every trade or business would be profit-making. However, the reality can be quite different. This is particularly true when trading circumstances are difficult, as the Covid-19 pandemic has keenly highlighted.

There are a number of trading loss relief provisions available to sole traders and individual partners in partnership, including claims for current year, prior year, and carry-forward relief.

There are also specific provisions governing the availability of trading loss relief when a trade commences or ceases, and when a trade is transferred to a company.

Certain trading loss claims can, subject to restrictions, be used to relieve a taxpayer's general, non-trading income (known as "sideways" loss relief), while other trading losses can only be used to relieve profits of the same trade.

This chapter examines:

- the different trading loss reliefs available;
- the additional loss relief restrictions facing partners in partnership; and
- the specific loss relief provisions applicable to property businesses.

The income tax rules for losses are mostly found in Pt. 4 of ITA 2007, and references in this chapter are to that Act unless otherwise stated.

17.2 Trade loss relief

17.2.1 Early years loss relief

If an individual makes a trading loss in the first four tax years of trade, relief can be claimed under s. 72 (a "s. 72 claim") to deduct the loss from the individual's general net income for the three tax years before the year in which the loss is made.

Put simply, under a s. 72 claim, earlier years take priority over later ones. The loss is first deducted from the individual's net income for the earliest of the three tax years. Any remaining loss is then deducted from the taxpayer's net income for the next tax year, with any remaining loss deducted from the individual's net income for the latest of the three tax years.

Example

In 2018-19, Shanaz started a business, which generated profits in the first few years of trading. However, due to ongoing problems stemming from the Covid-19 pandemic, the business made a loss in the 2021-22 tax year.

Shanaz has the following results over the first few years of trading:

2018-19	2019-20	2020-21	2021-22
£	£	£	£
Profit 5,000	Profit 20,000	Profit 35,000	Loss 35,000

Shanaz has no income other than that generated by her business, except that in 2018-19 she had other income of £5,000.

Under a s. 72 claim, loss relief would be applied as follows:

	2018-19	2019-20	2020-21	2021-22
	£	£	£	£
Trading profit	5,000	20,000	35,000	Nil
Other income	5,000	Nil	Nil	Nil
Loss relief (ITA 2007, s. 72)	(10,000) Applied first	(20,000) Applied second	(5,000) Applied third	N/A
Revised net income	Nil	Nil	30,000	

A s. 72 claim is "all or nothing" – the loss claimed must be used in full, or until all the available net income across the preceding three tax years has been relieved.

Any remaining losses following a s. 72 claim can be used as part of another loss relief claim, such as a s. 64 claim ("sideways" loss relief – see **17.2.2**).

Claims for loss relief under s. 72 or s. 64 can be made in any order. Where claims are made under both sections, the individual should specify which relief is claimed first.

There is no obligation on a taxpayer to make a s. 72 claim (for example, if it would be more advantageous to claim only under s. 64).

Note that a s. 72 claim is also subject to restrictions – see **17.5**.

Break in trade

An individual who carries on a trade may leave it for a period of time and then recommence it at a later date. A new s. 72 claim will not be available when the trade recommences as it is not "first carried on by the individual".

HMRC give the following example at BIM 85050:

> "A builder takes an extended holiday and then recommences; unless the break is regarded as the permanent cessation of the old business and commencement of a new one, relief under ITA 2007, s. 72 will only be due by reference to the original date of commencement."

Law: ITA 2007, s. 72-74
Guidance: BIM 85050

17.2.2   Current year/carry-back claim

An individual who makes a trading loss in a tax year can make a claim under ITA 2007, s. 64 to use the loss against his or her general income (i.e. as sideways loss relief) in three different ways. The loss can be deducted when calculating the individual's net income in:

- the loss-making year (i.e. the current tax year);
- the previous tax year; or
- both the previous and current tax years.

If making a claim for relief for both the loss-making year and the prior year, the claim must specify the tax year for which a deduction is made first.

However, a s. 64 claim may be made for only the prior year, or only the loss-making year, if the trader so chooses.

Again, an individual may choose not to make a s. 64 claim at all if another loss relief claim would be more beneficial.

Although a s. 64 claim is very flexible, it is an "all or nothing" claim – the loss must be used in full in a tax year, or until all the available net income in a specified tax year has been relieved.

In practice, this means that a s. 64 claim may lead to the loss of the individual's personal allowance.

Example

Tom has been trading for several years and makes a loss of £15,000 in the 2021-22 tax year. He has the following sources of income:

	2020-21 £	2021-22 £
Trading profit/loss	20,000	(15,000)
Property income	10,000	10,000

Tom could choose to relieve the loss in 2021-22 in any of the following ways:

- Solely against his property income of £10,000 in 2021-22, leaving £5,000 of loss to carry forward. However, this would simply waste his personal allowance for 2021-22, so he is unlikely to choose this form of relief.
- Solely against his total net income of £30,000 in 2020-21. If this is done, the full £15,000 of loss must be used up, leaving net income of £15,000. No loss would remain to carry forward.
- Against his total net income in both 2020-21 and 2021-22. In this example, if Tom wished to claim for both years, he would need to claim relief for 2021-22 first, wasting his personal allowance for that year. This would leave £5,000 of loss available to set against his net income in 2020-21. After relief for both years is claimed, no loss would remain to carry forward. Again, he is unlikely to choose this option.

Any remaining loss following a s. 64 claim may be used as part of another loss relief claim, for example for relief as an allowable capital loss (see **17.2.3**). Alternatively, the loss can be carried forward under ITA 2007, s. 83 (see **17.2.4**).

Note that a s. 64 claim is also subject to restrictions – see **17.5** below.

Law: ITA 2007, s. 64-65

Break in trade

As announced at Budget 2021, there is a temporary extension to the carry-back of trading losses for trading losses arising in the 2020-21 and 2021-22 tax years.

Such losses can be carried back and set against *profits of the same trade* for three years before the tax year of the loss, rather than the one year carry-back usually available under s. 64. Relief is given in priority to later years first.

In practice, this means that:

- Where a trader claims loss relief against general income under s. 64 for the prior year, the extended loss relief provisions can be used to carry back trading losses, to offset trading profits only, for a further two years.
- Where a trader only claims current-year relief against general income under s. 64, any trading loss carried back under the extension provisions can only be set against trading profits.

The amount of loss in 2020-21 and 2021-22 that an individual can carry back to the earlier two years (Y2 and Y3) is capped at £2 million of loss each year. There is no restriction on the amount of loss that can be relieved against profits of the same trade in the previous year (Y1).

In the 2021-22 tax year, for the extended carry-back to be available, a claim must first have been made under s. 64 to use a trading loss against general income in the current tax year and/or the previous year. A claim for extended loss relief is also available where a trader's loss would have been eligible for s. 64 relief, but no such claim is made as the trader has no income to claim against for either 2021-22 or 2020-21.

The operation and availability of other loss reliefs are unaffected by these provisions.

Law: *Finance Bill* 2021, cl. 18

Guidance: https://tinyurl.com/3affjbtm (Extended loss carry back for businesses)

17.2.3 Relief as an allowable capital loss

An individual who has a remaining trading loss following a s. 64 claim for a tax year (see **17.2.2**) may be able to treat the unused part as an allowable loss for CGT purposes to the extent that there are chargeable gains arising in the year in which the loss is to be relieved.

This loss relief is governed by TCGA 1992, s. 261B and 261C.

The amount of loss that can be claimed under s. 261B is broadly restricted to the lower of:

- the amount of remaining loss available following other loss relief claims (e.g. a s. 64 claim); and

- the "maximum amount", which is the amount on which the individual would be chargeable to CGT for the year of claim, ignoring the annual exempt amount.

In essence, the maximum amount takes into account the taxpayer's net capital gains in the year of the claim, less any capital losses brought forward (or, exceptionally, carried back).

Example – adapted from BIM 85040

A trader has chargeable gains of £100,000 in 2021-22. She returns the following income, losses and gains for 2021-22:

	£
Taxable income	40,000
Trading losses current year	50,000
Chargeable gains	100,000
Allowable capital losses current year	45,000
Capital losses brought forward	40,000
CGT annual exempt amount	12,300

The trader makes a claim under ITA 2007, s. 64 in respect of the current year trading losses. She also makes a claim under TCGA 1992, s. 261B to extend loss relief to chargeable gains.

First, we must determine the amount of remaining loss available once other loss relief claims have been made.

As a s. 64 claim has been made, this means that there is a remaining trading loss of £10,000 (£50,000 - £40,000). This is also known as the "relevant amount".

Secondly, we need to determine whether the £10,000 is limited to the "maximum amount".

In this example, the maximum amount is £15,000 (£100,000 - £45,000 - £40,000).

As the relevant amount of £10,000 is lower than the maximum amount of £15,000, the £10,000 can be treated as an allowable loss in full.

The capital gains computation is as follows:

	£
Chargeable gains	100,000
Capital losses:	
Current year	(45,000)
s. 261B relief	(10,000)
Brought-forward	(32,700)*
Net chargeable gains	12,300
Annual exempt amount	(12,300)
	Nil
Capital losses carried forward	7,300
Trading losses carried forward	Nil

* As this example illustrates, allowable losses brought forward can be restricted to the level of the annual exempt amount by virtue of TCGA 1992, s. 1F.

As is perhaps apparent, claiming loss relief under s. 261B will mean the individual wastes his or her personal allowance in the tax year for which relief is claimed. It is also possible for a s. 261B claim to result in the wastage of an individual's annual exempt amount, although this did not occur in the above example.

Law: TCGA 1992, s. 1F, 261B, 261C; ITA 2007, s. 71
Guidance: BIM 85030, 85040

17.2.4   Losses carried forward

If a trading loss in a tax year remains unrelieved (e.g. trading losses remain following a s. 64 claim (see **17.2.2**) or a trader chooses not to make a loss relief claim) the unrelieved loss can be carried forward under ITA 2007, s. 83.

Losses carried forward under s. 83 can only be deducted from profits arising from the same trade. The loss must be used in the next tax year in which a profit arises, with any balance then used in the next tax year in which a profit arises, and so forth until all the carried-forward loss is extinguished.

In other words, a taxpayer has no choice as to when to offset a carried-forward loss.

Law: ITA 2007, s. 83-84
Guidance: BIM 85060

17.2.5   Terminal loss relief

If an individual permanently ceases trading in a tax year and makes a "terminal loss" (defined below), terminal loss relief can be claimed under ITA 2007, s. 89 (a "s. 89 claim").

Terminal loss relief is deducted from the individual's profits of the same trade in the final tax year, with any remaining loss set against profits of the same trade in the three previous tax years, with later years relieved in priority to the earlier.

Calculating a terminal loss

A terminal loss will rarely be the same as the actual trading loss generated.

The definition of a terminal loss is provided in ITA 2007, s. 90, and the calculation is given at s. 91.

A terminal loss is the sum of:

- the trading loss made in the final tax year up to the cessation of trade, including any unused overlap relief; and
- the trading loss made in the previous tax year, to the extent it falls in the 12 months prior to the cessation of the trade.

Where either of the above parts represents a net profit, that part is taken to be nil for the purposes of calculating a terminal loss.

The example below shows how a terminal loss is calculated.

Example 1 – adapted from BIM 85055

A business which has been in existence for many years has an annual accounting date of 30 September. The business ceases on 30 June 2021. The accounts for the last two years are as follows:

12 months to 30 September 2020: £12,000.

9 months to 30 June 2021: (£9,000).

In addition, there is unused overlap relief of £2,500 to be taken into account. This will augment the loss of the final year, 2021-22.

The taxable profits (before any loss relief) are as follows:

2020-21	2021-22
£	£
12,000	Nil

A s. 89 claim can be made as follows:

Loss of final year (2021-22)	£
Loss for period 6 April to 30 June 2021 (3/9 x £9,000)	3,000
plus overlap relief	2,500
loss for 2021-22	5,500
Loss of the preceding year (2020-21)	
Loss for period 1 July 2020 to 5 April 2021, comprising	
loss from 1 October 2020 to 5 April 2021: (6/9 x £9,000)	6,000
less profit from 1 July to 30 September 2020: (3/12 x £12,000)	(3,000)
Loss for 2020-21	3,000
Total terminal loss under s. 89 = £5,500 + £3,000	**8,500**

As noted above, a terminal loss is unlikely to be the same as the actual trading loss generated.

Example 2 – adapted from BIM 85055 (cont.)

In the above example, the trading loss available to the business in its final accounting period is its trading loss of £9,000 plus the overlap relief of £2,500, a total loss of £11,500.

However, only £8,500 of this loss is available for terminal loss relief.

If the taxpayer elects to make a s. 89 claim, then the remaining £3,000 can be relieved using another form of loss claim (e.g. a s. 64 claim).

As the example above illustrates, a taxpayer can choose to make a terminal loss relief claim as well as a s. 64 claim where any loss remains unrelieved following the first claim.

Terminal loss/s. 64 claims can be made in any order (noting that loss relief under s. 89 is limited to the amount of terminal loss).

There is no obligation on a taxpayer to make a terminal loss claim (for example, if it would be more advantageous to claim only under s. 64).

However, a s. 89 claim is "all or nothing" (i.e. the terminal loss claimed must be used in full, or until all available trading profits across the relevant years have been relieved).

Law: ITA 2007, s. 89-94
Guidance: BIM 85055

17.2.6   Trade transferred to a company

Where an individual, or a partnership comprising solely individual partners, carries on a trade, and that trade is transferred to a company, ITA 2007, s. 86 allows any unrelieved trading loss to be carried forward and set against the income the individual derives from the company. This includes dividends, interest, remuneration and rent received.

To be eligible for relief under s. 86, the trade must have been transferred to a company, and the consideration for the transfer must have been wholly or mainly the allotment of shares.

Additionally, no relief under s. 86 is available for a tax year unless the individual retains all the allocated shares, and the company carries on the transferred trade at 5 April in that year.

BIM 85060 confirms that, in practice, relief should still be available provided the individual keeps shares which represent more than 80% of the consideration received for the business.

Law: ITA 2007, s. 86
Guidance: BIM 85060

17.2.7   Time limit for claims

Relief for trading losses requires a formal claim.

The normal time limits to claim relief for the losses outlined above are as follows:

Claim	Section	Time limit
Trade losses against general income	64	12 months after the 31 January following the loss-making year
Use of trading loss as CGT loss	71 (and TCGA 1992, s. 261B)	12 months after the 31 January following the loss-making year
Early trade losses	72	12 months after the 31 January following the loss-making year
Carry forward of trade losses	83	four years after the end of the year of assessment to which the claim relates
Trade transferred to company	86	four years after the end of the year of assessment to which the claim relates
Terminal trade losses	89	four years after the end of the year of assessment to which the claim relates

For example, a s. 64 claim for relief in respect of a trading loss arising in the 2021-22 tax year should be made by 31 January 2024. And a s. 83 claim to carry forward trading losses arising in that year should be made by 5 April 2026.

Ordinarily, a claim for loss relief is made in the individual's self-assessment tax return or amended return.

However, in certain cases, a standalone claim may be made. An example of when this may happen is a claim to carry forward losses: as the individual has four years after the end of the tax year of loss to claim, it may be the case that the loss is first claimed after the time limit to amend the individual's tax return has passed.

Further information on making a standalone claim can be found at HMRC Helpsheet HS227.

Guidance: BIM 85075; Helpsheet 227: Losses

17.2.8   Class 4 NIC

Schedule 2 of the *Social Security Contributions and Benefits Act* 1992 provides that trading losses are relieved for Class 4 NIC purposes in the same manner as for income tax under ITA 2007, s. 64, 72, 83, 89 and 93.

Sometimes, an income tax loss may be set against income that is not liable to Class 4 NIC (for example, when a trader claims sideways loss relief against employment income, which is liable to Class 1 NIC).

Where this occurs, it means that relief has not been given for Class 4 NIC purposes. That portion of the unused loss (for Class 4 NIC purposes) can be carried forward against Class 4 NIC profits of the same trade.

This can mean that an individual's income tax trading losses carried forward may differ from his or her NIC losses carried forward.

Example

2021-22

Caitlyn has employment income of £15,000 and a trading loss from her own business of £5,000.

Caitlyn claims sideways loss relief for the full £5,000 under s. 64.

For income tax purposes, her loss relief position looks as follows:

	£
Employment income	15,000
Less relief under s. 64	(5,000)
Income tax loss carried forward	0

For Class 4 NIC purposes, however, none of Caitlyn's income is eligible for relief (employment income being subject to Class 1 NIC). The full £5,000 of loss is carried forward.

2022-23

In 2022-23, Caitlyn has trading profits of £20,000, and no other income.

For income tax purposes, Caitlyn is assessable on the full £20,000.

For Class 4 NIC purposes, Caitlyn can offset the £5,000 brought forward from 2021-22. This leaves profits chargeable to Class 4 NIC of £15,000.

Legislation: SSCBA 1992, Sch. 2, para. 3
Guidance: NIM 24610

17.2.9   Summary of main loss reliefs

The following table is adapted from *Tax Losses*, by Katherine Ford, available from Claritax Books.

Relief available against	Guidance	Legislation	Subject to £50k/ 25% cap?	Class 4 relief given?	Time limit to claim
Future profits of same trade (c/fwd)	17.2.4	ITA 2007, s. 83-88	No	Yes	Four years from end of tax year
Net income of tax year of loss and/or previous year (either year first)	17.2.2	ITA 2007, s. 64	Yes	Only if there are other sole trade or partnership profits	12 months from 31 Jan following end of tax year
Capital gains of tax year of loss or previous year (NB must make a s. 64 claim for the same year first)	17.2.3	ITA 2007, s. 71 TCGA 1992, s. 261B, s. 261C	No	No	12 months from 31 Jan following end of tax year

Relief available against (cont.)	Guidance	Legislation	Subject to £50k/ 25% cap?	Class 4 relief given?	Time limit to claim
Net income of three tax years preceding the loss, earliest year first. Applies to losses arising in first four tax years of trading ("early years")	17.2.1	ITA 2007, s. 72-74	Yes	Only if there are other sole trade or partnership profits	12 months from 31 Jan following end of tax year
For losses in final 12 months of trading ("terminal losses"), relief against profits of same trade of tax year of cessation and three previous tax years, against latest years first.	17.2.5	ITA 2007, s. 89-94	No	Yes	Four years from end of tax year
For losses on incorporation, relief against income from the company (remuneration, dividend, interest, rent)	17.2.6	ITA 2007, s. 86	No	No	Four years from end of tax year

17.3   Post-cessation expenses/post-cessation trade relief

17.3.1   Introduction

A deduction is allowed for a loss, expense or debit arising after a trade has ceased, provided the expense would have been deductible had the trade not permanently ceased.

This means that any post-cessation expenses must still meet general deductibility principles, such as the "wholly and exclusively" rule (see **15.7.6**).

No deduction is permitted for any loss, expense or debit arising directly or indirectly from the cessation itself.

Equally, as expenses cannot be double counted, if relief can be given under another provision, then the expense is not a post-cessation expense and no further relief is available.

Law: ITA 2007, s. 96

17.3.2   Order of relief – deduction against post-cessation receipts

A post-cessation expense must first be relieved against post-cessation receipts arising in the same tax year from the same trade.

Where post-cessation expenses are incurred across more than one period, the deduction should be made from post-cessation receipts received in the earlier period in priority to a later period. However, no deduction is available for a period before the expense was incurred.

Exceptionally, no deduction can be made from any amount treated as a post-cessation receipt under ITTOIA 2005, s. 248(4) (debts paid after cessation) or s. 250 (receipts relating to post-cessation expenditure).

17.3.3   Additional relief available

If there are no post-cessation receipts, or excess post-cessation expenses, relief may then be given by way of post-cessation trade relief against total income.

Post-cessation trade relief is available where, after permanently ceasing to trade:

- a person makes a qualifying payment; or
- a qualifying event occurs in relation to a debt owed to the person.

The payment/event must occur within seven years of cessation.

The definitions of "qualifying payment" and "qualifying event" are provided at ITA 2007, s. 97 and 98 respectively.

A claim under s. 96 must be made on or before the first anniversary of the normal self-assessment filing date for the tax year for which the deduction is to be made.

If a person has excess post-cessation expenses after claiming s. 96 relief, he or she may be able to treat the excess as an allowable capital loss to be used against any chargeable gains arising in the tax year.

If excess post-cessation expenses still remain after all the above reliefs are applied, they are carried forward to be deducted from future post-cessation receipts from the same trade.

Similarly, if a person's post-cessation expenses do not meet the criteria for a qualifying payment or qualifying event for post-cessation trade relief, they are also carried forward to be deducted from future post-cessation receipts from the same trade.

For information on pre-trading expenses and post-cessation receipts, see **15.7.2**.

Law: TCGA 1992, s. 261D; ITTOIA 2005, s. 254-255; ITA 2007, s. 96-101
Guidance: BIM 90080, 90090, 90095

17.4   Miscellaneous losses

Relief is available where a loss arises on a transaction that, had it been a profit, would have been chargeable under the relevant provision within ITA 2007, s. 1016 (a "miscellaneous loss").

The list of s. 1016 transactions includes (but is not limited to):

- post-cessation receipts – trades, professions and vocations;
- post-cessation receipts – UK property businesses; and
- royalties and other income from intellectual property.

As HMRC note at BIM 100190:

> "There must have been a possibility of profit. For example, post-cessation expenses are not such a loss even though receipts would be chargeable under the post cessation provisions [...] This is because simply paying an expense is not a transaction which can yield a profit."

Miscellaneous losses can only be used against relevant miscellaneous income chargeable under s. 1016. Any unrelieved losses are carried forward to be used against such future miscellaneous income arising.

Where a miscellaneous loss is made by a partnership, relief is only available against relevant transactions entered into by the partnership.

A claim for miscellaneous loss relief is in two parts:

- First, the taxpayer must claim the quantum of loss within four years after the end of the tax year of loss.
- Second, a separate claim must be made to set the loss against particular income for a tax year. This must be done within four years after the end of the tax year in which the relief is given.

Law: ITA 2007, s. 152-155; 1016
Guidance: BIM 100190

17.5   Loss restrictions

17.5.1   No double counting of trade losses

Trading losses cannot be double counted. Where a loss, or part of a loss, is used, relief cannot be given for the same loss (or same part of the loss) in another claim.

Law: ITA 2007, s. 63

17.5.2   Restriction on relief unless trade is commercial

Trading losses made in a tax year cannot be used to relieve general income under s. 64 unless that trade/profession/vocation is carried on:

- a commercial basis; and
- with a view to the realisation of profit.

There is little statutory guidance as to what amounts to a trade. The question of whether a trade exists is primarily a question of fact (see **15.2**).

BIM 85705 draws from the *Wannell v Rothwell* case, where it was stated that:

> " 'Commercial' is not the same as 'profitable'. We take it to mean, conducted in the way that we would expect a business of the same type to be carried on."

Note that farming and market gardening losses are subject to further restrictions – see **18.2**.

As to whether there is a view to the realisation of profit, s. 66(3) states:

> "If at any time a trade is carried on so as to afford a reasonable expectation of profit, it is treated as carried on at that time with a view to the realisation of profits."

This means that "hobby trades" are at particular risk of not meeting the above tests.

Example – Patel (2015 FTT decision)

The First-tier Tribunal case of *Patel v HMRC* concerned Dipak Patel, a psychiatric social worker who started two separate trades. The first trade "Silver Spice" supplied ingredients and ran cookery workshops. The second trade "Art Sutra" sold art and photographic images of Indian culture. Both trades were conducted alongside his full-time employment.

The FTT found that Mr Patel's real motivation was not profit, but the enjoyment he got from working with people and conveying his passion for cookery and photography. As such, he was not carrying on the trades with a view to the realisation of profit and was not entitled to loss relief under s. 64 for the relevant years.

Early years loss relief under s. 72 is restricted by a slightly different test, namely that the trade should be carried on:

- on a commercial basis; and
- in such a way that profits of the trade could reasonably be expected to be made in the basis period or within a reasonable time afterwards.

There are also additional restrictions where an individual's spouse or civil partner previously carried on the trade – see s. 74(4).

Law: ITA 2007, s. 66, 74

Cases: *Wannell v Rothwell* (1996) 68 TC 719; *Patel v HMRC* [2015] UKFTT 13 (TC)

Guidance: BIM 85705

17.5.3 *Restriction on sideways loss relief*

Claims made under sections 64 (current year/carry-back), 72 (early years loss relief) and 96 (post-cessation trade relief) are subject to limits on the amount of sideways loss relief that may be claimed in a tax year.

The cap is the greater of:

- £50,000; or
- 25% of the taxpayer's adjusted total income for the tax year.

Broadly, adjusted total income is calculated as the taxpayer's total income for the tax year, adding back any payroll giving deductions, but deducting pension contributions. See ITA 2007, s. 24A(8) for the full calculation.

In practice, for loss restriction purposes, adjusted total income is only relevant where an individual's total income exceeds £200,000. If total income is below £200,000, the limit on relief will be £50,000.

The restriction applies to the aggregate of the relevant reliefs claimed for a tax year and is calculated separately for each tax year in which a relief is given effect.

Note that this restriction only applies in respect of sideways loss relief (i.e. relief against non-trade income). It does not apply to trading losses that are used against profits of the same trade.

While a s. 64 loss claim is subject to the above restriction, this restriction does not apply to losses that can be set against capital gains – see **17.2.3**.

Example

Penelope has been in business for a number of years. Her results for the past two years are as follows:

> 2021-22: £105,000 loss

> 2020-21: £60,000 profit

Penelope had property income of £55,000 in the 2021-22 tax year. She had no other income, other than her trading income, in 2020-21.

Penelope decides to claim loss relief under s. 64 for both the prior year and current year, with the current year claim to be made first.

Current year (2021-22)

As Penelope's trading losses exceed £50,000, consideration needs to be given to whether her claim for sideways loss relief must be restricted.

The cap is the greater of:

> £50,000; or

> 25% of Penelope's adjusted total income for the tax year.

25% of Penelope's adjusted total income for 2021-22 is £13,750 (£55,000 x 25%).

In this case, Penelope's sideways loss relief is capped at £50,000.

Penelope's tax position for 2021-22 looks as follows:

	£
Trading income	Nil
Other income	55,000
Less s. 64 loss relief	(50,000)
	5,000
Less: personal allowance	(5,000)
Taxable income	Nil

Penelope's remaining trading loss is £55,000 (£105,000 - £50,000).

Prior year (2020-21)

There are no restrictions on the amount of trading losses that can be used to offset profits of the same trade.

The full £55,000 of remaining trading losses from 2021-22 can therefore be used to offset trading profits in 2020-21.

Penelope's tax position for 2020-21 looks as follows:

	£
Trading income	60,000
Other income	Nil
Less s. 64 loss relief	(55,000)
	5,000
Less: personal allowance	(5,000)
Taxable income	Nil

Law: ITA 2007, s. 24A
Guidance: Helpsheet 204: Losses

17.5.4   *Tax-generated losses*

Where:

- an individual (alone or in partnership) carries on a trade, profession or vocation during a tax year, and makes a loss; and

- that loss arises directly or indirectly in consequence of, or otherwise in connection with, relevant tax avoidance arrangements,

no sideways relief or capital gains relief (see **17.2.3**) may be given.

Law: ITA 2007, s. 74ZA

17.5.5   Trade carried on in non-active capacity

This restriction applies if an individual carries on one or more trades in a non-active capacity and makes a loss in any of those trades (known as an "affected loss"). For loss restrictions for non-active partners, see **17.6.3**.

An individual is considered to carry on a trade in a non-active capacity during a tax year if he or she does not devote a significant amount of time to the trade during the tax year.

"Significant" is considered to be an average of at least 10 hours a week personally engaged in activities of the trade, with those activities carried on on a commercial basis and with a view to profit.

The total amount of the sideways relief and CGT relief available to the individual for all affected losses must not exceed the cap of £25,000 for any tax year. The cap does not apply to losses set against profits of the same trade.

Law: ITA 2007, s. 74A, 74C

17.5.6   Cash basis

If a person makes a trade loss in a tax year, and has elected to be taxed under the cash basis for that tax year, no sideways relief or CGT relief is available in respect of that loss.

Instead, the loss must be carried forward under s. 83 and offset against future profits of the same trade (see **17.2.4**).

Where the trade has ceased and has generated a loss, terminal loss relief under s. 89 is available (see **17.2.5**).

Law: ITA 2007, s. 74E

17.6   Partnership losses

17.6.1   *Overview*

Subject to a few exceptions, all partnerships are treated as transparent for tax purposes. This means that each partner in a partnership is taxable on his or her own allocation of profit or loss from the partnership; the partnership itself has no tax liability. See **Chapter 16** for more information on the taxation of partnerships.

For each tax year in which a partnership carries on a trade, each partner's allocation is treated for basis period purposes as though it is a profit/loss of a "notional trade" that is carried on by the partner alone. See **16.6.2** for more on notional trades and **15.4** and **16.6.3** for coverage of basis periods.

In practice, this means that where a partner is allocated a loss, loss relief is available to the partner much as if he or she were a sole trader (see **17.2**). Partners are responsible for their own loss relief claims.

Generally, when a partner joins a partnership, early years loss relief is available (see **17.2.1**). Similarly, a partner leaving a partnership may be entitled to terminal loss relief (see **17.2.5**). An individual partner can also make current year/carry-back (**17.2.2** and **17.2.3**) and carry-forward claims (**17.2.4**) as appropriate.

Example

Alfie and Bilal have been in partnership for a number of years. In 2021-22, the partnership makes a trading loss of £30,000.

Alfie and Bilal agree to share profits and losses of the partnership equally, meaning that each is allocated a partnership loss of £15,000 for the year.

Bilal has total net income of £30,000 in 2020-21 and property income of £10,000 in 2021-22.

Bilal may wish to claim loss relief under s. 64. Under this section, a taxpayer may claim relief for the prior year only, for the loss-making year only, or a combination of both.

As s. 64 is an "all or nothing" claim, Bilal is better off claiming relief solely for 2020-21, as relief in 2021-22 would waste his personal allowance.

After the s. 64 claim, Bilal's taxable profits for 2020-21 are £15,000 (£30,000 – £15,000). No losses remain to carry forward.

17.6.2   Notional losses

In certain circumstances, a partnership may have a trading profit but, due to the nature of the partnership's profit-sharing arrangements, a partner may be allocated a loss.

This is known as a notional loss, and it is not recognised for tax purposes. For more information see **16.6.4**.

17.6.3   Further partner restrictions on sideways loss relief – overview

Although there are no restrictions for partners when claiming loss relief against income derived from the same trade, there are additional restrictions placed on certain partners as to when sideways loss relief is available (i.e. loss relief against general, non-trade, income). The restrictions apply to:

- limited partners;
- LLP members; and
- non-active members of an LLP or other partnership (but not limited partners).

The following two sections are adapted from *Tax Losses* by Katherine Ford, from Claritax Books.

17.6.4   Restrictions to amount of capital contribution

For an individual partner, the amount of sideways loss relief is limited to the lower of:

- his or her "capital contribution" to the partnership at the end of the basis period for the tax year of the loss; or
- the amount of this loss plus any other sideways or capital gains relief given previously (whilst carrying on this trade or any other trade as a limited partner, LLP member or non-active partner), minus any relief that has been clawed back under s. 792 ITA (see below).

The definition of capital contribution varies slightly depending on whether you are dealing with a limited partner, LLP member or non-active partner, but in essence it means:

- the partner's capital contribution to the firm, at the end of the basis period for the tax year in question. (Loans from a partner to the partnership do not count as capital); *less*

- any amounts withdrawn or received back (unless those have been subject to income tax); *less*
- any "risk-free" capital contributions, where the partner does not personally bear the cost of making that contribution (see SI 2005/2017 and BIM 82655 onwards); *plus*
- any undrawn profits (per the accounts, not the tax-adjusted profits) not yet received in money or money's worth.

For LLP members, the amount of capital withdrawn (per the second bullet immediately above) includes any capital they withdraw in the following five years from the date their capital contribution is calculated. The aim of this is to prevent temporary increases in capital in order to obtain sideways loss relief.

Under ITA 2007, s. 792 (excess sideways relief), an individual partner in any type of partnership, who had previously claimed sideways loss relief and who then reduces his capital contribution, is treated as receiving a sum of miscellaneous (not trading) income, if his cumulative sideways loss relief claims exceed his remaining capital contribution. Losses set against profits of the same trade are not affected by this.

There is also anti-avoidance legislation (ITA 2007, s. 113A) that disregards, for the purposes of this restriction, any capital contribution by a limited partner or non-active partner, if it was made for a "prohibited purpose".

If loss relief has been restricted because of these provisions and the individual makes a further capital contribution in a later tax year, he can set off the unrelieved loss, up to the amount of the additional contribution, against his net income of that later tax year. This is a much better way of getting relief, as usually a loss carried forward can only be used against income of the same trade (ITA 2007, s. 109, 113, and see BIM 82135, 82635).

Example

Bob became a member of XYZ LLP on 1 July 2012 and made a capital contribution of £75,000 at that time. He has always drawn out his share of profits in full. In recent years, the partnership made trading losses which Bob wants to set against his other income. Bob's share of the losses is as follows:

	£
y/e 30 September 2019	(19,000)
y/e 30 September 2020	(36,000)
y/e 30 September 2021	(31,000)

The losses of 2019 and 2020 total £55,000. This is less than his capital contribution of £75,000 so there is no cap on his sideways loss relief under ITA 2007, s. 107. However, if Bob relieved both the 2019 and 2020 losses against his 2019-20 net income, the cap of £50,000/25% of adjusted net income would need to be considered. His sideways relief would be capped at £50,000 unless his adjusted net income was over £200,000, in which case the relief is capped to 25% of the adjusted net income, as that would be higher than £50,000.

For the September 2021 loss, only £20,000 of his capital contribution (£75,000 minus £55,000 of sideways loss relief given for earlier years – assuming the loss relief was not capped at £50,000 by s. 24A) has not been taken into account for sideways loss relief. So the sideways relief for that loss is capped at £20,000. That leaves £11,000 of the 2021 loss to carry forward to use against future trading profits of XYZ LLP, unless Bob makes an additional capital contribution and does not withdraw it within five years.

17.6.5   *The £25,000 cap*

For an individual limited member of a limited partnership or a non-active individual partner, the sideways relief for all trading losses for any tax year is capped at £25,000. The cap does not apply where the trading loss is used against profits of the same trade. Where there is other income in a tax year, any loss is deemed to be relieved against profits of the same trade first. The restriction does not apply either to losses deriving from "qualifying film expenditure" (see BIM 82610) or from Lloyd's underwriting.

Law: ITA 2007, s. 103C
Guidance: BIM 82611; PM 191000

17.7   Property losses

17.7.1   Introduction

When considering property losses for income tax purposes, there are two general principles to bear in mind:

1. Losses made in a property business (UK or overseas) can only be set against profits arising from the same property business.

2. Losses made in a property business (UK or overseas) are automatically carried forward to relieve future profits of the same business. In some cases, losses may also be set against general income.

These two principles are examined in further detail below.

17.7.2   What is a property business?

For loss relief purposes, it is important to keep a separate note of any losses arising in:

- a UK property business;
- an overseas property business; and
- a furnished holiday lettings (FHL) business.

This is because losses from one property business cannot be used against the profits of another.

This is also the case where a taxpayer has another rental business in a different legal capacity. For example, if an individual has let property of his own, and is also a partner in a partnership with a part share in a rental property, losses of his personal rental business cannot be set against his share of the partnership's rental income.

Law: ITA 2007, s. 117-127C
Guidance: PIM 1020, 4210

17.7.3   When does a property business commence?

Typically, a property business begins when letting first commences and it ceases when the last let property is disposed of or starts to be used for some other purpose (see **Chapter 26** for more information).

Knowing when a property business has commenced/ceased is important for loss relief purposes, because losses can only be carried forward and set against future profits of the same property business.

In other words, where one property business ceases and a new property business starts at a later date, any losses left unrelieved at the cessation of the first business cannot be used against profits of the second.

As to the question of whether a property business has temporarily paused or has permanently ceased, HMRC state at PIM 2510:

> "A general rule of thumb for rental businesses is that the old business stops where there is an interval of more than three years and different properties are let in the customer's old and new activities."

Guidance: PIM 2510

17.7.4   Property loss relief

As stated above, the default position is that property business losses are automatically carried forward to be relieved in priority against future profits of the same property business.

However, there are limited circumstances in which a property loss can provide sideways loss relief (i.e. relief against general income), namely when:

- the loss has a "capital allowances connection"; or
- the business has a "relevant agricultural connection".

A loss has a capital allowances connection if, in calculating the loss, the amount of the capital allowances treated as expenses of the business exceeds the amount of any charges under the *Capital Allowances Act 2001* treated as receipts of the business. This ignores any allowances under the structures and buildings regime.

A business has a relevant agricultural connection if it is carried on in relation to land that consists of or includes an agricultural estate, and allowable agricultural expenses deducted in calculating the loss are attributable to the estate.

Unusually, where sideways loss relief is available, the loss can be deducted from the taxpayer's net income for the loss-making year, or for the next tax year. The claim must specify the tax year for which the deduction is to be made.

A claim is "all or nothing", i.e. relief must be given in full up to the amount of the taxpayer's general income, or the amount of loss available for relief (whichever is less).

If there are excess losses after making a claim for one year, a separate claim may be made to set the excess losses against general income for the other year. Remaining losses can be carried forward, in the same way as other property losses.

Claims for property loss relief against general income must be made on or before the first anniversary of the normal self-assessment filing date for the tax year specified in the claim.

Example

Rosa is entitled to make a claim for sideways loss relief for the 2021-22 tax year. She should make her claim by 31 January 2024.

Examples of how sideways loss relief is calculated when the loss includes amounts relating to capital allowances or agricultural expenses are provided in PIM 4228.

No loss carry-back

For the avoidance of doubt, property losses cannot be carried back to relieve property business profits of an earlier year.

Law: ITA 2007, s. 120-124
Guidance: PIM 4220, 4222, 4228

17.7.5   Post-cessation property expenses/relief

Relief for post-cessation property expenses is given in much the same way as the provisions for post-cessation trading expenses (see **17.3**).

Legislation: ITTOIA 2005, s. 349-356; ITA 2007, s. 125-126
Guidance: PIM 3000

17.7.6   Furnished holiday lettings losses

Where a furnished holiday lettings (FHL) business makes a loss, the loss may only be carried forward and used against the profits of the same FHL business arising in a later year.

This means that losses arising in a UK FHL business may only be carried forward against a profit of the same UK FHL business, and a loss in an EEA FHL business can only be carried forward against a profit of the same EEA FHL business. So, if a taxpayer has both a UK FHL and EEA FHL business, losses must be tracked separately.

A loss in an FHL business cannot be used against profits of a non-FHL property business.

It is worth bearing in mind that, originally, the FHL legislation only applied to UK properties. It was extended in 2011 to include European Economic Area (EEA) properties.

It is not yet clear, following the UK's departure from the EU and the end of the transitional period, whether the provisions that extend the FHL regime to EEA properties will be repealed. There are no clauses to do this in *Finance Bill* 2021 (published on 11 March 2021), so for the time being, the *status quo* will continue. For further commentary see **28.1**.

Guidance: PIM 4120

17.7.7   Other property loss restrictions

Uncommercial losses

Where a property is let on uncommercial terms (typically to a family member or close friend, where below market or "peppercorn" rent is charged), then expenses can only be deducted up to the amount of the rent or other receipts generated by the uncommercially let property.

In other words, the "best case" result is that such expenses can be deducted so as to eliminate any taxable profit; if the deductions result in a loss, the loss cannot be carried forward for use in a future year.

If a property is occupied rent-free, it is completely outside the property income regime, as there is no exploitation of the property as a source of rents or other receipts.

PIM 2130 provides further guidance as to the tax treatment of properties that are not let at a commercial rent.

Legislation: ITTOIA 2005, s. 266(1)
Guidance: PIM 2130

Cash basis

If, in a tax year, a person makes a loss in a UK or overseas property business (whether carried on alone or in partnership), and the profits of the business are calculated on the cash basis for the tax year, no sideways loss relief is available.

Legislation: ITTOIA 2005, s. 127BA

Excess loss allocation to partners who are individuals

No loss relief is available if, in a tax year, an individual makes a loss in a UK or overseas property business as a partner in a firm, and his or her loss arises, wholly or partly:

- directly or indirectly in consequence of; or
- otherwise in connection with,

relevant tax avoidance arrangements, as defined.

Legislation: ITA 2007, s. 127BA, 127C

17.8   Pitfalls and planning points

Loss planning

A sole trader or individual partner in partnership has a number of options available when it comes to loss relief, all the more so when a business is starting or ceasing. Multiple computations may be required to see which relief gives the greatest tax benefit (see **17.2**).

Deadlines to claim losses

A trading loss must be claimed, even where it is carried forward under s. 83. However, not all loss claims have the same deadline by which to claim. See **17.2.7** for a summary of the time limits.

Class 4 NIC

Where an income tax loss is used against income that is not liable for Class 4 NIC (e.g. sideways loss relief claimed against employment income) an individual's income tax trading losses carried forward may differ from his or her NIC losses carried forward (see **17.2.8**).

Post-cessation expenses

There is a specific order in which post-cessation expenses can be relieved (see **17.3**).

Sideways loss relief

There are no restrictions on the amount of trading losses that can be used to offset profits of the same trade. However, if an individual claims sideways loss relief (i.e. loss relief against general income), there are certain restrictions on the amount of loss that may be used (see **17.5.3** and **17.5.5**). Individual partners in a partnership may be subject to further sideways loss relief restrictions (see **17.6.3**).

Property losses

For income tax purposes, losses made in a property business can only be used against profits arising from the same property business. Subject to limited exceptions, such losses are automatically carried forward to relieve future profits of the same business.

It is therefore important to keep a separate note of any losses arising in a UK property business, overseas property business, or a UK or overseas FHL business, as losses from one cannot be used against the profits of another (see **17.7**).

18. Farmers and creative artists

18.1   Introduction and key definitions

18.1.1   Farming

Farming is defined in the *Income Tax Act* 2007 as "the occupation of land wholly or mainly for the purposes of husbandry". This includes hop growing. It also includes the breeding and rearing of horses, and the grazing of horses in connection with those activities.

The cultivation of short rotation coppice is regarded as husbandry, not as forestry. Short rotation coppice is defined as:

> "a perennial crop of tree species planted at high density, the stems of which are harvested above ground level at intervals of less than 10 years".

For an activity to be within the definition of farming, the produce of the activity must have some husbandry origin in the land occupied by the person undertaking said activity. This means that intensive enterprises, where livestock are kept entirely separate from the land and fed entirely on purchased feed, are not considered farming under the statutory definition.

Market gardening

The definition of farming does not include market gardening, which itself is defined as "the occupation of land as a garden or nursery for the purpose of growing produce for sale".

Law: ITA 2007, s. 996
Guidance: BIM 55105

18.1.2   Farming trades

Regardless of whether the land is managed on a commercial basis and with a view to profit, farming or market gardening in the UK is treated as the carrying on of a trade or part of a trade for income tax purposes.

Further, all farming in the UK carried on by a person (other than farming carried on as part of another trade) is treated for income tax purposes as one trade.

Farming overseas

The automatic treatment of farming as a trade is restricted to land farmed within the UK.

Where husbandry is conducted on land outside the UK, such activity is not automatically deemed to be a trade. Instead, whether the activity constitutes trading is determined according to ordinary principles.

Market gardening

All market gardening in the UK is treated as the carrying on of a trade or part of a trade. While market gardeners can access the averaging provisions (see **18.1.3**) they are also subject to the rules that may restrict loss relief (see **18.2**).

Law: ITTOIA 2005, s. 9, 859
Guidance: BIM 55051, 62600

18.1.3   Averaging relief for farmers

Farming is an industry where profits can fluctuate markedly from year to year. To counteract this, farmers and market gardeners carrying on their trade in the UK may decide to claim averaging relief, which is designed to "smooth out" profits over a period of either two or five years.

Note that the intensive rearing in the UK of livestock or fish on a commercial basis for the production of food for human consumption, while outside the statutory definition of farming (see **18.1**), does qualify for averaging relief.

Two-year averaging

Two-year averaging relief is available in relation to two consecutive tax years where:

- the relevant profits of one of the tax years are less than 75% of the relevant profits of the other tax year; or
- the relevant profits of one (but not both) of the tax years are nil.

Five-year averaging

Five-year averaging relief is available in relation to five consecutive tax years where a "volatility test" is met, whereby:

- one of the following is less than 75% of the other:
  - the average of the relevant profits of the first four tax years to which the claim relates; or
  - the relevant profits of the last of the tax years to which the claim relates; or
- the relevant profits of one or more (but not all) of the five tax years to which the claim relates are nil.

Calculating average profits

For the purposes of two-year or five-year averaging relief, profit is taken to mean profits after capital allowances and balancing charges, and after any adjustment under the legislation for compensation for the compulsory slaughter of animals.

If a taxpayer makes a loss in a tax year, the relevant profits of that year are taken to be nil. Note that the taxpayer can still take advantage of loss relief provisions (see **Chapter 17**).

If a profit of a tax year has already been averaged, the figure to use in a later calculation is the averaged profit, not the actual result for the year.

Making the claim

Typically, a claim for averaging relief (whether two-year or five-year) must be made on or before the first anniversary of the normal self-assessment filing date for the last of the tax years to which the claim relates. So, a claim for averaging in the 2021-22 tax year should be made by 31 January 2024.

Sole traders should claim averaging relief in Box 72 of the self-employment (full) pages.

Partners should claim averaging relief in Box 11 of their partnership pages. Note that each partner in a partnership can make a personal choice as to whether to claim averaging relief, irrespective of what the other partners do.

Averaging does not affect the amount of tax or NIC that a taxpayer pays in earlier years – adjustments for years relating to an averaging claim are taken into account in the later year's tax return.

Restrictions

Averaging relief is available to sole traders and individual partners in partnership. It is not available to companies, including corporate partners in a partnership.

An averaging claim cannot be made in relation to a tax year in which the taxpayer starts, or permanently ceases, to carry on the trade.

Averaging relief is not available for taxpayers who use the cash basis to calculate their profit or loss.

Example 1 – two-year averaging

Priti's trading profits are £20,000 in 2020-21 and £10,000 in 2021-22.

As the trading profits in 2021-22 satisfy the 75% test, two-year averaging is available. Where averaging is claimed, the profit for each tax year is deemed to be as follows:

(£20,000 + £10,000) / 2 = £15,000

This means that Priti has a £5,000 increase in profit in 2021-22. This increase should be reported in Box 72 of the self-employment (full) pages of her return.

Note that the above example holds, even if Priti's trading profit of £20,000 in 2020-21 was the result of an averaging claim for 2020-21 and 2019-20.

Example 2 – five-year averaging

Paul has the following trading profits:

	£
2021-22	50,000
2020-21	30,000
2019-20	10,000
2018-19	20,000
2017-18	15,000

The average trading profit for the four tax years 2017-18 to 2020-21 is £18,750, being (£30,000 + £10,000 + £20,000 + £15,000) / 4.

As this average trading profit of £18,750 satisfies the volatility test when compared to the £50,000 trading profit in 2021-22, five-year averaging is available. Where averaging is claimed, the profit for each tax year is deemed to be as follows:

$$(£30,000 + £10,000 + £20,000 + £15,000 + £50,000) / 5 = £25,000.$$

This means that Paul has a £25,000 decrease in profit in 2021-22. This decrease should be reported in Box 72 of the self-employment (full) pages of his return.

As a five-year averaging claim has been made, Paul should also work out the overall increase/decrease in his tax and class 4 NIC for 2017-18 to 2020-21 as a result of the averaging claim, and report the adjustment in the tax calculation summary pages of his 2021-22 return. Box 14 is used to report an increase in tax due, and box 15 to report a decrease in tax due.

Law: ITTOIA 2005, s. 221-225
Guidance: Helpsheet 224: Farmers and market gardeners; BIM 84000

18.1.4   The herd basis election

As a general rule, farm animals are treated as trading stock.

However, farmers who keep a "production herd" for the purposes of their trade may elect for the herd basis to apply. The herd basis effectively treats a herd or flock of production animals as akin to a capital asset in most circumstances and excludes them from trading stock.

A production herd is defined in the legislation as:

> "... a herd of animals of the same species (irrespective of breed) kept by the farmer wholly or mainly for the products obtainable from the living animal which the animals produce for the farmer to sell."

"Products obtainable from the living animal" means the young of the animal, or any other product obtainable from the animal without slaughtering it (e.g. milk, eggs).

This means that some animals are excluded from the herd basis, whether by falling outside the above definition, or by specific exclusion. Examples of excluded animals include working animals, and animals kept primarily for fattening or slaughter.

Broadly, the effects of a herd basis election are that:

- The specified herd is not treated as trading stock, and so no deduction is allowed for the initial cost of the herd, nor for the cost of any subsequent increase in herd size.
- In calculating the profits of the trade, the value of the herd is not brought into account.
- The net cost of replacing animals in the herd is an allowable deduction.
- Where a few animals from the herd are sold and are not replaced, the profit/loss arising is brought into account as a receipt/deduction respectively.
- Where the whole or a substantial part of the herd is sold and not replaced, the profit/loss arising is not brought into account as a receipt/deduction.

There are a number of other legislative provisions that may apply depending on the situation. HMRC's guidance at BIM 55515 provides a useful summary of which rule to apply depending on the farmer's circumstances.

For the herd basis to apply, an election must be made in writing. The election should specify the class of production herd to which it relates, and separate elections may be made where there are different classes of production herds. The election is irrevocable.

Generally, for sole traders and partnerships, the election should be made within 12 months after the normal self-assessment filing date for the tax year which contains the end of the first period of account in which the farmer/partnership keeps a production herd of the specified class.

Example – time limit for claim

Isla, a sole trader, begins to keep an eligible production herd in June 2021. She prepares her accounts annually to 31 December.

Isla should make a herd basis election by 31 January 2024, being 12 months after the self-assessment filing date for her 2021-22 self-assessment tax return.

The election can be made by a sole trader, partnership, or a limited company. Where farming is carried on in partnership, a herd basis election is made at the partnership level. Any change to the membership of the partnership requires a new herd basis election.

Note that the herd basis rules do not apply where the farmer uses the cash basis.

Law: ITTOIA 2005, s. 111-129
Guidance: BIM 55500, 55515

18.1.5   Share and contract farming

A share farming agreement typically involves two parties who jointly farm the same land. This is usually a landowner who enters into a contract with a working farmer (the share farmer).

Where there is a genuine share farming agreement, both parties to the agreement may be accepted by HMRC as farming, as they have concurrent rights to the land, and both are contributing to an undertaking of husbandry thereon.

HMRC outline what they would *not* consider to be genuine share farming arrangements at BIM 55080 onwards.

Contract farming

Share farming should not be confused with contract farming, which is an arrangement where a contractor carries out operations of husbandry as agent for the landowner.

In such instances, the landowner is likely to be the occupier of the land and therefore farming. The contractor, by contrast, is not farming and is chargeable as a trader on his or her profits as a contractor.

Guidance: BIM 55050, 55080*ff.*

18.2   Loss restrictions for farming or market gardening

Legislation restricts when farming or market gardening losses can be used to offset non-farming income.

Uncommercial trades

There are trade loss relief restrictions against general income where the trade was not run on a commercial basis and with a view to the realisation of profit – see **17.5.2**.

The five-year rule

Trade loss relief against general income is generally restricted for farmers and market gardeners where a loss (without regard to capital allowances) was made in the trade in each of the previous five tax years (the "five-year rule").

In such instances, the loss cannot be used against general income or against capital gains, but it can be carried forward to be used against future profits of the same trade.

So if a farmer has had five consecutive tax years of trading losses, and makes a loss in tax year six, the five-year rule applies and denies loss relief against general income in the sixth tax year and onwards (there are exceptions to this – see below). Once a profit has been made, the five-year time limit is effectively reset.

Note that the legislation specifies that it is the tax year that is to be considered: an apportionment is required where a farmer/market gardener prepares accounts to a date other than 5 April.

Example – adapted from BIM 85630

Marjorie Brown makes up her accounts annually to 31 December. Her results were as follows:

Year ended	Trade profit or loss before capital allowances £
31 December 2015	Loss 3,700
31 December 2016	Loss 1,100
31 December 2017	Loss 4,800
31 December 2018	Loss 7,000
31 December 2019	Loss 2,600
31 December 2020	Profit 1,200
31 December 2021	Loss 4,400
31 December 2022	Loss 5,300

Marjorie claims trade loss relief against general income for 2021-22. At first sight it may appear that the five-year rule does not apply as she made a profit in the year ended 31 December 2020 (thereby "re-setting" the clock for the five-year rule). A different picture emerges when her profits and losses are computed by reference to tax years.

Tax year	Apportionment calculation	Profit/loss £
2016-17	$\left(\dfrac{270}{365} \times \text{L £1,100} = \text{L £814}\right)$ $plus \left(\dfrac{95}{366} \times \text{L £4,800} = \text{L £1,246}\right)$	Loss £2,060
2017-18	$\left(\dfrac{270}{366} \times \text{L £4,800} = \text{L £3,541}\right)$ $plus \left(\dfrac{96}{365} \times \text{L £7,000} = \text{L £1,841}\right)$	Loss £5,382
2018-19	$\left(\dfrac{270}{365} \times \text{L £7,000} = \text{L £5,164}\right)$ $plus \left(\dfrac{95}{365} \times \text{L £2,600} = \text{L £677}\right)$	Loss £5,841
2019-20	$\left(\dfrac{270}{365} \times \text{L £2,600} = \text{L £1,923}\right)$ $plus \left(\dfrac{95}{365} \times \text{P £1,200} = \text{P £312}\right)$	Loss £1,611
2020-21	$\left(\dfrac{270}{365} \times \text{P £1,200} = \text{P £888}\right)$ $plus \left(\dfrac{95}{366} \times \text{L £4,400} = \text{L £1,142}\right)$	Loss £254
2021-22	$\left(\dfrac{270}{366} \times \text{L £4,400} = \text{L £3,246}\right)$ $plus \left(\dfrac{96}{365} \times \text{L £5,300} = \text{L £1,394}\right)$	Loss £4,640

We can now see that Marjorie made a trading loss, computed without regard to capital allowances, in each of the five preceding tax years. The five-year rule therefore applies and the loss incurred for the year ended 31 December 2021 of £4,400 is not available for trade loss relief against general income.

Exceptions

This loss restriction does not apply in the year of commencement, so in practice a new business that has been continuously loss making would only fall under scope of the five-year rule in its seventh tax year.

Loss relief is also not restricted under the five-year rule in cases where the carrying on of the trade forms part of, and is ancillary to, a larger trading undertaking, or in instances where the farming or market gardening activities meet the "reasonable expectation of profit" test, which looks at the expectations of a hypothetical competent farmer or market gardener carrying on the activities.

The reasonable expectation of profit test is outlined in ITA 2007, s. 68 and is not always straightforward to interpret, as highlighted by the recent case of *Naghshineh*.

Law: ITA 2007, s. 67-70
Case: *HMRC v Naghshineh* [2020] UKUT 30 (TCC)
Guidance: BIM 85600, 85630

18.3   Creative artists – averaging relief

18.3.1   Introduction and overview

Farmers are not the only ones who are able to access income averaging relief. Creative artists may also claim the relief, as profits in this industry can also fluctuate significantly from year to year.

Eligibility

For a creative artist to make an averaging claim, the profits from his or her trade, profession, or vocation (hereafter shortened to "trade") must be derived wholly or mainly from creative works.

"Creative works" are defined as literary, dramatic, musical or artistic works, or designs created by the taxpayer personally. Where the qualifying trade is carried on in partnership, the creative works should be created by one or more of the partners personally.

HMRC regard this test as satisfied if more than 50% of the profit is derived from qualifying creative works.

Example

An author receives income from the sale of her written work, but also receives a small part of her income from personal appearances.

The author is still eligible to claim averaging relief (subject to meeting the 75% test – see below).

Someone who provides a service is not eligible to claim averaging relief, as the income comes from services, not from creative works. An example would be an architect whose income comes mainly from providing professional services.

Profits derived from works of craft (e.g. dress-making) are also excluded.

Two-year averaging

Unlike farmers, creative artists may only make a claim for two-year averaging relief.

This relief is available in relation to two consecutive tax years where:

- the relevant profits of one of the tax years are less than 75% of the relevant profits of the other tax year; or
- the relevant profits of one (but not both) of the tax years are nil.

Calculating average profits

For the purposes of claiming two-year averaging relief, profit is taken to mean profits after capital allowances and balancing charges.

If a taxpayer makes a loss in a tax year, the relevant profits of that year are taken to be nil. Note that the taxpayer can still access loss relief provisions to use the loss (see **Chapter 17**).

If a profit of a tax year has already been averaged, the figure to use is the averaged profit.

18.3.2   Making the claim

Typically, a claim for averaging relief must be made on or before the first anniversary of the normal self-assessment filing date for the last tax year to which the claim relates. So, a claim for averaging in the 2021-22 tax year should be made by 31 January 2024.

Sole traders should claim averaging relief in Box 72 of the self-employment (full) pages.

Partners should claim averaging relief in Box 11 of the partnership pages.

Averaging does not affect the amount of tax or NIC that a taxpayer pays in earlier years – adjustments for years relating to an averaging claim are taken into account in the later year's tax return.

18.3.3   Restrictions

Averaging relief is available to sole traders and individual partners in partnership. It is not available to companies, including corporate partners in a partnership.

An averaging claim cannot be made in relation to a tax year in which the taxpayer starts, or permanently ceases, to carry on the trade.

Further, averaging relief is not available for taxpayers who use the cash basis.

Example

Andy makes a profit of £30,000 in 2020-21 and a loss of £10,000 in 2021-22.

The loss of £10,000 is treated as nil for the purposes of averaging, meaning the average result for each year is taken to be:

   (£30,000 + nil) / 2 = £15,000

This means Andy's profit for 2021-22 increases to £15,000. This increase should be reported in Box 72 of the self-employment (full) pages of his 2021-22 return. The loss of £10,000 should be reported in Box 77.

Law: ITTOIA 2005, s. 221-225
Guidance: Helpsheet 234: Averaging for creators of literary or artistic works; BIM 84000

18.4   Pitfalls and planning points

Averaging relief

Some form of modelling is required to determine whether two-year averaging is beneficial for a taxpayer, rather than being taxed on the actual profits/losses of the given years.

When considering five-year averaging for farmers, this effectively means ten separate calculations are required to compute the averaged *versus* non-averaged position for each year under consideration.

See **18.1.3** for averaging relief for farmers, and **18.3** for averaging relief for creative artists.

Loss relief restriction – five-year rule

The five-year rule for farmers/market gardeners that restricts trade loss relief against general income is dictated by the profits/losses arising in a tax year, not an accounting period. A profit on the face of things may still result in a loss when computed by reference to the tax year. See Marjorie's example at **18.2** above.

19. Construction Industry Scheme

19.1 Introduction

Businesses operating in the construction industry – whether as a company, partnership, or self-employed individual – need to consider the Construction Industry Scheme (CIS).

The construction industry has a large, mobile workforce, and many subcontractors receive cash payments. This creates an environment that is potentially rife for non-compliance with tax obligations.

To counteract this, the CIS (in one form or another) has been in place for many years and requires "contractors" to deduct a percentage from payments to "subcontractors", on account of tax.

HMRC provide detailed CIS guidance for both contractors and subcontractors, on various websites and in the *Construction Industry Scheme Reform Manual* (CISR).

Guidance: https://tinyurl.com/mvuzvzks (HMRC guidance)

19.2 Definition of construction

"Construction operations" is defined to include:

- construction, alteration, repair, extension, demolition or dismantling of buildings or structures (whether permanent or not), including offshore installations;
- civil engineering work, such as on roadworks, railways, docks and harbours;
- installation of heating, lighting, air conditioning, ventilation, power supply, drainage, sanitation, water supply or fire protection systems;
- internal cleaning of buildings and structures (where carried out in the course of their construction, alteration, repair, extension or restoration); and
- painting or decorating the internal or external surfaces of any building or structure.

However, there are specific activities that are exempt, including:

- the professional work of architects or surveyors;
- the making, installation and repair of artistic works;
- installation of seating, blinds and shutters; and
- installation of security systems.

The CIS only covers construction works carried on in the UK (including UK territorial waters). However, an overseas business carrying out construction work in the UK does fall within the scope of the CIS and should comply with the scheme's requirements.

Law: FA 2004, s. 74

19.3 Contractor or subcontractor?

One of the more challenging aspects of the CIS is correctly identifying who is the contractor and who is the subcontractor, remembering that a business may sometimes be both.

19.3.1 Contractor

A contractor is a business that pays a subcontractor to carry out construction work.

A business is considered a "mainstream" contractor where it carries on a business that includes construction operations, for example builders or property developers.

A business can also be a "deemed" contractor where its business does not include construction operations. Previously, this test was met where the average annual expenditure of the business on construction operations over any three-year period exceeded £1 million. However, the test for a deemed contractor changed from 6 April 2021 – see **19.13.2**.

Bodies and businesses that may fall into this category of deemed contractor include government departments and local authorities.

Exceptions for contractors

The CIS does not apply to certain types of work.

For example, if the work is paid for by a charity or trust, or by a governing body or head teacher of a maintained school on behalf of a local education authority, the CIS does not apply.

There are also specific exceptions for mainstream and deemed contractors.

Mainstream contractors

If approval is obtained from HMRC, a mainstream contractor does not have to apply the CIS to small contracts or payments for construction operations amounting to less than £1,000 (excluding the cost of materials) in cases where the contractor is paying a subcontractor to undertake work that falls within the scheme:

- on the subcontractor's own property; or
- on any agricultural property of which the subcontractor is a tenant.

Deemed contractors

For deemed contractors, the CIS does not apply if the deemed contractor pays for work on property for its own business use. However, the CIS does have to be operated where construction work is undertaken on a property that is:

- not used for the purposes of the business;
- for sale or to let (except where the sale or letting is incidental to the business); or
- held as an investment.

A further "small payments" exception is available for deemed contractors where the contract for construction operations is less than £1,000, excluding the cost of materials. For this exception, the deemed contractor must seek approval from HMRC – this can be done by calling HMRC's CIS helpline (0300 200 3210).

Law: SI 2005/2045, reg. 18

Private householders

Private householders are not contractors for the purposes of the CIS. However, if work for a private householder is subcontracted, that contractor may still need to operate the CIS on payments to the subcontractor, depending on the work undertaken.

Example

Shelly undertakes some construction work on Paul's domestic home. She asks her colleague David to help with some of the repair works.

As Paul is a private householder, payments to Shelly are not subject to CIS. However, Shelly should operate the CIS on the payments she makes to David.

Law: FA 2004, s. 59; SI 2005/2045, reg. 21-24

19.3.2 Subcontractor

Broadly, a subcontractor is a business that carries out construction work for a contractor.

The works can be undertaken in any way: by the subcontractor personally, by engaging employees to carry out the work, or by making use of other subcontractors.

Examples of who can be considered a subcontractor include (but are not limited to) self-employed individuals, partnerships, companies and certain labour agencies.

Law: FA 2004, s. 58

19.3.3 Contractor and subcontractor

A business may be both contractor and subcontractor.

Example

Abby is self-employed and works in the construction industry.

She enters into a construction contract, and then subcontracts part of that work to another self-employed individual, Andy. In this scenario, Abby is both subcontractor (in respect of her original contract) and contractor (in respect of the parts of work subcontracted to Andy).

19.4 Employment status

The CIS does not apply to employees, as tax and NIC are accounted for via PAYE for such individuals.

The question of whether an individual is employed or self-employed for tax purposes is multifaceted and based on the individual's personal working arrangement. See **5.2** for a fuller discussion.

However, a key point is that it is not possible simply to choose whether an individual is employed or self-employed: it is a factual decision based on all the circumstances of the relationship between the person providing the work and the individual carrying it out.

19.5   Registration with HMRC

19.5.1   Introduction

Contractors must register for the CIS with HMRC.

While subcontractors are not required to register, higher rate deductions are taken from their payments if they do not.

19.5.2   Registering as a contractor

A contractor should register for the CIS when it is about to take on and pay its first subcontractor (regardless of the level of deduction, if any, that is to be taken from that subcontractor's pay).

The process to register as a contractor is broadly the same as registering as a new employer.

Once the contractor has registered, HMRC will set up a contractor scheme (and PAYE scheme if also requested).

Guidance: https://www.gov.uk/register-employer

19.5.3   Register as a subcontractor

A subcontractor should register when about to start work within the construction industry.

The registration process differs depending on whether the subcontractor:

- is self-employed and already has a Unique Taxpayer Reference (UTR) number;
- is self-employed but not registered for self-assessment; or
- is a limited company or partnership.

Further instructions on how to register are provided in HMRC's CIS guidance (see **19.14**).

19.6   Verification

19.6.1   Introduction

To ensure that subcontractors have the correct deduction taken from their payments, the registration status of the subcontractor is verified. This is a three-step process:

- The contractor provides HMRC with the subcontractor's details.
- HMRC will check whether the subcontractor is registered.
- HMRC will then tell the contractor what rate of deduction to apply, or that payments can be made gross (see **19.7**).

19.6.2   Information required for verification

HMRC require verification of both the contractor (so that HMRC can ensure the contractor's identity) and the subcontractor.

The contractor should provide details of its name, UTR number, HMRC Accounts Office reference and employer reference.

For the subcontractor, the details to be provided vary, depending on whether the subcontractor is an individual, a partner or a company. The required details will, however, include the subcontractor's name, UTR number, and NIC or company registration number.

After verifying a subcontractor, HMRC will provide the contractor with a verification reference number.

Once a subcontractor has been verified, the contractor should continue to pay the subcontractor in the same way unless instructed otherwise by HMRC (see **19.7.3**).

19.6.3   When verification is not required

There are some instances where a contractor does not need to verify a subcontractor.

Broadly, re-verification of the subcontractor is not required if the contractor has made a payment to the subcontractor in the current tax year or in either of the two previous tax years.

In such cases, the subcontractor should be paid on the same basis as before (unless HMRC have informed otherwise).

Example

A contractor engages the services of a self-employed subcontractor. The contractor last paid the subcontractor in June 2020, under a standard deduction of 20%. The contractor reported the payment in the relevant monthly return.

The contractor does not re-engage the subcontractor until March 2022. As the subcontractor was last paid in June 2020 – within the previous two tax years – the contractor does not need to verify the subcontractor, and should pay under deduction at 20%.

Law: FA 2004, s. 77

19.7   Deductions

19.7.1   Introduction

There are three rates of deduction that can be applied to a subcontractor's payment:

- no deduction (i.e. payments are made gross);
- a standard deduction of 20%; or
- a higher rate deduction of 30%.

A deduction may be taken at the higher rate if HMRC have no record of the subcontractor's registration, or are unable to verify that subcontractor's details.

If a subcontractor makes a false declaration, or submits any false documentation (e.g. to register for gross payment status), a penalty of up to £3,000 may apply.

From 2021-22, the scope of the false registration penalty has been expanded. See **19.13.4** for further information.

Law: FA 2004, s. 63-67, 72; SI 2007/46

19.7.2   Gross or net payment status?

HMRC will only grant gross payment status (i.e. with no deductions taken from payments to the subcontractor) where three tests are met:

- the business test;
- the turnover test; and
- the compliance test.

The business test

In essence, the purpose of the business test is to ensure that the subcontractor is carrying on a genuine business that includes carrying out construction operations (or providing labour for such operations). More specifically:

- the subcontractor should carry on a business in the UK;
- the business should consist of, or include, carrying out construction operations, or supplying labour for construction operations; and
- the business should be, to a substantial extent, carried on by means of an account with a bank.

The subcontractor needs to provide evidence to support the business test, including proof of the business address, and the business bank account details, including bank statements.

Law: FA 2004, Sch. 11; SI 2005/2045, reg. 27
Guidance: CISR 45000

The turnover test

Under the turnover test, the subcontractor's net construction turnover in the 12 months preceding the date of application should meet a minimum turnover threshold, excluding VAT and the cost of materials.

The threshold amount varies, depending on the type of business, the number of participants, and whether construction work is the main trading activity of the business.

Under the standard test, the thresholds are as follows:

- for an individual, £30,000;
- for each partner in a partnership, £30,000, or at least £100,000 for the whole partnership; and
- for each director of a company, £30,000, or at least £100,000 for the whole company.

The threshold amount cannot be pro-rated.

The subcontractor may be required to provide evidence that the turnover test is met.

Law: FA 2004, Sch. 11; SI 2005/2045, reg. 28-31; SI 2016/348, reg. 2(5), (6)
Guidance: CISR 44000

The compliance test

Broadly, to meet the compliance test the subcontractor must have complied on time with all tax reporting and payment obligations during the 12 months to the date of application (known as the "qualifying period").

HMRC must also have reason to expect that the subcontractor will continue to comply with his or her obligations.

HMRC will overlook a limited level of defaults (see CISR 46080 for details). This is a statutory provision, given at SI 2005/2045, reg. 32.

A summary of the main reasons subcontractors fail this test is provided at CISR 46060.

A subcontractor with gross payment status will be subject to an annual compliance review to determine if that status can be maintained.

Law: FA 2004, Sch. 11; SI 2005/2045, reg. 32-37
Guidance: CISR 46000*ff.*

19.7.3   Change in payment status

HMRC may change a subcontractor's payment status from gross payment (i.e. no deduction) to a payment under deduction, or *vice versa*. As HMRC's CISR 43030 summarises, a change in payment status may arise from:

- a request from the subcontractor;
- an appeal by the subcontractor against the tax treatment given;
- a scheduled review by HMRC; or
- a compliance officer changing the tax treatment if there is evidence of fraud.

Where gross payment status has been cancelled, a subcontractor wishing to reapply must wait a year from the date of cancellation before doing so.

Where HMRC change a subcontractor's payment status to gross, notification is given to both the subcontractor and any contractors who have verified or used the subcontractor in the current or previous two tax years. The change in payment status should be implemented for all subsequent payments to the subcontractor, as soon as it is practical for the contractor to do so.

Law: FA 2004, s. 66-68
Guidance: CISR 43030

19.7.4   Calculation of deduction

The amount of payment to a subcontractor that is subject to deduction (at the 20% or 30% rate, as applicable) excludes the direct cost of materials incurred by the subcontractor when carrying out the construction operations to which the payment relates.

While the subcontractor should be able to provide evidence of the direct cost of materials, it is the responsibility of the contractor to be satisfied that the cost has not been overstated.

Where a contractor cannot obtain satisfactory evidence of the cost of materials, a reasonable estimate may be used.

HMRC allow the following further deductions to be made provided they are paid by the subcontractor in order to carry out the construction work:

- consumable stores;
- plant and equipment hired from a third party;
- fuel (except fuel for travelling); and
- the cost of manufacture or prefabrication of materials.

Where the subcontractor is registered for VAT, the VAT-exclusive amount paid for materials should be used when calculating the CIS deduction.

The cost of any subsistence or travelling expenses paid to or on behalf of the subcontractor *are* included in the gross amount of payment and when calculating the amount of CIS deduction to be made.

The legislation in respect of materials deductions has been amended with effect from April 2021 (see **19.13.3**).

Example

Dev, a subcontractor, is registered for VAT.

He is engaged to carry out repair works to a building, and payments to him are subject to deduction at 20% under the CIS.

Dev sends his contractor an invoice for his labour and the materials he supplied, comprising £800 for labour (plus VAT of £160) and £200 for materials (plus VAT of £40). The total amount invoiced is therefore £1,200 (£1,000 plus VAT of £200).

The CIS deduction is calculated as follows:

	£
Payment to contractor (excluding VAT)	1,000
Less: cost of materials (excluding VAT)	200
Net amount subject to CIS deduction	800
CIS deduction at 20%	160
Net payment to subcontractor	1,040

The net payment to the subcontractor (Dev in this example) is £1,040, being his invoice of £1,200 less the CIS deduction to HMRC of £160.

If Dev had not been VAT-registered, the VAT-inclusive figure of materials would have been included as part of the deduction calculation.

Law: FA 2004, s. 61
Guidance: CISR 15000

19.8   Reporting to HMRC

19.8.1   Introduction

A CIS contractor has reporting responsibilities both to HMRC (considered here) and to its subcontractors (see **19.9**).

Contractors must submit a monthly return to HMRC, detailing all payments made to all subcontractors within the scheme in the preceding tax month, regardless of whether payments were made gross or under deduction.

A tax month begins on the sixth day of each month and ends on the fifth day of the following month. Monthly returns must be submitted not later than 14 days after the end of the relevant tax month (i.e. by 19th of the month in which the tax month ends).

Example

A contractor is making a CIS return for the tax month 6 July to 5 August 2021. The CIS return should reach HMRC by 19 August 2021.

A monthly return should contain the following:

- the contractor's name;
- the contractor's UTR and Accounts Office reference numbers;

- the tax month to which the return relates; and
- information relating to each subcontractor paid during the month, including:
  - o the subcontractor's name;
  - o the subcontractor's NI number or company registration number (if known);
  - o the subcontractor's UTR number;
  - o the total amount of contract payments made by the contractor to the subcontractor during the tax month; and
  - o where payments are made under deduction:
    - the total amount included in payments that represents the direct cost of materials used (or to be used) in carrying out the construction contract to which the contract payment relates; and
    - the total amount deducted from the payments.

The monthly return should also include a declaration by the contractor that the employment status of all subcontractors has been considered, and that all subcontractors that need to be verified have been.

Law: SI 2005/2045, reg. 4

19.8.2 Nil returns

If a contractor does not make any payments to subcontractors under the CIS in a tax month then a nil return should be submitted by the usual deadline (i.e. the 19th of the month). There is a box in the return to indicate that no payments have been made in the month. It is also possible to telephone HMRC to report that no payments were made.

If a contractor knows that it will not make payments to any subcontractors for an extended period, it can inform HMRC. HMRC will then mark the contractor's CIS status as inactive for six months, allowing an exemption from return submission during that time. If the situation changes during the inactive period, the contractor should inform HMRC.

19.8.3 Errors in monthly returns

If an error arises in a monthly return, HMRC have confirmed that they do not automatically look for penalties, or take away the contractor's own gross status as a subcontractor.

However, if HMRC believe that the error or omission has arisen from negligence or intent on the part of the contractor (i.e. the nature of the error/omission is more serious) HMRC will take action.

Errors arising from simple mistakes (e.g. a transposition error) can be corrected by contacting HMRC.

An amended return can also be submitted using HMRC's CIS online service or commercial software.

Subcontractor not in CIS

HMRC also recognise that, on occasion, a contractor may report a payment to a subcontractor in a monthly return, but that subcontractor may not be within the CIS.

Where this happens, HMRC do not usually regard the inclusion as giving rise to an incorrect return. However, contractors should ensure that deductions are not taken from payments to subcontractors for contracts that are outside the scope of the CIS.

19.8.4   Penalties for late monthly returns

If a monthly return is not submitted to HMRC by the deadline, a fixed penalty of £100 applies. Where the return remains unfiled, further penalties are applied:

- £200 where the return is outstanding two months after the first penalty date;
- a tax-geared penalty, being the greater of £300 or 5% of any CIS deductions shown on the return; where the return is outstanding six months after the first penalty date; and
- a further tax-geared penalty, being the greater of £300 or 5% of any CIS deductions shown on the return, where the return is outstanding 12 months after the first penalty date.

Where information has been deliberately withheld, the 12-month penalty will be higher.

An additional penalty can also be imposed where the return is more than 12 months late.

When penalties may be capped

A new contractor (i.e. one who has not previously filed a monthly return) is subject to "capped" CIS fixed penalties. Further information and illustrative examples are provided in CISR 65080.

Law: FA 2009, Sch. 55

19.9 Reporting to subcontractors

A contractor must give a written statement (a payment and deduction statement), not later than 14 days after the end of the relevant tax month, to every subcontractor from whom a deduction has been made.

The statement should include:

- the contractor's name and employer reference number;
- the tax month to which the payments relate, or the date of the payment;
- the subcontractor's name and UTR number;
- the total amount of contract payments made by the contractor to the subcontractor during the tax month;
- the direct cost of any materials; and
- the total amount deducted from the payments.

If the subcontractor is not registered, the verification reference should also feature on the statement.

If a subcontractor has gross payment status, it is best practice for a contractor to provide a statement but there is no obligation to do so.

Law: SI 2005/2045, reg. 4

19.10 Making payments to subcontractors

19.10.1 Introduction

The contractor may make a payment to the subcontractor directly, or the subcontractor may authorise payment to be made to a nominee.

Where payment is made to a subcontractor's nominee (e.g. a relative), the contractor must verify both subcontractor and nominee. For a payment to be made gross to the nominee, both the subcontractor and nominee must have gross payment status.

Regardless of who receives the payment, the payment and deduction statement (see **19.9**) should still be issued to, and in the name of, the subcontractor.

19.10.2 Underpayments to subcontractors

A contractor may make a payment error and underpay a subcontractor.

If this happens, and the underpaid amount is reported on the CIS monthly return, the error can be resolved by way of a balancing payment. The balancing payment (including any deductions made) should be reported in the CIS monthly return for the month in which it is paid.

19.10.3 Overpayments to subcontractors

If a contractor overpays a subcontractor, the CIS monthly return should report the amount actually paid.

If the subcontractor's engagement continues, the contractor and subcontractor may agree that the subcontractor will be paid less the following month, so that the subcontractor has received the correct amount overall. In this case, the contractor would report the actual amount paid in the second month in the relevant CIS return.

If the overpayment was the final payment made to the subcontractor, there are two ways to resolve the overpayment, depending on whether the payment has already been cashed and any deductions paid to HMRC:

- If the payment can be stopped, the contractor should reissue the payment in the correct amount. The contractor will then need to retrieve and reissue the subcontractor's payment statement and contact HMRC to report the error on the earlier return. The revised payment and any deductions should then be recorded on the next monthly return.

- If the payment has already been made (e.g. a cheque has already been cashed), and any deductions have been paid over to HMRC, the monthly return will be correct, as it will reflect what was actually paid in the month. Nevertheless, the contractor should phone HMRC to report the error and to advise the correct payments due to the subcontractor. HMRC are then likely to ask about whether and how the contractor proposes to recover the overpayment.

19.11 Self-assessment

This section applies only to subcontractors who are subject to income tax (i.e. a sole trader or a partner in a firm).

Such subcontractors should report their profits each year on a self-assessment tax return, with the tax liability based on the figures in the return.

Where a subcontractor has been subject to payments under deduction, and the tax payable is greater than the amount so deducted, the subcontractor should make a balancing payment to make up the shortfall by 31 January following the end of the tax year.

Conversely, if the subcontractor's tax payable is less than the amount of CIS deductions taken, HMRC will refund the excess.

19.12 Record-keeping

19.12.1 Contractors

Contractors must keep records of the gross amount of payments to subcontractors (excluding VAT), as well as records relating to the amount of deductions made from those payments.

Where a subcontractor's payment is subject to deduction, records should also be kept of the costs of materials for which the subcontractor has invoiced (excluding VAT where the subcontractor is VAT registered).

Such records should be kept for at least three years after the end of the relevant tax year.

If a contractor fails to produce records when requested by HMRC, penalties of up to £3,000 may apply.

19.12.2 Subcontractors

Subcontractors should receive monthly statements from the contractor that provide details of amounts received and deductions taken (if any).

A subcontractor who has not received all the monthly statements required to complete his or her tax return can ask the contractor to send a replacement copy of the statement(s).

If a contractor stops trading, a subcontractor who has not received all of his or her CIS statements can write to HMRC to request the information, providing the following details:

- the subcontractor's name, address and UTR number;
- the contractor's name, address and tax reference (where known);
- the dates of the payments (or the tax months when the contractor paid the subcontractor); and
- the reason why the subcontractor does not have the statements or duplicates.

19.13   Recent changes

19.13.1 Introduction

Following a 2020 consultation into tackling CIS abuse, the CIS regime has been amended in four areas, with those changes taking effect for the 2021-22 tax year onwards.

19.13.2 Test for deemed contractor

The previous rules relating to when a business became a deemed contractor were open to abuse. HMRC found indications that some contractors were manipulating both the amount and timing of construction payments, or were changing their accounting periods, to ensure that they did not fall within the deemed contractor rules.

As a result, a business will now become a deemed contractor when its expenditure on construction operations exceeds £3 million on a rolling 12-month basis.

19.13.3 Materials deductions

The provision relating to deductions for materials (FA 2004, s. 61) has been amended to make it clear that a materials deduction for CIS purposes can only be made from a payment under a construction contract where the subcontractor has directly purchased materials used or to be used in fulfilling that contract.

19.13.4 Penalties

Previously, HMRC could penalise a person for providing false information when registering for the CIS. However, that penalty only applied to the individual or business who had made the registration.

The scope of the false registration penalty has been expanded, so a penalty may now be levied on an agent, director, company secretary or anyone HMRC believe is in a position to exercise influence or control over the business, and/or on the person making the CIS registration.

19.13.5 CIS deductions claimed on an employer's return

Although outside the scope of this annual, it is worth noting that under the CIS, limited company subcontractors can set off CIS deductions against in-year employer liabilities.

HMRC became aware that some employers were using this process to reduce their tax liabilities falsely, or to create false repayments.

To tackle this, HMRC have a new amendment power, allowing them to correct certain CIS set-off claims.

19.14 Pitfalls and planning points

Types of contractor

A contractor under the CIS can either be a mainstream contractor (e.g. a builder) or a deemed contractor. The test for determining who is a deemed contractor changed from April 2021 (see **19.13.2**).

Contractor or subcontractor?

For the purposes of complying with the CIS, it is important to understand who is considered a contractor and who is considered a subcontractor. Some businesses are both (see **19.3**).

Applying for gross payment status

To receive payments gross, a subcontractor must meet three specific tests. Gross payment status is subject to annual review (see **19.7.2**).

CAPITAL ALLOWANCES

20. Plant and machinery allowances

20.1 Introduction and overview

20.1.1 Overview

Plant and machinery allowances (PMAs) are of value for virtually every business, and two key questions dominate: the amount of expenditure that can qualify for allowances, and the timing of relief.

As the name suggests, capital allowances are due only for capital expenditure, excluding any amount that may be deducted under other provisions in calculating the profits or gains. Qualifying expenditure includes VAT unless the VAT is allowable as input tax.

Statutory references in this chapter are to the *Capital Allowances Act 2001* (CAA 2001), unless otherwise stated. The main HMRC guidance is in the *Capital Allowances Manual*.

For more detailed guidance on this topic, see *Capital Allowances* 2021-22, from Claritax Books.

Law: CAA 2001, Pt. 2

Timing of expenditure

The legislation provides a general rule that expenditure is treated as incurred as soon as there is an unconditional obligation to pay it. This is the case even if actual payment may be deferred.

Various exceptions apply to the general rule, for example if payment is due after four months or more, or if there is an avoidance motive.

Pre-trading expenditure is treated as incurred on the first day on which the activity is in fact carried on.

Law: CAA 2001, s. 5, 12
Guidance: CA 11700, 11800, 23083

Claims

No allowances may be given unless a claim for allowances is made. Any claim must be included in a tax return, so the time limit for claiming is the same as that for submitting or amending a return. If a claim has been missed in an earlier year, it is not possible to go back and re-open computations from many years ago. However, the costs may be brought into account as qualifying expenditure in a later year, as long as the assets are still owned.

A claim may be for less than the statutory entitlement (e.g. to use up personal allowances), in which case the amount claimed must be specified.

Law: CAA 2001, s. 3, 565

20.1.2 General conditions for claiming allowances

PMAs are available if a person carries on a qualifying activity (see **20.2**) and incurs qualifying expenditure (see **20.3**).

If a person carries on more than one qualifying activity (e.g. a sole trader who also has an investment property), allowances must be calculated separately for each activity.

Law: CAA 2001, s. 11

20.2 Qualifying activities

The following are the main qualifying activities for the purposes of claiming PMAs:

- a trade, profession or vocation;
- an ordinary (UK or overseas) property business;
- a UK (or EEA) furnished holiday lettings business;
- special leasing of plant or machinery; and
- an employment or office.

"Special leasing" means the hiring out of plant or machinery otherwise than in the course of a trade or other qualifying activity.

Restriction re dwelling-houses

For ordinary property businesses, and for special leasing of plant or machinery (but not for trades, for example), allowances are denied for plant or machinery for use in a dwelling-house (see **20.3.7**).

Law: CAA 2001, s. 15, 35

20.3   Qualifying expenditure

20.3.1   Introduction

A fundamental condition for giving PMAs is that a person must incur qualifying expenditure. The "general rule" is that expenditure constitutes qualifying expenditure if:

"(a)   it is capital expenditure on the provision of plant or machinery wholly or partly for the purposes of the qualifying activity carried on by the person incurring the expenditure, and

(b)   the person incurring the expenditure owns the plant or machinery as a result of incurring it."

This general rule is, however, modified by various other provisions.

Law: CAA 2001, s. 11

20.3.2   Buildings, structures and land

Buildings

The legislation states that "expenditure on the provision of plant or machinery does not include expenditure on the provision of a building". For clarity, it goes on to state that "the provision of a building includes its construction or acquisition".

The concept of "building" is expanded to include assets actually or typically incorporated in the building and a whole range of specified assets (list A at s. 21) if they are merely in or connected with the building, including such assets as walls and floors, mains services, fire safety systems, and various others.

Law: CAA 2001, s. 21

Structures

Expenditure on the provision of plant or machinery does not include expenditure on the construction or acquisition of a structure or other asset in list B at s. 22 (e.g. roads, railways and bridges).

Section 22 also disqualifies expenditure on any works involving the alteration of land. The precise meaning of this restriction was considered in depth in the *SSE Generation* case. The Upper Tribunal stated that:

"List B does not in our view exclude expenditure on the alteration of land to the extent that it was required in the provision of a structure or other asset."

Law: CAA 2001, s. 22

Cases: *SSE Generation Ltd v HMRC* [2018] UKFTT 416 (TC); *HMRC v SSE Generation Ltd* [2019] UKUT 332 (TCC)

Exceptions

There could be no PMAs for any items caught by sections 21 or 22 if that were the end of the matter. In fact, however, the provisions for both buildings and structures are subject to very important exceptions given at s. 23.

Section 23 first lists particular provisions to which the restrictions for buildings and structures above do not apply. These provisions relate to thermal insulation, personal security, integral features, and software.

The rest of s. 23 works differently, providing a long list of assets (list C), being "expenditure unaffected by sections 21 and 22". List C includes a wide range of assets, including broad categories such as machinery and manufacturing equipment, and very specific items such as fish tanks, slurry pits and dry docks. Some of the terms were explored in depth in *Cheshire Cavity Storage*. A key principle is that the list does not operate by analogy – it is not possible to say that an asset is rescued because it is similar to one listed.

Inclusion in list C does not guarantee that the expenditure in question will qualify as plant or machinery; the effect of this part of s. 23 is merely to remove the automatic bar on claiming allowances on the items in question. The actual tax treatment of the asset can then be considered on its own merits, using case law precedents.

Law: CAA 2001, s. 23

Case: *Cheshire Cavity Storage 1 Ltd and EDF Energy (Gas Storage Hole House) Ltd v HMRC* [2019] UKFTT 498 (TC)

Interests in land

Expenditure on land does not constitute expenditure on plant or machinery. An "interest in land" has the meaning applied to it for the purposes of the fixtures legislation (s. 175: see **21.3**).

Law: *Interpretation Act* 1978, Sch. 1; CAA 2001, s. 24

20.3.3   *The meaning of plant and machinery*

The meaning of "plant" has been analysed in the courts for well over 100 years, with dozens of test cases. Together, these show that it is notoriously difficult to pin down the meaning.

Some assets are now categorised as "integral features", bringing certainty to the treatment of a few common types of expenditure, including electrical work and cold water systems.

The case of *Yarmouth v France*, heard back in 1887, defined plant as "whatever apparatus is used by a businessman for carrying on his business ... all goods and chattels, fixed or moveable, live or dead, which he keeps for permanent employment in his business". 95 years later, in the House of Lords ruling in *Scottish & Newcastle*, Lord Lowry confirmed that plant is a word "of comprehensive meaning".

In practice, particular focus has been given to the word "apparatus" and the courts have to some extent driven a wedge between apparatus on the one hand, and the setting or premises on the other. On this basis, electric lamps and fittings were held not to be plant in *J. Lyons & Co* (though today they would be treated as integral features), and a school laboratory and gym were held to be "only the structure within which" (as opposed to apparatus *with which*) the school activities were carried out. However, the concepts of setting and apparatus are not always mutually exclusive (*Jarrold v Good*). The more recent case of *Andrew* provides useful analysis of the distinctions to be considered.

Case law (e.g. *Wimpy*) has drawn out an extended meaning of "plant" (relating to the provision of *ambience*) for the hospitality or similar trades, largely preserved today by item 14 of list C at s. 23.

The meaning of "machinery" is generally more straightforward.

Cases: *Yarmouth v France* [1887] 4 TRL 1; *J. Lyons & Co Ltd v Attorney General* [1944] Ch 281; *Jarrold v John Good & Sons Ltd* (1963) 40 TC 681; *CIR v Scottish & Newcastle Breweries Ltd* [1982] BTC 187; *Cole Brothers Ltd v Phillips* [1982] BTC 208; *Wimpy International Ltd. v Warland* [1987] BTC 591; *Andrew v HMRC* [2010] UKFTT 546 (TC)
Guidance: CA 21100

20.3.4 Other qualifying expenditure

Building alterations

The cost of alterations to an *existing* building, if they are incidental to the installation of plant or machinery for the purposes of the qualifying activity, may qualify for allowances.

Law: CAA 2001, s. 25

Demolition costs

Tax relief, by way of PMAs, is available for costs incurred on demolishing plant or machinery that has been used for the purposes of a qualifying activity. The net demolition cost is the amount by which the cost of demolition exceeds any amount received for the remains of the plant or machinery.

Law: CAA 2001, s. 26

Thermal insulation

Expenditure on thermal insulation is in certain circumstances deemed to constitute capital expenditure on the provision of plant or machinery. HMRC take the view that the rules apply only to insulation added to an existing building.

Any costs qualifying by virtue of these rules are treated as "special rate" expenditure (see **20.6.1**). If there is a disposal event, the disposal value is treated as nil.

Law: CAA 2001, s. 28, 63(5), 104A(1)(a)
Guidance: CA 22220

Personal security

Assets provided for personal security may qualify for PMAs, but only in cases where there is an exceptional security risk.

Law: CAA 2001, s. 33
Cases: *Lord Hanson v Mansworth (HMIT)* (2004) Sp C 410
Guidance: CA 22270; EIM 21811

Shares in plant and machinery

A person may own part of an asset, or a share in an asset. Such a part or share is normally treated as an asset in its own right for the purposes of claiming PMAs. It is treated as used for the purposes of a qualifying activity so long as (but only so long as) the asset in question is used for the purposes of that activity.

Law: CAA 2001, s. 270, 571

20.3.5   Notional expenditure

Assets brought into use

A person may already own an asset (e.g. a computer or a car) before it is brought into use for the purposes of the qualifying activity. In such a case, the person is treated as incurring notional expenditure on the date on which the asset is brought into use for the purposes of the qualifying activity. The notional expenditure is generally the lower of market value or the actual cost incurred on the asset.

Law: CAA 2001, s. 13

Assets rotated between property businesses

Special rules may apply where plant or machinery is used in rotation for a variety of property-related activities (e.g. where a furnished holiday letting (FHL) activity becomes an ordinary property business). There is a deemed disposal and reacquisition at market value, and no fixtures election is possible in these cases. It will be necessary to watch the restriction (s. 35) for dwelling-houses, which applies to an ordinary property business but not to an FHL business.

Law: CAA 2001, s. 13B

Plant or machinery received as a gift

A person may be given an item of plant or machinery which he or she then brings into use for the purposes of a qualifying activity. In such a case, the market value of the asset, calculated on the day it is brought into use for the qualifying activity, is treated as qualifying expenditure.

The HMRC view is that the anti-avoidance rules beginning at s. 214 apply in these cases. These rules restrict allowances for transactions between connected persons, for transactions undertaken to gain a tax advantage, for sale and leaseback arrangements, and in certain other circumstances (see **20.6.10**).

Law: CAA 2001, s. 14, 213(3), 214, 218
Guidance: CA 28200

20.3.6 Integral features

Certain expenditure on integral features (IFs) is treated "as if" it were capital expenditure on the provision of plant or machinery. The person incurring the expenditure is treated as owning the plant or machinery as a result. This has several effects:

- An asset that would otherwise not qualify for relief (e.g. general office lighting) may now do so. The IF provisions overrule the various exclusions for buildings and structures.

- Tax relief given by way of writing-down allowances (e.g. for an air conditioning system) may be slowed down, as the expense will be "special rate" expenditure (see **20.6.1**).

- Some revenue expenditure (which would be fully deductible in the year) may be converted to capital expenditure (with tax relief possibly spread over many years). Expenditure on replacing all or most of an integral feature is automatically treated as new capital expenditure on the feature (even if it is actually revenue expenditure).

A short-life asset (SLA) election (see **20.6.5**) is not permitted for IFs. However, expenditure on IFs may be subject to a claim for annual investment allowances (AIAs). Indeed, if a business incurs expenditure in the same year on both IFs and general plant and machinery, it will normally wish to claim AIAs against the IFs first.

Law: CAA 2001, s. 23(2), 33A, 33B, 84 (table: item 4)
Guidance: CA 22310-22360, 23084

Definition of integral features

The statutory definition of integral features encompasses five categories of expenditure, as follows:

- an electrical system (including a lighting system);
- a cold water system;
- a space or water heating system, a powered system of ventilation, air cooling or air purification, and any floor or ceiling comprised in such a system;
- a lift, an escalator or a moving walkway; and
- external solar shading.

Assets provided mainly to insulate or enclose the interior of a building – or to provide a permanent wall, floor or ceiling – are excluded.

Law: CAA 2001, s. 33A(5), (6)
Guidance: CA 22320

20.3.7   Restriction for dwelling-houses

Expenditure is not qualifying expenditure if it is incurred on plant or machinery for use in a dwelling-house to be used for a (UK or overseas) property business. The restriction does not apply to FHLs.

The meaning of "dwelling-house" is complex and reference should be made to the HMRC guidance as necessary. Particular care should be taken in relation to houses in multiple occupation, where allowances are *not* generally available, and to student accommodation.

In some cases where no capital allowances are available, relief may instead be given for the cost of replacing certain domestic items (see **26.6**).

Law: CAA 2001, s. 35; ITTOIA 2005, s. 311A
Guidance: CA 11520, 20020, 23060

20.3.8   Other restrictions

The following non-exhaustive list shows other restrictions that may apply:

- assets used by MPs and others (s. 34);
- assets used for long funding leasing (s. 34A);
- assets where a depreciation subsidy is received (s. 37);
- production animals (s. 38); and
- assets of qualifying care providers (ITTOIA 2005, s. 824*ff*.).

20.3.9   Employments and offices

There are limited opportunities for employees and office-holders to claim PMAs, allowances being given as a deduction from earnings.

HMRC do not expect employees to capitalise very small items of office equipment (e.g. calculators or staplers), or "small tools, such as electric drills, or protective clothing such as safety boots or helmets". A deduction for such items should instead be claimed under ITEPA 2003, s. 336 (see **8.2** above).

No PMAs are given for a car, van, motorcycle or bicycle owned by the employee. Any other expenditure incurred by the holder of an office or employment will be qualifying expenditure if it is "necessarily provided" for use in the performance of the duties. Reference should be made, as necessary, to the extensive case law and HMRC guidance.

No PMAs are given for plant or machinery used by employees for the purposes of business entertaining.

Law: CAA 2001, s. 36(1), 205*ff.*
Cases: *Hillyer v Leeke* (1976) 51 TC 90; *Williams v HMRC* [2010] UKFTT 86 (TC); *Telfer v HMRC* [2016] UKFTT 614 (TC)
Guidance: EIM 36560

20.4 Allowances and charges

20.4.1 Introduction

PMAs are normally given by way of annual investment allowances (AIAs – see **20.4.2** below) or writing-down allowances (WDAs – see **20.4.3**). First-year allowances (FYAs – see **20.4.5**) or balancing allowances (**20.4.7**) may also be available. Detailed rules determine which allowances may be claimed and when.

Balancing charges (see **20.4.7**) are, in effect, a negative allowance.

Giving effect to allowances

Allowances and charges are given effect in calculating income (or profits, as the case may be) of a chargeable period. As such, allowances are deducted as part of the calculation of the taxable income or profits, and may create or increase a loss. This is done before any apportionment between income tax basis periods.

Law: CAA 2001, s. 2, 247*ff.*; ITTOIA 2005, s. 198*ff.*
Guidance: CA 11110

20.4.2 Annual investment allowances

Introduction

AIAs give immediate tax relief for certain types of expenditure, up to a defined limit. They are available for most capital expenditure on plant and machinery, including integral features. Key points are:

- AIAs may be claimed by businesses of any size.
- There is an annual limit, which has to be shared between associated businesses (and complex transitional rules apply when that limit changes).
- The claimant must incur "AIA qualifying expenditure" and must own the plant or machinery at some time during the chargeable period for which the claim is made.
- AIAs can only be claimed for the period in which the expenditure is incurred, and never for expenditure incurred in an earlier period.
- An AIA claim may convert a profit to a loss, or may augment an existing loss, to be relieved in the normal way.
- A person may choose not to claim AIAs, or only to claim at a lower level (e.g. to avoid wasting a personal allowance), in which case a higher amount will be carried forward to attract future WDAs.

The *Tevfik* case illustrated other issues that can go wrong with a claim for AIAs.

Example

Deborah spends £20,000 in June 2015 on some fixtures in her office. She only becomes aware in April 2021 that she can claim PMAs on those fixtures. She draws accounts up to 31 December.

As long as she still owns the fixtures in question, Deborah may make a capital allowances claim for a later year – perhaps for the year to 31 December 2020 or by amending the return for the previous year. However, she will be able to claim WDAs only, as the AIA claim was only possible for the year in which she actually incurred the cost. Unless her accounts are under HMRC enquiry, it is too late now for Deborah to change her claim for the year to 31 December 2015.

Law: CAA 2001, s. 51A
Case: *Tevfik v HMRC* [2019] UKFTT 600 (TC)
Guidance: CA 23080*ff.*

AIA qualifying expenditure

AIAs are only available for expenditure on plant or machinery incurred by an individual, by a partnership whose members are all individuals, or by a company.

Partnerships that have a corporate member, even if dormant, may not claim. Nor may partnerships with another partnership as a member. AIAs are not available for trusts, or for partnerships with a trust as a member.

Although there are a few "general exclusions" (see below), the AIA is available for a wide range of expenditure, including integral features and other fixtures, special rate expenditure, and general plant and machinery. AIAs are thus available for all vehicles except cars, for fixtures in property, business machinery, office equipment, etc.

Law: CAA 2001, s. 38A
Cases: *Hoardweel Farm Partnership v HMRC* [2012] UKFTT 402 (TC); *Drilling Global Consultant LLP v HMRC* [2014] UKFTT 888 (TC)
Guidance: CA 23084

General exclusions

Expenditure is not AIA qualifying expenditure if a claim is precluded by any of various "general exclusions", including:

- expenditure incurred in the chargeable period in which the qualifying activity is permanently discontinued (see below);
- expenditure on a car;
- where an item of plant or machinery provided for other purposes starts to be used for the qualifying activity; and
- where an asset has been received as a gift.

In contrast to the rules for FYAs, there is no general exclusion for leased assets.

Law: CAA 2001, s. 38B
Guidance: CA 23084

Amount of allowances

A cap is set on the amount of allowances that may be claimed for expenditure incurred in any given period. Businesses that are associated with one another have to share a single amount.

From 1 January 2019 to 31 December 2021, the maximum amount is set at £1 million, reducing to £200,000 from the start of 2022, unless further extended. However, transitional rules mean that in reality the reduction takes effect for expenditure incurred during 2021 – see below.

If a chargeable period is greater or less than one year, the relevant figure is increased or reduced *pro rata*.

If a person incurs AIA qualifying expenditure in excess of the threshold, AIA is simply claimed on an amount up to the limit. Any excess may be subject to a claim for WDAs in the same period.

Transitional rules apply when the maximum rate changes. So if the cap falls, as expected, from 1 January 2022, two separate calculations will be needed.

First, there will be a maximum AIA calculation for the *whole* of the chargeable period spanning the date of the change, made by a simple apportionment of the maximum figures for each part of the overall period. So, for example, for a chargeable period ending on 30 April 2022, the overall maximum AIA will be £733,333 (i.e. eight months at £1 million per year and four months at £200,000 per year).

But a second calculation will restrict the amount of AIA for expenditure in the period from 1 January 2022 to the end of the transitional chargeable period. For expenditure in this period, the maximum AIAs that can be given are those that would be available for a notional standalone period covering that period. For example, if accounts are drawn up to 30 April 2022, and expenditure is incurred in the last four months of that period, maximum AIA for that expenditure will be just £66,667 (i.e. 4/12 of the new maximum annual amount of £200,000).

For related businesses (as defined, and see CA 23089 for examples), a single amount must be shared. The question of being related is determined in various ways, including by reference to shared premises or shared activities in the tax year.

Law: CAA 2001, s. 38A(5), 51A; FA 2014, Sch. 2, para. 4; FA 2019, s. 32 and Sch. 13(2)
Guidance: CA 23083, 23085, 23089

20.4.3   *Writing-down allowances*

Introduction

The basic principle of the WDA is that tax relief for capital expenditure is given over a number of years, roughly mirroring the accounting concept of depreciation.

WDAs for plant and machinery are calculated year by year on the reducing value rather than on the original cost of an asset. If, for example, a trader has just one asset, costing £10,000 and attracting allowances at 18% per year, allowances would be £1,800 in year one, with the balance of £8,200 carried forward. In the second year, allowances would be calculated as £1,476 (£8,200 at 18%) and so on.

Law: CAA 2001, s. 53*ff.*

Pooling

In reality, allowances are rarely given for a single asset in isolation. Instead, the concept of pooling ensures that allowances are calculated collectively on a group of assets, adding in any additional purchases in the year, and deducting any disposal proceeds.

Most businesses will have at least two separate pools, one for ordinary ("main rate") expenditure, attracting allowances at 18% per year, and the other ("special rate") for certain assets where WDAs have to be restricted to just 6% per year (see **20.6.1** below).

Example 1

Sabina runs a consultancy business with three employees, each of whom is provided with a company car. All of these cars have higher emissions and therefore attract WDAs at just 6% (see **20.5** below).

At the start of the year, the special rate pool has a value of £20,000. In the year, Sabina buys one further car for £30,000 and sells another for £8,000. The pool value is therefore calculated as £42,000.

Allowances for the year on this pool (at 6%) are £2,520, and the balance of £39,480 is carried forward. If there are no additions or disposals in the following year, allowances will then be £2,369, calculated as 6% of the balance brought forward.

Some businesses, especially those that are not incorporated, will also have one or more single-asset pools (discussed below). These are needed for any assets that are used partly for private purposes by a sole trader or a partner (but not for assets, such as company cars, provided for employees). SLAs must also be allocated to a single-asset pool.

In practice, most assets other than cars will attract AIAs, as discussed above, rather than WDAs.

Law: CAA 2001, s. 53, 54
Guidance: CA 23210

Entitlement to WDAs

The allowances for each pool are calculated separately. As long as the available qualifying expenditure – including any additions in the year not covered by AIAs – exceeds any disposal proceeds, a WDA will be given on the balance at either 6% or 18%.

If the business is continuing, allowances will continue to be claimed on any remaining value even if all the assets have been sold or scrapped. In the final chargeable period (usually, but not invariably, when the business ceases – see **20.4.7**), WDAs are not given, but a balancing allowance will instead be available.

If disposal proceeds, in any period, exceed the available qualifying expenditure, a balancing charge will be imposed of the excess.

Law: CAA 2001, s. 55

Rate of WDAs

As mentioned above, the standard rate is 18% but a lower rate of just 6% applies for special rate expenditure (see **20.6.1**).

In each case, the maximum allowance is proportionately reduced or increased if the chargeable period is less or more than a year. It is (further) reduced if there is any non-business use of the asset – see "single-asset pool" below.

If the value of any pool does not exceed £1,000 – after adding amounts brought forward to any additional qualifying expenditure in the year, and deducting any disposal proceeds – the whole amount may be written off in one go (as a "small pool"). The £1,000 figure is adjusted if the period of accounts is more or less than one year.

A person claiming WDAs may always require the allowance to be reduced to a specified amount, so as to carry forward a higher figure to the following period. This may be appropriate, for example, in the case of a sole trader who only needs to take his or her income down to the level of the personal allowance.

Law: CAA 2001, s. 56, 56A

Guidance: www.gov.uk/guidance/capital-allowances-accounting-periods-which-are-more-or-less-than-a-year

Single-asset pool

The most common use of single-asset pools is where an asset is used partly for private purposes, e.g. a sole trader (or partner) who makes private use of a car. This enables WDAs to be restricted to reflect private or other disqualifying use.

The amount carried forward must, however, be calculated as if full allowances had been given.

Example 2 – unincorporated business

Julie runs a bakery business as a sole trader. She has a van on which WDAs are claimed annually. WDAs are available at 18%.

In Year 1, the brought-down value of the van is £14,000. Julie has used the van 90% for business purposes. Her WDAs are calculated as £2,268 (£14,000 x 18% x 90%). The amount carried forward is £11,480, calculated as £14,000 less an unrestricted amount of £2,520.

In Year 2, just 75% of Julie's use of the van is for business purposes. Her allowances for the year are calculated as £1,550 (£11,480 x 18% x 75%). The amount carried forward is £9,414.

For a single-asset pool, a balancing adjustment will be made as soon as the asset is sold.

Example 3 – unincorporated business (cont.)

Continuing the example above, the van is sold in Year 3 for £5,000.

Julie will be entitled to a balancing allowance, before private use adjustment, of £4,414. This must be adjusted for the extent of non-business use in the year in question, or on a different basis if that would not be "just and reasonable".

Law: CAA 2001, s. 53, 54, 65, 206, 207
Guidance: CA 27005

Available qualifying expenditure

In simple terms, available qualifying expenditure (AQE) consists of new qualifying expenditure allocated to a pool for a period, plus any unrelieved amounts brought forward from the previous period.

If expenditure was incurred many years previously, but has never before been added to a pool, it may be brought in at a later date, without time limit. However, this may only be done if the asset in question is still owned at some point in that later period. This arises most frequently in relation to property fixtures (see **Chapter 21**).

Law: CAA 2001, s. 57

20.4.4   Assets used for business entertainment

No PMAs are given for an asset to the extent that it is used for providing business entertainment. This includes any kind of hospitality, but does not extend to anything provided for employees of the person carrying out the qualifying activity.

Law: CAA 2001, s. 269

20.4.5   First-year allowances

Introduction

The ability to claim AIAs means that few payers of income tax need to worry about FYAs. However, for those with exceptionally high expenditure, exceeding the AIA threshold, FYAs may be claimed for various categories of expenditure, including:

- cars with zero CO_2 emissions (s. 45D);
- zero-emission goods vehicles (s. 45DA);
- plant or machinery for a gas refuelling station (s. 45E); and
- electric vehicle charging points (s. 45EA).

The plant or machinery in question must be new and unused.

In each case, 100% FYAs are available, so the full cost may be claimed as a deduction for the chargeable period in which the cost is incurred (though a person may claim a reduced allowance if preferred). Private use does not stop FYAs altogether, but the amount must be reduced on a just and reasonable basis.

As for AIAs (but not for WDAs), FYAs may *only* be claimed for the chargeable period in which the expenditure is incurred.

Unlike the treatment of AIAs and WDAs, the rate of FYAs does not change for shorter or longer accounting periods.

The March 2021 Budget introduced the concept of the "super-deduction" (and an associated "SR allowance"), a form of temporary FYA. However, the scheme is only available for companies within the charge to corporation tax, so it has no relevance for income tax purposes.

Enhanced plant and machinery allowances for freeport sites are also restricted to companies within the charge to corporation tax (though the freeport rules for structures and buildings allowances (see **Chapter 22**) apply also to those paying income tax).

Law: CAA 2001, s. 39, 50, 52, 58, 205(1)
Guidance: CA 23155

General exclusions

No FYAs are available in various circumstances, including for:

- the chargeable period in which the qualifying activity is permanently discontinued;
- cars (as defined) – except that this does not apply to certain electric or zero-emission cars (see **20.5** below);
- plant or machinery for leasing (s. 46) – some complex rules apply here (see CA 23115); or
- plant or machinery received as a gift (s. 14).

Law: CAA 2001, s. 52, 52A

20.4.6 Disposals

A person who has claimed PMAs on a particular asset may have to bring a disposal receipt into account. This may either reduce current or future allowances, or create a balancing charge.

There is a disposal not only if the person ceases to own the plant or machinery, but also in various other circumstances, including when the qualifying activity is permanently discontinued, or where the asset starts to be used for other purposes.

The disposal value is normally the amount of disposal proceeds received (net of any selling costs). In rarer circumstances, market value or an alternative figure may have to be used instead.

The disposal value is capped at the amount of qualifying expenditure previously taken into account. So if an asset bought for £100 is later sold for £120, the amount to bring in as a disposal value is capped at £100 (with the excess ignored for capital allowances purposes). The effect is that the person will – over the years – obtain no net allowances on the asset in question. The rule is modified only where there is a connected party transaction.

Law: CAA 2001, s. 61, 62, 64, 66, 577(1)

Apportionments

When two or more items are sold together, the net proceeds of sale of any given item must be calculated as "so much of the net proceeds of sale of all the property as, on a just and reasonable apportionment, is attributable to that item".

Law: CAA 2001, s. 562

Nil-value disposals

If a disposal of plant and machinery is by way of gift, and gives rise to an employment tax charge under ITEPA 2003, the disposal value for capital allowances purposes is nil.

There is also a nil disposal value where a person makes a gift of plant or machinery (used in the course of the qualifying activity) to certain charitable or other institutions.

Again, the disposal value is taken to be nil where the expenditure has been treated as incurred on plant or machinery by virtue of s. 27(2) (thermal insulation, personal safety, etc.).

Law: CAA 2001, s. 63
Guidance: CA 23250

20.4.7   Balancing allowances and charges

Balancing allowance

A balancing allowance will arise for the "final chargeable period" (see below) if, for any given pool, the available qualifying expenditure exceeds any disposal receipts that have to be brought into account. The balancing allowance is given in lieu of any AIA, FYA or WDA that might otherwise have been given.

Example 1 – balancing allowance

Joanna is retiring from her business. She has drawn accounts up to 30 June each year but now has a final set of accounts for the six months to 31 December.

At the start of the final chargeable period, she has a value brought down in the main pool of £2,400. She buys a paper shredder in the year for £150 and she sells some office equipment for £300.

She cannot claim any FYAs, WDAs or AIAs, but she obtains a balancing allowance of the net amount of £2,250.

There is no automatic balancing adjustment simply because a business no longer owns any assets in the pool.

Example 2 – no balancing allowance

Greg operates a simple business that requires one large machine. He has had the machine for some years and its written-down value is £20,000. He sells it for £3,000, and he then hires a new machine.

Greg is not entitled to any balancing allowance. Rather, he can simply claim WDAs on £17,000, carrying the remaining balance forward and claiming on the reducing balance year by year thereafter.

Adjustments to the allowances will be needed where there is private use of the asset by a business proprietor (or family member).

Law: CAA 2001, s. 55(2), (4)

Final chargeable period

For the main pool, and for the special rate pool, the final chargeable period is the period in which the qualifying activity is permanently discontinued.

For a single-asset pool, it is normally any period in which there is a disposal of the asset in question. However, this is modified if plant or machinery starts to be used partly for other purposes, and in relation to SLAs after eight years.

Law: CAA 2001, s. 65

Balancing charges

A balancing charge is the method whereby allowances that have been given are partially or wholly clawed back. Such a charge arises fairly rarely for an ongoing business, as disposal proceeds will normally simply reduce the balance in the continuing pool of expenditure.

A balancing charge will arise, however, if the proceeds (capped at original cost) exceed the total of expenditure brought forward and new expenditure in the year.

Example 3 – balancing charge

Petra, with a balance of £1,200 brought forward in her main pool, incurs no further expenditure but sells some old items for £1,500 (being less than their original cost).

The £1,500 is offset against the balance brought forward and a balancing charge is imposed of £300.

Law: CAA 2001, s. 55(3)

20.5   Cars and other vehicles

20.5.1   Introduction

PMAs are generally available for cars and other vehicles used for the purposes of a qualifying activity. The rate at which relief is given for cars is dictated mainly by the level of CO_2 emissions. More detail is given in the following pages but, in summary, the following is the position from April 2021:

- most cars attract WDAs at just 6%;
- higher WDAs (at 18%) are given for cars with emissions not exceeding 50g/km;
- FYAs are given for most new cars (and new goods vehicles) with zero emissions, including electric cars;
- AIAs are not given for any vehicle classified as a car, but are available for other vehicles.

Most expenditure on cars today goes into the special rate pool, though it may occasionally still go into the main pool. In either case, the cars will thus be merged with other assets (e.g. air conditioning systems or computers) in one or both of these pools. Where there is private use of a vehicle (e.g. by a sole trader) it is allocated to a single-asset pool (though private use by a director or employee is not treated as such for capital allowances purposes).

Law: CAA 2001, s. 38B, 268A
Guidance: CA 23510

20.5.2   Definition of car

A "mechanically propelled road vehicle" is treated as a car for capital allowances purposes unless it is:

- a motorcycle;
- a vehicle of a construction primarily suited for the conveyance of goods or burden of any description; or
- a vehicle of a type that is not commonly used as a private vehicle and that is unsuitable for such use.

441

By default, therefore, a mechanical vehicle designed to drive on the roads is treated as a car, even if it would not be so treated under any normal definition (e.g. if it is a quadbike or – see *Morris* – a motor home). An invalid carriage is also treated as a car for these purposes.

HMRC interpret these provisions tightly, but accept that neither dual control vehicles nor emergency vehicles are to be treated as cars. It is thought that hearses would also escape the definition, though the treatment of funeral limousine vehicles is less clear cut.

Taxis are cars, but HMRC accept that "traditional 'London black cab' type vehicles" fall outside the definition.

Law: CAA 2001, s. 268A
Case: *Morris v R & C Commrs* [2006] BTC 861
Guidance: CA 23500

Conveyance of goods or burden

A vehicle is not treated as a car for capital allowances purposes if it is "of a construction primarily suited for the conveyance of goods or burden of any description" (i.e. a goods vehicle). What matters is therefore the construction, rather than the use, of the vehicle. Much of the case law relates to employee benefits (for company cars) but the tests are similar, with one or two exceptions.

The following points, based largely on HMRC guidance, may be relevant:

- People are not "goods or burden" (*Bourne v Norwich Crematorium*).
- The manufacturer's description is relevant but not determinative.
- HMRC interpret the word "primarily" in a literal way, arguing that if "neither purpose predominates with regard to the construction of the vehicle, the vehicle is not primarily suited for either purpose and this means that it does not escape from being a car".
- A vehicle with side windows behind the driver and front passenger doors will normally be treated as a car.
- Similarly, the HMRC view is that the vehicle will usually be a car if it is fitted (or is capable of being fitted) with additional seating behind the driver's row of seats.

It is difficult to fault the following HMRC comments:

"Most estate cars (or indeed cars with some sort of boot) are suited to the dual purpose of carrying passengers and some cargo or luggage. But it is clear that what they are primarily suited for is the conveyance of passengers.

In contrast, a standard transit van is also capable of carrying a driver plus a passenger (occasionally two) as well as cargo, but it is clear that what it is primarily suited for is the conveyance of goods or burden.

A vehicle will not automatically satisfy this test simply because it has only one row of seats. There are certain sports cars and leisure vehicles that can only seat a driver and one passenger, but that are quite clearly not primarily suited for carrying goods or burden."

The dividing line between cars and vans was explored in some depth in the Upper Tribunal *Coca-Cola* decision (and in the earlier hearings in that case).

A vehicle may change its status through permanent, substantial modification, but HMRC do not accept that painting a vehicle in a particular way (e.g. to include an advertisement for the business products) would change the type of vehicle.

Law: *Road Traffic Act* 1988, s. 185(1); CAA 2001, s. 268A; ITEPA 2003, s. 115(2)

Cases: *Bourne (HMIT) v Norwich Crematorium Ltd* (1964) 44 TC 164; *Payne, Garbett and Coca-Cola European Partners Great Britain Ltd v HMRC* [2017] UKFTT 655 (TC); *HMRC v Payne, Garbett and Coca-Cola European Partners Great Britain Ltd* [2019] UKUT 90 (TCC)

Guidance: EIM 23110-23125

Not suitable for use as a private vehicle

A vehicle is not treated as a car for capital allowances purposes if it is:

- of a type not commonly used as a private vehicle; *and*
- unsuitable to be so used.

Both conditions must be met if the vehicle is to avoid being treated as a car for these purposes.

Law: ITEPA 2003, s. 115(1)(d)

Cases: *Bourne (HMIT) v Auto School of Motoring (Norwich) Ltd* (1964) 42 TC 217; *Gurney (HMIT) v Richards* [1989] BTC 326

Guidance: EIM 23135, 23140

20.5.3   Annual investment allowances

No AIAs are available for cars, but they are given for other vehicles.

AIAs are therefore available for motorcycles, vans and black London cabs (but not other taxis).

Law: CAA 2001, s. 38B, 268A

20.5.4   First-year allowances

As a general principle, no FYAs are available for cars. However, FYAs are available (until April 2025) for new (i.e. unused) cars if:

- the car is not bought for leasing; and
- it is electrically propelled or otherwise has zero CO_2 emissions (with a less stringent emissions test applying before April 2021).

FYAs are also available for zero-emission goods vehicles, which cannot in any circumstances emit CO_2 by being driven, again subject to the condition that they are not used for leasing.

Zero-emission vehicles used for a variety of specified activities are also precluded from qualifying for FYAs. The restrictions apply to businesses engaged in fisheries, aquaculture and (where performed for third parties) certain waste management activities.

Law: CAA 2001, s. 45D, 45DA, 45DB, 46, 268A
Guidance: CA 23153

20.5.5   Writing-down and other allowances

In practice, allowances for cars are nearly always given by means of WDAs. A "main rate car" is allocated to the main pool (and therefore attracts allowances at the standard rate). Most cars today, however, go to the special rate pool, but subject to a complication where there is private use.

The following vehicles are (from April 2021) classified as main rate cars:

- cars with an official CO_2 figure that does not exceed 50g/km;
- any car first registered before March 2001; and
- cars that are propelled *solely* by electrical power.

Any car that is not a main rate car, as so defined, is normally allocated to the special rate pool, attracting allowances at a slower rate. In practice, most new cars (other than electric cars) therefore now attract allowances at just 6% per year, such that the tax relief lags way behind commercial depreciation.

As the expenditure is pooled with other assets, the sale of a car will not normally produce any balancing allowance or charge; instead, the proceeds will simply reduce the value in the ongoing pool. The practical effect of this is often to delay the timing of tax relief, as cars (especially those cars with higher emissions) generally depreciate faster than the rate of WDAs.

Law: CAA 2001, s. 104A, 104AA, 268B

Private use

A car (whatever the level of emissions) is allocated instead to a separate single-asset pool if there is any private use by the business proprietor. WDAs are calculated using the same rate as would otherwise apply (i.e. depending on the level of emissions) but allowances are then restricted to reflect the level of private use.

Example

Pete is a sole trader who buys a car for £20,000. It has emissions of 123g/km and it is therefore a special rate car. One quarter of the use is for private purposes.

The car must be kept out of the main pool. With a WDA rate of 6%, Pete's allowances for Year 1 will be £900 (£20,000 x 6% gives £1,200, from which one quarter is deducted). The amount carried forward to the next year is, however, calculated by subtracting the full £1,200 from the cost, rather than the amount as amended for private use. So the figure carried forward is £18,800.

Using the same principles, allowances for Year 2 will be £846, and the amount carried forward will then be £17,672.

Although the private use restriction permanently reduces the allowances that are given, the effect can be partially countered by an advantage in terms of timing of relief. This is because an asset with private use is allocated to its own single-asset pool and the disposal will therefore trigger a balancing adjustment. For cars, that adjustment will normally be a balancing allowance (as the tax relief tends to lag behind the real depreciation rate of the car).

Law: CAA 2001, s. 65(2), 104A
Guidance: CA 23535

445

Very expensive cars

The HMRC view (not necessarily accepted by the author) is that very expensive cars may still be subject to a restriction of capital allowances if "there is a blatant incongruity between the asset provided for the director or employee and the commercial requirements of the business". This is based on the principles brought out in the *Northiam Farms* case.

Case: *G H Chambers (Northiam Farms) Ltd v Watmough* (1956) 36 TC 711
Guidance: CA 27100

Short-life assets

A car can never be treated as an SLA (see, generally, **20.6.5** below) but there is no reason in principle why a van should not be so treated (unless it is used partly for purposes other than those of the qualifying activity).

Law: CAA 2001, s. 84

20.5.6   Employees

Employees claim mileage relief – rather than capital allowances – for business mileage. The claiming of capital allowances by employees for their cars is specifically prohibited.

Employers, of course, may claim allowances for cars owned by the business but driven by directors or employees (and no adjustment is made to the capital allowances computation for private use of the vehicle in such circumstances).

Law: CAA 2001, s. 36, 59; ITTOIA 2005, s. 94E

20.5.7   Car hire

The treatment of car hire costs is not strictly a capital allowances issue. In broad terms, however, there is a fixed 15% disallowance of car hire costs if emissions exceed a given threshold, set at 50g/km from April 2021. The disallowance is not applied to maintenance or similar costs, if identified separately in the rental agreement.

Law: CAA 2001, s. 104AA; ITTOIA 2005, s. 48*ff*; SI 2017/740

20.5.8   Fixed-rate deduction

As an alternative to claiming capital allowances, some unincorporated businesses have the option of claiming mileage allowances.

As a general principle, no mileage allowances may be claimed if the car has already been subject to a capital allowances claim. Once mileage allowances are claimed, any residual capital allowances value is written off. The effect of this was expressed in the *Explanatory Notes* to the *Finance Bill* 2018 as follows:

> "This prevents unrelieved capital expenditure on a particular vehicle, being carried forward for capital allowances purposes for that property business, when mileage rates have been used for that vehicle for that same property business."

Law: CAA 2001, s. 59; ITTOIA 2005, s. 94E

20.6   Other matters

20.6.1   Special rate expenditure

The special rate expenditure rules apply to slow down the rate at which tax relief is given for certain classes of asset. The most important categories of special rate expenditure are integral features (see **20.3.6**) and most cars (see **20.5**). The concept also covers thermal insulation, solar panels and long-life assets.

Special rate expenditure is allocated to a special rate pool. If an asset falls into one of the categories of special rate expenditure, but is used partly for private or certain other purposes, it is allocated to a single-asset pool but WDAs are still given at the slower rate.

Law: CAA 2001, s. 104A-104G
Guidance: CA 23220

Reduced allowances

WDAs for the special rate pool are given at just 6% (rather than 18%), adjusted for shorter or longer periods. A lower amount may be claimed (e.g. to prevent wastage of the personal allowance).

The "small pools" rule (see **20.4.3**) allows the balance to be written off once it falls below a given threshold.

AIAs are generally available for special rate expenditure, subject to normal rules, but are not given for cars.

Law: CAA 2001, s. 104D

20.6.2   Property fixtures

Valuable tax relief is available (and is all too often missed or underclaimed) for property fixtures. This topic is covered in depth in **Chapter 21**.

Law: CAA 2001, Pt. 2, Ch. 14

20.6.3   Apportionments

When two or more items are sold together, the net proceeds of sale of any given item must be calculated as "so much of the net proceeds of sale of all the property as, on a just and reasonable apportionment, is attributable to that item".

Law: CAA 2001, s. 562
Guidance: CA 12100*ff.*

20.6.4   Hire purchase and assets provided by lessees

One of the conditions for claiming PMAs is that the person who incurs the expenditure must, as a result, own the asset in question. This can cause problems for hire purchase (HP) contracts.

The nature of an HP arrangement is that the lessee has use of an asset but the lessor retains ownership until a final instalment has been paid. The capital allowances rules ensure that the lessee rather than the lessor is entitled to allowances, as long as the lessee has the right to acquire the asset at the end of the contract. HMRC use the terms "hire purchase" and "lease purchase" synonymously.

A special provision applies if the contract is one which, in accordance with generally accepted accounting practice (GAAP), falls (or would fall) to be treated as a lease. The special HP rules outlined above will in such a case apply only if the contract falls (or would fall) to be treated by the lessee in accordance with GAAP as a finance lease.

The HP rules do not apply to fixtures (as defined for capital allowances purposes: see **Chapter 21**).

Law: CAA 2001, s. 11(4)(b), 67, 69; FA 2019, Sch. 14
Guidance: CA 23310-23350

Timing of expenditure

As soon as the plant or machinery is brought into use for the purposes of the qualifying activity, the person is treated for capital allowances purposes as incurring all the capital expenditure that is to be incurred by him under the HP contract thereafter.

Deemed disposals

A person treated as owning plant or machinery under the HP rules may cease to be entitled to the benefit of the contract without actually ever owning the asset in question. Such a person is treated as making a disposal of the plant or machinery at that time. The disposal value will consist of any "relevant capital sums", as defined.

Law: CAA 2001, s. 67(4), 68, 229
Guidance: CA 23310

Assets provided by lessees

A lessee is treated as owning plant or machinery (if he does not in fact do so) if he is required to provide the asset under the terms of a lease, and he incurs capital expenditure in doing so for the purposes of his qualifying activity. This rule does not apply to fixtures.

Law: CAA 2001, s. 70
Case: *Inmarsat Global Ltd v HMRC* [2019] UKFTT 558 (TC)

20.6.5   Short-life assets

The SLA rules are always optional, but can speed up tax relief in certain circumstances. For most businesses, AIAs provide a simpler and better alternative, so use of the SLA rules is now relatively rare, other than for the largest businesses.

Where an SLA election is made, the asset is removed from the main pool. Capital allowances are instead calculated on the asset in isolation, within a single-asset pool. Any tax advantage comes only when the asset is sold or scrapped, at which point there may be an acceleration of the allowances that would otherwise have been given. An SLA election only has any beneficial effect if the asset is disposed of within a given period of approximately eight years.

Example – effect of election

Amir buys some machinery in Year 1 for £20,000 and sells it in Year 3 for £7,000. He has already used up his AIA for Year 1 on other purchases. He has a range of other assets in his main capital allowances pool. Assume a WDA rate of 18% throughout.

If Amir simply adds the new machine to his main pool, he will obtain allowances of £3,600 in Year 1, £2,952 in Year 2 and £2,421 in Year 3. By the time the asset is sold, therefore, he will have had tax relief on just £8,973, even though the actual depreciation is £13,000. He will eventually receive allowances on the rest of the £13,000 but this will be by way of ever reducing amounts over future years.

By making an election for SLA treatment, Amir will receive the same allowances in Year 1 and Year 2, but will receive a balancing allowance in Year 3 instead of the WDA of £2,421. This balancing allowance will be calculated by starting with the original cost of £20,000 and deducting the allowances already received in Years 1 and 2 (£6,552). From this net amount of £13,448, the disposal proceeds of £7,000 are deducted and he can claim a balancing allowance in Year 3 of £6,448.

An SLA election may occasionally be disadvantageous. If Amir had sold the machine for £17,000 instead of £7,000, he would have suffered a balancing charge of £3,552.

The SLA election (which must be made within normal self-assessment time limits) will only have an effect if the asset is disposed of within a specified period (broadly eight years) from the end of the chargeable period in which it was acquired. In simplified terms, the asset is transferred back into (normally) the main pool if there is no disposal of the asset within that eight-year period. The tax effect is usually then the same as if no election had been made.

An SLA election may not normally be made for cars, for special rate expenditure, for leased assets, or in various other circumstances. Certain exceptions apply, however.

Law: CAA 2001, s. 83-86

20.6.6   Long-life assets

Certain assets are categorised as long-life assets (LLAs), and are then subject to the slower rate of tax relief for special rate expenditure (see **20.6.1** above).

Plant or machinery is an LLA if, when first brought into use, it can reasonably be expected to have a useful economic life of at least 25 years. It is necessary to look at the life of the asset as a whole, not at its component parts, some of which may be replaced sooner.

Law: CAA 2001, s. 90-104

Fixtures

Fixtures are exempt from the LLA regime if they are for use in a building used mainly as a dwelling-house, hotel, office, retail shop or showroom. Fixtures in other premises will be subject to the LLA rules in the same way as any other assets (based on the expected life of the asset, and not of the building as a whole).

Law: CAA 2001, s. 93
Guidance: CA 23720, 32221, 32311

Other particular assets

Cars and motorcycles are never treated as LLAs.

HMRC provide detailed guidance in relation to certain jet aircraft.

Greenhouses, formerly subject to a special agreement, must now be considered on their own merits.

Most printing equipment will *not* be an LLA.

Law: CAA 2001, s. 96
Guidance: CA 23781-23783, 23790

Monetary limit

The legislation includes a "monetary limit". The idea is to provide a *de minimis* exemption from the effects of the LLA restrictions. The limit is £100,000, reduced or increased for shorter or longer chargeable periods. So a trader who spends £80,000 in a given year will not normally have to apply the LLA rules.

Care is needed with second-hand assets, however. Once an asset is classed as an LLA, that treatment continues for future owners as well, unless it is a fixture used for one of the excluded types of trade.

The monetary limit exemption does not apply for trusts, for assets for leasing, for shares in plant or machinery, or for contribution allowances (see **20.6.9**).

The rules are more complex where (broadly) an individual carries on more than one activity, and for partnerships where (broadly, again) at least half of the partners are engaged in other activities.

Law: CAA 2001, s. 97-100
Guidance: CA 23740

20.6.7 Software

Computer software, whether bought or developed, is specifically treated as constituting plant or machinery. For capital expenditure (determined on ordinary principles), a person paying for the right to use software is treated as owning it, so that PMAs may be given. If the person owning the software receives a capital payment, e.g. by granting a licence for its use, a disposal value is brought into account.

Law: CAA 2001, s. 71-73
Guidance: CA 35800*ff.*

20.6.8 Partnerships and successions

Partnership changes are generally ignored for the purposes of claiming PMAs, as long as at least one person carrying on the activity before the change continues to do so thereafter. The ongoing partnership continues to claim allowances (and to be subject to balancing charges) as if anything done by former partners had been done by the present partners.

Law: CAA 2001, s. 263

Property owned by partner

Assets owned by partners individually, but used for the partnership business, are treated as partnership property. For example, where partners own cars personally but use them for the partnership business, allowances are claimed as part of the partnership return. This rule does not apply if the asset in question is let by the partner to the partnership, or if the partner receives a payment that is deductible in calculating the taxable partnership profits.

Law: CAA 2001, s. 264
Guidance: CA 29020

Successions

The term "succession" is used where one person takes over (succeeds to) a qualifying activity previously carried on by someone else (as distinct from a partnership change, where at least one person continues from before).

The general rule for successions is that any relevant property *given* by the old owner to the new is treated as sold at market value by the predecessor to the successor at the time of the succession. The person acquiring the assets can claim WDAs but not AIAs or FYAs. "Relevant property" means assets used by the predecessor before the transfer and by the new owner for the purposes of the activity immediately after the transfer. This could therefore arise for a gift or for a business incorporation if certain assets are gifted to the newly formed company.

Where assets are sold, normal principles will therefore apply. For non-fixtures, the disposal value will generally be determined by item 1 of the table at s. 61(2). For fixtures, an election under s. 198 will usually be needed to determine the transfer value.

Law: CAA 2001, s. 265
Guidance: CA 29030

Connected persons

Where there is a succession to a business, the predecessor and the successor may jointly elect for different treatment if they are connected with each other (see s. 575) and if each is within the charge to tax on the profits of a qualifying activity (and whether or not the plant or machinery has actually been sold or transferred). The joint election must be made within two years from the date of the succession.

Where such an election is signed, relevant plant or machinery is treated as sold by the predecessor to the successor at a price that gives rise to no balancing adjustment (i.e. at the capital allowances written-down value). For fixtures, this election should routinely be accompanied by an election under s. 198 (see **Chapter 21**).

If there is no succession to the business, no election is possible and normal principles are applied, even between connected parties (but subject to general anti-avoidance considerations).

Example

John has decided to incorporate his business. He owns a machine that cost £60,000 and that is now worth £40,000. John was not able to claim AIAs because of other expenditure. The written-down value of the machine is £25,000. John may:

- sell the machine to the company for a notional figure of £1, potentially gaining a balancing allowance (as item one in the table at s. 61 will apply to give a disposal value of just £1);

- transfer the machine at its written-down value of £25,000, and sign an election, thus avoiding any balancing adjustment; or

- give the asset to the company but sign no election, in which case he will have to bring in the market value of £40,000, potentially producing a substantial balancing charge.

Law: CAA 2001, s. 265-267, 575
Guidance: CA 29030-29040

20.6.9   Contributions

If someone contributes to the costs of an asset for a second person (e.g. a landlord contributing to fit-out costs for a tenant, or a grant given by the NHS to a medical practice) there are potential implications for both parties.

Treatment of the recipient

The recipient is treated as not having incurred expenditure to the extent that it is met directly or indirectly by a public body or by another person, whether the grant (for example) is capital or revenue in nature. A repayable loan is not a contribution, but if part of a grant is returned the original recipient cannot then claim allowances.

If the person making the payment cannot claim any form of tax relief, the recipient may be able to ignore the contribution and claim unrestricted capital allowances. This relaxation applies as long as the contributor:

- is not a public body;
- is unable to claim relief under the rules for contributions (considered below); and
- cannot deduct the contribution in calculating the profits of a trade or other "relevant activity" that he or she carries on.

Law: CAA 2001, Pt. 11
Guidance: CA 14100-14300

Treatment of the contributor

A person who makes a contribution to someone else's capital expenditure may be entitled to claim PMAs for some or all of the expenditure. The parties must not be connected, and the contribution must be made for the purposes of the contributor's trade.

HMRC example

Johnny runs a restaurant. June has a market garden where she grows herbs that Johnny uses in the restaurant. June buys new equipment for the market garden and Johnny makes a contribution towards her costs. Johnny's contribution is deducted from June's expenditure qualifying for PMA ... and Johnny can claim PMA on the contribution.

But if Johnny and June are married Johnny cannot claim capital allowances on his contribution because they are connected persons. However June can then claim capital allowances on all of her expenditure – the contribution is within the exception for contributions by someone other than a public body who cannot get relief for it.

Law: CAA 2001, s. 537, 538
Guidance: CA 14400

Different rules

Special rules apply for:

- insurance receipts (s. 535); and
- reverse premiums (ITTOIA 2005, s. 100(1)).

20.6.10 Anti-avoidance

The PMA rules are peppered with anti-avoidance measures, including (among others) the following:

- allowance buying (s. 212A-212S);
- restrictions for certain connected persons (s. 213-218);
- transactions to obtain tax advantages (s. 213-218A);
- certain sale and leaseback transactions (s. 216-218ZA, and s. 230); and
- certain hire purchase transactions (s. 229).

There are also measures that apply in more restricted circumstances, for example:

- for integral features sold to connected parties;
- the prevention of additional AIAs;
- the prevention of accelerated allowances for cars;

- sales of SLAs at less than market value; and
- disposal values for special rate expenditure.

20.6.11 Additional VAT liabilities and rebates

There may be capital allowances implications when a person incurs an "additional VAT liability" or receives an "additional VAT rebate".

Broadly speaking, additional VAT paid by the owner of an asset is qualifying expenditure, and AIAs, FYAs or WDAs may all be given, as appropriate.

There is a disposal event if a person receives an additional VAT rebate while owning the asset at some time in the chargeable period in which the rebate is made.

Law: CAA 2001, s. 234-246
Guidance: CA 29230

20.6.12 Partial depreciation subsidy

Allowances are restricted if the person claiming is entitled to receive a "partial depreciation subsidy". HMRC give the example of an employee who uses an asset owned personally for work purposes, and who receives a payment from his or her employer to cover some or all of the depreciation.

Law: CAA 2001, s. 209-212
Guidance: CA 27500

20.6.13 Long funding leases

The complex long funding leases regime applies for income tax as well as for corporation tax purposes. The broad effect is to give PMAs to the lessee (as economic owner) rather than to the lessor (the legal owner).

Law: CAA 2001, s. 34A; FA 2006, Sch. 8, para. 15-27
Guidance: CA 23805

20.7   Pitfalls and planning points

Qualifying expenditure

The definition of plant and machinery is very broad, but subject to certain statutory restrictions.

Annual investment allowances

AIAs offer relief for substantial amounts of qualifying expenditure, but severe restrictions apply when the AIA thresholds change (see **20.4.2**).

Cars

Most cars now attract allowances at just 6%, such that they lag far behind commercial depreciation rates. Better allowances are available for very low emission cars and, especially, for electric vehicles. Sole traders may paradoxically obtain much faster allowances if they make some small element of private use of their cars (see **20.5**).

21. Fixtures

21.1 Introduction

21.1.1 Overview

Fixtures (in their capital allowances sense – see **21.2** below) are by definition plant or machinery, so the rules described in **Chapter 20** above (plant and machinery allowances (PMAs)) apply. However, those rules are modified and extended by special provisions found at Chapter 14 of Part 2 of the *Capital Allowances Act* 2001. In particular, the special rules for fixtures are needed to determine ownership, which is in turn a fundamental condition for claiming PMAs.

For more detailed guidance on this topic, see *Capital Allowances* 2021-22, available from Claritax Books.

Law: CAA 2001, s. 172

21.1.2 When the fixtures rules need to be considered

The fixtures legislation is relevant for those who incur capital expenditure on property, whether buying or improving it.

Allowances are not generally given for residential property, though this is subject to certain exceptions. Fixtures claims can be made for communal areas (e.g. the reception area for a block of flats), and for other parts of residential accommodation that do not themselves form part of any dwelling. See also **20.3.7** above.

The fixtures rules should be considered as early as possible if a client:

- is buying a new or existing property, or extending or improving a property;
- is granting, or is being granted, a lease over a property, if the client is paying a capital sum (lease premium);
- is assigning, or is accepting the assignment of, an existing lease (i.e. sideways to or from another tenant), again if there is a capital payment;
- acquired an interest in a property in the past and did not fully consider the fixtures rules at that earlier time; or
- is planning to sell a property (or otherwise to dispose of a property interest), or has done so in the past two years.

21.2   Definition of fixture

The term "fixture" is defined to mean "plant or machinery that is so installed or otherwise fixed in or to a building or other description of land as to become, in law, part of that building or other land".

This statutory definition differs from the term "fixtures and fittings" that is used more loosely in the accountancy sense. Tables and chairs in a restaurant are certainly plant and machinery but they are not usually fixtures. By contrast, the ceiling lighting in the restaurant will normally be shown in the accounts as part of the cost of the property, but this lighting is a fixture (and therefore by definition also plant or machinery) for capital allowances purposes. HMRC guidance explains that the term "fixture" has the same meaning here as it does for property law purposes.

As such, the fixtures rules relate specifically to assets (such as lighting or central heating) that qualify for PMAs despite being part of the property.

HMRC's *Stamp Duty Land Tax Manual* gives examples of items that will normally be treated as fixtures rather than as moveable chattels, including fitted cupboards, fitted bathroom sanitary ware, central heating systems and intruder alarm systems.

Law: CAA 2001, s. 173(1)
Guidance: BIM 46910; CA 26025; SDLTM 04010

21.3   Interests in land

In most cases, a person can only claim allowances for fixtures in property if he has some underlying interest in the land. The interest will normally be either a freehold or a leasehold, but the concept also includes a licence to occupy land, an easement or servitude.

A lease of land is defined to include any leasehold estate in the land, or any agreement to acquire such an estate.

The meaning of "licence to occupy" was considered in *J C Decaux*, and HMRC guidance is that:

> "A licence to occupy is a permission to enter and remain on land for such a purpose as enables the licensee to exert control over the land."

Law: CAA 2001, s. 174(4), 175
Case: *J C Decaux v Francis* (1996) Sp C 84
Guidance: CA 26100

21.4   Ownership of assets

21.4.1   Introduction

A key condition for obtaining PMAs is that the person who incurs the capital expenditure should own the plant or machinery as a result. This usually poses no problems, but particular issues arise in relation to fixtures. Suppose, for example, that a tenant installs air conditioning in a property. Legally, the building belongs to the landlord; as the air conditioning – once installed – forms part of the property, it immediately belongs to the landlord. Without special rules, the landlord could not obtain allowances (as he has not incurred the cost) and the tenant could not claim allowances (as he does not own the air conditioning system).

The point came to a head in the *Costain Property* case. Although it felt compelled to rule against the taxpayer, the court could see no reason of principle to justify the outcome. Special rules were therefore introduced from 1985. Those provisions, as amended, are now at CAA 2001, Pt. 2, Ch. 14.

Law: CAA 2001, s. 11, 172*ff.*

Case: *Costain Property Investments Ltd v Stokes* [1984] BTC 92

21.4.2   Deemed ownership

To overcome the problem of ownership identified above, the fixtures rules create a legal pretence of ownership so that PMAs may be given for fixtures in certain defined circumstances.

The following are identified in the legislation as potential claimants of capital allowances by virtue of the special fixtures rules:

- persons with an interest in relevant land;
- equipment lessors and energy service providers;
- purchasers of land giving consideration for fixtures;
- purchasers of land discharging the obligations of an equipment lessee, or under an energy services agreement; and
- incoming lessees (with different rules according to whether or not the lessor is entitled to allowances).

In practice, some of these categories arise much more frequently than others, and the key ones are considered below.

Law: CAA 2001, s. 172, 172A

21.4.3   Persons with an interest in relevant land

A person is treated as owning fixtures, for the purposes of claiming PMAs, where:

- he incurs capital expenditure on plant or machinery, for the purposes of a qualifying activity he is carrying on;
- the plant or machinery becomes a fixture; and
- the person has an interest in the relevant land at the time the item in question becomes a fixture.

If a tenant pays to add an air conditioning system, for example, he will in principle be able to claim PMAs on the costs.

Where there are different interests in the same land, the legislation broadly gives the right to claim allowances to the person with the lowest interest – e.g. the tenant rather than the landlord.

Law: CAA 2001, s. 173(2), 176
Guidance: CA 26150

21.4.4   Purchasers of land with fixtures

This is another important category, covering the ordinary purchase of a commercial property. It applies where:

- plant or machinery has become a fixture;
- a person thereafter acquires an interest in the relevant land (which must exist before the purchaser acquires it, so the granting of a new lease is not covered under this section);
- the amount paid is, or includes, a capital sum; and
- that capital sum falls to be treated as expenditure on the provision of a fixture.

In such cases, the new owner can in principle claim allowances on an amount paid for the fixtures in the property. Determining that amount can be straightforward (where an election is made) or complicated (where a valuation apportionment is needed).

The new owner is not, however, entitled to claim allowances to the extent that someone else has a prior right to the allowances. It is therefore important when acquiring a tenanted property – whether from the landlord or the tenant – to be clear about which parties have a right to claim allowances on which fixtures.

Law: CAA 2001, s. 181, 562
Guidance: CA 26250

21.4.5 Tenants

For leased property, the landlord, the tenant, or possibly someone else, may be entitled to claim the allowances. The intention of the legislation is therefore to resolve the question of who is entitled to claim where two or more persons have an interest in the land.

To apply the fixtures rule it is necessary to be clear about the distinction between two different concepts:

- granting a new lease; or
- assigning an existing lease.

For tax purposes in general, and for capital allowances purposes in particular, these two options are treated very differently.

21.4.6 Granting a new lease

An incoming tenant (lessee) may incur capital expenditure (a lease premium) on land that contains fixtures. Where the necessary conditions are met, the tenant may then be treated as owning the fixtures for the purposes of claiming PMAs.

The legislation draws a distinction between:

- cases where (broadly) the lessor is entitled to claim allowances, in which case a conscious decision must be taken by both parties to transfer (by election) the right to claim allowances from landlord to tenant; and
- other cases, where the tenant's right to claim allowances is automatic in certain cases.

Law: CAA 2001, s. 183-184
Guidance: CA 26350

21.4.7 Assigning an existing lease

Different issues arise where an existing lease is assigned by an outgoing tenant to a new one. This scenario does not come within either s. 183 or s. 184 (above) because both of those sections only apply where a person "grants a lease" (i.e. a new lease).

Example

ABC is a legal partnership that took on a lease of an old office block in 2010. The property was extensively refurbished at the time, and all the old fixtures were stripped out. ABC installed new heating and electrical systems, as well as a variety of other new fixtures. It quantified the expenditure qualifying as fixtures at £450,000 and has since been claiming PMAs on those fixtures.

In May 2021, ABC sells ("assigns") the lease to DEF, an accountancy LLP, receiving a capital payment of £1 million. This constitutes a disposal of the fixtures by ABC and an acquisition of those fixtures by DEF. An election under CAA 2001, s. 198 will be required (not s. 199 as this is not the *grant* of a lease).

Law: CAA 2001, s. 173, 174

21.5   New construction costs

21.5.1   Introduction

Where a person incurs capital expenditure on constructing, improving or extending a commercial property (see below) a part of that cost will normally qualify as expenditure on fixtures. PMAs can then be claimed for the cost of those fixtures, including lighting and electrical costs, hot and cold water systems, toilets and other sanitaryware, central heating, lifts, and much else besides.

Example

Janet and Jo Care LLP buys some land for £500,000 and then pays £1 million to build a new care home. Equipping the home with moveable furniture (beds, chairs, tables, etc.) costs a further £40,000. Analysis shows that £425,000 of the build cost and the whole of the additional costs qualify for allowances, the former category qualifying as "fixtures" in the capital allowances sense.

If the partners have a marginal income tax rate of 40%, the £465,000 has the potential to save them tax of £186,000.

The figures *cannot* simply be lifted from the accounts. Most or all of the fixtures will be shown in the accounts under some such heading as "land and buildings"; items shown in the accounts as "fixtures and fittings" or as "plant and machinery" will qualify for PMAs but are not fixtures in the tax sense (see **21.2** above).

Integral features

Any fixtures claim will include an amount for integral features. These are a subset of fixtures, and are subject to their own modification of the normal fixtures rules. The most common integral features are hot and cold water systems, heating and ventilation systems, general electrical and lighting systems, and lifts. The concept is fully defined at CAA 2001, s. 33A.

Commercial property

The reference above to "commercial" property is important. This term is not a statutory one, but is a useful shorthand, essentially to be contrasted with residential property, for which allowances are much more restricted (see **20.3.7**). It should nevertheless be remembered that PMAs are in principle available for qualifying expenditure (including fixtures) in communal parts of residential property blocks. See **21.1.2** above.

21.5.2 Quantifying the qualifying expenditure

A fixtures claim should give rise to substantial levels of legitimate tax relief. The methodology for calculating the claim will in practice depend on the size of the project.

For most sizeable projects, the surveyor will have prepared a bill of quantities. This will include a detailed breakdown of the pricing of the project, prepared before work is begun. As the bill of quantities has been prepared in advance of the work carried out, it will contain provisional sums, and these will have to be resolved. Similarly, there will inevitably be variations along the way as the work is put into practice and as complications arise.

In other cases, the paperwork will not be adequate to prepare a claim for allowances. This may be the case, for example, if the work was undertaken many years previously. In such situations, a specialist capital allowances valuer will be able to survey the property and create a proper computation of the costs incurred.

21.5.3 Professional fees

A proportion of professional fees will be treated as expenditure on plant or machinery. Broadly speaking, if a more accurate approach can be obtained from a reasonable amount of work then that should be done, but a *pro rata* apportionment is acceptable where the work involved for a more accurate assessment would be disproportionate.

Fees of a mechanical or electrical engineer may well qualify in full, but will need apportionment between general plant and integral features. On the other hand, some legal fees may be too remote from the provision of plant or machinery to qualify at all. Fees for a structural engineer, a quantity surveyor or an architect are all examples of professional costs where some apportionment will usually be required between qualifying and non-qualifying elements.

Cases: *J D Wetherspoon plc v HMRC* (2007) Sp C 657; *J D Wetherspoon plc v HMRC* [2009] UKFTT 374 (TC); *J D Wetherspoon plc v HMRC* [2012] UKUT 42 (TCC)
Guidance: CA 20070

21.5.4   Overheads and preliminary costs

These categories of expenditure are likely to arise in almost any project, and it is important to identify the part of the costs that may be claimed as qualifying expenditure on plant and machinery.

Overhead costs should be apportioned in a reasonable way between the different categories of expenditure: those qualifying as standard plant or machinery, those qualifying as special rate expenditure (e.g. integral features) and those not qualifying at all (or, perhaps, now qualifying for structures and buildings allowances).

In the various *Wetherspoon* appeals, it was held that businesses should not be expected to spend a disproportionate amount of time on the exercise. In the Upper Tribunal, this approach was "unhesitatingly" approved, such that the HMRC appeal on the question of preliminaries "entirely fails".

If a project proves to be abortive, no relief will in principle be due. This is because no tangible asset will come into existence. See also the case of *ECC Quarries* discussed at BIM 35325.

Cases: *ECC Quarries Ltd v Watkis* (1975) 51 TC 153; *J D Wetherspoon plc v HMRC* (2007) Sp C 657; *J D Wetherspoon plc v HMRC* [2009] UKFTT 374 (TC); *J D Wetherspoon plc v HMRC* [2012] UKUT 42 (TCC)
Guidance: BIM 35325; CA 20070

21.5.5 Extensions

For any capital expenditure on an existing building, the same principles apply as they do for newly constructed property. Once more, it will be necessary to divide up the total cost between elements that qualify as fixtures and those that do not.

Care is needed if integral features are being replaced on a significant scale, as such expenditure may be automatically treated as capital for these purposes (s. 33A).

21.6 Fixtures elections

21.6.1 Introduction

The fixtures election fixes for capital allowances purposes the transfer value of fixtures on the sale of a property. It is binding on both parties and on HMRC.

An election is essential for anyone buying a property and intending to claim capital allowances for fixtures. The election also offers vital protection for a taxpayer who is selling a property containing fixtures that have been the subject of a capital allowances claim.

This section explains the principles. Their practical application is then considered for buyers at **21.7** and for vendors at **21.8**.

Example

Javeed has a portfolio of commercial properties and is selling one of these properties to Propco (an unrelated party).

Javeed has made all appropriate claims, on fixtures costing £350,000 forming part of the property in question. The property to be sold is unfurnished, so there are no items of plant or machinery except for fixtures.

As Javeed has other properties, it is not possible to say that a given pool value exists in relation to this particular property (as allowances for all properties have correctly been merged into two pools – one for special rate expenditure and one for main rate expenditure – without separation between the properties). Javeed's overall pool values are £400,000 for the main pool, and £120,000 for the special rate pool.

Javeed and Propco both recognise that a fixtures election is needed, but whereas Javeed wants the elected figures to be as low as possible, Propco wants to maximise its claim. In the end, the parties agree an overall fixtures value of £100,000, split £1 to main rate expenditure and £99,999 to special rate expenditure. The election reflects these figures, and Javeed brings those amounts into his tax computations as disposal figures, reducing his pool values but not triggering any balancing charges. Propco claims annual investment allowances (AIAs) on the whole of the £100,000.

The election is made under s. 198 where (broadly) the property is sold at not less than market value. An election may instead be made under s. 199 where an incoming tenant pays a lease premium to the landlord so as to acquire a subsidiary interest in the property.

Figures for the election

There is no requirement for the values in the election to be "commercial" or "market value". The figures cannot exceed the amount being paid for the property. Nor can the figure for any given fixture exceed its historic cost. Subject to these restrictions, however, the parties can agree any figure from £1 upwards.

In the example above, note the split between special rate and main rate expenditure, which is permitted by the rules. This works to the benefit of Javeed (as he would prefer to reduce his special rate pool rather than the main rate pool, so as to receive faster tax relief in future on the reducing balances), but at no cost to Propco (as it is claiming AIAs on the whole cost anyway).

Effect of no election

In the absence of a valid fixtures election, Propco (and also all future owners of the property in question) would be completely barred from claiming allowances for all those fixtures on which Javeed *claimed or could have claimed* allowances.

Javeed would still have to bring into account a disposal value, using an apportioned amount. A valuation exercise would be needed to determine that amount but it could well be as high as the historic £350,000 cost of the fixtures.

Wording in the sale and purchase agreement is *not* an alternative way of achieving the same result. In the absence of a valid election (or, exceptionally, any alternative way of meeting the fixed value requirement – see **21.7.4** below), the legislation unambiguously shows that the tax relief is permanently lost.

Law: CAA 2001, s. 198, 199

21.6.2 Legal requirements

A fixtures election should be signed jointly by seller and purchaser and must be submitted within two years of the date of sale (or of the grant of the lease). It must specify the amount fixed as the sale price for a particular fixture (but see below where, as is almost certainly the case in practice, there are multiple fixtures). This must be an actual figure rather than a formula or algorithm.

The election must include all of the following and will (at least in principle) be invalid if any of these items is missing:

- the amount fixed by the election;
- the name of each of the persons making the election;
- information sufficient to identify the fixture(s) covered by the election;
- information sufficient to identify the relevant land;
- particulars of the interest acquired by the purchaser (or, as the case may be, particulars of the lease granted); and
- the unique taxpayer reference (UTR) of each of the parties, or a statement that one or both does not have a UTR.

The taxpayer must include a copy of the election when subsequently making a tax return.

The election is irrevocable, but if the figure included in the election proves – because of circumstances arising after the making of the election – to be higher than the statutory maximum, the election is treated as having been made in the maximum allowable amount.

The normal income tax rules relating to claims and elections (TMA 1970, s. 42 and Sch. 1A) are disapplied for these purposes.

A person is obliged to notify HMRC if a return becomes incorrect as a result of making a fixtures election under s. 198 or s. 199.

The notice must be given (in writing – s. 577(1)) within three months of the person becoming aware that something has become incorrect. All such assessments and adjustments may then be made as are necessary to rectify the matter.

Law: CAA 2001, s. 203

21.6.3   Election not possible in some circumstances

An election under s. 198 is only possible where the disposal value of the fixture has to be brought into account in accordance with items 1 or 9 of the table at s. 196. Normally, this means that it may be made when there is a sale of a property at not less than market value. No election is possible if the vendor is a non-taxpayer (such as a pension fund) or if the vendor has held the property on trading account rather than as a capital asset. A *purchaser* who is a non-taxpayer should still sign an election, however.

An election is also normally possible if the sale is at less than market value as long as it is to a person who can claim allowances under CAA 2001, Pt. 2 (plant and machinery) or Pt. 6 (research and development). Again, an election is possible if the permanent discontinuance of the qualifying activity is followed by a sale of the qualifying interest in the property.

An election is not possible in relation to other, less common, types of disposal. No election may be made, for example, if the fixture starts to be used wholly or partly for private purposes, or if the permanent discontinuance of the qualifying activity is followed by the demolition or destruction of the fixture.

Law: CAA 2001, s. 196, 198(1), 199(1)

21.6.4   Multiple fixtures in one election

A typical property may contain thousands of different fixtures. Strictly speaking, an election is made on a fixture-by-fixture basis (s. 198 referring to "the provision of *the fixture*") but this would be wholly impractical in reality.

As such, HMRC will allow "a degree of amalgamation of assets where this will not distort the tax computation". It is important, however, to ensure that nothing breaches the validity of the election. For this reason, HMRC normally require some apportionment of value between integral features and other fixtures.

Good practice dictates that the distinction between integral features and other fixtures should be taken a step further by including in the election separate schedules, and separate figures, for three categories of expenditure:

- assets that have always been general fixtures (e.g. toilets);
- assets that were general fixtures for the seller but that are now special rate (e.g. lifts); and
- assets (bought by the seller since 6 April 2008) that are special rate expenditure for both seller and buyer.

If the seller could not claim for particular assets, because they were bought before April 2008 and did not then qualify, they will not be included in the election. The buyer will nevertheless claim for these, in addition to any amounts included in the election.

HMRC never allow a single election to cover the fixtures in more than one property.

Law: CAA 2001, s. 198
Guidance: CA 26850

Fixtures only

The election must include information sufficient to identify the fixtures covered, and the amount fixed for those fixtures.

If the election purports to include "all fixtures and fittings" or "all plant and machinery" then this will create problems because that category could include plant or machinery other than fixtures (e.g. beds in a hotel or care home, or possibly desks in an office building), even though such moveable items (chattels) should be totally excluded from a fixtures election. If there is just one figure allocated for everything, then it is certainly arguable that no amount has been "fixed" for the fixtures, and that the election is therefore invalid.

An election could arguably be valid if worded to cover "all the fixtures in the property" but best practice involves the use of one or more schedules in which the fixtures are more specifically identified. In any case, care would be needed to ensure that a prior claim had been made for all the fixtures in the property, as the inclusion of an item for which no claim had previously been made (e.g. a replacement item where the cost had been claimed as revenue expenditure) would again risk invalidating the election.

21.6.5 Restrictions on amounts claimed

If a previous owner has claimed PMAs in relation to any given fixture, the claim by the new owner is restricted to the disposal value brought into account by a previous owner (s. 185), or to the figure that should have been brought into account if the tax computations had been prepared correctly (see *Glais House*). That disposal value will in turn be capped at the cost incurred by the previous owner.

It is quite possible, of course, that the property will have had more than one previous owner. In principle, it is then necessary to cap the qualifying expenditure at the lowest historic disposal value.

Equivalent restrictions apply if a previous owner claimed industrial buildings allowances, business premises renovation allowances or research and development allowances.

Law: CAA 2001, s. 62, 185
Case: *Glais House Care Ltd v HMRC* [2019] UKFTT 59 (TC)
Guidance: CA 26400

21.6.6   Amounts to include in election

Beyond the statutory restrictions, the question of what figures to include in an election is one of negotiation, and will depend in part on the relative negotiating strength of the two parties, on whether the vendor has unused losses, on whether the buyer is a non-taxpayer, and on who is in fact driving the whole capital allowances exercise.

21.6.7   Sample election

The following is an example of an election that might be used in the case where a freehold property is sold by a limited company to an unconnected partnership.

The election includes three different categories of asset, which have been given names for identification (main rate fixtures, special rate fixtures, changed status fixtures). These non-statutory terms help to achieve the clarity for both parties that the legislation demands.

Election under CAA 2001, s. 198

We hereby elect under section 198 of the *Capital Allowances Act 2001* to fix the amount that is to be treated for the purposes of Part 2 of that Act as the part of the sale price that is on the provision of the specified fixtures.

In this election:

- "main rate fixtures" means fixtures correctly allocated to the main pool by both parties;

- "special rate fixtures" means fixtures correctly allocated to the special rate pool by both parties;
- "changed status fixtures" means fixtures that were main rate expenditure for the seller but that are special rate expenditure for the buyer.

The property: the whole of the premises at [address].

Title number: ANY12345.

Interest acquired: freehold.

Price paid: £1.2 million

Date of transaction: 1 February 2021.

Seller: Yellow Ltd, whose registered office is [address]. Unique Tax Reference: 11111 22222.

Buyer: The Green Partnership, [address]. Unique Tax Reference: 33333 44444.

Main rate fixtures covered by this election: as listed in the attached Schedule 1.

Special rate fixtures covered by this election: as listed in the attached Schedule 2.

Changed status fixtures covered by this election: as listed in the attached Schedule 3.

Amount fixed for main rate fixtures: £25,000.

Amount fixed for special rate fixtures: £50,000.

Amount fixed for changed status fixtures: £5,000.

Signature of seller (with date) ....

Signature of buyer (with date) ....

The schedules will be an important part of the election, and must only include fixtures (in their capital allowances sense – see **21.2** above) so there should be no mention of any moveable chattels such as chairs or tables. The third schedule will not be needed if the vendor bought the property since April 2008.

21.7   Buying property

21.7.1   Introduction

Every commercial property contains fixtures (e.g. lighting systems and toilets). When the property changes hands, ownership of the fixtures forming part of the property will by definition be transferred. The transaction therefore constitutes (a) the sale of fixtures by the vendor and (b) the acquisition of the same fixtures by the purchaser. This raises capital allowance considerations for both parties.

This section explains the legalities and the practical issues that arise from the buyer's point of view. The seller's perspective is covered at **21.8** below.

21.7.2   Conditions for claiming allowances

For most property acquisitions, two specified conditions must be met if the buyer is to obtain any allowances: the "pooling requirement" and the "fixed value requirement".

If these two requirements apply in the circumstances of the deal but are not met, the purchaser – and all future owners of the property – will be denied allowances for the fixtures in question (but the past owner must still bring in a disposal value – see **21.8** below.)

A third requirement – the "disposal value statement requirement" – is imposed in much rarer circumstances, as explained at **21.7.7** below.

These various requirements are often referred to as the "FA 2012" rules, as they were introduced by that Act.

Law: CAA 2001, s. 187A(3)

When the requirements are imposed

The FA 2012 rules are imposed in most but not all cases. The conditions for them to apply may be summarised as follows:

- The buyer of the property ("the current owner") must own a fixture as a result of incurring capital expenditure for the purposes of a qualifying activity.
- A previous owner (usually but not necessarily the seller in the current transaction) must have owned the fixture as a result of incurring capital expenditure for the purposes of a qualifying activity.

- It is not the case that the fixture was treated as owned only by virtue of the special rules for contribution allowances.
- That previous owner must have been entitled to claim PMAs on the fixture in question (whether or not he in fact did so).

The last condition above may prevent the imposition of the FA 2012 restrictions in various circumstances. This may be the case, for example, for certain integral features acquired before April 2008. Some items now classified as integral features did not normally qualify for relief if they were already owned before that date.

Example

Charlie bought an office building in 2002 and is now selling it. He meets all the conditions in respect of most of the fixtures in the property, so the pooling and fixed value requirements must be met if the purchaser is to claim allowances. However, Charlie is not entitled to claim allowances for the cost of the general lighting, for example.

It follows that the pooling and fixed value requirements do not apply to the lighting costs. The new owner (Deborah), however, is entitled to claim for the costs, and the quantum of the claim must be established by applying apportionment principles. Charlie has no interest in this part of the claim, but he will need to cooperate with Deborah regarding all the remaining fixtures in the property.

Another circumstance in which this condition will not be met is when the vendor has owned the property since before April 2012 (the date from which, broadly speaking, the FA 2012 rules apply) and is a non-taxpayer, such as a charity or pension fund. (But if a charity bought the property in 2015, for example, it will now be necessary to look back to the details of that earlier transaction.)

Law: CAA 2001, s. 187A(1)

21.7.3   Pooling requirement

Allowances will be denied to the buyer of a property (and to future owners) if the pooling requirement is imposed on the seller, but is not met. In essence, the pooling requirement simply means that the seller must have added the qualifying expenditure to his own capital allowances computations – to the extent that he is permitted to do so.

Example

A Ltd bought a property in 2009 and is now selling it to Ella. Ella can only claim allowances for fixtures in the property if A Ltd has added them to its own computations first.

However, this only applies if A Ltd is entitled to claim, and each fixture must in principle be considered separately. If A Ltd had bought the property before April 2008, for example, it will probably not be entitled to claim allowances for certain integral features. These fixtures would not be covered by the pooling requirement.

Law: CAA 2001, s. 187A

21.7.4   Fixed value requirement

If the general conditions at **21.7.2** above are met, allowances will be denied to the buyer, and to all future owners, if the fixed value requirement applies but is not satisfied.

In practice, the fixed value requirement is nearly always met by signing an election (a "fixtures election") under s. 198 (see **21.6** above).

The requirement may instead be met by obtaining a determination from "the tribunal" (i.e. the First-tier Tribunal). A further way in which the fixed value requirement may be met arises only where there is an intermediate owner (e.g. a charity or a pension fund) who is not entitled to claim PMAs. Exceptionally, allowances may be given if evidence can be provided that a disposal value was brought into account by an earlier owner.

Law: CAA 2001, s. 187A(5)-(9)

When the requirement must be met

The fixed value requirement has to be met only where the disposal value is given by items 1, 5 or 9 of the Table at s. 196. These cover respectively a sale at market value; an incoming lessee paying a lease premium; and a property sale following permanent discontinuance of a business.

Law: CAA 2001, s. 187A(5)-(9)

21.7.5   Apportionments

There is a statutory requirement to find a "just and reasonable apportionment" when a property containing fixtures is sold. This applies even if the single transaction is supposedly split into several separate parts or if separate prices are agreed for particular assets.

475

The fixtures election is often the only permitted way of determining the apportioned value, but an apportionment is still required if no election is possible. So if a valid election is signed, that will determine the transfer value of the fixtures, but an apportionment may still be needed for other items of plant or machinery (chattels).

What is a just and reasonable apportionment?

The question of what is a "just and reasonable apportionment" is far from intuitive but valuation specialists have for years had an agreement in place with HMRC that requires a particular approach.

The non-statutory approach gained approval in the FTT *Bowerswood House* case in 2015. HMRC's guidance also refers to the much earlier case of *Salts v Battersby* to support the assertion that "the underlying aim of any method of apportionment should be to apportion the purchase price in proportion to the values of the constituent parts that go to make up the property".

The key point is to use *replacement* values rather than the market value that the items would have if they were stripped out and sold individually, so the fact that a property is old does not mean that the values are low. Indeed, the value apportioned to the plant and machinery is often much higher than the (possibly negligible) amount it would attract if sold separately from the property.

Most accountants will wish to engage specialist valuers for all but the smallest cases, to ensure that the client is properly looked after and that the valuation can withstand HMRC scrutiny. It will also be necessary to consider other capital allowances rules, which may impose other statutory restrictions on the values.

Law: CAA 2001, s. 562

Cases: *Salts v Battersby* [1916] 2 KB 155; *Bowerswood House Retirement Home Ltd v HMRC* [2015] UKFTT 94 (TC)

When is the apportionment needed?

An apportionment will be needed in various circumstances.

First, a person may acquire a property from someone who bought it before April 2008. In such a case, the vendor will not normally have been able to claim for certain integral features that did not then qualify (typically, cold water systems, general lighting systems and other general electrical costs). In addition to any amounts included in the fixtures election, the buyer will in principle be able to claim on an apportioned valuation basis for such assets.

Second, a vendor may not have made a full capital allowances claim for the fixtures. Even though the values now will be determined by making a fixtures election, the vendor's right to pool the expenditure in the first place may require an apportionment as at an earlier date.

Example

Joe is buying a property from Donna in 2021. The transfer value of the fixtures must be determined by signing an election.

Enquiries made by Joe's advisers, however, make it clear that Donna has never made a full capital allowances claim since she bought the property back in 2006. No election was signed at that earlier time.

An apportionment exercise will be needed now to determine the amounts (if any) of qualifying expenditure incurred by Donna at that earlier time. Various entitlement checks will be required (e.g. restrictions from the time of purchase; whether some fixtures have since been stripped out). Subject to those, Donna will be able to add further qualifying expenditure to her capital allowances pools and the two parties can negotiate a higher figure for the fixtures election.

Another case where an apportionment may be needed is if a property is being bought from a non-taxpayer, such as a local authority, a pension fund or a charity. Such vendors are not able to sign a fixtures election, and the rules that apply depend on when they acquired the property in their turn; broadly speaking, the capital allowances figures for the buyer will be determined by apportionment if the vendor acquired the property before April 2012, or in some cases April 2014, but subject to a cap for claims made by previous owners.

A further example of where an apportionment could be required is if the vendor incurred revenue expenditure on an asset that is nevertheless clearly capital expenditure for the buyer. Here, too, the buyer can make a claim using an apportionment approach.

21.7.6   Commercial property standard enquiries

Accountants or others advising in relation to property transactions will often be asked by the legal teams to respond to capital allowances queries on the commercial property standard enquiries (CPSE) form. This form is normally sent by the solicitor acting for the buyer as a way of gathering essential information from the vendor.

CPSEs cover much more than just capital allowances, but the final section deals with capital allowances. The accountant advising the buyer may be asked to review the replies received from the vendor's side, and a critical evaluation of the answers is essential to protect the buyer's interests.

In practice, CPSE replies provide a useful starting point but can almost never be relied on to give all the information the buyer needs, so an appreciation of the implications of each question and answer is essential. Given the substantial amounts of expenditure at stake, this is an area where non-specialist tax advisers may wish to engage a competent capital allowances specialist to work alongside them.

21.7.7   Disposal value statement requirement

The "disposal value statement requirement" is (according to HMRC guidance) likely to apply only very infrequently.

A taxpayer may be required to bring a disposal value into account even though the property has not been sold: for example, if the qualifying activity simply comes to an end but without a disposal of the property. If he then does sell the property some years later, it will not be possible to enter into an election with the buyer to fix the value of the fixtures (as the requirements of s. 198(1) will not be met and it may in any case be too late). Instead, the new owner can ask the past owner for a written statement giving details of the disposal value that that past owner was required to bring into account. However, the past owner should not delay making the statement: even though it may not be needed until some years after the disposal is brought into account, there is a two-year time limit for the past owner to make the written statement.

Law: CAA 2001, s. 187A(11)

21.7.8   Summary for buyer

The main claim to be made by the purchaser of a property will therefore be determined by the fixtures election.

In some circumstances, the purchaser will also need to consider a claim based on an apportionment approach.

Certain professional and other costs may also qualify for allowances.

Finally, relief may be due also for moveable items of plant and machinery (chattels).

Law: CAA 2001, s. 11, 187A, 187B

21.8   Disposals

21.8.1   Introduction

Whenever a (non-residential) property is sold, there are likely to be important capital allowances considerations.

Tax relief for the fixtures in the property is valuable. A vendor needs to recognise that potential value and to build it in to negotiations from an early stage – the price of the property should not be agreed without factoring in the tax relief.

It may be that the vendor retains the entire amount of tax relief, or passes it all to the buyer, or (more probably) the parties may agree to share the relief between them in some way.

The pooling and (especially) the fixed value requirements are also important considerations for the vendor (see **21.7.3** and **21.7.4** below respectively). First, however, it is necessary to consider what constitutes the disposal of a fixture for capital allowances purposes.

21.8.2   Types of disposal

Introduction

Most disposals of fixtures come about when a property is sold; if an owner sells the property, this will by definition constitute a disposal of the fixtures it contains. If the vendor has claimed allowances for any fixtures, a fixtures election will be essential. If there are fixtures for which the vendor could have claimed allowances, but did not, the pooling requirement may also need to be considered (see **21.8.5**).

The concept of a disposal of fixtures is broader than just a sale, however. As we have seen, allowances are often given for fixtures by means of a statutory sleight of hand: the legislation creates a pretence of ownership, and a tenant claims allowances *as if* he were the owner of the property. In such cases, the normal disposal rules cannot apply to fixtures as a person cannot dispose of something he does not really earn. The fixtures rules therefore have an expanded definition of what constitutes a disposal.

The general principle is that a person who has been treated as the owner of a fixture under the fixtures provisions is treated as ceasing to own the fixture at the time he ceases to have the qualifying interest (as defined at s. 189).

If, on the termination of a lease or licence, the outgoing lessee or licensee is treated under these rules as ceasing to be the owner of a fixture, the lessor or licensor is treated as the owner of the fixture from the time of the termination of the lease or licence.

Law: CAA 2001, s. 188, 190, 192-195B
Guidance: CA 23150

21.8.3   *Disposal values*

The disposal value to be brought into account depends on the nature of the event triggering the disposal.

For a normal sale of the qualifying interest at or above market value, the sale price for the vendor is specifically linked to the part of the price on which the buyer can claim PMAs as expenditure on fixtures. In certain other cases, market value is substituted, or a different value is used.

A detailed table is given at s. 196, and the HMRC version, at CA 26700, may be preferred as it is easier to digest than the table itself.

When the figure to be used for the disposal value is the figure of net proceeds of sale, the apportionment rules of s. 562 should not be overlooked. In particular, where two or more items are sold together, the net proceeds of sale of any given item must be calculated as "so much of the net proceeds of sale of all the property as, on a just and reasonable apportionment, is attributable to that item".

Anti-avoidance provisions provide for a different value if the disposal event is linked to a scheme or arrangement of which a main purpose is the obtaining of a plant and machinery tax advantage.

Law: CAA 2001, s. 35, 197, 562
Guidance: CA 26700

21.8.4   *Pooling requirement*

The pooling requirement generally has been considered in detail at **21.7.3** above. The vendor of a property cannot be forced, by HMRC or by a tax tribunal, to pool expenditure before a property is sold, and there are no tax penalties for failing to do so.

The result of such failure, however, is to surrender permanently to HMRC the tax relief that could otherwise be enjoyed by the new owner or by the vendor (or that could be shared between them). From a commercial point of view, therefore, a vendor will almost certainly wish to understand the principles and to pool expenditure as far as it is legitimate to do so. If done correctly, the effects can only be positive, whether the vendor reduces his own tax bill or whether he enhances the real value of the property for the buyer, which is likely to make the sale proceed more readily.

In some cases, the vendor of a property on which there is valuable tax relief to be claimed will be able to command a higher price than an equivalent property that does not offer such potential tax savings.

Practicalities for the vendor

The pooling requirement means that the vendor is asked to add to his or her capital allowances computations any qualifying expenditure that has previously been left out. In practice, this may mean adding one figure to the main pool and another to the special rate pool. Having made these additions, it is open to the vendor to negotiate a disposal value for the fixtures (the fixed value requirement – see the next section below), and this will determine how the tax relief for the qualifying expenditure is to be shared between the parties.

Example

Janice has run a successful village pub for a number of years, but is now selling out as she wishes to retire.

She is advised that there was unclaimed qualifying expenditure of around £40,000 from the time of purchase, including some additional capital expenditure incurred at that time. The expenditure is properly analysed and, in the event, she is able to add £25,000 to her special rate pool and £17,000 to her main pool. Her pool values before this exercise were nil and £5,000 respectively.

Having worked out her potential tax liabilities, her accountant advises her that she needs to retain £32,000 of these allowances, so she agrees to sign a fixtures election whereby:

- she transfers the special rate assets to the buyer for £1; and

- the main rate assets for £14,999.

This will give her allowances of £24,999 for the special rate pool (value brought down of nil, plus expenditure added of £25,000, less disposal value of £1).

Janice will also have allowances of £7,001 for the main rate pool (value brought down of £5,000, plus expenditure added of £17,000, less a disposal value of £14,999).

Combining these, she achieves her desired target allowances of £32,000.

The split between special rate and main rate assets has no impact for Janice, as she will obtain a balancing allowance in her final year, but will be helpful for the buyer (who can claim WDAs at the higher rate).

21.8.5   Fixed value requirement

The fixed value requirement nearly always involves the signing of a fixtures election under s. 198 (or s. 199 where a new lease is granted) (see **21.6** above). There are potentially disastrous consequences for *both* parties if this is not done.

For the vendor, the consequences depend on the extent to which allowances have been claimed for fixtures in the property. In the absence of an election, the vendor is likely to have to bring into account a disposal value that could be very high. This will reduce the vendor's pool value and may result in a balancing charge, which could be substantial. The underlying principle here is that in the absence of a fixtures election the vendor will have to bring in a disposal value on a "just and reasonable" basis, and this could well reverse most or all of the allowances given for the fixtures in question.

Example

Roger and Martina have run a nursing home as a partnership. They are now planning to sell the business.

Over the years, they have incurred qualifying expenditure on fixtures in the property amounting to £400,000. Through a combination of annual investment allowances and writing-down allowances, the value remaining in their capital allowances pools is just £35,000.

The buyer is asking for a minimum transfer value of £50,000, to be reflected in a fixtures election. This will give them a balancing charge of £15,000 and they are considering their options.

- They may decide simply to sign the election as requested, and to take the hit on the balancing charge. It will not be huge in the overall context of the sale and may be a price worth paying to secure the sale.

- They may negotiate the figure down, and say that they are willing to sign an election for £35,000, but no more. If that is agreed, the outcome is likely to be acceptable to them (even though they would ideally have had an election for just £1, if they could use the extra allowances, as this would reduce their income tax liability).

- They may agree to meet somewhere in the middle.

They should categorically *not* simply refuse to sign a fixtures election. If they refuse, but the sale goes ahead anyway, there are two possible outcomes, both of which are likely to prove very expensive for Roger and Martina.

The first possibility is that the buyers do not go to the tax tribunal. In this case, the buyers will be denied allowances for all the fixtures in question (though they may be able to claim for certain integral features for which the vendors could not claim). The partners will still have to bring in a disposal value, however (per s. 187B(6)). This disposal value will have to be calculated on a just and reasonable basis, using agreed apportionment principles. The figure is likely to be much higher than the £50,000 that was asked for, and could be as high as £400,000.

The buyers could go to the tribunal and ask it to determine an appropriate figure (per s. 187A(7)(a)). The outcome will be uncertain, but the *Bowerswood House* case gave approval to the methodology that is well-established practice, and the result is again likely to be more than £50,000 and could still be as high as the full figure of £400,000. The buyers will be able to claim accordingly and the partners will have to bring in the appropriate disposal value.

In summary, it is always better to reach a negotiated figure, to remove the uncertainties and costs of going to tribunal, and to ensure that the parties can between them enjoy the full tax relief.

Case: *Bowerswood House Retirement Home Ltd v HMRC* [2015] UKFTT 94 (TC)

Guidance: https://tinyurl.com/y2v75xjo (Valuation Office Agency manuals)

21.9   Interaction with CGT

It is sometimes thought that if, say, £50,000 of costs are allocated to fixtures rather than to the property, the base cost of the property is reduced accordingly and a higher capital gain will eventually ensue.

Despite the apparent logic, this is simply incorrect; this is because the division between property on the one hand, and fixtures on the other, is a false one. Making a claim for capital allowances does not increase any CGT charge when the property comes to be sold. The only impact a claim for PMAs for the fixtures can have is if the property is later sold at a loss, in which case there is a restriction on the tax relief that might have been given at that time.

The interaction of CGT with the newer structures and buildings allowances (SBAs) works differently, however (see **22.8**). This distinction between SBAs (on the one hand) and the allowances available for fixtures under the plant and machinery code (on the other) is one of several reasons why the latter will be the more attractive allowances to claim where possible.

Law: TCGA 1992, s. 39, 41; CAA 2001, s. 2, 247
Guidance: CG 15400*ff.*

21.10   Claims and amendments

A person is said to make a claim in respect of a fixture if he or she makes an actual claim or includes the cost in a tax return (or an amendment to a return) as qualifying expenditure.

Law: CAA 2001, s. 202

Amending a return

A person is obliged to notify HMRC if a return becomes incorrect for any of the following reasons:

- withdrawal of approval for the purposes of s. 180 (affordable warmth programme);
- any of sections 181(2), 182(2), 182A(2) or 184(2) (where another person has a prior right to claim) applies;
- s. 185 applies (restriction on qualifying expenditure where another person has claimed an allowance);
- a fixtures election is made under s. 198 or s. 199; or

- s. 200(4) applies (reduction in amount which can be fixed by an election).

The notice must be given within three months of the person becoming aware that something has become incorrect. All such assessments and adjustments may then be made as are necessary to rectify the matter. The notice must be in writing (s. 577(1)).

Law: CAA 2001, s. 203

21.11   Pitfalls and planning points

Fixtures elections

Both parties to a commercial property should sign a fixtures election, as failing to do so can be very expensive for either party. The amounts to go into the election need to be negotiated as early in the process as possible. Care is needed as an election can be invalid for numerous different reasons. See **21.6** above.

The two-year time limit for making the election is strictly enforced.

Pooling requirement

The buyer of a commercial property must ensure that the vendor has met the pooling requirement as fully as possible, as failure to do so will be expensive for the buyer. See **21.7.3** above.

Claiming allowances for historic expenditure

Opportunities remain for claiming allowances for fixtures in properties bought many years ago. Dates are critical, with different rules applying depending on whether the property was bought before 6 April 2008, 2012 or 2014, or on or after those dates. See **21.5** above.

Due diligence

It is easy to focus on valuations before checking that there is any entitlement to claim at all, potentially causing risk to the client for years to come (e.g. in the event of a future discovery assessment). A good capital allowances specialist will always put entitlement first, and will create a full audit trail to show the basis for the claim.

22. Structures and buildings allowances

22.1 Introduction

Structures and buildings allowances (SBAs) offer tax relief for the construction costs of non-residential properties and other structures.

The allowances are a poor relation of the plant and machinery regime, in that the relief is given slowly and there is a potential capital gains tax (CGT) cost at the point of disposal. Nevertheless, the allowances are a welcome additional form of relief, offering cash-flow benefits and in some cases permanent tax savings.

SBAs are not given for construction expenditure incurred before 29 October 2018, even if the building is acquired after that date. Allowances are available for UK taxpayers for buildings and structures in the UK or overseas.

For SBA purposes, the term "building" is specifically defined to include any "structure". References in this chapter to buildings are therefore to be read as including structures. Structures include (among other assets) roads, hard-surface car parks, fences, parts of golf courses and bridges.

For more detailed guidance on this topic, see *Capital Allowances* 2021-22, available from Claritax Books.

Law: CAA 2001, s. 270AA-270IH; FA 2019, s. 30
Guidance: CA 90250, 90300

22.2 SBAs at a glance

The key features of the SBA regime are as follows:

- Allowances are given at a flat rate of 3% per year, so typically over a period of 33.33 years.
- Allowances are not given for residential property or for land costs.
- There are no first-year allowances, annual investment allowances or balancing adjustments.
- The right to claim allowances until they are exhausted passes to the new owner when a building is sold. The new owner is required to obtain appropriate documentation to underpin the right to claim.

- The person claiming the allowances must have the relevant interest in the building. Special rules apply for certain leases of 35 years or more.
- SBAs are not given for property fixtures.

22.3   Conditions for claiming

22.3.1   Overview

Three core conditions must be met for these allowances to be available:

- The construction of a building must begin on or after 29 October 2018.
- Qualifying expenditure must be incurred on or after that date on its construction or acquisition.
- The first use of the building, after the qualifying expenditure is incurred, must be non-residential.

A person is entitled to an allowance for a given chargeable period if the person has the relevant interest (see **22.3.4**) in the building, in relation to the qualifying expenditure, in respect of any day in the chargeable period.

Allowances cease if the building is demolished.

Law: CAA 2001, s. 270AA; FA 2019, s. 30(1)
Guidance: https://tinyurl.com/ycw7vlos (HMRC Technical Note)

Highway undertakings

SBAs may be available for a person who is carrying on a highway undertaking, but who cannot claim the costs as revenue expenditure.

Law: CAA 2001, s. 270FA-270FC
Guidance: CA 94510, 94525

22.3.2   Date of construction

Construction is treated as beginning before 29 October 2018 (so that allowances are denied) "if any contract for works to be carried out in the course of the construction of that particular building or structure ... is entered into before that date".

The HMRC view is that a contract may consist simply of "an email exchange confirming works will take place".

A person who incurs pre-trading expenditure is treated as incurring it on the commencement date. This provision does not, however, allow expenditure incurred before 29 October 2018 to qualify.

Law: CAA 2001, s. 270AB, 270BN; FA 2019, s. 30
Guidance: https://tinyurl.com/ycw7vlos (HMRC Technical Note)

22.3.3   Evidence of expenditure (allowance statement)

No SBAs are given unless the person claiming (the "current owner") meets the "allowance statement requirement". The allowance statement must be made by (broadly speaking) the person incurring the qualifying expenditure. It must show, in relation to that expenditure:

- the date of the earliest contract for construction;
- the amount of qualifying expenditure; and
- the date on which the building was first brought into non-residential use.

HMRC state that for extensions or renovations completed after the structure is first used, "you can record separate construction costs on the allowance statement or create a new allowance statement".

Law: CAA 2001, s. 270IA
Guidance: CA 91400, 94650, 94700; https://tinyurl.com/yxjh2f8r (HMRC guidance: *Claiming capital allowances for structures and buildings*)

22.3.4   Relevant interest

SBAs are, broadly speaking, claimed by the person who has the relevant interest in the building.

The general principle is that the relevant interest, in relation to any qualifying expenditure, is the interest in the building or structure to which the person was entitled when the expenditure was incurred.

Different people may each have their own relevant interests in a building, each then claiming for his or her own qualifying expenditure. See **22.6** below for the special rules for leases.

Good record-keeping will be essential to meet the evidence requirement, as explained above.

Law: CAA 2001, s. 270DA-270DE
Guidance: CA 90510

22.4   Qualifying use

22.4.1   Introduction

Qualifying use means non-residential use for the purposes of a qualifying activity carried on by the person with the relevant interest.

The use must not be "insignificant". A building or structure that is only used for the purposes of a particular activity to an insignificant extent is not treated as used for those purposes. This must be determined on a just and reasonable basis.

Law: CAA 2001, s. 270CE; FA 2019, s. 30
Guidance: CA 92100, 92200; https://tinyurl.com/ycw7vlos (HMRC technical note re SBAs)

22.4.2   Residential use

A condition for claiming allowances is that the property must be in non-residential use. Entitlement to claim ends when a building or structure is brought into residential use.

Furthermore, it is a condition that the *first use* of the building, after the qualifying expenditure is incurred, must be non-residential. If this condition fails, no allowances are due under the SBA code. For this reason, it is essential to understand when qualifying expenditure is treated as being incurred.

The most common residential use will be as an ordinary dwelling-house. No allowances are given for *any part* of a building or structure that is used as a dwelling-house, even if it is used for other purposes as well. Allowances are not given for work spaces within domestic properties, such as home offices. A hotel is not a dwelling-house, but a serviced apartment is.

Reference should be made, as needed, to extensive HMRC guidance on other properties that may constitute residential use, including provision for school pupils or students, members of the armed forces, residential accommodation for children or adults, and prisons and similar establishments. With a growing range of options for housing and caring for older people, there are grey areas around the boundary between residential and non-residential accommodation.

Buildings are treated as in residential use if they are ancillary to a residential building, or situated on land intended to be occupied with such a building.

Law: CAA 2001, s. 270AA(3), 270CF; FA 2019, s. 30
Guidance: CA 92500-92800

22.4.3   Periods of disuse

Once entitlement to claim has been established, and as long as the building or structure is neither demolished nor turned to residential use, allowances will continue to be available. (The building or structure must be in actual (non-residential) use to trigger the initial ability to claim allowances, but allowances continue thereafter without the need for continuing actual use.)

Law: CAA 2001, s. 270AA, 270CE
Guidance: CA 92100, 92900

22.4.4   Qualifying activities

The main qualifying activities for SBA purposes are trades, professions, vocations and property businesses (though residential property letting is excluded). Furnished holiday lettings (in the UK or abroad) are *not* a qualifying activity.

Law: CAA 2001, s. 270CA-270CG
Guidance: CA 90450, 92300

22.4.5   Demolition

No further claims may be made for qualifying expenditure once the property is demolished in its entirety. HMRC have confirmed that:

"Demolition only applies to the demolition of an entire building. Where parts of a building, such as a single wall, are demolished, any capital costs of demolition or restoration works are covered under the capital renovation and conversion provisions."

Law: CAA 2001, s. 270AA(4)
Guidance: CA 91500

22.5   Qualifying expenditure

22.5.1   General principle

The legislation distinguishes between two types of qualifying capital expenditure:

- expenditure incurred on construction (see **22.5.2**); and
- expenditure incurred on a purchase (see **22.5.4** and **22.5.5**), where the rules depend on whether the person selling is a developer or someone else.

Certain other amounts (renovation costs, conversion costs, incidental repairs, and site preparation costs) are treated as construction costs for these purposes (see **22.5.6**).

Various costs are specifically excluded from qualifying. And if the first use of a building is residential use, the qualifying expenditure is nil.

Law: CAA 2001, s. 270BA

22.5.2   Construction costs

Construction costs include capitalised renovation and conversion costs, and site preparation costs (including demolition of an existing building), as well as professional fees relating to design and construction (as long as the building work does go ahead).

Capital expenditure is qualifying capital expenditure where it is incurred on the construction of a building; and

- the relevant interest (see **22.3.4**) in the building has not been sold; or
- it has been sold only after the building has been brought into non-residential use.

Where subsequent qualifying expenditure is incurred on the property, allowances will be claimed separately for that later expenditure, for a new 33.33-year period beginning from that time. Some flexibility is allowed in determining the date of new expenditure incurred after the property has been brought into use.

Law: CAA 2001, s. 270BB
Guidance: CA 93110

22.5.3   Burden of proof

The legislation puts the onus firmly on the taxpayer to prove that the qualifying construction expenditure has been incurred.

So the qualifying expenditure consists only of "the sum of those items of expenditure the actual amount of which can be shown". This means that estimates are not permitted (though a proper apportionment of expenditure actually incurred will sometimes be needed).

Law: CAA 2001, s. 270BM
Guidance: CA 91800, 91900

22.5.4   Sale by someone other than a developer

Unused buildings or structures

Where a building is sold by someone other than a developer, but before the building is first used, the qualifying capital expenditure incurred by the purchaser is the lesser of the amount paid and the actual construction costs.

The purchaser is treated as incurring qualifying expenditure when the capital sum is paid. If the buyer pays a deposit, with the balance on completion, the entire amount is treated as being incurred on the date of completion.

Land costs must be excluded (by apportionment). Stamp duty land tax (SDLT), and legal and surveyor costs, may be claimed if attributable to the building, but not to the land.

Guidance: CA 93500, 93550

Used buildings or structures

The sale of a used building (other than by a developer – see **22.5.5** below) does not give rise to new qualifying expenditure for the buyer. Rather, the buyer continues to claim by taking over the residue of qualifying expenditure previously incurred by the seller or by a previous owner.

This has an important implication for residential property. Even if the buyer will use the property for commercial purposes, no allowances will be available for the earlier construction costs, as this condition was not met when that earlier qualifying expenditure was incurred.

Law: CAA 2001, s. 270AA(1)(c), 270BC
Guidance: CA 91300

22.5.5   Sale by a developer

A "developer" is defined as "a person who carries on a trade which consists in whole or part in the construction of buildings or structures with a view to their sale".

Where property is bought from a developer, an apportionment will be needed to exclude land costs.

Law: CAA 2001, s. 270BD-270BL, 562
Guidance: CA 93600, 93650

Unused buildings or structures

In most cases, the sale of the relevant interest by the developer will be the only sale of that interest before the building is first used. Where this is the case, and where the purchaser pays a capital sum to acquire the relevant interest, that capital sum will be the qualifying capital expenditure. The construction cost is not relevant.

It is possible, however, that the sale by the developer will not be the only sale before first use of the building. In this case, if the purchaser pays a capital sum for the relevant interest on the last sale, the qualifying capital expenditure will be the lesser of the amount so paid and the amount paid for the relevant interest on its sale by the developer.

In either case, the qualifying expenditure is treated as incurred by the purchaser when the capital sum is paid.

Used buildings or structures

If the building is used before the relevant interest is sold by the builder, the construction expenditure is treated as the qualifying capital expenditure (even though it was in reality revenue expenditure). This then determines the tax position for the person to whom the relevant interest is first sold and for any person who subsequently acquires the relevant interest.

493

Example

A builder constructs a small office block. The land cost was £200,000 and the construction costs amounted to £350,000.

The builder is unable to sell the property. He therefore leases it out on a short lease with a three-month notice period. Two years later, a buyer is found and the property is sold for £600,000.

Although the buyer is in reality the first to incur capital expenditure, the rules are applied as if the £350,000 costs incurred by the builder had been capital rather than revenue expenditure. SBAs for the new owner will therefore be based on this figure.

22.5.6 Renovations, conversions and repairs

Renovation, conversion and repair costs – if not deductible because they are capital in nature – are treated as "capital expenditure on the construction of that part of the building or structure for the first time". So if a property is built in 2010 and renovated in 2020, no SBAs can ever be claimed for the original costs, but allowances are in principle available for the renovation costs.

Applying the same principle, if capital expenditure is incurred on residential accommodation in 2020, but the property is converted to business use some time later, the original construction costs cannot qualify for SBAs, but the conversion costs can.

Law: CAA 2001, s. 270BJ
Guidance: CA 91200, 93200

22.5.7 Excluded expenditure

Land

Allowances are specifically *not* available for the costs of acquiring or altering land (including land remediation). The exclusion extends to expenditure on seeking planning permission (including related fees and costs), and to SDLT (and equivalent Scottish and Welsh taxes) insofar as these relate to land rather than to the building.

Law: CAA 2001, s. 270BG
Guidance: CA 94010, 94100

Plant and machinery

SBAs may not be claimed to the extent that allowances are available under the plant and machinery rules for property fixtures (see **Chapter 21**), whether such allowances are in fact claimed or not.

Dividing qualifying expenditure between fixtures (the costs to be claimed under the plant and machinery regime) and non-fixtures (to be claimed under the SBA rules) will be a key element of tax planning. The former will give much faster tax relief, protection against higher taxation of capital gains (see **22.8**), and greater flexibility as between seller and buyer on disposal of the property.

Law: CAA 2001, s. 270BI
Guidance: CA 90250, 94300

Other restrictions

Capital expenditure on preparing land as a site for constructing a building may qualify, but not if it amounts to the alteration of land.

There is a broad principle that qualifying expenditure is restricted to market value.

HMRC list various non-qualifying costs, including financing and loan costs, capitalised interest, legal expenses, marketing costs and costs for which any grant or contribution is received.

Some fairly standard anti-avoidance rules are included to counter transactions involving "avoidance arrangements", as widely defined.

Law: CAA 2001, s. 270BH, 270BK, 270IB; FA 2019, s. 30(8)(b)
Guidance: CA 93250, 94200, 93110, 94810; https://tinyurl.com/yxjh2f8r (HMRC guidance: *Claiming capital allowances for structures and buildings*)

22.6   Leases

22.6.1   General principles

For SBA purposes, a lease is defined to include any tenancy and also an agreement for a lease if the term to be covered by the lease has already begun. It does not include a mortgage.

Both lessor and lessee may claim for their respective qualifying expenditure, as long as each is carrying on a qualifying activity. Typically the landlord will have a property investment business and the tenant may be carrying on a trade or profession.

Various rules apply where leases are terminated or extended.

Law: CAA 2001, s. 270IG, 270IH

22.6.2 Creation of new lease

As a general principle, the granting of a lease does not extinguish the existing relevant interest. So a freeholder, who grants a 10-year lease to a tenant, will continue to claim SBAs as before (though the tenant will claim for qualifying expenditure it then incurs).

Where a very long lease is granted, however, this becomes more akin to a sale. Modified rules therefore apply where:

- qualifying capital expenditure has been incurred;
- a lease is granted out of the relevant interest; and
- the "effective duration of the lease" is at least 35 years.

If the market value of the retained interest is less than one third of the capital sum paid, then the lessee is treated as acquiring the relevant interest in the building or structure on the grant of the lease. When the lease later expires, or is surrendered, the lessor is treated as re-acquiring the relevant interest from the lessee.

Where a lease premium is paid, part of the amount may be treated as a revenue (rather than capital) sum received, for the purposes of calculating the lessor's profits (ITTOIA 2005, s. 277 – see **27.3.2**). In such cases, any amount so treated is excluded for these SBA purposes from the capital sum when making the comparison with the market value retained.

The effective duration of a lease is to be determined in accordance with the rules at ITTOIA 2005, s. 303 (property income – calculation of profits of property business – lease premiums).

Example

Scarlett owns the freehold of a commercial property and grants an 80-year lease to Amber, charging a premium of £300,000 and an annual rent of £50,000. The value of the retained interest is calculated as £75,000.

A calculation must be made as the lease exceeds 35 years.

The market value of the retained interest (£75,000) is less than one third of the capital sum paid (£300,000). Amber is therefore treated as acquiring the relevant interest at the time the lease is granted. She

therefore takes over from Scarlett the right to claim allowances from that
date.

Law: CAA 2001, s. 270DC, 270DD
Guidance: CA 90600, 90800

22.6.3   Merger of leasehold interest

The relevant interest may be a leasehold interest that is extinguished
because the person entitled to the interest acquires the interest that is
reversionary on it. Where this happens, the interest into which the
leasehold interest merges becomes the relevant interest.

The natural ending of a lease does not, however, constitute the merger
of a leasehold interest.

Law: CAA 2001, s. 270DE
Guidance: CA 90700, 90800, 90900

22.7   Calculation and claims

22.7.1   General principles

The "basic rule" is that SBAs for a given chargeable period are 3% (2%
before 6 April 2020) of the qualifying costs, giving relief on a straight-
line basis over 33.33 years (formerly 50 years). There are no annual
investment allowances, first-year allowances or balancing allowances.

The 3% allowance is proportionately increased or reduced if the
chargeable period is longer or shorter than 12 months.

An apportionment is needed if:

- the conditions for giving allowances are only met for part of the
  year;
- a property is sold part way through a chargeable period;
- the property is demolished; or
- the building is put to multiple uses.

If relief is not claimed for a given period, that relief is then lost; it cannot
be deferred until a later period. It may occasionally be appropriate not
to claim the relief because of the interaction with the calculation of a
capital gain (see **22.8**).

Although the legislation refers to apportioning by reference to days,
HMRC have confirmed that "a reasonable adjustment by reference to

months in the period may be acceptable, provided it is used consistently throughout the period of ownership".

Chargeable periods spanning 6 April 2020 had allowances calculated on an apportioned basis, partly at 2% and partly at 3%.

The rate of allowances for structures and buildings in "freeport tax sites" will be 10% rather than 3% (for income tax as well as corporation tax purposes), once the designated sites have been confirmed.

Law: CAA 2001, s. 270AA, 270EA, 270EB; FA 2019, s. 30; FB 2021, cl. 109

Guidance: CA 91100, 91400; https://tinyurl.com/yxjh2f8r (HMRC guidance re SBAs)

22.7.2   No balancing adjustments

A property sale will not give rise to any balancing adjustment for the vendor. Instead, the purchaser steps into the vendor's shoes, as it were, and may start to claim allowances in respect of the residue of the qualifying expenditure. The purchaser's claim is based on the earlier construction cost, and not on the price paid to the vendor.

Allowances for the period in which the sale takes place will be apportioned between the two parties.

Guidance: https://tinyurl.com/yxax6ds8 (*Capital allowances for structures and buildings* – CIOT comments)

22.7.3   Interaction with R&D allowances

In some circumstances, research and development allowances (RDAs) will be claimed in relation to part or all of a property.

A "general rule" requires the deduction of any RDAs. So if a person buys a property for £1 million but can claim £300,000 of RDAs for part of the property, then the maximum figure on which SBAs could otherwise have been claimed is reduced by £300,000. This cannot, however, reduce the expenditure eligible for SBAs below nil.

A further restriction is applied where a person entitled to claim RDAs has sold the property, and where the buyer pays less than the total remaining SBAs available at the time of sale.

Law: CAA 2001, s. 270EC

22.7.4   Giving effect to allowances

Where the qualifying activity is a trade, profession or vocation, allowances are given in calculating the profits or gains of the activity in question, treating the allowances as an expense of the trade, profession or vocation in question.

Where the qualifying activity is an ordinary (UK or overseas), property business, allowances are given in calculating the profits of that business. No SBAs are allowed for an FHL business.

Law: CAA 2001, s. 270HA-270HC

22.7.5   Additional VAT liabilities and rebates

The legislation specifies how SBAs are to be calculated for the chargeable period in which an additional VAT liability accrues and for any subsequent chargeable period. In essence, the amount of qualifying expenditure is treated as increased, at the beginning of the chargeable period in which the additional VAT liability accrues, by the amount of the liability.

Conversely, the amount of qualifying expenditure is treated as reduced, at the beginning of the chargeable period in which an additional VAT rebate accrues, by the amount of the rebate.

Law: CAA 2001, s. 270GA-270GC
Guidance: CA 94555, 94570, 94580

22.8   Capital gains

When calculating any capital gain on disposal, the allowable cost of the asset is reduced by the amount of relief the vendor has claimed.

This is an important distinction from the way the rules operate where plant and machinery allowances are claimed, where a capital gain is not increased by virtue of having claimed allowances (though a capital loss may be restricted).

Law: TCGA 1992, s. 37B, 39(3B), 41(4A)

INVESTMENT INCOME

23. Taxation of interest

23.1 Introduction

Savings and investment income are taxable under ITTOIA 2005, Pt. 4. "Savings income" comes in different forms, including interest (covered in this chapter) and dividend income (see **Chapter 24**). There may also be chargeable event gains from life policies (see **Chapter 25**).

23.2 Definition of interest

There is no statutory definition of "interest". Rather, the concept of interest derives from contract and common law. Halsbury's *Laws of England* (quoted at SAIM 2030) defines it as:

> "... the return or compensation for the use or retention by one person of a sum of money belonging to or owed to another. Interest accrues from day to day even if payable only at intervals, and is, therefore, apportionable in respect of time between persons entitled in succession to the principal."[1]

And in *Westminster Bank*, interest was defined as:

> "... a payment which becomes due because the creditor has not had his money at the due date. It may be regarded either as representing the profit he might have made if he had had the use of the money, or, conversely the loss he suffered because he had not had that use. The general idea is that he is entitled to compensation for the deprivation."

The logic behind this concept is that there must be a capital or principal amount involved, being a sum of money from which the interest can be calculated and accrued as payable by the party liable to return the principal.

However, a principal amount will not earn interest unless there is either an implication through custom or the nature of the transaction, or an express agreement to do so. Interest may also be received where there are damages for breaches of contract, where the wronged party would have been able to receive interest if the contract had not been breached.

---

[1] © 2021 RELX (UK) Ltd.

If a payment of an "interest-like" sum is voluntary, it cannot be defined as interest (*Seaham Harbour*). This is because interest is always received as a result of a right (to receive) or an obligation (to pay). Where no such right or obligation exists, any receipt is not interest. Interest cannot be backdated if there was no agreement to pay interest at the time of the contract and, even when interest is wrapped up in an indivisible sum, it will retain its nature.

Interest cannot be negative. For example, where a creditor (one who has loaned the capital) pays a sum to a debtor (one who owes the principal back) this is defined by HMRC as "a fee paid to the debtor to hold the creditor's money" rather than negative interest. Not only is this arrangement not "interest", it may also not be set off against interest in creating a "net" interest received figure.

Example

Rafaele loaned £10,000 to his brother Rogier. Rogier paid £400 in interest to him in 2021-22. Rafaele then repaid Rogier £50 of the interest.

In this case it would not be possible for Rafaele to declare income tax payable on only £350 interest, having offset the £50 he paid to Rogier against the £400 interest he received from him. The whole £400 would be subject to income tax in 2021-22.

The legislation concerning the taxation of interest includes, in its definition:

- interest from UK banks and building societies;
- interest on gilts and other government securities;
- interest received on both private and corporate loans;
- interest on refunds or delayed payments; and
- interest on all of these sources coming from abroad.

Discounts (except deeply discounted securities) are also taxed as interest. Such interest is classified under the blanket of "savings income" and is taxed on individuals and trustees after "non-savings income" such as employment, trading and property income.

Interest does not need to be named, or formally considered, "interest" in order to be so. Where a sum has been received for damages, there may be an element of interest even if it is not called "interest". For instance, if there is some kind of payment for the time value of money in cases of compensation receipts, this is likely to be interest. Conversely, payments made may not be interest just because they are called "interest" and may simply be an entirely capital sum.

Law: ITTOIA 2005, s. 369; ITA 2007, s. 18

Cases: *Seaham Harbour Company v Crook* (1932) 16 TC 333; *Westminster Bank v Riches* (1948) 28 TC 159

Guidance: SAIM 2060

23.3   Taxing interest arising

23.3.1   *The arising basis and the rate of tax*

Interest is not taxed in the same way, or at the same rates, as non-savings income so, generally, it is sensible to keep the two elements separate when calculating tax payable.

Interest is taxed on an arising basis at 0%, 20%, 40% and/or 45% depending on the income tax band into which the individual with the beneficial interest to the interest falls.

"Arising" means received either in cash or into a bank account that the taxpayer is free to draw from. Further than this, it can mean "the swelling of a person's assets" even if the recipient is not able to enjoy the interest right now, as defined in the case of *Dunmore v McGowan*. For example, interest received on a fixed-term deposit – where access to the fund is prohibited until maturity – would not usually be taxable until the end of the fixed period, as it cannot be accessed until then. However, if the funds can be accessed, albeit with the payment of a penalty, the interest will be taxable in the year in which it is credited – even if the interest will not in fact be withdrawn or enjoyed until the maturation of the deposit.

There is a tax rate for interest which non-savings income does not have; the 0% rate. This is applicable in two situations. Firstly, where the individual qualifies for the personal savings allowance (**see 23.6**), and secondly if the starting rate band is available (**see 23.8**).

UK banks and building societies pay interest to savers in the UK gross, so no tax is deducted at source. This includes all high street banks and building societies and government savings products such as government gilts and National Savings and Investment (NS&I) products. Therefore, all savers with interest above the personal allowance, the personal savings allowance and the starting rate band (if applicable) will have to pay income tax on their interest received. As this is unlikely to have been deducted at source, HMRC will need to be informed of a new source of such income by 5 October following the end of the tax year in which the interest is first received.

Cases: *Dunmore v McGowan* (1978) 52 TC 307

23.3.2 *Interest on dormant bank accounts*

In November 2008, the UK government introduced a scheme to redistribute the funds in dormant bank accounts into a "reclaim fund" which could be used for good causes. This was legislated through the *Dormant Bank and Building Society Accounts Act* 2008. Accounts were classified as dormant when there had not been any customer-initiated activity for over 15 years.

If the customer reclaimed a balance in an account that the scheme had taken as dormant, any interest accumulated in respect of the account would be treated as not received by the owner of the funds until such time as he or she reclaimed the dormant account balance under the terms of the Act.

23.3.3 *Joint accounts*

Generally, the person liable for income tax is the person receiving or entitled to the interest. This will usually be the beneficial bank account holder, who will remain liable even if the money cannot be withdrawn immediately, for example if the interest credited is required to remain in the account as security or as a guarantee for the bank, or it is held under an escrow account with a charge over it.

If there is a joint account, the proportion of the interest taxed on each party will depend on whether the holders of the account are married or in a civil partnership. Where the holders are married or in a civil partnership, HMRC the parties will be treated as holding the principal sum equally and the interest will be taxed accordingly, so 50:50, irrespective of how much each party contributed to the balance.

If they wish to be taxed in the actual percentage of their beneficial interest in the capital, the parties can inform HMRC of the actual split and be taxed on their corresponding precise ownership. However, this will not be the case if the interest is being received on a business trading partnership account. Even if the joint holders are married or in a civil partnership, trading interest will be received by each in accordance with the partnership agreement rather than on a 50:50 basis.

If the joint account holders are not married or in a civil partnership there will be no automatic 50:50 basis; they will always be taxed on the percentage to which they are beneficially entitled. This is generally an equal proportion as long as each party is, on his or her own, entitled to and liable for 100% of the bank account. They may, however, request to be taxed in proportion to the funds that each has contributed to the account.

If the account is held as tenants in common rather than joint tenants (very rare in the UK) each account holder will have his or her own share of the capital funds and, as such, will be entitled to their own interest based on the capital amount of their own respective shares.

Law: ITTOIA 2005, s. 371; ITA 2007, s. 836-837

23.3.4   Children under 18

Minor children earning interest on funds given to them by their parents will not be personally taxed. Instead, the interest will be taxed on their parents under ITTOIA 2005, s. 629, the "settlements rules". The only exception to this is if the interest is £100 or less in the tax year.

Law: ITA 2007, s. 12B, 16, 836
Guidance: SAIM 2030, 2400, 2440

23.4   Other income chargeable as interest

23.4.1   Interest in kind

Interest may be paid in some other form than cash, such as in goods and services, or by way of a redeemable voucher. Although it is still considered to be interest-like (having been paid to compensate for the time value of money on the principal), the valuation of the amount to be taxed may be complicated. The provisions state that if the interest in kind is goods or services, the value will always be the market value of such goods or services. If the payment is in the form of a voucher, the value will be the highest of:

- the face value of the voucher;
- the amount of money that the voucher can be exchanged for; and
- the market value of goods and services that the voucher can be exchanged for, at the time the "interest" is paid.

Interest in kind paid under an instrument is not treated as a funding bond (see **23.4.3**).

23.4.2 Dividends and bonuses

"Dividends" paid by building society "share accounts" are treated as interest for the purposes of UK taxation. So too are distributions from units held in authorised unit trusts (AUTs) and shares held in open-ended investment companies (OEICs) if the distributions are classified as interest rather than dividends. Even if the holder has accumulation units or shares which automatically re-invest, he or she will still be taxable on the interest notwithstanding the fact that it is automatically re-invested.

There are also "dividends" or "bonuses" received by credit unions or registered industrial and provident societies such as registered societies within the meaning of the *Co-operative and Community Benefit Society Act* 2014, which are treated as interest per the legislation. Likewise, a UK agricultural or fishing co-operative dividend or bonus received is interest for income tax purposes.

Law: ITTOIA 2005, s. 372, 373
Guidance: SAIM 2200, 2600

23.4.3 Funding bonds

Funding bonds arise when an entity cannot afford to pay the interest due on a debt security that the taxpayer had invested in and is expecting a return from. Whether it is a company, a public authority (such as a local council) or another similar entity, where it is unable to pay the interest, a funding bond may be issued instead. Examples of funding bonds are shares in the entity, or further loan notes, bonds or other kinds of promissory notes or indebtedness. The issue of such types of funding bonds is treated as interest received by the lender, the value of which is the market value of the product issued.

Law: ITTOIA 2005, s. 380
Guidance: SAIM 2210

23.4.4 Loan and credit transactions and disguised interest

Anti-avoidance legislation applies where interest becomes "disguised". Transactions where money is lent or credit is given, or where there is a variation in the terms of such loans or credit, may lead to disguised interest. Further "enabling or facilitating" of any of these loans or variations, by either the lender or the borrower or connected parties on either side, may also lead to disguised interest.

Disguised interest is a "return" as a result of an "arrangement", (which includes any agreement, understanding, scheme, transaction or series of transactions, whether or not legally enforceable) on a principal amount, which is substantially the same in definition and substance and "economically equivalent" to interest, but is not called interest. It is also not charged to income tax under any other provision (unless it is only non-chargeable because of an exemption).

Disguised interest is chargeable on the full amount of the return received in the tax year, and is taxed on the taxpayer in receipt (or entitled to the receipt) of such returns. Detailed rules apply.

Law: ITTOIA 2005, s. 381A-381E; ITA 2007, s. 809CZA, 809CZB
Guidance: SAIM 2770

23.5   Interest that is not taxable

Some interest is not taxable, as detailed below.

23.5.1   National savings income

Income from certain authorised savings certificates are exempt from UK taxation. These are:

- savings certificates issued under:
    - s. 12 of the *National Loans Act* 1968;
    - s. 7 of the *National Debt Act* 1958; or
    - s. 59 of FA 1920;
- war savings certificates (defined in the *National Debt Act* 1972); and
- savings certificates issued under Northern Ireland law, and Ulster savings certificates.

Although Ulster savings certificates have not been in issue since March 1997, there are still some in circulation which have not been redeemed and any interest on these is still exempt from income tax.

Law: ITTOIA 2005, s. 692

23.5.2   Individual investment plans

These are investments created by HM Treasury for UK residents to be able to invest in free of income tax. There are currently two main forms of investment, which are:

- individual savings accounts (ISAs); and
- child trust funds (CTFs).

ISAs are divided into normal and junior ISAs. Investment income from both is exempt from tax. A junior ISA can be purchased by a child born after 2 January 2011 and the child (alone) must have the beneficial ownership of the product. He or she may withdraw the capital from age 18.

CTFs are also in the beneficial ownership of a child. Eligible children must have been born between 1 September 2002 and 2 January 2011 and they too can withdraw the capital after they reach their majority at 18 years old. The oldest children will have reached their majority in September 2020 and the scheme will run until the last child becomes 18 on 2 January 2029.

Holders of these accounts do not have to notify HMRC of the source of income arising, as long as the annual investment limits have been observed.

There are various limitations and regulations on the amount and type of holdings – see the link below.

Law: ITTOIA 2005, s. 692

Guidance: https://www.gov.uk/individual-savings-accounts

23.5.3 SAYE and other employment share scheme interest

Save As You Earn (SAYE) is a type of HMRC government employment share scheme (see also **11.5**). The goal is to save through deposits with a certified contractual savings scheme over a period of either three or five years. At the end of the period the investor employee can buy shares with the funds saved, for a pre-agreed fixed price. The scheme is advantageous as there is no charge to income tax on the interest or on any bonus at the end of the scheme.

If the employee receives interest from another type of employee share scheme, this interest too will be exempt.

Law: ITTOIA 2005, s. 702, 752

23.5.4 FOTRA securities

"Free of tax to residents abroad" (FOTRA) securities offer advantages for taxpayers who are not resident in the UK (per the statutory residence test – see **Chapter 34**) who receive interest from beneficially holding investments in certain UK government-issued securities, namely:

- securities issued with an exemption condition authorised by F(No. 2)A 1931;
- gilt-edged securities (without the exemption condition) issued before 6 April 1998 (except 3½% war loans 1952 or later); and
- 3½% war loans (1952 or later).

In addition to FOTRA securities, interest received on foreign currency securities – such as those issued by local authorities or statutory corporations and foreign currency loans made to a statutory corporation – will be exempt from UK income tax for non-UK resident individuals.

Law: ITTOIA 2005, s. 713-716, 755

23.5.5   Repayment supplements

A repayment supplement is a form of recompense paid to a taxpayer by HMRC. If HMRC have to repay any income tax to a taxpayer, for example, there may be an interest-like supplement included in the repayment. This is not chargeable to income tax.

Law: ITTOIA 2005, s. 749

23.5.6   Personal injury damages

If an individual receives a payment of damages for personal injury by order of a UK court, there is usually interest which is generated from the date of the cause of the action to the date of the award of the damages to the injured party. "Personal injury" includes both disease and any impairment of the individual's physical or mental condition. Any interest received is not chargeable to income tax in the UK.

If the award was made by a court abroad, and the interest is exempted in that country, no income tax charge will be made in the UK either.

The legislation goes even further in the exemption of the interest in that, even if the case is settled out of court, or if there is a payment into the Court which never actually gives a judgment, the interest is still exempt.

There is no exemption for the interest generated after the date of the award but before the date of the payment.

> **Example**
>
> Rohan is a retired postman. On 5 May 2020 he was knocked off his bike while on the way to buy milk and sustained a broken pelvis. Rohan took legal action against the driver and was awarded damages by the court on 18 October 2021 for personal injury. Rohan receives £62,160 in damages. £60,000 represents the damages for the injury and £2,160 is the interest from 5 May 2020 to 18 October 2021. This interest is not chargeable to income tax.
>
> Rohan receives the damages and interest on 13 December 2021, when a bank transfer is made to his personal bank account for £62,460. The additional £300 in interest received from 19 October to 13 December, alongside any interest generated on the £62,460 from 14 December 2021 to 5 April 2022, is chargeable to income tax in 2021-22 as interest.

Law: ITTOIA 2005, s. 751
Guidance: SAIM 2330

23.5.7 Student loan repayments

Where student loans (made under the appropriate legislation) are overpaid, a refund will be made to the taxpayer with interest covering the period between the date of the overpayment and the date of the repayment of this. The interest is not taxable.

Law: ITTOIA 2005, s. 753
Guidance: SAIM 2320

23.5.8 Redemption of funding bonds

As outlined above (**see 23.4.3**), an entity that is unable to pay interest may issue a funding bond in lieu. Where the taxpayer has been charged to income tax as interest on the issue of funding bonds (under ITTOIA 2005, s. 380), if there is any interest payable on the consequent redemption of these funding bonds it will be exempt from income tax.

Law: ITTOIA 2005, s. 754
Guidance: SAIM 2210

23.5.9 Interest from deposits made by victims of Nazi persecution

Where interest is paid to a victim of National-Socialist persecution under a qualifying constituted compensation scheme for a qualifying purpose in respect of a qualifying deposit, no income tax will be due on the interest. A qualifying deposit is one made either directly for the victim or on his or her behalf before 6 June 1945. This interest will be exempt whether it is genuine interest or whether it is "interest counteracting the effects of inflation" on the principal.

Law: ITTOIA 2005, s. 690, 754, 756A
Guidance: SAIM 2210, 2310

23.6   The personal savings allowance (savings nil rate)

Called the "savings nil rate" by the legislation, but generally known as the "personal savings allowance", this is a means-tested figure of up to £1,000 interest which a taxpayer may earn without incurring any liability to income tax.

Taxpayers with taxable income in the basic rate band are eligible to earn £1,000 interest a tax year at a tax rate of 0%, but this falls to £500 for taxpayers who have any income in the higher rate band. For those taxpayers with income in the additional rate tax band, there is no eligibility to the personal savings allowance at all. The band limits are considered before having applied any personal savings allowance.

It is important to understand that all interest is taxable. This allowance is not a tax reducer or an exception or a deduction from taxable income. It is simply the rate that is different; so 0% rather than 20%, 40% or 45%. The interest earned will continue to form part of taxable income in calculating the basic rate, higher rate, and additional rate bands despite being taxed at 0%. Once the interest has exceeded the personal savings allowance the normal income tax rates for interest will apply.

Law: ITA 2007, s. 12A, 12B
Guidance: SAIM 2310

Example 1 – basic rate taxpayer

Ringo is a retired supermarket checkout operator without a private pension. His annual income consists of the state pension, some rental income from a buy-to-let he owns and interest on his savings "nest egg". In 2021-22 Ringo receives the following:

	£
State pension income	9,340
Property income	21,000
Bank interest	6,500

He will always be taxed on his non-savings income first, and then his savings income.

	Total income	Non-savings income	Savings income
	£	£	£
State pension income	9,340	9,340	
Property income	21,000	21,000	
Bank interest	6,500		6,500
	36,840	30,340	6,500
Personal allowance	(12,570)	(12,570)	
Taxable income (Total under £37,700 so basic rate taxpayer)	23,270	17,770	6,500

	Total income	Tax due
	£	£
Tax on non-savings income £17,770 x 20%	17,770	3,554
Tax on savings income Personal savings allowance £1,000 x 0%	1,000	0
Other savings income (£6,500 – £1,000) = £5,500 x 20%	5,500	1,100
Total income and tax payable	24,270	4,654

Ringo will have to pay £4,654 in income tax for 2021-22.

Example 2 – higher rate taxpayer

Roddy is a driving school teacher. He was previously in the armed forces and has substantial savings built up over the years. In 2021-22 Roddy receives the following:

	£
Trading income	43,000
Bank interest	16,500

He will always be taxed on his non-savings income first, and then his savings income.

	Total income	Non-savings income	Savings income
	£	£	£
Trading income	43,000	43,000	
Bank interest	16,500		16,500
	59,500	43,000	16,500
Personal allowance	(12,570)	(12,570)	
Taxable income (Total over £37,700, but under £150,000 so higher rate taxpayer)	46,930	30,430	16,500

	Total income	Tax due
	£	£
Tax on non-savings income £30,430 x 20%	30,430	6,086
Tax on savings income Personal savings allowance £500 x 0%	500	0
Other savings income (37,700 – 30,930) = £6,770 x 20%	6,770	1,354
Balance of (£16,500 – £500 – £6,770) = £9,230 x 40%	9,230	3,692
Total income and tax payable	46,930	11,132

Roddy has to pay £11,132 in income tax for 2021-22.

Example 3 – additional rate taxpayer

Ryland is a marketing executive at a large firm. In addition to a healthy salary, he also has a portfolio of rental properties and a substantial savings deposit at the building society. Ryland receives the following in 2021-22:

	£
Employment income	130,000
Property income	74,000
Building society interest	26,500

He will always be taxed on his non-savings income first, and then his savings income.

	Total income £	Non-savings income £	Savings income £
Employment income	130,000	130,000	
Property income	74,000	74,000	
Building society interest	26,500		26,500
	230,500	204,000	26,500
Personal allowance (abated as total income exceeds £125,000)	0		
Taxable income (Total £150,000 so additional rate taxpayer)	230,500	204,000	26,500

	Total income £	Tax due £
Basic rate tax on non-savings income £37,700 x 20%	37,700	7,540
Higher rate tax on non-savings income £112,300 (£150,000 – £37,700) x 40%	112,300	44,920

(Cont.)	Total income £	Tax due £
Additional rate tax on non-savings income £54,000 (£204,000 – £150,000) x 45%	54,000	24,300
Tax on savings income Personal savings allowance £0 x 0% (Not entitled as additional rate taxpayer) Other savings income £26,500 x 45%	26,500	11,925
Total income tax payable	230,500	88,685

Roddy has to pay £88,685 in income tax for 2021-22.

23.7   Offsetting the personal allowance

In this scenario, the personal savings allowance is taxable at 0% anyway so some of the basic rate band would be wasted. It will therefore be better to allocate only so much of the personal allowance as is needed to bring the total taxable figure of the non-savings income to the basic rate band (£37,700 in 2021-22). The balance is then set against the savings income. This means that less of the savings income is taxed at 40% and more at 20%, saving up to £100 in income tax.

Example – higher rate taxpayer with savings income only just in higher rate band

Rudd is a trainee accountancy student in his third year at a large London firm. Rudd's grandfather died last year, leaving him a substantial savings deposit account at the bank. Rudd receives the following in 2021-22:

	£
Employment income	40,000
Bank interest	13,500

He will always be taxed on his non-savings income first, and then his savings income, and usually the personal allowance is taken from non-savings income first and then savings income. If this is done, the tax due will be:

	Total income	Non-savings income	Savings income
	£	£	£
Employment income	40,000	40,000	
Bank interest	13,500		13,500
	53,500	40,000	13,500
Personal allowance	(12,570)	(12,570)	
Taxable income (Total over £37,700 but under £150,000, so higher rate taxpayer)	40,930	27,430	13,500

	Total income	Tax due
	£	£
Tax on non-savings income at basic rate £27,430 x 20%	27,430	5,486
Tax on savings income Personal savings allowance £500 x 0%	500	0
Other savings income at basic rate (£37,700 – £27,430-£500) £9,770 x 20%	9,770	1,954
Other savings income at higher rate £3,230 (£13,500 – £500 – £9,770) x 40%	3,230	1,292
Total income tax payable	40,930	8,732

On the above basis, Rudd has to pay £8,732 in income tax for 2021-22. However, if Rudd chooses to allocate the personal allowance to non-savings income to the extent that it only brings it to the basic rate band the tax payable will be reduced as follows:

	Total income	Non-savings income	Savings income
	£	**£**	**£**
Employment income	40,000	40,000	
Bank interest	13,500		13,500
	53,500	40,000	13,500
Personal allowance	(12,570)	(2,300)	(10,270)
Taxable income (Total over £37,700 but under £150,000, so higher rate taxpayer)	40,930	37,700	3,230

	Total income	Tax due
	£	**£**
Tax on non-savings income at basic rate £37,700 x 20%	37,700	7,540
Tax on savings income Personal savings allowance £500 x 0%	500	0
Other savings income £2,730 (£3,230 – £500) x 40%	2,730	1,092
Total income tax payable	41,000	8,632

Rudd now has to pay only £8,632 in income tax for 2021-22, a saving over the first calculation of £100.

23.8 The starting rate band

The starting rate band is available to those taxpayers with lower amounts of taxable non-savings income, to be applied against their taxable savings income.

The perfect example is a retired individual in receipt of the state pension. The new state pension is currently completely covered by the personal allowance, so this type of individual would have no taxable non-savings income. He may, however, have been able to accumulate savings over his life, and therefore may have savings income.

Where taxable non-savings income is under £5,000, the difference between the level of the actual *non-savings* income and £5,000, is available to tax the *savings* income at 0%. It is an interesting concept as the 0% rate, although being used to tax savings income, is not dependent on the level of savings income but on the level of non-savings income.

For example, if the taxpayer's non-savings income is, say, £3,500, the capacity to tax the savings income at 0% is £1,500 (the difference between £5,000 (an absolute number in the legislation) and the level of taxable non-savings income of £3,500, so £1,500. If the taxpayer's non-savings income is, say, £2,000, then £3,000 of the savings income can be taxed at 0%. Again, this is the difference between the £5,000 and the level of the taxable non-savings income, so £5,000 less £2,000.

This interest will not use the personal savings allowance. The starting rate band, if available, should always be used before the personal savings allowance. Again, as above with the personal savings allowance, the starting rate band is simply a 0% tax rate rather than a reduction or exemption, so will always still use the basic rate band.

Example

Rita is a retired hairdresser earning the state pension. She has been a keen saver all her life and has a comfortable balance at the bank. In addition, as Rita penned a book on hairdressing techniques in the 1960s, now a standard textbook in hairdressing training throughout the UK, Rita receives a royalty cheque four times a year. She receives the following in 2021-22:

	£
State pension	9,340
Royalties	4,070
Bank interest	12,260

Once Rita's personal allowance is taken off her non-savings income, her taxable non-savings income will be £840 (£9,340 + £4,070 – £12,570). This means that there will be £4,160 (£5,000 – £840) of the starting rate band available to tax her savings income at 0%.

	Total income £	Non-savings income £	Savings income £
State pension	9,340	9,340	
Royalties	4,070	4,070	
Bank interest	12,260		12,260
	25,670	13,410	12,260
Personal allowance	(12,570)	(12,570)	
Taxable income (Total under £37,700 so basic rate taxpayer)	13,100	840	12,260

	Total income £	Tax due £
Tax on non-savings income at basic rate £840 x 20%	840	168
Tax on savings income Starting rate band (£5,000 – £840) = £4,160 x 0%	4,160	0
Personal savings allowance £1,000 x 0%	1,000	0
Other savings income £7,100 (£12,260 - £4,160 - 1,000) x 20%	7,100	1,200
Total income tax payable	13,100	1,368

Rita has to pay £1,368 in income tax for 2021-22, a mere 5.33% effective tax rate due to a combination of the personal savings allowance and the starting rate band.

23.9   Tax planning investments between spouses and civil partners

Purely from a tax point of view, ignoring other considerations, it is generally good practice either to equalise income (of couples that have roughly the same income), or to split income between couples in the most advantageous manner (if they have substantially different incomes). For example, it is good planning for a spouse without an income (typically staying at home to raise children) to receive enough income from investments to cover his or her personal allowance, starting rate band, personal savings allowance and dividend allowance (see **24.2**). Altogether, the stay-at-home partner could earn passive income of over £20,000 without paying tax and this could benefit the couple with tax savings of over £9,000 a year.

Example

Rosalind and her husband Reginald married in 2017. He has a rental property earning £25,140 profit annually, and a variety of investments in banks and in the UK stock market. Reginald is a salesman on a salary of £57,500 and is a higher rate taxpayer due to the investments. Rosalind is much younger and did not have any savings built up when they married. Rosalind is a doctor but went on maternity leave to have their first child in March 2021. No financial planning was undertaken, and their joint tax payable (all paid by Reginald as Rosalind had no income) in 2021-22 was forecast to be £44,041, calculated as follows:

	Total	Non-savings income	Savings income	Dividend income
	£	£	£	£
Employment income	57,500	57,500		
Property income	25,140	25,140		
Bank interest	20,000		20,000	
Dividends	35,000			35,000
Personal allowance (abated as total income exceeds £125,000)	137,640	82,640	20,000	35,000
	137,640	82,640	20,000	35,000

	Total taxed £	Tax due £
Non-savings income at basic rate (£37,700 x 20%)	37,700	7,540
Non-savings income at higher rate (£82,640 – £37,700 x 40%)	44,940	17,976
Personal savings allowance (£500 x 0%)	500	0
Savings income at higher rate (£20,000 – £500 x 40%)	19,500	7,800
Dividend allowance £2,000 x 0%	2,000	0
Dividends charged at upper rate (£35,000 – £2,000) x 32.5%	33,000	10,725
Total tax payable	137,640	44,041

After meeting with their tax consultant in March 2021, Reginald gifted some of his investments to Rosalind. He was advised to give her enough of the bank investments to yield £6,000 of the interest, and £31,700 of the dividends generated by the stocks and shares. Rosalind would then have taxable income up to the basic rate band of £37,700.

He was also advised to give half the rental property to Rosalind so that she earned half of the rental income, which would be covered by her personal allowance.

The bank interest would be covered by both the starting rate band and her personal savings allowance. Finally, £2,000 of the dividend income would be covered by the dividend allowance. It would only be the remaining dividends given that would exceed the dividend allowance of £2,000 (of £29,700) that would be taxable. These would be taxable at the dividend ordinary rate of 7.5% rather than the upper rate of 32.5%, so a total tax payable figure of £2,227.

Reginald	Total	Non-savings income	Savings income	Dividend income
	£	£	£	£
Employment income	57,500	57,500		
Property income	12,570	12,570		
Bank interest	14,000		14,000	
Dividends	3,300			3,300
	87,370	70,070	14,000	3,300
Personal allowance – no longer abated as income is now under £100,000	(12,570)	(12,570)		
	74,800	57,500	14,000	3,300

	Total taxed	Tax due
	£	£
Non-savings income at basic rate (£37,700 x 20%)	37,700	7,540
Non-savings income at higher rate (£57,500 – £37,700 x 40%)	19,800	7,920
Personal savings allowance (£500 x 0%)	500	0
Savings income at higher rates (£14,000 – £500 x 40%)	13,500	5,400
Dividend allowance £2,000 x 0%	2,000	0
Dividend income at upper rates (£3,300 – £2,000) x 32.5%	1,300	423
Total tax payable	74,800	21,283

Rosalind	Total	Non-savings income	Savings income	Dividend income
	£	£	£	£
Property income	12,570	12,570		
Bank interest	6,000		6,000	
Dividends	31,700			31,700
	50,270	12,570	6,000	31,700
Personal allowance	(12,570)	(12,570)		
	37,700	0	6,000	31,700

	Total taxed	Tax due
	£	£
Non-savings income at basic rate (0 x 20%)	0	0
Starting rate band (£5,000 x 0%)	5,000	0
Personal savings allowance (£1,000 x 0%)	1,000	0
Dividend allowance £2,000 x 0%	2,000	0
Dividends above allowance at basic rate (£31,700 – £2,000) x 7.5%	29,700	2,227
Total tax payable	37,700	2,227

Although Rosalind must pay tax when previously she did not, Reginald's tax bill reduces significantly. Reginald would have only £21,283 of income tax to pay.

The tax saving for the couple is the previous tax payable of £44,041 less the total payable after the changes of £23,510 (£2,227 + £21,283), which is £20,531 – a significant difference indeed.

This is made up of:

	£
Rental income previously taxed on Reginald at 40% but now covered by each spouse's personal allowance £25,140 x 40%	10,056
Interest previously taxed on Reginald at 40% now covered by Rosalind's starting rate band and PSA £6,000 x 40%	2,400
Dividends previously taxed on Reginald at 32.5% now covered by Rosalind's dividend allowance £2,000 x 32.5%	650
Dividends previously taxed on Reginald at 32.5% and now taxed on Rosalind at 7.5% £29,700 x (32.5% – 7.5%) 25%	7,425
	20,531

One pitfall to be aware of when considering planning involving changes to a spouse or civil partner's salary or bonus, or changes in the percentages of profits in a jointly owned business or partnership, is that these kind of amendments and manipulations could be seen as tax avoidance and challenged by HMRC. However, HMRC are quite relaxed about certain aspects of this type of approach and state at PIM 10500:

> "Spouses and civil partners can enter into partnership with each other. Sometimes this is done for tax planning reasons as it may be advantageous for a person to share their business profits with his or her spouse to maximise the use of their personal allowances and basic rate tax bands. HMRC [are] unlikely to challenge such an arrangement."

Of course, if entering into a business or partnership with spouses, civil partners (or indeed other family members), it should always be for genuine business reasons and monetary rewards should be attained according to the contribution to such a business.

Another pitfall to avoid is a failure to make "outright gifts". A gift must be outright otherwise the gifting spouse will continue to be charged tax on the income under the settlements rules. An outright gift is not conditional on anything, and must carry the right to *all* the income, as well as the right to capital.

Finally, if the asset transferred (or income derived from it) can be used for the donor spouse's benefit this would not be an outright gift. This is obviously problematic inside a marriage or civil partnership as most assets are enjoyed by both of the couple. However, HMRC look kindly on this and state that:

> "In most everyday situations involving gifts, dividends, shares, partnerships, etc. the settlements legislation will not apply. If there is no 'bounty' or if the gift to a spouse or civil partner is an outright gift which is not wholly, or substantially, a right to income, then the legislation will not apply."

As long as the transfer is a *bona fide* legal transfer from one partner's name to another, HMRC should normally be satisfied that an outright gift has been made.

Law: ITTOIA 2005, s. 625, 626

Guidance: BIM 82065; PIM 10500; TSEM 4205

23.10 Pitfalls and planning points

See also section **23.9** above regarding investment tax planning for spouses and civil partners.

Using the personal savings allowance

Taxpayers should ensure that they get the most out of the personal savings allowance (and dividend allowance – see **Chapter 24**). If all income is in the form of dividends for instance, they could diversify some of the capital to an interest-bearing investment in order to make the most of the personal savings allowance.

Having income in the form of interest becomes even more important when the individual has less than £5,000 from non-savings income sources, such as employment, trading and property income.

Watch out for the cliff-edge pitfalls

Having encouraged all taxpayers to ensure they exploit the personal savings allowance above, care must be taken among those whose total income tips them into the higher or additional rate bands.

The worst position for a taxpayer to be in, with respect to this, is to have £1 more than £50,000 total income and then to be classified as a higher rate taxpayer and so lose £500 of the personal savings allowance. A similar problem will arise when total income rises £1 to be over

£150,000, causing the individual to lose the personal savings allowance altogether.

In both these cases, a gift aid donation, or a personal pension contribution, can increase the basic rate band by the gross amount of the donation or contribution, ensuring that the taxpayer remains in the lower band. Alternatively, income-generating assets may be passed between spouses or civil partners (see next planning tip).

Remember also that the personal allowance is abated once adjusted net income is between £100,000 and £125,140, such that the marginal rate of tax in this bracket is 60%. Again, gift aid donations or personal pension contributions can be employed to counter this. Qualifying loan interest payments may also reduce the income to below the cliff-edge amount.

Mortgage interest

As there is no longer any tax relief for mortgage interest against income tax, a good use for cash lump sums may be to pay off (wholly or in part) the mortgage on the family home. If this is done, any interest saved on the capital paid off can often be more than the return after tax of the capital invested.

Some types of mortgage attract early redemption penalties, however, and for others there is a maximum amount (e.g. 10% of the original mortgage) that can be repaid every year. Sometimes there is a restricted time period when the payment can be made.

Gifts of capital to others

If the other party is not the donor's spouse or civil partner, there are other taxes to consider when gifting in order to reduce income tax, such as inheritance tax, capital gains tax (CGT) and stamp duty land tax. Again, as above, taxpayers must be careful that gifting is outright so that the settlements legislation does not bite, causing the income tax liability to remain with the donor.

Minor children may be recipients of gifts into a bare trust. The amounts are unlimited except that parents are limited to gifting amounts generating no more than £100 income a year. At the tiny interest rates currently available this could mean that thousands can be tucked away for the next generation, transferring the tax liability from parent to child. Any relevant gift would use the *child's* personal allowance and save tax in the family at the marginal rate of the donor. In addition, gifts can be made on behalf of the child by a parent to friendly societies up to £270 a year and parents may contribute up to £3,600 into a personal pension plan for the child.

Gifts to a charity or community amateur sports club are likewise tax-free for both cash donations and gifts of investment assets. This is effected by reducing income tax payable through either the gift aid scheme or in the case of assets gifted, a direct reduction to taxable income.

Law: FA 2002, Sch. 18; ITTOIA 2005, s. 629

Individual savings accounts (ISAs)

ISAs are free of income tax and CGT for UK residents (or non-UK resident Crown servants), so they are an excellent vehicle for tax-free investment. All ISAs have a limit on the maximum savings per tax year of £20,000 for (2021-22). ISA savings can be taken out in cash by any individual over 16 years old. If the ISA consists of stocks and shares investments, or if innovative finance or lifetime ISAs are preferred, the holder must be over 18. An additional restriction on opening a lifetime ISA is that the saver must be under 40.

Law: ITTOIA 2005, s. 694
Guidance: SAIM 2310

Friendly societies

Friendly societies essentially issue insurance contracts. These may be specific provident benefits or certain insurance policies such as for life, health, or loss of income. Any increases in value in the society's funds are not chargeable to income tax or CGT. These societies may also offer tax-exempt saving policies (TESPs) to their members. Although investment in the funds is not unlimited (only £270 a year can be invested in such a tax-free policy) they can last for a significant period, often between ten and 25 years, and any growth accumulated at maturity will be free of tax.

Law: FA 2012, s. 155
Guidance: IPTM 8410

Credit unions

Credit unions can also offer a source of tax-free income. These are run on a co-operative not-for-profit basis and are historically comprised of "members" that all have something in common. They might work for the same employer or all be in the same family.

Credit unions offer similar products to those of an ordinary bank, such as current and savings accounts and loans. From October 2019 there has been a "win while you save" account called a "PrizeSaver". Savers are entered into a draw to win up to £5,000 a month with regular savings deposits into their accounts from only £1 a month. HMRC have confirmed to the CIOT's Low Incomes Tax Reform Group (LITRG) that the prizes won through these savings accounts are not taxable income. Other income from credit unions, whether referred to as interest or dividends, is interest for income tax purposes and can benefit from the personal savings allowance and the starting rate band if applicable.

Guidance: https://tinyurl.com/yxlfouwa (LITRG information on PrizeSaver accounts)

National Savings and Investments products

National Savings and Investments (NS&I) is effectively the government's bank and all products offered are guaranteed by the government, making them very interesting to risk-averse investors. In addition, some of the products offer tax-free income. For these reasons, the interest rates are usually lower than those found elsewhere in the market. Recently, however, with a general reduction in interest rates, the interest paid by these products has been more on a par with other investment products. The current prospectus can be found at the NS&I website or at the post office, but generally the tax-free products are the NS&I savings certificates or their premium bonds.

Law: ITTOIA 2005, s. 692

Guidance: SAIM 2300; https://www.nsandi.com/tax-free-saving/

24. Taxation of dividends

24.1 Introduction

24.1.1 Dividends and distributions

Dividends are income in the hands of company shareholders from the distribution of the company's profits and, in the case of individual shareholders, are chargeable to income tax in the UK. Dividends include distributions from UK companies and from foreign companies. The shareholder does not have to provide any consideration for the dividend; it is a return on capital for investing in the company.

If the company is a "close" company, CTA 2010, s. 1000 defines a distribution as being any amount paid to a participator in a close company, so this may include expenses as well as formally declared dividends.

Law: ITTOIA 2005, Pt. 4, Ch. 3

24.1.2 The person liable

The person liable to the income tax on the dividend is the individual receiving it, or entitled to receive it. Usually, the person in receipt of the dividend is the shareholder.

Distributions from open-ended investment companies (OEICs) are treated as dividends and given to the owners of the shares. Distributions from authorised unit trusts (AUTs) are also treated as dividends and given to the owners of the units.

Sometimes, as a result of trust or similar arrangements, the recipient will not be the legal shareholder. If the distribution legally belongs to, or is treated as belonging to, someone other than the recipient then that party will be liable for the tax. As an example, personal representatives are liable for the tax due on dividends received by the deceased in the period of the administration of an estate.

24.1.3 The amount taxed

The amount subject to tax is the full amount of the gross dividend and any other distributions paid to the shareholder (apart from distributions from share incentive plans – see **11.6**). "Distributions" encompass a broad range of transfers, including:

- dividends;
- bonus shares;
- transfers of assets and liabilities to the shareholders;
- interest payments exceeding market rates;
- interest on securities; and
- any other distributions made out of the capital employed in the company which are distributed in relation to, and in proportion to, the shareholdings in it.

There is one exception to this, which is a transfer to the shareholder of the original share capital. This is not a distribution unless there is a premium included.

A dividend does not always have to be in cash and can also be received *in specie* or "in kind", for example by the transfer of an asset of equivalent value.

There is no longer any tax credit or any income tax deducted at source from dividends received in the UK. The tax credit was abolished for dividends received after 5 April 2016.

Sometimes building societies give "dividends". These amounts are taxable as interest (see **Chapter 23**).

24.1.4   The rate of tax for dividends

Dividend income is often referred to as the "top slice" of income. This means that it is taxed after non-savings income and savings income. It is taxed at four different income tax rates which are:

- 0% for the dividend allowance (dividend nil rate);
- 7.5% for the ordinary rate (basic rate);
- 32.5 for the upper rate (higher rate); and
- 38.1% for the additional rate.

Law: ITTOIA 2005, s. 383, 386, 389
Guidance: SAIM 5010, 5020

24.2   The dividend allowance (the dividend nil rate)

Like the personal savings allowance, which allows certain amounts of savings income to be taxed at 0%, the dividend nil rate or dividend allowance does the same for dividend income. For dividends, however, the amount is £2,000 whether the taxpayer is paying at the basic, higher or additional rate.

Again, this is not exempt income and will be counted when establishing whether the taxpayer has exceeded the basic, higher, or additional rate bands. It is taxable income; it is merely taxed at 0%. Once the £2,000 dividend allowance has been exhausted, the taxpayer's level of other income and his or her marginal rate of tax will determine the rate at which any remaining dividends are taxed (7.5%, 32.5% or 38.1%).

Example 1 – Rupert

Rupert is a retired barber with a state pension, some property income (from a double garage he lets out in central London), and some bank interest. Rupert's income in 2021-22 is as follows:

2021-22	£
State pension income	9,340
Property income	4,070
Bank interest	13,000

Rupert's tax computation analyses the income as follows:

	Total income	Non-savings income	Savings income
	£	£	£
State pension income	9,340	9,340	0
Property income	4,070	4,070	0
Bank interest	13,000	0	13,000
	26,410	13,410	13,000
Personal allowance	(12,570)	(12,570)	0
Taxable income (Total under £37,700 so basic rate taxpayer)	13,840	840	13,000

His tax calculation will then be:

	Total income	Tax due
	£	£
Tax on non-savings income at basic rate £840 x 20%	840	168
Tax on savings income Starting rate band (£5,000 – £840) = £4,160 x 0%	4,160	0
Personal savings allowance £1,000 x 0%	1,000	0
Other savings income £7,840 (£13,000 – £4,160 - £1,000) x 20%	7,840	1,568
Total income tax payable	13,840	1,736

In the following year, Rupert is the beneficiary of a friend's estate. He invests the legacy and receives £8,000 in dividends. His income in 2022-23 is as follows:

2022-23	£
State pension income	9,340
Property income	4,070
Bank interest	13,000
Dividends	8,000

The existence of dividend income will not affect Rupert's tax rate calculated for his non-savings income or savings income, as these categories are always taxed first before dividend income. However, the dividend income may have an impact on whether Rupert is eligible for a personal savings allowance of £1,000 or only £500, as the dividend income increases the overall taxable income. In Rupert's case, the addition of £8,000 dividend income increases his taxable income to £21,840 but as this is still under £37,700, the basic rate band, Rupert is still entitled to the full £1,000 personal savings allowance.

Rupert's income for 2022-23 is analysed as follows:

	Total income £	Non-savings income £	Savings income £	Dividend income £
Employment income	9,340	9,340		
Property income	4,070	4,070		
Bank interest	13,000		13,000	
Dividends	8,000			8,000
	34,410	13,410	13,000	8,000
Personal allowance	(12,570)	(12,570)		
Taxable income (Total under £37,700 so basic rate taxpayer)	21,840	840	13,000	8,000

His tax calculation for the year will be as follows:

	Total income £	Tax due £
Tax on non-savings income at basic rate £840 x 20%	840	168
Tax on savings income Starting rate band (£5,000 – £840) = £4,160 x 0%	4,160	0
Personal savings allowance £1,000 x 0%	1,000	0
Other savings income £7,840 (£13,000 - £4,160 - £1,000) x 20%	7,840	1,568

(Cont.)	Total income £	Tax due £
Tax on dividend income		
Dividend allowance		
£2,000 x 0%	2,000	0
Other dividend income taxed at basic rate		
£6,000 (£8,000-£2,000) x 7.5%	6,000	450
Total income tax payable	21,840	2,186

Rupert has to pay £2,186 of income tax for 2022-23, a mere 6.35% effective tax rate due to a combination of the personal savings allowance, the starting rate band, and the dividend allowance.

The amount of dividend income may have an impact on the tax paid on the taxpayer's savings income. This is because having an amount of dividend income in addition to non-savings and savings income can push a taxpayer above the basic or higher rate bands, meaning a lower amount of (or no) personal savings allowance. Dividend income is included in establishing which income tax band the individual will fall into *before* any dividend allowance is taken off. Therefore, it is always important to establish the level of "taxable income" (total income after the personal allowance) and determine the band into which the individual falls, before taxing the income.

Illustrating this point, we can return to the Rupert example.

Example 2 – Rupert (cont.)

Instead of £8,000 dividends, Rupert receives £25,000 in dividends, so his income is now as follows:

	£
State pension income	9,340
Property income	4,070
Bank interest	13,000
Dividends	25,000

As Rupert has total taxable income of £38,840, he is now in the higher rate band and so is only entitled to £500 of personal savings allowance rather than £1,000 in the previous example:

	Total income £	Non-savings income £	Savings income £	Dividend income £
Employment income	9,340	9,340		
Property income	4,070	4,070		
Bank interest	13,000		13,000	
Dividends	25,000			25,000
	51,410	13,410	13,000	25,000
Personal allowance	(12,570)	(12,570)		
Taxable income	38,840	840	13,000	25,000

The tax computation is now as follows:

	Total income £	Tax due £
Tax on non-savings income at basic rate £840 x 20%	840	168
Tax on savings income		
Starting rate band (£5,000 – £840) = £4,160 x 0%	4,160	0
Personal savings allowance (higher rate taxpayer) £500 x 0%	500	0
Savings income at basic rate £8,340 (£13,000 – £4,160 – £500) x 20%	8,340	1,668

(Cont.)	Total income	Tax due
	£	£
Tax on dividend income Dividend allowance £2,000 x 0%	2,000	0
Basic rate band used	15,840	
Other dividend income – balance of basic rate £37,700 – £15,840 = £21,860) x 7.5%	21,860	1,639
Other dividend income – higher rate £25,000 – £2,000 – £21,860 = £1,140 x 32.5%	1,140	370
Total income tax payable	38,840	3,845

Rupert will have to pay £3,845 in income tax for 2022-23, increasing his overall tax rate to 7.6% due to the extra dividends being taxed at the upper rate coupled with a reduction in the personal savings allowance.

Law: ITA 2007, s. 16, 13A

24.3   Stock dividends

24.3.1   Introduction

Dividends are a distribution of the reserves of a company to its shareholders, but there are occasions where a company intends to make a dividend distribution, but does not wish to deplete its cash reserves to do so. In these instances, which generally arise in quoted companies, it is possible for the company to give the shareholders additional shares in the place of cash for their "dividend". These dividends are called "stock" or "scrip" dividends and are effectively dividends in kind as "stock dividend income".

The rates for the income tax charge to stock dividends are the same as for ordinary cash dividends. For example, a higher rate taxpayer receiving stock dividends will use the dividend upper rate for dividend income regardless of whether cash or stock dividends are received.

Stock dividends are also sometimes known as "bonus issues" but not all bonus issues are stock dividends. Ordinary bonus issues made by a company – i.e. where reserves are capitalised and bonus shares given to shareholders in their ownership proportions – arise from a special resolution made by the shareholders and not from any right inherent in the share itself. The bonus issues that are stock dividends will instead derive their rights from the terms of the shares. Although both are chargeable to income tax, they are chargeable under different parts of ITTOIA 2005 and therefore have subtly different rules.

The shareholder will usually have a choice as to whether to accept the dividend in the form of a share or in the form of cash. If the shareholder was intending to buy more shares in the company anyway, stock dividends are a very interesting option as they avoid the need to pay dealing costs in purchasing shares afresh. If the shareholder opts for the additional shares, the tax will be based on the cash value of the dividend that he or she did not opt to take, or the "dividend forgone". Once the shareholder has made that decision, the dividend forgone is simply treated like a normal cash dividend for taxation purposes.

24.3.2   Large differences in value between cash and stock dividend

Sometimes, however, there may be a significant difference between the value of the cash dividend and the stock dividend. Companies often offer a higher value stock alternative to tempt the shareholders into accepting the extra shares. If the difference in value between the two alternative dividend forms is equal to, or more, than 15%, the market value of the share dividend will be taken rather than the value of the equivalent cash dividend.

For example, the market value of the share offered may be more than 15% higher than the value of the alternative cash dividend. However, the requirements of the provisions in ITTOIA 2005, s. 412 work in the same way for shortfalls in value. If the share offered to the shareholders as a stock dividend has a value at least 15% *less* than the cash dividend, the lower value of the shares will be taken as the value of the dividend (rather than the value of the cash dividend) if the shareholder opts for the dividend alternative.

Example

Russo owns 100,000 shares in R Ltd. R Ltd declared a 30p dividend per share on 9 October 2021. However, the company offered the shareholders a stock dividend at the same time. The offer was a 1-for-5 share alternative. The price of the shares on 9 October 2021 was £1.55.

If Russo opts for the cash dividend, he will receive £30,000 (100,000 x 30p = £30,000) in cash.

If Russo opts for the stock dividend, he will receive 20,000 shares (100,000/5 x 1) at £1.55 each so they will be valued at £31,000.

At this price, the difference between the stock dividend and the cash dividend is not great enough to require a dividend value amendment to the stock dividend price (as the difference is not more than 15%). So, if Russo opts for either the stock dividend or the cash dividend, the amount of dividend to be declared for income tax purposes will be 30p per share.

If the share price was, for instance, £1.80 instead of £1.55, the total value of the stock dividend would be £36,000 (20,000 x £1.80). As the value of this dividend would be more than 15% higher than that of the cash dividend, there would be a difference in the amount of the dividend for taxation purposes depending on what form of dividend Russo chooses. A cash dividend would be taxed at the value of the dividend (£30,000) but the stock dividend would be taxed at the market value of the shares, i.e. £36,000.

If, on the other hand, the share price was £1.25 a share instead of £1.55, the total value of the stock dividend would be £25,000 (20,000 x £1.25). As the value of this dividend would be more than 15% lower than that of the cash dividend, there would be a difference in the amount of the dividend for taxation purposes depending on what form of dividend Russo chooses. A cash dividend would be taxed at the value of the dividend (£30,000) and the stock dividend would be taxed at the market value of the shares (£25,000).

Law: ITTOIA 2005, s. 409, 412
Guidance: SAIM 5150

24.4 Foreign dividends

24.4.1 Introduction

Individuals who are tax resident in the UK are liable to pay income tax on their worldwide income, including dividends received from overseas companies (ITTOIA 2005, s. 402).

Although s. 402 goes on to state that dividends do not include "distributions of a capital nature", it does not include the more extensive definition for UK dividends received (s. 383, which states that dividends "and other distributions" will be taxable as dividends).

HMRC conclude that such other foreign distributions are not taxed as dividends and may instead be taxed under "interest income", "income not otherwise charged" or the "miscellaneous income" provisions of s. 687-689.

Under ITA 2007, s. 19, the definition of dividends to be taxed includes "a relevant foreign *distribution*" (italics added). So a distribution from a non-UK resident company, even if it is not a dividend, is still taxable as if it were a dividend, but just under a different category.

24.4.2   *Dividends of a capital nature*

Section 402 excludes dividends of "a capital nature". Whether foreign dividends are of a capital nature is determined by the means by which they are distributed in the overseas territory (according to the law of that territory) and the impact that this has on the overseas distributing company. This "territory" is where the company is incorporated or registered.

For example, if, as a result of the distribution, the capital is reduced, all or part of the distribution will be of a capital nature.

In a case concerning dividends received from a US company, *Rae v Lazard*, a partial liquidation was held to be a distribution of a capital nature rather than a dividend. The recipient in this case was a company that owned 2,000 $1 shares in an American paper products and roofing company. The US company transferred the paper products business to a new company in a share-for-share exchange, and these shares were then distributed among its members, including the recipient company. Lord MacDermott was quoted in the case as saying:

> "The question is, whether 'the corpus of the asset' or 'shares of the company' or 'the capital of the possession' did or did not remain intact after the ... shares were distributed."

The distribution was effected under the law of the State of Maryland by what was defined as a "distribution on partial liquidation". The corpus of the asset had not remained intact and there was therefore a distribution of a capital nature.

Case: *Rae (HMIT) v Lazard Investment Co. Ltd* (1963) 41 TC 1

24.4.3 Taxing foreign dividends

Although foreign dividends are taxed at the same rates as dividends received from UK resident companies, dividends from overseas are taxed on the arising basis rather than the receipts basis.

Withholding tax is a form of retention tax that is taken from an amount of income by the party that is to pay the income to the beneficiary, which is usually the company invested in or an agent thereof. The tax withheld is paid to the government of the country or territory in which the dividend arose, before the dividend is paid to the UK resident taxpayer. The UK resident recipient, therefore, receives the dividend net of foreign withholding tax.

In the UK, the tax is always calculated on the *gross* dividend. Where tax has been paid twice, there may be the option for tax relief on the "double tax" paid (see double tax relief at **Chapter 35**) but, at the outset, tax on the full gross dividend will need to be calculated at the appropriate tax rate in the UK.

Example

Romeo, a UK resident, received a dividend from a share on the Borsa Italiana of £3,861. It has been converted at 1.15 euros to the pound on the day it was received. The withholding tax on dividends at the time of the receipt was 26%.

The first step is to convert the dividend to euros on the day it was received:

£3,861 x 115/100 = €4,440

The next step is to gross this up to the value of the dividend before the withholding tax:

€4,440 x 100/74 = €6,000

This now has to be converted back to sterling to be included in the tax computation:

€6,000 x 100/115 = £5,217

A quicker step is simply to ignore the exchange rate and gross up the net dividend in sterling:

£3,861 x 100/74 = £5,217

The gross dividend of £5,217 will be entered into Romeo's self-assessment tax computation as "dividends received".

Law: ITTOIA 2005, s. 402
Guidance: SAIM 5020, 5210

24.5   Shares in approved share incentive plans

24.5.1   Introduction

Shares held in approved share incentive plans (SIPs) are a method of incentivising employees and encouraging their ownership of shares in the company. See **11.6** for more information on SIPs and their workings.

24.5.2   Dividends reinvested in shares in the SIP

Shares in the employee's company are held on behalf of the participant employee by the SIP scheme trustee. When dividends are received, they are paid directly into the scheme. If dividends are paid in cash these can be used to purchase more shares to be invested back into the scheme. These dividends then become "dividend shares". Such dividends are exempt from income tax.

24.5.3   Dividend shares cease to be part of an approved SIP

If the dividend shares cease to be part of an approved SIP scheme within three years of their acquisition, they will be taxable as a dividend distribution in the year in which the plan no longer qualifies as a SIP. The amount of the dividend will be the cash equivalent of the original cash dividend that was then converted into the dividend shares.

The only exception to this is if the shares cease to be in the SIP because they are required to be sold (ITEPA 2003, Sch. 2, para. 65). In such a case, the value of the distribution will be the lower of the cash dividend used to buy the shares or the market value at the time of the sale multiplied by the "relevant fraction". The relevant fraction is A/B, where:

> **A** is so much of the amount of the cash dividend applied to acquire the shares on the participant's behalf as represents a cash dividend paid in respect of plan shares in a UK company; and

> **B** is the amount of the cash dividend applied to acquire the shares on the participant's behalf.

If tax has already been paid on these shares under ITEPA 2003, s. 501 (charge on capital receipts of plan shares) this will reduce the tax due on the dividend shares.

24.5.4   Dividend paid over to employee participant in cash

If the dividend is paid over to the employee in cash, this is treated as a normal dividend and is subject to income tax as if it were a regular dividend from any other company in the tax year in which it was paid.

If the dividend is paid out to the participant in a later tax year than the one in which the dividend arose, the participant will nevertheless have a tax liability in the later year when it was *received* and not the earlier year when it arose.

The scheme can only hold a cash dividend for three years before it must be paid out to the participant.

Law: ITTOIA 2005, s. 392, 393, 395, 770
Guidance: SAIM 5080

24.6   Dividends taxed as trading income

Some dividends received are taxed as trading income rather than investment income. This would apply to financial traders, for example, and also to Lloyd's underwriters. In each case, ITTOIA 2005, Pt. 2 has priority over Pt. 4, which means that the dividends are taxable under the trading income provisions.

Law: ITTOIA 2005, s. 409, 412
Guidance: CTM 48580, LLM 1040, 8170

24.7   Loans by close companies to participators

If a close company (or indeed a company controlled by a close company) makes a loan to a participator or to an associate of a participator (i.e. a relative or partner of a shareholder), there is a "s. 455 charge" (i.e. under CTA 2010, s. 455) of 32.5%, payable by the company. When the loan is repaid by the participator, this charge is paid back to the company by HMRC.

However, if the loan is not paid back by the participator, the company may decide to "release" or write off the loan. In these situations, the company is reimbursed in the same way by HMRC but a tax charge is imposed on the participator. This charge to tax will be deemed to be on a dividend from the company to the participator at his or her marginal rate. Income tax will thus be due on a "dividend" which is the value of the loan that has been released or written off.

The person liable for the tax on the written-off loan is either the individual to whom the loan was made or any partner who is an individual, if the loan was made to a partnership. If there is more than one person liable, the liability should be apportioned in a just and reasonable manner.

Even if the original debt has been passed to a third party, the liability for the tax will remain. Under English law the concept of "novation" is where a debtor can transfer both contractual rights and obligations to a new debtor. It will thus be at the point of the transfer of said rights and obligations by the participator to the new debtor that the liability to pay the income tax on the "dividend" due on the release will arise. It will be payable by the participator because it is at this point that the debt has been "released" (even though the company will still be able to receive the payment of the loan outstanding from a third party).

In *Collins v Addies* it was held that "release" under ITTOIA 2005, s. 287 should bear its plain and ordinary meaning and that:

"If Parliament had intended to qualify the application of that term 'released' under s. 287 it would have done so expressly. It was therefore not permissible to read into that section the qualification that a release ought to be confined to one which was either wholly voluntary or made for less than adequate consideration."

The income tax on the "dividend" representing the written-off, or released, loan will not be chargeable if the person liable to it has died and the liability has passed to his or her personal representatives. Nor is it taxable under the settlements legislation if the person liable is acting as a settlor of a trust (subject to further rules on the taxation of beneficiaries).

Law: ITTOIA 2005, s. 415-419; ITA 2007, s. 19
Guidance: SAIM 5200
Case: *Collins v Addies (HMIT)* and related appeal [1991] BTC 244

24.8   Real estate investment trusts

24.8.1   Introduction

A UK real estate investment trust (REIT) is a type of investment product that specialises in exploiting real property assets to generate property rental profits.

In the UK, REITs have to satisfy a number of conditions, but there are many tax benefits for both the company and the investor where these are met. UK REITs are quoted companies with a balance sheet that contains a minimum amount of residential and/or commercial properties that are let to generate rental property income.

REITs are easy for investors to trade (through the stock market) and allow a straightforward investment in property through shares without having to own property directly. They allow investors the benefit of investing in property that they would not generally have access to, such as shopping malls and industrial buildings. Investors are not required to be "landlords" with all the liabilities, risks and challenges associated with this role. Transaction costs of purchasing shares are also lower than for purchasing property, e.g. stamp duty rather than SDLT.

24.8.2   Requirements for the REIT

To satisfy the requirements of a tax-efficient REIT, the company must have at least 75% of its business involved in renting property. REITs are then exempt from corporation tax as long as they distribute at least 90% of the rental profits to the shareholders.

The catch is that, while distributing the minimum of 90% of the profits, the REIT has to pay the income tax on behalf of the shareholders directly to HMRC at the time of the distribution, such that the shareholder receives the "dividends" net of basic rate tax. Shareholders will, of course, have a basic rate tax credit (20%) to offset against their self-assessment tax liability, which is calculated on the gross amount of the REIT.

24.8.3   Requirements for the investor

The practical advantages of REITs have a cost in that the returns made are taxed as if they were property income, despite the fact that they are legally dividends. The "relevant profits" in the REIT are therefore not taxed in the REIT itself but in the hands of the investors.

The REIT is deemed to distribute the 90% of the profits first. These are the "relevant profits". If it distributes profits above the 90%, the REIT will need to decide the nature of these remaining profits.

If the excess profits are deemed to have come out of profits from activities which are not tax exempt, these will be classified as dividends in the hands of the shareholders, and income tax will not be deducted at source. If the excess profits are deemed to have come out of profits from activities which are tax exempt, these will be classified as property income in the hands of the shareholders – just like the first 90% – and likewise, will have the tax credit attached. The split will be set out on a dividend voucher which the shareholder will be entitled to on receipt of the income.

24.8.4   Property income business

As the qualifying profits and any capital gains (that are tax exempt inside the company) from a REIT are treated as property income, they are taxed in accordance with ITTOIA 2005, Pt. 3 as property income rather than dividends. However, they will create a new UK property business and, although the receipts from a number of different REITs can be grouped together, the new property business will be separate from any other UK property businesses a taxpayer might already have. Losses on other such businesses cannot be offset against gains on the REIT property business (whether the individual is holding the REIT share in his or her own name or as a partner in a partnership).

If the recipient of the REIT income is a taxpayer for whom dividends are already treated as trading income rather than dividends, such as financial traders and Lloyd's underwriters (see **24.6**), the property income from a REIT will continue to be treated as trading income rather than property income.

Example

In 2019, Rutherford, a higher rate taxpayer, invests in Y Ltd, a UK resident REIT quoted on the UK stock exchange. He purchases 10,000 shares and receives a net dividend of £16,000 in 2021-22. The whole of the dividend is a qualifying dividend for CTA 2010 purposes.

Rutherford will have to gross up the dividend at the basic rate, as this is what has been deducted at source. He will then declare £20,000 (£16,000 x 100/80) property income in his tax return for 2021-22. Tax on this at Rutherford's marginal rate is 45%, so his income tax on the property business of his REIT is £9,000 (of which £4,000 has already been paid by the REIT). This leaves Rutherford with a net income received after tax of £11,000 (out of gross income of £20,000), so 55%.

If Rutherford is employed, the additional tax can be collected through his PAYE code or included in his self-assessment tax return.

When completing a tax return, although the income is classified as property income, it does not go into the property income page. Instead it is declared as other income and the net amount will be inserted into box 13.1, the tax from the dividend voucher in box 13.2 and the total in box 13.3. If the distribution is not from relevant income it will be treated as an ordinary dividend receipt and will be shown in boxes 10.15 to 10.17.

Law: CTA 2010, s. 548, 550

Guidance: SAIM 5300-5340

24.9 Pitfalls and planning points

Using the dividend allowance

The dividend allowance is available to all taxpayers and is not means tested, so those seeking a tax-efficient investment should always consider dividend-paying stocks and shares, as the first £2,000 dividends received will be tax free.

Other planning points

Reference may also usefully be made to the planning points at the end of **Chapter 23** regarding the taxation of interest.

25. Taxation of life policies

25.1 Introduction

Life policies are products that either insure someone's life so that, should they die, an amount will be payable to the person who insured the life, or act as an investment vehicle to provide a return.

Any "chargeable events" that cause "chargeable gains" arising on life policies are subject to income tax in the UK, but not all gains are chargeable gains. Whether such a gain is chargeable or not will depend on whether the policy is qualifying or non-qualifying, and the type and amount of income received by the taxpayer.

The distinction between a qualifying and non-qualifying policy is important, as events relating to qualifying life policies never lead to a chargeable gain whereas those relating to non-qualifying policies often do. One specific type of non-qualifying policy is a personal portfolio bond (see **25.5**).

25.2 Qualifying life policies

A qualifying policy has a minimum term of ten years. The policy generally requires premiums to be paid regularly (say every week or every month) for approximately the same amount from year to year (adjusted for inflation).

Policies taken out (or varied) since 21 March 2012 will not be qualifying if premiums exceed £3,600 in a 12-month period.

The "sum insured" must be a high amount compared to the premiums. A qualifying policy can therefore be thought of as the first type from the definition above; one where someone genuinely insures a life such that there is a pay out if that person dies.

For qualifying policies, unless the policy is cancelled within ten years or before 75% of the term of the policy has been completed, there is no tax liability when the policy matures.

The detailed definitions are at ICTA 1988, Sch. 15. They are complex but, as HMRC point out, the responsibility for ensuring that policies are qualifying will normally lie with the insurers themselves.

Law: ICTA 1988, Sch. 15; ITTOIA 2005, s. 461, 485
Guidance: IPTM 2020, 2076

25.3 Non-qualifying life policies

25.3.1 Introduction

The blanket definition of a non-qualifying policy is that it is one that does not satisfy the definition of a qualifying policy. However, the characteristics of these policies are that they are more like an investment vehicle. They are typified by a one-off payment of a single premium and tend to be entered into for the investment potential rather than life insurance. These may also be referred to as "single premium life insurance" bonds or policies. These policies are liable to income tax under the rules in ITTOIA 2005, Pt. 4, Ch. 9, "Gains from contracts for life insurance".

25.3.2 Gains on non-qualifying policies

A gain arises if, during the tax year, cash benefits are received or the policy is surrendered, either fully or in part. There will also be a gain if the policy matures or is partly or fully sold or assigned. This is subject, however, to rules deferring a tax charge if the policyholder draws down no more than 5%, per tax year, of the amount invested – see **25.4.4** (partial surrenders) below.

The gain is the difference between the market value of the policy at the time of the maturation or surrender and the payments that have been made into the policy.

On the occasion of a gain, the insurer is required to send the policyholder a "chargeable event certificate" which will show the gain that has arisen. This gain is a "chargeable event gain" and will need to be reported on the supplementary pages of the individual's tax return under "Gains from life insurance policies, capital redemption policies and life annuity contracts". A chargeable event gain is subject to income tax rather than capital gains tax.

In cases where the policyholder has not received a chargeable event certificate, it may be that a gain has still arisen but the certificate has been sent to the trustees of a trust (bare or otherwise), a nominee for the policyholder, or a bank or other lender who has taken the policy as security for a policyholder debt. In these cases, the responsibility remains with the policyholder, so he or she should contact the insurer to see whether a certificate has been issued.

25.3.3   Taxing the gain on non-qualifying policies

If the taxpayer is the beneficial owner of the rights under the policy, whether this has been assigned as security for a debt or not, the gain will be treated as arising on the taxpayer.

If the beneficial owner is the trustee of a charitable trust, the gain will be treated as the income of the trustees.

It will also be treated as the income of the trustees if the trust is not charitable but there is an "absent settlor". An absent settlor is one who is either:

- non-UK resident (or UK resident but the gain occurs in the overseas part of a split year);
- deceased (unless the gain arises in the year of the death); or
- a company or foreign institution that has been dissolved or wound up, such that it no longer exists.

If the trust is not charitable but the absent settlor conditions do not apply, the gain will be treated as the income of the trustees if no other individuals or personal representatives are chargeable on it.

Any gain will also be charged as income on the personal representatives of a deceased estate if the deceased was not treated as the owner of the income, having been charged at the basic rate. For example, if there was a life policy in the estate taken out by the deceased on another person who is still alive and the personal representatives surrender this policy or it matures during the period of the administration.

25.3.4   The gain charged to income tax

The chargeable event certificate will show whether the tax has been taken off at source or whether the policyholder needs to pay the tax on the gross gain. The date of the event on the certificate is the date of chargeability. For example, if the event is 1 April 2022, it will be charged in the 2021-22 tax year.

If two dates are shown on the certificate, which can sometimes occur if a part-surrender or sale is made during the year, it is the later date that is relevant. This is because all part surrenders are treated as being made at the end of the insurance year or policy year, which is usually the period from the date of the inception of the policy to 12 months following that date.

Example

Rose was the beneficial holder of a non-qualifying single premium insurance bond. She took out the policy on 3 October 1998. In July 2022 she received a chargeable event certificate showing that the policy had been part surrendered on 3 March 2021.

Although the part surrender occurred in the 2020-21 tax year, because a part surrender is always deemed to occur on the last day of the policy year, the actual date considered as the chargeable date would be the last date of the "insurance year" which is 2 October 2021. As 2 October 2021 is in the 2021-22 tax year, Rose will be charged to income tax on the gain one tax year later than the tax year of the actual gain.

Where more than one certificate is received by the policyholder, the most recent one will be deemed to be the most correct and valid for the self-assessment.

The order of taxation

Income tax will be due at the taxpayer's marginal rate, so is treated as the "top slice" of income tax. It will, however, be charged as savings income at the savings income tax rates, so 20%, 40% or 45%.

For example, if a policyholder had employment income, interest from a building society, dividends from a UK company and a gain on a non-qualifying life policy, the order would be:

- non-savings income first (the employment income); then
- savings income (without the policy gain, so just the interest part); then
- dividends income; and
- finally, so at the individual's highest rate, the rest of the savings income, i.e. in this case the policy gain.

When performing the calculation, it is a good idea to include an extra column for the policy gain so that it is correctly taxed in the right order.

The chargeable event policy gain is paid over to the taxpayer with a notional tax credit of 20%. This can be offset against any tax due in the tax year, but cannot create a repayment. A basic rate taxpayer will therefore have no more tax to pay on a non-qualifying life policy gain.

The impact on the tax rate of the individual

However, in the year of maturity or surrender of the policy, if a chargeable gain on the policy is large, it could push a taxpayer into the higher or additional rate band. To counter this, a claim for "top slicing relief" may be made (see **25.4** below).

The personal and married couple's allowances

The other thing that might happen when a large chargeable event policy gain is received in a tax year is that it might cause an individual to lose his or her personal allowance, either in full or in part. The personal allowance is abated fully if adjusted net income is more than £125,140 and reduced by £1 for every £2, if adjusted net income is above £100,000 and below £125,140.

A taxpayer born before 6 April 1935 may also be eligible for the married couple's allowance which also relies on the level of adjusted net income, and this too may be reduced as a result of a policy gain (though this allowance is never fully lost).

Top slicing relief ensures that only the "annual equivalent" gain is considered when calculating the tax. There will be no loss of allowances as long as the annual equivalent does not push the income beyond the threshold levels.

Law: ITTOIA 2005, s. 467, 484, 530

25.4   Top slicing relief

25.4.1   Introduction

A gain may accrue across a number of tax years but is taxable only in the year of the chargeable event. Top slicing relief applies a spreading mechanism to mitigate the impact of this on the individual's marginal tax rate and on any personal or married couple's allowances (see above).

For example, if the net chargeable event gain was earned over five years, it will be "sliced" or divided over the five years the policy has earned the gain. This would end up theoretically adding another one fifth of the gain to every year. If the taxpayer is a basic rate payer in the year of charge, and the one fifth proportion of the gain allocated to that tax year does not lead to his income increasing into a higher rate band, he will be charged at the basic rate, rather than the marginal rate, for all of the gain.

Law: ITTOIA 2005, s. 535

25.4.2   The mechanics

The first thing to do is to calculate the tax ignoring top slicing relief, and isolate the tax calculated on the policy gain after the tax credit or the notional amount. Then the top slicing relief is applied. The legislation divides the process for applying top slicing relief into steps:

Step one

Find the "annual equivalent" of the amount of the total gain. This is done by taking the total chargeable gain and dividing it by the number of complete years for which the policy has been held. This will give the income chargeable as the "top slice" every year (referred to in the legislation as the "annual equivalent" or "N").

Step two

Establish the tax that would be due on this top slice (N) in isolation, by adding N to the other income in the tax year. The individual's liability to income tax on just that top slice is then calculated in that year, with N being included as the marginal income.

Step three

Deduct the tax credit of 20% from this tax due.

Step four

Add all the tax on the annual equivalents (Ns) for all the appropriate number of years the policy has been held. This will give what the legislation refers to as the "relieved liability".

Step five

Calculate the final tax paid. This will be a reduction in tax, equal to the difference between the net tax calculated normally (so at the marginal or top slice rate) and the "relieved liability" which is the net tax calculated on only the annual equivalent multiplied by the number of years of the policy.

Law: ITTOIA 2005, s. 536

Example

Ragnar is a hospital night nurse employed by the NHS at a salary of £48,070 a year. He took out a single premium life policy on 1 January

2018. The policy matured five years later in January 2023. Ragnar received a chargeable event gain of £40,000 on 3 March 2023.

Without the top slicing relief steps, the whole gain would be taxed at Ragnar's marginal rate, as below.

	£	Non savings income £	Life policy gain £
Employment income	48,070	48,070	
Life policy total gain	40,000		40,000
Personal allowance	(12,570)	(12,570)	
	75,500	35,500	40,000

Tax	£	Tax on slice £	Total £
Tax on non-savings income £35,500 x 20%	35,500		7,100
Tax on savings income			
Personal savings allowance (higher rate) £500 x 0%	500	0	0
Tax on balance of savings income at basic rate (£37,700 - £35,500 - £500) £1,700 x 20%	1,700	340	340
Tax on savings income at higher rate (£40,000 - £500 - £1,700) £37,800 x 40%	37,800	15,120	15,120
Total liability before tax credit	75,500	15,460	22,560

Tax (cont.)		Tax on slice	Total
	£	£	£
Tax credit (nominal tax) £40,000 x 20%		(8,000)	(8,000)
Total liability after tax credit		7,460	14,560

As can be seen above, Ragnar's policy gain pushes him well into the higher rate band, with £37,800 of the £40,000 gain being charged at 40% if top slicing is not given. In reality, however, the application of the steps will mitigate the tax liability significantly.

Step one

The total gain is £40,000 and this is divided by five years to give the "annual equivalent" or the "top slice" of £8,000 per year.

Step two

This annual equivalent must now be added to Ragnar's other income.

		Non savings income	Life policy gain
	£	£	£
Employment income	48,070	48,070	
Life policy annual equivalent gain	8,000		8,000
Personal allowance	(12,570)	(12,570)	
	43,500	35,500	8,000

		Tax on slice	Total
	£	£	£
Tax on non-savings income £35,500 x 20%	35,500	0	7,100
Tax on savings income Personal savings allowance (higher rate) £500 x 0%	500	0	0
Tax on balance of savings income at basic rate (£37,700 - £35,500 - £500) £1,700 x 20%	1,700	340	340
Tax on savings income at higher rate (£8,000 - £500 - £1,700) £5,800 x 40%	5,800	2,320	2,320
Total	43,500	2,660	9,760

The total amount of the tax on the "annual equivalent" is £2,660.

Step three

Remove the tax credit or notional tax of 20%.

$$£8,000 \times 20\% = £1,600$$

	£
Total tax on the annual equivalent	2,660
Tax credit	(1,600)
Net tax on the annual equivalent	1,060

Step four

Multiply the net annual equivalent by the number of tax years for which the policy has been held, in this case five.

$$£1,060 \times 5 = £5,300$$

This is the "relieved liability".

Step five

The final tax liability can now be calculated. This is a reduction in tax equal to the difference between the tax calculated normally and the relieved liability.

The tax on the total gain (after the tax credit) was originally calculated as £7,460. The relieved liability will reduce this to find the top slicing relief.

	Tax £
Tax calculated normally after the tax credit	7,460
Relieved liability	(5,300)
Top slicing relief	2,160

The total tax for the year 2021-22 can now be calculated for Ragnar.

	Total £
Total liability after tax credit (as normal, as above)	14,560
Less: top slicing relief	(2,160)
	12,400

The tax on the policy gain, calculated normally, would have meant a net tax charge after the tax credit of £14,560. £7,460 of this was due to the gain and £7,100 due to the employment income. As the tax on the annual equivalent gain calculated was £5,300, there should have been a £2,160 fall overall in the tax liability, which through the steps there has been. It fell from £14,560 to £12,400.

What the top slicing relief has achieved is that – instead of having the benefit of the £500 personal savings allowance, and the balance in the basic rate band of £1,700 being charged tax at 20% rather than 40% for only one year – Ragnar has been able to have it for the whole five years, giving him an extra four years of benefit.

	Total saved £
Extra four years of £500 personal savings allowance at 0% instead of being taxed at 40% (£500 x 4 x 40%)	800
Extra four years of £1,700 balance of basic rate band at 20% instead of being taxed at 40% (£1,700 x 4 x 20%)	1,360
Reconciliation with top slicing relief	2,160

25.4.3   More than one chargeable event in one tax year

Where there is more than one chargeable policy gain in the tax year, an individual's annual equivalent income tax on the chargeable events, calculated together, must then be pro-rated in order to establish the top slicing relief specific to each one. The steps are similar up until the end, when the tax credit has been taken off the total annual equivalent. It is here, in between the original step three and step four, where the two or multiple gains are pro-rated. This is necessary, as each annual equivalent value (N) will need to be multiplied by a different number of years in order to arrive at the correct top slicing relief total.

Law: ITTOIA 2005, s. 537

Example

Ralph runs his own business. In 2021-22, his profits from his trade earn him taxable income, after his personal allowance, of £36,500. During the year he receives policy gains from two chargeable events. The first, received in June 2021, is £9,000 from a six-year-old policy. The second, in February 2022, is from a policy taken out on 1 September 2019 for £10,000.

Without the top slicing relief steps the whole gain would be taxed at Ralph's marginal rates as below.

	£	Other taxable income £	Life policy gain £
Taxable income	35,500	36,500	
Life policy total gains	19,000		19,000
Total taxable income	54,500	36,500	19,000

	£	Tax on slice £	Total £
Tax on non-savings income £36,500 x 20%	35,500		7,300
Tax on savings income			
Personal savings allowance (higher rate) £500 x 0%	500	0	0
Tax on balance of savings income at basic rate (£37,700 - £36,500 - £500) £700 x 20%	700	140	140
Tax on savings income at higher rate (£19,000 - £500 - £700) £17,800 x 40%	17,800	7,120	7,120
Total liability before tax credit	54,500	7,260	14,560
Tax credit (nominal tax) £19,000 x 20%		(3,800)	(3,800)
Total liability after tax credit		3,460	10,760

As can be seen above, Ralph's policy gains push him into the higher rate band, with £17,800 of the £19,000 gains being charged at 40%. Once more, however, top slicing relief will mitigate this.

Step one

The total gains are as follows.

The first gain, £9,000 is divided by six years to arrive at the annual equivalent, or top slice, of £1,500 per year.

The second gain, £10,000, is divided by two complete years to arrive at the annual equivalent, or top slice, of £5,000 per year.

Step two

These annual equivalents, totalling £6,500, must now be added to Ralph's other income.

	£	Non savings income £	Life policy gain £
Taxable income	36,500	36,500	
Life policy annual equivalent gain	6,500		6,500
	43,000	36,500	6,500

	£	Tax on slice £	Total £
Tax on non-savings income £36,500 x 20%	36,500		7,300
Tax on savings income Personal savings allowance (higher rate) £500 x 0%	500	0	0

(Cont.)	£	Tax on slice £	Total £
Tax on balance of savings income at basic rate (£37,700 - £36,500 - £500) £700 x 20%	700	140	140
Tax on savings income at higher rate (£6,500 - £500 - £700) £5,300 x 40%	5,300	2,120	2,120
Total	43,000	2,260	9,560

The total tax on the annual equivalent of both gains is £2,260.

Step three

Remove the tax credit or notional tax of 20%.

> £6,500 x 20% = £1,300

	£
Total tax on the annual equivalent	2,260
Tax credit	(1,300)
Net tax on the annual equivalent	960

Step four

Now the two gains need to be apportioned in order to multiply the net annual equivalent of each gain by the number of complete years for which each policy has been held.

For Ralph's first gain this is six years.

> £960 x 1,500/6500 = £221.54 x 6 years = £1,329.24

For Ralph's second gain this is two years.

> £960 x 5,000/6,500 = £738.46 x 2 years = £1,476.92

These total £2,806.16, and this is the "relieved liability".

Step five

The final tax liability can now be calculated. This is a reduction in tax equal to the difference between the tax calculated normally and the relieved liability.

The tax on the total gain was originally calculated as £3,460 as below.

	Tax £
Tax calculated normally after the tax credit	3,460
Relieved liability	(2,806)
Top slicing relief	654

The total tax for the year 2021-22 can now be calculated for Ralph.

	Total £
Total liability after tax credit (as normal as above)	10,760
Less: top slicing relief	(654)
	10,106

The tax on the policy gain, calculated normally, would have meant a net tax charge after the tax credit of £10,760. £3,460 of this was due to the gain and £7,300 due to the trading income. As the tax on the annual equivalent gain calculated was £2,260, there should have been a £654 fall overall in the tax liability, which through the steps there has been. It fell from £10,760 to £10,106.

25.4.4   Partial surrenders

Sometimes value can be extracted from a policy without surrendering the whole policy. These partial surrenders are known as "excess events" and can occur either when cash is taken from a policy that continues (partial surrenders) or from a policy that is partly sold (a part-assignment). Policyholders may cash in to liquidate some of the funds out of the policy for specific life events. If the policy is only partially surrendered or sold, the amount surrendered will determine whether there is a charge or not.

An immediate income tax charge will only arise if the amount surrendered is more than 5% of the initial investment (premiums paid) in the policy. The 5% is calculated per policy year but is also cumulative. For example, after four years the policyholder can surrender 20% of the value of the initial investment tax free.

If a part surrender has been made, and the amount is under the 5% deferral allowance, the event that is not chargeable at the time of the surrender will be deferred to the point when the policy matures. It will then be added with the chargeable event gain at that time.

For example, if a policyholder invested £100,000 into a life insurance policy, he could make a part surrender every year of £5,000. On a cumulative basis over ten years £50,000 could be part surrendered. None of these part surrenders would be immediately chargeable to income tax unless they were more than 5% of the initial investment. For example, if £7,000 was withdrawn one year, this would become a chargeable event of £2,000.

However, this is only a deferral; the income tax is still chargeable on the gain and eventually, when the policy matures, the cash that has been withdrawn through the years will be added to the chargeable event at the point of the maturity of the policy and taxed. In the example above of the policyholder withdrawing £7,000, the £2,000 income tax charge in the year of the withdrawal will, however, reduce the tax on the final policy gain.

Law: ITTOIA 2005, s. 498, 507

25.5   Personal portfolio bonds

25.5.1   Introduction

Personal portfolio bonds (PPBs) may be a life insurance policy, a contract for a life annuity or a capital redemption policy which must meet certain conditions at ITTOIA 2005, s. 516. In reality, most PPBs are single premium investment bonds.

These products are subject to stricter tax rules than other non-qualifying life policies, as the holder is able to choose the investment "property" and, as such, there is a much wider choice for the property that determines the benefits under the scheme. The most common example is where a policyholder transfers shares in his or her private trading company to the insurer and it is these shares that are the underlying property. Other less common examples may be the transfer of fine wines, vintage cars, or racehorses into the policy.

25.5.2   Conditions

A PPB must meet a number of conditions.

The first condition is that the benefits under the policy are determined by either the value of, or the income from, property, or by changes in an index which represents this property.

The second condition is that the holder of the policy, under the terms of the policy, is able to choose the property or index. If the only property or index that can be selected is from the following list, the policy will not be a PPB:

- property appropriated by the insurer to an internal linked fund;
- units in an authorised unit trust and shares in an open-ended investment company (as defined);
- shares in an approved investment trust, or an overseas equivalent;
- cash (including in banks and building societies but excluding cash held for speculation);
- certain life policies and so on;
- interests in certain collective investment schemes;
- shares in a UK real estate investment trust (REIT) or an overseas equivalent;
- interest in an authorised contractual scheme; and
- indices such as:
  - o the retail prices index;
  - o any similar general price index; or
  - o any index of share prices published and quoted on the official list of a recognised stock exchange.

25.5.3   Taxation

PPB schemes are taxed differently and have an *annual* charge to income tax. This is applied to all PPBs at the end of the insurance year unless it is the final insurance year. Any gain calculated under this regime is in addition to any made under the chargeable event regime for other non-qualifying policies.

The choice of the property being invested in must be made either by the holder of the policy, or by the holder together with his or her connected persons, or by a person acting on behalf of these parties in any combination. If the policyholder or his or her connected persons cannot themselves select the property from which the benefits will derive, the policy will not be a PPB even if the "permitted investment" condition is satisfied.

As already noted, the policyholder must be able to choose the property being invested in. This is interpreted broadly by HMRC, however, so allowing a third party to choose the investments may not always disqualify the policy from being a PPB. For example, HMRC accept that a broker or adviser may be:

> "no more than a conduit or agent through whom the policyholder gives the insurer its instructions."

As such, the policy would remain a PPB.

25.5.4   Gains

Unlike non-qualifying policies, which are only taxed when cash is received or the policy is brought to an end, PPBs have an income tax charge every year. This is essentially an anti-avoidance provision.

Law: ITTOIA 2005, s. 516-521

Guidance: IPTM 3320, 3600; https://tinyurl.com/y53y9tz3 (guidance on personal portfolio bonds)

25.6   Pitfalls and planning points

Maximum investment plans (MIPs)

MIPs are investment vehicles that are considered qualifying life policies as they have regular contributions and do provide life cover (albeit a small amount). No income tax is payable on any gains over the term of the policy on maturity, despite the fact they are primarily used for investment purposes.

Guidance: IEIM 401660

Annuities

If an amount is invested and the capital is valued at higher than it was when it was paid in (either by a lump sum or regular payments), the "annuity" is the regular payment of the excess made to the product owner. Usually annuity income is taxable, but a set proportion of every instalment paid into a purchased annuity is exempted from income tax. The exempt element is computed using mortality tables and represents the return on capital. Typically, such annuities are purchased annuities that comply with the terms of a will or settlement, or superannuation or pension scheme, or those that recognise a person's service in an office or employment.

Law: ITTOIA 2005, s. 717-724
Guidance: IPTM 7065

PROPERTY INCOME

26. Taxation of rental profits

26.1 Property businesses

26.1.1 UK property businesses

In the UK, income from the exploitation of land owned by the taxpayer is considered as "property income" and is taxed as non-savings income. For income tax purposes, the taxpayer owning the property could be an individual, a partner in a partnership, a trustee or a personal representative of an estate. Furthermore, an individual may carry out more than one property business in different capacities. For example, he or she may have a buy-to-let as an individual taxpayer, jointly own a let commercial property through a partnership, and be a trustee of a trust letting out a property. Such an individual would have more than one rental business on which to be taxed in each different capacity.

This property income may be generated from the letting of land or buildings or may be from more diverse sources, such as income from shooting rights over land or fishing rights over rivers and lakes. If the let land includes buildings, they may be residential or commercial. Where a taxpayer has property income from any of these sources in the UK, he or she is said to have an income from a "UK property business".

In addition to regular rental income received from the tenant for the use of land or buildings, any premiums received to pay for the right to use the property will be taxed. Premiums are usually received at the start of the lease and represent a one-off payment to the landlord on the granting of the lease.

Special rules apply to lease premiums (see **Chapter 27**).

Example

Roger lets a commercial warehouse to Petra to store her stock for her retail business. Petra agrees to pay £34,000 a year for the next 20 years. In addition, at the commencement of the lease, Petra pays Roger a one-off payment of £5,000, a premium, for the right to let the property.

Tax on property income is payable by the owner of the property – irrespective of whether the owner employs an agent to collect the rental income. Strictly, in law, the person due to pay the tax is "the person receiving or entitled to the profits".

Generally, these two parties are the same person, but in some cases, such as where tax is due through the non-resident landlord scheme, agents or tenants become liable for the tax on behalf of the person entitled to the profits (see **38.7**).

Law: ITTOIA 2005, s. 264, 266, 276, 277
Guidance: PIM 1020

26.1.2   Overseas property businesses

The profits of an overseas property business (i.e. for property outside the UK), carried on by a UK resident, are calculated in exactly the same way as those of a UK property business. The income is classified as foreign source income.

The profits and losses of a UK property business must be kept separate from those of an overseas property business; by law, the two sources are treated as two separate businesses. The profits of each business are taxed separately and, more importantly, losses from a UK property business cannot be set against profits of an overseas property business, or *vice versa*. Any overseas property losses can therefore only be carried forward against future profits of that overseas business. Furthermore, a different accounting basis (i.e. either cash or accruals) may be used for calculating the profits of a UK and an overseas property business, as each is considered a separate business.

The favourable rules for furnished holiday accommodation (see **Chapter 28**) do not apply to property overseas unless the land or buildings generating the property income are in the European Economic Area (EEA). The property allowance (see **26.8** below), however, will be available to both UK and overseas businesses, though there is only one property allowance per taxpayer so this will be shared between both businesses if applicable. At the time of writing, this does not appear to have changed following Brexit (and the end of the associated transitional period).

Law: ITTOIA 2005, s. 265, 269

26.2   Income classification

26.2.1   Trading or non-trading income?

Although rental income profits are *computed* in much the same way as income from a trading business, property rental businesses are not treated as trading unless the taxpayer is running an actual trading business such as a hotel or a guest house. This has been confirmed in several court cases over the years, including *Salisbury House Estates*. Consequently, whereas trading businesses attract inheritance tax (IHT) and capital gains tax (CGT) reliefs, e.g. business asset disposal relief, property rental businesses will not be able to benefit from these.

Property income

If an individual has a trading business, but with property income as a part of that business, it will generally fall to be taxed as property income. For example, if a business was trading as a retail shop but there was a residential flat above the shop, owned and let out by the trading business, all the income from the residential letting would be chargeable to tax under the property income category, not the trading income category.

This is reversed if the trading business is an overseas business. In these cases, any income from property as a part of a trading business will be taxed as trading income.

If there is a right to use a caravan or houseboat, this will derive from an interest in land and, as such, will be considered property income.

Exceptions to property income

However, some types of income that would appear to be property income are in fact taxed as trading income. These include:

- farming income and income from market gardening;
- income from quarries and other extraction sources such as mines;
- water, iron and gas works;
- markets and fairs;
- fishing activities (but only substantial commercial activity; smaller fishing rights are property income);
- toll bridges and ferries;
- railways;
- other commercial uses of land;
- commercial woodlands (letting woodlands is included);

- hotels and guesthouses; and
- rental from tied premises.

Law: ITTOIA 2005, s. 261, 266, 267
Case: *Salisbury House Estates Ltd v Fry* (1930) 15 TC 266
Guidance: PIM 1051

26.2.2 Types of property income

All "income generated from land" from a property business will be chargeable to income tax. This will include rent and "other" receipts. Usually, income from property will be in the form of cash or a bank transfer; however, payments in kind, such as the painting and redecorating of rooms, will also be counted as property income based on the value of what is being provided.

Rent

Rent consists of payments received by the landlord for the right to use the land and the term specifically includes:

> "payments by a tenant for work to maintain or repair leased premises which the lease does not require the tenant to carry out".

This is an anti-avoidance provision which stops the landlord asking the tenant to pay personally for repairs and maintenance to keep the "official" (taxable) rent lower (ITTOIA 2005, s. 266(2)).

Example

A landlord has an agreement with a tenant that the tenant pays £2,000 rent a month by bank transfer. However, outside the rental contract, the tenant agrees to paint and redecorate every room in the house for the landlord every year. The value of this painting and redecoration (by reference to what it would cost the landlord to employ a third party to complete) would be deemed to be a rent payment made by the tenant to the landlord "for work to maintain or repair leased premises, which the lease does not require the tenant to carry out".

This would not achieve the landlord's objective of having lower rent to pay tax on, as the value of the tenant's work has to be added to the rental income actually received as additional rent.

Rents will be property income regardless of whether the property is commercial or residential, furnished or unfurnished.

Other receipts

Other receipts could include receipts for licences to occupy or use land. A licence is more restricted than a lease in that a lease usually gives the lessee exclusive possession of the property, whereas a licence grants permission to perform a particular act at the property and therefore prevents only the permitted act from being a trespass. For example, a licence may be given for a car parking space. The only thing the licensee can do is park his car there; he cannot live or camp there, for example. A licence does not normally give an interest in land (CG 70250), though tax law overrides this in some circumstances (e.g. in relation to fixtures).

Other receipts also include payments for the exercise of other rights over land, e.g. allowing storage, or the burial of waste on the land. Film crews using the land for making a movie would also be exploiting a right to use the land, and the payment for this would be included in property income. If the property is let furnished, but there is a separate charge for the furniture, or other "service" charges for, say, laundry or cleaning or gardening, this is also property income unless, exceptionally, these amount to a trade in their own right.

Any refunds or rebates for items that, when paid, were offset or deducted from taxable rental income, will be treated as rental receipts when received. Likewise, if a landlord has rent protection insurance, and the tenant defaults on the rental payments, so that the policy pays out for non-payment, the insurance receipts will be rental property income.

Bonds and premiums

The treatment of deposits and bonds paid to the landlord on the commencement of the rental will differ depending on whether the cash or the accruals basis of accounting is being used, and whether the deposits are left with the landlord or lodged with a deposit scheme.

If the landlord receives the deposit directly and he or she is operating the cash basis (see **26.4.2**), all receipts are taxable including the deposit or bond.

However, if the accruals basis (see **26.4.3**) is being operated, deposits and bonds will only be chargeable if the landlord is actually entitled to the deposit. This will be the case if the deposit is kept and matched against costs, to make good rent arrears or damage done by tenants.

Likewise, if the deposit is given directly to one of the three government deposit schemes (Deposit Protection Service, MyDeposits, or the Tenancy Deposit Scheme) the deposit is legally the property of the tenant, and will only be chargeable if the landlord becomes legally entitled to it.

See **Chapter 27** for details of how lease premiums are dealt with.

Guidance: PIM 1051, 1052, 1094

26.3 Ownership structures

26.3.1 Introduction

A taxpayer can own property in his or her own name as an individual, jointly with another individual, or as a partner in a partnership. Jointly owned property can be held legally:

- as "joint tenants" – where the property held passes directly to the other joint owner on the death of one of the owners; or
- as "tenants in common" – where the half owned can be left to whomever the joint owner wishes.

However the property is legally owned, owning property jointly with another individual does not automatically make the structure a partnership. It is important to know whether a partnership exists, as the taxation of the income will be different depending on the structure of the entity.

If the structure is considered to be a true partnership, the income belongs to the partnership and not the individual. The income will be grouped with any other partnership income and the partner will be taxed on his or her partnership share of the total income under the tax rules for partnerships (see **26.3.3** and **Chapter 16**).

On the other hand, if the income is derived merely from a joint ownership of property, and not a formal partnership, it will be taxed as property income in the hands of the individual under the property income legislation to the extent of that individual's ownership share of the property.

26.3.2 Where no partnership exists

Two or more individuals

If two or more individuals own a rental income source jointly, but there is no formal partnership, they will share the profit depending on the share of the property they own. There may be occasions where the joint owners agree between themselves to share the profits in a different way to their actual ownership, but if this has been agreed, they must also be taxed on this share.

Example 1

Raul, Rabi and Rajak are triplets who were left a legacy of a commercial storeroom by their late aunt, and which they let out. They legally own a third each, but as Raul and Rabi are both working full-time as a doctor and dentist respectively, and Rajak is unemployed, they decided between them to share the profits 20:20:60 rather than one third each.

Because the brothers are sharing the profits in a percentage different from their actual ownership, they will need to declare to HMRC the actual share of profits that they receive, rather than the share of profits based on ownership. They will then be taxed accordingly.

Spouses and civil partners

If the joint owners are husband and wife or civil partners, HMRC will initially and automatically tax both taxpayers on 50% of the profits of the property business. The only time this will not be the case is if a true partnership is being run (see below) or if the income is trading income such as from qualifying furnished holiday accommodation (see **Chapter 28**).

If the couple do not own the property in equal shares, they may inform HMRC of the actual split and ask to be taxed according to these percentages. They will do this by signing a declaration on Form 17 stating their actual beneficial interest. The form may be accessed at https://tinyurl.com/hy4zj64.

However, if they genuinely do own the property on a 50:50 basis they are not permitted to split the profits in any other way than 50:50.

Example 2

River and Ruby are married and own, in equal shares as tenants in common, a residential apartment in London which they let out at £4,000 a month. The total net income after all allowable deductions for 2021-22 was £40,000. River is an architect on a salary of £160,000 a year whereas Ruby has no income.

To prevent River paying 45% tax on £20,000 of the income, River and Ruby decide that Ruby is to receive 70% of the income and River 30%, and both will be taxed accordingly. However, unlike the triplets in Example 1, this is not possible as River and Ruby are married.

River could genuinely gift 20% of the apartment to Ruby – formally, by making a CGT no-gain no-loss disposal and changing the deeds with the Land Registry – and they could then inform HMRC of the *actual* legal split of the property. If they do not do this, the couple will continue to receive and be taxed on 50% of the rental profits each.

Law: ITA 2007, s. 837
Guidance: PIM 1030

26.3.3 Where a partnership exists

A partnership exists when "… persons [are] carrying on a business in common with a view to a profit".

It is essential, therefore, to have a business in order to have a partnership and although the definition of "business" is wider than "trade", simply holding a rental property from which rental income is derived is not enough to constitute a trade. Rental profits are thus calculated using the same principles as calculating profits from a trade, but the taxpayer is not actually treated as carrying out a trade.

An existing trading partnership

If two or more individual taxpayers are already in a trading or professional partnership, and that trading partnership happens to let out property while also making profits from the core trading activities, a partnership for recording property income will exist. Any property income arising from the partnership will be declared under partnership profits rather than under profits from a property business in the partners' self-assessment tax returns.

Losses cannot be deducted from profits from a property business made in a different capacity (e.g. as an individual).

A separate self-assessment tax return page will be required for each different capacity in which property income arises.

Example 1

Riley and Ryan are brothers who are both solicitors. Their partnership RR Law is trading as a law firm. However, as the partnership owns a large office building that is surplus to RR Law's requirements, the firm also receives income from letting out offices.

Riley also has a buy-to-let property in Worthing that he lets out in his own individual capacity. Any property income Riley receives in his capacity as a partner of RR Law will be reported separately from the property income he receives personally from the Worthing property. He will have one property business (Worthing) and one trading business (his share of the profits from RR Law, which will include the property income from the rental of the offices). Losses made on either of Riley's rental businesses cannot be set off against profits made on the other.

If the partnership is a trading partnership that also happens to have property income, any profits will be taxed according to the partners' basis periods rather than the actual profits of the tax year. Special rules exist for the taxing of the opening and closing years of partnership profits (see **Chapter 16**).

Law: *Partnership Act* 1890, s. 1

An investment partnership business

There is another partnership structure which may cause the property income to be classified as partnership income rather than property income. This is where the partnership is running an investment business rather than a trading business.

It will be extremely unlikely that two or more individuals, who do nothing more than let out their share of a jointly owned property, will be considered to be running an investment partnership business.

If, on the other hand, the partners supply several additional paid services, and there is significant "business" activity, this may be considered an investment partnership business. If the partnership resembles more a regular commercial business than a convenient structure within which to hold let property, it may fall within the definition, but these types of partnership are rare.

A property business can never be a trading business even though it is treated as if it is trading for calculating the profits.

Example 2

Rory and Rhys have a partnership that lets a block of residential flats in Enfield, North London. They have an estate agent that manages the property and finds tenants for them.

Rubin and Ronnie also have a let property in Enfield, but theirs is a commercial office building, fully managed by them. Rubin looks after the ground floor and manages the reception staff, the vending machines, the café that the partnership also provides, the lockers and shower rooms and the rented plants. Ronnie manages the rest of the floors and the external area. He organizes the cleaning of the offices for the tenants, the rubbish removal, window cleaning and the gardening and car parks. Rubin and Ronnie both work full time in the office building managing their share of the office tasks.

Although each case will be decided on its merits, it is likely that Rory and Rhys will not be considered to have an investment partnership business, but that Rubin and Ronnie will be.

Again, even if the partnership is an investment partnership business, this will not amount to a trade so will not be taxed by reference to basis periods. The rental profits will be taxed for the tax year from 6 April to 5 April.

Guidance: PIM 1030

26.4   The cash and accruals bases

26.4.1   Introduction

As with all other income chargeable to income tax, the calculation of taxable rental profits will generally be based on profits from 6 April to the following 5 April, i.e. for the tax year.

The cash basis is used by default for all UK resident individuals where the gross property income in the tax year is £150,000 or less. If the gross property income does not exceed £150,000 there is an option to elect to use the alternative method of calculation, the accruals or "generally accepted accounting practice" (GAAP) basis (see **26.4.3**). Where the £150,000 limit is exceeded, the accruals method becomes obligatory.

"Gross property income" is the total of all the rental income received by the individual in the tax year calculated on a cash basis.

The £150,000 limit is pro-rated if the individual has not carried on the property business throughout the whole year.

Example

Richard decides to let out his two Cornwall beach properties. He has the properties ready for the summer of 2021, and both cottages are let to a company for their various directors from 6 June 2021.

Under the cash basis, Richard receives rents of £130,000. Usually, the cash basis will operate as the default method, as Richard has not received gross cash rents exceeding £150,000. However, as he has only operated his UK property business for ten months of the year, the £150,000 maximum is adjusted to £150,000/12 x 10 = £125,000. As

Richard has pro-rated property receipts in excess of this maximum he will be unable to use the cash basis and will be required to calculate the profits according to GAAP.

As mentioned above, the cash basis is the default where the gross rental income is £150,000 or under but, if desired, a taxpayer may make an election to use the accruals or GAAP basis. This could be the case where historically the taxpayer has always used the accruals basis and anticipates that the fall in rental income to below £150,000 is only temporary.

Any such election to use the accruals basis must be made by the anniversary of the 31 January following the year in which the rental profits have been generated. For example, if calculating the profits for the tax year 2021-22, the election would need to be made by 31 January 2024. Elections are only applicable to the tax year they specify, and so need to be made every year if the business wishes to continue using the accruals basis.

Spouses and civil partners

Within a marriage or a civil partnership, the way the profits are split will determine whether the taxpayer can use his or her own chosen method (cash or accruals) on his individual share of the profits.

If the property is genuinely held in equal shares, or if HMRC have not been given any alternative basis, each spouse or partner must use the same basis of calculation.

If the property is held unequally by each spouse or civil partner, and they have informed HMRC of their wish to be taxed on their actual owned share, a precise split of the profits taxed can be made. The spouses will then be taxed on their own respective shares of the profits and each may use the cash or accruals basis.

Other joint owners

If the property is jointly owned by individuals *outside* a marriage or civil partnership, it will be for each individual taxpayer to decide which basis to use on their respective shares of the profits. It will be irrelevant what the other joint owners opt to do.

Law: ITTOIA 2005, s. 271A, 271C

26.4.2 The cash basis

The cash basis involves calculating the profits to be taxed on the basis of actual receipts and expenses during the tax year, with subsequent adjustments to profit for income tax purposes. See also **15.9**.

If the landlord is entitled to receive accrued rent, but this rent has not yet been received, it will not be counted, or therefore taxed. This means that bad debt relief is achieved automatically.

If an estate or letting agent has been used, and the agent receives rents, the applicable date for taxation purposes is the date *the agent* receives the rental income, and not the date the agent eventually pays it over to the landlord.

If expenses such as insurance and council tax have been incurred but not yet paid by 5 April, these will not be deductible from the taxable income for the tax year.

Security deposits are dealt with differently. The deposit is not legally the property of the landlord unless and until the tenant leaves the property and the landlord needs to use some of the deposit to make good any rent arrears or damage that the tenant has made to the property. Until that time, as they are not legally the property of the landlord, the landlord will not be taxed on the receipt of the deposit.

Example

Rachel's employer has requested she move from London to Manchester. She lets out her Kilburn flat from 6 August 2021. The rent charged is £1,800 a month and is paid directly into her bank account by direct debit monthly. In calculating her profits for 2021-22, Rachel is entitled to eight months' rental income but has only *received* six months income as the last two months were still outstanding at 5 April 2022 due to the tenant's cash-flow problems.

£14,400 (£1,800 x 8) is the total amount of rent entitlement in the year, using the accruals basis.

£10,800 (£1,800 x 6) is the actual amount that Rachel has received, using the cash basis.

As Rachel has not opted for the accruals basis, she will be taxed on the cash basis, so £10,800 will be the amount of rental income (less qualifying deductions) that she is taxed on in 2021-22.

The balance of £3,600 will be taxed if and when it is received, probably in the tax year 2022-23.

26.4.3   The accruals basis

The accruals or GAAP basis will apply if the gross rental income exceeds £150,000, or (where the profits are lower) if the taxpayer has elected for it (see **26.4.1** above). The accruals basis must also be used if the landlord is a company, an LLP, a mixed partnership (where at least one partner is not an individual) or a trustee.

Rather than using the cash income and expenditure as the cash basis does, the accruals basis taxes the income accruing and the expenses incurred during the tax year, irrespective of whether the actual amounts have been collected or paid over. The income and expenditure are thus matched to the period to which they relate.

If rents have accrued and are due to the landlord, but have not yet been received, these will still be included and taxed under the accruals basis. If eventually the rents receivable go unpaid, an adjustment may be made in future years to recognise the bad debt, reducing tax payable in that future tax year.

If expenses, such as insurance and council tax, have been incurred but not yet paid over, these will be deductible in the tax year to which they relate, even if paid later. This is obviously beneficial for the taxpayer. If they are not in fact paid, an adjustment will be needed.

Example

Rodney owns a large residential apartment block in Bristol, which he lets out to several university students. The first year of the property business was 2021-22 and the students signed the tenancy agreement on 1 September 2021. Rodney received £13,500 in rent every month up to 5 April 2022. Four of the students were in arrears and Rodney had £6,000 of rent unpaid to him at 5 April 2022.

£94,500 (£13,500 x 7) is the total amount of rent entitlement in the year on an accruals basis.

£88,500 (£94,500 less the £6,000 rent not paid) is the amount received in the year, on which Rodney would have been taxed if using the cash basis.

Because Rodney only operated the property business for seven months in 2021-22, the £150,000 limit for using the cash basis will need to be pro-rated. This means that as he has gross rental income of more than £87,500 (£150,000 x 7/12) he will need to use the accruals basis.

£94,500 will be the amount Rodney is taxed on in 2021-22. There will be no allowance made for the £6,000 of rent that has not yet been received. If this rent remains outstanding and is not eventually paid, this can be deducted from rental income in a future tax year as a bad debt, reducing any tax payable, or increasing a loss.

Law: ITTOIA 2005, s. 271A

26.4.4 Changing between the cash and the accruals bases

There are some occasions when a landlord must change between the cash and the accruals basis, e.g. if the gross rental income from the rental business increases to above £150,000, or if the receipts fall to £150,000 or less and the landlord does not wish to continue to use the accruals basis. In both cases, adjustments may be required to ensure that income is charged to tax (but only once) and that expenses are relieved (but again only once).

If the landlord switches from the accruals basis to the cash basis, the business will have rental income and debtors recorded at the end of the year prior to the change which will have been taxed (under the accruals basis). Without adjustment, these will be taxed again when the rent is received the following year (under the cash basis). In addition, there may be expenses and creditors that have been relieved (under the accruals basis) which, without adjustment, will be relieved again when paid (under the cash basis).

Both of these must be adjusted for.

The rental expenses and creditors will need to be removed at the beginning of the first year using the cash basis, which will require an adjustment increasing the rental profits for that first cash basis year. In addition, the rental income and debtors will need to be removed at the beginning of the first year using the cash basis, which will require an adjustment decreasing the rental profits for that first cash basis year.

On the other hand, if the business changes from the cash basis to the accruals basis, the business would have had no debtors at the end of the previous year. The related rental income and debtors that would have been recorded for the previous year under the accruals method will need to be instated, at the beginning of the first year for which the landlord uses the accruals method. Likewise, the related expenses and creditors will need to be instated. Again, adjustments will be required.

Overall, the net of these two adjustments will either be an increase to the profit or an expense.

If it is an expense, it is an allowable deduction in the first year of using the accruals basis. No spreading is required.

If it is an increase in profit, additional tax will be due. This tax is by default spread over six tax years in order to avoid an overly large income tax burden for the taxpayer. However, the taxpayer may elect to take the adjustment expense earlier. Any portion of the adjustment expense can be accelerated and the remaining part is taxed equally over the rest of the six-year period. Such an election must be made by 12 months after the 31 January following the tax year in which the change in basis was made and the adjustment started to be charged.

Law: ITTOIA 2005, s. 239, 239B, 330, 334A

26.5   Deductibility of expenditure

26.5.1   Introduction

The normal rules and commercial principles for a rental business are almost identical to those of a trading business, including the need for a distinction between capital and income (or "revenue") expenditure.

Income expenditure is usually deductible in full in calculating rental profits, as long as it is incurred "wholly and exclusively" for the purposes of the rental business – see **26.5.3** below. Tax relief may be given immediately, and at the owner's highest marginal rate of income tax. However, there is an important exception for certain interest and other finance costs (see **26.9** below). Motor expenses also have particular rules (see **26.5.7**).

If an expense is of a capital nature, on the other hand, it will not be taken into account until the property is disposed of, when it will in principle lead to a smaller CGT charge – as long as the enhancement is still in existence at the disposal date. For some properties, however (broadly speaking, those that are not residences) capital allowances may be available for certain qualifying expenditure – see **Chapter 21** (Fixtures).

26.5.2   Income or capital expenditure

The distinction between income and capital expenditure is considered in greater depth at **15.7.3**. In brief, income expenses maintain the value of an asset rather than enhancing its value.

Examples of common income expenses for a property business are:

- accountancy, legal, and estate agent fees;
- advertising and insurance costs;
- replacement of domestic furnishing and appliances;
- costs of travelling to visit the property; and
- repairs and redecoration.

Specific examples of expenses that HMRC indicate can be treated as deductible as a revenue rather than a capital expense in the context of rental properties are:

- painting/decorating inside and outside the home;
- cleaning external stones and pavements;
- treatment for damp and rot;
- repairs of broken windows and doors, and of furniture and appliances in the home such as washing machines, ovens and lifts;
- re-pointing the bricks;
- replacing roof tiles and slates; and
- replacing roof flashing and gutters.

A capital expense leads to a new asset being acquired or brought into existence, or more capital value being added to an existing asset (e.g. by extension or improvement). HMRC state that it will be a "question of fact if expenditure on a property leads to improvement".

HMRC give the following examples of expenditure that would be classified as capital items in a rental property business:

- converting an old unoccupied barn into a holiday home;
- refurbishment costs of repairing a property purchased in a derelict or run-down state;
- costs of demolishing a derelict factory to clear space for a new office building;
- new buildings;
- costs of a car park or garage next to a let property;
- expenditure on a new access road to a property; and
- any new land next to a let property.

Improvements to the property will also be considered to be capital.

Guidance: PIM 2025, 2030

26.5.3   Wholly and exclusively

As for other sole trader and partnership businesses, expenses may only be deducted from rental profits if they are wholly and exclusively incurred for the purpose of the property business. Any personal expenses, or expenses that have a duality of purpose, cannot reduce the taxable profits. See, generally, **Chapter 15**.

Common expenses deducted from rental income include estate or management agent letting fees, house insurance and repairs. The house insurance will be for the structure of the home. Any contents insurance is the liability of the tenants rather than the landlord.

If the landlord has contracted to pay charges that are normally paid by the tenant – such as water charges, sewage charges, WiFi or council tax – these too will be allowable deductions.

If there is a dual purpose to the expense, it will not usually be deductible. For example, if a landlord travels to inspect a rental property, but also to meet friends for dinner at a restaurant next door, the costs of the travel to the rental property will be for a dual purpose, and not deductible. However, for some expenses, an obvious and identifiable part will be for the business. For example, an individual may have an itemised mobile phone bill. Calls relating to the rental business, such as calls to the agent, insurance broker, local council etc., may be aggregated separately from private calls and deducted as a business expenses.

26.5.4   Finance costs for dwelling-related loans

The treatment of interest and other finance costs for residential property (excluding furnished holiday accommodation) has been subject to important changes in recent years. The more restrictive rules apply to individuals, partnerships and trusts.

Instead of claiming a full deduction in computing rental profits, landlords receive a basic rate (20%) deduction from their income tax bill. See **26.9** below.

Law: ITTOIA 2005, s. 272A

26.5.5   Repairs

Repairs can be problematic, as they can sometimes be of an income nature and sometimes of a capital nature. HMRC define a repair as "the restoration of an asset by replacing subsidiary parts of the whole asset".

For example, the repair of one or two broken cupboard doors in a kitchen would be classified as an income expense repair; it does nothing more than maintain the value of the property by replacing subsidiary parts. On the other hand, the installation of a completely new kitchen might well be a capital improvement, enhancing or improving the value of the property.

The question as to whether an item of expenditure is an income or a capital expense often centres around whether the property now has "additional" assets. This can often be quite difficult to establish.

For example, if the property had a tiled roof, and this was replaced with another roof of the same kind, the property has not benefited from any additional assets. Even if the new roof incorporated some more modern features – such as using more up-to-date materials, greater durability, flexibility or ability to withstand weather – it would still be considered to have replaced an existing asset, on a like-for-like basis. HMRC give examples of replacing wooden beams with steel girders, lead pipes with plastic ones, or single glazed windows with double glazing, none of which represent additional assets being introduced, despite the assets being updated for modernity or function. Indeed, it would be difficult to make direct replacements of some assets, for example where particular materials are no longer in use.

However, if an improvement is significant, it would constitute an additional asset. Keeping with the example of the tiled roof in the previous example, if a designer roof is built onto the property with turrets and an extra chimney, and is made with a quality that is drastically enhanced compared to the original roof, an additional asset will have been added to the property. Similarly, and despite HMRC's girder and pipe examples, if the new steel girders take a substantially heavier load, or if the new plastic pipes take considerably more pressure or heat, an additional asset would be evident. The expenditure would then be classified as capital, and not deductible from rental income.

It is possible to incur both income and capital expenses together. Continuing with the roof example, if the designer roof was built, but the contractor repaired some of the guttering at the same time and issued only one invoice, it would contain two types of expenses – revenue for the guttering repair and capital for the new roof. An apportionment may be appropriate.

Guidance: PIM 2030

Property unusable until repairs are carried out

If repairs are made very soon after a property is purchased, landlords must take care before classifying subsequent expenses as income.

If the price paid at purchase reflected a dilapidated and unusable state, any repairs to make it "fit for purpose" will be capital expenditure because the property price would probably have been higher if it had been in a ready-to-use state.

Two well-known conflicting cases show this principle well: *Law Shipping* and *Odeon Associated Theatres*. These are considered at **15.7.3** above.

Cases: *Law Shipping Co Ltd v IRC* (1923) 12 TC 621; *Odeon Associated Theatres Ltd v Jones* (1971) 48 TC 257

26.5.6   Capital allowances

Tax relief for some capital expenditure will be available by way of capital allowances. See:

- **Chapter 21** for detailed coverage of property fixtures;
- **Chapter 28** for furnished holiday lettings; and
- **26.6** below for the relief for the replacement of domestic items.

26.5.7   Motor expenses

Landlords may use their own vehicle to visit the property for a variety of reasons, including repairs and periodic checks. There are two options for claiming tax relief.

The landlord can claim capital allowances on the cost of the vehicle as well as an annual deduction for the actual running costs. Alternatively, the landlord may opt to use a fixed rate mileage deduction using rates provided by HMRC. This choice is available whether the landlord uses the cash or the accruals basis of accounting. Once the decision is made for a given vehicle, it cannot be changed for as long as that particular vehicle is used in the business.

The fixed, or flat rate, allowance enables the landlord to claim a certain amount per mile driven for the purposes of the rental property business.

The rate remains the same irrespective of how many people are in the vehicle.

The allowance covers all the costs of the vehicle including the initial purchase and the running and maintenance costs such as fuel, MOTs, servicing and insurance. The amounts that can be claimed for cars and goods vehicles in 2021-22 are 45p per mile for the first 10,000 miles, and 25p per mile thereafter. For motorcycles, the rate is 24p per mile, whatever the level of mileage. See **Appendix 8.**

The "wholly and exclusively" rule and motor expenses

Whichever method is chosen, the deduction is only available for business journeys, so the definition of a "business journey" is crucial.

When considering income from property, almost all of the rules and provisions concerning expenses are the same as those for general trading income expenses. These rules rely on the concept that a tax deduction is only allowed if the expenses are wholly and exclusively for the purpose of the business. It follows that journeys carried out entirely and only for the purpose of the rental business will *prima facie* attract allowable deductions.

In some cases it will be obvious that an expense is wholly and exclusively for the business, but in other cases it will be less clear cut.

Example 1

Reem lives in Swindon. In May 2021 she drives to inspect her rental property in Oxford, taking roughly an hour. If Reem drives directly from Swindon to Oxford and back, stopping only to view the residence, this journey is clearly wholly and exclusively for the rental property business.

If Reem is driving to London to do some shopping, but on her way home she stops in to inspect her Oxford property, this journey is clearly not wholly and exclusively for the business. It is a private journey where the inspection was incidental to it.

If Reem's journey was at the outset genuinely only driving to inspect the property, but after the inspection she decided to take advantage of the fact she was near Bicester village to do some shopping there on a whim, this subsequent stop was not the whole point of the journey. So, although the visit to Reem's rental property in this example is not *incidental* to the journey, it still cannot be said that the entire trip was wholly and exclusively for the property business. In this case, it would be likely that the stop at the shopping village would render this trip as one with a dual purpose, and as such the journey would not be a wholly and exclusively business journey, and therefore not deductible. Although the *intention* may have been originally just to view the rental property, the actual facts must determine the tax outcome.

Note that a landlord can still meet the wholly and exclusively test if the personal benefit received is only incidental.

Example 2

In August 2021, Reem makes the same journey to inspect her rental property in Oxford. On her way home this time, rather than stopping off to shop at Bicester village, she goes directly home, but stops off at a motorway services to buy fuel. While she is in the services she visits the supermarket (located inside the services) to buy bread and milk. It is likely that the stop to purchase the bread and milk would be considered incidental to the visit to the property and the journey would still be wholly and exclusively for the business, and deductible.

HMRC give the example of a landlord stopping on the way to collect a newspaper as being incidental.

Another example of an incidental benefit is where the journey itself could offer the landlord some benefit.

Example 3

Reem has had a very difficult week. She has had work deadlines and her father is ill. She makes the same one-hour journey to inspect her rental property in Oxford. Reem spends the two hours driving to and from the rental property in her car listening to a stress-releasing podcast and classical music. By the time she gets home she feels much better; the journey broke up her day and was of huge value to her mental health. This benefit to Reem, however valuable, would not prevent the journey from being wholly and exclusively for the business.

Because this continuum exists, it is good advice for a landlord to retain evidence proving that such journeys were in fact wholly and exclusively for the business. Evidence could be in the form of agreements and arrangements for meetings, such as emails or texts, notes of meetings, photos, receipts and other such verification, including mileage records. This evidence can assist the landlord in demonstrating that the expense of the journey can be justified as being wholly and exclusively for business.

Case law

The question of whether a travelling expense is wholly and exclusively for the rental business is the same as the test for trades and, as such, settled case law from trades and professions is relevant here.

The concept that the journey must be for business purposes was highlighted in the 2018 case of *Daniels*. Miss Daniels was an exotic dancer in London and had claimed her travel from home to the club in which she worked. She justified this by claiming that she carried on her profession from her home. It was found that the travel expenses were partly incurred because of where she chose to live and partly for her to get from her home to her place of work. Travel between her home and the club in which she worked was therefore not wholly and exclusively for the purposes of her profession.

An earlier case, *Horton v Young*, considered a taxpayer who did genuinely carry on his trade from home, travelling to various sites on an *ad hoc* basis to perform his physical work of bricklaying. As it was held that his home was his workplace, the miles he travelled from his home to the many and varied sites at which he worked were for the purposes of the trade and deductible.

Applying these cases to a rental property business, if the business is genuinely carried out at the landlord's home, then journeys from his or her home to the location of the rental property will in principle be deductible.

If, however, there is another location from which the property business is being managed, travel from home to the rental property will not be business travel, and is not deductible. In these cases, travel from this other location to the rental property will be wholly and exclusively for the business and allowed. Landlords should therefore take care if the rental property is managed by a letting agent or property management company as, in these cases, the landlord's home will almost certainly not be the property business's base.

Split use of the vehicle for private and property business use

Usually, if an expense is not incurred wholly and exclusively for the purposes of the rental business, it is not allowable as a deduction. However, there are some expenses where the proportion used by the business can clearly be identified and in these cases, an apportionment can be made. So as long as mileage can be clearly split between business and private usage, the costs of running the car may be apportioned on a just and reasonable basis. For example, if 40% of the car mileage is for business use, a landlord could deduct 40% of the running costs.

Capital allowances

The initial purchase cost of a vehicle is not deductible in a rental property business, even if the car is being used wholly for the purpose of the business, and even if the cash basis is being used. Nor is there an annual deduction available for depreciation. However, capital allowances (under the plant and machinery category) may be applicable. These allowances will be adjusted to take account of non-business use.

See **20.5** for detailed guidance on capital allowances for cars.

Capital allowances cannot be claimed if the landlord has opted to deduct the fixed rate mileage allowance.

Cases: *Horton v Young* (1971) 47 TC 60; *Daniels v HMRC* [2018] UKFTT 462
Guidance: PIM 2220

26.6   Replacement of domestic items

26.6.1   Introduction

For residential property landlords, it is not possible to deduct the cost of domestic items initially purchased for use in a rental property. "Domestic items" here include such chattels as:

- furniture, such as sofas, beds, tables and chairs;
- furnishings, such as carpet and rugs, curtains and cushions;
- appliances, such as ovens, fridges and washing machines; and
- kitchenware, such as plates and cutlery.

For example, if a landlord prepares a house for letting for the first time and purchases a fridge and a washing machine, the cost of these items cannot be deducted from his or her rental profits.

26.6.2   The conditions of the replacement

However, relief may be given for the cost of replacing such domestic items, by way of the "replacement domestic items relief". The former "wear and tear" allowance is no longer available.

For landlords running a residential letting business, as long as there was an existing "old" item and the landlord has incurred expenditure replacing this with a "new" item, which was provided wholly and exclusively for the rental property, an allowable deduction is available for the cost of the new item.

This deduction is available whether the landlord uses the accruals or the cash method, but is not allowed where the property satisfies the conditions of furnished holiday accommodation (see **Chapter 28**), or if rent-a-room relief is being claimed (see **26.7**). Further, if there is any element of personal use by the landlord, the relief is not available.

Example

Radley has a residential apartment in Penzance. He lets it on a six-month shorthold assured tenancy every winter, but uses it himself between lettings during the summer months. Although in 2021-22 Radley replaced the fridge-freezer and an armchair, no deduction is available as there is personal use by the landlord.

The old item must no longer be available to the tenant, and no capital allowances must have been claimed on the item during its ownership. Fixtures – such as baths, basins, toilets and boilers – do not qualify for replacement of domestic items relief. Replacing these types of items would generally be considered a repair to the building, i.e. deductible under general principles anyway.

Law: ITTOIA 2005, s. 311A

26.6.3 Restrictions

If the item is replaced on a like-for-like basis (so with the same size, quality and functionality), there are no restrictions on the deduction and the new cost of the item will be fully deductible – even if the price has increased over time. However, if the new item is a significant improvement in capacity, quality or function from the old item, the replacement cost deductible will be limited to the lower of either the cost of the new item or the value of the old item at the time of the replacement (including inflation).

Example 1

Raquel has a residential property in York. She provides a basic budget washing machine costing £200 in the dwelling when she starts letting it out in 2018. In 2022 the tenant informs her that it has stopped working so she replaces it with a top of the range washing machine, with many more features and cycles and costing £1,000. The cost of replacing the budget brand machine directly would have been £300 in 2022.

Raquel's deduction from her property income in 2022 is restricted to the lower figure of £300.

If there is an expense associated with the disposal of the old item, this can be added to the allowable cost. Likewise, if there are expenses associated with purchasing the replacement item, such as the costs of plumbing in a new washing machine, these too will be deductible.

Example 2

Rebecca lets out her penthouse apartment in Manchester. When she commenced her rental property business in 1996 she bought a leather Chesterfield sofa for the property at a cost of £2,000. At the last checkout it was found to be beyond repair, so Rebecca purchased an equivalent new leather Chesterfield sofa for £2,500, paying another £150 for delivery, and a further £100 to recycle the old one.

The total allowable cost of the replacement is £2,750.

If the landlord receives any proceeds for the old item, the value of the proceeds must reduce the amount that can be claimed on the new one. If the purchase was made with the old item in part-exchange, the amount allowable will be the net purchase cost.

Example 3

Rory owns a large fifth floor apartment in London which is on two levels. Over the staircase he had installed a Venetian chandelier costing £600. When new tenants moved in during 2021 they did not like the chandelier and, as a condition of the tenancy, asked Rory to replace it. He did as the tenants requested and purchased a new Empire chandelier costing £500. He sold the Venetian chandelier for £350.

Rory can offset the net amount of £150.

Law: ITTOIA 2005, s. 311A
Guidance: PIM 3210

26.7   Rent-a-room relief

26.7.1   Introduction

The rent-a-room scheme is designed to allow property owners in the UK to have one or more tenants or lodgers to enjoy furnished accommodation in their home, without incurring a tax bill, or at least mitigating it. Although primarily designed for property owners, the rent-a-room scheme may also be used by tenants of a property, as long as the rental agreement does not prohibit sub-tenancy. Both owners and tenants may need to check their insurance and/or mortgage documents to ensure sub-letting or taking in a lodger is not forbidden.

The rent-a-room scheme was introduced in 1992 with the intention of increasing the:

> "quantity and variety of low-cost rented housing, giving more choice to tenants and making it easier for people to move around the country for work".

The benefits to the landlord of rent-a-room relief are twofold.

Firstly, the relief allows a standardised (and generous) amount to be deducted as expenses, irrespective of the amount of actual expenses incurred.

Secondly, if the gross rental income from the lodger does not exceed £7,500 in a tax year, there is no need to report the income received to HMRC and there is no tax to pay. For higher figures of gross income, the scheme can reduce the tax bill.

All taxable rental income from renting the room(s) is categorised as property income, taxable at 20%, 40% or 45% depending on the level of the landlord's taxable income.

Law: ITTOIA 2005, s. 784-802

26.7.2 The mechanics

Usually, if rental income is received, the landlord will use the cash or accruals basis to establish, and pay tax on, the net profits.

Under the rent-a-room scheme there is another option. Rather than needing to determine the exact costs of all the deductible expenses, a fixed figure of £7,500 per property (not per lodger) may instead be offset per relevant period. If the property is owned by more than one landlord, the amount is restricted to 50% of the £7,500, so £3,750, for each lessor – even if there are more than two.

The relevant period is usually the tax year, but if the individual has a trading business such as a B&B or a guest house, and has chosen an accounting date other than 5 April, the relevant period will be the taxable basis period for that tax year.

Per property

Although the £7,500 is per property and not per lodger, a taxpayer will not accrue a new £7,500 if moving to a new house in the year. The £7,500 will be for all the properties that an individual has in succession in a tax year, as long as each qualifies for rent-a-room relief.

If the landlord moves to a new property but still owns the previous residence and the lodger remains there, HMRC will accept that rent-a-room relief still applies until the end of the basis period during which the landlord moved – even if the lodger subsequently uses the whole of the previous residence and not just a room. If the landlord then starts to let a room in the new property during this period, relief will be available in respect of both income streams, but is restricted to £7,500 in total.

The logic behind the relief

This relief is intended to overcome the difficulty and time required for a "casual" landlord to determine the exact costs associated with the room a lodger is occupying. Costs that may need to be split will be those such as light, heat, telephone, WiFi, council tax, water rates and other such domestic expenses. While it may be possible to apportion light and heat by reference to floor area or room volume, the question of how much of the WiFi or council tax or water rates bills to attribute to the lodger may be more problematic.

Gross rents below £7,500

Where the gross rents are £7,500 or less, there is no need to notify HMRC of the source of income or to register for self-assessment. The landlord is effectively exempt from income tax on any profits. The way this works is that the rent-a-room relief automatically applies up to £7,500 in costs to cover the rental income, so there will be deemed to be no profit to tax.

Gross rents above £7,500

If the gross rental income exceeds £7,500 and the actual expenses are less than £7,500 it will always be in the landlord's favour to claim the rent-a-room scheme if the letting qualifies. An election must be made (see below), as the rent-a-room scheme does not apply automatically where rents are above £7,500. An election is not needed every year as, once the taxpayer has claimed, the election will continue until it is withdrawn.

If the actual expenses are more than £7,500, the landlord may be better off taking the time to apportion the expenses and deduct the precise amounts in order to reduce the taxable profits and, ultimately, to pay less tax.

Losses

The standard expense deduction of £7,500 cannot create or increase a loss – it merely reduces the taxable rental profits to nil. Any shortfall is not carried forward as a loss.

Example

Raymond receives £6,000 gross rents and incurs £300 expenses a year from renting a room in his home. The rent-a-room scheme will apply automatically to him as he has less than £7,500 in gross rental receipts. By claiming the £7,500 rent-a-room deduction, though, Raymond will not obtain a loss of £1,500. Instead, the whole £6,000 will simply be exempt.

Raymond's sister Rhonda also has a lodger in her home, and she also receives £6,000 gross income annually from renting the room. Rhonda's actual costs during the year were much higher than Raymond's at £7,000. Rhonda would thus be best advised to disclaim the automatic rent-a-room relief and use the actual costs incurred of £7,000. This would allow Rhonda to use the £1,000 loss to offset against any taxable profits from other UK rental income sources in the same tax year, or against such profits arising in future tax years.

If property income losses have been made in previous years, but have not yet been offset, they can be carried forward indefinitely. If the landlord makes an election for the rent-a-room scheme to apply from a subsequent year, the losses will only be used if, and to the extent that, the profits exceed £7,500. If future profits do not exceed this within the scheme, the profits are recorded as nil, so there is nothing to offset, and the losses can be carried forward once more.

Capital gains tax

If a landlord has let part of his or her main residence, a CGT charge may apply to the part of the property that was not the individual's main residence for the period in question. This is no different if the landlord is letting a room to a lodger.

However, Statement of Practice 14/80 is intended to give an indication of whether the landlord would in fact be liable to CGT on an eventual sale. The Statement of Practice states that where there is a lodger living with the homeowner "as a member of the owner's family, sharing their living accommodation and taking meals with them...", then no charge to CGT would arise in respect of the part of the property used by the lodger. A landlord must therefore keep evidence of the interactions between the landlord's family and the lodger to ensure that this close relationship can be substantiated.

Guidance: PIM 4001; SP 14/80

26.7.3   The election

Once a relevant letting commences, no special form or application needs to be made. It is sufficient to report the profits on the chosen basis. The basis used will be obvious to HMRC by the way the profits have been calculated.

However, if a *change* in the basis is required, HMRC must be informed. This would apply, for example, if the taxpayer wishes to start using the rent-a-room scheme for an existing letting, having not used it previously, or wishes to disclaim it after using it.

If the change is an election for the rent-a-room relief, rather than the actual cost basis which the taxpayer has been using to date, the time limit for submission is the first anniversary of 31 January following the tax year in which the income arises, i.e. the normal amendment deadline for the tax return for the year in question. For example, if a landlord who has not previously used the rent-a-room scheme decides that he wishes to start using it for 2021-22, he will need to inform HMRC by 31 January 2024. The election has to be made in writing, but there is no prescribed format. It lasts indefinitely until it is disclaimed.

The election to withdraw is subject to the same time limit. The withdrawal also has to be made in writing, and it does not last indefinitely – only for one year.

If the gross rental income drops below the £7,500 threshold, this will also lead to a change to the basis used if the landlord was not previously using rent-a-room relief, as the scheme will then apply automatically. If the taxpayer was already using the scheme and wishes to continue using it, there will be nothing to notify to HMRC. However, a landlord who was previously using the actual cost method, or who no longer wishes to use the rent-a-room scheme, will need to make a notification.

HMRC have discretion to extend the time limits for these elections, and may do so in cases of illness, or other serious personal difficulties, or possibly if the taxpayer was abroad.

26.7.4   The conditions to qualify

The individual

An individual landlord will qualify for the rent-a-room scheme if:

- he has taxable gross rents (see below) from letting furnished accommodation in his main residence; and
- he does not have any other taxable income from that property, for example through a trade or any other letting or agreement.

For example, if a landlord lets an unfurnished room (which would not meet the conditions of the rent-a-room scheme), he or she could not also rent a furnished room at the same time and opt into the rent-a-room scheme.

The scheme can also apply to individuals running a B&B or guest house as long as the property is also the main residence of the taxpayer and the other rent-a-room conditions are met. Although this individual may well also be running a trade, the trading profits should be excluded from the rent-a-room profits and declared as trading income.

Gross rents

The concept of "gross rents" is mentioned several times in the legislation. Gross rents include all the rental income for the room in addition to any other payments that are made to the homeowner for other services. For example, the landlord may allow the lodger a part of the garage as well as the room, or may charge separately to do the laundry, or cook meals for the lodger.

Furnished accommodation

The legislation states that the relief is available for the provision of furnished accommodation in the UK. Accommodation in this sense means home living. Normal activities performed at home such as sleeping, reading, eating meals, surfing on the internet and watching TV would all be acceptable activities.

This distinction is important, as the rent-a-room relief is not available for any commercial use of the room. If a tenant uses the room as an office, or for other business purposes such as a warehouse or storeroom, the landlord cannot use the rent-a-room scheme. However, HMRC also state that this restriction:

> "does not apply to genuine lodgers such as students who are provided with study facilities in their lodgings. In such cases, we would not want to deny relief where a lodger living in the home is provided with a desk, or the use of a room with a desk, which he or she uses for work or study".

Law: ITTOIA 2005, s. 785
Guidance: PIM 4002

26.7.5   The residence

The property in question could be a building in its entirety or only a part of a building, but it must be a structure being used and occupied as a residence. If a building is divided into several residences, such as a house with a self-contained annexe or basement, it can be treated as a single residence if the split is only temporary. For example, it may be the lodger's residence now, but in a few years when the landlord's children are older it may be planned to become the eldest's bedroom and become a part of the residence again.

The residence does not have to be a traditional residence and could be an alternative to a building such as a caravan or houseboat.

Sometimes a taxpayer will have more than one home and will have elected for one of them to be his or her main home for CGT main residence relief. HMRC have stated that they would usually expect the rent-a-room relief election to relate to the individual's main home *based on the facts*. This may not be the home that the landlord has elected to be his main residence for CGT purposes, but might instead be the home that he actually uses as his main home for the majority of the time; this may even be a rented property, and not one owned by the rent-a-room claimant. HMRC will:

> "look critically at any claim for rent-a-room treatment for second homes and holiday homes".

Frost v Feltham, a case from 1981 considering the deductibility of interest, summarised how a residence is considered a "main" residence for income tax purposes, starting with the *Oxford English Dictionary* definition of "main" which included "principal" and "most important". Nourse J stated that although the taxpayer's opinion of which property was most important to him was significant, it did not carry as much weight as *how* he lived in it objectively by reference to the facts. In this

601

case, it was the only home that the taxpayer owned. It was furnished and used as a home and was visited every month, and so it was concluded that it was the taxpayer's main residence.

Case: *Frost v Feltham* (1980) 55 TC 10
Guidance: PIM 4001

26.7.6   Leaving the main residence

If a landlord is no longer living in the residence as his only or main residence with the lodger, rent-a-room relief is not usually available.

However, if the landlord has to move during the year, either because his employment has caused him to relocate overseas or because he needs to occupy job-related accommodation, he may continue to claim rent-a-room relief until the end of the basis period for that tax year. He must have been using the rent-a-room scheme prior to his departure in the year in order to have the relief continue.

Rarely, a taxpayer will not have an alternative main residence overseas and will still be using the UK property as his or her main residence – for example, if secondments are short and, on the facts, the main residence remains the UK home. Even if this taxpayer is not living in the home for the whole year, relief under the rent-a-room scheme may still apply. In PIM 4015, HMRC give the example of a taxpayer on several four-month secondments which cause him to have only eight months in his UK home with the lodger every year. This is enough to allow the landlord to continue to be eligible for the rent-a-room scheme.

Example 1 – Rachel

Rachel, who is recently divorced, owned a large four-bedroomed townhouse in Chelsea, central London. On 6 April 2021 she decided to take in a lodger. The lodger took the largest bedroom and had access to the communal kitchen where he cooked and ate his own meals. Rachel charged him £850 a month. Rachel asked her accountant to establish the following apportioned costs between her and the lodger:

	£
Gas	2,200
Electricity	3,000
Council tax	1,240
WiFi	300
Phone line	120
Re-painting room	500
Repair radiator in room	340
Total costs	7,700

As the deductions that Rachel actually incurred and can offset from her rental income are above £7,500, she is unlikely to opt into the rent-a-room scheme. Instead, she will deduct the actual costs incurred, leading to a net profit on the let of £2,500 (£10,200 - £7,700). If she used the rent-a-room scheme, the net taxable profit on the letting would be more, i.e. £2,700.

Example 2 – Robert

Rachel's ex-husband Robert also took in a lodger from 6 April 2021. He had bought a three-bedroomed cottage on the outskirts of Norwich after their divorce and charged his lodger £350 a month. His lodger cooked his own meals and generally kept himself to himself. Robert estimated his expenses associated with the room were £800 for the year as the house was well insulated and his bills were low.

Because Robert's income from the lodger is below £7,500 he will not have to notify HMRC of the new source of income from April 2021. There will be no tax to pay on the net income of £3,400 (£4,200 (£350 x 12) less £800) as the rent-a-room scheme will apply automatically and deem the net income to be zero. Robert is unlikely to disclaim the rent-a-room relief, as without it he would be taxed on profits of £3,400 and would need to declare the income on an annual self-assessment tax return.

Example 3 – Roz

Roz is Rachel and Robert's adult daughter. She rents a two-bedroomed apartment in Cambridge as she is at university there. Her rental agreement with her landlord allows her to sub-let, so she brings in a lodger, another student, into her spare room from 6 April 2021.

Roz charges her lodger £250 a month but she has to redecorate the room fully before the student moved in at a cost of £5,000, and this, alongside the normal expenses she incurs on the lodger's costs of £100, meant that she made a loss of £2,100 in 2021-22.

Roz has a small property profit on a studio apartment she rents out in London and wishes to offset her loss on the spare room against her other UK property profit in the same year. She therefore wishes to disclaim the rent-a-room relief which would otherwise apply automatically to her as her receipts were under £7,500 a year. Roz will need to do this by claiming the loss on her self-assessment tax return.

Law: ITTOIA 2005, s. 309, 784-802

Guidance: PIM 40001; https://tinyurl.com/y6j487vp (Responses on consultation on rent-a-room relief)

26.8 The property allowance

26.8.1 Introduction

Landlords with low levels of property income may save both tax and administration time by using the property allowance. In brief:

- If gross income receipts from the property business do not exceed £1,000, no income tax is payable and there is no need to report the income on the landlord's tax return. Relief is automatic.

- If gross receipts exceed £1,000, the landlord may elect to pay tax on the excess, rather than deducting expenses in the usual way under either the cash basis or the accruals basis.

Exclusions

The property allowance is not available on income that has qualified for the rent-a-room scheme, even if the landlord does not decide to use it (see **26.7**). Adjustment income (see **26.4.4**) – where an individual has moved from the cash basis to the accruals basis – will also not be counted as income for the property allowance.

The property allowance is also not available for a landlord who wishes to claim interest relief via a tax reducer (see **26.9**). Landlords can still choose to use the property allowance but no interest offset can then be given. They will have to decide which method gives the lower tax bill.

Anti-avoidance legislation, introduced to ensure landlords do not artificially "create" property income in order to take advantage of the property allowance, means that the property allowances cannot be used to cover property income from:

- close companies where the landlord is a participator;
- a partnership where the landlord is a partner; or
- the individual's employer (or the employer of the individual's spouse or civil partner).

Furthermore, the property allowance is not available to offset income from a connected party (see **Appendix 2**).

Law: ITTOIA 2005, s. 783B-783BQ

26.8.2   The calculation of the allowance

Income from property does not exceed £1,000

Where the landlord's income from all property lettings (both in the UK and overseas) does not exceed £1,000, no profits are declarable to HMRC. This is referred to in the legislation as "full relief".

Example 1

Rhys runs a letting business renting out two garages close to Folkestone town centre for £35 each a month. The annual income from the garages is £840 and his expenses each year, including painting one of the garage doors, are £140.

Although Rhys does actually make a profit letting the garages of £700 in each tax year, he will not need to pay tax on this, as the property allowance will mean that his taxable profit will be nil.

It is not mandatory to use the property allowance, but it applies automatically if the income is under £1,000 so an election must be made by the landlord if he or she wishes not to apply the allowance. By doing this, the taxpayer is instead able to use the exact expenses incurred rather than the £1,000 standard allowance. In the example above this would mean that Rhys would be chargeable to £700, but electing not to use the property allowance is usually beneficial if a loss has been made.

Guidance: PIM 4434

Income from property exceeds £1,000

A landlord whose income from property exceeds £1,000 can elect to use the property allowance ("partial relief"). If actual expenses are less than

£1,000 it will probably be advantageous to use the (higher) property allowance. The property allowance cannot create or increase a loss.

Example 2

Ronnie's letting business consists of one three-bedroomed cottage in Bournemouth. The rental income was £9,600 in 2021-22, but there were very few expenses apart from the buildings insurance as Ronnie managed the property himself and had no mortgage on it. His annual expenses were £260.

Although Ronnie's net taxable profits from letting the cottage were £9,340 (£9,600 – £260), by electing to use the property allowance of £1,000, this reduces the taxable profits to £8,600 (£9,600 – £1,000).

Landlords with overseas properties

A landlord may have rental properties in the UK and overseas. In these cases, there will be two separate property businesses, one UK and one overseas. As there is only one property allowance per taxpayer, the landlord will need to decide how to allocate the property allowance between the two property businesses. This can be done in any proportion the taxpayer wishes up to £1,000, as long as the landlord remembers that no actual expenses can be deducted if even part of the property allowance is used, and no loss can be created on either business.

Example 3

Robin has studio apartment rental properties in London, New York and Paris. He starts his lets in New York and Paris in March 2022 and receives only one month's rent for each in the tax year 2021-22, totalling £900 in overseas property receipts in the year. Actual expenses were £300.

In London he commences letting in September 2021 and has total UK property receipts of £1,200 with expenses of £200. Overall profits from his two property businesses before the property allowance would be £1,600 (£900 – £300 = £600 and £1,200 – £200 = £1,000).

Robin will need to decide how to allocate the property allowance between the two property businesses. For example, if he chooses to allocate £900 to his overseas property business, he will reduce the profits to nil. He then has £100 of the property allowance left to allocate to his UK property business, bringing the taxable profit to £1,100. Although the UK profit is higher than it would have been prior to the allocation (he would have been able to have offset the actual expenses of £200 rather than the property allowance of £100) overall, he will have total profits of £1,100 (nil and £1,100 respectively for the overseas and UK property businesses), rather than £1,600 without the property allowance.

Guidance: PIM 4436, 4438, 4484

26.8.3   Elections

An election to apply or disapply the property allowance must be made by one year after 31 January following the tax year. For example, for the tax year 2020-21, the election must be made by 31 January 2023.

Once an election has been made it does not continue every year. A decision can be made every tax year as to whether to use the property allowance or not, though it automatically applies if profits are below £1,000 unless specifically disapplied.

26.8.4   Property owned jointly

Where the let property is owned jointly, it is the amount of profit allocated to the taxpayer that is compared to the £1,000 and not the whole income from the property. Each taxpayer has his or her own property allowance of £1,000.

Example 1

Reuben and Rose are twins and are both married. Reuben lets a garage close to Reading town centre and owns it outright. Rose lets a garage out close to Brighton town centre and owns it jointly with her husband. Both garages generate £1,500 a year in gross rental income and have £200 in expenses.

Reuben would be well advised to elect to use the property allowance as his expenses are under £1,000 and if he elected for the property allowance he would be charged to income tax on £500 rental profits rather than £1,300 without the property allowance.

As Rose owns her property jointly with her husband she is only receiving 50%, so £750 in gross rental income. As this is under £1,000 the property allowance applies automatically and she is neither chargeable to income tax on the income, nor does she have to notify HMRC of the source of the income. The same applies to her husband, who will have his own property allowance of £1,000.

Overall, on the same source and amount of income Reuben will pay tax if he holds the garage in his sole name whereas by splitting ownership between them, Rose and her husband will have no tax liability.

Law: ITTOIA 2005, s. 783B-783BQ
Guidance: PIM 40001

26.9 Interest and related charges

26.9.1 Introduction

Many landlords find it tax-efficient to take out a mortgage or other dwelling-related loans to purchase rental properties. This was particularly advantageous prior to April 2017 if the landlord was a higher or additional rate taxpayer, as any payment for interest was deductible from the rental property business profits directly and therefore attracted tax relief at the landlord's marginal tax rate. If the mortgage was high enough, the interest offset could even create a loss.

Since 2017, however, a residential property landlord who pays interest can no longer deduct it directly from profits, and only gains relief at the basic rate of 20%. The same applies to amounts that are commercially equivalent to interest, including fees and commissions.

The legislation applies to interest on any amounts borrowed to finance the purchase of a residential property by a property business that is receiving rental income from letting residential property. The loan does not have to be for the whole of the property, and can be used for the building, purchase or extension of the property.

The restriction, however, is only for landlords of individually owned or partnership-owned residential property (and trustees and personal representatives). Property rental businesses with furnished holiday accommodation (see **Chapter 28**) or commercial property, and companies carrying out a property business, are not subject to the restriction and can offset their qualifying interest in full.

The letting of residential caravans in mobile homes parks would not be included in the restriction as these tend to be considered a trade rather than a property business.

Law: ITTOIA 2005, s. 272A, 272B
Guidance: PIM 2054

26.9.2   The mechanics of the relief

The loan interest is deductible at only the basic rate of 20%, whatever the marginal rate of the taxpayer. The interest is not deducted in calculating the taxable profits but is given instead as a 20% tax reducer when calculating the overall tax due.

In addition to the restriction of the rate, the 2017 changes also limited the amount of interest that could be offset, albeit at the basic rate. Relief is limited to the lowest of:

- the amount of eligible interest;
- the total property income for the tax year less property losses brought forward (i.e. no loss can be created by the interest offset); and
- adjusted total income.

"Adjusted total income" is the landlord's net income less his or her savings and dividend income and personal allowance.

Example 1

Regina is employed as a solicitor earning £60,070 a year and also has a residential property which she lets out in Canterbury. In 2021-22 her rental profits for the year were £18,000 before paying mortgage interest of £9,000. She also receives £5,000 dividends.

To establish how much mortgage interest Regina can set off, the amount of the interest (£9,000) is compared with her rental property income for the year (£18,000) and her adjusted total income. She can offset the lowest of the three amounts.

Her adjusted total income is her total net income less savings and dividend income, less the personal allowance, which comes to £65,500 (see below).

The lowest of the three of these figures is the total amount of the interest, £9,000.

	Non-savings income £	Savings income £
Employment income	60,070	
Dividends		5,000
Rental profits	18,000	
Net income	78,070	5,000
Personal allowance	(12,570)	
Taxable income	65,500	5,000

The next step is to complete the tax computation by calculating the tax on the non-savings and the savings income and to reduce the tax payable by the tax reducer. The tax reducer will be the amount of the interest of £9,000 multiplied by the basic rate of 20%, so £1,800.

	Non-savings income £	Savings income £
Taxable income (as above)	65,500	5,000
Tax calculation		
Non-savings income		
Basic rate band		
£37,700 x 20%		7,540
Higher rate band		
£27,800 (£65,500-£37,700) x 40%		11,120
Dividend allowance		
£2,000 x 0%		0
Higher rate band dividends		
£3,000 x 32.5%		975
Interest tax reducer		
£9,000 x 20%		(1,800)
Total income tax liability		17,835

If the interest cannot be offset in full in the year, for example if it is more than the total property income or the adjusted net income, it can be carried forward to the following year and (added to the interest incurred in the following year) can be offset in that year.

Example 2

Ria is employed as a coffee barista earning £22,070 a year and also has a residential property which she lets out in Nottingham. In 2021-22, due to significant repairs she needed to make to the roof of her rental property, her rental profits for the year were only £1,800 before paying mortgage interest of £4,000. She also received £2,000 dividends.

To establish how much mortgage interest Ria can set off, the amount of the interest (£4,000) is compared with her rental property income for the year (£1,800) and her adjusted total income. The lowest of the three amounts will be the amount she can offset.

Her adjusted total income will be her total net income less savings and dividend income, less the personal allowance, which comes to £11,300 (see below).

The lowest of the three of these figures is Ria's rental property income of £1,800.

	Non-savings income £	Savings income £
Employment income	22,070	
Dividends		2,000
Rental profits	1,800	
Net income	23,870	2,000
Personal allowance	(12,570)	
Taxable income	11,300	5,000

The next step is to complete the tax computation by calculating the tax on the non-savings and the savings income and to reduce the tax payable by the tax reducer. The tax reducer will be the amount of the rental property profits of £1,800 multiplied by the basic rate of 20%, so £360.

	Non-savings income £	Savings income £
Taxable income (as above)	11,300	2,000
Tax calculation		
Non-savings income Basic rate band £11,300 x 20%		2,260
Dividend allowance £2,000 x 0%		0
Interest tax reducer £1,800 x 20%		(360)
Total income tax liability		1,900

Regina's final tax liability is £1,900. The rental profit element of this is the taxable rental profits before the interest of £1,800, taxed after the personal allowance, and the tax reducer offsetting the tax deduction on £1,800 of the interest at the basic rate. The remaining interest of £2,200 (£4,000 - £1,800), which could not be deducted in 2021-22, will be carried forward to the following tax year and added to the qualifying interest paid in 2022-23.

26.9.3   Restriction on loans

Restrictions on the capital employed in the business

Interest on loans taken out in a property business will still attract relief even if the capital is later extracted from the business. However, the amount of the loan outstanding must not exceed the remaining capital employed in the business.

The "capital employed" for these purposes is the value of the rental properties at the time of commencement of the business or when the property is first used in the property business, plus any other capital used in the business at commencement, such as fixtures and fittings and plant and machinery.

For example, a landlord may take out a loan of £400,000 to purchase two apartments worth £400,000 each, but then a few years later, sell one of the apartments without paying off the loan. As long as the capital employed in the business – in this example, the remaining apartment alongside any other assets such as white goods, furniture and any plant and machinery at the commencement of the business – is worth at least the amount of the loan of £400,000, all the interest can still be used to calculate the reducer.

If the landlord makes further borrowings subsequent to the initial borrowings, these too can be relieved as long as the total loan does not exceed the capital employed in the business at commencement. The more recent HMRC view is that the new borrowings must be wholly and exclusively for the purposes of the letting business, though there has been some discussion in the professional press about whether a different interpretation of the legislation might be more correct.

Guidance: https://tinyurl.com/y9gvctex (HMRC guidance: *Work out your rental income when you let property*)

Restrictions on interest offsets while using the cash basis

If the property business is using the cash basis to calculate profits, the amount of interest that can be offset is restricted under ITTOIA 2005, s. 307C-307D. The legislation looks at the value of the rental property at the time it was first let out (and any associated capital expenditure not offset through deductions from income tax) and compares this with the value of the loan at the end of the applicable tax year. The resulting percentage is applied to the interest paid during the year, creating the maximum amount of interest deductible under the cash basis.

Example

Reece purchased a property in 2000 for £450,000 and lived in it with his family. He had a 90% interest-only mortgage at 2.9% of £405,000. Reece's job moved to Italy eight years later so he let his house out. Unfortunately, this was right in the middle of the 2008 crash, so the property was only worth £350,000 at this date but bounced back and was worth £700,000 in 2021-22. Reece has only one let property and used the cash basis to calculate his rental profits. The mortgage interest paid in 2021-22 was £11,745.

The percentage to be used is:

$$\text{Interest paid} \times \frac{\text{Value of the property when first used in the property business}}{\text{Total loans of the property business remaining}}$$

which in Reece's case is:

$$£11,745 \times £350,000/£405,000 = £10,150$$

The maximum amount Reece can offset against his rental income profits is £10,150.

Law: ITTOIA 2005, s. 307C, 307D
Guidance: PIM 1094

26.10 Non-commercial lets

26.10.1 Introduction

If a letting is not made on an arm's length basis for a fully commercial rent, it is likely that there is another reason for the let rather than being a property business carried on to make a profit. For example, a landlord may provide a property at a lower rent to a friend or relative, or may allow a charity rent-free use of a premises.

In these cases, expenses are not likely to be deductible against any property income received, as the expenses will not be wholly and exclusively incurred for the business. Some of the expense will be for personal, charitable or philanthropic purposes.

26.10.2 Expenses

Strictly, no expenses can be offset if the rental contract is not commercial. However, a landlord who does charge rent, albeit not at the market rate, may in practice charge the appropriate fraction of the expense incurred. Such deductions are made only to the extent of the amount of rent the landlord receives. So, if the deductions were to result in a loss, the loss cannot be carried forward for use in a future year.

If a property is let commercially for some of the year, but then to friends or relatives for other times in the year, the expenses in the year must be apportioned between the allowable and disallowable weeks. Any loss made in the commercial periods can be offset in future periods, but any loss made in the uncommercial periods cannot. These rules cannot be manipulated. For example, if friends use a holiday cottage from September to June, and it is let out for July and August, it would not be possible to offset repairs from damage incurred during the non-commercial use period, just because said damage became evident during the two-month commercial period.

Replacement of domestic items relief is not usually available on properties that are not let commercially, as this relief requires the expenditure to be wholly and exclusively for the purpose of the rental property business.

Guidance: PIM 2100

26.10.3 House-sitting

If a friend or relative is staying in the house between commercial lets, as long as the property is genuinely made available during this time for letting on a commercial basis, any expenses incurred during this period can be offset as normal. If the property is taken off the rental market, however, the expenses during this period are not deductible. HMRC further define this by stating:

> "Ordinary house sitting by a relative for, say, a month in a period of three years or more will not normally lead to a loss of relief. On the other hand, relief will be lost if, say, a relative is really just taking a month's holiday in a country cottage."

Law: ITTOIA 2005, s. 266, 272
Guidance: PIM 2130

27. Leases and lease premiums

27.1 Introduction

The taxation of rental profits has been considered in depth in **Chapter 26**. This chapter looks at the particular issues that arise in relation to leases and lease premiums, a complex sub-topic that often requires joint consideration of both income tax and CGT provisions. For the CGT perspective, see the companion volume to this book, *Capital Gains Tax*, from Claritax Books.

For a more detailed analysis of all aspects of rental income, including leases and lease premiums, see *Property Investment: A Tax Guide*, from Claritax Books.

Statutory references in this chapter are to ITTOIA 2005, unless otherwise stated. HMRC guidance can be found in the *Property Income Manual*, starting at PIM 1200.

27.2 Granting versus assigning a lease

27.2.1 The two concepts

When considering the taxation of capital sums paid in relation to leases, the first step is to determine whether a premium has been paid for the *grant* of a lease, or whether the sum has been paid on the *assignment* of a lease. The distinction is important, as the terms have different meanings with different tax implications.

Where a lease has been granted (say, from landlord to tenant) the tenant may only occupy the property for a set period of time. Once the tenant's lease expires, the property reverts to the landlord.

Compare this to an assignment of a lease (e.g. where a tenant wishes to leave the property and finds someone else to take over the lease). Where a lease is assigned, the tenant's interest in the lease is transferred for the rest of the term of the lease.

27.2.2 Tax treatment

Where a premium is paid for the grant of a lease, the income tax treatment depends on the length of the lease. A short lease is subject to the rules covered at section **27.3.2**.

Where the lease is a long lease (generally, one that exceeds 50 years in duration), the premium paid is considered a capital sum and is taxed wholly within the CGT provisions, which are outside the scope of this annual.

An assignment of a lease is also subject to the CGT provisions. The exceptions to this treatment are where the taxpayer is carrying on a property dealing trade, or if any of the following legislative provisions apply:

- s. 282 (assignments for profit of lease granted at undervalue) – see **27.5.1**;
- s. 284 (sales with right to reconveyance) – see **27.5.2**; or
- s. 285 (sale and leaseback transactions) – see **27.5.3**.

Guidance: PIM 1204

27.3   Lease premiums

27.3.1   What is a lease premium?

A lease may be granted on terms that require the payment of a premium (a lump sum) as well as regular payments of rent. Alternatively, payment of rent may be all that is required.

Again, it is important to distinguish between any premium paid for the grant of a lease and any rent due under the lease. This is because a premium is, according to ordinary principles, capital in nature. On the other hand, rental payments are of an income nature.

"Premium" is defined at s. 307 to include any similar sum (including the value of any consideration) payable to the immediate landlord, to a superior landlord or to a person connected with either.

In the past, landlords would sometimes offer to take premiums in place of rent, with the aim of avoiding taxation. Such tax avoidance measures are no longer effective, following the introduction of s. 277-283.

Rent or premium?

Sometimes, it can be difficult to determine whether a payment is a premium or is simply rent payable in advance. HMRC provide additional guidance around unusual patterns of rental payments, including where a landlord grants a lease with an initial rent-free period, at PIM 1102.

Law: ITTOIA 2005, s. 276-283, 307
Guidance: PIM 1102, 1202

27.3.2 How are lease premiums taxed?

To determine how a lease premium is taxed, it is important to identify the length of the lease in question. The shorter the lease, the greater the likelihood the premium has an income nature.

As a general principle:

- a premium paid for a long lease is a capital sum, and so is subject to CGT; but

- a premium paid for a short lease is more like rent paid as a lump sum, and so is more akin to income, which is subject to income tax.

The deciding factor for whether a lease is long or short is whether it will last for more than 50 years. If it will, it is broadly considered a long lease, and all the premium is subject to CGT.

Leases with a duration of 50 years or less (broadly referred to as short leases) have a proportion of the premium charged to tax as income, the amount of which is dependent on the length of the lease.

Broadly, where a premium is required under a short-term lease, the person to whom the premium is due (for example, the landlord) must bring into account a receipt in calculating the profits of a property business for the tax year in which the lease is granted.

Calculation

The amount to be brought into account as a receipt is determined by the following formula:

$$P \times \frac{(50 - Y)}{50}$$

where:

P = the premium; and

Y = the number of complete periods of 12 months (other than the first) comprised in the effective duration of the lease.

Example

Melissa grants a 30-year lease to Rupert at the start of the 2021-22 tax year.

Under the terms of the lease agreement, Rupert pays Melissa a premium of £50,000. There is also annual rent of £5,000.

As the lease is a short lease, part of the premium Melissa receives – as well as the rent payable under the lease – is subject to income tax. The element of the premium subject to income tax is calculated as follows:

$P \times ((50 - Y)/50)$

where:

$P = £50,000$

$Y = 29$ (being $30 - 1$)

So £50,000 x $((50 - 29)/50) = £21,000$

Melissa should report property income of £26,000, being the £21,000 of the premium taxable as income, plus the £5,000 of rental receipts.

The effect of this formula is that the shorter the lease is, the more of it is charged as property income (i.e. effectively taxed as rent). The remainder is charged to CGT (unless the taxpayer has a property dealing trade, in which case it will be treated as trading income).

The above does not apply where a taxpayer receives a lump sum for assigning an existing lease. See **27.2** for an explanation of the distinction.

For further information on the tax position from the point of view of the tenant, see **27.4.4**.

Law: ITTOIA 2005, s. 277
Guidance: PIM 1203, 1205

27.3.3   Adjusting lease terms for tax purposes

In most cases, the length of a lease is simply the term for which it was granted.

However, anti-avoidance legislation (at s. 303 onwards) counteracts any attempts to obtain a tax advantage from the lease premium provisions, though the imposition of three "rules". Where these rules apply, the effective duration of the lease for tax purposes will be treated as other than the stated term.

Term of lease treated as shorter than stated (rule 1)

Rule 1 applies if:

- the terms of the lease or any other circumstances make it unlikely that the lease will continue beyond a date before the end of the term for which the lease was granted; and
- the premium was not substantially greater than it would have been had the term been one ending on that date.

Where rule 1 applies, the lease is treated as having an expiry date on the earlier date.

Term of lease treated as longer than stated (rules 2 and 3)

A term of a lease may be treated as longer than stated.

Rule 2 applies where the terms of the lease include provision for the extension of the lease beyond a given date by notice given by the tenant. In such cases, account may be taken of any circumstances making it likely that the lease will be so extended.

Example – rule 2 – adapted from PIM 1207

On 13 June 2021, Zenab grants a one-year lease of a property to Oskar for a premium of £500,000 and a rent of £100. Under the terms of the lease, Oskar has the right to extend the lease for a further 55 years without premium at a rent of £100 a year.

As Oskar is likely to exercise his right to the extension, the duration of the lease is treated as 56 years. In consequence:

- There is no chargeable amount included as property income, since the lease is for more than 50 years.
- Oskar gets no relief for the premium paid.

Rule 3 applies where the tenant, or a person connected with the tenant is, or may become, entitled to a further lease or the grant of a further lease (whenever commencing):

- of the same premises; or
- of premises including the whole or part of the same premises.

In such cases, the term of the lease may be treated as continuing until the end of the term of the further lease.

Law: ITTOIA 2005, s. 303-304
Guidance: PIM 1206, 1207

27.3.4   Subleasing a short lease

It is possible for a landlord, who holds a leasehold interest of less than 50 years (i.e. a short lease) to grant a sublease to a tenant. Such a sublease is also, by virtue of the landlord's leasehold interest, very likely to be a short lease.

In such instances, the lease premium rules may need to be considered twice – once in respect of the headlease and again in respect of the sublease.

The taxation of subleases can become highly involved and is considered in depth in *Property Investment: A Tax Guide* (see **27.1**).

27.4   Other amounts treated as lease premiums

27.4.1   Overview

Various other receipts (and different forms of consideration) relating to short leases are also treated as premiums. Such amounts are to be included in the landlord's rental business in the same way as an ordinary premium (see **27.3.2**). This principle applies to:

- amounts treated as a lease premium where work is required;
- sums payable instead of rent;
- sums payable for the surrender of a lease; and
- sums payable for a variation or waiver of terms of the lease.

Each item is considered in turn below.

Guidance: PIM 1210

27.4.2   Amounts treated as a lease premium where work required

Under the lease terms, a tenant may be obliged to carry out work on the premises. In such cases, the lease is treated as requiring the payment of a premium to the landlord (in addition to any other premium).

The amount of the premium is the amount by which the value of the landlord's estate or interest immediately after the commencement of the

621

lease exceeds what its value would have been at that time if the terms of the lease did not impose the obligation on the tenant.

Obligations relating to "excepted work" are ignored. Work is excepted "if the payment for carrying it out would, if the landlord and not the tenant were obliged to carry it out, be deductible as an expense in calculating the profits of the landlord's property business".

HMRC example

Jozef lets a shop to Milka from 6 January 2007 for 11 years at a rent of £300 per month. She is also required to have tarmac laid on the area at the rear of the premises to be used as a new car park, and it costs her £5,000.

Jozef could not have deducted the cost of laying the tarmac in his rental income computation since it is capital expenditure. He is treated as if he had received a premium equal to the extra value of his interest in the property immediately after the commencement of the lease. The increase in value is agreed to be £3,000 (not the cost of the work) to reflect the wear and tear that the improvement will have suffered by the time the lease falls in and the restating of that reduced amount to present value. Jozef's rental income computation must include the following:

	£
Deemed premium receivable	3,000
Less £3,000 x (11 – 1)/50	600
Chargeable amount of premium	2,400
Add actual rent for three months	900
Total	3,300

If the terms of the lease also require her to redecorate the premises every three years, this does not result in a charge under this provision. Jozef could have deducted the cost if he had paid it.

Law: ITTOIA 2005, s. 278
Guidance: PIM 1212

27.4.3 Sums payable instead of rent/sums payable for the surrender of a lease

Section 279 (sums payable instead of rent) applies if, under the terms subject to which a lease is granted, a sum becomes payable by the tenant in lieu of the whole or a part of the rent for a period, and the period is 50 years or less.

Similarly, s. 280 (sums payable for surrender of lease) applies if, under the terms subject to which a short-term lease is granted, a sum becomes payable by the tenant as consideration for the surrender of the lease.

In such cases, the landlord (or person to whom the sum is due) is treated as though the lease had required payment of a premium.

The amount of the receipt to be taken into account for income tax purposes is given by the formula:

$$S \times \frac{(50 - Y)}{50}$$

where:

> **S** = the sum payable instead of rent, or as consideration for the surrender of the lease; and
>
> **Y** = the number of complete periods of 12 months (other than the first) comprised in the period in relation to which the sum is payable.

Law: ITTOIA 2005, s. 279, 280
Guidance: PIM 1214

27.4.4   *Sums payable for variation or waiver of terms of lease*

Tax is charged as if a premium had been paid if:

- a sum becomes payable by the tenant (otherwise than by way of rent) as consideration for the variation or waiver of a term of a lease;
- the sum is due to the landlord or to a person connected with the landlord; and
- the period for which the variation or waiver has effect is 50 years or less.

The calculation is broadly similar to that at **27.4.3** immediately above, being:

$$S \times \frac{(50 - Y)}{50}$$

where:

> **S** = the sum payable as consideration for the variation or waiver; and

> **Y** = the number of complete periods of 12 months (other than the first) comprised in the period for which the variation or waiver has effect.

A charge may still arise even where the original lease is a long lease (i.e. more than 50 years). See HMRC's PIM 1216 for an example.

Law: ITTOIA s. 281
Guidance: PIM 1216

27.4.5   Tax position for tenant

The above sections (**27.3 to 27.4.4**) are mainly relevant from the landlord's perspective (or the perspective of another person receiving the lease premium, as the case may be).

From the tenant's point of view, there are also tax implications on the payment of lease premiums.

From an income tax perspective, there are two main reliefs available:

- when the tenant uses the property in connection with a trade; and
- when the tenant uses the property in his or her own rental business (other than as a source of rents).

Tenant uses property for trade

Where the landlord is subject to income tax on a lease premium received, the tenant is treated as incurring revenue expenditure, and may claim an equivalent deduction in calculating trading profits.

The deduction for the trading tenant is based on the landlord's "taxed receipt". This is normally the part of the premium that is treated as an income receipt for the landlord, but this is subject to adjustment if the landlord is also paying a lease premium.

The taxed receipt is spread across the receipt period (normally the term of the lease), calculated on a daily basis. The trader is then treated as incurring a daily revenue expense. In some circumstances, relief for a premium paid by a previous tenant can continue to be given to a new tenant.

Various complicating factors can be at play, so reference should be made to the legislation and/or to the detailed HMRC guidance, as appropriate.

Law: ITTOIA 2005, s. 61
Guidance: BIM 46250*ff.*

Tenant uses property for rental business

Broadly similar principles apply if the tenant uses the property for his or her own rental business. Relief is again available for part of the premium, if treated as a revenue receipt for the superior landlord, and this is once more calculated on a daily basis.

Again, this basic principle is subject to various complications.

Law: ITTOIA 2005, s. 292

27.5   Anti-avoidance

27.5.1   Lease granted at undervalue

Where there has been an assignment of a short-term lease that was granted at an undervalue, and a profit is made on the assignment, the person who assigns the lease is treated as receiving an amount. That amount is brought into account as a receipt in calculating the profits of the property business for the tax year in which the consideration for the assignment becomes payable.

Law: ITTOIA 2005, s. 282
Guidance: PIM 1222

27.5.2   Sales with a right to reconveyance

A charge to tax may arise if an estate or interest in land is sold subject to terms that provide that it may be reconveyed in the future to the seller or to a person connected with the seller at a lower price.

The seller is treated as receiving an amount that is brought into account as a receipt in calculating the profits of the property business for the tax year in which the estate or interest is sold.

Where the period between sale and repurchase exceeds 50 years, the charge will not arise.

Law: ITTOIA 2005, s. 284, 286
Guidance: PIM 1224

27.5.3   Sale and leaseback transactions

A further anti-avoidance provision is designed to counteract attempts to avoid the charge on sale with a right to reconveyance (see above) through a sale with a right to lease back.

Where the legislation applies, the seller is treated as receiving an amount that is brought into account in calculating the profits of the property business for the tax year in which the estate or interest is sold. Where the period between sale and leaseback exceeds 50 years, the charge does not apply.

Law: ITTOIA 2005, s. 285, 286
Guidance: PIM 1226, 1232

27.6   Reverse premiums

27.6.1   Overview

A reverse premium is, broadly, a payment or other benefit from a landlord to a prospective tenant to incentivise the latter to take on a lease or other interest in land.

For income tax purposes, a reverse premium is treated as a receipt – by the person receiving it (e.g. the tenant) – that is revenue in nature. Where the recipient enters into the transaction for the purposes of a trade, the reverse premium is treated as a trade receipt. Otherwise, it is considered a receipt of a property business.

Recognition

Unless avoidance arrangements are present (see **27.6.7**) the tax treatment of a reverse premium typically follows generally accepted accounting practice (GAAP), so a reverse premium is usually brought into account for tax purposes as it is credited in the accounts. Under both Financial Reporting Standard (FRS) 102 and International Accounting Standards (IAS), the receipt is spread on a straight-line basis over the term of the lease.

Law: ITTOIA 2005, s. 101, 311
Guidance: BIM 41055

27.6.2   Commercial context

At first sight, a reverse premium may seem like an odd concept. However, there is a commercial rationale behind reverse premiums, as HMRC's BIM 41052 elaborates:

> "Developers have long been prepared to offer inducements to so-called anchor tenants. The presence of a major department store in a shopping mall will attract shoppers and permit smaller concerns to enjoy their custom. This will enable the owner to charge higher rents."

Inducements to potential tenants may take various forms. The most obvious are to offer the tenant a reduced rent, or a rent-free period of occupation. Increasingly, however, tenants have come to receive lump sum payments, either to spend as they choose or as a contribution to specified expenditure. Another possibility is that sums are paid to a third party in satisfaction of some liability of the tenant.

The commercial benefit of actual payments from the payer's perspective is that, unlike the reduced rent or rent-free period, they leave the rental flow unimpaired. This is particularly important for a developer, who will normally be seeking to sell the property to a prospective landlord, typically a financial institution such as a life assurance company. The rental flow from the property will determine the sale price. Even for a landlord with no immediate intention of selling, the maintenance of a rental flow may be vital, for example in relation to the ability to borrow funds.

Guidance: BIM 41052

27.6.3   Definition

A payment or other benefit is generally considered a reverse premium if conditions A to C are met.

Condition A

A person ("the recipient") receives the payment or other benefit by way of inducement in connection with a transaction being entered into by the recipient, or by a person connected with the recipient.

Condition B

The property transaction is one under which the recipient, or the person connected with the recipient, becomes entitled to an estate, interest or right in or over land.

Condition C

The payment or other benefit is paid or provided by:

- the person ("the grantor") by whom the estate, interest or right is granted or was granted at an earlier time;
- a person connected with the grantor; or
- a nominee of, or a person acting on the directions of, the grantor or a person connected with the grantor.

Exclusions

Certain excluded cases are not treated as reverse premiums. This includes where a payment or other benefit is:

- brought into account under CAA 2001, s. 532 to reduce the recipient's expenditure qualifying for capital allowances;
- received in connection with a property transaction, where the person entering into the transaction is an individual, and the transaction relates to premises occupied or to be occupied by the individual as his or her only or main residence; or
- consideration for the transfer of an estate or interest in land which constitutes the sale in a sale and lease-back arrangement (under ITA 2007, s. 681AA, 681AB or 681BA).

Law: ITTOIA 2005, s. 99, 100
Guidance: BIM 41051

27.6.4 Examples of reverse premiums

The definition of a reverse premium includes the term "a payment or other benefit".

This could be a simple payment of cash from landlord to tenant, but it is equally possible that a landlord gives a tenant a benefit other than cash, or pays a sum to a third party in order to meet a liability of the tenant. BIM 41075 states:

> "Broadly, only benefits procured by actually laying out money are within the meaning of the term 'reverse premium' for tax

purposes. Inducements that represent amounts forgone or deferred by the operator, such as rent-free periods or reduced rents, are not reverse premiums. The smaller deduction for rent payable will reflect such inducements in the tenant's taxable profits."

HMRC's manual goes on to outline common forms of inducement that are considered reverse premiums, which include:

- cash payments directly to the tenant;
- cash payments by indirect means, for example writing off a loan that is a liability of the tenant;
- certain contributions towards the tenant's fitting-out costs (unless exempted – see **27.6.5**);
- assumption by a landlord of the tenant's liabilities under an existing lease, such as a continuing obligation to pay rent, or the payment of a lump sum to terminate it; and
- other sums paid to third parties to satisfy some obligation of the tenant.

By contrast, the following are not considered to be reverse premiums:

- granting the tenant a rent-free period or reduced rent;
- replacement, by agreement, of an existing lease at an onerous rent by a new lease at a lower rent; and
- replacement, by agreement, of an existing lease with some other provision the tenant has found onerous by a new lease without the onerous condition.

Example

A property developer agrees to make a partially completed building available to its tenant, Janet. The developer pays Janet a sum to complete the building on the landlord's behalf.

The amount paid to Janet is not a reverse premium, as the expenditure relates to the cost of producing a completed building (as opposed to being a payment as an inducement for Janet to take on the lease).

Guidance: BIM 41075

27.6.5   *Fitting-out costs*

A landlord may meet the tenant's fitting-out costs (i.e. the costs relating to the provision of fixtures and chattels to equip the building to serve the tenant's needs). This may be achieved directly (by paying any suppliers or installation costs) or indirectly (by reimbursing the tenant).

Provided that the costs being met by the landlord relate to costs that are, properly, the tenant's expenses of fitting-out, the tenant is considered to receive a reverse premium. However, where a landlord covers fitting-out costs that are necessary to make a building ready to let, the payment is not considered a reverse premium.

Where reimbursements relate to fitting-out costs, the contribution may be deducted from expenditure otherwise qualifying for capital allowances in the tenant's hands, under CAA 2001, s. 532. To the extent that it reduces the recipient's expenditure qualifying for capital allowances in this way, the sum is not considered a reverse premium.

Law: CAA 2001, s. 532; ITTOIA 2005, s. 100(1)
Guidance: BIM 41085, 41090

27.6.6 Tax treatment of reverse premiums for payer

Although a reverse premium is treated as a receipt of income in the hands of the recipient, this has no bearing on how it should be taxed from the perspective of the payer (who could be, for example, a landlord, builder, or developer).

Instead, the tax treatment for the payer is determined by reference to ordinary principles.

Typically, where the payer is a landlord, the premium is considered capital, as the purpose of the payment is to enhance the value of the asset in question by securing an income stream for it. In such cases, the premium is not allowable as a deduction in the landlord's rental business.

It is possible, however, for a reverse premium to be treated as a deduction in the hands of the payer. This may apply, for example, if a developer pays the reverse premium in the course of its trade. In such cases, the reverse premium is part of the cost of realising trading stock, and so should be allowable as a deduction when calculating trading profits.

Law: ITTOIA 2005, s. 33
Guidance: BIM 41060

27.6.7   Anti-avoidance

To prevent connected parties from taking advantage of the reverse premium rules, for example by creating extremely long leases and spreading the reverse premium over an unrealistically long period, anti-avoidance provisions are in place.

Broadly, the anti-avoidance provisions apply if two or more of the parties to the property arrangements are connected persons, and the terms of those arrangements are not such as would reasonably have been expected if those persons had been dealing at arm's length.

The definition of "connected persons" is taken from ITA 2007, s. 993 (see **Appendix 2**).

Where the provisions apply, the general rule is that the whole amount or value of the reverse premium is brought into account in the period of account in which the property transaction is entered into. This means that spreading, which ordinarily would be applied in accordance with GAAP (see **27.6.1**), is denied.

Law: ITTOIA 2005, s. 102-103, 311; ITA 2007, s. 993
Guidance: BIM 41130, 41135

27.7 Pitfalls and planning points

Determining the tax treatment

To determine how a lease premium should be taxed for income tax purposes, a few steps should be taken:

- Determine whether the lease in question has been granted or assigned (**27.2**).
- If granted, determine whether the lease is long or short (**27.3.2**).
- Consider whether anti-avoidance provisions have been triggered (**27.5**).

Tenant versus landlord

When considering the lease premium and reverse premium provisions, the tax position is different for landlord and tenant. This position can become more complex where a sublease is granted.

Remember CGT

This annual provides an overview of the taxation of leases from an income tax perspective. Any CGT implications must also be considered.

28. Furnished holiday lettings

28.1 Introduction

The furnished holiday lettings (FHL) rules were originally introduced in FA 1984, although the regime has seen its fair share of changes since then. The biggest shift came in FA 2011, which introduced loss relief restrictions for FHLs, altered the day count tests, and introduced the period-of-grace election.

Brexit

When originally introduced, the FHL legislation only applied to UK properties. This was extended in 2011 to include European Economic Area (EEA) properties, following concerns that the rules were discriminatory under EU law.

It is not yet clear, following the UK's departure from the EU and the end of the transitional period, whether the provisions that extend the FHL regime to EEA properties will be repealed. There are no clauses to do this in *Finance Bill* 2021 (published on 11 March 2021), so for the time being, the *status quo* will continue.

However, FHL businesses located overseas – and their professional advisers – should keep a close eye on this area for any developments, as there is no guarantee that the special taxation regime for FHLs will continue to apply to non-UK properties.

It is also worth noting that all of a taxpayer's furnished holiday lettings in the UK are taxed as a single UK FHL business, while all of a taxpayer's non-UK FHLs located in the EEA are taxed as a single EEA FHL business (see **28.5**). The EEA comprises the EU states plus Iceland, Liechtenstein and Norway.

Further guidance

The FHL rules are covered in greater depth in the specialist title *Furnished Holiday Lettings* from Claritax Books. See also HMRC's *Property Income Manual*, beginning at PIM 3200.

28.2   Income tax treatment

The tax treatment of a qualifying FHL is more advantageous than other types of property letting, as an FHL is treated as though it were a trade for certain tax purposes.

This special treatment affords FHLs several advantages that are unavailable to other property businesses. For example:

- there are capital allowances benefits (see **28.5.3**);
- certain restrictions to which let properties are ordinarily subject do not apply (see **28.5.5** – interest deductibility); and
- FHL profits are counted as relevant UK earnings for pension purposes.

FHLs may also take advantage of certain CGT reliefs, including business asset disposal relief (formerly entrepreneurs' relief), rollover relief and holdover relief. Discussion of these reliefs is outside the scope of this annual, but see the equivalent *Capital Gains Tax* title from Claritax Books.

Law: ITTOIA 2005, s. 322; ITA 2007, s. 127, 127ZA

28.3   Qualifying criteria

28.3.1   Introduction

There is a "commercial letting of furnished holiday accommodation" where all of the following conditions are met (ITTOIA 2005, s. 323):

- The accommodation is let on a commercial basis, and with a view to the realisation of profits.
- The person entitled to the use of the accommodation is also entitled, in connection with that use, to the use of furniture. The furnishing must be to a standard that allows "everyday occupation".
- The accommodation is qualifying holiday accommodation by virtue of meeting the three occupancy tests (see below).

In addition, to be a FHL a property must be located in the UK or EEA.

There is no "opt-out" from the FHL regime; where accommodation qualifies by meeting the above criteria (or where the test of qualifying holiday accommodation is met by virtue of an averaging and/or period-of-grace election – see **28.4**) the property must be treated as an FHL.

Once a property qualifies as an FHL, all the income from that property qualifies for the special tax treatments afforded to FHLs for that year, including lettings outside the period when the FHL conditions are met.

It is important to note that FHL status is applied to each property individually; it is not a "substantially" type of test such as applies to trading status, for example. If an individual owns ten properties, nine of which are qualifying FHLs and one is a long-term letting there will be two separate businesses: a qualifying FHL business consisting of nine properties, and a property rental business. There is no scope to include the profits from the letting business with the FHL profits on the basis that, taken as a whole, the properties are substantially qualifying.

Commercial letting

In respect of commercial letting, HMRC help sheet HS253 confirms that there must be an intention to make a profit.

Where a taxpayer lets a property out of season to cover costs but does not make a profit, the letting will still be treated as commercial.

Law: ITTOIA 2005, s. 323-325
Guidance: HS253 *Furnished holiday lettings*

28.3.2   Qualifying holiday accommodation

Accommodation let by a person is "qualifying holiday accommodation" for a given tax year if three conditions are met:

- availability;
- letting; and
- pattern of occupation.

All three conditions refer to a "relevant period", and the meaning of this is considered below.

Availability

The availability condition is that, during the relevant period, the accommodation is available for commercial letting as holiday accommodation to the public generally for at least 210 days.

A property is not available for letting if the person operating the property business is staying there.

Letting

The letting condition is that, during the relevant period, the accommodation is commercially let as holiday accommodation to members of the public for at least 105 days.

Note the term "commercially". This condition is not met where the property is let to friends or relatives at below-market rates.

Periods of longer-term occupation (see below) are also not counted, unless the longer-term occupation is a result of unforeseen or unusual circumstances. This may be relevant in years affected by the Covid-19 pandemic.

Pattern of occupation

The pattern of occupation condition is that, during the relevant period, no more than 155 days fall during periods of longer-term occupation.

A "period of longer-term occupation" is a continuous period of more than 31 days during which the accommodation is in the same occupation otherwise than because of circumstances that are not normal (e.g. if a holidaymaker falls ill and cannot leave the accommodation on time).

Relevant period

The relevant period is determined as follows:

- If the accommodation was not let by the person as furnished accommodation in the previous tax year, the relevant period is 12 months beginning with the first day in the tax year on which it is let by the person as furnished accommodation.
- If the accommodation was let by the person as furnished accommodation in the previous tax year, but is not let by the person as furnished accommodation in the following tax year, the relevant period is taken to be 12 months ending with the last day in the tax year on which it is let by the person as furnished accommodation.
- In other cases, the relevant period is taken to be the tax year.

Example1

Carrie owns furnished holiday accommodation, which is let on a commercial basis for the first time on 20 December 2021. The three qualifying conditions are applied to the period of 12 months beginning with 20 December 2021.

Example 2

Doug owns a cottage that has been let furnished on a commercial basis for many years. The letting ceases on 1 February 2022. The three qualifying conditions are applied to the period of 12 months ending with 1 February 2022.

Example 3

Mary has a continuing furnished holiday let. For the 2021-22 tax year, the three qualifying conditions are applied on a tax year basis (i.e. 6 April 2021 to 5 April 2022).

Law: ITTOIA 2005, s. 323-325
Guidance: PIM 4110

28.4 Elections

28.4.1 Introduction

Where a taxpayer has a property that would qualify as an FHL, save for the fact that the letting condition is not met, there are two potential elections that may resolve the matter:

- the averaging election (see **28.4.2** below); and
- the period-of-grace election (see **28.4.3**).

See **28.4.4** for a discussion of the interaction between the two elections.

A taxpayer who is eligible to use either election (or both) can effectively treat the property with the failed letting condition as an FHL.

28.4.2 Averaging election

If, during a tax year, a person lets accommodation that qualifies as an FHL, and also lets accommodation that would qualify as an FHL except for the fact that it did not meet the letting condition, the person may elect to apply the letting condition to the average rate of occupancy for all the FHL properties.

The election must be applied separately to UK FHL and EEA FHL businesses, i.e. the occupancy of a UK property cannot be used to average the occupancy of an EEA property, or *vice versa*.

An election for a tax year must be made on or before the first anniversary of the normal self-assessment filing date for the tax year.

Example

Bailey lets out the following furnished UK properties within a holiday complex in the 2021-22 tax year. There were no periods of longer-term occupation for any property:

	Days let
Property 1	110
Property 2	135
Property 3	100

If no averaging election is made, property 3 would not meet the letting condition, as it has been let for fewer than 105 days. However, if an averaging election is made, all three properties satisfy the letting condition: (110+135+100)/3 = 115 days.

The election must be made by 31 January 2024.

Law: ITTOIA 2005, s. 326
Guidance: PIM 4110

28.4.3   Period-of-grace election

Where a person has let accommodation that qualifies as an FHL in one tax year, but fails to do so the following tax year on the sole basis that the letting condition is not met, an election may be available. The legislation uses the description "Under-used holiday accommodation: letting condition not met" but the election is commonly referred to as a "period-of-grace election".

Where such an election is made, the accommodation is treated as an FHL for the relevant tax year.

The election can be made in respect of the tax year following the one in which the accommodation qualified as an FHL, or for the next two tax years. For the election to be claimed over two tax years, it must have been made for the first tax year.

There must have been a genuine intention to meet the letting condition for the tax year(s) in question (e.g. marketing the property to the same level as in previous years where the letting condition was met, or if lettings have been cancelled due to unforeseen circumstances).

HMRC have confirmed, for the 2020-21 tax year, that unforeseen circumstances include cases where the letting condition is not met because of Covid-19 measures, such as enforced closure due to lockdowns or travel bans. Although yet to be confirmed at the time of writing, it would be reasonable to assume that such restrictions would still be accepted as unforeseen circumstances to the extent that Covid-19 restrictions remain in place in 2021-22.

An election for a tax year must be made on or before the first anniversary of the normal self-assessment filing date for the tax year.

Example

In 2020-21, Sarah's property qualified as an FHL. In 2021-22, the property was marketed throughout the tax year, but it was only let for 90 days in total. Using the period-of-grace election, the property can continue qualifying as an FHL in 2021-22.

The election should be made by 31 January 2024, either as a standalone claim, or in the UK property pages of the taxpayer's self-assessment tax return.

Law: ITTOIA 2005, s. 326A
Guidance: PIM 4110

28.4.4   Interaction between the averaging election and period-of-grace election

Where a taxpayer lets more than one property as an FHL, it is possible to make use of both the above elections to maximise the time that a property qualifies as an FHL.

HMRC example – from PIM 4110

Emma has four cottages that she lets as furnished holiday lettings. In some years cottage 3 doesn't meet the letting condition.

	Year 1	Year 2	Year 3	Year 4	Year 5
Cottage 1	qualifies	qualifies	qualifies	qualifies	qualifies
Cottage 2	qualifies	qualifies	qualifies	qualifies	qualifies
Cottage 3	qualifies	averaging	period of grace	period of grace	qualifies
Cottage 4	qualifies	qualifies	qualifies	qualifies	qualifies

Emma uses averaging in year 2 and period of grace in years 3 and 4 to make sure that cottage 3 qualifies for the whole period.

Guidance: PIM 4110

28.5 Calculation of profit and loss

28.5.1 Introduction

Although an FHL is treated as a deemed trade for certain tax purposes, FHLs are subject to the property income rules, meaning that the usual principles for calculating rental business profits should be applied (see **Chapter 26**).

All FHLs in the UK are taxed as a single UK FHL business, while all FHLs located outside the UK in the EEA are taxed as a single EEA FHL business. As a result, separate records need to be kept for each UK/EEA FHL business. This is also relevant when it comes to matters such as loss relief (see **28.7**).

In addition, where a UK or overseas property business consists of both the commercial letting of FHL accommodation and other businesses or transactions, separate calculations should be made of the profits of the FHL part and the other part. Capital allowances also have to be kept separate for each element.

While an overall profit of an FHL business is included in the taxpayer's general property business result, there are restrictions on how FHL losses can be used – see **28.7**.

Covid-19

A number of support measures have been introduced by the government as part of its response package to the Covid-19 pandemic, one such measure being the Self-Employment Income Support Scheme (SEISS) – see **15.7.4**.

However, as many FHL owners report the results of their FHL business in the property pages of their self-assessment tax return (see above), such taxpayers are unlikely to benefit from the SEISS in practice.

There are other potential options, such as grants, which may be available for qualifying FHL businesses, including the one-off grant announced in January 2021 (see link in guidance below).

Alternatively, FHL businesses may need to make use of averaging and/or period-of-grace elections where available to maintain FHL status during this time (see **28.4**).

Law: ITTOIA 2005, s. 327-328B

Guidance: PIM 4115; https://tinyurl.com/yn9kv3ky (Covid-19 support for business)

28.5.2   *Pre-trading expenses*

The date on which a rental business begins is a question of fact, dependent on the nature of the rental business. Usually, a rental business begins when letting first commences.

Relief for pre-trading expenditure incurred within seven years before the date of commencement may be given to the extent that:

- no deduction would otherwise be allowed for the expenses; but
- a deduction would have been allowed for them if they had been incurred on the start date.

Such expenses are treated as if they were incurred on the day of the trade commencing.

Law: ITTOIA 2005, s. 57

Guidance: PIM 2505

28.5.3   *Capital allowances*

One of the more generous aspects of the taxation of FHLs is that the remit to claim capital allowances is greater than that afforded to other residential property businesses.

Ordinarily, for capital allowances purposes, expenditure is not qualifying expenditure if it is incurred on plant or machinery for use in a dwelling-house (see **20.3.7**). This restriction applies for an ordinary (UK or overseas) property business.

However, the restriction does not apply to FHLs, so plant and machinery allowances can be claimed for qualifying expenditure relating to furniture and furnishings in an FHL property. Such allowances may also be claimed for integral features and other fixtures within an FHL, and for qualifying plant and machinery used outside the property (e.g. a van). However, no capital allowances may be claimed for the land on which the property stands.

As with any capital allowance claim under income tax principles, the amount of available allowances is restricted where there is an element of private use.

Structures and buildings allowances (see **Chapter 22**) are not given for FHL properties.

When a property ceases being an FHL

If a property ceases to be an FHL (see **28.6**), the taxpayer should technically calculate any balancing allowance or charge (as appropriate) for capital allowances purposes. See **Chapter 20** for further information.

However, PIM 4115 states that:

> "Strictly, if a property qualifies in one year but does not do so in the next, the disposal value of plant and machinery should be brought into account. If income from a property temporarily ceases to qualify solely because not all the tests are satisfied for that year, capital allowances may be continued. But if a property is let on a long-term basis, or sold, or otherwise seems unlikely to qualify in the foreseeable future, disposal value should be brought into account."

Law: CAA 2001, s. 15, 35
Guidance: PIM 4105, 4115

28.5.4   Replacement of domestic items relief

FHLs cannot use the replacement of domestic items relief (see **26.6**). However, in most cases capital allowances will give relief anyway.

Law: ITTOIA 2005, s. 311A

28.5.5   Interest deductibility

FHLs are not subject to the rules restricting the deductibility of finance costs related to residential property (see **26.5.4**).

Law: ITTOIA 2005, s. 272A-272B

28.5.6   Private use adjustments

There is no set type of property that can be an FHL – the property could be a cottage in a seaside town that is exclusively let on a short-term basis, or it could be a property within an apartment complex that is let out during peak holiday seasons.

It could also be a property that is let as an FHL for only part of the tax year and is used as private accommodation for the remaining part (as long as the various conditions are met).

Where an FHL property is used privately for part of the tax year, or only part of the property is let as an FHL, it will be necessary to determine the amount of income and expenses to bring into account when calculating the FHL profits. Any apportionment should be made on a just and reasonable basis.

HMRC confirm in HS253 that where a property is only used as an FHL, and is closed for part of the year because there are no customers, the taxpayer can deduct all the expenses, such as insurance and loan interest, for the whole year, provided the taxpayer does not live in the property (i.e. there is no private use).

Law: ITA 2007, s. 127
Guidance: HS253: *Furnished holiday lettings*

28.6   Ceasing to be an FHL

If a property meets the conditions to be treated as an FHL, the special tax treatment afforded to FHLs is automatic.

However, this does not mean that once a property qualifies as an FHL it will always do so, as the qualifying conditions need to be assessed for each relevant period. For continuing FHL businesses this period is the tax year (see **28.3.2**).

Where a property ceases to qualify for special tax treatment as an FHL, but is still let out, it is thereafter taxed according to ordinary principles for rental property (see **Chapter 26**).

Guidance: PIM 4115

28.7   Loss relief

Where an FHL business makes a loss, the loss may only be carried forward and used against the profits of the same FHL business arising in a later year. A loss in an FHL business cannot be used against profits of a non-FHL property business (see **Chapter 17**). If the property ceases to qualify as an FHL, it will not be possible to carry losses forward against future non-FHL rental profits from the same property.

28.8   Pitfalls and planning points

Qualifying criteria

There are several qualifying criteria that let accommodation must meet in order to be considered an FHL (see **28.3**).

Where accommodation would qualify as an FHL, but the letting condition is not met, it may nevertheless be possible to qualify by virtue of the averaging or period-of-grace elections (see **28.4**).

Special tax treatment

FHLs are subject to more advantageous tax treatment than other residential let properties. Additional capital allowances are available (see **28.5.3**), as well as certain CGT reliefs. FHL profits are also counted as relevant UK earnings for pension purposes.

Separate businesses

All of a taxpayer's FHLs in the UK are taxed as a single UK FHL business, and all of his or her EEA FHLs are taxed as a single EEA FHL business. Separate records should be kept of the profits/losses arising to each UK and/or EEA FHL business. Profits of an FHL business should also be kept separate from profits arising from other rental businesses.

Covid-19

To the extent that an FHL business reports its results in the property pages of a self-assessment tax return, relief under Covid-19 support measures such as the Self-Employment Income Support Scheme (SEISS) is unlikely to be available (see **28.5.1** and **15.7.4**).

Grants may be available for qualifying FHL businesses.

An averaging election and/or period-of-grace election may need to be considered to ensure that FHL status is maintained (see **28.4**).

PENSIONS AND STATE BENEFITS

29. Introduction to pensions

29.1 Introduction

Although pension benefits are paid by the state after retirement (see **Chapter 32**), many people supplement their post-retirement income through additional arrangements. Since 2012, employers are required to provide workplace pensions (see **29.5**), and numerous private or personal pension products are available on the market.

From an income tax perspective, much depends on whether a pension scheme is:

- a registered pension scheme (see **29.3**);
- an employer-financed retirement benefits scheme (see **29.4**); or
- an unregistered scheme.

An unregistered scheme may be set up to provide retirement benefits outside the restrictions imposed on a registered scheme. Unregistered schemes do not attract any special tax reliefs, are not subject to particular rules, and are not considered further in this chapter.

The key legislation for pension tax issues is to be found in FA 2004. HMRC's guidance is primarily available in the *Pensions Tax Manual*. Further useful information may be found on the website of the Pensions Regulator, the official UK regulator of workplace pension schemes.

Guidance: https://www.thepensionsregulator.gov.uk

29.2 What is a pension scheme?

A pension scheme is defined as essentially a scheme or arrangement that can provide benefits to, or in respect of, a person in any one or more of the following circumstances:

- retirement;
- death;
- reaching a particular age; and
- serious ill-health or incapacity.

This is potentially very wide in scope, although in practice most pension schemes are either defined contribution arrangements, defined benefits arrangements or a combination of the two.

Defined contribution schemes

Defined contribution schemes (sometimes referred to as money purchase schemes) involve contributions being invested on behalf of the individual concerned until the fund can be accessed, and usually also thereafter. The value of pension benefits depends on the scheme's performance and, as such, there are no guarantees as to the amounts that will be received. Most personal pension schemes are defined contribution schemes.

Defined benefits schemes

With a defined benefits scheme, the size of the fund is irrelevant in determining the level of eventual benefits. Instead, the individual receives a pension amount based on a formula, typically involving salary and length of service, as set out in the scheme documents. Defined benefits schemes are typically established by employers for employees (often referred to as "occupational schemes"), but they are less common now than in the past because of the potential costs for the employer.

Law: FA 2004, s. 150(1)

29.3   Registered pension schemes

A registered pension scheme is one registered with HMRC under FA 2004, Pt. 4, Ch. 2. HMRC will have to be satisfied that:

- the scheme exists for the purposes of making authorised payments of pensions and lump sums to members (s. 164(1)(a)-(b), and see **Chapter 30**);
- the scheme administrator is a fit and proper person; and
- all appropriate documentation and declarations (see s. 153) have been completed.

If the pension scheme is registered, investments in the pension will grow tax-free.

Certain tax reliefs are also available on contributions to the scheme (see **Chapter 30**) and on payments from the scheme (**Chapter 31**).

HMRC can withdraw registration at any time, if the rules are not complied with.

Law: FA 2004, s. 153-159D, 164; TCGA 1992, s. 271(1A)

29.4   Employer-financed retirement benefit schemes

An employer-financed retirement benefit scheme (EFRBS) is a type of unregistered scheme set up by employers to provide relevant benefits to former employees and their families. "Relevant benefits" are defined by ITEPA 2003, s. 393B and include any lump sum, gratuity or other benefit (including non-cash benefits) provided on death, on or in anticipation of retirement, in connection with past service or by virtue of a pension-sharing order.

If a scheme is classified as an EFRBS, payments to members are treated as employment income. In other words:

- Employer contributions to an EFRBS on behalf of an employee are not taxable benefits for the employee unless a third party is involved and ITEPA 2003, Pt. 7A applies (see **13.3**).
- Employee contributions to an EFRBS (if permitted) do not attract any income tax relief.
- Payments out to individuals will be taxed as employment income (assuming they are not otherwise taxable under ITEPA 2003, Pt. 7A or general earnings provisions). PAYE is due but NIC liability will depend on the nature of the payment.

If the employee is non-UK resident for tax purposes, foreign service relief may be available to exempt or reduce the taxable amount when a payment is received from a EFRBS that is taxable under ITEPA 2003, s. 394. This depends on the extent to which the EFRBS payment relates to overseas duties (s. 395B).

Since the introduction of ITEPA 2003, Pt. 7A – which can give rise to a charge before employees receive the funds, e.g. if assets within are earmarked for particular employers – the use of EFRBS has diminished.

Law: ITEPA 2003, s. 393-399A, Pt. 7A
Guidance: NIM 02765

29.5   Auto-enrolment

The rules set out in the *Pensions Act* 2008 impose a duty on employers (whether or not situated in the UK) to arrange for the automatic enrolment of all eligible workers into a workplace pension and to make contributions on their behalf.

A detailed consideration of the obligations of the employer under auto-enrolment is beyond the scope of this book, but see the *Pension Tax Guide* from Claritax Books. However, in assessing liability to income tax, it is important to note that a workplace pension must have been certified as a qualifying pension scheme by the Pensions Regulator. Qualifying pension schemes include registered pension schemes (see **29.3**). Alternatively, employers can use the National Employment Savings Trust (NEST), set up by the government and designed to operate on a defined contribution basis. The practical consequence of this is that contributions made or payments received under auto-enrolment are subject to the same tax reliefs and rules as any other registered pension scheme (see **Chapters 30** and **31**).

To fall within auto-enrolment, an individual must be a "worker". This is defined in *Pensions Act* 2008, s. 88(3) and extends beyond employees to include agency workers (see **13.2.2**). However, there are a number of exclusions set out in the legislation, including:

- workers who do not work, or ordinarily work, in the UK;
- company directors, except those who have a contract of employment with the company and where the company has at least one other employee; and
- members of the armed forces.

Each worker within the legislation will fall into one of three categories:

- An eligible jobholder – a worker aged between 22 and state pension age (see **32.1**) who earns more than £10,000 per year. Eligible jobholders must be automatically enrolled in a qualifying pension scheme, although they do have the right to opt out.
- A non-eligible job holder – a worker aged between 22 and state pension age who earns between the lower earnings threshold for NIC (£6,240 for 2021-22) and £10,000 per year; or a worker aged between either 16 and 21 or state pension age and 74 who, in each case, earns more than £6,240 per year. Non-eligible jobholders have a right to be enrolled in a qualifying scheme on request, but there is no obligation to enrol them automatically.

- An entitled worker – a worker who is aged between 16 and 74 and who earns less than £6,240 per year. Entitled workers have a right to join a pension scheme on request, but the scheme offered does not have to be a qualifying scheme, and the employer is not required to make contributions on their behalf.

For the purposes of auto-enrolment, a worker's qualifying earnings are those that attract Class 1 NIC (see **14.5**) and are calculated by reference to the pay period applicable to them (usually monthly).

Employers should monitor the situation on an ongoing basis, and automatically enrol anyone who becomes an eligible job-holder, although the worker always has the right to opt out. In addition, the employer has a cyclical re-enrolment duty at three-yearly intervals to review the workforce and re-enrol any eligible jobholders who have previously opted out (again, these jobholders can opt out at any time). After each such review, the employer has to re-certify compliance with the automatic enrolment rules to the Pensions Regulator.

A minimum level of pension contribution must be made in respect of each enrolled eligible and non-eligible job holder. For defined contribution schemes, this is currently 8% of earnings between the lower earnings limit and upper earnings limit for NIC purposes (£6,240 and £50,270 respectively, for 2021-22). The employer must pay at least 3% of this.

For defined benefits schemes and hybrid schemes, minimum contributions are calculated by reference to a hypothetical benchmark (or "test scheme") standard (see *Pensions Act* 2008, s. 21-24 and SI 2010/772, Pt. 11).

Law: *Pensions Act* 2008, s. 20, 21-24, 88(3); SI 2010/772, Pt. 11

29.6   Pitfalls and planning points

Termination payments

HMRC will treat an *ex gratia* payment made on termination of employment as a relevant benefit within ITEPA 2003, s. 393B (and therefore fully taxable) if the recipient is retiring. A formal scheme is not required. See **9.4** for more details.

Law: ITEPA 2003, s. 393B

Re-enrolment

When dealing with cyclical re-enrolment under the auto-enrolment rules, the employer does *not* have to re-enrol a worker who has previous opted out if:

- the re-enrolment date is during an employee's period of notice to end the worker's employment; or
- the employer has reasonable grounds to believe that the worker has registered for one of the varieties of lifetime allowance protection that have been offered each time the lifetime allowance has reduced (see **31.2**).

This can avoid unnecessary administration due to re-enrolling followed by immediate opting out.

30. Contributions to registered pension schemes

30.1 Introduction

Contributions to a registered pension scheme can be made by:

- the scheme member;
- a third party on the member's behalf (such as a parent on behalf of a child); or
- an employer or former employer.

Where a pension scheme is registered, the scheme member is entitled to income tax relief in respect of contributions to the scheme, subject to a maximum limit.

How this relief is given depends on who makes the contributions, on the type of scheme, and on whether or not it is an occupational pension scheme.

30.2 Tax relief for individual contributions

30.2.1 Introduction

All pension contributions made to a registered pension scheme by, or on behalf of, a member of that scheme potentially qualify for income tax relief provided:

- the member is a relevant UK individual (see **30.2.2**);
- contributions do not fall within an exclusion set out in FA 2004, s. 188 (see **30.2.3**);
- the contributions do not exceed the greater of £3,600 and the individual's relevant earnings (see **30.2.4**); and
- the contributions do not exceed the annual allowance (see **30.4**).

Contributions to overseas pension schemes may also attract tax relief in certain circumstances (see **39.5**).

Law: FA 2004, s. 188-195

30.2.2 Relevant UK individuals

Tax relief for contributions is only available under s. 188 if the individual is a "relevant UK individual", defined as an individual who:

- is resident in the UK for tax purposes at some point during the tax year;
- was resident in the UK for tax purposes both at some point during the preceding five tax years *and* at the point the individual became a member of the pension scheme;
- has relevant UK earnings (see **30.2.4**) chargeable to income tax in the tax year;
- has earnings from an overseas Crown employment subject to UK tax in the tax year; or
- has a spouse or civil partner who has earnings from an overseas Crown employment subject to UK tax in the tax year.

Law: FA 2004, s. 188-189

30.2.3 Non-relievable pension contributions

Contributions do not attract tax relief for the individual if they:

- are made after the individual has reached the age of 75;
- constitute the payment of life assurance premiums; or
- are made by the individual's employer (but see **30.3** for the tax treatment of employer contributions).

Law: FA 2004, s. 188, 195A

30.2.4 The meaning of relevant UK earnings

The maximum amount of pension contributions for which a taxpayer can obtain tax relief in any one tax year is the greater of £3,600 (gross) and 100% of relevant UK earnings (s. 190).

Relevant UK earnings include:

- earnings within ITEPA 2003, s. 7(2), such as salary, bonuses, taxable benefits in kind and statutory payments;
- income from a trade, profession or vocation that is chargeable under ITTOIA 2005, Pt. 2;
- income from a furnished holiday lettings business that is chargeable under ITTOIA 2005, Pt. 3;

- certain types of patent income chargeable under ITTOIA 2005, s. 579, 587 or 593; and
- amounts on which tax is payable under CAA 2001, s. 472(5) or Sch. 3, para. 100 (again in relation to patents);

For the avoidance of doubt, income from a pension is not classed as earnings and cannot be included in the definition of relevant earnings.

Law: FA 2004, s. 189(2), 190

30.2.5   Relief-at-source schemes

Tax relief is given on individual contributions through "relief at source" (RAS) where the scheme is a personal pension scheme. This may have been set up by the employer as a group personal pension scheme or may be a private arrangement entered into by the individual with one of the commercially available registered schemes.

Under RAS, payments made to the pension scheme are deemed to be made net of 20% basic rate tax. HMRC will then top up the tax element of the contribution.

Example 1

Xavier contributes £400 into his personal pension scheme. He is deemed to have made this payment net of basic rate tax of £100. HMRC will pay the sum of £100 into the scheme, making a total contribution of £500.

If the individual is a higher rate or additional rate taxpayer, further tax relief is given by increasing the basic rate and higher rate upper thresholds by the gross amount of the pension contribution.

Example 2

In 2021-22, Olive makes contributions of £3,200 to her personal pension scheme. This is deemed to be net of basic rate tax and so the gross payment is £4,000. HMRC will pay £800 into her personal pension scheme, by way of basic rate tax relief. In calculating her income tax liability for 2021-22, her basic rate limit will be increased from £37,700 to £41,700 and her higher rate limit to £154,000.

It is important to note that the annual maximum contribution eligible for tax relief (£3,600 or, if greater, 100% of relevant UK earnings) relates to the gross amount of contributions. This means that the maximum contributions that the taxpayer can actually pay, and still gain tax relief, is 80% of the annual maximum.

HMRC have confirmed that scheme administrators who operate relief at source should continue to claim income tax relief at 20% for Scottish taxpayers, despite the starter rate being 19%.

Law: FA 2004, s. 191-192A

30.2.6   Net pay arrangements

Net pay arrangements may be used as an alternative to RAS provided:

- the scheme is an occupational scheme, a public service pension scheme or a marine pilots' benefit fund; and

- in the case of occupational schemes, the individual is an employee of the sponsoring employer and all employees in the scheme are subject to net pay arrangements.

To give tax relief, the employer calculates PAYE on employees' pay net of the pension contribution.

There may be circumstances where insufficient relief is given through the net pay arrangement, for example where the amount of relievable pension contributions exceed the employment income received from the sponsoring employer(s) for the relevant tax year. In this case, the individual can claim the remaining tax relief through self-assessment.

Pension contributions do not receive relief from NICs, which continue to be calculated on gross salary. However, salary sacrifice arrangements are not caught by the optional remuneration rules (see **6.10**), so salary sacrifice can save NIC for the employee.

Law: FA 2004, s. 191-195

30.3   Employer contributions

A contribution by an employer to an employee's pension scheme is treated as a tax-free benefit where the scheme is registered. This extends to qualifying overseas pension schemes where the employee is eligible for migrant member relief (see **39.5**).

In each case, the employee is not entitled to any further tax relief on the contributions.

The exemption is restricted to payments in respect of an employee. Therefore, employer contributions in respect of an employee's family member are taxed as employment income of the employee.

Law: ITEPA 2003, s. 308-308A

30.4   Impact of the annual allowance

30.4.1   Introduction

Where the total pension input in any tax year exceeds the individual's available annual allowance (see **30.4.3**), this will give rise to an annual allowance charge.

This charge is calculated by reference to the individual's marginal rate of income tax and the amount of excess contributions over the available annual allowance.

The calculation is carried out after the end of the tax year and does not affect the amount of contributions that can be made. It is the responsibility of the individual to check whether the pension input in a tax year exceeds his or her annual allowance and, if so, to declare it through self-assessment.

Law: FA 2004, s. 227-238A

30.4.2   Calculating pension inputs

For a defined contribution scheme, the "pension input" in a tax year is the gross amount of all contributions made by or on behalf of the individual.

The position is slightly more complicated for a defined benefits scheme. Here, pension input means the increase in the value of the rights under the scheme in the tax year. This is calculated by comparing the accrued annual pension entitlement at the end of the tax year with the equivalent figure at the beginning of the tax year. In each case, the amount is multiplied by an actuarial factor of 16.

Example

Antonia is a member of her employer's defined benefits scheme and her pension benefits accrue at a rate of 1/80 of final pay for each year of employment. On 6 April 2021, she has 15 years' accrual and a salary of £32,000. During the tax year, her salary increases to £34,000.

At the start of 2021-22, her accrued pension rights are:

15/80 x £32,000 x 16 =   £96,000

At the end of 2021-22, her accrued pension rights are:

>   16/80 x £34,000 x 16 =   £108,800

Antonia's total pension input is the difference of £12,800.

Law: FA 2004, s. 233-234

30.4.3   Computation of annual allowance

The standard annual allowance for 2021-22 is £40,000. However, where the individual is classed as a "high income individual", the annual allowance is reduced. The amount of the reduction is equal to £1 for every £2 of the individual's adjusted income in excess of £240,000, although the annual allowance cannot fall below £4,000.

An individual is a high income individual if annual threshold income exceeds £200,000 and annual adjusted income exceeds £240,000.

"Threshold income" is defined as taxable income less the gross amount of any pension contributions attracting RAS. Any salary sacrifice arrangements or flexible remuneration arrangements entered into after 8 July 2015, and designed to swap employment income for pension provision, must be disregarded, and the pay given up added back.

If (but only if) threshold income exceeds £200,000, it is necessary to go on to consider adjusted income. This is the individual's taxable pay plus any pension contributions relieved through net pay arrangements and any employer contributions.

Example 1

Charlotte is a member of a personal pension scheme. She makes a personal contribution of £16,000 net each year. Her employer also contributes £10,000 a year. Her gross salary is £220,000 and she has taxable benefits totalling £8,000.

Charlotte also receives income (after allowable expenses) of £10,000 a year from her holiday letting business.

Calculation of threshold income	£
Employment income (£220,000 + £8,000)	228,000
Holiday letting income	10,000
Net taxable income	238,000
Less: gross pension contributions (£16,000 × 100/80)	(£20,000)
Threshold income	218,000

As Charlotte's threshold income exceeds £200,000, her adjusted income needs to be calculated:

Calculation of adjusted income	£
Net taxable income (as calculated above)	238,000
Add: employer pension contribution	£10,000
Adjusted income	248,000

As adjusted income exceeds £240,000, the tapering provisions apply.

Annual allowance of £40,000

Less restriction (£248,000 - £240,000)/2 = £4,000

Revised annual allowance = £36,000

In addition to the current year's annual allowance (tapered or otherwise), s. 228A provides that any unused annual allowance from the preceding three years can be brought forward and used against current year contributions provided that the individual was a member of a registered pension scheme during the years to which the unused annual allowance relates.

The oldest year's unused annual allowance is used before later years.

Example 2

Leanne has been in a personal pension scheme since 6 April 2017. Her relevant earnings are £80,000 per year. Her pension inputs are:

Tax year	Contribution £
2017-18	10,000
2018-19	30,000
2019-20	60,000
2020-21	40,000

Leanne's unused allowances can be summarised as follows:

	2017-18 £	2018-19 £	2019-20 £	2020-21 £
Contribution	10,000	30,000	60,000	30,000
CY allowance	(40,000)	(40,000)	(40,000)	(40,000)
Unused allowance	(30,000)	(10,000)	nil	nil
Excess contribution	nil	nil	20,000	nil
Used 2019-20	(20,000)			

In 2021-22, Leanne will have £10,000 to bring forward from 2018-19 as well as her current year allowance of £40,000, giving her a total allowance of £50,000. The unused allowance of £10,000 from 2017-18 is no longer available for use.

Anti-avoidance provisions prevent an individual from entering into an arrangement to reduce or eliminate the effect of the tapering provisions by reducing threshold or adjusted income in one year, but then increasing it in another. The annual allowance is calculated as if the arrangements had not been made.

When calculating the amount of any unused allowance to carry forward, only the unused amounts of the tapered annual allowance can be carried forward.

Law: FA 2004, s. 228A, 228ZA(1)-(5), 228ZB

30.4.4 *The annual allowance charge*

Where total pension input in the tax year exceeds the available annual allowance (and any qualifying unused annual allowance brought forward), the excess is charged to income tax. This is referred to as the annual allowance charge.

The rate of the tax charge will be the rate which would apply if the excess were the top slice of taxable income for the tax year.

Liability to the annual allowance charge must be reported on the individual's tax return. If the annual allowance charge exceeds £2,000 and the pension savings in the year are more than £40,000, the individual can elect for the charge to be paid from the pension scheme, with benefits in the pension scheme being reduced accordingly. The election must be made by 31 July following the anniversary of the end of the tax year in which the charge arises.

Law: FA 2004, s. 227(4A), 237B

30.4.5   The money purchase annual allowance

The annual allowance applicable to all defined contribution schemes is reduced to £4,000 on certain trigger events (essentially when an individual starts to access benefits consisting wholly or partly of income under a defined contribution scheme, but see FA 2004, s. 227G). This reduced annual allowance is referred to as the money purchase annual allowance (MPAA).

An individual may have pension arrangements other than defined contribution arrangements (essentially defined benefits arrangements). In such cases, the standard annual allowance less the MPAA will continue to apply to those other arrangements (but with the standard allowance tapered for a high-income individual, in accordance with the usual rules).

Unused annual allowances from previous years cannot be brought forward to enhance the MPAA in the current year (although they can continue to be set against non-defined contribution arrangements).

Law: FA 2004, s. 227ZA, 227B-227G

30.4.6   Lifetime allowance

In addition to the annual allowance, individuals may incur a charge if total pension savings exceed a lifetime allowance, frozen at £1,073,100 up to and including 2025-26.

Although the tax charge where the lifetime allowance is exceeded does not apply until there is a benefit crystallisation event, usually at the point benefits can be paid from the pension scheme (see FA 2004, s. 216), consideration should be given to this when determining the levels of contributions. The rate of charge depends on how the excess amounts are taken (see **31.2**).

Law: FA 2004, s. 214-226

30.5   Pitfalls and planning points

Contributions received later than the contribution date

Any delay between payment and receipt could be important where the payments are made near to the beginning or end of the tax year or a pension input period. The tax rules do not require schemes to accept contributions (though there may be other statutory requirements), or to accept them at a particular time or in a particular amount. HMRC confirm at PTM 052000 that each individual case may require a review to establish exactly why the payment was not received on the date expected, including who expected it and why.

Consequently, care should be taken to make payments well in advance of the end of the tax year.

Guidance: PTM 052000

Bringing unused annual allowances forward

Prior to 2020-21, the adjusted and threshold income levels were £150,000 and £110,000 respectively. This should be kept in mind when calculating any unused allowance to be brought forward and set against current-year contributions (see **30.4.3**).

# 31.	Payments from registered pension schemes

## 31.1	Introduction

This chapter considers the income tax position of an individual when value is received from a registered pension plan.

When determining the tax treatment, much depends on:

- the value of the fund;
- the nature of the payment; and
- whether or not the payment is an authorised payment.

Although payments are occasionally made to employers or sponsors of pension schemes, consideration of the tax treatment of these payments is outside the scope of this book.

For more detailed coverage of this topic, see *Pension Tax Guide* from Claritax Books.

Statutory references are to FA 2004, unless otherwise stated.

## 31.2	Value received above the lifetime allowance

In addition to the annual allowance (see **30.4**), a lifetime limit is placed on the total value of the pension fund that can benefit from tax relief. When there is a "benefit crystallisation event" (as defined in s. 216), the value available to the individual is assessed against this lifetime limit or allowance and any excess is subject to the lifetime allowance charge.

For 2021-22, this lifetime allowance is £1,073,100. The 2021 Budget on 3 March 2021 confirmed that this will be frozen until at least 6 April 2026.

The level of the tax charge imposed depends on how the excess over the lifetime allowance is dealt with. If it is taken out of the fund as a lump sum, a tax charge of 55% will arise. If the individual chooses to leave the excess in the pension fund, two tax charges arise:

- a 25% tax charge on the retained amount; and
- a charge at the individual's marginal income tax rate when the amount is ultimately withdrawn.

The individual and the scheme administrator are jointly and severally liable for the lifetime allowance charge. In practice, however, the scheme administrator tends to deduct the relevant tax from the fund and pay it over to HMRC, reducing the individual's retirement benefits accordingly.

The lifetime allowance was first introduced on 6 April 2006 and since then there have been a number of reductions. Each reduction has been accompanied by a limited opportunity for individuals with pension funds already over the new limit to elect for lifetime allowance protection. The consequence is that the individual keeps the lifetime allowance prior to the reduction as long as no further contributions are made to the fund.

Law: FA 2004, s. 214-226

31.3 Value received within the lifetime allowance

The types of payments authorised to be made out of pension schemes are limited to those listed in s. 164-168. Generally, an individual becomes entitled to access benefits at the age of 55 (scheduled to rise to 57 from 2028 under current government plans) and can choose how to receive benefits. For example, the fund could be taken out as a lump sum, used to buy an annuity, or partially drawn down from year to year. The pension administrator may also be able to use the fund to pay benefits to the individual's dependents or nominated person in the event of the individual's death.

Where a defined benefits scheme has a total fund value equal to or less than 20 x annual pension entitlement (ignoring any separate tax-free cash lump sum), it is possible under trivial commutation rules to take all benefits in a single lump sum. Various conditions apply, including the following:

- the individual must be at least 55, or be retiring early due to ill health;
- no benefit can already have been paid from the scheme; and
- the total value of benefits under all schemes (ignoring any state pension entitlement) cannot exceed £30,000.

The tax treatment of authorised payments made from a pension scheme will depend on the nature of the payment and who receives it. Generally, however, up to 25% of the fund may be taken by the individual as a tax-free lump sum. The remainder will be treated as non-savings income and will be subject to income tax as and when payments are drawn. This income tax will be accounted for by the pension scheme administrator through PAYE.

There are some limited situations where pensions will be treated as exempt and free of tax. For example, pensions relating to awards of bravery, deaths or wounds received during military service, and certain overseas pensions. A full list is included in ITEPA 2003, Pt. 9, Ch. 17-18.

Similarly, some lump sums are tax-free, such as serious ill-health lump sums and refunds of excess contributions.

Pension income from a UK-registered plan is regarded as UK source income, so individuals living abroad remain subject to UK income tax on amounts received. This is, of course, subject to any contrary provision in any applicable double taxation agreement (see **Chapter 35**).

Law: FA 2004, s. 164-171, 212, Sch. 29, para. 7-9; ITEPA 2003, s. 636A, and Pt. 9, Ch. 17-18

31.4   Unauthorised payments to members

If a payment is made, to or in respect of a member, by a registered pension scheme which is not an authorised payment within s. 164-168, it is by default an unauthorised payment.

An unauthorised payment can give rise to up to three separate tax charges:

- the unauthorised payments charge – an income tax charge at a flat rate of 40% (regardless of the marginal rate at which the individual pays tax), based on the value of the unauthorised payment;
- the unauthorised payments surcharge – where unauthorised payments reach or go above 25% of the total value of the individual's rights in the fund over a set period of time, an additional income tax charge at a rate of 15% will be due, based on the value of the unauthorised payment; and
- the scheme sanction charge – this is a charge on the scheme administrator at a rate of 40% (reduced to as low as 15% where the unauthorised payments charge has been paid).

It can also lead to de-registration of the pension scheme.

Law: FA 2004, s. 160, 208-212, 238-239

31.5   Pitfalls and planning points

Changes to annual allowance after drawdown from defined contribution schemes

Certain trigger events will lead to a reduced annual allowance for defined contribution arrangements, with no ability to bring forward unused allowances from previous years (see **30.4.5**). Consideration should be given to the impact of this when planning drawdown.

32. State pension provision

32.1 Introduction

There have been a number of important changes to the state pension regime since its introduction, the most recent being in April 2016. As such, the nature and level of state pension paid varies from individual to individual depending on the date of birth. Essentially, though, there are a number of common features:

- The state pension is not available before state pension age is reached. This is currently 66 for men and women, although it will increase to age 67 between 2026 and 2028.

- Entitlement to state pension generally relies on the number of qualifying years an individual has. The exact meaning of a qualifying year varies, depending on which scheme is being considered, but fundamentally it is linked to paying sufficient NIC or receiving NIC credit.

- It is not necessary to stop working when state pension age is reached.

- If an individual moves overseas, it is still possible to receive a state pension providing sufficient qualifying years exist, although the amount paid will not be increased during years of absence unless in the EU, EEA, Switzerland or countries with which the UK has a reciprocal agreement (excluding New Zealand and Canada).

Special provision is made in relation to pensions for members of the armed forces, and other personnel killed or injured in military action. Further details can be obtained from Veterans UK, part of the Ministry of Defence.

Law: SSCBA 1992, Pt. 2-6; *Pensions Act* 2014, Pt. 1-3

32.2 Pre-2016 state pension

For men born before 6 April 1951, and women born before 6 April 1953, the state pension consists of two components:

- basic state pension; and
- additional state pension.

The full basic state pension is £137.60 per week for 2021-22, and is based on having at least 30 qualifying years. A qualifying year is defined in SSCBA 1992, s. 21-23A and Sch. 3, para. 5-5A, but essentially will depend on the individual having paid sufficient NIC (either through working or by paying voluntary contributions) or, in certain circumstances, receiving NIC credits while in receipt of state benefits.

Men born before 1945, and women born before 1950, need 44 and 39 qualifying years respectively to get a full state pension. Men with fewer than 11 qualifying years, and women with under ten years, do not have any entitlement at all.

Where an individual does not qualify for the full basic state pension, voluntary contributions can sometimes be made. Top-ups may also be available based on contributions by a spouse or civil partner.

The basic state pension increases every year (under the so-called "triple lock") by the highest of:

- the average percentage growth in UK wages;
- the percentage growth in prices in the UK as measured by the consumer prices index (CPI); and
- 2.5%.

The additional state pension is paid on top of the basic state pension. If eligible, it is paid automatically (i.e. with no need to submit a claim). The computation of the amount payable is complex and dependent on a number of factors including:

- the number of years for which a sufficient amount of NIC was paid or credited;
- prior to 6 April 2016, whether the individual had "contracted out" of the scheme and, as such, paid a lower NIC rate;
- whether an individual has the right to inherit entitlement for a deceased spouse or civil partner;
- whether there is a pension-sharing arrangement in force following divorce; and
- whether the individual qualifies for old age, dependent children or disability enhancements.

More details can be found in SSCBA 1992, Pt. 3.

Recipients may have chosen to defer their pensions for an enhanced rate or, in certain circumstances, a lump sum. See SSCBA 1992, s. 55 and Sch. 5 for more details.

Law: SSCBA 1992, s. 21-23A, 43-61A, 78; Sch. 3, Pt. 1; Sch. 5

32.3   New state pension

The "new" state pension regime applies to men born on or after 6 April 1951 and women born on or after 6 April 1953. To have any entitlement, an individual has to have a minimum of ten qualifying years.

To obtain the full new state pension (£179.60 per week for 2021-22), an individual must be at or above state pension age and have at least 35 qualifying years.

A qualifying year has the same definition as for the basic and additional state pension (see. **32.2** and SSCBA 1992, s. 22-23).

The new state pension has to be claimed in order to be payable and can be deferred for an increased amount in the future (PA 2014, s. 16-17).

Transitional provisions apply where qualifying years have accrued prior to 6 April 2016 (typically those born before the year 2000 or becoming UK resident before 2016). In summary, a "starting amount" of the new state pension is calculated based on the higher of:

- the amount under the old state pension rules (which includes basic state pension and additional state pension); and
- the amount if the new state pension had been in place at the start of working life (but subject to a deduction if contracted out prior to 6 April 2016).

If the starting amount is above the full new state pension, any excess is a "protected payment" and will be paid on top of the full new state pension. Where the starting amount is less than the full new state pension, qualifying years after 6 April 2016 can continue to increase entitlement until either the full amount or state pension age is reached.

The new state pension increases every year by the highest of:

- the average percentage growth in UK wages;
- the percentage growth in prices in the UK as measured by the CPI; and
- 2.5%.

A protected payment increases each year in line with the CPI.

Law: *Pensions Act* 2014, Pt. 1-3

32.4   Other main state pension benefits

32.4.1   Graduated retirement benefit

This depends on the graduated NIC paid by employees when the graduated pension scheme existed (from 1961 to 1975).

Law: *National Insurance Act* 1965, s. 36-37

32.4.2   Industrial death benefit

If an individual died before 1988 as a result of an industrial accident, industrial death benefit is paid to the surviving spouse until he or she re-marries or forms a civil partnership.

Law: SSCBA 1992, s. 94 and Sch. 7, Pt. 6

32.4.3   Widowed parent's allowance

Widowed parent's allowance applies if an individual:

- died between 9 April 2001 and 5 April 2017, having paid sufficient NIC (or as a result of an industrial accident or disease); and
- leaves a surviving spouse or civil partner who is below state pension age, and who is pregnant or entitled to child benefit (see **33.5.7**) for at least one child.

Where applicable, it is paid until the earlier of the surviving spouse or civil partner reaching state pension age or ceasing to be entitled to child benefit.

Widowed parent's allowance replaced widowed mother's allowance. The latter should no longer have any active participants.

Law: SSCBA 1992, s. 39A

32.4.4   Widow's pension

Where an individual died before 9 April 2001, the surviving spouse may have been entitled to widow's pension. The amount varies according to the age of the survivor and the amount of NIC paid by the deceased. Where applicable, it is paid until the survivor reaches pension age or, if earlier, re-marries or starts living with a partner. It is not paid at the same time as widowed mother's allowance.

Law: SSCBA 1992, s. 38

32.5 Taxation of pension benefits

UK social security pensions are chargeable to income tax as pension income under ITEPA 2003, Pt. 9, Ch. 5.

Section 577 specifies that the following are treated as pension income:

- the state pension (**32.2** and **32.3** above);
- graduated retirement benefit (**32.4.1**);
- industrial death benefit (**32.4.2**);
- widowed parent's allowance (**32.4.3**); and
- widow's pension (**32.4.4**).

The person liable for the tax is the person receiving or entitled to the pension, benefit or allowance (see ITEPA 2003, s. 579).

Where an old-style pension has been deferred in return for a lump sum, the whole sum will be taxable at the recipient's top rate of income tax in the year of receipt. When the lump sum is paid, the Pensions Service deducts tax at the rate its records show to be the individual's top rate, but this may not be correct, and can result in an overpayment or a shortfall.

Any tax is calculated on an arising basis, i.e. when there is an entitlement to the pension payment as opposed to when it is received.

Tax may be accounted for through self-assessment, or under PAYE if the individual is also receiving a private pension or ongoing employment income. Another possibility is that it will be collected directly by HMRC through simple assessment.

Law: ITEPA 2003, s. 577-579; F(No. 2)A 2005, s. 7-10

32.6 Pitfalls and planning points

HMRC online checking system

The various changes to the state pension regimes (and the complexity of the rules) means that a person's entitlement and consequential tax liability must be assessed on an individual basis.

To assist, HMRC have created a useful online service which an individual can use to check his or her likely entitlement, based on NIC and credits, though mistakes in the NIC record are not uncommon.

Guidance: https://www.gov.uk/check-state-pension

33. Non-pension state benefits

33.1 Introduction

In addition to state pension provision (see **Chapter 32**) and statutory payments (see **Chapter 12**), various benefits and payments are available to support those on a low income. These change and evolve on a regular basis to meet the needs of the population, for example the additional support provided to meet the challenges posed by Covid-19 (see **Appendix 11**).

An overall cap applies in certain circumstances to the amount of benefits that can be received (see **33.3**).

Various sources of guidance are available (see below).

The tax treatment of the amounts paid depends on the nature of the payment and is set out in ITEPA 2003, Pt. 10. Other key statutory provisions referred to in this chapter include the *Social Security Contributions and Benefits Act* 1992 (SSCBA 1992), the *Jobseekers Act* 1995 (JSA 1995) and the *Welfare Reform Act* 2012 (WRA 2012).

Guidance: https://www.gov.uk/benefits-calculators; https://revenue benefits.org.uk (HMRC guidance); https://tinyurl.com/4xjv7my7 (LITRG guidance to state benefits); https://www.entitledto.co.uk (for calculation of benefit entitlement)

33.2 Taxation of benefits

ITEPA 2003, s. 660(1) and Pt. 10, Ch. 4 provide that the following payments are subject to income tax:

- carer's allowance;
- carer's allowance supplement;
- employment and support allowance (ESA);
- income support except to the extent it is attributable to a child maintenance bonus (s. 666); and
- jobseeker's allowance (JSA).

Income support, income and contribution-related ESA, and income-related JSA have now been replaced by universal credit (see **33.5.1**) for new claimants, although previous awards continue to be paid where relevant. More details on the benefits currently available are set out in **33.4** below.

In each case, the taxable amount for any tax year is the amount a person becomes entitled to in that tax year.

Payments received from overseas jurisdictions are taxable if they are equivalent to a taxable UK payment.

Any tax due can usually be dealt with by an adjustment to the individual's tax code if he or she has other sources of income taxable under PAYE. Simple assessment is also designed to address circumstances like these. In other cases, a self-assessment return will be needed, although there will only be tax to pay if annual taxable income exceeds the available personal allowances.

A list of exempt benefits can be found at s. 677(1). Of particular note is child benefit. Although included in s. 677(1), a high income individual will suffer additional tax which effectively claws back the child benefit paid (see **33.5.7** below). Further details of other key exempt benefits can be found in **33.5**.

Law: SSCBA 1992, s. 24, 28, 30A-30B, 40-41, 70, 124; JSA 1995 s. 1; ITEPA 2003, s. 658, 660-681A; WRA 2007, s. 1; *Social Security (Scotland) Act 2018*, s. 24, 28

33.3   Benefit cap

The benefit cap is a limit on the total amount of benefits an individual can receive in any one week. The cap applies to most people aged 16 or over who have not reached state pension age. An individual's state pension age will depend on his or her date of birth, as the age is being raised over a period of years.

There are exceptions; for example, the cap does not apply where there is a disability or health condition that prevents an individual from working, or where the benefits being paid relate to military service. The most common exceptions in practice are for people in work; the cap does not apply, for example:

- to SEISS or to Covid-19 furlough payments;
- to individuals who are in work and who are entitled to working tax credits (whether or not they are actually receiving them);
- where the claimant and his or her partner are between them earning at least the amount they would receive for 16 hours a week if claiming universal credit; or

- for certain disability benefits or for carer's allowance and related allowances.

Furthermore, the benefit cap will not apply for a grace period of nine months following an application for universal credit (see **33.5.1**) where earnings (including any partner's earnings) were at least equivalent to 16 hours of work per week at the level of the national minimum wage for the 12 months prior to the application.

Law: WRA 2012, s. 96-97; SI 2013/376, Pt. 7

33.4   Key taxable benefits

33.4.1   Employment and support allowance

Employment and support allowance (ESA) may be available if:

- an individual has a disability or health condition that affects the ability to work; or
- an individual is self-isolating or shielding because of Covid-19.

A claimant can be employed, self-employed or out of work, although he or she must:

- be under state pension age;
- not be claiming JSA (see **33.4.3**) or statutory sick pay (see **12.2**);
- be working fewer than 16 hours a week and earning less than £140; and
- have paid enough NIC, or have sufficient NIC credits, over a prescribed period (usually in the preceding two years).

The amount depends on personal circumstances and the reason for needing ESA.

Law: WRA 2007, Pt. 1

33.4.2   Carer's allowance and carer's allowance supplement

If an individual cares for someone for at least 35 hours a week, and the person being cared for is in receipt of certain other benefits, carer's allowance is available of £67.60 per week (in 2021-22). However, the allowance is not available if weekly earnings exceed £128 (2021-22).

The carer does not have to be related to, or live with, the person he or she is caring for, although only one carer's allowance is available if that person has more than one carer.

For individuals living in Scotland, a carer's allowance supplement is available, which is payable twice a year to anyone receiving carer's allowance.

Law: SSCBA 1992, s. 70; SS(S)A 2018, s. 24, 28

33.4.3   Jobseeker's allowance

Income-related jobseeker's allowance (JSA) has been replaced by universal credit. A new style JSA is, however, available if an individual:

- is 18 or above but below state pension age, although there are some limited circumstances where 16 to 17 year-olds qualify;
- is available for work;
- is not in full-time education;
- is working fewer than 16 hours per week on average;
- is taking reasonable steps to look for work or additional work;
- is living in England, Scotland or Wales;
- is entitled to work in the UK; and
- has paid sufficient Class 1 NIC or received NIC credits (usually in the last two to three years).

Self-employed individuals who have only paid Class 2 NIC are usually ineligible.

Where payable, the amount of JSA depends on age and other income. The income and savings of any partner are ignored in determining eligibility.

Law: *Jobseekers Act* 1995, s. 1-2

33.5   Key exempt benefits

33.5.1   Universal credit

For new claimants, universal credit has replaced working tax credit, child tax credit, housing benefit, income support, income-based JSA and income-related ESA. Tax credits are, however, still given for many existing claimants (see **33.5.2** below).

To be eligible for universal credit, an individual must:

- be 18 or above, but below state pension age, although there are some limited circumstances where 16 to 17 year olds qualify;
- be on a low income or out of work;
- have £16,000 or less in savings (including the savings of any partner); and
- live in the UK.

Ordinarily, individuals in full-time training or education are excluded, but they may still be eligible if they are:

- 21 or under, and do not have parental support and are not in local authority care; or
- they are responsible for a child.

Universal credit consists of a standard allowance with a series of enhancements and deductions depending on the exact circumstances, for example, the number of children in the family, whether help with housing costs is needed, or whether the claimant has a disability or health condition.

The standard allowance for 2021-22 can be found at the link given in **Appendix 11**. Various amounts may be added to the standard allowance, together adding up to the "maximum amount". Details are given in the *Universal Credit Regulations* 2013 (SI 2013/376), but the websites listed at the end of **33.1** above probably offer a more practical resource.

Universal credit is designed to encourage people to work, but payments reduce by £0.63 for every pound of earnings above the "work allowance". This work allowance is £515 per month, unless assistance with housing costs is also being given, in which case it reduces to £293. However, the work allowance only applies if the claimant has one or more children or qualifying young persons, or has limited ability to work.

For employed people, the data used for universal credit is fed across directly from the RTI PAYE system, so employers should be aware that the data they provide via RTI can affect their employees' benefits. A particular point is that the timing of pay days can cause problems if two pay days fall into the same month for universal credit. This can happen if (for example) the payroll is run early because of a bank holiday – an employee who receives double the pay in one month but none the next will have wild fluctuations in his or her entitlement to universal credit.

For the self-employed, there is no relief for universal credit purposes for trading losses (in contrast to the tax credits rules). Also, the self-employed can be affected by the minimum income floor (though this has been temporarily relaxed in response to the Covid-19 pandemic).

Law: WRA 2012, Pt. 1; SI 2013/376

33.5.2   Tax credits and the transition to universal credit

Working tax credit (WTC) and child tax credit (CTC) were introduced for the tax year 2003-04. The *Welfare Reform Act* 2012 replaced them with universal credit (see **33.5.1**), but tax credits will continue to be paid to existing claimants until:

- they make a claim for universal credit, or for another benefit that has been replaced by universal credit; or
- a change of circumstances brings their tax credits claim to an end (see below).

Meanwhile, no new claims are permitted. In due course, all remaining tax credit claimants will be transferred to universal credit by a process known as "managed migration". Before the pandemic this was expected to be completed by September 2024, but in March 2020 the pilot to test the process was suspended, so the timetable is now uncertain.

WTC is payable to people in work who are on a low income, whether or not they have children. They must normally work for more than a certain number of hours a week, depending on their circumstances. CTC is payable to people with responsibility for a child or children, whether or not they are in work. Depending on hours worked, lone parents and couples who both work can get help with up to 70% of their childcare costs by claiming the childcare element of WTC, which is paid to the main carer along with CTC.

Tax credits, along with child benefit (see **33.5.7**) and guardian's allowance, are administered by HMRC. Entitlement is for the whole or part of a tax year, and is dependent on the eligible person (or persons) making a claim for them. A claim may be made jointly, by members of a couple, or by a single person, and comes to an end automatically if:

- the couple can no longer claim as such (for example, one of them dies or goes abroad for any length of time, or they separate or divorce); or

- a single person can no longer make a single claim (for example, because he or she enters into a relationship and forms part of a couple).

A couple can be married or unmarried, of opposite sexes or the same sex.

Tax credits entitlement is assessed on the basis of the claimants' circumstances and income during the course of a tax year. The claimants' circumstances include their age, their usual hours of work, whether they have certain disabilities, whether they are responsible for a child or children and whether a child has a disability. The claimants' income for the tax year is taken as a whole and is deemed to accrue from day to day throughout the year. Changes of circumstances must be reported promptly. HMRC may recover any overpayments, either by reducing the ongoing award or by direct collection, and underpayments can be made good when identified.

Administrative aspects such as information powers, enquiries, penalties and appeals are based on their equivalents in the tax system, but appeals are routed to the Social Entitlement Chamber of the First-tier Tribunal rather than to the Tax Chamber, and onwards to the Administrative Appeals Chamber of the Upper Tribunal.

Law: *Tax Credits Act* 2002, and associated regulations
Guidance: https://revenuebenefits.org.uk

33.5.3   *Personal independence payment*

A personal independence payment (PIP) is available to meet additional costs where an individual has long-term ill-health or disability.

To be eligible, an individual must:

- be aged 16 or over and usually not have reached state pension age;
- have had difficulties with daily living or getting around (or both) for three months as a result of a health condition or disability, and expect these difficulties to continue for at least nine months;
- be living in England, Scotland or Wales at the time of the claim; and
- have ordinarily lived in England, Scotland or Wales for at least two of the last three years.

PIP may be available sooner if the individual is terminally ill (expected to have less than six months to live).

The amount of PIP is between £23.70 and £152.15 a week in 2021-22, depending on the impact the health condition or disability has on the individual. This is determined by a health professional and regularly reviewed.

Law: WRA 2012, Pt. 4

33.5.4   Attendance allowance

Attendance allowance is payable to individuals living in the UK over state pension age where there is a physical or mental disability that requires carer support or help.

The allowance is paid at two rates (£89.60 and £60 per week in 2021-22) depending on the level of care needed.

Law: SSCBA 1992, s. 64-66

33.5.5   Industrial injuries disablement benefit

Industrial injuries disablement benefit (IIDB) is available if an individual becomes ill or disabled as a result of an accident at work or an occupational disease such as asbestosis.

The amount received depends on the extent of the disability, as assessed by a health professional.

SSCBA 1992, Pt. 5 contains details on eligibility.

Where IIDB is paid, other non-pension benefits will be reduced accordingly.

Law: SSCBA 1992, Pt. 5

33.5.6   Maternity allowance

Maternity allowance may be payable when a pregnant woman does not qualify for statutory maternity pay (see **12.3**).

The amount of maternity allowance is the lower of 90% of average weekly earnings or £151.97 in 2021-22. To qualify for the maximum pay period of up to 39 weeks, the woman must:

- in most cases, be employed or self-employed at the eleventh week before the baby is due;

- during the 66 weeks before the baby is due, have been employed or self-employed for 26 weeks;
- have earned at least £30 a week in at least 13 weeks (which do not need to be consecutive); and
- if self-employed, have paid Class 2 NIC for at least 13 of the 66 weeks before the baby is due.

If the individual does not qualify for the full amount, a reduced period of up to 14 weeks may still be available in some circumstances.

Maternity allowance will stop when the woman returns to work. Where paid, it will reduce entitlement to other non-pension benefits payable at the same time.

Law: SSCBA 1992, s. 35-35B

33.5.7   Child benefit

Child benefit is available if the individual is responsible for bringing up a child who is either:

- under the age of 16; or
- under the age of 20 and in approved education or training (for example, GCSEs or A levels or equivalent).

Child benefit is paid every four weeks. For 2021-22, the level of benefit is:

- £21.15 a week for the eldest (or only) child; and
- an additional £14 a week for each additional child.

Only one person can get child benefit for a child. Where a child lives with a couple one of whom works, the other should claim the benefit as the main carer in order to secure the NIC credits (which are not needed by the member of the couple who is in work).

Everyone who qualifies can obtain child benefit, although there is a "high income child benefit charge" (HICBC) where the adjusted net income of either the claimant or his or her partner exceeds £50,000. This charge effectively claws back 1% of the child benefit for every £100 of adjusted net income in excess of £50,000. This is paid to HMRC through the self-assessment process.

"Adjusted net income" is essentially taxable income less the gross amount of any personal pension contributions and gift aid donations but before personal allowances.

Example

Iris is a single mother with two children (aged 14 and 10). She has employment income of £60,000 and pays personal pension contributions of £150 per month.

Her child benefit for the year is 52 x (£21.15 + £14) = £1,827.80.

Her net income for the purpose of the HICBC is £60,000 less gross pension contributions of £2,250 (£150 × 12 × 100/80) = £57,750.

The excess over £50,000 is £7,750.

$£7,750/100 \times 1\% = 77.5\%$.

Therefore the clawback is 77.5% of the child benefit claimed.

$77.5\% \times £1,827.80 = £1,416.55$.

As an alternative to paying the HICBC, an election can be made not to receive the child benefit. This may avoid the administration of completing a self-assessment tax return and repaying the child benefit where income is above £60,000 (and therefore the full 100% of child benefit is repayable).

Some care is needed here. The process of claiming child benefit, and then opting out of receiving it, provides the individual claimant with NIC credits. These NIC credits are not available if child benefit is not claimed at all.

It is obviously important that a person who opts out should remember to opt back in again if income falls to a level where the HICBC no longer applies.

It will not usually be advantageous to opt out of receiving child benefit unless adjusted net income for the year is £60,000 or more.

Where there is a couple in the same household (whether married, in a civil partnership or co-habiting), the charge rests with the person with the higher income.

Law: SSCBA 1992, s. 13A; ITEPA 2003, Pt. 10, Ch. 8

33.6 Pitfalls and planning points

Child benefit

The HICBC is based on the income of one of the partners only (not on combined income). Therefore, a household with two partners each earning £50,000 will be able to claim the full child benefit without any clawback, but a household with one partner with income of £60,000 will lose it all. Therefore, if it is possible to equalise income between spouses/partners, this should be considered.

Furthermore, increasing pension contributions (subject to obtaining appropriate financial advice) has the effect of reducing adjusted net income and may decrease the charge if it can bring adjusted net income to below £60,000 (see **33.5.7** above).

Impact of Covid-19

There have been a number of adjustments to state social security provision as a result of the Covid-19 pandemic. These are drawn together in **Appendix 11**.

INTERNATIONAL ASPECTS

34. Residence

34.1 Introduction

A person's tax residence status is fundamental in determining how he or she will be taxed in the UK. Residents are taxed on their worldwide income, whereas non-residents are taxed only on their UK-sourced income, such as dividends from UK companies (UK incorporated and resident), interest from UK bank accounts and earnings from work physically performed in the UK.

When establishing whether income is taxable in the UK, an individual has to look at his or her residence status at the time the income arises and not when it is received, even though that is when it is taxed in the UK.

Example

Marvin has been assigned to the US for a few years by his UK employer. He is not resident for the 2022-23 tax year, but was resident for 2021-22.

Every May, Marvin receives an annual bonus in respect of his work, generally for the previous year to 31 December.

His bonus for the year to 31 December 2021, which he receives in May 2022, will remain taxable in full in the UK even though he received it when he was not resident, as he was resident throughout all of the year to 31 December 2021 when the bonus was earnt and so was taxable on his worldwide income during this year.

The bonus for the year to 31 December 2022 will need to be apportioned between the time he is resident and not resident, the former being taxed in the UK, the latter not being taxed (assuming he did not perform any work in the UK while not resident).

Home

For the statutory residence test (see **34.2**) and split-year treatment (see **34.3**), reference is frequently made to "home". This is perhaps one of the more ambiguous areas of the residence rules, as there is no real definition of the concept in the legislation.

A person's home will be determined broadly by the facts of his or her situation and circumstances, with the term taking on its normal everyday meaning. It is a place where someone stays with a reasonable degree of stability and permanence. It can be a building, vessel, vehicle or some other structure used by an individual as a home, and can still be a home even if it is temporarily unavailable (e.g. if it is being renovated).

Residential accommodation is not treated as an individual's home if the accommodation is being commercially let and the individual has no right to live there. Furthermore, it is not a person's home if the property is advertised for sale or let and the individual lives in another residence.

A property does not need to be owned by the individual for it to be regarded as his or her home, so rented or employer-provided accommodation, would also count as a home. Similarly, a home can be a place where someone is simply living with a family member, relative or friend.

Guidance: RDRM 13020-13060

34.2   Statutory residence test

34.2.1   Basic rule

Since 2013-14, tax residence in the UK is established under the statutory residence test (SRT).

The basic rule under the SRT is that an individual is resident in the UK for a tax year if he or she meets:

- the automatic residence test (which is made up of automatic overseas and UK tests); or
- the sufficient ties test.

Law: FA 2013, Sch. 45
Guidance: RDRM 11000; RDR3

34.2.2   The automatic residence tests

Legislation gives priority to the automatic overseas tests first, and then the automatic UK tests over the sufficient ties test (see **34.2.3**). This means that an individual should consider the tests in that order.

An individual will be resident in the UK if he or she meets one of the automatic UK tests and none of the automatic overseas tests.

Automatic overseas tests

If any one of the automatic overseas tests is satisfied, the individual is automatically not resident.

The automatic overseas tests are that the individual:

- was resident in one or more of the previous three tax years but is present in the UK for fewer than 16 days in the current tax year;

- was not resident in the UK in all the previous three tax years and is present in the UK for fewer than 46 days in the current tax year; or

- leaves the UK to work sufficient hours overseas (often referred to as full-time work overseas or the third automatic overseas test), providing he or she is in the UK for fewer than 91 days in the tax year and no more than 30 days are spent working in the UK during the tax year (the 91 and 30 days are reduced on a *pro rata* basis if split-year treatment (see 34.3) is applicable in the tax year). In addition, there must be no significant break in the overseas work.

An individual who does not meet any of the above tests progresses to the next part of the SRT and the automatic UK tests.

Automatic UK tests

An individual will be regarded as resident in the UK if he or she meets any one of the following automatic UK tests (and none of the automatic overseas tests is met).

The automatic UK tests are that the individual:

- is present in the UK for 183 or more days in a tax year;

- has a home (see **34.1** above) in the UK, spends at least 30 days in that home during the tax year and there is a period of at least 91 consecutive days (of which at least 30 days must be in the tax year concerned) throughout which he or she:

  o has no home overseas; or

  o has one or more homes overseas but spends fewer than 30 days in these homes during the tax year (a day of presence at a home being a day on which any time at all is spent in the home); or

- works sufficient hours in the UK (again often referred to as full-time work in the UK).

An individual who does not satisfy any of the above tests will progress to the third and final part of the SRT, the sufficient ties test.

Law: FA 2013, Sch. 45, para. 1-16
Guidance: RDRM 11100-11380, 13010

34.2.3   Sufficient ties test

An individual who is not automatically resident under the automatic residence test will need to see if he or she is resident under the sufficient ties test.

This test is met if an individual does not meet any of the automatic overseas tests, or any of the automatic UK tests, and has sufficient ties with the UK. For the sufficient ties test, the individual considers the number of days spent in the UK and the number of specific ties he or she has with the UK. These ties are considered in turn below.

Family tie

An individual has family in the UK if, at any time during the tax year:

- his or her spouse/civil partner (including couples living together, but not separated couples) is resident in the UK; or
- he or she has a minor child who is resident in the UK and the individual spends time with him or her in the UK for at least 61 days (including part days) in the tax year.

For the purposes of the latter test, a child can be disregarded if his time in the UK is because of time spent at a UK educational establishment (full-time) *and* he spends fewer than 21 days in the UK in the tax year when not attending the educational establishment (half terms are regarded as term-time).

Accommodation tie

The individual has UK accommodation if:

- he has a place to live in the UK (regardless of whether it is owned), and this can include a holiday home or some other similar temporary place or other accommodation that is "available" to the individual and where he can live);

- it is available to be used by the individual for a continuous period of at least 91 days in a tax year; and
- he spends at least one night in that place during the tax year.

Where, in the tax year, there is a gap of fewer than 16 days between periods for which a particular place is available, that accommodation will continue to be regarded as being available to the individual during the gap.

Other than accommodation held by an individual's spouse, partner or minor child, accommodation that is the home of a close relative (parent, grandparent, adult child or grandchild, sibling) will only count as a tie if the individual spends more than 15 nights there during a tax year and it is available to him or her for a continuous period of at least 91 days.

Short stays in hotels or guesthouses will be excluded, provided the individual has not booked a room at the same hotel, etc. that covers at least 91 days continuously in a tax year, subject to the 16-day rule mentioned above. Accommodation let out commercially is also excluded.

An accommodation tie has less permanence and degree of stability than a "home" has for the purposes of the automatic UK test. For example, a holiday home does not count for the home automatic UK test, but does for the accommodation tie test.

Guidance: RDRM 13070-13090

Work tie

An individual has a work tie if he or she works in the UK for 40 days or more in a tax year, a working day being a day on which more than three hours of work are performed. There is a separate rule for international transport workers (see FA 2013, Sch. 45, para. 36).

90-day tie

This is when an individual has spent more than 90 days in the UK (present at midnight) in either or both of the previous two tax years. The deeming rule (see **34.2.5**) does not apply for this tie and days spent in the UK during transit or as a result of exceptional circumstances (up to a maximum of 60) can be excluded.

Country tie

This is applicable if the individual spends more days (midnights) in the UK during a tax year than in any other country, or if he or she spends the same number of days in the tax year in more than one country, of which the UK is one, and this is the greatest number of days spent in any country during the tax year. Days spent in the UK during transit or as a result of exceptional circumstances *are* included (see **34.2.5**).

The above ties are then taken into account, together with the number of days spent in the UK. It is also necessary to determine whether a person is an "arriver" or a "leaver".

Arriver

If an individual has not been resident in the UK for the previous three tax years, all the above ties except the country tie are taken into account, along with the number of days spent in the UK during a tax year, as shown in the table below:

Days spent in the UK during a tax year	Residence status depending on ties
Fewer than 46	Not resident
46-90	Resident if individual has four ties
91-120	Resident if individual has three or more ties
121-182	Resident if individual has two or more ties
183 or more	Resident

Leaver

If an individual has been resident in one or more of the previous three tax years, then all the above ties are taken into account, as well as the number of days spent in the UK during a tax year, as shown below.

Days spent in the UK during a tax year	Residence status depending on ties
Fewer than 16	Not resident
16-45	Resident if individual has four or five ties
46-90	Resident if individual has three or more ties
91-120	Resident if individual has two or more ties
121-182	Resident if individual has one or more ties
183 or more	Resident

Law: FA 2013, Sch. 45, para. 17-20, 31-38
Guidance: RDRM 11500-11580, 13300

34.2.4   SRT definitions

Working sufficient hours

This will be met where an employee or self-employed individual works either overseas or in the UK (depending on which test is being considered) and works more than 35 hours or more per week on average. The legislation sets out precisely how this average is calculated for both overseas and UK work.

The reference period over which the average working hours per week are calculated is a tax year for overseas work, but is any 365-day period for UK work falling either wholly or partly in a tax year (with fewer than 25% of total work days performed overseas). The figure may be reduced by:

- reasonable work days on annual, sick or parental leave;
- certain time spent working in the UK (for overseas work) and overseas (for UK work), known as disregarded days – see **34.2.5** below. (Days spent working in both the UK and overseas will also be disregarded for this purpose.);
- gaps between employments of up to 15 days per gap (maximum for the year of 30 days if there is more than one change in employment) – not relevant for self-employment; and
- embedded days, which are non-working days such as public holidays and weekends while on leave, which are preceded and followed by three consecutive days on the above leave.

The resultant number of days in the reference period is divided by seven, and rounded down to the nearest whole number. The number of hours worked overseas or in the UK (depending on the test being looked at) is divided by the result to give the average number of hours per year.

The above reference period is modified if a split year – see **34.3**.

Law: FA 2013, Sch. 45, para. 9(2), 14(3), 28

Significant break

This is where an individual does not carry out more than three hours of work on a day for at least 31 consecutive days – overseas for full-time work overseas or in the UK for full-time work in the UK. If this were to occur, and the gap was not due to annual, sick or parenting leave, the individual will not qualify for full-time work (overseas or in the UK, as the case may be). Care should be taken in this respect of employees working on a rotational basis who return to the UK on their days off shifts, and of individuals returning to the UK on compassionate leave or unexpectedly working in the UK for a period of time, e.g. employees stranded in the UK following the Covid-19 lockdowns.

Law: FA 2013, Sch. 45, para. 29

Working day

A working day is a day where more than three hours' work is performed. Depending on the circumstances, travelling time can count as time spent working. Travel time is considered as time spent working if UK tax relief is available for the individual in respect of the cost of that journey.

Training is counted as time working if paid for or provided by the employer.

Law: FA 2013, Sch. 45, para. 26

Location of work

This will be where a person physically performs the work. Any work done on a journey to or from the UK will be regarded as overseas work according to the following rules:

- For journeys to the UK, the overseas work ceases when a person disembarks from his or her plane, ship, train, etc.
- For journeys from the UK, the overseas work starts when an individual embarks on his or her plane, ship, train, etc.

Law: FA 2013, Sch. 45, para. 27

Exceptional circumstances

For the purposes of the SRT, special rules apply if an individual dies during a tax year or is an international transport worker (see **38.6.4**). The legislation should be referred to in these situations.

Law: FA 2013, Sch. 45, para. 10, 15-16, 30
Guidance: RDRM 11900

34.2.5   Counting days

For all tests, an individual is treated as present in the UK if in fact present in the UK at midnight. However, midnights are excluded for those in transit through the UK at midnight who do not perform any activities (such as attending a business meeting or a social event with friends or family) that are unrelated to the journey.

Deeming rule

There is an anti-avoidance rule, known as the "deeming rule", for those individuals who spend a large number of days in the UK, without being present at midnight.

This deeming rule will apply to individuals who:

- have been resident in the UK for one or more of the three previous tax years;
- have at least three ties for a tax year; and
- are present in the UK on more than 30 days at some point, but not at midnight, during the tax year concerned.

If an individual meets all of the above, any days in excess of 30 days where he or she is present in the UK at any point but not at midnight, will be treated as a day of presence and so will be included when establishing the number of days an individual has spent in the UK during a tax year.

Exceptional circumstances

For certain aspects of the SRT, days spent in the UK due to exceptional circumstances which are beyond the individual's control and which were unforeseen – such as national or local emergencies (e.g. natural disasters, civil unrest or war) or sudden or life-threatening illness or injury – may be disregarded when counting days. However, the number of days that can be disregarded due to exceptional circumstances is restricted to 60 in any tax year.

The individual must intend to leave the UK after the exceptional circumstances have ended, and HMRC have indicated that if someone actually does leave after the exceptional circumstances have ceased, this is evidence that that person had this intention.

HMRC tend to have a very narrow view as to what is an exceptional circumstance. Travel problems such as traffic congestion, or delayed or cancelled trains that cause a flight to be missed, will not be regarded as exceptional.

HMRC have indicated that if a person unexpectedly remains in the UK because of the Covid-19 pandemic, the resultant days in the UK may be disregarded when establishing the person's residence status if, as a result of the virus:

- the individual is quarantined or advised by a health professional or by public health guidance to self-isolate in the UK;
- official government advice is not to travel from the UK;
- the individual is unable to leave the UK as a result of the closure of international borders; or
- the individual's employer requests him or her to return to the UK on a temporary basis.

However, the above 60-day limit is still in place. Furthermore, some of the SRT tests do not recognise exceptional events and still include such days when counting. For example, the automatic full-time work overseas test does include days from exceptional events when looking at whether there is a significant break in the overseas work and whether more than 30 days' work have been performed in the UK.

Law: FA 2013, Sch. 45, para. 22-24
Guidance: RDRM 11005, 11700, 13200, 13400

34.2.6 Examples

Example 1 – British individual moving to work abroad

Sam is a British citizen who has lived all his life in the UK.

He leaves the UK to work in Germany at the end of March 2021, working 7.5 hours per day. As soon as he arrives, he rents an apartment in Germany, which is his home there and is available for his use throughout all of 2021-22.

Sam is married and has two young children. Because of the Covid-19 pandemic, they decide that it is safer and provides more stability for the children if his wife and children remain living in the UK in the family home, which Sam stays in when he visits the UK.

He leaves his job in Germany on 2 June 2021, and on 26 June goes to work for a competitor company, also in Germany and with the same working conditions. He does not visit the UK between jobs. From 25 November 2021, he visits the UK on compassionate leave for his mother's funeral, returning to Germany on 1 December.

From 23 December to 1 January 2022 he takes a holiday in Tanzania with his family, returning to work the next day. From 17 February to 18 March 2022 he takes sick leave with malaria, which he contracted in Tanzania, and during this time spends two weeks recuperating in the UK with his family. He returns to work in Germany on 19 March 2022 until the end of the UK tax year 5 April 2022.

The number of overseas hours worked, after taking into account 11 public holidays within those work days, was 1,447.50 (193 days x 7.5 hours per day).

For 2021-22, Sam does not satisfy the first automatic overseas test (see **34.2.2** above), as he has been present in the UK for more than 15 days. The second automatic overseas test is not applicable as he was resident up to and including 2020-21. Sam therefore needs to see if he has satisfied the third automatic overseas test, and has worked sufficient hours overseas. In this respect, he needs to calculate his days in the UK, which are fewer than 91, so he passes that test, and he has not spent any days working in the UK, passing that test as well.

Sam also has to look at whether he has satisfied the "sufficient hours worked overseas" test, and see whether there is a significant break in his overseas work during the 2021-22 tax year. For the former, Sam needs to establish how many days there are in the reference period. The starting point in this respect is 365 days, being the number of days in the 2021-22 tax year. From this he can deduct certain days as follows.

The change-of-work period is 23 consecutive days, so there is no significant break (being less than 31 days). However, it does exceed the maximum 15 days that can be deducted when looking at the reference period for the sufficient hours worked overseas test, so only the maximum of 15 days can be deducted from the total number of days during 2021-22 of 365 days.

His visit back to the UK for his mother's funeral (of five work days) was compassionate leave, which cannot be deducted. However, Sam's five days of holiday in Tanzania can be (work days excluding weekends and public holidays over the Christmas and new year period). His sick period was 30 days, which again can be deducted, but only up to 22 days, i.e. the days on which he should have been working but was off sick.

Sam can also deduct six embedded days. These are days on which he would not normally be expected to work, and does not actually work, such as weekends and public holidays, and which are embedded in a period of annual, sick or parenting leave. To be embedded the day must both be preceded and followed by three consecutive days of leave. In Sam's case he can deduct six days which were embedded in his block of sick leave. There were no embedded days in his holiday to Tanzania.

The relevant period is, therefore, as follows:

	Days
Total number of days in 2021-22	365
Less:	
Days on annual leave	(5)
Days on sick leave	(22)
Gap between employments – maximum	(15)
Embedded days	(6)
Days in reference period	317

The above figure of 317 days is then divided by 7 to give 45.29 which is round down to 45. The overseas hours of 1,447.50 are rounded up to 1,448 (as they are .5 and above) and this figure is divided by 45 to give 32.17 hours per week on average, which is less than the required figure of 35 hours per week. Sam has not, therefore, met the "sufficient hours worked overseas" test and needs to consider the automatic UK tests.

As an aside, if Sam had performed some work in the UK during 2021-22, then these UK work days would be treated as disregarded days and deducted from the 365 days above, when looking at the number of days in the reference period.

Sam does not satisfy any of the automatic UK tests. He was only present in the UK for 20 days during 2021-22. He does have a home in the UK, but there is no period of at least 91 consecutive days when he does not have a home overseas, so he fails the automatic UK home test. He has not performed any work in the UK during 2021-22, so the full-time work in the UK test does not apply. Sam therefore needs to establish his residence status under the sufficient ties test.

The ties Sam has in the UK during 2021-22 are family, accommodation and the 90-days tie, so three ties. As he was resident in all the three tax years prior to 2021-22 he is a leaver and so can spend up to 45 days in the UK before becoming resident. Sam in total has spent 20 days in the UK and so is not resident for 2021-22 under the sufficient ties test.

Had Sam been working in the UK, such that he had spent 45 days working there during 2021-22, he would still have failed the full-time work overseas test (working more than 30 days in the UK) and acquired the work tie. With four ties, he could only spend up to 16 days in the UK, which would mean he was resident in the UK.

Example 2 – Non-British individual moving to UK

Raj has lived in India all his life.

In June 2021, he visits family in London and decides to emigrate to the UK. He spends the next few months preparing for the move. He ceases his employment in India on 30 November 2021 and sells his Mumbai house (his only home) on 10 January 2022, arriving in the UK on 25 January 2022. He finds a flat in London and moves in on 1 February 2022. The London flat is now his only home and he lives there for a year. He does not find employment in the UK until after 5 April 2022 (so during the 2022-23 tax year).

During the tax year 2021-22, Raj is present in his Mumbai home on 250 days and in his London flat on 55 days. In 2021-22 Raj has a home in the UK from 1 February 2022 and is present in it on at least 30 days during the tax year. Also from 1 February 2022, there is a period of at least 91 consecutive days, of which at least 30 fell in 2021-22, when Raj has a UK home and no overseas home.

As Raj does not meet any of the automatic overseas tests, he is resident in the UK under the second automatic UK test (having a home in the UK) from 6 April 2021, and so taxable on his worldwide income from this date, unless one of the Cases of split-year treatment (see **34.3**) applies.

Example 3 – Non-British individual on secondment to UK

Chloe is a French citizen who has lived all her life in France.

Her French employer sends her on secondment to the UK for a year and she travels to the UK on 1 July 2021 to start work the following day. Her posting finishes on 1 July 2022 and she leaves the UK on 6 August 2022 to return to work full-time in France. While working in the UK she rented out her home in France from 1 July 2021, so it was not available for her own use.

Over the 365-day period to 30 June 2022 (which falls over two tax years, 2021-22 and 2022-23), Chloe calculates that she has worked full time in the UK (in accordance with the sufficient hours worked in the UK test) and has not taken a significant break from her UK work during this period. In addition, over this 365-day period Chloe works for over three hours on 240 days, 196 (82%) being days on which she works for more than three hours in the UK. There is at least one day when Chloe does more than three hours' work per day in the UK in both 2021-22 and 2022-23.

Under the full-time work in the UK test (the third automatic UK test), Chloe is resident in the UK for both 2021-22 and 2022-23, so she is resident for UK tax purposes from 6 April 2021 to 5 April 2023. As a result, she is potentially taxable in the UK on her worldwide income from 6 April 2021 to 5 April 2023.

See **34.3.4** for continuation of this example.

34.3   Split-year treatment

34.3.1   Introduction

If it is established – under the automatic residence or sufficient ties tests – that a person is resident in the UK for a tax year, this will be for the whole tax year. However, split-year treatment may apply to split a tax year between:

- a UK part, when the individual is taxed as a resident and so on his or her worldwide income; and
- an overseas part, when he or she is taxed as if not resident and just on UK-sourced income.

Note that the individual is still regarded as resident for the whole of the tax year, but is *taxed* as if non-resident for the overseas part.

Split-year treatment will apply when a person satisfies one of the following "Cases" (situations).

Law: FA 2013, Sch. 45, para. 39-56
Guidance: RDRM 12000

34.3.2   Relevant Cases for when an individual leaves the UK

Case 1 – starting full-time work overseas

For this Case to apply, all of the following conditions must be satisfied:

- An individual commences working full-time overseas during a tax year and the overseas criteria mentioned below are met between the start date (first day on which more than three hours of work overseas are performed) and the end of the tax year.

   The overseas criteria are:

   ○ The individual works sufficient hours overseas over the above period of overseas work. This will be calculated in accordance with the sufficient hours worked overseas calculation explained at **34.2.3**.

- o During this period of work there are no significant breaks in the individual's overseas work, as explained at **34.2.4**.

- o The number of days in the above work period on which the individual does more than three hours of work per day in the UK, must not exceed the permitted limit set out in a specific HMRC table (see RDRM 12070), which is dependent upon the month in which the start date falls.

- o The number of days spent in the UK during the overseas part of the tax year cannot exceed the permitted limit, which is again set by HMRC's table at RDRM 12070 and which is dependent upon the month in which the start date falls.

- The individual is a tax resident in the UK for the tax year of departure and the previous tax year.

- The individual is non-resident in the UK for the tax year following the year of departure, as a result of meeting the sufficient hours worked overseas test under the automatic overseas tests (see **34.2.1**). It does not matter if the individual is non-resident under any other test of the SRT, the key thing is that he or she must be non-resident for the following tax year because of the sufficient hours worked overseas test.

Case 2 – the partner of someone starting full-time work overseas

A partner is an individual's:

- spouse or civil partner; or

- partner, if living together as husband and wife or civil partners.

This Case applies to an individual if his or her partner satisfies Case 1. In addition:

- He must have been resident for the tax year before the year of departure.

- He must be not resident under any of the SRT tests for the tax year following the year of departure.

- There is a day during the tax year of departure when the individual leaves the UK to live with his partner, who left during the same tax year. The individual could also leave to live with his partner in the tax year following that of the partner's year of departure.

- They must have been living together in the UK before leaving the UK.

- For the period from the deemed departure day (see below) to the following 5 April, the individual has no home in the UK or (if he or she has a home in both the UK and overseas) the individual spends the greater part of his or her time living in the overseas home and does not spend more than the permitted level of days in the UK during this period, as per an HMRC table (see RDRM 12070).

See **34.1** above for the meaning of "home".

The deemed departure day mentioned above depends on when the individual's partner qualifies for split-year treatment under Case 1. If the individual leaves the UK during the same tax year as the partner, this will be the later of when he or she leaves the UK and the first day of the overseas part of the year under Case 1 for the partner. If the individual leaves during the following tax year, the deemed departure day will be the day that he or she moves overseas to live with the partner.

The overseas part of the tax year will be from the deemed departure day until the following 5 April.

Case 3 – ceasing to have a home in the UK (and living overseas)

This Case will apply if all of the following apply:

- An individual was resident for the tax year prior to the year of departure.

- He or she is not resident for the tax year following the year of departure.

- At the beginning of the tax year of departure, the individual has a home in the UK, but ceases to have one in the UK at some point during the year of departure and continues not to have one from this day until the following 5 April.

- From the date of ceasing to have a home in the UK, until the following 5 April, the individual spends fewer than 16 midnights in the UK.

- One of the following conditions is met:
    - within the six-month period commencing from this date, the individual's only home (or homes) is (or are) in the country to which he or she has moved, or the individual is regarded as tax resident in that country; or
    - the individual has spent every midnight during this six-month period in the country to which he or she has moved.

The last requirement is particularly onerous to meet, as the individual has to spend every single night of this six-month period in the country to which he or she has moved (the host country). It follows that he will not satisfy this if he were to visit another country, say on holiday or a business visit, and spend a midnight there.

Similarly, if there is a gap between the individual ceasing to have a home in the UK and moving to the host country, then again this last condition will not be met, for example if he or she ceases to have a home in the UK before leaving. This would be a problem if the person were to leave the UK and take a holiday in another country on the way to the host country, or even if the flight left the UK before midnight but arrived after midnight in the host country so that he or she is not in the host country at the midnight following the last midnight in the UK.

For Case 3 to apply in this scenario, it is advisable for the individual to be sure of satisfying one of the other sufficient link tests, of either having his or her only home in the host country or becoming tax resident there within six months.

Another issue may be what constitutes a "home". Generally, holiday homes do not, but this could become an area of dispute with HMRC as to whether or not a property is a home, especially for properties in different countries. See also **34.1** above.

The above 16-day rule remains the same regardless of when the individual leaves the UK, so it will potentially be more difficult for an individual to satisfy this test the earlier in the tax year he or she leaves.

Under this Case the individual is required to cease having a home in the UK, so the Case will not apply if he maintains the UK home and it is available for his own use, for example:

- the individual's spouse and family remain living there; or
- the spouse and family do move to the host country with the individual, but the home is not rented out, so that they can stay there when visiting the UK.

If this Case were to apply, the overseas part of the split year will be from when the individual ceases to have a UK home until the following 5 April, with the UK part being from the previous 6 April until the day before he or she ceases to have a UK home.

If more than one Case above applies, Case 1 always takes precedence over the other two Cases, and Case 2 takes priority over Case 3.

Law: FA 2013, Sch. 45, para. 44-46
Guidance: RDRM 12040-12140

34.3.3   *Relevant Cases for when an individual arrives in the UK*

Case 4 – *starting to have a home only in the UK*

This Case will apply if an individual's only home starts being in the UK some time during the tax year of his or her return and continues to be so for the rest of that tax year.

The individual must have been non-resident in the tax year prior to the year of arrival and must not have met the only-home-in-the-UK test (see below) at the start of the tax year of arrival.

The individual must also not meet the sufficient ties test (see **34.2.3**) for the overseas part of the tax year, i.e. from 6 April to the day before he or she starts to satisfy the only home test. In this respect, the days in the tables under **34.2.2** are modified as per RDRM 12150.

The only home test in this respect is different from the only home test under the automatic UK tests at **34.2.1**. The test is satisfied if a person's only home is in the UK (or, if there is more than one home, they are all in the UK).

The date the individual potentially first satisfies the only home test will be when his only home is in the UK (or if more than one home these are all in the UK) and he has ceased having an overseas home.

The overseas part will be from 6 April to the day before the individual first has a home in the UK.

Case 5 – starting full-time work in the UK

This Case will apply if an individual:

- starts to have a period of 365 days in the tax year of his or her arrival where the full-time employment in the UK test as explained at **34.2.1** is satisfied;

- is non-resident in the tax year prior to the year of arrival; and

- does not meet the sufficient ties test in the overseas part of the tax year, i.e. from 6 April to the day before he or she starts working full-time in the UK under the third UK test at **34.2.1**.

The tables at **34.2.3** are modified by RDRM 12170.

The UK part will start on the first day on which more than three hours' work in the UK is done, and will run to the following 5 April.

Case 6 – ceasing full-time work overseas

This Case will apply if an individual:

- returns to the UK following a period of working full-time abroad;

- is resident in the tax year following that of his or her return;

- was not resident in the tax year prior to the year of return as a result of the full-time work overseas test under **34.2.1**; but

- was resident in one or more of the four tax years prior to that previous tax year (e.g. if an individual returned during 2021-22 this four-year period would be for 2016-17 to 2019-20).

There also needs to be a period – starting on 6 April for the tax year of return until the last day on which the individual does more than three hours of work overseas – during which he or she:

- has worked sufficient hours overseas (see **34.2.3**);

- has no significant break in his or her overseas work; and

- has not spent or worked for too many days in the UK. For these permitted days in the UK, reference should be made to a specific HMRC table at RDRM 12200. The result will depend on when the individual returns to the UK during the tax year.

Case 7 – partner of someone who is ceasing to work full-time overseas

This case applies if the individual:

- is not resident for the tax year prior to the year of arrival;
- is resident for the tax year following the year of arrival;
- has a partner who satisfies Case 6 split-year treatment either in the same or the previous tax year;
- moves to the UK to be able to live with his or her partner upon arrival in the UK;
- for the period between 6 April and the deemed arrival day (see below):
  - has no home in the UK; or
  - has homes in both the UK and overseas, and spends the greater part of his or her time living in the overseas home; and
- for the above period, spends no more than the permitted level of days in the UK, in accordance with the specific HMRC table at RDRM 12220, which is dependent on the month of the deemed arrival day.

The deemed arrival day referred to above is the later of the day the individual moves back to the UK to live with his or her partner or the day the partner's UK part of the tax year commences.

The overseas part of the year under this Case ceases on the day before the deemed arrival day.

Case 8 – starting to have a home in the UK

This case differs from Case 4 in that it refers only to having a home in the UK, as opposed to Case 4 which refers to a person's *only* home being in the UK.

This case will apply if all of the following conditions are met:

- An individual is non-resident in the tax year prior to the year of arrival, and is resident for the tax year following the year of arrival, with split-year treatment not applying for that year.
- At the beginning of the tax year of arrival, the individual has no home in the UK, but during this tax year acquires a UK home and continues to have a UK home until the following 5 April

and throughout the following tax year. So, for example, an individual arriving in the UK during 2021-22 would need to have a UK home until 5 April 2023.

- From 6 April until the day before acquiring a UK home, he or she has no sufficient ties with the UK. The days shown at **34.2.3** are modified by RDRM 12150.

The year is split from when the individual first acquires a home in the UK, so the overseas part is until the day before this happens.

Issues with this Case may arise if the individual returns to the UK and acquires a home, but then ceases to have that home during the tax year of arrival or the following tax year, even if acquiring another UK home later in the tax year – for example, if a person stays in rented accommodation initially but then buys a house to move to. In this scenario there must be no gap between moving out of the rental property and into the purchased property until the end of the tax year following that of an individual's arrival. If there is such a gap between the two homes then this Case will not apply.

In addition, this Case will not apply if an individual has maintained a home in the UK for his or her own use while living overseas.

Where more than one case applies

If more than one Case applies:

- Case 6 has precedence over all the other Cases unless Case 5 has an earlier date.
- If Case 6 does not apply, Case 7 will have priority over the other Cases, unless again Case 5 has an earlier date.
- If the only Cases that apply are Cases 4, 5 and 8, the Case with the earliest date will take priority.

Law: FA 2013, Sch. 45, para. 47-51
Guidance: RDRM 12150-12280

34.3.4   The Cases in practice

Example 1 – Chloe (cont.)

Following on from Example 3 under **34.2.6**, Chloe is resident under the SRT for the whole of the tax years 2021-22 and 2022-23. As such, she is potentially taxable in the UK on her worldwide income between 6 April 2021 and 5 April 2023, even though she was only present in the UK between 1 July 2021 and 6 August 2022. This means she is facing double taxation (i.e. being taxed for a time in both the UK and France on the same income), so she will need to see if split-year treatment applies to alleviate this double tax.

Split-year treatment for 2021-22

Looking at split-year treatment for 2021-22, the year of Chloe's arrival in the UK:

Case 4

Chloe was not resident for the previous year, 2020-21.

On 6 April 2021, her only home was not in the UK but France. Her only home started being in the UK on 1 July 2021.

Between 6 April and 30 June 2021, Chloe had no sufficient ties with the UK (as she did not visit the UK prior to 1 July 2021 and had none of the ties under the sufficient ties test).

Case 4 therefore applies.

Case 5

Chloe is not resident for 2020-21, the previous tax year.

There is a period of 365 days starting in the tax year on 2 July 2021 upon which she performs more than three hours of work.

Chloe has worked sufficient hours in the UK during this 365-day period, with no significant breaks, and at least 75% of the days she has worked during the period have been performed in the UK.

Between 6 April and 1 July 2021, Chloe has no sufficient ties with the UK.

Case 5 therefore applies.

Cases 6 to 8

These Cases do not apply as:

- there was no year between 2016-17 and 2019-20 when Chloe was resident (Case 6);
- Chloe is single (Case 7); and
- Chloe did not have a home in the UK through to 5 April 2023 (Case 8).

Summary for 2021-22

Cases 4 and 5 are the only cases that apply, with Case 4 taking priority, so 2021-22 is split between a UK part (6 April to 30 June 2021) and an overseas part (1 July 2021 and 5 April 2022).

Split-year treatment for 2022-23

It is now necessary to consider the treatment for 2022-23, the tax year of Chloe's departure from the UK.

Case 1

Chloe was resident for 2021-22, the previous tax year.

Chloe establishes that she satisfies the full-time work test (the third automatic overseas test) for 2023-24.

Chloe starts working again in France on 8 August 2022 (more than three hours per day).

Between 8 August 2022 and 5 April 2023 Chloe, works sufficient hours overseas, there are no significant breaks in her overseas work and she is below the permitted limits of days she can work in the UK and generally spend in the UK (she does not visit the UK after leaving).

Case 1 therefore applies.

Case 2

This Case does not apply as Chloe is single.

Case 3

Chloe is resident for 2021-22, but she is not resident for 2023-24.

On 6 April 2022 she had a home in the UK, but she ceased to have a home on 6 August 2022 and continued not to have one up to 5 April 2023.

She spent fewer than 16 midnights in the UK between 6 August 2022 and 5 April 2023.

Within six months of leaving she had a home in France and was resident there for tax purposes.

Case 3 therefore applies.

Summary for 2022-23

Both Cases 1 and 3 apply to 2022-23, with Case 1 taking priority.

2022-23 is therefore split between a UK part (6 April 2022 to 7 August 2022) and an overseas part (8 August 2022 to 5 April 2023).

Suppose that during 2023-24 Chloe decided to have a break from work and to travel the world for a few months. Case 1 would not then apply and 2022-23 would be split under Case 3, so the overseas part would be from 6 August 2022 to 5 April 2023.

If Chloe had decided instead to travel the world after leaving the UK for the rest of 2022-23, then neither Case would apply, so 2022-23 would not be a split year. In this situation, Chloe would need to look at the double tax treaty between the UK and France to see if exemption or relief from double tax is available.

The UK part of a tax year will not necessarily start on the day of an individual's arrival in the UK. It will start when the conditions for each particular Case are first met. For example, if a person arrives in the UK for full-time work, it may be the day he or she commences working more than three hours per day in the UK, which may be before or after the day of arrival in the UK.

Example 2 – Sandra

Sandra returns to the UK to live during May 2021, but actually starts performing some work in the UK for her new UK employer (more than three hours per day) in April. She may be treated as being resident before she actually moves to the UK.

Similarly, if a person ceases to have a home overseas before returning to the UK, the UK part of the tax year may start prior to the individual's return to the UK. This could potentially cause some of the overseas earnings to be taxed in the UK.

The overseas part of the year of departure from the UK may not be from when an individual leaves the UK but may be later. For example, if Case 1 applies, it will be the day the individual first starts working overseas, which is likely to be after the day he or she leaves the UK.

Other practicalities

If an individual qualifies for any of the Cases for split-year treatment, there is no choice in the matter and split-year treatment will apply, and the individual needs to show this on his or her self-assessment tax return if filing one (on the "Residence, remittance basis etc." pages).

If an individual needs to rely on a double tax treaty between the UK and another country, it is important to realise that the above split-year treatment does not apply when using double tax treaties, so for treaty purposes the individual will be regarded as being resident in the UK for all of the tax year even though it may be a split year. This will be relevant when an individual is trying to establish in which country he or she is resident for double tax treaty purposes only (known as treaty residence – see **35.2**).

Guidance: RDRM 12000-12280

34.4   Record-keeping

Detailed records are necessary as a result of the SRT and for an individual to be able to prove his or her situation, especially in negative terms, e.g. showing that he or she did not perform more than three hours' work on a given day in the UK or overseas.

If a person is working, various parts of the SRT refer to the number of hours worked. Records will not only have to show where an individual spends his days, and what he was doing on that day, but will also need to be detailed enough to show how many hours are worked on a particular day, so that it can be established whether or not it is a work day, and whether a person is working full-time. Only then will it be possible to calculate a person's average number of hours per week in order to satisfy the sufficient hours worked tests.

Even though a person may know that he or she is working full-time, without the need to keep records, it will be necessary to back up the claim for full-time work with documentary evidence if HMRC query this. In addition, the legislation can lead to some surprising and unexpected results, sometimes with a person not being regarded as working full-time even though he may think he is. For example, most people would think an employee working 9 to 5, five days a week, with standard holidays of four weeks, would satisfy the full-time work tests, but the reality is that he or she is unlikely to do so.

Similarly, an individual needs documentary evidence to back up a claim for days on which he or she has and has not worked. It will also be necessary to record the time the individual embarks and disembarks on journeys to and from the UK (together with the entry and exit points to and from the UK) and to show separately any internal journeys within the UK. Where a person stays will also need to be recorded to help establish where his or her home is.

HMRC list in great detail, at RDRM 12900, the records and details they expect individuals to keep. Similar details may be needed for the individual's spouse or partner, and for any minor children. One way to show many of the above details is by using a diary system, possibly in a spreadsheet format, which will enable a person to include notes to cover many of the above details. However, it will also be essential to keep much documentation.

It is difficult in negative situations to show that something has not been done, e.g. that a person has not done more than three hours of work in the UK. Any documentation that can show this must be kept, as this area of the SRT may cause disputes with HMRC. Detailed evidence must be kept in respect of work days and hours, of where these are performed and what work activity was performed, including training and travelling, as HMRC may scrutinise this area in great detail. HMRC can request details such as work calendars and diaries, notes of meetings, email records etc., so it is important that these records are kept as well. This will be particularly important if an employee were to change employers, after which it becomes more difficult to obtain all the necessary records if needed.

For busy expats, keeping this amount of detail will be a challenge. In response, some now arrange for personal assistants to keep a diary of the expat's travelling and other details.

The expat should keep records in respect of the SRT for at least a year after the filing deadline for a self-assessment tax return (see **2.1.6**) and penalties may be charged for inadequate records (see **Appendix 1**).

Guidance: RDRM 12900

34.5   Dual residents

Each country's domestic tax legislation (which can vary significantly between countries) establishes an individual's residence status for its own tax purposes – regardless of that person's residence status elsewhere.

This often leads to individuals being dual residents, i.e. resident for tax purposes in two countries at the same time. The individual is then in a potential double tax situation, with his income and gains taxed in both countries, as most countries tax their residents on their worldwide income and gains. An individual would then need to see if there is a double tax treaty (see **35.2**) between the two countries concerned, so as to establish if relief or exemption from one country's tax is available.

For UK tax purposes, as was mentioned above, a person is resident for all of a tax year, which means from 6 April to the following 5 April. This can very often lead to individuals being dual resident until 5 April after leaving the UK, or from 6 April before arriving if coming to the UK. The date from which the person is regarded as resident in the country to which he or she is moving, and the date from when the individual ceases to be resident in the country he or she has left, will both depend on that country's domestic tax legislation.

In the UK, a dual resident may be rescued from double taxation by the application of split-year treatment (see **34.3**). However, this may not always be the case, in which case the person would then need to look at any relevant double tax treaty to establish if relief is available (see **35.2**).

34.6   Residence prior to 2013-14

34.6.1   *Ongoing relevance*

The earlier rules for determining residence can still be important in certain situations, such as for an employee who has worked many years overseas and has been made redundant – this may become increasingly common following the Covid-19 pandemic and the economic turmoil this has caused. If he is not resident for the tax year in which his redundancy or other termination fell then he may wholly or partially escape UK tax on his termination package if foreign service relief applies (see **38.8.6**). This involves going back throughout the employee's time in employment with the employer and establishing what his UK residence status was for these years.

Another situation in which the old residence rules may be relevant is when establishing whether a person has become a deemed domicile (see **36.3**), i.e. if he or she has been resident in the UK for 15 out of the 20 years immediately before the tax year in question.

34.6.2   *Tests that formerly applied*

Prior to the introduction of the SRT on 6 April 2013, the establishment of a person's residence status was much less clear and a great deal of uncertainty existed. This was further complicated by there being two types of residence – residence on its own and ordinary residence, the former being more of a temporary type of residence, whereas ordinary residence was a more permanent type of residence.

Whether an individual was resident or not was a question of fact and circumstances, and depended on whether a distinct break from the UK had been made. The circumstances surrounding an individual all had an important bearing (albeit in varying degrees depending on the individual) when establishing residence status, including his or her:

- pattern of life;
- habits;
- ties with the UK and the nature of these ties (including family, business, social, economic and property connections);
- purpose for being in the UK or overseas;
- intentions;
- duration of presence, and how many days were spent in the UK;
- frequency and regularity of visits to the UK;
- availability of accommodation; and
- nationality.

There was no statutory definition of residence in the UK tax legislation, so a body of well-established practice arose over the years, largely originating from case law and based on HMRC's interpretation of this and the legislation. This guidance was included in IR20, which was later replaced by HMRC 6.

The result of the above was a mishmash of rules and much confusion could exist when establishing an individual's residence status for UK tax purposes. In response to this, the SRT was introduced from 2013-14.

Guidance: HMRC publications IR20 and HMRC6 (accessed via the National Archives website)

34.7 Pitfalls and planning points

Statutory residence test

In respect of the third automatic overseas test and working sufficient hours overseas, the requirement that there is no significant break in an individual's overseas work can often trip individuals up. For instance, an employee usually working overseas may be working in the UK for more than 30 consecutive days, or an employee working on a rota basis may spend his or her time off in the UK and this is not regarded as annual leave.

The sufficient hours worked overseas calculation may not always be satisfied, even though the employee is considered full-time.

The only home in the UK test (the second automatic UK test), can often cause individuals to be resident for the tax year, particularly in the year of arrival or departure from the UK.

Detailed records need to be kept, particularly in respect of hours worked. For many individuals this will be a challenge.

Split-year treatment

If split-year treatment does not apply, the individual will need to refer to a double tax treaty, to see if relief or exemption from UK tax is available for the period after leaving or before arriving in the UK.

Events happening in the tax year following the year of departure from, or arrival in, the UK can have an effect on split-year treatment for the year of departure or arrival.

35. Double taxation

35.1 Introduction

Double taxation will arise if an individual is a dual resident (see **34.5**) or if he or she has income arising in one country (the source state), but is resident in another country (the residence state) and so is taxed in both. Double tax treaties exist between countries to try and minimise or eliminate this double tax.

35.2 Double tax treaties

35.2.1 Introduction

The UK has treaties in place with most countries around the world (see https://www.gov.uk/government/collections/tax-treaties).

The treaties do not give new taxing rights, but try to allocate taxing rights between the two countries and to alleviate double taxation. Care needs to be taken when a federal system, such as the USA, is involved, to see whether all the states making up the federation acknowledge double tax treaties. For example, some states in the USA do not.

Care also needs to be taken if a country taxes its residents on a remittance basis, or does not tax their overseas income. For example:

- Australia does not tax its residents on their foreign income if they are on temporary visas; and

- Japan taxes the foreign income of certain types of residents on the remittance basis.

In these types of situation, it is very unlikely that the treaty will allow exemption or relief from UK tax if the income is not taxed in the other country.

Example

Beryl and Bert have lived and worked in the UK all their lives.

Their son moved to live in Australia with his family, so after retiring Beryl and Bert decide to move to Australia to be closer to their grandchildren. Bert receives a pension from his UK employer.

They enter Australia under temporary residence visas, so Bert's UK pension is not taxed in Australia. Under the double tax treaty between the UK and Australia, pensions are just taxed in the state of residence, i.e. Australia in this case, so Bert's pension would be exempt from UK tax under the treaty. However, because the pension has not in fact been taxed under Australian tax laws, exemption from UK tax is not available under the treaty. As such, Bert's pension will remain taxable in the UK until he becomes a permanent resident in Australia, from which point it will be taxed in Australia.

35.2.2   Residence requirement

An individual has to be resident in one of the countries party to the double tax treaty, so if he is not resident in either country, that treaty cannot be used. This is a particular issue for an individual who is not resident anywhere in the world, as he may find himself bearing the cost of income being double taxed with no relief for this under a treaty or under UK tax law; an individual has to be resident in the UK or in the other country in which the tax is paid, to be able to obtain a credit for the foreign tax against the UK tax due.

35.2.3   Model treaties

Most of the UK's treaties follow the OECD or UN model treaties. These are templates for treaties between developed countries (OECD) and developing countries (UN). Even though the basics of a treaty may follow the OECD or UN model, it is vital that the actual treaty is referred to, as many of the UK's treaties differ in some way from the model treaties. Commentaries on both model treaties exist, to help in interpreting them.

Guidance: https://tinyurl.com/s3eb79e8 (model OECD treaty); https://tinyurl.com/wtahhzy8 (UN model treaty)

35.2.4   Interpreting treaties

When interpreting double tax treaties, it is important to distinguish between an individual being "liable to tax" and being "subject to tax". A person may be liable to tax in a country on all of his or her income, but not subject to tax on all of it because of (say) a tax relief. This difference can be key in correctly interpreting double tax treaties and understanding what an individual is *liable to tax on* in the country he has moved to, and not just what he actually ends up being taxed on (subject to tax). Liaison with the overseas tax adviser will be important so as to understand the tax situation of the individual in the country to or from which he has moved.

The first step is to establish where the individual is resident for the purposes of the treaty, known as "treaty residence". In this respect, the individual will look to see in which country he or she is resident under domestic tax law. If this is just one country, he is treaty resident in that country. If he is resident in both countries, i.e. a dual resident, then the treaty is likely to have a "tie-breaker" clause that establishes, through a number of tests, which country the individual is resident in for the purposes of the treaty only. In this respect, it is often necessary to look at where the person's permanent home is, and to determine his or her centre of vital interests, habitual abode and nationality, but the actual test depends on the treaty being considered. Again, it is vital to liaise with the overseas tax adviser to establish the residence status under domestic tax legislation of the individual in the country he moves to or from.

35.2.5   *Different types of income*

Various treaty articles cover specific types of income in certain situations. If a particular item of income is not covered by a specific article, it is often covered by an "other income" article, e.g. the UK's state pension is often not covered by the pensions article, so it is covered instead by the other income article – this usually states that the income is taxable only in the state of residence.

The more common articles in respect of income tax include:

- residence;
- dividends;
- interest;
- royalties;
- immoveable property (rental income);
- business profits if self-employed;
- employment (sometimes called "dependent personal services");
- directors' fees;
- pensions;
- government service;
- teachers, professors, etc. and students; and
- other income.

Any limitation-of-relief (or similar) article should be referred to, to establish if there is a restriction of treaty relief or exemption in certain circumstances, such as those mentioned in the example at **35.2.1** above.

A brief overview of the some of the above articles is as follows:

Dividends and interest

These are often taxable in both countries, but the amount of tax that a source state can charge is generally restricted to between 5% and 15%, depending on the treaty.

Royalties

The treatment of these is similar, and very often there is a maximum rate of tax that the source state can charge, though some treaties do state that royalties are just taxed in the residence state.

Rental income

This is generally taxable in both states, with no restriction on the amount of tax the source state can charge.

Business profits

Income falling under this article is generally taxable only in the state of residence, unless the profits arise from a permanent establishment (e.g. an office or branch) in the other state. In some treaties, independent professional services – such as those of lawyers, doctors, accountants, scientists, engineers and teachers – are covered by an independent personal services article, and are taxed in the country of residence unless the professional has a base (such as an office) in the other state.

Income from employment

Employment income is usually taxable only in the residence state, unless work is physically performed in the other state. If it is, then the earnings from these work days can be taxed in the other state as well.

However, if certain conditions are satisfied, the earnings from the work performed in the other state are only taxable in the residence state. These conditions are typically that:

- the employee is not present in the other state for more than 183 days over a certain period of time (usually over any 12-month period commencing or finishing in the other state's tax year);

- the employer is not resident in the other state; and
- the employee is paid by an employer who is not resident in the other state, and the employee's remuneration is not borne by a permanent establishment in the other state.

This means, for example, that an employee who is assigned overseas by his UK employer may not be exempt from UK tax under this article on the earnings from work performed in the UK while non-resident, if his employment contract remains with his UK employer or if he is employed on a local contract in the residence state but his remuneration costs are recharged to and borne by a UK permanent establishment.

Government service

For an employee who is employed by a government, local authority, etc., but working in the other country, earnings are covered by the government services article and are usually just taxed in the country where the government or local authority is located. However, there are exceptions to this, for example if the individual is not only a resident but also a national of the other state. In this case, the earnings are taxed in the other state.

Directors' fees

This article generally allows both states to tax fees when a director resident in one state is on the board of a company resident in the other state. So, for example, this article allows the UK to tax the fees of a non-resident director on the board of a UK resident company (but under UK domestic tax rules, if certain circumstances are satisfied then these may not be taxed in the UK – see **38.6.2**).

Pensions

Pension income is often taxed only in the residence state, but this provision only covers pensions from past employment. It therefore excludes pensions from government service (which are covered by the government service article) and usually also the state pension (which is often covered by the other income article). Some treaties, such as that between the UK and the USA, cover pension contributions and allow a deduction against taxable income, in the residence state, for pension contributions into a pension scheme located in the other state.

Teachers and professors

Teachers and professors may be exempt from tax in the country they are visiting if they are generally present in that country for under two years.

35.2.6   Other considerations

As mentioned above, all treaties vary in some respects, so it is important to refer to the relevant treaty.

Double tax treaties generally also have an article explaining how relief for double tax is given in the countries party to a treaty. If the UK is required to give relief for foreign tax under a treaty, the main method of giving this relief is the credit method, whereby relief for foreign tax is set off against the UK tax due on the double taxed income (see **35.3**).

A double tax treaty will also have an article specifying what taxes a treaty covers. i.e. "admissible taxes". For instance, Germany not only charges income tax on an individual's income, but also has a solidarity surcharge and sometimes a church tax. Switzerland has cantonal and communal income taxes in addition to federal income tax, similar to the USA, which also has federal and state taxes (and, with the latter, state taxes are not covered by the UK/US double tax treaty). It is important to check this article to establish which country's taxes are covered, particularly when claiming double tax relief in the UK.

When claiming relief or exemption from UK under a double tax treaty (for individuals treaty resident overseas), the individual needs to claim this either on form HS302 (dual residents who are treaty resident in another country) or HS304 (non-residents resident in another country), if filing self-assessment tax returns. A residence certificate is required from the overseas country's tax authorities (other than for the US), confirming the individual's residence there for the purpose of the double tax treaty. This certificate is attached to the individual's tax return, along with the form HS302 or HS304.

In other cases, the individual should complete form DT-Individual, requesting a repayment of tax and applying for relief at source on pensions, purchased annuities, interest or royalties. The form is sent to the relevant overseas tax authority, who will confirm the individual's residence status on the form and then send it directly to HMRC.

35.3   Double tax relief

35.3.1   *Principles*

As mentioned above, double tax treaties explain how double tax relief is given, usually by the credit method in the UK.

If an individual is resident in the UK and is taxed on income from a country with which the UK does not have a double tax treaty, then relief for any foreign tax on the double taxed income may be available under UK tax law and is known as unilateral relief. Unilateral relief is only available if there is no relief under a treaty (this would also include taxes not covered by a treaty such as USA state taxes) and is not additional to relief that is available under a treaty, even if the individual fails to claim relief under a treaty.

HMRC will only give relief for foreign tax if the tax is legally due in the other country, so care needs to be taken if, for example, tax is deducted at source in the other country but it turns out not to be actually due or only partially due.

Example 1

Norman is working for a Dutch employer and performs most of his work in the Netherlands. His family have remained living in the family home in the UK, so he commutes weekly between the UK and the Netherlands, travelling back on a Thursday evening, working from home in the UK on a Friday and then travelling to the Netherlands on a Monday morning. He has remained resident in the UK under the SRT (see **34.2**) and so taxable on his worldwide income, but he is also taxable in the Netherlands on his earnings.

It is established that Norman is treaty resident (see **35.2**) in the UK, so the UK must give relief for the Dutch tax paid on his earnings against his UK tax. Norman's Dutch employer withholds £50,000 Dutch tax from his salary under a system similar to PAYE.

In January 2023, Norman prepares and files his UK tax return for the 2021-22 tax year and takes a credit of £50,000 against the UK tax due on his earnings of £60,000 for all the Dutch tax that was deducted from his salary for 2021-22 by his Dutch employer. He pays the balancing payment due for 2021-22 of £10,000 before the due date of 31 January 2023.

Norman prepares and files his Dutch tax return in April 2023. He discovers that too much tax was deducted from his 2021-22 salary by his employer, so he is due a refund of £5,000 in this respect, his actual tax liability in the Netherlands being £45,000. However, this means that too much credit was taken against his UK tax, resulting in an underpayment of UK tax. This will result in not only the additional UK tax of £5,000 having to be paid, but also penalties and interest for the late payment of tax. The longer the delay after the UK tax return filing and balancing payment deadline, the higher the penalties and interest will be.

Example 2

Norma, an Australian, has retired to England where she has lived and been resident for a number of years and where she is regarded as treaty resident for the purposes of the double tax treaty between the UK and Australia.

During 2021-22 she starts receiving a pension from Australia and pays Australian tax on this. She prepares her 2021-22 UK tax return, declaring her Australian pension, and she sets off the Australian tax paid on this against her UK tax due on the income (it is not beneficial for Norma to claim the remittance basis – see **Chapter 37**).

Under the UK/Australia double tax treaty, pension income is only taxed in the country where Norma is treaty resident, the UK in her case. Norma's UK tax adviser advises her of this and that she should make the appropriate claim for exemption from Australian tax. Norma prepares and files her own UK tax return and completely ignores her tax adviser's advice – her view is that tax has been paid on the pension, so it does not matter where it is paid.

A few years later, HMRC open an enquiry into her UK tax affairs and disallow the Australian tax credit against her UK tax, on the grounds that her pension was exempt from Australian tax under the double tax treaty. By this time it is too late to claim back the tax in Australia, so Norma in the end suffers double tax for which she is unable to obtain any tax relief.

Similarly, Norma had received dividends from a US company which had withheld US tax at 30%. Norma had claimed a foreign tax credit (FTC) for the full amount of the US tax withheld against the UK tax due on the dividends. Again, HMRC disallowed some of this credit, as the US – under the double tax treaty between the UK and US – can only tax the dividends up to a maximum rate of 15%, so Norma should have claimed back the excess tax from the IRS in the US.

35.3.2 Methods of relief

There are two methods by which the UK gives relief for double tax:

- foreign tax credit relief (FTCR, but also known as the credit method); and
- deduction of the foreign tax as an expense against the foreign income.

Foreign tax credit relief

FTCR is by far the more common method as it is usually more beneficial. It is the lower of:

- the foreign tax paid on the double taxed income; and
- the UK tax due on that income.

Relief is given by deducting the FTC against the UK tax due. The foreign tax cannot be repaid.

The first step is to establish the maximum amount of foreign tax that can be relieved – see the above examples. Once this is established, the UK tax payable on the double taxed foreign income is calculated by comparing the UK tax liability:

- including all the individual's income; and
- excluding that particular source of foreign income.

If there is more than one source of foreign income, the UK liability is calculated in this way for each such source by excluding it from the tax calculation. In this respect, the taxpayer may choose in which order to exclude foreign income from the tax calculation; usually, the foreign income suffering the highest rate of foreign tax should be excluded first.

HMRC have working sheets that can assist in calculating FTCR in the most beneficial way for most situations.

Example

Following on from the second example above, Norma's income for 2021-22 is:

- UK earnings from a part-time job of £25,000, with £2,500 in tax deducted under PAYE;
- Australian pension of £30,000, with £9,750 Australian tax paid;

- US dividends of £10,000 (gross), of which £3,000 has been withheld in US tax;
- Spanish dividends of £5,000 (gross), with £950 Spanish tax withheld;
- UK rental income of £20,000, on which no tax has been paid; and
- UK interest of £1,000, again no tax paid.

Under the double tax treaties the UK has with these countries, the Australian pension is only taxed in the UK and the maximum rates of tax that the USA and Spain can charge on dividends are 15% and 10% respectively.

The first calculation is to establish what the UK tax is, including all of Norma's income and before any double tax relief:

	£
UK earnings	25,000
Australian pension	30,000
US dividends	10,000
Spanish dividends	5,000
UK rental income	20,000
UK interest	1,000
	91,000
Less: personal allowance	(12,570)
Taxable income	78,430
Tax liability	
Tax on interest covered by personal savings allowance of £500 at 0%	Nil
Tax on dividends covered by dividend allowance of £2,000	Nil
Tax at 20% on £37,700 (earnings and pension)	7,540
Tax at 32.5% on dividends of £13,000	4,225
Tax at 40% on pension, rental and interest of £25,230	10,092
UK tax due before double tax relief	£21,857

The next step is to exclude each source of foreign income so as to establish the FTC:

	£	£
Taxable income as above	78,430	78,430
Less: foreign income (highest taxed first)		
(i) US dividends taxed at a maximum of 15% under the double tax treaty	(10,000)	(10,000)
(ii) Spanish dividends taxed at a maximum of 10% under the double tax treaty		(5,000)
Revised taxable income	68,430	63,430
Tax liability:		
Tax on interest covered by personal savings allowance of £500 at 0%	Nil	Nil
Tax on Spanish dividends covered by dividend allowance of £2,000	Nil	Nil
Tax at 20% on £37,700 (earnings and pension)	7,540	7,540
Tax at 32.5% on Spanish dividends of £3,000	975	Nil
Tax at 40% on pension, rental and interest of £25,230	10,092	10,092
Revised tax liability	18,607	17,632
Previous tax liability	21,857	18,607
Double tax relief the lower of:		
(i) UK tax liability on US dividends (£21,857 – £18,607)	3,250	–
UK tax liability on Spanish dividends (£18,607 – £17,632)	–	975
(ii) Foreign tax paid and legally due on US dividends (£10,000 x 15%)	1,500	–
Foreign tax paid and legally due on Spanish dividends (£5,000 x 10%)	–	500
Double tax relief (FTC)	1,500	500

(Cont.)	£	£
Original tax liability before double tax relief		21,857
Less: FTC		(2,000)
UK tax liability		19,857
Less: tax deducted under PAYE		(2,500)
Tax due for payment		17,357

Notes:

1. There is no relief for the Australian tax paid on Norma's pension, as under the UK/Australia double tax treaty this is taxed in the UK only. Norma will need to claim a repayment of the Australian tax from the Australian tax authorities.

2. Similarly, the maximum rate of US and Spanish tax that can be taken into account when calculating the FTC is 15% and 10% respectively, as stated in the relevant double tax treaties. The excess tax that has been deducted will need to be claimed back from the US and Spanish tax authorities.

Care needs to be taken when an individual is not resident anywhere – see **35.2.2** above.

Expense deduction

Double tax relief as an expense deduction is rarely beneficial compared to FTCR. There are exceptions, however, such as when there is insufficient or no UK tax against which to set off the foreign tax.

One example might be an individual who has a foreign rental property which under UK tax law is making a loss, but in the source country is making a taxable profit. Another might be an individual with a number of overseas rental properties, one of which is loss-making, with the result that no UK tax is due on the overseas rental business, but foreign tax has arisen on the profit-making properties.

In these situations, as no UK tax will arise on the income, there is no FTCR, but the foreign tax as an expense deduction can increase the allowable loss that is either carried forward or set off against the profits from any other overseas rental properties.

A third situation in which relief as an expense deduction is more beneficial, is if the individual concerned is not resident in either the UK or the relevant overseas country, but has incurred a tax liability on income in both countries. Relief under a double tax treaty is not possible (as an individual needs to be resident in one of the countries party to a double tax treaty to benefit from the agreement).

FTCR cannot be claimed for tax deducted on dividends from the following countries, so double tax relief can only be obtained by deducting the foreign tax from the dividend as an expense:

Antigua	Isle of Man
Australia (franked dividends only)	Jersey
Belize	Kiribati
Cayman Islands	Malaysia
Cyprus	Malta
The Gambia	Montserrat
Guernsey	Singapore

Relief as an expense deduction is not available if the income concerned is taxed on the remittance basis (see **Chapter 37**).

If the deduction proves to be excessive due to tax adjustments in the other country, the individual must inform HMRC within a year of these tax adjustments or risk a maximum penalty of 100% of the additional tax that becomes due.

Law: TIOPA 2010, Pt. 2
Guidance: DT 2140PP; INTM 150000, 160000; Helpsheet HS260

35.4   Special withholding tax

Under a revised EU Savings Directive, some EU countries (along with some non-EU countries under separate arrangements) may charge a special withholding tax (SWT) on savings and certain investment income (as defined under the directive, or arrangement with the non-EU country) paid to UK residents, in addition to any foreign tax that may also be due. This SWT is deemed to be income tax deducted at source for UK tax purposes and is not treated in the same way as foreign tax and credit relief, so it is not restricted as foreign tax may be, and any excess above the UK tax liability on the income will be repaid by HMRC.

Law: TIOPA 2010, Pt. 3; Council Directive 2014/107/EU

35.5   Pitfalls and planning points

Dual residents

An individual who is a dual resident must establish the country in which he or she is regarded as treaty resident for the purposes of a double tax treaty. This then dictates how the double tax treaty is interpreted, which country has primary taxing rights and which must give relief for double tax.

Some of the most complex situations are where an individual lives overseas for a short period of time, but does not break residence in his or her home country. Such an individual will remain taxable there on worldwide income, while either becoming resident in the host country or taxable on the income sourced there (e.g. earnings if working there). This is further complicated if the individual's family and home remain in the home country, so that it is not easy to establish (under the tie-breaker clause of a double tax treaty) the country in which his or her permanent home or centre of vital interests is. It may also be more difficult to establish the habitual abode of an individual who commutes regularly between the home and host countries.

If an individual is working in many countries, it can be complex to establish the countries in which he or she is taxable and the countries that have to give tax relief.

Planning will be vital in such situations, including liaison with a relevant tax adviser in the countries concerned.

Resident in just one country

For an individual who is resident in only one country, but who has a source of income in another, it is important that any double tax treaty between the two countries is referred to, to establish how the income is taxed. Some types of income, such as pensions, are taxed in the country in which the individual is treaty resident, and not in the source state.

UK double tax relief

When claiming a foreign tax credit (FTC) against UK tax, it is important that credit is only taken for tax that is legally due. If too much tax has been paid in the overseas country, the excess cannot be included in the FTC and must be reclaimed from the overseas country's tax authority.

36. Domicile

36.1 Introduction

The concept of domicile is important for certain areas of tax law, in particular inheritance tax (outside the scope of this publication) and the taxation of foreign nationals.

Everyone has a domicile at any stage of life, and an individual generally can only have one domicile at any one time.

Domicile is not the same as nationality or citizenship. It is basically where an individual wishes to live permanently or indefinitely, where his or her permanent settled life is.

Domicile is not defined by tax law, but by common law, and is associated with a country's legal system. That system may not apply to the country as a whole, but instead to individual states if they have their own legal system, e.g. the states making up the US or Australia.

Strictly speaking, an individual does not have a UK domicile, but instead has a domicile in England and Wales, in Scotland or in Northern Ireland. However, it is common to see references to a person having a UK domicile including under tax legislation.

There is much case law surrounding the concept of domicile.

The main HMRC guidance can be found in the *Residence, Domicile and Remittance Basis Manual*.

Guidance: RDRM 20000

36.2 Types of domicile

There are three types of domicile, as below.

36.2.1 Domicile of origin

When an individual is born he immediately takes on the domicile of his father, known as his domicile of origin. This domicile remains with him until it changes, either through his father changing his domicile before the individual reaches the age of 16 or through choice once he has reached 16.

If the child was born after his father's death, or is illegitimate, he takes on his mother's domicile. An adopted child will take on his or her adoptive father's domicile, or that of the adoptive mother if there is no adoptive father.

36.2.2   *Domicile of dependence*

This now applies largely to children; the individual will follow the domicile of his or her father until the age of 16. So (for example) if a UK domiciled man successfully acquires a domicile of choice in France, then his child (under the age of 16) will also acquire a French domicile.

Domicile of dependence also applies to an individual of any age who lacks sufficient mental capacity, i.e. does not have full legal capacity.

Prior to 1 January 1974, the concept also applied to married women.

36.2.3   *Domicile of choice*

Once an individual reaches 16, he or she can acquire a domicile of choice. However, it is very difficult for a UK domicile to shed his domicile of origin: there must be a fixed intention to change domicile, and action must accompany this intention.

A vague intention to move to another country is not enough. The individual must actively be seen to sever ties with the domicile country of origin and reside and set up home in the new country of domicile indefinitely. There must be a genuine intention to abandon the domicile country of origin. HMRC will look at various factors in this respect including:

- the individual's intentions;
- his or her social, family and financial interests;
- ownership and location of property;
- the individual's will; and
- any other relevant circumstances.

If an individual abandons the domicile country of choice, then his or her domicile reverts back to the domicile of origin, unless and until a new domicile of choice is acquired. This is particularly relevant for countries that are made up of states with their own legal system.

Example

Kath, who has UK domicile, emigrates to New South Wales in Australia and adopts a domicile of choice there. However, she then moves within

731

Australia to Victoria. Her domicile of origin will revert back to the UK until she can show that she has adopted a domicile of choice in Victoria.

Guidance: RDRM 22000

36.3   Deemed domicile

Since 6 April 2017, a foreign domicile may become a deemed domicile in the UK for a tax year, if he or she has been resident in the UK (including split years – see **34.3**) for 15 out of the previous 20 tax years (condition B under the tax legislation). There is, though, an exception if a non-UK domicile is not resident for a tax year and was not resident for any of the preceding tax years starting after 5 April 2017. An individual who becomes a deemed domicile will lose this status if he or she is non-resident for at least six consecutive tax years.

In addition, a non-UK domicile who was born in the UK and has a domicile of origin there, will be a deemed domicile for any tax year for which he is resident in the UK (condition A under the legislation).

Law: ITA 2007, s. 835BA
Guidance: RDRM 25000

36.4   Pitfalls and planning points

Foreign domiciles resident in the UK

Domicile is important for foreign domiciles who are resident in the UK for a number of reasons, in particular the taxation of their overseas income, which can be taxed on the remittance basis if they so claim – see **Chapter 37**.

UK domiciles overseas

Care should be taken with an individual who has not lived in the UK, but was born to a father who had a UK domicile at the time of his or her birth, e.g. the individual's parents were British and emigrated to a country such as Australia or New Zealand. The individual may have a UK domicile of origin but may well believe he has a foreign domicile, as he has never lived in the UK.

This will also be the case for an individual who was born in the UK to a UK domicile father if the family moved to live permanently overseas very early on in the individual's life. Such a person may feel no association with the UK and may regard himself or herself as a foreign domicile.

An individual with a UK domicile of origin may move permanently overseas and adopt a domicile of choice in another country. If the individual moves to another country (or even to another state within a federal system) his or her domicile will revert back to the UK domicile of origin, until the individual can show that a new domicile of choice has been acquired in another country.

An individual trying to shake off a UK domicile of origin must show that he or she has moved permanently overseas with no intention of returning to the UK, and must sever all ties with the UK wherever possible. For this reason, some individuals obtain burial plots overseas, but this is just one of many factors that are looked at when establishing a person's domicile status.

37. Remittance basis

37.1 Introduction

The remittance basis is an extremely complex area of tax law. It refers to the taxation of foreign income ("relevant foreign income" as defined by ITTOIA 2005, s. 830, and relevant foreign earnings as per ITEPA 2003, s. 22 and s. 26) received by foreign domiciles, who are resident in the UK at the time the income arises. As such, it does not apply to UK domiciles (including deemed domiciles – see **36.3**) or foreign domiciles who are not resident in the UK.

For split years (see **34.3**), if an individual remits income to the UK during the overseas part of the tax year, this will not be a taxable remittance.

The remittance basis still applies even if the source of the foreign income is no longer in existence at the time of the remittance. The remittance basis does not apply to certain foreign income, such as income from offshore life bonds.

37.2 Mechanics

A resident foreign domicile can choose, for each tax year, to be taxed on his or her foreign income on:

- the arising basis, i.e. on worldwide income as and when it arises and regardless of whether or not it has been remitted to the UK; or

- the remittance basis, where only the income remitted to the UK is taxed in the UK.

There are, however, some downsides to claiming the remittance basis, the main one from an income tax perspective being the loss of allowances such as the personal allowance (see ITA 2007, s. 809G).

A comparison therefore needs to be made each tax year between taxing the foreign income on the arising basis and on the remittance basis, to establish which method is the more beneficial in producing the lowest tax liability.

It is not always beneficial to claim the remittance basis as a lower liability will often result from using the arising basis, especially if the individual is paying tax in the source country, for which he can receive a foreign tax credit against the UK tax due (see **35.3**), or the remittance basis charge (RBC) applies (see **37.9**). Claiming the remittance basis is likely to be beneficial if the individual's taxable income is at such a level that he has already lost his personal allowance (see **3.4.2**), unless again the RBC applies.

An individual can swap each tax year between the remittance basis and the arising basis.

If an individual is a dual resident and is treaty resident (see **35.2**) in another country, then for foreign domiciles who are treaty resident in certain countries, it may be possible for the individual to claim the remittance basis, but still be entitled to the personal allowance under a double tax treaty – see RDRM 32050 for further details and the countries involved. For individuals treaty resident in other countries, the arising basis may be more beneficial if treaty relief from UK tax is available.

The default position is that a non-domicile's foreign income is taxed on the arising basis. If the remittance basis is to be used instead, a claim must normally be made, via an individual's self-assessment tax return, within four years of the end of the relevant tax year.

Law: ITA 2007, s. 809B

37.3   Automatic application

There are, however, situations in which the remittance basis applies automatically, so that a claim in not necessary. These are:

- If the non-domicile's unremitted overseas income and gains (ignoring foreign capital losses) are less than £2,000 for the tax year concerned. Unremitted overseas income and gains for a tax year are amounts that arise in a tax year and that are not remitted in the same tax year. This can also apply to deemed domiciles.
- If the individual is not a deemed domicile and:
  - has been resident in the UK for six or fewer years out of the nine tax years immediately preceding the tax year concerned, or is under 18 for all the tax year;
  - has less than £100 in UK *taxed* investment income;
  - has no other UK income or gains; and
  - does not remit any foreign income or gains to the UK.

The individual does not lose his or her allowances (e.g. the personal allowance) if one of the above situations arise and the remittance basis applies automatically. The individual also does not incur the remittance basis charge (see **37.9** below).

In any of the above situations, the individual can claim for the remittance basis not to apply, i.e. to be taxed on the arising basis instead. This may, for example, be beneficial for an individual in the first scenario, who is remitting income such as foreign dividends that cannot take advantage of the lower dividend tax rates if taxed on the remittance basis.

Law: ITA 2007, s. 809D, 809E

37.4　Definition of remittance

Remittances to the UK are not just the simple transfer of funds into the UK, but can also include more indirect methods, such as:

- the use of overseas credit cards in the UK;
- paying for a UK product, service or any other liability with overseas money;
- gifting overseas funds to a spouse (or any other person), who then remits the funds into the UK, if the individual either wholly or partly benefits from the remittance;
- the recipient of the above gift purchasing an asset overseas that is then brought into the UK, which the individual or his spouse enjoy the benefit of;
- bringing assets into the UK that were purchased overseas with foreign income or gains;
- bringing the finance from overseas loans into the UK; and
- paying off UK loans with overseas funds.

Overseas funds do not have to be physically transferred to the UK for a remittance to occur, but can be used merely to pay for a service in the UK. Care should therefore be taken with anything that the individual or anyone close to him (such as a spouse, child etc. – a "relevant person") benefits from in the UK, if that has been funded by overseas income or gains that can be traced back directly or indirectly to the individual. See RDRM 33000 and 33050 for HMRC examples of remittances.

Example

Stefan, a Danish national who is a foreign domicile resident in the UK, gifts some money in Denmark to his adult son Kenny, who uses this to travel around the world during his gap year between school and university. On his travels, Kenny visits his parents in London and treats them to an expensive dinner and theatre trip using the money that he was gifted by Stefan. This would be a remittance for Stefan.

Law: ITA 2007, s. 809L, 809M

37.5   Taxable remittances

Remittances become taxable in the UK if income that has arisen since the individual became resident is remitted to the UK. Income that arose when the individual was not resident will not be taxed in the UK even if the remittance occurs when the individual is resident.

Similarly, a taxable remittance will still occur if the individual remits income while not resident which relates to a time when he was resident in the UK and was claiming the remittance basis. Care is needed so that the individual who has claimed the remittance basis never remits to the UK taxable income that was not taxed because of the remittance basis (remittance basis income), even if the person has long since departed the UK and has been not resident for many years.

If an individual is a UK domicile (e.g. he or she becomes a deemed domicile), and remits income that arose previously when he or she was a foreign domicile and was not taxed because the remittance basis was claimed, then this will still be taxed in the year of remittance.

A taxable remittance may also occur if a resident individual who was taxed on the remittance basis leaves the UK for a short period, becomes not resident and is covered by the temporary non-residence rules (see **38.3**). In this situation, the remittance(s) made during a period of temporary non-residence will become taxable in the UK when the individual returns to the UK within the five-year rule (a period of non-residence starting from when the individual's *sole* period of UK residence ceases and which is less than five years) and becomes resident again.

37.6   Mixed overseas accounts

Many individuals will have just one or two bank accounts overseas into which various sources of income are paid. This results in a "mixed account", which makes it difficult to establish what type of income has been remitted to the UK. In this scenario, the legislation sets out a deemed order of remittances.

Example 1

Johanna was assigned to the UK for a few years by her German employer in January 2021 and works both in the UK and Germany. She is resident for 2020-21, but with split-year treatment applying from 3 January 2021.

Johanna's income is at such a level that she no longer has a personal allowance and so she has claimed the remittance basis for taxing her overseas income. She is taxed in Germany on her overseas earnings as all her overseas work is performed there.

All her salary is paid into her German bank account from which she remits income into the UK. German dividends and interest, along with the rental income from renting out her home in Berlin, are also paid into the same account. She pays German tax on her rental income but not on her dividends or interest.

Johanna previously worked in London and so already has a UK bank account in which she has left bonuses, etc. from her previous time working in the UK, along with rental income from a London flat she rents out.

The transactions of her German bank account for 2021 (from when Johanna is taxed as a resident) and 2022 are as follows:

Date	Income	Funds in £	Funds out £
31 January 2021	UK salary	5,000	
	German salary (in respect of German work days)	2,500	
15 February 2021	Berlin rental income	1,325	
14 February 2021	German dividends	1,000	
28 February 2021	UK salary	5,000	
	German salary	2,500	
15 March 2021	Berlin rental income	795	
31 March 2021	UK salary	5,000	
	German salary	2,500	

Date (cont.)	Income	Funds in £	Funds out £
15 April 2021	Berlin rental income	1,350	
30 April 2021	UK salary	5,000	
	German salary	2,500	
14 May 2021	German dividends	750	
15 May 2021	Berlin rental income	825	
31 May 2021	UK salary	5,000	
	German salary	2,500	
15 June 2021	Berlin rental income	1,350	
30 June 2021	UK salary	5,000	
	German salary	2,500	
15 July 2021	Berlin rental income	1,200	
31 July 2021	UK salary	5,000	
	German salary	2,500	
14 August 2021	German dividends	925	
15 August 2021	Berlin rental income	1,100	
31 August 2021	UK salary	5,000	
	German salary	2,500	
15 September 2021	Berlin rental income	1,350	
30 September 2021	UK salary	5,000	
	German salary	2,500	
15 October 2021	Berlin rental income	965	
31 October 2021	UK salary	5,000	
	German salary	2,500	
14 November 2021	German dividends	1,010	
15 November 2021	Berlin rental income	1,350	
30 November 2021	UK salary	5,000	
	German salary	2,500	

Date (cont.)	Income	Funds in £	Funds out £
15 December 2021	Berlin rental income	1,050	
28 December 2021	Transfer to UK bank account		85,000
31 December 2021	UK salary	5,000	
	German salary	2,500	
31 December 2021	German interest	100	
15 January 2022	Berlin rental income	680	
31 January 2022	UK salary	5,000	
	German salary	2,500	
14 February 2022	German dividends	1,250	
15 February 2022	Berlin rental income	1,350	
28 February 2022	UK salary	5,000	
	German salary	2,500	
15 March 2022	Berlin rental income	1,275	
31 March 2022	UK salary	5,000	
	German salary	2,500	
15 April 2022	Berlin rental income	1,115	
30 April 2022	UK salary	5,000	
	German salary	2,500	

The following process has to be followed to establish what income has been remitted during 2021-22:

Step 1 – For each of the categories of income and capital in paragraphs (a) to (i) below, Johanna needs to find the amount of income or capital per category for the relevant tax year (the tax year in which the remittance occurred – 2021-22) in the mixed fund immediately before the transfer, so between 6 April and 28 December 2021.

ITA 2007, s. 809Q(4)	Johanna's income	£
(a) employment income (other than income within paragraph (b), (c) or (f))	UK salary	40,000
(b) relevant foreign earnings (other than income within paragraph (f))	None	Nil
(c) foreign specific employment income (other than income within paragraph (f))	None	Nil
(d) relevant foreign income (other than income within paragraph (g))	German dividends	2,685
(e) foreign chargeable gains (other than chargeable gains within paragraph (h))	None	Nil
(f) employment income subject to a foreign tax	German salary	20,000
(g) relevant foreign income subject to a foreign tax	Berlin rental income	10,540
(h) foreign chargeable gains subject to a foreign tax	None	Nil
(i) income or capital not within another paragraph of this subsection.	None	Nil
Total		73,225

Step 2 – Find the earliest paragraph for which the amount determined under step 1 is not nil – this is Johanna's UK salary of £40,000.

Step 3 – Reduce the amount of the transfer (£85,000) by the amount taken into account under step 2 (£40,000), i.e. £85,000 less £40,000 = £45,000.

Step 4 – As the amount of the transfer (as reduced under step 3) is not nil, Johanna needs to repeat the process at steps 2 and 3 for each category of income shown above for the period 6 April to 28 December 2021, so:

	Johanna's income	£
Amount of transfer		85,000
Less:	UK salary	(40,000)
		45,000
	German dividends	(2,685)
		42,315
	German salary	(20,000)
		22,315
	Berlin rental income	(10,540)
Amount of transfer left		11,775

Step 5 – As there is still an amount of the transfer left, Johanna needs to repeat steps 1 to 4 again only, in respect of the 2020-21 tax year from January 2021 (when she first started being taxed as a resident in the UK).

Category (a) and Johanna's UK salary amount to £15,000 for the UK part of 2020-21, which covers the balance of the above transfer, so Johanna does not need to continue with steps 2 and 3 for other categories of income.

The remittance of £85,000 that Johanna made on 28 December 2021 is made up as follows:

	£
UK salary (2021-22 £40,000 plus 2020-21 £11,775) – already taxed in the UK, so not a taxable remittance	51,775
German dividends (2021-22)	2,685
German salary (2021-22)	20,000
Berlin rental income (2021-22)	10,540
	85,000

The above is a straightforward example. In reality, establishing what has been remitted from a mixed overseas account is often more complex and can become very laborious, especially if several overseas accounts are involved, with transfers between the accounts. See also "segregation of bank accounts" at **37.10** below.

With regard to transfers between offshore accounts, the transfer is deemed to be made up in proportion to the nature of the income in the account from which the transfer was made immediately before it is made.

Example 2

Brit has two Swedish accounts. One is made up of £50,000 of foreign taxed earnings, £1,000 of interest and £5,000 in Swedish dividends, so total income of £56,000. If she were to transfer £25,000 to her other Swedish account, then this transfer would be made up as follows:

Foreign taxed earnings £22,322 (i.e. 25,000 x (50,000/56,000))

Foreign interest £446 (i.e. 25,000 x 1,000/56,000))

Swedish dividends £2,232 (i.e. 25,000 x (5,000/56,000))

The exchange rates to be used are those on the day income is credited into the account and the date remittances to the UK are made.

Anti-avoidance rules are in place with regard to mixed accounts and arrangements that are entered into to minimise the amount of taxable remittances made to the UK, if the main or one of the main purposes of such arrangements is to gain a tax advantage. The mixed fund is regarded as containing any of the income under (a) to (i) above on a just and reasonable basis.

Law: ITA 2007, s. 809Q, 809S

37.7   Overseas workday relief and exemptions

Special relief applies to foreign domiciles who are working both in the UK and overseas in respect of earnings from overseas work days and who are eligible for overseas workday relief, if bank arrangements are set up in a particular way and these earnings are not remitted to the UK – see **39.2**.

There are exemptions from UK tax on certain remittances to the UK. These are remitting funds to the UK to:

- invest in a "qualifying company" – referred to as "business investment relief" in the legislation;

- gift to the nation certain works of art; and
- pay HMRC in respect of UK tax liabilities.

37.8   Investment income

The special income tax rates and allowances (personal savings and dividends allowances) that apply to investment income such as savings and dividends, which are taxed on the arising basis, do not apply to foreign investment income that has been taxed on the remittance basis. The usual income tax rates apply in this situation.

For foreign dividends remitted to the UK after 5 April 2016, if these were paid before 6 April 2016, the 10% associated tax credit is still available even though tax credits on dividends paid to UK tax residents were abolished from 6 April 2016.

37.9   Long-term residents – remittance basis charge

Special rules apply if a foreign domicile aged 18 or over has been resident for at least seven out of the nine years immediately preceding the tax year concerned (the "relevant tax year"). For these purposes, it is necessary to include split years, years where the individual was below 18, and years when an individual was dual resident and treaty resident in another country (see **35.2**)). The legislation refers to such an individual as a long-term UK resident.

In such cases, a remittance basis charge (RBC) of £30,000 will be charged for each tax year for which the individual claims the remittance basis.

If the individual has been resident for 12 out of the 14 tax years immediately preceding the relevant tax year, an RBC of £60,000 will be charged for each tax year for which the remittance basis is claimed. (At the time of writing, HMRC's RDRM refers to £50,000, but this is out of date.)

An individual to whom the remittance basis applies automatically (see **37.3** above) will not be subject to this RBC, no matter how long he or she has been resident in the UK.

Nominating income and gains for the RBC

A long-term UK resident who claims the remittance basis for a tax year, and who is subject to the RBC, is required to nominate offshore income and gains arising in the same tax year to which the RBC will apply, resulting in the RBC being made up of income or capital gains tax or both, depending on what is nominated. This nominated income is taxed on the arising basis (Scottish and Welsh tax rates are ignored) and if the tax liability is less than the RBC, an additional amount is charged to bring it up to the RBC. For these purposes, the tax liability includes any foreign tax credit, so an individual may want to nominate foreign income or gains that are subject to tax in another country, so that a foreign tax credit is available.

The reason for this nomination is so that the RBC can be classed as an income or capital gains tax charge, and so become eligible for double tax relief. The maximum that can be nominated is the amount that will produce a UK tax liability equal to the RBC. See RDRM 32340 and 32350 for examples.

An individual only needs to nominate part of his foreign income or gains, so can nominate as little as £1. In situations such as this, where there is insufficient nomination, the legislation deems sufficient foreign income to be added so that the RBC of £30,000 or £60,000 in the form of tax is achieved. This will always be income rather than gains, and so in respect of income tax (see RDRM 32370 for an example). However, care is needed as any double tax relief in other countries may not be available as this topping-up element of the RBC will relate to notional rather than actual income.

When the nominated income is remitted to the UK and, becomes taxable in the UK, this will be taxed; however a tax credit can be claimed for any part of the RBC that is nominated to actual income. Where an individual's nominated income or gain is less than the RBC, there is no credit for the element of the RBC that tops up the tax liability to the full RBC amount, as this relates to notional rather than actual income.

The legislation sets out a deemed order of remittances of this nominated income and unremitted income, in such a way that produces the greatest tax liability by ensuring that un-nominated amounts are deemed to be remitted first before nominated amounts – see RDRM 35130 and RDRM 35150, and 35160 for an example. However, if the individual remits £10 or less of nominated income for a tax year, this deemed order of remittance does not apply.

37.10   Pitfalls and planning points

Segregation of bank accounts

Taxable remittances can be minimised by segregating different sources of income and gains into separate offshore bank accounts. In this way, an individual can remit first from accounts that will produce a lower UK tax liability.

Funds in an overseas account previously used by an individual should be "ring-fenced" prior to becoming resident in the UK, with no income or gains being deposited into the account. In this way, the funds become "capital" and can be remitted without causing a tax liability to arise. (As all the income and gains in the account arose prior to becoming resident in the UK, they are not taxable assuming there is no UK source of income.)

Law: ITTOIA 2005, s. 829-845; ITA 2007, s. 809A-809Z10

Guidance: RDRM 30000; RDR1 (HMRC's Guidance note for residence, domicile and the remittance basis)

38. Non-residents

38.1 Introduction

In the UK, a non-resident is only taxed on his or her UK-sourced income. This is also the case for the overseas part of a split year (see **34.3**).

There are no specific tax rates for non-residents and the income of a non-resident individual is taxed in broadly the same way as that of a resident, although there are some rules specific to non-residents, such as the disregarded income rules that limit the amount of tax a non-resident pays (see **38.4**).

Double taxation may arise when an individual's UK-sourced income is also taxed in the country where he or she is resident. In this situation, the individual needs to see if relief from UK tax is available under a double tax treaty (see **35.2**).

See also **Chapter 40** for non-residents assigned overseas.

38.2 Personal reliefs

To be eligible to claim personal reliefs (e.g. the personal allowance), an individual must be resident in the UK or, if not resident, must:

- from 1 January 2021, be a UK national (previously a national of an EEA state);
- be resident in the Isle of Man or the Channel Islands;
- have previously resided in the UK and be resident abroad for the sake of the health of the individual, or of a member of the individual's family who is resident with the individual;
- be or have been employed in the service of the Crown;
- be employed in the service of any territory under Her Majesty's protection;
- be employed in the service of a missionary society; or
- be a person whose late spouse or late civil partner was employed in the service of the Crown.

If a non-resident does not fall within any of the above, personal reliefs may still be available under a double tax treaty. HMRC's *Digest of Double Tax Treaties* is a useful source in this respect. A notable example of a treaty which does *not* allow a non-resident access to the personal allowance is the double tax treaty between the UK and the US, so a US national resident in the US with UK-sourced income (such as rental income) will not be entitled to a personal allowance.

Law: ITA 2007, s. 56

Guidance: RDRM 10300; https://tinyurl.com/ecwp7nte (HMRC Digest of Double Taxation Treaties)

38.3 Temporary non-residence

Provisions have been introduced to tax an individual on certain types of income while overseas, if he or she is regarded as being temporarily non-resident.

A person will be regarded as being temporarily non-resident if the period of non-residence is less than five years. This period does not always begin as soon as a person leaves the UK, as the period of non-residence starts when the individual's *sole* period of UK residence ceases; a person may often be a dual resident for a time when leaving or arriving in the UK, e.g. if a person is not entitled to split-year treatment and is treated as resident for all of the tax year.

The types of income covered include:

- foreign income remitted to the UK during a period of temporary non-residence by a non-UK domicile, if the person's overseas income was previously taxed on the remittance basis when he or she was resident in the UK;
- distributions to participators in close companies in the UK;
- gains from contracts such as life insurance, annuities etc.;
- certain pension income;
- offshore income gains; and
- income taxable under the disguised remuneration regime.

If the above types of income arise in a period of temporary non-residence, they will be taxed in the year of return to the UK, when the individual becomes resident again.

Law: FA 2013, Sch. 45, Pt. 4, and Pt. 5, para. 157
Guidance: RDRM 12600

38.4   Disregarded income rules

Legislation, known as the "disregarded income" rules, limits the amount of tax a non-resident pays in the UK. These rules apply to individuals who are non-resident for the whole of the tax year, so they do not apply to the overseas part of a split year (see **34.3**).

Two tax computations need to be prepared:

> The first calculates the tax due as normal on all the non-resident's taxable income in the UK, taking account of the personal allowance if the individual is entitled to this (and any other personal reliefs the individual may be entitled to as a non-resident – see ITA 2007, s. 811(6)).

> The second computation calculates the tax due excluding certain types of income (disregarded income – see below) and also the personal allowance (and any other personal reliefs available), and adds to this liability any tax that has been deducted at source on the disregarded income.

Whichever computation produces the lower tax liability is used. If the non-resident is filing self-assessment tax returns, then whichever calculation is more beneficial is claimed (tax return software should calculate this automatically when preparing the individual's tax computation). Helpsheet HS300 is available to assist in these calculations.

ITA 2007, s. 813 defines disregarded income to include:

- interest;
- income from annual payments such as royalties;
- dividends from UK-resident companies;
- purchased life annuity payments;
- profits from deeply discounted securities;
- income from some unit trusts;
- some social security benefits (such as the state pension); and
- retirement annuities.

Tax credits are generally no longer associated with UK dividends. However, non-residents are still entitled to a 7.5% tax credit (not repayable), and dividends continue to be treated as disregarded income for the purposes of this limit.

Law: ITTOIA 2005, s. 399; ITA 2007, s. 810-814
Guidance: INTM 269180; SAIM 1170

38.5   Incidental duties

If a non-resident individual physically performs work in the UK, then the earnings from these UK work days are taxable in the UK under ITEPA 2003, s. 27, unless they are earnings from duties incidental to the individual's overseas duties. There is no statutory definition of incidental duties, but they are regarded as being subordinate to (and more minor and less important than) the employee's overseas duties. HMRC have a very narrow view of what they regard as incidental duties, and give examples such as attending a training course or arranging a business meeting while in the UK. On the other hand, answering emails while in the UK may well not be regarded as being incidental duties.

If work performed in the UK is not in respect of incidental duties, then relief from UK tax on the earnings from these UK work days may be available under a double tax treaty (see **35.2**).

Law: ITEPA 2003, s. 39
Guidance: EIM 40203-40204

38.6   Particular occupations

38.6.1   Self-employment

If a non-resident individual is a sole trader, and carries out all of his business overseas, then none of the profits will be taxable in the UK. If he does carry out part of his business in the UK, then the profits from this will be taxable in the UK. In this situation, the business profits article of any relevant double tax treaty should be referred to. To "carry out" for these purposes means to manage and control the business, and care is needed as to the place where contracts are concluded, as those concluded in the UK may cause some of the business profits to be taxed in the UK.

The specific rules on cessation and commencement of a business (see **15.4**) will apply if a sole trader:

- is resident in the UK but then becomes not resident and continues to run the same business overseas; or
- is not resident but then becomes resident in the UK and continues to carry on his or her overseas business in the UK.

Similar rules apply for a partner of a partnership whose residence status changes; the person is treated as ceasing to be a partner and then as immediately becoming a partner. As a UK resident partner, the individual is taxed on his or her share of the partnership's worldwide profits, whereas a non-resident partner is only taxed on a share of the partnership's UK profits.

Most of the employment parts of the statutory residence test (SRT) apply to self-employed individuals. However, there are exceptions, such as parts of the calculation used to establish whether an individual has worked sufficient hours in either the UK or overseas.

38.6.2   Directors

Fees paid to a non-resident individual, for carrying out his or her statutory duties as a director of a UK-registered company, are taxable in full unless *all* of the duties are performed overseas. HMRC do not regard these statutory duties as being incidental duties to the director's overseas duties (see **38.5**), so they are taxed in the UK.

There is usually a separate article in respect of directors in double tax treaties, which should be referred to.

38.6.3   Consulting through a limited company

If a non-resident, self-employed consultant operates through a limited company, the IR35 ("off-payroll") rules (see **13.2**) need to be considered. However, if the consultant's income would not have been taxed in the UK had he or she been an employee, these rules should not apply.

An individual moving overseas has to consider certain corporate tax issues if continuing to use, while overseas, the UK company through which he or she operated when in the UK. These include:

- the residence status of the company under a double tax treaty, which may be overseas if it is managed and controlled from abroad, and which will affect the company's residence status for UK corporation tax; and
- the compliance obligations if the company is regarded as migrating (and there are hefty penalties if these are not met).

These are not income tax issues, and are therefore outside the scope of this publication.

Any salary paid to the consultant will not be taxable in the UK if the individual has not performed any work in the UK. If work is performed in the UK, the employment article of any relevant double tax treaty needs to be referred to.

Dividends may still be taxable in the UK, depending on the circumstances. If they are, the consultant will still receive the dividend allowance. Furthermore, the disregarded income rules may mean that none of the dividend is taxed in the UK, depending on the individual's other UK-sourced income (see **38.4**).

38.6.4 Seafarers and transport workers

Specific rules apply to international transport workers and seafarers, including workers in the oil and gas industry.

International transport workers are referred to for the purposes of the SRT as "relevant jobs on board vehicles, aircraft or ships" (as defined by FA 2013, Sch. 45, para. 30). Such a worker is excluded from the full-time work (overseas and in the UK) tests of the SRT (see **34.2.1**), if he or she has, during the tax year, made at least six "cross-border trips" that either start or end in the UK. A cross-border trip is one that crosses an international border.

The work performed in the UK by non-resident international transport workers is excluded from being incidental duties (see **38.5**).

The following types of work performed by an individual are considered to have been performed in the UK, so the earnings from such work are taxed in the UK:

- work performed on a vessel on voyages that do not extend to a port outside the UK, regardless of the individual's residence status;
- work performed by a resident individual on a vessel or aircraft on a voyage that starts or ends in the UK, or part of such a journey that starts or ends in the UK; and
- an individual working in the UK sector of the continental shelf if in respect of the exploration or exploitation of the seabed or subsoil and their natural resources.

A seafarer is anyone who performs work on a ship, including not just sailors but also (for example) cooks and entertainers on cruise ships.

Crown employees, however, are excluded – e.g. members of the Royal Navy.

Offshore installations are not ships for this purpose (ITEPA 2003, s. 385), even though such installations can use navigation. HMRC's view of a ship is that it is a vessel that is capable of navigation and used in navigation. This therefore excludes structures that do not move about, such as fixed production platforms, accommodation barges, light and weather ships, and similar structures.

If certain conditions are satisfied, a special deduction of 100% is available against a seafarer's general earnings taxed under ITEPA 2003, s. 15, 22, 26 or 27 if the individual is resident in another EEA state and liable to tax there. Non-resident seafarers are not entitled to this deduction.

This 100% deduction is available against a seafarer's non-UK earnings, if the individual works wholly or partly outside the UK during an eligible period that:

- falls wholly or partly in a tax year and consists of at least 365 consecutive days of absence from the UK; or
- is a combined period, as defined at ITEPA 2003, s. 378(3).

Specific expenses can be claimed by offshore gas and oil workers on their transfer costs, including accommodation and transport costs (s. 305). Travel costs borne by an employer can also be claimed by employees working partly on a vessel outside the UK, subject to conditions being satisfied (s. 370(5)), as can travel expenses for family to visit a worker (s. 371), again subject to conditions being satisfied and the expense being borne by the employer.

Detailed guidance and examples can be found from EIM 33000 onwards and in HMRC Helpsheet HS205.

Law: ITEPA 2003, s. 40-41, 305, 370-372, 378-385; ITA 2007, s. 1001; FA 2013, Sch. 45, para. 9(3), 14(4), 30
Guidance: EIM 33000, 34090-34110, 70200-70245; HMRC Helpsheet HS205

38.6.5   Commuting employees

An employee may commute, perhaps on a weekly basis, from his or her home in the UK to work in another country, very often in Europe. This often leads to the individual remaining resident in the UK and potentially becoming a dual resident.

Example

George is a British national and lives in London with his family. He works in the Netherlands for a Dutch IT company and flies from London to Amsterdam on a Monday morning and then returns home on a Thursday evening, working from home in London on the Friday. So he spends four nights a week in the UK and three in the Netherlands.

His home and family remain in the UK, and he lives in temporary accommodation while working in the Netherlands. He typically spends 200 midnights in the UK per tax year and so is automatically resident in the UK under the 183-days test (see **34.2.1**).

George will remain taxable in the UK on his worldwide income. The Netherlands may also treat him as a resident there for tax purposes and tax him on his worldwide income. Even if he is not resident there, the earnings from the work he performs in the Netherlands may still be taxable there, subject to any relief that may be available to him under any special expatriate scheme under Dutch tax law.

In this scenario, George would need to look at the double tax treaty between the UK and the Netherlands. The first step would be to see which country he is regarded as being resident in for the purposes of the treaty under article 4. Assuming he is resident in both the UK and the Netherlands, it is likely that his permanent home is in the UK and so he will be regarded as treaty resident in the UK. Even if he is not regarded as resident in the Netherlands, he will still be regarded as treaty resident in the UK, as he is resident in the UK under the UK's domestic tax legislation.

If George had a more permanent home in Amsterdam, such as renting accommodation on a long-term basis or owning another property that he lived in, then there would be grounds to argue that he has a permanent home in each country. In this case, under article 4, he would need to look at where his personal and economic relations are closer (centre of vital interests). This may not be so clear cut, given that his family and home are in the UK but his work is in the Netherlands, so a full review of all his social and economic activities would have to be performed. If his centre of vital interests cannot be determined, then his habitual abode and finally his nationality are considered.

Assuming that George is treaty resident in the UK, he will not be able to claim exemption from Dutch tax under article 14(2) of the double tax treaty, because his employer is resident in the Netherlands. He will therefore be taxed both in the UK and the Netherlands on some or all of his earnings, depending on his residence status in the Netherlands and on what tax reliefs are available to him under Dutch tax law.

Assuming the Dutch tax is less than the UK tax, the UK will have to give George relief for the Dutch tax he has paid on his earnings. This relief will be given by way of a credit against his UK tax on the double taxed income, usually via a claim on his UK tax return. In this respect, George will need to be careful as to the credit he claims against his UK tax for the Dutch tax he has paid. It is a common mistake for employees in this situation to deduct all the Dutch tax that was deducted from their salary under the Dutch equivalent of PAYE.

George files his UK tax return first and then files his Dutch tax return later, at which point he discovers that too much Dutch tax was deducted from his salary and so he is due a refund. In this situation, too much credit will have been taken against the UK tax, so the UK tax return must be amended, resulting in more UK tax being due. As this will invariably be after the payment deadline for outstanding tax for a tax year, it will result in late payment penalties and interest arising on a daily basis. George will therefore need to make sure that he only deducts, against his UK liability, the Dutch tax that is actually due and not refundable.

George will also need to consider his social security contributions. These may be at least as complicated as his tax situation.

With regard to PAYE, George's Dutch employer (being a foreign employer) may not have an obligation to operate PAYE on George's salary. Strictly speaking, George should operate a PAYE scheme himself. However, he can request agreement from HMRC that he can pay his UK tax via self-assessment rather than having to set up a PAYE scheme. If he does this, he needs to take into account the cash-flow implications, particularly in the first year when payments on account may first arise.

As can be seen from the above example, the taxation of such commuters can be complicated, with double tax commonly arising.

Tax relief may be available for travel and accommodation expenses incurred by such commuting employees who have remained resident in the UK. Relief for these costs under the standard employee travel rules (ITEPA 2003, s. 337 and 338) is unlikely to apply, as an individual's travel expenses will most likely be to a permanent workplace. However, that should still be the starting point when looking at relief for travel and subsistence expenses.

Relief may also be available under ITEPA 2003 for the following:

- Travel costs at the start and end of overseas work if all the work is performed overseas and none in the UK. If the employer is a foreign employer then the employee needs to be a UK domicile (see **Chapter 36**). There is no requirement for the employer to have borne the costs of these expenses (s. 341).

- Travel costs to overseas work, but only if borne by the employer. The employee's absence from the UK must be wholly and exclusively to perform work that can only be performed overseas, although other work can be partly performed in the UK. There is no limit to the number of journeys that can be made, but any private element will prevent relief for the whole journey (s. 370).

- Accommodation and subsistence expenses borne by an employer while a resident employee is working wholly overseas (so there is no relief if the employee is partly working in the UK). If a foreign employer, then the employee must be a UK domicile (s. 376).

- Travel costs for a resident employee's spouse/civil partner and minor child to visit him or her while working overseas. The employer must bear the cost and there is a maximum of two return journeys per tax year per person. Also, the employee must be absent from the UK for work overseas for a continuous period of at least 60 days, so a commuting employee like George in the above example would not obtain relief (s. 371).

Law: ITEPA 2003, s. 341, 370, 371, 376
Guidance: EIM 34001-34200

38.6.6   *Crown employees*

Employees with overseas Crown employment (as defined by ITEPA 2003, s. 28(2)) include members of HM Armed Forces, diplomats, and civil servants such as those with the Foreign, Commonwealth and Development Office. The earnings of such employees, if they have been resident and then posted overseas, remain taxable in the UK and the individuals concerned continue to be eligible for the personal allowance and other allowances.

A Crown employee's residence status is still established under the SRT, so he or she can be regarded as not resident. Other income is taxed like that of any other individual and is based on the person's tax residence status (see **Chapter 34**).

Double tax is unlikely to arise in respect of the earnings of these types of employee, as the government services article 19 of the OECD model treaty exempts the employee from the host country's tax. Double tax may arise on his or her other income, though, so the relevant article of a double tax treaty needs to be referred to as normal in this respect.

Certain allowances that a Crown employee may receive are not taxable:

- a foreign service allowance paid to cover the additional cost of living expenses that an employee may incur while working overseas;
- an operational allowance paid to armed forces personnel operating in dangerous locations; and
- other tax-free allowances and termination payments as defined by the tax legislation.

Law: ITEPA 2003, s. 28, 296-299; ITA 2007, s. 56(3)(c)
Guidance: EIM 40205, 40209, 50100-50125

38.6.7   *Non-resident entertainers and sportspeople*

Special rules apply for entertainers and sportspeople who perform in the UK, but who are not resident for UK tax purposes.

Income from an activity performed in the UK is treated as a separate UK trade (or profession or vocation), unless the individual already has a UK trade or the activity is part of an employment. Income tax is paid on the profits from this deemed trade, unless relief is available under a double tax treaty (article 17 of the OECD model treaty).

UK tax at basic rate has to be deducted from income paid to a non-resident entertainer or sportsperson, and then accounted for to HMRC, regardless of whether the income is exempt from UK tax under a double tax treaty.

Law: ITA 2007, s. 965-970; SI 1987/530
Guidance: https://www.gov.uk/guidance/pay-tax-on-payments-to-foreign-performers; HMRC Helpsheet 303

38.7   UK letting income – non-resident landlord scheme

Anyone living overseas, and renting property out in the UK, will fall under the non-resident landlord scheme (NRLS). The individual does not have to be non-resident under the SRT (see **34.2**) to fall under this scheme, but merely living overseas. In this respect HMRC view anyone living overseas for more than six months as falling under the scheme.

Under this scheme, a tenant or letting agent (if one is engaged), paying rental income to an overseas landlord, is required to deduct tax at basic rate from the rental income and to account for this to HMRC. If a property is jointly owned, and one owner is resident in the UK and the other not resident (under the NRLS rather than the SRT), the payer of the rental income only needs to deduct tax from the share of rental income of the landlord who is not resident.

A landlord can apply to HMRC for his rental income to be paid gross by completing form NRL1. For rental properties that are jointly owned, such as by a husband and wife, each person must complete an NRL1 form. If the application is successful, HMRC will contact the tenant or letting agent and instruct them that tax no longer has to be deducted from a specific date. The rental income is still taxable, however, so it must be declared on the non-resident landlord's tax return and any tax due must be paid via the self-assessment system.

If tax is deducted under the NRLS, the tenant or letting agent will provide the landlord with a certificate (NRL6) that shows how much tax was deducted at source for a tax year.

Law: ITA 2007, s. 971, 972; SI 1995/2902

Guidance: INTM 370000, PIM 4800; https://tinyurl.com/dkcdu5zx (HMRC guidance for non-resident landlords)

38.8   Other matters

38.8.1   *Individual savings accounts (ISAs)*

A person who becomes non-resident is unable to open an ISA or contribute into an existing one. The individual can keep any existing ISA, and still benefit from the tax benefits, but the income and gains arising are likely to be taxable in the country in which he or she is resident.

Law: SI 1998/1870, reg. 10(2)(d)

Guidance: https://www.gov.uk/individual-savings-accounts/if-you-move-abroad (HMRC guidance on ISAs)

38.8.2   *Personal portfolio bonds*

A personal portfolio bond (PPB – see **25.5**) is usually a life assurance policy, life annuity contract or capital redemption policy. If the policyholder has the ability to invest in assets outside the tax legislation, anti-avoidance rules subject the policyholder to income tax on deemed gains when resident in the UK. The deemed gain is calculated at the end of each insurance year, and top slicing relief is not available.

Non-residents are not subject to this rule, so an individual needs to take care when moving to the UK and becoming resident. A hefty income tax charge will arise if the individual does not "endorse" the policy (restrict the assets within the policy to permissible assets under the tax legislation) by the end of the insurance year in which he or she became resident in the UK.

Law: ITTOIA 2005, s. 515-526
Guidance: IPTM 3600-3670, 7700-7835

38.8.3   Life insurance policies

Life insurance gains arising on chargeable events – such as upon the surrender of the policy – that are subject to income tax, are not taxable if the individual is not resident for the tax year concerned or if the chargeable event arises in the overseas part of a split year (see **34.3**). See also **25.3** for a broader discussion of life policies.

For individuals who are resident, but who have been not resident for previous tax years, the gain is reduced for the periods of non-residence. The method for calculating the reduction depends on whether the policy was issued before, or on or after, 6 April 2013.

Many non-resident individuals have life assurance policies that have been issued by a foreign resident company. These policies are not normally regarded as "qualifying" for the purposes of establishing which events are chargeable to income tax.

The temporary non-residence anti-avoidance provisions (see **38.3**) cover chargeable events that occur during a period of non-residence, so these will become taxable in the tax year in which the individual becomes resident again.

Law: ITTOIA 2005, s. 461-546
Guidance: IPTM generally

38.8.4   Pensions

Pensions are a large and complex area, especially in respect of cross-border issues, so a detailed analysis is outside the scope of this publication (but see **Chapters 29-32**). For a much more detailed analysis, see *Pension Tax Guide* from Claritax Books.

The main income tax consideration for non-residents is that tax relief is available for contributions made into a UK registered scheme if the individual is an active member of that scheme and is a "relevant UK individual" during the tax year in which the contributions are made. A relevant UK individual:

- has relevant UK earnings chargeable to income tax for that year;
- is resident in the UK at some time during that year;
- was resident in the UK both at some time during the five tax years immediately before that year and when the individual became a member of the pension scheme; or
- has general earnings for the tax year from overseas Crown employment subject to UK tax, or the individual's spouse/civil partner has such earnings.

If a non-resident individual falls under the third category above, and has no chargeable earnings, HMRC have confirmed that he or she can obtain tax relief on annual contributions up to £3,600 (gross). However, this tax relief will only be given at source.

If a UK registered pension scheme is transferred to an overseas pension scheme, this will be regarded as a recognised transfer (and so an authorised payment) if it is to a qualifying recognised overseas pension scheme (QROPS). A QROPS is a recognised overseas pension scheme (ROPS) that becomes qualifying, which is largely where the scheme manager of the ROPS undertakes to report certain details to HMRC.

This is a complex area and advice from a pension adviser suitably experienced in international transfers should be sought.

Law: FA 2004, s. 188-190; 221-226, 242A-242E; FA 2013, s. 53-54
Guidance: PTM 044100, 095300, 095400, 101999, 103500, 110000; https://tinyurl.com/3w2xje65 (HMRC list of ROPS)

38.8.5 *Employees' share-based income*

The legislation includes specific rules for the taxation of share-related income for internationally mobile employees (IME). Under these rules, the relevant period – from the day securities are acquired (usually upon grant or award) to the day of a chargeable event (e.g. vesting) – is time-apportioned between resident (taxable) and non-resident (not taxable) periods.

Example

Freda, a Brit living and working in the UK, was granted some share options by her UK employer on 1 January 2020.

She was then sent on assignment to Singapore for a few years, leaving the UK on 1 January 2021 and becoming not resident for UK tax purposes from 2021-22 onwards. Split-year treatment applied from when she left during 2020-21, and she did not perform any work in the UK while on assignment.

On 31 December 2022, Freda exercises her options when they vest for a gain of £10,000. The relevant period (the period over which the share income is regarded as being earned) will be three years, with one year when Freda was resident in the UK and two when she was resident in Singapore.

Being an IME (as defined at ITEPA 2003, s. 41F(2)), Freda will be taxed in the UK as follows:

	£
Total gain on exercise	10,000
Less: unchargeable foreign securities income for two years when not resident	(6,667)
Taxable income (year when resident)	3,333

Law: ITEPA 2003, s. 41F-41L
Guidance: ERSM 162000

38.8.6   *Termination payments*

If an employee is not resident for the tax year in which the termination of his or her employment occurs, foreign service relief may be available for periods when the employee was working overseas for an employer (this can include different employers in one group) and was not resident. This therefore applies if the individual's earnings were not assessable under ITEPA 2003, s. 15, or were not taxable because of the seafarers' deduction. See **9.6.4** for details.

If an employee's employment is terminated in a tax year in which he or she is resident, then all the termination package will be taxed, even if the individual spent all or part of his or her time working overseas and not resident.

For the definition of foreign service for this purpose see s. 413(2) (and EIM 13690); and for foreign seafaring service see s. 414B(2) (and EIM 13685).

When looking at termination payments and cross-border workers, double tax treaties need to be referred to. In particular, the OECD's commentary on this should be considered, as most treaties are silent in respect of termination payments.

Law: ITEPA 2003, s. 413, 414, 414C
Guidance: EIM 13680-13705, 13970-13985

38.8.7   Compliance

An individual leaving the UK needs to consider whether a P85 departure tax form is required. This form notifies HMRC that the individual has left the UK, and what sources of UK income he or she will still be receiving after leaving. The individual can also use the form to claim back any overpayment of tax that has arisen in the tax year of departure. An individual who is filing self-assessment tax returns is not required to complete a P85 form.

Guidance: https://tinyurl.com/6s99xzuv (guidance on form P85)

38.8.8   Covid-19

HMRC have confirmed that if a non-resident employee is stuck in the UK as a result of the Covid-19 pandemic, and is unable to leave because of the pandemic, the earnings from work performed in the UK as a result (from the date the employee originally planned to leave to the date he or she actually leaves) will not be subject to UK tax. The relaxation only applies if the earnings from the UK work days are taxed in the country in which the employee is normally resident, and if he or she left the UK as soon as it was possible to do so.

Despite this exemption, days upon which the employee works for more than three hours in the UK will still count as a UK work day when looking at the SRT (see **34.2**). Also, the above exemption does not help an individual who is resident in a country where he does not pay tax on his earnings, such as many of the Middle Eastern countries.

Guidance: https://www.gov.uk/tax-uk-income-live-abroad

38.9   Pitfalls and planning points

Personal allowance

When completing self-assessment tax returns, it is common for an individual not to complete the Residence, remittance basis etc. pages and so not to claim to be non-resident.

If the pages are completed, the individual very often fails to claim the personal allowance as a non-resident. If HMRC pick up on this they will deny the personal allowance, causing a tax liability to arise. The individual will then need to amend the tax return or make an overpayment relief claim.

A non-resident who is not a British citizen will not be entitled to the personal allowance unless it can be claimed under a double tax treaty

Working in the UK

A non-resident will often not realise that earnings from any work he or she physically performs in the UK are taxable in the UK unless exemption is available under a double tax treaty. Conditions must be satisfied for this treaty exemption and often these are not, resulting in a tax liability in the UK, for example if a non-resident continues to be employed by a UK employer.

Temporary non-residence

If an individual receives any of the income listed at **38.3**, and is not absent from the UK for the required five years, then any of this income received while absent and not resident may be taxed in the year in which the individual returns and becomes resident again.

Non-resident landlords scheme

It is a common misunderstanding among non-residents that when HMRC agree to rental income being paid gross (i.e. with no deduction of tax at source), the income is exempt from UK tax. This is not the case – the income is still taxable in the UK, it still needs to be declared on a tax return and any tax liability must be paid under self-assessment.

39. Foreign nationals coming to the UK

39.1 Introduction

There are some specific points relating to foreign nationals living and working in the UK. See also **Chapter 40** for foreign nationals assigned to the UK.

A foreign domicile has the opportunity for his or her overseas income to be taxed on the remittance basis if this is beneficial (see **Chapter 37**).

For foreign domiciles working in the UK who have claimed the remittance basis, the remittance of their earnings from overseas work will be taxed under ITEPA 2003:

- s. 22 (UK resident with a non-UK employer/contract where all work from that contract is performed overseas – see **39.3**); or
- s. 26 (UK resident, with both UK and overseas earnings – see **39.2**).

An exemption from UK tax on foreign earnings (up to £10,000 per tax year) exists for foreign domiciles who have a UK-based employment and who meet all of the following conditions:

- they are resident in the UK for a tax year;
- they have an employment the duties of which are either wholly or partly performed in the UK;
- their foreign earnings are subject to foreign tax;
- they are not taxed at the higher or additional rates;
- they have less than £100 in relevant foreign income (as defined by ITTOIA 2005, s. 830) that is subject to foreign tax;
- they have no other foreign income or gains during the relevant tax year;
- they do not file a self-assessment tax return; and
- they have not claimed the remittance basis under ITA 2007, s. 809B.

Law: ITA 2007, s. 828A-828D
Guidance: EIM 40102, 40301-40303; RDRM 32070

39.2   Overseas workday relief

An employee who is a resident foreign domicile, and so able to claim the remittance basis (see **Chapter 37**), may perform work outside the UK while resident in the UK, generating foreign earnings.

For such an individual, foreign earnings while resident in the UK (including during the UK part of a split year – see **34.3**) are not taxed in the UK if not remitted to the UK in a tax year. This is referred to by HMRC and others as "overseas workday relief" (OWR).

The individual must meet the following conditions, which are illustrated by taking 2021-22 as the relevant tax year. He or she must be either:

- not resident for all three previous tax years (so for 2018-19 to 2020-21);
- resident for the previous tax year, but not resident for the three years prior to that previous year (so resident for 2020-21 but not resident for 2017-18 to 2019-20);
- resident for the two previous tax years, but not resident for the three tax years prior to the first of those two previous tax years (so resident for 2019-20 and 2020-21 but not resident for 2016-17 to 2018-19); or
- not resident for the previous tax year, but resident for the tax year prior to that and not resident for the three tax years prior to this year (so not resident for 2020-21, resident for 2019-20, but not resident for 2016-17 to 2018-19).

If the foreign earnings are remitted, they are taxed in the year of remittance (ITEPA 2003, s. 26).

The apportionment of earnings between the UK and overseas is usually done on a workday time apportionment basis, unless it is clear that that basis is unsuitable, or that earnings relate to specific duties – see EIM 77020.

There is no limit to the number of times an individual can claim OWR in his or her life, as long as there is a consecutive period of at least three tax years for which the individual is not resident.

For dual residents, being treaty resident (see **35.2**) in another country will not affect the individual's eligibility to OWR.

It does not matter whether the employee is employed by a UK or foreign employer.

Mixed fund rules and OWR

With regard to the remittance of foreign earnings, special rules apply (ITA 2007, s. 809RA-809RD) to determine the order in which earnings are remitted from a qualifying mixed account. These rules only apply to foreign earnings assessed under ITEPA 2003, s. 26, and not to overseas earnings under s. 22 (dual contracts – see **39.3**), so any mixed account with earnings not assessed under s. 26 and the OWR rules will not be a qualifying account for this purpose.

These special mixed fund rules apply when an individual has general earnings for a tax year, some of which are taxed under ITEPA 2003, s. 15 and some are taxed on the remittance basis under s. 26 and which are paid into the individual's account that is qualifying at the time of payment.

A qualifying account must be nominated to HMRC under ITA 2007, s. 809RB. Other than a *de minimis* balance of less than £10, such an account must be cleared of funds immediately prior to the qualifying date (the first date mixed s. 15 and s. 26 earnings of more than £10 are paid into the account) referred to in the nomination notice. The account must be an ordinary bank account, i.e. a current or savings account.

The account becomes disqualified if no s. 26 remittance basis earnings are paid into the account during the tax year in which the qualifying date falls, such as when the employee is actually not resident for the tax year or decides to be taxed on the arising basis instead.

The employee can only have one nominated account, and joint earners cannot have the same nominated account and so must have separate qualifying accounts.

Where an account is a qualifying account, the transaction-by-transaction basis for determining what has been remitted from mixed funds under ITA 2007, s. 809Q and 809R does not apply. Instead, ITA 2007, s. 809RA sets out in four steps how the composition of each transfer from the account is established.

Where an employee's earnings are paid both into a UK account and an overseas qualifying account, the amounts paid into the UK account are deemed to be remittances, with UK taxed earnings deemed to have been remitted first under ITA 2007, s. 809Q(4).

For examples of these special mixed funds rules see HMRC's Joint Expatriate Forum meeting note of 29 January 2014 and numbers 3 and 4 of the forum's Q&A log at https://tinyurl.com/afyybk8f.

Covid-19

HMRC have confirmed that if, as a result of Covid-19 travel restrictions, an employee works in the UK more than he or she had intended, the earnings from these additional UK work days will be taxed in the UK, despite the fact that had it not been for these travel restrictions, the work would have been carried out overseas.

Law: ITEPA 2003, s. 26, 26A, 41ZA; ITA 2007, s. 809RA-809RD

Guidance: HMRC RDR4; EIM 40102-40103, 77020; https://www.gov.uk/government/publications/rdr4-overseas-workday-relief-owr

39.3   Dual contracts

If a resident foreign domiciled employee does not meet the conditions for OWR under ITEPA 2003, s. 26A, his or her earnings from overseas work days may be taxed under ITEPA 2003, s. 22 (overseas earnings, as opposed to foreign earnings assessed under s. 26) if the remittance basis is claimed.

ITEPA 2003, s. 23 sets out the conditions that need to be satisfied for earnings to be treated as overseas earnings and so taxed under s. 22 if remitted to the UK. The individual's employment must be with a foreign employer (an employer resident outside of the UK and not in the UK) and all the work in respect of the employment must be performed *wholly* outside the UK.

If the employee performs any work at all in the UK, then *all* the earnings will be regarded as not overseas earnings and will be taxable in the UK on the arising basis under s. 15. Work performed in the UK that is merely incidental to the overseas work, as described in EIM 40203 (see **38.5**), may be possible without causing the employee's overseas earnings status to be lost; but as mentioned in **38.5**, HMRC take a very narrow view of what incidental duties are.

ITEPA 2003, s. 23 also sets out how the overseas earnings are calculated (see an HMRC example at EIM 31771), with a limit for any employment performed in the UK for an associated employer, as set out under the anti-avoidance rules of s. 24 in respect of artificial dual contracts.

The special mixed funds rules for OWR and qualifying overseas bank accounts (see **39.2**) do not apply to overseas earnings.

Dual contracts and HMRC's view

A common tax planning technique is for a foreign domiciled employee resident in the UK to have two employment contracts – one for a UK employer, covering work performed in the UK, and another for a foreign employer, usually associated with the UK employer (under common control), covering all work performed outside the UK.

Very often, particularly in the past, the difference between the two employment contracts was purely geographical and not in respect of the actual duties performed. This scenario led to the introduction of the anti-avoidance provisions of s. 24 and 24B, which limit the amount of earnings that can be classed as overseas. HMRC will invoke s. 24 if they feel the split between the two contracts is disproportionate – s. 24 allows the reapportionment of earnings on a more commercial basis. If the overseas country involved has a low rate of tax, HMRC may invoke s. 24A and s. 24B, which allow all the remuneration under the overseas contract to be classed as UK earnings. See HMRC document *Restrictions on the remittance basis – dual contracts*.

HMRC's view is that dual contracts should be based on the actual facts and that the employee must genuinely be performing different duties under the contracts with differing responsibilities. If the contracts are split purely on where the duties are performed, such that there is no real distinction in the employee's work and role, there is a high chance that HMRC may enquire into the situation and try to treat the employment as one and so assess all the earnings in the UK under s. 15.

Appendix 3 at EIM 77030 sets out in detail HMRC's approach to dual contracts. See EIM 40108 for an example, where HMRC confirm that if an employee was carrying out one employment in the UK, but at a later date that contract was sub-divided into two contracts to take advantage of s. 22, HMRC will challenge the situation and will seek evidence that there are in reality two employments.

Law: ITEPA 2003, s. 22-26A

Guidance: EIM 31770-31771, 40102, 40105-40109, 77030 (but note that HMRC still make reference to ordinary residence, which ceased to exist from 6 April 2013); https://tinyurl.com/2fw5jct4 (HMRC document – *Restrictions on the remittance basis – dual contracts*); https://www.gov.uk/government/publications/dual-contracts

39.4   Employees of foreign governments and international organisations

Various categories of employee working in the UK are exempt from UK income tax, even though they may be resident in the UK. These categories include the following.

Diplomatic staff

Diplomatic staff enjoy exemption from income tax on official emoluments and private income arising outside the UK, even if remitted to the UK (see INTM 860230). This applies to those members of diplomatic missions set out in INTM 860210, but not for:

- those permanently resident in the UK (someone who was living in the UK at the time of appointment or has made the UK his or her permanent home); or
- a British citizen, British Dependent Territories citizen, British National (Overseas) or British Overseas citizen.

UK-sourced private income is still taxable. The tax residence status of such individuals is established as normal under the SRT (see **34.2**), so an individual who is resident will be entitled to the personal allowance.

Consular staff

In the same way as above, consular staff are exempt from UK income tax on official remuneration and private income arising outside the UK (see INTM 860310). Exemption applies to staff of foreign states' consuls in the UK.

INTM 860300 sets out those members of staff who are entitled to tax exemption and those who are not.

Agents-general

Agents-general have the same tax exemption as staff on diplomatic missions if they are representatives of:

- any state or province of a Commonwealth country, or the Republic of Ireland; or
- any colony certified by the appropriate Secretary of State to be self-governing.

INTM 860420 states which staff are entitled to tax exemption.

Commonwealth and Republic of Ireland offices

Certain officers and their staff in the above offices have the same exemptions as consular staff (see INTM 860450).

Armed forces

Certain visiting armed forces personnel are exempt from UK income tax on their emoluments (see INTM 860600 and 860610).

Military officers of Commonwealth governments are also exempt from UK income tax on their service pay and allowances, if they are present in the UK for training purposes.

An individual who is exempt from UK income tax will not become resident in the UK under the SRT (see **34.2**) just because of his service in the UK. However, if any income is chargeable to UK tax, he will still be eligible for the personal allowance if he would otherwise have been resident.

International organisations

Exemption from income tax depends on the relevant Order in Council in place under the *International Organisations Act* 1968, which generally provides exemption from tax for individuals working for international organisations of which the UK is a member. The exemption also covers the individual's family, household and staff.

British citizens employed by certain organisations (see INTM 860750) are not exempt from UK tax, although normal rules apply and they will not be taxed in the UK if not resident for UK tax purposes and not performing any of their work in the UK.

Consultants (often described as "experts on mission") who are independent contractors are not entitled to exemption from tax.

There are many international organisations whose employees are covered by this exemption, some of the main ones being:

The Commonwealth Foundation	The International Monetary Fund
The Council of Europe	NATO
The European Central Bank	The OECD
The European Court of Human Rights	The United Nations
The European Court of Justice	The World Health Organisation

The International Court of Justice

The International Development
Association

The World Trade Organisation

The World Bank

Law: *International Organisations Act* 1968; ITEPA 2003, s. 300-303; ITA 2007, s. 833
Guidance: INTM 860000-860870

39.5 Pensions

Pensions are a large and complex area, especially in respect of cross-border issues, so a detailed analysis is outside the scope of this publication (but see **Chapters 29-32** for coverage of pensions from a UK perspective). For a much more detailed analysis, see *Pension Tax Guide* from Claritax Books.

Some of the main points to watch for in respect of foreign nationals in the UK are as follows.

If an overseas pension scheme is not registered/approved for UK tax purposes, this will mean that any employer contributions paid for an employee will be taxable; the employer will need to consider the PAYE consequences and the employee the self-assessment implications. In addition, the employee will not benefit from any tax relief for the contributions he or she may make into the pension scheme.

However, under ITEPA 2003, s. 307 a tax charge on the above benefit may not arise if the provision made by the individual's employer is for a "retirement or death benefit" (a pension, annuity, lump sum, gratuity or other similar benefit) which will be paid or given to the employee in the event of the employee's retirement or death, regardless of whether or not the pension scheme is registered.

If the overseas scheme is a registered pension scheme, or a qualifying overseas scheme and the employee is a relevant migrant member for UK tax purposes, there will be no tax liability on employer contributions into such a scheme. The employee will be able to claim tax relief (subject to the usual limits) on contributions he makes into the scheme providing:

- he is resident in the UK at the time they are paid;
- he has relevant earnings chargeable to UK income tax; and
- he has notified the scheme manager that he intends to claim tax relief.

FA 2004, Sch. 33, para. 4 defines "migrant member" and para. 5 defines "qualifying overseas pension scheme". Both definitions are long and quite complex.

Care needs to be taken, however, when considering whether or not an employee claims tax relief in the UK, as this may mean that any unauthorised payments from the overseas scheme could lead to an unauthorised payment charge/surcharge, regardless of the residence and domicile status of the individual at the time.

Some double tax treaties, e.g. that between the USA and the UK, allow relief on pension contributions paid by or for employees working in the host country, subject to certain conditions.

Law: ITEPA 2003, s. 307-308A; FA 2004, s. 242A-249, Sch. 33, 34
Guidance: PTM 110000-114000

39.6 Travel and subsistence expenses

39.6.1 Detached duty relief

If a foreign employee is working in the UK for his foreign employer, "detached duty relief" may be available if his time in the UK is less than two years. This is relief under ITEPA 2003, s. 338 for his travel and subsistence expenses while assigned to the UK, which may be very generous if available, as it will cover all costs of his travel when in the UK. This therefore includes commuting costs (but not private travel), accommodation costs and associated expenses such as utilities, and also living costs such as food, as long as these are reasonable.

It is important that the employee's secondment to the UK is expected to be less than two years, so that the UK workplace is regarded as a temporary workplace and the individual's usual workplace overseas is regarded as his or her permanent workplace. In this respect it is also important that the employee's employment contract remains with the foreign employer. In practice, however, detached duty relief is often not available, because the individual's employment contract is transferred to the UK entity to which he or she has been seconded.

If an employee's secondment to the UK is extended beyond two years, it may still be possible to claim detached duty relief up until the point at which the employee's intentions about staying in the UK changed, i.e. the point at which there was an intention to stay in the UK for more than two years. It is important to keep documentation showing when this change in intention happened and why, along with documentation showing what the original intentions were, as there is a higher chance that HMRC will enquire into any detached duty relief claim in these circumstances. HMRC may well argue that the individual had always had the intention to work in the UK for more than 24 months.

If the time spent in the UK makes up the whole of the employee's period of employment, detached duty relief will not be available.

If detached duty relief is claimed, then relocation relief under ITEPA 2003, s. 271 (see **7.2**) cannot be claimed as well.

Relief is available for expenses incurred by the employee (as a deduction against taxable earnings) and also for those borne by the employer.

See also sections **8.2.8** to **8.2.13**.

Law: ITEPA 2003, s. 337-339
Guidance: EIM 31800

39.6.2   Other reliefs

The table below shows some of the most common reliefs for travel expenses that may be available for foreign nationals working in the UK. Once more, see sections **8.2.8** to **8.2.13** for further coverage.

Relief is available only if the costs are borne by the employer, apart from travel costs between employments (s. 342 – first row of table below), where relief is available for costs met by the employee.

Description/ITEPA 2003/ EIM ref.	Residence/ domicile status	Deduction against earnings under ITEPA
Travel costs between two or more employments, one of which is performed wholly or partly overseas, and costs are in respect of performance of work at destination. s. 342* – EIM 34080	Must be resident. If foreign employer, must be UK domicile.	s. 15
Travel costs in respect of employment duties performed overseas that can only be performed there. s. 370* – EIM 34025, 34040, 34090	Must be resident. Can be a UK or foreign domicile.	s. 15

Description/ITEPA 2003/ EIM ref. (cont.)	Residence/ domicile status	Deduction against earnings under ITEPA
Travel costs (including inoculations and certain visas) within a five-year period for qualifying journeys to UK from home country in order to perform work in UK, and journeys back to home country. No limit to number of qualifying journeys. Often known as home leave. s. 373, 375 – EIM 35000	Foreign domicile only (not deemed domiciles).	s. 15 or 27
Travel costs of employee's family (spouse/civil partner and minor child) if employee works in UK for at least 60 continuous days. Limited to two return trips per tax year per person. Often known as home leave. s. 374 – EIM 35000	Foreign domicile only (not deemed domiciles)	s. 15 or 27
* Meaning of travel costs – EIM 354130		

39.7   Termination payments

Any termination payment that a foreign national receives, covering years worked in the UK when resident, may be taxed in the UK depending on the circumstances at the time. See **Chapter 9** for detailed coverage of the termination payment rules.

Full or partial foreign service relief, as explained at **38.8.6**, will be available if the foreign national is not resident for the tax year in which the termination falls. If the individual is resident, then there will be no foreign service relief and all the termination payment will be taxed in the UK, even if the individual performed most of his employment overseas when not resident.

In respect of foreign service relief, the remittance basis needs to be considered (see example 2 of EIM 13985). If OWR (see **39.2**) applies, the overseas work days count as foreign service if the earnings from these work days have not been remitted to the UK.

39.8   Share-based remuneration

As with non-residents, for internationally mobile employees (IME), the relevant period is time-apportioned between periods when resident and not resident (see **38.8.5**).

In addition, the remittance basis (see **Chapter 37**) also needs to be considered. Any of the share income taxed on the remittance basis is excluded and taxed in the tax year of remittance if remitted to the UK.

Example

Greta, a Dane, was granted share options by her Danish employer while working in Denmark on 6 April 2018.

Greta was assigned to the UK on 1 April 2020 for five years and became resident for 2020-21, so from 6 April 2020. She exercised her options on 5 April 2022 with a gain arising of £10,000. She was entitled to OWR (see **39.2**) for 2020-21 and 2021-22, and works 60 days a year overseas out of a total of 240 work days per year. The relevant period is four years from 6 April 2018 to 5 April 2022.

	£
Total gain on exercise	10,000
Less: unchargeable foreign securities income for 2018-19 and 2019-20 when not resident	(5,000)
	5,000
Chargeable foreign securities income taxed on the remittance basis in respect of 2020-21 and 2021-22 (£5,000 x 120/480)	(1,250)
Taxable income for 2021-22	3,750

39.9   Pitfalls and planning points

Planning prior to arrival

Planning opportunities are available for foreign nationals coming to the UK in respect of overseas workday relief, detached duty relief and the remittance basis (see **Chapter 37**).

The planning should take place well before the individual becomes resident in the UK, which may be before he or she arrives. The structure of the individual's employment/assignment contract may also have an important part in planning, for example in relation to detached duty relief. Bank accounts overseas may need to be opened to meet the conditions for overseas workday relief and the remittance basis.

Dual contracts

Extreme care should be taken when dual contracts are used, ensuring that they reflect a genuine difference between the duties of employments overseas and in the UK, and that they are not artificially created just to reduce tax.

40. International assignments

40.1 Remuneration packages for international assignees

40.1.1 Principles

In addition to the issues raised in **Chapters 38** and **39**, specific issues arise for employees who are assigned either from or to the UK.

When sending employees on an international secondment, the employer must consider various additional elements when making up the assignee's remuneration package. These will in turn affect how the individual will be taxed.

The first step is for the employer to decide whether to adopt a home country approach or a host country one (the host country being the one the employee is moving to), or potentially a combination of both.

A home country approach is where the employer tries to keep the employee in the same position as he or she would have been, had the individual remained living in the home country, so that the individual neither gains nor loses from being assigned overseas. This approach will involve paying the employee additional amounts, such as a cost of living allowance (COLA), and will include tax equalisation.

Under tax equalisation, the employer will try to ensure that the employee has the same net salary as he or she did while living in the home country, and will be responsible for the payment of the employee's tax in the host country. This will cause tax complications, including potentially the need to gross up the tax, as the payment of an employee's tax is regarded as a benefit in kind in the UK.

A host country approach is to treat the employee in the same way as a locally recruited employee in the host country. The individual will be paid the level of remuneration paid to a local employee at a similar grade, although additional allowances may be paid to compensate the individual for living away from his or her home country. The employee will be responsible for his or her own tax affairs, including paying taxes in the host country.

There are various methods when it comes to constructing an expatriate's remuneration package, and these are shown in **Appendix 12**. The method or methods selected will dictate how the employee is taxed, both in the host country and also in the home country if the individual remains taxable there.

40.1.2   UK employees assigned overseas

For UK employees assigned overseas, tax equalisation is carried out as follows.

- UK hypothetical (or "hypo") tax is calculated by taking those elements of the employee's usual remuneration while living in the UK and that are to be included, according to the employer's tax equalisation policy.

- UK tax is calculated on these as normal, taking into account personal adjustments, such as relief for pension contributions, etc. (again as set out in the tax equalisation policy).

- This hypo tax is then deducted from the employee's gross salary in each pay period and is kept by the employer as a contribution towards the overseas tax, although complications can arise if the employee remains taxable in the UK and UK tax is still due, which the employer also pays.

The employer pays the employee's overseas tax by one of two methods: the gross-up method or the reimbursement method.

The gross-up method

The employee's salary is grossed up so that after the host country's tax, the individual receives his or her net salary after the deduction of hypo tax, i.e. the net salary the employee would have been receiving in the UK had he or she not left on assignment. This will involve:

- calculating what the employee's net salary after hypo tax should be;

- calculating what the host country tax is;

- establishing by how much the host country tax exceeds the hypo tax;

- grossing up this excess by the employee's marginal rate of tax in the host country (the gross-up, sometimes called a tax equalisation allowance) which is then added to the employee's gross salary; and

- applying the host country tax rates to this, which should produce the net salary required after hypo tax.

An alternative, shorter approach (which is often used in practice), is to gross up the net salary by the employee's marginal rate of tax in the host country to give the gross salary required.

Specialist tax return software, which includes tax equalisation and gross-ups, is required for completing the tax returns of tax-equalised employees.

The reimbursement method

The employee's net salary after hypo tax is treated as the gross salary for the host country's tax, and the employee either pays this tax personally, and is reimbursed by the employer, or it is paid directly by the employer.

This is then a taxable benefit in kind on the employee in the tax year it is reimbursed or paid. A tax gross-up may be required in the final year of assignment to collect any tax that may be due on tax that is reimbursed or paid for that year.

This will depend on the circumstances and whether the benefit is taxable. For example, if the employee is reimbursed after he has left, it may not be taxable in the host country and may also not be taxed in the UK if he returns there, because it relates to earnings arising when he was not resident and for work not performed in the UK.

Reconciliation

At the end of the relevant tax year, a tax reconciliation is carried out (often via specialised tax return software), which compares the hypo tax calculated using actual figures with the hypo tax deducted during the year. An appropriate adjustment is then made, resulting in either the employer or employee having to pay the other an additional amount.

40.1.3   Foreign employees assigned to the UK

For a foreign employee assigned to the UK, the same steps above will be taken, only with the UK being the host country. So the hypo tax will be the tax the employee normally pays in his or her home country. It will be UK tax that will then have to be grossed up on the individual's UK tax return if the gross-up method is used. If the reimbursement method is used, the assignee's gross salary that is taxed in the UK will be his or her net salary after foreign hypo tax, with UK tax also being due on the resultant benefit in kind of the employer reimbursing the employee for the cost of the individual's UK tax.

Example – tax equalisation

Hans was assigned to the UK from Germany and was tax equalised.

His gross salary for 2021-22 is £75,000 and the German hypo tax on this is £15,000, meaning that the required net salary is £60,000.

Using the gross-up method, the UK tax for 2021-22 is calculated as follows:

	£
Gross salary	75,000
Less: personal allowance	(12,570)
Taxable income	62,430
Tax at 20% on £37,700	7,540
Tax at 40% on £24,730	9,892
Total tax	17,432
The above UK tax liability exceeds the German hypo tax by (£17,432 – £15,000)	2,432
This amount therefore needs to be grossed up (2,432 x 100/60).	4,053
This grossed-up figure is then added to the original gross salary of £75,000 to give a revised gross salary of £79,053 (£75,000 + £4,053). This is the amount taxed in the UK	79,053
Check:	
Revised gross salary	79,053
Less: Personal allowance	(12,570)
Revised taxable income	66,483
Tax at 20% on £37,700	7,540
Tax at 40% on £28,783	11,513
Revised UK tax liability	19,053
Revised net salary, which is the net salary required (£79,053 less £19,053)	60,000

(Cont.)	£
A shorter method which is often used in practice is to gross up the required net salary by the individual's marginal rate of tax in the UK (19,053/79,053 = 24.102%), so £60,000 x 100/75.898, to calculate the required gross salary that is taxed in the UK	79,053

The above is a very simple example to highlight the basic principles involved with tax equalisation. In practice, these calculations are considerably more complex, which is why specialised tax return software is required.

If the reimbursement method was used, then Hans would be taxed in the UK as follows (using 2021-22 tax rates throughout):

Example – tax equalisation (cont.)

2021-22	£
Net salary treated as gross salary	60,000
Less: Personal allowance	(12,570)
Taxable income	47,430
Tax at 20% on £37,700	7,540
Tax at 40% on £9,730	3,892
Tax due and reimbursed by employer during 2022-23	11,432
2022-23	
Gross salary (£60,000 net salary plus £11,432 2021-22 tax reimbursed by employer)	71,432
Less: personal allowance	(12,570)
Taxable income	58,862
Tax at 20% on £37,700	7,540
Tax at 40% on £21,162	8,465
Tax liability reimbursed by employer during 2023-24	16,005

The same process will be used for 2023-24 onwards.

40.2 PAYE

Employers need to be aware of specific PAYE issues for expatriate employees assigned to the UK or overseas.

40.2.1 UK employees assigned overseas

Employees of UK employers, who have been assigned overseas, will need to obtain an NT (no tax) PAYE code from HMRC if they:

- become not resident;
- remain on a UK payroll; and
- do not intend to perform any work in the UK.

This code will ensure that no tax is deducted from the employee's salary under PAYE while he or she is assigned overseas.

If the non-resident employee does not have an NT code, and is partially performing work in the UK (such that the earnings from these UK work days are taxable under ITEPA 2003, s. 27), the employer should consider obtaining a direction from HMRC under ITEPA 2003, s. 690 (the employee cannot apply for this direction). This reduces the amount of tax collected under PAYE, which will otherwise need to be operated on *all* the employee's earnings, causing potential cash-flow issues for the individual.

If an employee has remained resident but is working overseas, his or her PAYE code can be amended to take account of any foreign tax that has been withheld from his or her salary. In this way, double tax relief is obtained via the individual's PAYE code (known as a net-of-tax credit relief arrangement – see EP Appendix 5, PAYE 82001). This will be particularly important from a cash-flow perspective for the employee, if the host country's tax is also being withheld from his or her salary.

Guidance: https://tinyurl.com/ybaw6tew (online application for s. 690 direction)

40.2.2 Employees assigned to the UK

The above s. 690 direction can also be applied for on behalf of employees who are resident and claiming overseas workday relief (see **39.2**).

Complications arise when operating PAYE on salaries of assignees to the UK who are tax equalised, in particular obtaining the relevant details from foreign entities in a timely manner for PAYE and RTI purposes. A modified payroll scheme can be applied for under EP Appendix 6 (PAYE

82002), whereby PAYE is operated on estimates of the employee's earnings and benefits which are grossed up; the actual figures are then declared on the employee's self-assessment tax return, with any additional tax paid through the self-assessment system.

If an employee is assigned to the UK by a foreign employer who does not have a presence or a place of business in the UK (see PAYE 81605 and 81610), the employer does not need to operate a PAYE scheme. In this situation, the onus falls on the employee to operate a PAYE scheme on his or her own earnings (a direct scheme), and the employee is unlikely to have the knowledge or experience to run this successfully. It may be possible to agree with HMRC that the tax due on the earnings is paid instead via self-assessment, but the employee must then be aware of the cash-flow implications, especially in the first year when payments on account start.

For employees of foreign employers with no presence or place of business in the UK, the host employer rules under ITEPA 2003, s. 689 need to be considered. It is necessary to see whether these cause a PAYE obligation on a host employer, if that UK entity has control over the employee.

UK employers operating internationally may have non-resident employees visiting and working for them in the short-term (known as short-term business visitors (STBV)). In such cases, HMRC may agree to relax the PAYE obligations in respect of these STBVs, either under EP Appendix 4 (PAYE 82000) or under EP Appendix 8 (PAYE 82008), depending on the circumstances. The concept of an "economic employer" is relevant – this is where the employee is legally employed by one employer, but another employer benefits from and bears the risks of the work the employee performs, with some of the employee's remuneration being recharged to the economic employer (see *Tax Bulletins* 17 and 68). This concept is applied when looking at the employment article of double tax treaties.

Employees assigned to the UK are generally dealt with by HMRC's specialist Expatriate Team in Bootle.

Law: ITEPA 2003, s. 689-690; SI 2003/2682, Pt. 7, Ch. 4

Guidance: PAYE 81500-82008; https://tinyurl.com/3re6hb7n (HMRC Helpsheet on tax equalisation)

40.3   Pitfalls and planning points

Assignment structure

It is essential to understand how an assignee's package and assignment are structured, in order to establish the correct tax treatment in both the home and host countries.

Involvement in the early stages of formulating an employee's assignment will present potential tax planning opportunities – e.g. detached duty relief (see **39.6.1**) and ensuring the assignment is for less than two years and that the employment contract remains with the home country employer.

PAYE

Employers should ensure the PAYE procedures covering expatriate employees are correctly followed, to avoid potential enquiries from HMRC.

Appropriate actions should be taken to avoid potentially significant cash-flow issues for the employee, such as tax in both countries being withheld from salary, which would undoubtedly lead to a very unhappy employee!

Tax-equalised employees

If the employer is responsible for paying the employee's tax, it is important to ensure that this is paid on time. Some tax authorities around the world are not as "nice" as HMRC, and again there will be an unhappy employee if bailiffs arrive on his or her doorstep, demanding the payment of tax.

TRUSTS AND ESTATES

41. Taxation of trusts

41.1 Introduction

41.1.1 Historical context

Trusts have a long history reaching back to the Middle Ages when from around the eleventh century the concept of "use" was born. A use was given to allow the legal title of land to be conveyed to another owner (called the "*feoffee* to uses") but the transferor or another third party could use the land (called the "*cestuis que use*" equivalent to the modern day beneficiary). The use was exploited for various reason, including ensuring that land could be disposed of rather than automatically passed down over generations and to circumvent feudal estate and capital taxes. In addition, it is thought the crusaders conveyed their ownership to a *feoffee* while they went to fight, and Franciscan monks used them to retain the use of their property while not undermining their vow of poverty.

However, common law, the only law that existed at the time, did not recognise that the ownership of land could be divided into such parts. According to common law, the beneficial owner was always also the legal owner and it was this owner, and only he, who had any power or control over the land. This meant that if the "use" had any problems or difficulties, he had no legal recourse or "*seisin*" to correct such problems.

This was deemed not just, and its eventual solution gave birth to the modern rules of equity. In those times, when something appeared not to be fair, a petition was placed for the consideration of the king. The king received so many of these petitions that around the 15th century, he started referring them to the Lord Chancellor, who formed the Court of Chancery to make remedial decisions as to the fairness of situations. For the "use petitions" the Lord Chancellor was to establish who the real owner was "in equity"; in other words, who (he felt) the true owner was, "in all fairness and in the name of good consciousness".

Usually the Lord Chancellor's court would side with the use and find that the legal owner was only holding the land for the benefit of the use and it was unconscionable to claim anything different. This created the split between legal owner (the trustee) and beneficial owner (the beneficiary) that still exists today.

41.1.2   Definitions

The settlor

The settlor is the person who creates the trust, by transferring ownership of the trust property to the trustees. The settlor is genuinely giving both the legal title and the beneficial interest away, so is making a gift or transfer. The process of transferring the property to the trustees is often called "settling" a trust, or "making a settlement".

There can be more than one settlor, but this is uncommon in practice.

The trustees

The trustees are the party that *legally* own the assets transferred into the trust by the settlor.

The trustees have the responsibility to deal with the trust property for the benefit of those who have beneficial ownership, i.e. the beneficiaries. They have a duty of care under the *Trustee Act* 2000 to exercise reasonable care and skill when dealing with the trust property and this duty increases where the trustees are professional trustees.

The trustees are not able to benefit from the trust property themselves; in fact, there is a general rule under equity that trustees may not profit from the trust.

The individual trustees form a single and continuing body, which is a separate legal entity with a separate legal personality from those individuals that make it up. For instance, trustees can be liable to income tax as trustees, as well as being liable to income tax in their own capacity as individuals. These two liabilities are separate and will be disclosed on entirely separate tax returns. Any changes in the make-up of the trustee body (for instance, trustees resigning and new trustees being appointed) will therefore have no effect on the tax treatment of the trust (unless the change causes the trust to change tax residence – see **Chapter 34**).

The settlor can choose as many trustees as he or she wishes for the trust, but usually there is a minimum of two. Trustees can be anyone the settlor choses, including the settlor, but they must have mental capacity.

If the settlor choses to make himself a trustee, he will have additional control over the trust and the destination of the income and capital. This is not prohibited and in fact is one of the advantages of setting up a trust, as a modicum of control may be retained. Generally, in these cases, the settlor will also have the power within the trust deed to add or remove trustees. Settlors must ensure that they keep their settlor and trustee roles separate.

The beneficiaries

The beneficiaries are the *beneficial* owners of the property transferred into the trust, and will be named in the trust deed. The named beneficiaries are the only people that can benefit from the trust. No one else, including the settlor (but see below) and the trustees, can benefit from the trust. This goes back to the 1734 case of *Robinson v Pett* where it was held that "the court never allows ... a trustee for his time and trouble."

There is one exception to this, which is if the trustees are professional trustees. They may benefit by being paid remuneration for performing the trust duties but only if this is either allowed under statute or provided for in the trust deed.

The settlor may also be a beneficiary of the trust. If the settlor, or his or her spouse, is also a beneficiary, the trust is known as a "settlor-interested trust". Anti-avoidance provisions prevent a settlor from benefiting from tax advantages by being a beneficiary and a settlor at the same time. This is therefore usually advised against unless there are strong non-fiscal reasons.

Whether the settlor is a settlor and a trustee, or a settlor and a beneficiary, or more rarely a settlor, a trustee and a beneficiary, each role must be kept separate.

The trust

The existence of the trustees and the beneficiaries creates an entity defined as a "trust". The word trust here is used in the ordinary way. The settlor is entrusting the assets that he or she transfers to the trustees, for them to hold and protect on behalf of the beneficiaries. A trust may also be known as a settlement.

The trust deed

The trust deed is a legal document that sets out the details of the trust. It will contain the following information:

- the name of the settlor;
- the names of the trustees;
- the names of the beneficiaries;

- the type of trust;
- the date the trust was set up; and
- the ages of the beneficiaries, and what kind of interest they have.

Law: TA 2000, s. 1, 29

Case: *Robinson v Pett* (1734) 2 Eq Cas Abr 454

Guidance: *Trusts, Settlements and Estates Manual,* TSEM 6237

41.1.3 Creating an express trust

A trust deed is not always essential to create a trust. A trust will arise in all instances where the legal title and beneficial interest are separated, whether there is a trust deed or not (see resulting and constructive trusts at **41.6.5**).

The most common type of trust is one that has been set up by a positive intention. This is called an express private trust, and is set up either by the settlor creating a trust deed, or by creation in the will of the testator or testatrix.

A trust requires three certainties in order to be valid. These are:

1. Certainty of words and intention. This means that it must be clear from the trust deed that the intention is to set up a trust. Where insufficient certainty of intention exists, there is a risk that the intended trustee could keep the trust property for him or herself.

2. Certainty of subject matter. The property that is to be held in the trust must be clearly identified. This isn't so much a problem with cash, but with other assets. For example, in the case of *Palmer v Simmonds*, it was not certain enough to state: I gift "the bulk of my estate". "The bulk" was not a measure that could accurately be put into a trust.

3. Certainty of objects. The "objects" are the beneficiaries. In order to have a valid trust it is essential to have sufficient knowledge of those to whom the trust property is intended, either individually or as a class. For example, "my grandchildren" is a certain class, whereas "my friends" is not. It is not necessary to name the beneficiaries individually if a class is used as long as there is at least one living person in the class at the commencement of the trust.

Case: *Palmer v Simmonds* (1854) 2 Drew 22

41.1.4   *Scope of this chapter*

This chapter offers a practical analysis of the tax consequences of using trusts in the UK. The complexities of offshore trusts are beyond the scope of a volume of this nature and are not covered.

For a more in-depth guide to the practicalities of using trusts for tax and financial planning purposes, see *Financial Planning with Trusts* by John Woolley and Marcia Banner, from Claritax Books.

41.2   Taxing a trust

Once the trustees have the trust property legally in their hands, they are liable as one legal body to pay income tax on any income the trust generates during the tax year.

The trust will not have employment income or any trading income (normally), or other income that can only be earned by a real person, but can have passive income, such as property income, royalty income and investment income such as interest and dividends. In practice, trusts may typically have income from letting residential or commercial property, interest from government stocks and shares, and other secure share investments.

These categories of income are calculated for tax purposes in the same way for the trustees as they are for individuals, so see also **Chapters 23** (interest), **24** (dividends) and **26** (rental profits).

The trustees will (usually, but see below) need to register for self-assessment as a chargeable taxable body for the income received inside the trust and will be taxed for income arising in the tax year (6 April to 5 April). The self-assessment tax return will be due by 31 January in the year after the tax year ends (31 October if filed on paper), and the penalties for late filing, late payment, errors and failure to notify are the same as those for individuals.

Trustees do not need to notify HMRC if the only source of income they have is from savings income in the form of interest (not dividends) as long as the tax calculated on that income does not exceed £100 in the tax year. This is a concession that began in 2016.

Trustees are "persons in the law" and not individuals and, as such, they are not entitled to a personal allowance. They are also not entitled to the starting rate band, the personal savings allowance, or the dividend allowance.

Trust management expenses

Trust management expenses (TMEs) and overheads often need to be incurred in the running of the trust. Examples of TMEs are the costs of preparing the trust accounts and tax returns, lawyers' fees, bank charges for distributing the income to beneficiaries, travelling costs and the costs of trustees attending meetings.

TMEs cannot be offset in calculating income tax inside the trust. In fact, no expenses can be deducted for tax purposes from a trust except for expenses that are properly associated and chargeable with a source of income. For example, house insurance of a rental property let by the trustees can properly be offset against the rental income to form the profits to be taxed.

The reasoning for this is explained very well in the comments made in the 1894 tax case *Aikin v Macdonald's Trustees:*

> "The only kind of deduction allowed is expenditure incurred in earning the profit. There is no deduction under any circumstances allowable for expenditure incurred in managing profits which have already been earned and reduced into money."

TMEs will, however, need to be removed before the income is paid to the beneficiary – although they are not tax-deductible, they were actually paid out, so the funds are not there to pay the beneficiary. For these purposes, the TMEs are always deemed to have been paid from dividend income in priority and then from savings income, and finally non-savings income.

Law: TMA 1970, s. 8A; ITA 2007, s. 34, 474, 486, 503
Case: *Aikin v Macdonald's Trustees* [1894] 3 TC 306
Guidance: TSEM 3036, 11000; https://tinyurl.com/y6y7r4ad (HMRC Trusts and Estates Newsletter)

41.3 Interest-in-possession trusts

41.3.1 Overview

Trusts tend to be classified into two categories:

- those in which the trustees can accumulate the income; and
- those in which the income must be paid out to the beneficiaries.

An interest-in-possession (IiP) trust is the latter. The definition usually used for an IiP trust arose from *Pearson* in 1980, where a beneficiary was defined as having an interest in possession if he or she has:

> "a present right of present enjoyment or an immediate right to the income or enjoyment of property (irrespective of whether the property produces income)".

The power of the trustees to accumulate income destroys an interest in possession, so if the trust is an IiP the trustees have no ability to accumulate the income. Legally, to be an IiP trust the income must be paid out to the beneficiary. Such trusts are also known as life interest trusts.

A trust that does not produce income can still be an IiP. Likewise, a life tenant beneficiary enjoying the use of an asset rather than the income will also have an interest in possession.

Law: IHTA 1984, s. 50
Case: *Pearson v IRC* [1980] BTC 8113
Guidance: IHTM 16066

41.3.2   The structure of an IiP trust

The following is a pictorial representation of an IiP trust.

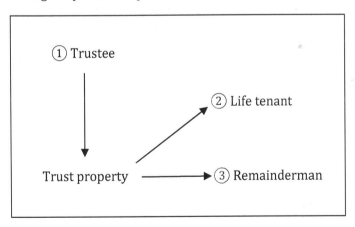

1. The trustee holds the trust property for two beneficiary groups: the life tenant and the remainderman. The trustee receives income from holding the trust property. The life tenant is entitled to the income and the remainderman is entitled to the capital remaining.

2. The life tenant (or life tenants if there are more than one of them) must be given all the income in the trust that the capital or the trust property has generated in the year. The trustees are not able to retain or accumulate any of this income for the trust or for the remainderman. The life tenant has no rights over the trust capital and cannot call for any capital instead of income (unless the trust deed specifically permits this).

3. At some point in the future, on the occasion of an event detailed in the trust document, the life tenant will no longer have the right to the income from the trust property and the capital will be transferred to the remainderman. Usually, at this point, the trust will end. The end may be because of the death of the life tenant (this is why it is often called a life interest trust, as the life tenant has the interest for his or her life). However, it does not always have to end on the death of the life tenant. It may end when the life tenant marries, or reaches a certain age, or if another significant event occurs, such as having a baby or moving to a new country.

4. It is always up to the settlor to define the parameters under which the trust deed operates, so it will have been the settlor's decision when the trust was formed, as to when, and in what circumstances, the trust will end. It may even go on to another life tenant and not end at all. In any case, before the event that ends the (current) life tenant's right to the income, that person is said to have a "present right to enjoy the income of the settlement". The remainderman is the residual beneficiary or reversionary beneficiary of this type of trust. That is because when the life interest ends, for whatever reason, the residual capital will "revert" to that beneficiary.

The workings of each individual trust are unique and are defined by the terms of the trust deed. In some trust deeds, there are clauses that allow trustees to distribute a share of the capital or the trust property to the life tenants. In others, capital distributions may be made to the remainderman before the life tenancy comes to an end. The terms of the trust must be studied carefully to see the exact working of the specific trust involved.

41.3.3 The taxation of the trustees of an IiP

Trustees of an IiP trust are treated as the owners, under common law, of the underlying trust property and are charged to income tax on income arising in the trust from the trust property at basic rates. In 2021-22 these rates are:

Non-savings income	20%
Savings income	20%
Dividend income	7.5%

There are no basic, higher or additional rate bands for IiP trustees, so, irrespective of the level of income coming into the trust, the income will always be taxed in the trust at the applicable basic rates.

Property income and interest are received by the trustees gross and are taxed at the basic rate of 20%. Dividends are also received gross and are taxed on the trustees at the dividend ordinary rate of 7.5%.

The IiP trust can be seen as a process, almost like a conveyor belt. The income from the trust assets flows onto the conveyor belt, expenses properly associated with this income are deducted, tax is calculated and deducted, then the balance is counted, and any trust expenses are deducted, before it leaves the belt and is paid out to the life tenant beneficiary.

The capital remains unchanged, safe, and secure for the remainderman.

Example – Rihanna

Rihanna was the only life tenant of the Diamonds trust. The income received by the trust in the tax year 2021-22 is as follows:

	£
Property income	30,000
Bank interest	7,000
Dividend income	8,000

There were £4,000 of expenses to be offset against the property income and £925 of other trust expenses.

The tax is calculated as follows:

	Total income	Non-savings income	Savings income	Dividend income
	£	£	£	£
Property income (£30,000 - £4,000)	26,000	26,000		
Savings income	7,000		7,000	
Dividend income	8,000			8,000
Taxable income	41,000	26,000	7,000	8,000
Tax at basic rates	(7,200)	(5,200)	(1,400)	(600)

Note that there was no deduction for the TMEs as these are not deductible in arriving at taxable income. The £4,000 of property expenses could be offset, however.

Law: TMA 1970, s. 8A; ITA 2007, s. 34, 474

41.3.4 The taxation of the beneficiary from an IiP

The life tenant beneficiary is, as outlined above, entitled to all the income arising in the IiP trust over the tax year in line with his or her equitable beneficial ownership of the trust property. When this income is distributed to the beneficiary it will already have been taxed in the hands of the trustees, but the taxing of this income does not stop there. The beneficiary will be taxed, not at the basic rate that is applied in the trust, but at his or her own rate.

To achieve this, the beneficiary is given a summary of the tax that has been paid on the income by the trust, using form R185 (Trust Income). This shows the net income, the gross income and the tax paid on that income by the trust. The life tenant beneficiary initially ignores the income tax paid by the trust and inserts the gross income totals into his or her own tax computation for the year. This allows the tax due to be calculated at the individual's own marginal tax rate. Once the tax has been calculated at this rate, the beneficiary can offset the tax already paid by the trustees as a tax credit. This should leave a basic rate taxpayer with no tax to pay or reclaim.

For example, if the only thing received by an IiP trust was £10,000 of interest in a tax year, the trustees would pay £2,000 tax on that income, using the 20% basic rate. They would then pass the net income of £8,000 to the beneficiary. That beneficiary would gross up the £8,000 by 100/80 to £10,000, and then multiply this by his or her personal rate of tax. If the recipient beneficiary was a basic rate taxpayer, this would be 20%, making £2,000 income tax due by the beneficiary. The beneficiary can then offset the tax credit (representing the tax paid by the trustees) of £2,000, leaving the beneficiary with no tax due or receivable on the income.

It does not always work out so neatly though. The amount of income tax payable by the beneficiary could be more or less than the trust paid, depending on the tax status of the beneficiary.

For example, if the life tenant was a baby and had no other income, income arising up to the personal allowance would not be taxable at all. The whole £2,000 would be repayable to the baby. Alternatively, if the life tenant was an additional rate taxpayer, the tax due on the £10,000 interest would be £4,500 (at 45%) and he or she would therefore need to pay HMRC a further £2,500 after offsetting the £2,000 tax credit.

Other factors may also need to be taken into account, such as the savings starting rate.

Trust management expenses

Once the trustees have calculated the tax due on the income and found the income after tax, they need to calculate how much income there is left to pay out to the beneficiary. Although the TMEs cannot be deducted for tax purposes, they were still paid out, so the income from which they were paid is not available for distribution to the beneficiaries.

The order of offset for TMEs is treated as coming from dividend income first, then savings and finally non-savings income. This means that TMEs will be deducted from dividend income in priority.

If TMEs deplete the income due to the beneficiary down to nil, any excess TMEs can be carried forward to future years, reducing distributable income in those years.

Example 1 – Rihanna (cont.)

Continuing the example in **41.3.3**, the following 2021-22 income would be available to distribute to Rihanna:

	Total income £	Non-savings income £	Savings income £	Dividend income £
Taxable income (as before)	41,000	26,000	7,000	8,000
Tax at basic rates	(7,200)	(5,200)	(1,400)	(600)
TMEs	(925)			(925)
Total available to distribute to the beneficiary	32,875	20,800	5,600	6,475

Rihanna will have to pay income tax on the amount of income that has arisen in the year and is payable to her. Form R185 from the trustees will set out how much income she is entitled to gross and net, and the associated tax paid by the trustees. Rihanna's R185 would look as follows:

	Gross £	Net £	Tax £
Non-savings income	26,000	20,800	5,200
Savings income	7,000	5,600	1,400
Dividend income	7,000	6,475	525

Note that the tax on the non-savings and the savings income is the same as that which was actually paid out to HMRC by the trustees. However, the tax on the dividend income is different. This is because the TMEs were deemed to have come from the dividend income in priority, so the actual dividend income received by Rihanna was less than the amount received and taxed by the trustees.

The beneficiary's income tax

Form R185 certifies the tax the trustees have paid on the income they received in the trust which was then paid out to the beneficiary. Whether or not interim payments have been made by the trustees to the beneficiary during the year, the figures on the form R185 must be used to calculate the beneficiary's tax.

The gross amounts will be entered into the beneficiary's tax computation and then the tax calculated at his or her appropriate rates. Finally, the tax credit – representing the tax already paid over to HMRC by the trustees on the amounts of income they received – is offset against the beneficiary's tax due.

In the hands of the beneficiary, the income retains its character. For example, if the trust received rental income on a let property, the beneficiary will also declare the receipt of rental income as non-savings income. As the character of the income paid to the beneficiary by the trustees is retained, the beneficiary has the use of the personal savings allowance and the starting rate band (if eligible for this – see **Chapter 23**) for the savings income, and of the dividend allowance for dividend income (see **Chapter 24**).

Example 2 – Rihanna (cont.)

Assume that Rihanna is a higher rate taxpayer, enjoying property income of £20,000 a year after deductible expenses, and employment income of £40,070 a year. During the year, Rihanna also earned £4,000 from interest on her savings and £2,100 in dividends. She paid £5,500 of income tax through PAYE.

The trustees provided Rihanna with a form 185 (Trust Income) for the tax year 2021-22, as in the example at **41.3.4** above.

Rihanna's tax computation for 2021-22 would show her employment income, property income, interest and dividends, in addition to the income from the IiP trust.

	Total income	Non-savings income	Savings income	Dividend income
	£	£	£	£
Employment income	40,070	40,070		
Savings income	4,000		4,000	
Dividend income	2,100			2,100
Income from the IiP trust	40,000	26,000	7,000	7,000
Taxable income	86,100	66,000	11,000	9,100

(Cont.)	Total income	Non-savings income	Savings income	Dividend income
	£	£	£	£
Personal allowance	(12,570)	(12,570)		
Taxable income	73,600	53,500	11,000	9,100

Her tax calculation will then look like this:

	Total income	Total tax due
	£	£
Tax on non-savings income at basic rate £37,700 x 20%	37,700	7,540
Tax on non-savings income at higher rate £53,500 – £37,700 x 40%	15,800	6,320
Personal savings allowance (higher rate taxpayer) £500 x 0%	500	0
Savings income at higher rates £11,000 – £500 x 40%	10,500	4,200
Dividend allowance £2,000 x 0%	2,000	0
Other dividend income at higher rate £9,100 – £2,000 = £7,100 x 32.5%	7,100	2,307
Tax liability	73,600	20,407
Offset PAYE paid	(5,500)	(5,500)
Offset tax credit (£5,200 + £1,400 + £525)	(7,125)	(7,125)
Tax payable	60,975	7,782

The special rate applicable to trustees

Where the trustees have the ability to accrue the income inside the trust, different tax rates apply, sometimes referred to as the rates applicable to trusts (RATs – see **41.4.3** below). As outlined above, IiPs must pay income out to the beneficiary, so usually the trustees of an IiP do not need to concern themselves with the RAT.

However, there are some types of income that do have to be taxed at the RAT. These receipts are actually classified as capital in trust law but are treated as income for tax purposes. As they are not income in trust law, the income does not normally flow through to be received by the life tenant beneficiary and as such, will not be included on the form R185. If TMEs are chargeable to this income, they can be extracted, and the associated income taxed at basic rates.

The most common examples of such capital items under trust law treated as income for tax purposes are a gain made under the accrued income scheme, and the income element of any premium received on the granting of a short lease. Income from these sources into an IiP will be charged at the RAT.

Mandating income

If the trustees send the income directly to the beneficiary without taxing it, this is called "mandating the income". In these situations, as it has not been taxed in the trust, there is no form 185 and no tax credit to be offset against any tax payable by the beneficiary. This was confirmed in the case of the *Paul Hogarth Trust*. This is often seen with investment income such as dividends, where an investment manager sends the income directly to the beneficiary rather than through the trustees.

Law: ITA 2007, s. 481, 482, 484

Guidance: TSEM 3011, 3040, 3201, 8315

Case: *Trustees of the Paul Hogarth Life Interest Trust 2008 v HMRC* [2018] UKFTT 595 TC

41.4   Discretionary trusts

41.4.1   Overview

Discretionary trusts do not have two parties as the IiP trust does (the life tenant and the remainderman). Instead there are only the trustees and one class of beneficiaries. The trustees decide if they distribute any income, to whom they may distribute it, and how much they may distribute. The beneficiaries have no automatic right to distributions. Legally, a discretionary trust is one in which the trustees have the power to accumulate the income should they choose to do so.

The following is a pictorial representation of a discretionary trust:

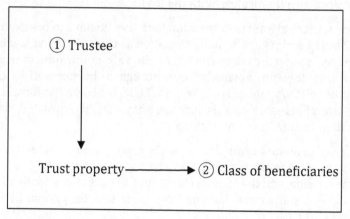

1. The trustee holds the trust property for the class of beneficiaries under common law. The equitable interest in the property is in abeyance. The trustee receives income from holding the trust property. No beneficiary is entitled to the income or the capital.

2. If, and only if, the trustees make a decision to distribute some of the income to the beneficiary, it will be distributed. Only at this point will the recipient beneficiary be taxed on the income received.

Law: ITA 2007, s. 479
Guidance: TSEM 3011, 3019, 3025

41.4.2   *The taxation of the trustees of a discretionary trust – overview*

The taxation of income for a discretionary trust is far more complex than that of an IiP. There are always four things to consider when taxing a discretionary trust, considered in the sections below:

- the rate applicable to trusts (RAT);
- the standard rate band;
- the treatment of TMEs; and
- the tax pool.

41.4.3   The rate applicable to trusts

As set out in **41.3** above, the trustees of an IiP trust must distribute all the income arising in the trust to the beneficiaries. So, for example, an additional rate taxpayer, entitled to £100 gross interest income from an IiP trust, will receive £80 net from the trust (as £20 will have already been paid by the trust), and will pay another £25 over to HMRC. HMRC have received £45, which represents tax at the correct rate for the taxpayer.

Consider now, if this same system were in place for a discretionary trust with an additional rate beneficiary. Suppose that the trustees use their discretion and decide not to pay any income over to the beneficiary. HMRC would only receive £20 in tax. If this continued year after year, there could be a significant tax gap between the income tax that would be paid if the trustees distribute the income to the additional rate beneficiary, and if they do not.

To close this gap, a different tax rate is applied to income tax arising in discretionary trusts. This may be referred to as the rate applicable to trusts (RAT). This essentially means that all income in a discretionary trust is deemed to be taxed at the additional rate. In this way, HMRC will always receive the amount that they would have received if the income had been paid out to an additional rate taxpayer every year, rather than being accumulated in the trust.

If it is eventually paid out to a person who is not an additional rate taxpayer, e.g. one paying tax at the basic rate, the recipient will be entitled to a repayment from HMRC for the year the income is received. In practice, this system transfers the cash-flow disadvantage, described above, from HMRC to the trustees.

The RAT has two rates of income tax:

On non-savings and savings income	45%
On dividend income	38.1%

These are equal to the additional rates for individuals.

Accumulated income for these purposes is income that may either be accumulated or paid out to beneficiaries at the discretion of the trustees. If all the income *must* be paid out to the beneficiaries (as in an IiP trust), the RAT will not be applicable.

HMRC specify certain exemptions from the RAT:

- income of trusts set up for charitable purposes;
- income of flat management company trusts (funds not within s. 42 of the *Landlord and Tenant Act* 1987); and
- some dividends from approved profit-sharing schemes.

Law: ITA 2007, s. 479, 480
Guidance: TSEM 3025

41.4.4   The standard rate band

The second feature of taxing income in a discretionary trust is the standard rate band. This is a nod to the fact that discretionary trusts do have necessary expenses, so not all income can in reality be accumulated and paid out to beneficiaries. As the RAT only applies to income that can be paid out to beneficiaries, a £1,000 blanket figure may be taxed at basic rates and at the ordinary rate for dividends. This can be increased if actual TMEs are incurred – see **41.4.5**.

This £1,000 is to apply to the first "slice" of the trustees' income and is applied in the order of non-savings and savings income first, and then dividend income. The tax rates to be used are the basic rate (20%) and the dividend ordinary rate (7.5%).

If the settlor of the trust has made more than one settlement, there is an anti-fragmentation rule, which means the £1,000 standard rate band will be divided among the number of settlements created. The band can never be less than £200, so settlors with more than five trusts can get more aggregate standard rate band depending on how many "current settlements" they have made. A current settlement is defined as one in existence at a time during the tax year, so if a trust had already been wound up before the start of the current tax year, it would not be counted.

If the trust is a mixed trust (see **41.5**) – with income being received both for beneficiaries that can be accumulated and those that have a life interest – the £1,000 may only be used against the part of the trust where income can be accumulated.

If the trust has more than one settlor, the £1,000 will be split on the basis of the settlor with the highest number of trusts. For example, if A and B settle a trust, but A has already settled three other trusts, the trust will only have £250 of standard rate band, despite B only having one trust.

Example – Ross

Ross is the trustee charged with the tax computation for the Aikman family discretionary trust. The trust was set up by Ross's father Logan who also set up an IiP trust for Ross five years ago. The discretionary trust received the following income in 2021-22:

	£
Property income (letting a garage)	650
Interest income	500
Dividend income	1,000

Ross will need to use the RAT, as the trust is a discretionary trust. However, the first £1,000 of income can be charged at the basic rate or dividend ordinary rate. As Logan, the settlor, had set up two trusts, this will fall to £500 in the Aikman family discretionary trust.

The income will be categorised as follows:

	Total income £	Non-savings income £	Savings income £	Dividend income £
Property income	650	650		
Savings income	500		500	
Dividend income	1,000			1,000
Taxable income	2,150	650	500	1,000

The tax computation will then be:

	Total income £	Total tax due £
Tax on non-savings income at basic rate £500 x 20% (standard rate band)	500	100
Tax on non-savings income at the RAT £150 x 45%	150	67

(Cont.)	Total income £	Total tax due £
Savings income at the RAT £500 x 45%	500	225
Other dividend income at the RAT £1,000 x 38.1%	1,000	381
Tax liability	2,150	773

The standard rate band allows £500 to be taxed at basic rates, rather than the whole income being charged to the RAT.

Law: ITA 2007, s. 479, 491, 492

Guidance: TSEM 3012

41.4.5 Trust management expenses

As already noted, a discretionary trust allows the trustees to accumulate the income or to distribute it to the beneficiaries. Where such power is held over the income, the income must be charged at the RAT.

However, not all income can be accumulated or paid out to beneficiaries. If the trustees have trust expenses they need to pay, the income received will not be available either to be accumulated or to be paid to the beneficiaries. In this case, the income representing these expenses is taxed at the applicable basic rate and not at the RAT. The legislation states that these TMEs are deemed to be paid out of dividend income first and then savings and, finally, non-savings income.

However, two practical issues have to be addressed.

First, when TMEs are paid, they are paid out of *net* income. In other words, if a trustee pays a professional for services provided to the trust, the invoice must be paid out of taxed funds. As the income that paid for this invoice can be taxed at basic rates rather than the RAT, the net amount paid must be grossed up to find the total amount due to be taxed. The rate of grossing up will depend on the source of income.

For example, say that an invoice of £925 was paid. This is to be taxed at basic rates, and is deemed to have been paid out of dividend income first. If the trustees have enough dividend income, £1,000 of this dividend income (£925 x 100/92.5) will be taxed at the dividend ordinary rate, representing the amount received that paid for the TME invoice. If the trustees do not have enough dividend income to cover this expense, and it has to come from savings income, it will be grossed up at 100/80, so £1,156 of the savings income would be taxed at basic rates.

The second practical problem is the need to separate the income used to pay the TMEs at the basic rate from the rest of the income. This is done by extracting the TMEs at the gross value from the rest of the gross income, leaving the amount in each category due to be taxed at the RAT.

TMEs are the only trust expenses that can be removed from trust income before it is paid out to the beneficiaries. Expenses that are defined as being charged against capital cannot be deducted.

If we revisit the Ross example at **41.4.4** above, we can consider what happens if the trust incurs some TMEs.

Example – Ross (adapted)

The facts and income are as in the previous example, but this time the trustees incurred properly deductible income TMEs of £1,245.

Ross will need to use the RAT, as the trust is a discretionary trust. However, for the first £500 of income, tax can be charged at the basic rate due to the standard rate band. In addition, as the trustees have incurred TMEs, the income that paid for these can instead be taxed at the dividend ordinary or basic rate.

The TMEs were £1,245 net. These will be assumed to have been paid out of dividend income first. However, as there is only £1,000 of dividend income, only £925 (£1,000 x 92.5%) can be offset against the dividend income. The balance will be offset against the savings income.

	Net	Gross	
	£	£	
Total TMEs	1,245		
Offset against dividend income	(925)	1,000	(£925 x 100/92.5)
Balance to be offset against savings income	320	400	(£320 x 100/80)

The income will be categorised as follows:

807

	Total income	Non-savings income	Savings income	Dividend income
	£	£	£	£
Property income	650	650		
Savings income	500		500	
Dividend income	1,000			1,000
TMEs			(400)	(1,000)
Taxable income	2,150	650	100	0

The tax computation will then be:

	Total income	Total tax due
	£	£
Tax on non-savings income at basic rate £500 x 20% (standard rate band)	500	100
Tax on non-savings income at the RAT £150 x 45%	150	67
TMEs taxed as savings income at basic rate £400 x 20%	400	80
Savings income at the RAT £100 x 45%	100	45
TMEs taxed as dividend income at basic rate £1,000 x 7.5%	1,000	75
Tax liability	2,150	367

The standard rate band allows £500 to be taxed at basic rates, rather than the whole income being charged to the RAT. And as a result of £1,245 net income being spent on TMEs, £1,000 of dividend income (£925 net) and £400 of savings income (£320 net) were also charged to income tax at the basic or dividend ordinary rate.

Law: ITA 2007, s. 484, 491

41.4.6   The tax pool

As explained, the RAT is applied to income in discretionary trusts. When the beneficiary receives income from the trust, a tax credit is applied of 45%, meaning that the beneficiary receives the taxed income net of 45% tax from the trust. This tax credit is set out on the form R185 and can be used to reduce any tax payable by the beneficiary in his or her personal tax computation.

The tax credit, however, does not depend on the form in which the income has been received in the trust. It is a standard tax credit of 45% irrespective of whether the trustees received non-savings, savings or dividend income. This can cause problems depending on what kind of income the trustees receive, and a tax pool must be kept to resolve these problems.

Purpose of the tax pool

To understand the purpose and function of the tax pool, it helps to put ourselves into the shoes of HMRC. Consider the following simplified example.

The trustees of a discretionary trust earn £1,000 of property income. The trustees pay £450 (£1,000 x 45%) in tax to HMRC. The trustees then have £550 left to pay over to the beneficiary, which they do. The beneficiary must gross up this receipt for the net plus the tax credit, and calculate tax at his or her own personal rate.

The total to be taxed would be £1,000 (£550 x 100/55). If the beneficiary was a child with no other income, for instance, the tax calculated would be £0. HMRC would then need to pay the tax credit of £450 back to the child beneficiary. In the end, the child pays no tax and HMRC do not receive any tax.

But imagine it was not so neat. Suppose the trustees received £1,000 in dividends instead of property income. The trustees pay £381 (£1,000 x 38.1%) in tax to HMRC. They then have £619 left to pay over to the beneficiary, which they do. The beneficiary needs to gross up this receipt for the net plus the tax credit of 45%.

If, again, the beneficiary was a child with no other income, the tax calculated would be £0. HMRC would then have to pay the tax credit of £450 back to the child beneficiary However, HMRC only received £381 from the trustees. The child should not have paid tax. He or she should have received £1,000 but cannot get the whole amount back from HMRC

809

as HMRC only have £381 to give. If HMRC give the child the whole £450, HMRC are £69 out of pocket.

This is the problem that the tax pool resolves.

How the tax pool works

Every trustee in a discretionary trust must keep a tally of all the tax paid to HMRC on income available to be distributed to a beneficiary (i.e. income that could be used to guarantee a tax credit). This income tax might have been a result of basic rates, if it fell within the standard rate band, or the RAT of 45% or 38.1%. If the amounts paid over to HMRC are lower than the amount that can be claimed by the beneficiaries as a tax credit, additional tax will be payable by the trustees. This tally is called the tax pool.

In the first year, the tax pool will start at zero. Every year, the tax on income received that can be distributed to the beneficiaries is added to the tax pool. The highest potential amount the beneficiary can claim is subtracted from that amount. A positive balance at the end of the tax year becomes the opening balance for the following tax year.

If the balance is negative, or has "gone overdrawn", this will mean that more tax credits have been guaranteed to the beneficiaries than the trustees have paid to HMRC. The trustees must make an additional tax payment (a "section 496 charge") to HMRC.

The only tax that goes into the tax pool is tax paid on income that could be paid out to the beneficiaries or accumulated. If income was used to pay TMEs, for instance, the tax on that income cannot be used to guarantee a tax credit made to a beneficiary. Tax paid on TMEs therefore does not go into the tax pool. If there are receipts into the trust that, although treated as income for tax purposes, are actually capital receipts, (such as lease premiums, chargeable event gains on certain life policies and profits from the accrued income scheme – see TSEM 3018 for a full list), the tax paid on these items is limited to 25% of the chargeable income. This represents only the additional amount of tax over the basic rate tax paid (45% - 20% = 25%).

Any tax payable under ITA 2007, s. 496 cannot itself go into the tax pool. Nor can tax paid on income arising to a settlor-interested trust.

The trustees must send the tax pool calculation to HMRC, alongside the self-assessment tax return, and this has the same reporting deadlines.

If the trustees decide to wind up the trust, they will need to distribute all the remaining capital and income to the beneficiaries. This may be as a result of the beneficiary reaching a certain age or some other term in the trust deed, or at the discretion of the trustees. In any case, the tax pool alongside the trust will finish when the trust is closed. Any credit amount on the tax pool will be lost at that point if not used. It will not be repaid by HMRC.

Example – Roxy

Roxy is the trustee charged with the tax computation for the Avalon family discretionary trust. The trust was set up by Roxy's mother Olympia. It was the only trust Olympia had set up. The discretionary trust received the following income in 2021-22:

	£
Property income	36,500
Interest income	50,000
Dividend income	1,000

During 2021-22, the trustees incurred TMEs of £1,445, and they distributed income to Roxy's youngest child Kitty of £5,000 to help her purchase a musical instrument, and £10,000 each to her three cousins to help with university payments. The tax pool brought forward was £1,400.

Roxy will have to use the RAT, as the trust is a discretionary trust. However, the first £1,000 of income can be charged at the basic rate due to the standard rate band. In addition, as the trustees have incurred TMEs, the income used to pay these can be extracted from the gross income to be taxed at the RAT, and instead be taxed at basic rates.

The TMEs were £1,445 net. These will be assumed to have been paid out of dividend income first. However, as there is only £1,000 of dividend income, only £925 (£1,000 x 92.5%) can be offset against the dividend income. The balance will be offset against the savings income.

	Net	Gross	
	£	£	
Total TMEs	1,445		
Offset against dividend income	(925)	1,000	(£1,000 x 92.5%)
Balance to be offset against savings income	520	650	(£520 x 100/80)

Roxy will also need to establish the tax pool. The first step is to calculate the tax to go into the tax pool.

The income can be categorised as follows:

	Total income	Non-savings income	Savings income	Dividend income
	£	£	£	£
Property income	36,500	36,500		
Savings income	50,000		50,000	
Dividend income	1,000			1,000
TMEs			(650)	(1,000)
Taxable income	87,500	36,500	49,350	0

The tax calculation is then as follows:

	Total income	Total tax due
	£	£
Tax on non-savings income at basic rate £1,000 x 20% (standard rate band)	1,000	200
Tax on non-savings income at the RAT £35,500 x 45%	35,500	15,975
TMEs taxed as savings income at basic rate £650 x 20%	650	130

(Cont.)	Total income £	Total tax due £
Savings income at the RAT £49,350 x 45%	49,350	22,207
TMEs taxed as dividend income at basic rate £1,000 x 7.5%	1,000	75
Tax liability	87,500	38,587

Although £38,587 has been charged to tax on income in the discretionary trust, not all of this can go into the tax pool. Only the tax on the income that was *available for distribution* can go into the tax pool, so this will be:

	£
Tax on the non-savings income at the basic rate	200
Tax on the non-savings income at the RAT	15,975
Tax on the savings income at the RAT	22,207
	38,382

This is the same as taking the total tax and subtracting the tax paid on the income used to pay for TMEs:

	£
Total tax paid in the tax year	38,587
Less: tax on TMEs – savings income	(130)
– dividend income	(75)
	38,382

813

The 2021-22 tax pool is therefore:

	£
Balance at 6 April 2021	1,400
Tax added to the tax pool	38,382
Tax credits guaranteed through distributions (£35,000 x 45/55) (see below)	(28,636)
	11,146

The tax credits guaranteed are £5,000 to Kitty and £10,000 each to her three cousins. It is possible to gross all of these up and then multiply them by 45% (£35,000 x 100/55 = £63,636, x 45% = £28,636), or simply multiply them by 45/55 to see directly the tax guaranteed on these payments.

Because there *has* been enough income tax paid over to HMRC to cover the potential £28,636 tax credits guaranteed to Kitty and her cousins, the trustees have no additional tax for 2021-22.

Law: ITA 2007, s. 496-498
Guidance: TSEM 3013, 3020, 3021

41.4.7 The taxation of the beneficiary of a discretionary trust

Unlike the beneficiaries of the IiP trust, who are treated as owning an equitable beneficial interest in the trust property, beneficiaries of a discretionary trust have no such interest. The equitable interest in the discretionary trust property is "in abeyance", or on hold, so the beneficiaries are only entitled to such income as the trustees, using their discretionary power, choose to give them.

As mentioned above, the payments to a discretionary beneficiary are received with a 45% tax credit. This means that the beneficiary must first gross up the income received at 45%, but can then offset the tax credit against the amount of income tax payable for that tax year.

The beneficiary will see the tax credit on the form 185 that the trustees provide, showing the gross and net income paid and the tax that the trustees have paid on that income.

Unlike IiP trusts, the income received from a discretionary trust does not keep its character once in the hands of the beneficiary. All the income is taxed as non-savings income, irrespective of how the trustees received it. One effect of this is that the beneficiaries of a discretionary trust cannot benefit from the personal savings or dividend allowances.

If a beneficiary is an additional rate taxpayer, no further tax will be payable to HMRC as a result of income from the trust. However, the majority of taxpayers in the UK are not additional rate taxpayers, so most beneficiaries will be able to claim a repayment for the tax paid through the trustees.

Example – Rufus

Rufus is 19 years old and has just accepted an offer into the university of his choice in Bristol. He had a job at a local bar part time. He is one of Roxy's nephews and one of the discretionary beneficiaries of his grandmother Olympia's Avalon family discretionary trust who were each paid £10,000 in 2021-22 (see the example of Roxy above).

In 2021-22 Rufus received the following income:

	£	£
P60 "Peal of Bells" Bristol – gross	1,990	
– tax deducted	0	1,990
Interest		1,750
Dividends		2,300

In addition, Rufus was given the following form R185 (Trust Income):

	Gross £	Net £	Tax £
Income from trust	18,181	10,000	8,181

Rufus will need to declare all his sources of income on his self-assessment tax return for 2021-22. His income may be summarised as follows:

	Total income	Non-savings income	Savings income	Dividend income
	£	£	£	£
Employment income	1,990	1,990		
Savings income	1,750		1,750	
Dividend income	2,300			2,300
Income from discretionary trust	18,181	18,181		
Personal allowance	(12,570)	(12,570)		
	11,651	7,601	1,750	2,300

His tax computation will then look like this:

	Total income	Total tax due
	£	£
Tax on non-savings income at basic rate £7,601 x 20%	7,601	1,520
Personal savings allowance (£1,000 as basic rate taxpayer) £1,000 x 0%	1,000	0
Balance of savings income at basic rates £750 x 20%	750	150
Dividend income (dividend allowance) £2,000 x 0%	2,000	0
Balance of dividend income at basic rates £300 x 7.5%	300	22
Tax liability	11,651	1,692
Tax credit from trust		(8,181)
Tax repayment due from HMRC		(6,489)

Rufus is entitled to a tax refund of £6,489 from HMRC. Of the income he received from the trust, he was only due to pay £1,520 on it once the personal allowance was taken into account. Add the small amounts of tax due on the savings income (£150) and the dividend income (£22), and his total tax liability for the year was only £1,692. The trust, however, had paid £8,181 on his behalf to HMRC for the £10,000 he received, and of this £6,489 can be refunded to Rufus.

Law: ITA 2007, s. 493, 494

41.5   Mixed trusts

41.5.1   Overview

Mixed trusts are trusts that have beneficiaries with an interest in possession and discretionary beneficiaries inside the same settlement. There is therefore a combination of income that must be paid out to one or more life interest beneficiaries, and income that can be accrued or paid out on a discretionary basis.

Although there are no separate provisions in the legislation that cover mixed trusts, they can sometimes be challenging as the income must be apportioned between the different beneficiaries. The income subject to the IiP will be taxed at the basic rate and the dividend ordinary rate. But for the income subject to the discretionary rules, the trustees will have to consider the standard rate band, use the RAT, deal with the identification and grossing up of any TMEs, and keep a tax pool.

Example 1 – Rochelle

Rochelle was asked to be one of the trustees for a settlement for her three nieces, the Foster family settlement. The nieces are Frankie, Una, and Mollie and they are aged 25, 23 and 19 respectively in 2021-22.

The terms of the trust are that each beneficiary is entitled to a third of the trust income from the age of 20, and then once they reach 30 a third of the capital. Before the age of 20, income can be discretionally accumulated or distributed by Rochelle and the other trustees to the girls.

As Mollie has not yet reached the age of 20, her third of the income is a discretionary trust, and will be taxed accordingly. The other two thirds of the income will be an IiP trust. All the income available for Frankie and Una must be paid out to them. Once Mollie is 20, she too will have an interest in possession and the trust will be taxed accordingly.

Complications can occur when the beneficiary attains his or her majority such that an IiP is created mid-way during a tax year. In these instances the income needs to be apportioned not only between the beneficiaries, but also between the months for the beneficiary acquiring the IiP. Depending on how the income is made up, the income may be split in different ways.

Rental profits are split according to time. For example, a beneficiary obtaining an IiP two months into a year for which her share of the annual rental profits was £12,000, would have £2,000 taxed as a discretionary trust and £10,000 as an IiP.

Interest and dividend income is taxable in the period in which it was actually received.

Expenses can be deducted evenly during the year if they cover a whole year, such as the costs for preparing the tax return. Other expenses can be allocated to the period to which they relate if this is obvious.

Example 2 – Rochelle (cont.)

Using the data from the example above, it is now 2021-22 and Mollie has turned 20 on 5 September 2021.

The income in the trust in 2021-22 is as follows:

	£
Net rental income	32,000
Building society interest	3,000
Dividends	10,000

The dividends were received as an interim dividend of £3,000 on 30 April 2021, and a final dividend on 31 October of £7,000. The interest is credited annually on 31 December 2021. TMEs, occurring evenly through the year, were £1,850.

The first thing that must be done is to establish the percentage of interest and dividends that each of the beneficiaries will be entitled to.

Interest

As the interest was received in the second part of the year, when all three of the beneficiaries had an IiP trust, it is all income of the IiP trust.

Dividend

The dividend income, however, will need to be split. The £3,000 received on 30 April will be split in thirds for each beneficiary, such that one third

(Mollie's third) will be in the discretionary trust and two thirds (Frankie and Una's) in the IiP. The dividend received in October, however, will be received at a time when all three beneficiaries had an IiP, so it will be entirely for the IiP trust.

Trust management expenses and rental income

The TMEs and the rental income accrue evenly over the year. They are therefore apportioned according to the percentage each beneficiary has of the trust fund multiplied by the percentage of the year for which he or she has it. These calculations can get quite complex with several beneficiaries and several dates, so are best done in a table such as below.

	Discretionary trust	Interest-in-possession trust
Frankie 33% x 100% (12/12)		33%
Una 33% x 100% (12/12)		33%
Mollie 33% x 41.67% (5/12) months of DT 33% x 58.33% (7/12) months of IiP	14%	20%
Total	14%	86%

The expenses and the profits then need to be apportioned accordingly.

	Discretionary trust £	IiP trust £
Trust management expenses £1,850 x 14% £1,850 x 86%	259	1,591
Property income £32,000 x 14% £32,000 x 86%	4,480	27,520

Finally, the two tax computations must be completed: one for the IiP and one for the discretionary trust.

IiP trust

	Total income £	Non-savings income £	Savings income £	Dividend income £
Property income	27,520	27,520		
Savings income	3,000		3,000	
Dividend income £9,000 (2/3 of £3,000 = £2,000 + all of the £7,000)	9,000			9,000
	39,520	27,520	3,000	9,000
Tax thereon at basic rates	(6,779)	(5,504)	(600)	(675)
TMEs	(1,591)			(1,591)
Amount distributable to beneficiaries	31,150	22,016	2,400	6,734

Discretionary trust

The income categories are as follows:

	Total income £	Non-savings income £	Savings income £	Dividend income £
Property income	4,480	4,480		
Savings income	0		0	
Dividend income 1/3 of £3,000 = £1,000	1,000			1,000
TMEs (grossed up £259 x 100/92.5)				(280)
Taxable income	5,480	4,480	0	720

The tax computation will then be:

	Total income £	Total tax due £
Tax on non-savings income at standard rate £1,000 x 20%	1,000	200
Tax on non-savings income at RAT £3,480 x 45%	3,480	1,566
TME dividends at ordinary rate £280 x 7.5%	280	21
Dividends at RAT £720 x 38.1%	720	274
Total income tax payable	5,480	2,061

The total amount of tax payable by the trust will be £8,840, made up of £6,779 from the IiP part of the settlement and £2,061 from the discretionary part of the settlement.

41.6   Other types of trust

41.6.1   Accumulation and maintenance trusts

Accumulation and maintenance (A&M) trusts were often known as "grandparent trusts" and had various tax benefits. Although they can no longer be set up, they were very common before the trust tax regime changes in March 2006.

There are various important issues that A&Ms bring to IHT, but for income tax purposes they are simply a kind of hybrid between a discretionary trust and an IiP. Usually they would be discretionary trusts used only for the maintenance, education or benefit of the child until the grandchild turned 25, when the child would either get the capital or the trust would convert to an IiP. They would often be subject to the issues discussed above with mixed trusts.

Guidance: IHTM 42807; TSEM 1567

41.6.2   Bare trusts

Bare trusts are the most uncomplicated of all trusts. In fact, some argue that they are not really trusts but are more "nominee arrangements". This is because in a bare trust arrangement, the trustee simply has the legal title. The beneficiary has no limited or discretionary interest but is absolutely entitled to the trust property; the trust property has "indefeasibly vested" in the beneficiary. This means that there are no conditions for the beneficiary to meet, such as reaching a certain age or surviving anyone.

As the beneficiaries have an absolute interest in the trust, the trustees do not have to submit any tax return or pay income tax. Rather, the beneficiary is charged personally, and in the first instance, for all income arising in the trust. This has to be reported to HMRC by the normal income tax reporting deadlines on a form 40.

In practice, bare trusts are often used for minors. A child cannot legally hold real property in the UK and, for this reason, where a child is either given or inherits real property, a bare trust is set up to hold it for the child, who will be entitled to the trust property at his or her majority at age 18.

Where the beneficiary is a minor, the provisions of the *Trustee Act* 1925 apply. These allow for the use of the income for the maintenance, education and benefit of the child until the age of 18 but must accumulate any income not used for these purposes. Benefit is defined widely and can include providing a house not only for the beneficiary but for his or her parents to live in (*Re Lesser*), paying beneficiaries' debts (*Re Moxon's Will Trusts)* and making charitable donations if the beneficiary feels a moral obligation to do so (*X v A*).

If the child is gifted the trust property by a parent, the settlement rules apply (see **41.7** below).

Cases: *Re Lesser* [1947] VLR 366; *Re Moxon's Will Trusts* [1958] 1 WLR 165; *X v A* [2005] EWHC 2706 (Ch), [2006] 1 WLR 741
Guidance: TSEM 4512

41.6.3 *Charitable trusts*

Charities are usually set up as a trust including a "board" of trustees to consider the uses of donations received. Charitable trusts are normally simply discretionary trusts. The trust property of a charitable trust can be distributed according to the discretion and direction of the trustees, but it must be applied only for charitable purposes, which means either within the legal meaning of charity or to promote the public benefit. Charitable trusts are generally exempt from income tax and from most other taxes.

Guidance: TSEM 6273

41.6.4   *Protective trusts*

A protective trust may be set up to protect and safeguard the right to the life interest from any attempts by the life tenant to sell or otherwise dispose of it. Protective trusts start out as IiPs. However, if the life tenant does anything to threaten his or her share of the income by "prejudicing" it, the trust will switch to become a discretionary trust. Prejudicing the income could include arrangements that seek to sell, exchange or give away the interest. The bankruptcy of the life tenant would also be seen as prejudicing his or her right to income.

Protective trusts are generally set up where there is some concern about the mental state of the beneficiary, perhaps due to age, impairment through substance abuse, or mental health issues.

Protective trusts will be taxed as either an IiP or a discretionary trust, depending on what form they take during the tax year in question. In cases where the trust converts from an IiP to a discretionary trust during the tax year, they will be taxed as a mixed trust (see **41.5**).

Law: TA 1925, s. 33
Guidance: TSEM 4512

41.6.5   *Implied trusts*

Express trusts are set up intentionally. Examples are trusts made by testators in their will, or trusts set up by older generations for younger generations. There are also formal trusts set up by statute (statutory trusts).

However, trusts can also be set up unintentionally, by actions. These are not express trusts, but implied trusts, and are defined through case law as trusts that have "not been expressly created" (*Cowcher*).

There are two categories of implied trust.

Resulting trusts

A resulting trust occurs where the trust property results, or reverts back to the settlor, because it was obvious that the intention was not there for the settlor to create a beneficial interest for the supposed beneficiary. In the 1964 case of *Vandervell,* reference was made to two eminent trust manuals, *Underhill on Trusts* and *Lewin on Trusts. Underhill* was quoted as saying:

"When it appears to have been the intention of a donor that the donee should not take beneficially there will be a resulting trust in favour of the donor."

And in *Lewin on Trusts*, Lewin was quoted as saying that the general rule is that a resulting trust will arise whenever:

"...it appears to have been the intention of a donor that the grantee, devisee or legatee was not to take beneficially...".

This is explained in the case of *Pettit,* in which the equitable presumption of a person funding part of the consideration to purchase property, is that the person is entitled to a corresponding proportionate beneficial interest in that property by way of a resulting trust.

Constructive trusts

Lord Millett gave a good definition of a constructive trust in the Court of Appeal decision in *Paragon Finance* where he stated:

"[A] constructive trust arises by operation of law whenever the circumstances are such that it would be unconscionable for the owner of property (usually the legal estate) to assert his beneficial interest in the property."

An excellent illustration of this is the *Bannister* case from 1948. The defendant was allowed to live in a property purchased by her brother-in-law, on a verbal understanding that she could live there for life. The brother-in-law later reneged on his verbal agreement and tried to take possession of the property. The Court of Appeal held that the brother-in-law's attempt to take possession was unconscionable and the court imposed a constructive trust in order to allow the defendant a lifetime interest in accordance with the oral agreement.

Virtually all implied trusts are bare trusts and any income arising is taxed on the beneficiary.

Cases: *Bannister v Bannister* [1948] 2 All ER 133; *Vandervell v CIR* (1966) 43 TC 519; *Pettit v Pettit* [1970] AC 777; *Cowcher v Cowcher* [1972] 1 WLR 425; *Paragon Finance v DB Thakerer & Co* [1998] EWCA 1249

Guidance: TSEM 6263; *Underhill on Trusts*, 11th edition, at page 172; *Lewin on Trusts*, 16th edition, at page 115

41.7   The settlement rules

41.7.1   Overview

The settlement rules are anti-avoidance provisions that prevent taxpayers from diverting income to children or legal partners so as to make use of additional personal allowances, reliefs, deferrals and lower tax rates or bands.

For example, without the settlement rules, a mother could transfer up to £12,570 of her property income to each of her three minor children using a bare trust. As bare trust income is taxed on the beneficiary, each child would be able to use his or her personal allowance (otherwise lost if the child has no other income) and save a total of up to £16,970 in income tax for the mother (three amounts of £12,570 taxed at 0% rather than at 45%).

41.7.2   Definitions

There is no reason why a settlor cannot legally also be a beneficiary, but in such cases, there are income tax implications. The provisions for the settlement rules come from ITTOIA 2005.

Both a settlor and a settlement are defined quite widely, a settlement being where a person directly or indirectly makes "... any disposition, trust, covenant, agreement, arrangement or transfer of assets ...".

A disposition is the provision of funds, an undertaking to provide funds, or a reciprocal arrangement for another person to do so.

A settlor is "any person by whom the settlement was made".

These definitions cover the kind of settlements where the person making the settlement uses an intermediary instead of settling it directly, and also situations where friends may make reciprocal settlements for each other's children. Absolute gifts without conditions are not covered.

Law: ITTOIA 2005, s. 620, 624, 626
Guidance: TSEM 4100, 4120

41.7.3   The implications

The settlor or the spouse can benefit

If the settlor or his or her legal partner (spouse or civil partner) is able to benefit from the trust, either now or in the future, it is a settlor-interested trust. A legal partner does not include a former or a future legal partner, or a spouse or civil partner from whom the taxpayer is separated, under either a court order or a separation agreement or where it is likely to be a permanent separation.

All income arising in the trust during the life of the settlor will be taxed on the settlor irrespective of the person or persons to whom the trustees pay this income out. As with the examples above, it will still be taxed on the trustees first, but rather than then being taxed on the beneficiaries when they receive the income, it will be taxed on the *settlor's* personal tax return.

Even if the trust is a discretionary trust, the income will keep its character and be taxed in the same category as it arrived in the trust, i.e. non-savings, savings or dividend income. This means that the settlor may use the personal savings allowance or the dividend allowance when taxing such trust income. The settlor will also have the tax credit issued by the trustees to offset against this tax burden. However, if the settlor receives a tax repayment, due to having a marginal tax rate lower than that of the trustees, it must be repaid to the trustees and cannot be retained by the settlor.

Example

Rafferty set up a discretionary trust for his golfing friends. He was not one of the class of beneficiaries, but the trustees have the option to add him to the class of beneficiaries. Because ITTOIA 2005, s. 625 (1)(c) refers to income that "... may become so payable or applicable" (rather than to income actually payable to the settlor), Rafferty will be chargeable personally on all the income in the trust as if it were his own, irrespective of whether or not he actually receives any of the income.

If the settlor-interested trust does pay out income to a beneficiary other than the settlor, the trustees will need to issue a form R185 to the recipient but the tax credit cannot be used by the beneficiary and is not repayable.

Law: ITTOIA 2005, s. 619, 622-625
Guidance: TSEM 4100, 4120, 4573

Parental settlements

If income is *actually paid* to a minor child of the settlor, this will also cause a settlor-interested trust. A minor child is one without a legal partner and below the age of 18. A child includes step-children. See also **22.3.4**.

There is a subtle difference between the tax treatment of a parental settlement and one where the settlor (or his or her spouse) can benefit. In the latter, the settlor is taxed on all the income arising in the trust in the tax year in which it is settlor-interested. However, in the case of parental settlements, only amounts paid out to the child, or used for the benefit of the minor, are taxable on the settlor. Any amounts accumulated in the trust are taxed only on the trustees (unless they are distributed).

Finally, there is an exception to the settlement rules for small amounts of income distributed. If the income distributed is no more than £100, s. 629 sets out a *de minimis* exception so that this can be taxed as the child's income rather than the settlor's. It is a cliff-edge reprieve, though, and £101 distributed to the child will be entirely taxed on the settlor rather than just the £1 excess.

Law: ITTOIA 2005, s. 619, 622-625, 629
Guidance: TSEM 4100, 4120, 4573

41.8   Trust registration

If a trust is liable to pay UK taxes, it must be registered with HMRC. This is achieved through the online Trust Registration Service (TRS).

Information that must be provided to HMRC includes:

- the name of the trust;
- the date the trust commenced;
- the territory in which the trust operates;
- the value and type of the trust property, including addresses if the property consists of land or buildings; and
- the identity details of the settlor, the trustees, all the beneficiaries and anyone else that has control over the trust assets. Such identity details include:
  o names and addresses;
  o dates of birth; and
  o National Insurance or passport numbers.

Registration has the same deadlines as the notification of a new source of income for individuals, so before 6 October in the year following the tax year in which the trust first has a source of income liable to income tax.

Guidance: https://www.gov.uk/guidance/register-your-clients-trust

41.9   Pitfalls and planning points

Reasons to use a trust

Generally, due to the complexities of the income tax regime and also the IHT impact, it is advisable to use a trust only where an outright gift is not appropriate. As an income-protection vehicle, however, a trust may be appropriate for individuals looking to ensure that their family is provided for while protecting their wealth at the same time. Good reasons include:

- providing for children too young to manage the trust property, or unstable beneficiaries;
- providing for second wives, while allowing the capital to go to children of a first marriage;
- protecting assets in the event of the taxpayer's divorce, or from their children's legal partners; and
- protecting vulnerable beneficiaries.

The tax pool

As tax pool credits are lost when the trust is closed, it is good planning for the trustees to make income distributions (enough to use the remaining balance in the tax pool) before the trust is wound up. This enables the beneficiaries to use the 45% tax credits, often leading to a tax repayment.

Avoiding a s. 496 charge

Where the trust income is mostly dividends, trustees should be extremely careful that they do not distribute more than the balance in the tax pool, so as to avoid additional tax charges under ITA 2007, s. 496. In addition, if there are significant TMEs in a trust year, the distributions should be monitored carefully because the tax paid on the TMEs does not enter the tax pool.

Allocation of expenses

Trustees must ensure that they can split expenses between those that can properly be offset against income (such as house insurance for a rental property) and TMEs such as accountancy fees for producing the trust accounts. The latter cannot be deducted for income tax purposes.

The standard rate band

Where the settlor has settled more than one trust, the standard rate band will be correspondingly apportioned between them. However, there is a minimum standard rate band, so even if the settlor has more than five trusts, each trust will always have a standard rate band of £200.

Cash-flow considerations of the trustees

Although the type of trust is usually decided on for reasons other than tax, the IiP trust will have a cash-flow advantage compared to the discretionary trust. This is because, in an IiP, all income is taxable at the basic or dividend ordinary rate, whereas in a discretionary trust only income falling into the standard rate band and any income used to pay TMEs is charged at basic rates. All other income is chargeable at the RAT.

Taxation considerations of the beneficiaries

When deciding whether to set up an IiP or a discretionary trust, the settlor should consider whether the beneficiaries may be eligible for the starting rate band and the personal savings or dividend allowances. If so, they may consider an IiP rather than a discretionary trust due to the ability of the income to retain its character. A discretionary trust will always be deemed to provide non-savings income (unless it is a settlor-interested trust) and, as such, these allowances would not be available.

42. Taxation of estates

42.1 Introduction

Once an individual dies, his or her affairs will obviously need to be conducted by someone else, in terms both of the period up to death, and of the period from death until the grant of probate is obtained.

The grant of probate permits the assets of the deceased to be distributed. The interim period is referred to as the period of administration. If the deceased has made a will, there will normally be at least one specified executor. If the deceased died intestate or did not name an executor, or if the executor named refuses to take office, the estate will have an administrator. Generally, the term "personal representative" can be used, whether the individual is in fact an executor or an administrator. In Scotland, all personal representatives are known as "executors".

In this chapter the person who holds the office will be referred to as a personal representative (PR).

After the death and once probate has been granted (see **42.3.4**), the assets left by the deceased are transferred to become the legal property of the PRs. It is the responsibility of the PRs to pay any tax due on these assets in the estate at the date of the death and to deal with this property during the period of administration, eventually distributing the assets to the rightful beneficiaries of the estate.

42.2 The legalities of the administration period

42.2.1 The period of administration

The period of administration starts on the day after death and ends when the PRs have completed all their duties in relation to the estate. Their duties include ascertaining the assets and liabilities, paying all the liabilities including debts, taxes, and specific gifts (**see 42.6.2**), and taking all the steps to ensure that the residue balance (**see 42.3.5**) is left for the residual legatees. The period of administration is typically about a year, often referred to as the "executor's year", but can extend to a longer period if required.

Law: ITTOIA 2005, s. 653
Guidance: TSEM 7360

42.2.2   The will and the PRs

A testator may include in his or her will words such as these:

> "I appoint (someone) to be my executor and trustee. I give and bequeath all my goods and possessions to the said (someone) upon trust."

This does not create a legal trust (see **Chapter 41**). The words used just emphasise that the deceased trusts the executor to deal with his or her property and to perform the tasks and responsibilities required of the executor office. A PR merely stands in the shoes of the deceased to deal with all their assets.

PRs are generally not entitled to remuneration for the duties performed during the administration period unless the will specifically allows for this. If the executor is a professional, no income tax need be deducted by the PRs on the payment. If they are not a professional, any payments to them from the estate will be paid net of income tax from the estate. However, if a professional agent is instructed by the non-professional PRs this will be paid gross and no income tax will need to be deducted.

If the will has not been completed correctly and is thus invalid, or if a will has not been written at all, the deceased is said to have died "intestate". Specific rules set out in the *Administration of Estates Act* 1925 determine who will inherit the deceased's property and how much each beneficiary will receive.

Law: *Administration of Estates Act* 1925, s. 46; *Inheritance and Trustees' Powers Act* 2014
Guidance: TSEM 6034-6036, 6040, 6061, 6071, 6079

42.3   The process of the administration period

42.3.1   Check if there is a will and if so, check the will

Once the PRs have been advised that they must act (and they accept), they must ensure they have the latest copy of the will and any codicils. The first formal act is to establish the extent of the estate – i.e. the property owned by the deceased – and to determine the amount of any liabilities.

The will does not routinely have to be sent to HMRC. However, this may be necessary if HMRC need to check time limits for an instrument of variation, including a statement of intent under IHTA 1984, s. 142 (an

IHT statement) or under TCGA 1992, s. 92 (a CGT statement). Or HMRC may open a formal self-assessment enquiry.

However, HMRC must be informed of the death. Note that HMRC have established specialist bereavement teams.

A basic accounting system will need to be employed to establish all the assets and the liabilities at the date of the death.

Law: IHTA 1984, s. 142; TCGA 1992, s. 92

Guidance: https://taxagents.blog.gov.uk/2014/10/23/bereavement-service/

42.3.2   Split income properly

The PRs must ensure that any income received is separated into that to which the deceased was beneficially entitled *before* death, and that which is received during the period of the administration. Usually, the requirements of the *Apportionment Act* 1870 are excluded by modern wills in accordance with the standard provisions of the Society of Trust and Estate Practitioners (STEP), which state:

> "Income and expenditure shall be treated as arising when payable, and not from day to day, so that no apportionment shall take place."

For income tax purposes, income is taxable when it is due to be paid.

42.3.3   Probate

To manage the assets of the deceased, the PRs must apply to the court for authority to do so. The court will give either a grant of probate (if the PR is an executor) or a grant of letters of administration (if the PR is an administrator). This is called confirmation in Scotland.

Often shortened to just "probate", the grant of probate gives the PRs the legal power to deal with the deceased's assets, but probate may only be applied for once all inheritance taxes have been paid. This can cause a circular problem for the PRs. PRs cannot get probate before they have paid the inheritance tax (IHT). However, the IHT cannot be paid before the PRs have access to the bank accounts or assets of the deceased, though it is understood that banks will sometimes release funds for a direct payment (i.e. to HMRC) of any IHT due.

In other cases, loans may be needed for this purpose. Any interest paid on a loan by the PRs to meet an IHT liability is tax deductible during the period of administration, against any income chargeable to income tax.

Guidance: https://www.gov.uk/paying-inheritance-tax/deceaseds-bank-account

42.3.4   Deal with the assets

After making any specific gifts, paying tax and other liabilities, and paying any pecuniary legacies, the PRs will pay any remaining amount, the residue, to the residual beneficiaries.

The residual beneficiaries will require a statement in writing giving them the amount of their share of the income and the residue, and the amount of tax that has been borne on this by the PRs. This is usually given on a form R185 (Estate Income).

If the will creates any trusts, these will have to be registered online using the trust registration service. A separate agent authority will be required for dealing with any trusts.

42.3.5   Distribute the assets

Finally, the PRs must distribute the assets to the residual beneficiaries. The administration period ends when all the assets have been collected, all the debts paid, and the estate has been ascertained and distributed.

Law: *The Trustee Act* 1925, s. 27

Guidance: TSEM 6052, 6057, 6073, 7256; https://tinyurl.com/yxu3rswc (STEP Standard Provisions)

42.4   Income tax payable in tax year of death

42.4.1   Overview

It is the responsibility of the PRs to calculate the income tax or CGT due by the deceased from 6 April in the tax year of the death until the date of the death. This is separate from any tax payable in the period after death – even if this falls into the same tax year.

In addition, if the deceased had any self-assessment tax returns outstanding for previous tax years, it is the PRs' responsibility to complete these and to bring the deceased's tax affairs completely up to date. All tax calculated as due at the date of death will need to be included as an additional liability in the death estate.

Only income actually received up to the date of death is included in the individual's tax computation, even if income is due at the date of death but received later. For example, if an individual is self-employed and has debtors at the date of the death, the debt payments will be counted as income during the period of administration if they are received after death. Likewise, if the deceased was an employee, any earnings received after the date of the death will be accounted for by the PRs.

42.4.2   Employment and self-employment income

If the deceased had his own self-employed or partnership business, his interest in this will have ceased at the date of the death. Unless the PRs were given specific powers in the will to carry this business on, they should be merely realising the assets in the best manner for the estate.

If the deceased had only employment income or pension income, and died close to the start of the tax year, there is generally a repayment of tax due to the estate. This is because PAYE is calculated on a cumulative basis, assuming only one twelfth of the personal allowance every month. A person who dies in May, for example, would still have the whole personal allowance for the year available and a repayment would be due (which would be an asset of the estate at the date of death).

Guidance: TSEM 6056, 6112

42.4.3   Interest and other investment income received and paid

Any interest accrued, but not received, at the date of death will be taxed on the PRs during the period of administration. According to case law, it is *not* apportioned into the pre-death and post-death periods.

Likewise, qualifying interest paid and other similar charges will only be allowable during the period of administration if they fell due to be paid prior to or on the date of the death but were paid out after the death.

42.4.4   Personal allowance

The deceased has a full year's personal allowance for the tax year of death – even if he or she died only on 6 April.

42.4.5   The process

If HMRC know who the PRs are (which they should do, as the details are generally requested by the HMRC bereavement team – see **42.3.1**), a formal self-assessment return will be sent to them to cover income of the deceased from 6 April to the date of the death. The return will be due back by the standard filing date, and normal taxing principles apply.

HMRC must make an assessment – within four years of the end of the year of assessment in which the person died – of any tax due up to and including the date of death, even if the deceased had caused a loss of tax carelessly or deliberately. However, within that four-year time limit HMRC may assess the PRs for tax lost in any year of assessment ending up to six years before the death.

If the deceased had incurred penalties during his or her life, HMRC's guidance states that these should be cancelled as a result of an appeal from the PRs. If such penalties are due to dishonest conduct attributable to the PRs after the death, these will be issued by HMRC as usual.

Law: *Apportionment Act* 1870; TMA 1970, s. 40

Case: *IRC v Henderson's Executors* (1932) 16 TC 282

Guidance: TSEM 7252, 7260, 7270; CH 54200; SAM 6170; https://tinyurl.com/yxu3rswc (STEP Standard Provisions)

42.5 Income tax payable by the PRs during the period of administration

42.5.1 Overview

The PRs will need to pay income tax on income received in the period of the administration. This is paid at basic rates, and the method is similar to that of an individual taxpayer, but with some important differences.

42.5.2 Allowances and reliefs

PRs are not liable to any higher or additional rates of tax so, unlike an individual, there are no basic rate, higher rate, or additional rate bands to consider. Nor are they entitled to any allowances such as the personal allowance, the starting rate band, the savings allowance, or the dividend allowance.

However, they are allowed to claim tax reliefs that are not restricted to individuals. Examples would be:

- loss relief if the PRs are conducting a business; and
- interest paid on loans to finance inheritance tax.

Any reliefs available should be offset first against non-savings income such as property income or business profits. If the reliefs cause a repayment of income tax, a formal self-assessment tax return will be required rather than the informal process (see below).

42.5.3   Residence of the PRs

The statutory residence test does not apply to PRs.

The body of PRs is treated as a single "office" and its residence is dependent on the residence of each individual making up the body.

If all the PRs are resident abroad the estate is a non-resident estate.

In mixed-residence cases, where some of the PRs are resident in the UK and some outside the UK, the PRs are only regarded as non-UK resident (with the result that offshore income arising is not chargeable to UK income tax) if the deceased was himself or herself:

- not resident in the UK at the time of death; and
- not UK domiciled at the time of death.

If the PRs are collectively resident in the UK, income tax is chargeable on the worldwide income of the estate.

Law: ITA 2007, s. 834
Guidance: TSEM 7356, 7358, 7406, 7407, 7410, 7376; INTM 340080

42.5.4   Income to be taxed

All income received in the period of the administration is taxable on the PRs in their capacity as PRs, from the day following the date of the death until the date of the end of the period of administration. This may cover more than one tax year and, if it does, more than one tax return will be needed.

If the estate has only savings income, on which the tax charge would be less then £100, there is no requirement to advise HMRC of the income. This is a concession and does not include dividend income. Originally introduced in 2016, HMRC state on their website:

> "These arrangements have been extended to include the 2019-20 to 2020-21 tax years, and we will continue to review the situation longer term."

Virtually all the income received by the PRs will be received gross. The types of income received will vary, and may include some from the categories discussed below.

Guidance: HMRC *Trusts and Estates Newsletter* April 2016, December 2017, August 2019 (https://tinyurl.com/y6y7r4ad)

Income from property

Income from property will be calculated as outlined in **Chapter 26**. Once the net profit has been obtained, this will be taxed on the PRs.

Interest and other investment income

Interest and dividends are taxed in the same way as for individuals. However, the complications of the starting rate band and the personal savings and dividend allowances are not in point as these allowances are not available to PRs.

The deceased may have had an individual savings account (ISA). This does not need to be closed as a result of the death of the investor. Although no more funds may be added to the account, it can continue to enjoy the benefits of tax-free income and growth during the period of administration. The ISA will continue to be tax-free until the earlier of the end of the period of the administration, the date the ISA is closed or a period of three years from the date of the death. No income tax will therefore need to be calculated on any ISAs held by the deceased.

Guidance: TSEM 7413

42.5.5   Expenses deductible

Estate management expenses

Estate management expenses (EMEs) can be offset against the income distributed to the beneficiaries (see **42.7.2**) but are not tax deductible in the income tax calculation of the estate (even though they appear to be similar to, say, the trading expenses of a business).

The first loan to cover inheritance tax payable

Tax relief is available if the PRs have had to take out a loan to pay any IHT (including any interest payable on that tax) due under IHTA 1984, s. 226. As s. 226 is the liability due at the time of the IHT return, the loan must only be for this purpose, so interest on future loans taken out for corrective amounts cannot be offset.

For such initial loans, interest is only tax-deductible if paid during the first 12 months of the loan being outstanding.

Relief is also given for interest on a replacement loan, taken out to pay off a former loan to pay IHT due under s. 226. However, it is only eligible for 12 months from the issue of the *first* loan.

If the relief for the loan interest cannot be offset as there is insufficient income, the relief can be either carried back or carried forward. The statutory order of the set-off is to preceding years (on a LIFO basis) first and then to following years (on a FIFO basis).

Example

Rosalie was named in the will as the executor for two death estates, Barry's and Jane's.

Barry's estate

Barry died on 4 May 2020. Rosalie was unable to access Barry's bank account until she acquired the grant of probate on 13 December 2020. She therefore took out a loan to pay the IHT on 1 October 2020. On computing the income tax of the estate for 2020-21 she was able to offset £200 of interest that had been paid on the outstanding loan. Further IHT liabilities were discovered in May 2021 and a second loan was taken out on 3 June 2021. The administration was completed on 13 October 2021 and both loans was paid off on that date.

In the estate income tax computation for 2021-22, Rosalie can only offset the loan interest from 6 April 2021 to 30 September 2021, and only that arising on the first loan.

Any loan interest incurred from 4 June 2021 to the end of the period of administration on the second loan could not be offset for tax purposes as it was a *subsequent* loan and therefore not one to cover a liability arising at the time of the IHT return.

Interest arising from 1 October 2021 to the end of the period of administration was also ineligible as it was outside the 12-month period of the loan being outstanding.

Jane's estate

Jane had died on 4 May 2018, but the administration of the estate was still ongoing in July 2020. A loan for the payment of the IHT had been taken out on 5 November 2019, and interest charged of £500 could be offset in 2019-20. However, as there was no income in the estate, this deduction could not be used in 2019-20. It could, however, be used (first) against income in the previous year of 2018-19. As there was also no income from 5 May 2018 to 5 April 2019, the loan interest could then be carried forward to the tax year 2020-21 where there was sufficient taxable income to claim the tax deduction.

Law: ITTOIA 2005, s. 666; ITA 2007, s. 403-405
Guidance: TSEM 7908, 7910, 7912, 7914; SAIM 10350

42.5.6   Calculating the tax due on the PRs

Chapter 3 explains how to perform an income tax calculation for an individual. The process is the same for a PR, apart from the differences explained above.

Example

Raegan was the executor of his friend Jeff's death estate. The period of administration started on 1 October 2020, when Jeff died, and ended on 1 December 2021. The income received in the two tax years was as follows:

	2020-21 £	2021-22 £
Property income (net of all allowable expenses)	2,200	3,000
Building society interest (received gross)	700	900
Dividends	3,200	1,800

Raegan incurred some income expenses for professional fees for the estate and these totalled £700. As the period of administration has spanned two tax years, Raegan will need to prepare two tax computations for the estate: one for 2020-21 and one for 2021-22.

2020-21	Total income £	Non-savings income £	Savings income £	Dividend income £
Property income	2,200	2,200		
Building society interest	700		700	
Dividend income	3,200			3,200
Taxable income	6,100	2,200	700	3,20

	Total income £	Total tax due £
Tax on non-savings income at basic rate @ 20%	2,200	440
Tax on savings income @ 20%	700	140
Tax on dividend income @ 7.5%	3,200	240
Total income tax payable	6,100	820

2021-22	Total income £	Non-savings income £	Savings income £	Dividend income £
Property income	3,000	3,000		
Building society interest	900		900	
Dividend income	1,800			1,800
Taxable income	5,700	3,000	900	1,800

	Total income £	Total tax due £
Tax on non-savings income at basic rate @ 20%	3,000	600
Tax on savings income @ 20%	900	180
Tax on dividend income @ 7.5%	1,800	135
Total income tax payable	5,700	915

As can be seen, the calculation of the income tax from the perspective of the PRs is quite straightforward.

42.5.7   The formal process

If HMRC send the PRs a trust and estate self-assessment tax return to file, they must file this return and pay any tax through the formal self-assessment procedure. This, however, will be the exception not the rule, as the tax office will normally only issue a self-assessment tax return to PRs if there is an existing open enquiry into the deceased's tax affairs.

In practice, HMRC will accept a tax return before the end of the year in which the period of administration was completed.

HMRC can enquire into self-assessment tax returns, normally for up to 12 months after the day on which the return was filed (as long as it was not late).

The PRs may ask HMRC for confirmation that the return has been accepted, without having to wait for the formal enquiry window to expire. If such confirmation is given, the PRs can then finalise all the tax liabilities and distribute the remainder of the estate. However, if the return was incorrect or incomplete, HMRC reserve the right to re-open an enquiry.

Guidance: TSEM 7418

42.5.8   The informal process

The tax affairs of deceased estates are usually uncomplicated and the period of administration normally lasts for under a year. As the tax payments being made by the PRs are not ongoing, it is easier for both HMRC and the PRs to settle any tax payable outside the self-assessment system.

The informal payment procedure is only available where no return has been requested by HMRC and where all of the following conditions are satisfied:

- the total tax liability for both income tax and CGT is under £10,000;
- the probate value of the estate is less than £2.5 million; and
- any proceeds for any assets in the estate sold in any one tax year are less than £500,000.

Where these conditions are satisfied, the PRs can make an informal payment of the total liability without the need for a formal self-assessment.

An estate that fails any of the above conditions is considered "complex" and will require a formal return. Furthermore, an informal payment will not be allowed if income tax is due on any of the following specific receipts into the estate:

- those that fall within ITA 2007, s. 946 (specific payments to the estate such as building society securities, UK public revenue dividends, patent royalties, and certain other categories);
- a recovery of tax overpaid under TMA 1970, s. 30; or
- the recovery of excessive tax credits under ICTA 1988, s. 252.

42.5.9   Administration

If the informal procedure is being used, the PRs should send HMRC a computation of the tax liability towards the end of the period of administration. Even if the administration has spanned more than one tax year, only one payment is required.

Guidance: TSEM 7413

42.6   Types of legacy from deceased estates

42.6.1   Overview

A beneficiary or legatee of an estate is either a recipient of a specific legacy from the deceased or a part of, or all of, the residue of the estate.

A residual beneficiary may have:

- an absolute interest in both the capital and the income of a part of the estate;

- a limited interest (e.g. entitlement to the income but not the capital); or
- a discretionary interest, where any income paid to the beneficiary is at the discretion of the PRs.

Payment to the beneficiaries includes a direct cash payment, a transfer of assets, paying a beneficiary's personal liabilities, or releasing his or her debts.

Beneficiaries may receive a gift specifically stated in the will or it may be from other sources. It might be received through a *donatio mortis causa*, a secret trust, a will trust or a statutory trust – see **42.6.6** below for an explanation of these terms. Irrespective of the vehicle that provides the legacy, it will be either a specific legacy or a share, or all, of the residue.

Law: ITTOIA 2005, s. 650, 652, 654, 655, 666, 681
Guidance: TSEM 7904

42.6.2   Legatees of specific legacies

A legacy is an amount of money or a particular asset left to a legatee or recipient or beneficiary of the estate.

There are two types of specific legacies: pecuniary and specific assets.

Pecuniary legacies

Pecuniary legacies are monetary amounts. They represent a specific sum of either cash or a direct bank transfer.

Unless the will says otherwise, the recipient legatee is not usually eligible for interest on the sum unless there is a delay of more than 12 months from the date of death in the PRs paying the legacy. If interest is payable, it is taxable in the hands of the recipient legatee. They cannot offset any such interest against the income tax due in the estate.

The rate of interest payable by the PRs on such late payments is 0.05% at the time of writing (March 2021).

Specific assets

A specific asset is any other specific gift left to a legatee in the will that is not cash. These gifts can be any asset the deceased wished to gift such as cars, jewellery, land, buildings, and shares.

Where the asset is not income-producing (e.g. a violin) there will be no income tax impact as a result of the receipt of the gift.

Where, on the other hand, the asset produces income (e.g. a rental property), the legatee beneficiary is entitled to any income generated by that asset from the date of the death and is taxable thereon.

Usually, the PRs (rather than the specific legatee) receive the income arising on such an asset during the period of the administration. The PRs then periodically pay this income over to the relevant beneficiary.

The PRs are not required to pay tax on the income received for the specific beneficiaries as this is not legally their income during the period of the administration. If the PRs have mistakenly paid income tax on this income, they should issue a form R185 (Estate Income) showing the income tax deducted so that the recipient can use this as a tax credit against any income tax that he or she is due to pay on the income. There are some instances where the PRs are legally able to use the income for other purposes; in these cases, the legatee will not be taxed on the income not received.

Irrespective of whether the PRs have paid over the income receivable to the beneficiary, the legatee must pay income tax on the income *arising* on the asset, not only when the income is actually received from the PRs; this is made clear in case law, specifically *Hawley*. This means that a delay in the PRs paying the income over to the beneficiary may lead to cash-flow problems for the beneficiary, who will have the tax liability but not the income.

Example

Rosa's mother died on 1 February 2019. Rosa had been left a buy-to-let house as a specific gift from her mother's estate. The property generates income of £25,000 a year after deductible expenses.

In 2018-19, 2019-20 and 2020-21 the administration was ongoing.

Despite the PRs sending Rosa a letter instructing her of the income received by them in 2018-19 and 2019-20, they did not pay her any of this income. They did not send Rosa a form R185 either, as they had no obligation to deduct any tax on income received from the specific gift and did not do so. Rosa therefore had the liability for the income tax on the rents received by the PRs in 2018-19 and 2019-20, despite not having received any of the rental income herself.

When the administration was completed on 31 July 2020, Rosa received all the rent due to her that had accumulated over the administration period. As she has already paid the tax on the rental income for 2018-19 and 2019-20, she only has to declare the 2020-21 share of rental income in her tax computation for that year.

However, in this case, the tax due on the 2018-19 rental income was due on 31 January 2020, some six months before the rental income was paid to Rosa from the PRs at the end of the administration.

Law: *The Wills Act* 1837, s. 33
Case: *IRC v Hawley* (1928) 13 TC 327
Guidance: TSEM 6060, 6074, 7490;
https://www.lawgazette.co.uk/download?ac=95213 (sample data page)

42.6.3   Legatees with a limited interest in the residue

If the beneficiary is entitled only to the income, and not to the whole or any share of the capital in the residue, this represents a "limited interest" in the residue.

This situation is usually created through an interest-in-possession (IiP) trust at the end of the period of administration (see **41.3**). In an IiP trust there is a life tenant (life renter in Scotland) who is entitled to the income arising in the trust and a remainderman who will be entitled to the capital after some event described in the trust deed (e.g. the death of the life tenant, or any other event the settlor may wish to specify).

The limited interest beneficiary is taxed on the gross income paid in the tax year of assessment. When the administration is completed, the beneficiary is treated as having received the balance of income to which he or she was entitled.

The income is treated as being paid from the PRs in the following order:

* non-savings and savings income; then
* dividend income.

The year of assessment of the income could follow the statutory or the conventional basis.

Statutory basis

The statutory basis arises from ITTOIA 2005, s. 654-656. Where the limited interest *and* the administration are ongoing in the tax year, the beneficiary is taxed on the income received in the tax year of receipt. However, if only the limited interest is ongoing throughout the tax year and the administration has been completed in the tax year (e.g. where a formal IiP is created at the end of the administration period), the total to be taxed in that tax year is all income paid before the administration period ends *as well as* any amount still due to the beneficiary at the end of the administration period, whether this is in the tax year or not.

Example

Romina died on 13 January 2020. She left her entire estate to her civil partner Taylor on a limited interest and the capital to their two children. The administration ended on 2 February 2022.

The income received by the PRs in the applicable tax years was as follows:

	2019-20 £	2020-21 £	2021-22 £
Property income	2,000	12,000	10,000
Bank interest	200	800	100
Dividend income	120	400	80

The estate incurred EMEs of £150 in 2019-20, £350 in 2020-21 and £120 in 2021-22.

The PRs paid the income to Taylor as follows:

	£
26 September 2020	11,000
13 December 2021	5,000
2 February 2022	3,500
14 June 2022	515

The first step is to establish the tax paid by the PRs on the income received in the three tax years the administration spanned. From this it can be seen from which source of income the PRs are distributing.

2019-20	Total income	Non-savings income	Savings income	Dividend income
	£	£	£	£
Property income	2,000	2,000		
Savings income	200		200	
Dividend income	120			120
Taxable income	2,320	2,000	200	120
Tax at basic rates	(449)	(400)	(40)	(9)
EMEs	(150)	(150)	0	0
Amount available to distribute to beneficiary	1,721	1,450	160	111
Paid to beneficiary	0	0	0	0
Carried forward to 2020-21	1,721	1,450	160	111

2020-21	Total income	Non-savings income	Savings income	Dividend income
	£	£	£	£
Property income	12,000	12,000		
Savings income	800		800	
Dividend income	400			400
Taxable income	13,200	12,000	800	400
Tax at basic rates	(2,590)	(2,400)	(160)	(30)
EMEs	(350)	(350)	0	0
Total net income in 2020-21	10,260	9,250	640	370
Add total net income from 2019-20	1,721	1,450	160	111

2020-21 (cont.)	Total income	Non-savings income	Savings income	Dividend income
	£	£	£	£
Total available to distribute to beneficiary	11,981	10,700	800	481
Paid to beneficiary	(11,000)	(10,700)	(300)	0
Carried forward to 2021-22	981	0	500	481

2021-22	Total income	Non-savings income	Savings income	Dividend income
	£	£	£	£
Property income	10,000	10,000		
Savings income	100		100	
Dividend income	80			80
Taxable income	10,180	10,000	100	80
Tax at basic rates	(2,026)	(2,000)	(20)	(6)
EMEs	(120)	(120)	0	0
Total net income in 2021-22	8,034	7,880	80	74
Add totals from 2019-20 and 2020-21	981	0	500	481
Amount available to distribute to beneficiary	9,015	7,880	580	555
Paid to beneficiary	(9,015)	(7,880)	(580)	(555)
Balance remaining	0	0	0	0

Taylor's income distributions in 2020-21 would represent the payment on 26 September 2020 as follows:

2020-21	Gross	Net	Tax
	£	£	£
Non-savings income	13,375	10,700	2,675
Savings income	375	300	75
Dividend income	0	0	0

Taylor's declaration of income in 2021-22 would include *all* the distributions from the estate (up to and including 2021-22) and the £515 paid to him in the following tax year (2022-23). This is because the statutory method requires *all* payments to the limited interest from the estate to be taxed in the tax year the administration ends; both those paid before and after the end of that tax year. For Taylor, this means that the payment in June, despite it being in the following tax year, should be declared, and tax should be paid on it, in 2021-22.

2021-22	Gross	Net	Tax
	£	£	£
Non-savings income	9,850	7,880	1,970
Savings income	725	580	145
Dividend income	600	555	45

Taylor will also have income from the IiP created at the end of the period of administration. The income received from this in 2021-22, earned from the end of the administration period to 5 April in the following tax year (3 February 2022 to 5 April 2022), will also be taxable in 2021-22.

Conventional basis

The conventional basis (an alternative to the statutory basis) is that the legatee is taxed on income in the tax year in which he or she receives it. This income may well have arisen over several years if the administration period spanned more than one tax year and the income was paid as one final payment at the end of the administration. HMRC state that they are unlikely to insist on taxpayers using the statutory basis.

In Taylor's case this would mean that the final payment of income of £315 from the estate could be declared in the 2022-23 tax year rather than the 2021-22 tax year and HMRC would not challenge this. However, the beneficiary can insist on using the statutory basis.

Law: ITTOIA 2005, s. 650, 654
Guidance: TSEM 7652, 7654

42.6.4 Legatees with a discretionary interest in the residue

If the deceased did not specify to whom the residue is to go, but instead asked the PRs to use their discretion, a discretionary trust will be set up. This may or may not be formalised in the will.

If the will specified that the income and/or capital were to be distributed at the PRs' discretion to selected beneficiaries, any payments made from the trust to the beneficiaries during the period of administration is treated as paid from the discretionary trust in the year of the payment.

If the will merely asked the PRs to exercise their discretion in selecting which beneficiaries to distribute the estate to, with no indication that an ongoing trust is desired, reliance is instead made on Statement of Practice SP 4/93.

SP 4/93 explains that this is taxable as a discretionary trust and that the "trustees" (actually the PRs) may be liable to tax at the rate applicable to trusts on the payments. Beneficiaries may therefore be treated as receiving the payments after deduction of tax at the rate applicable to trusts (see **41.4.3**).

Law: ICTA 1988, s. 686; ITTOIA 2005, s. 650, 655
Guidance: TSEM 7660; SP 4/93

42.6.5 Legatees with an absolute interest in the residue

Most beneficiaries have an absolute interest in the residue. Essentially, this means that they can have their share of the residue without any strings attached.

The residue is simply what is left in the estate after all the liabilities of the estate have been settled, including any tax, pecuniary liabilities and specific assets.

When the PRs pass the residue to the beneficiaries, they are in law passing a capital asset. Despite this, however, it may be that the estate received income during the period of the administration, and (if so) the part of the capital that is made up of this income is deemed to be taxable income for the beneficiary (*Barnardo's Homes*). Essentially, this means that whether the PRs pass capital or income to the beneficiary, the lower of the amount received and the income not distributed in the estate will be taxed as income.

"Income" for these purposes includes:

- any UK taxable income received by the PRs in their capacity as such after allowable deductions, including income gains from life policies if treated as the income of the PRs; and

- any taxable income that would have been charged to UK income tax if it had been UK source income arising to a UK resident, taking into account allowable deductions.

Income specifically does *not* include any income that is due to the legatee of a specific legacy, or an income-producing asset that is due to the beneficiary through the law of intestacy. Nor does it include income from any assets that are not available to pay the deceased's debts.

Law: ITTOIA 2005, s. 411, 419, 466
Case: *Barnardo's Homes v IRC* (1921) 2 AC 1
Guidance: TSEM 7678

Allowable deductions

Once income has been identified, the legislation only taxes the beneficiary on the net income after allowable deductions. Allowable deductions are:

- interest paid by the PRs in that capacity (e.g. interest paid on unpaid legacies and (commercial rate) interest paid on the debts of the deceased); interest on overdue tax and unpaid IHT are not deductible for these purposes;

- "annual payments" for the year which are properly payable out of residue;

- any EMEs (see below); and

- excess deductions brought forward from the previous tax year.

Expenses may only be deducted once, so if the PRs deduct an expense the beneficiary must take care not to do so again. Deductions in the amounts distributed to the beneficiaries are assumed to have come from non-savings income and savings income first, then dividend income.

If the deductions exceed the income, a negative amount cannot be given to the beneficiaries to offset against their other income. Any excess expenses are carried forward until the following tax year.

Estate management expenses

EMEs are payments made from the estate by the PRs, in their capacity as such, which represent income expenses incurred. The EMEs are taken from the taxed income before the income is passed to the beneficiaries.

There is no statutory order for the deduction of EMEs. HMRC state:

> "The deduction for allowable expenses is given against aggregate income and not against any specific income source."

However, of the three main types of income that PRs receive (i.e. non-savings income, savings income and dividend income), it would normally be most beneficial to set the expenses off against the non-savings income as far as possible. This allows the taxpayer a higher tax saving (20%) for the EMEs than if it were deducted from dividend income (7.5%).

These expenses can only be deducted if they are income expenses ("properly chargeable to income"), ignoring any specific direction in the will. Although the term "properly chargeable to income" is not defined in the legislation, and no courts have considered it, the HMRC view is that the term covers expenses that on ordinary legal and accountancy principles are applicable to the administration of trust estates. Examples are professional fees, such as those of accountants and lawyers (but only for income-related issues such as income tax), and testamentary and administration expenses that are related to income. Note that only the residual beneficiaries incur the expenses; recipients of income from specific legacies do not take a share of these expenses.

Expenses that pay for costs associated with identifying, collecting, realising or preserving the assets in the estate are capital and cannot be deducted from income received. If an expense has both an income and a capital element, such as professional advice for both income tax and capital gains tax, the invoice should be split on a reasonable basis.

The following expenses, which may appear to be income-related, must in fact be deducted against capital instead:

- funeral expenses;
- probate (confirmation) fees;

- the costs of collecting in the assets and preserving them once collected;
- any debts of the deceased at death (plus interest due); and
- other testamentary fees, including professional fees relating to capital.

Other expenses, such as insurance on a rental property, are already taken into account elsewhere.

Guidance: TSEM 7684, 7912

42.7 Income tax on the beneficiaries of the residue

42.7.1 Overview

Income arising during the course of the administration is assessed on the PRs not the beneficiaries. However, once the beneficiaries are in receipt of this income from the deceased's estate, they will pay tax at their own tax rate, offsetting any tax already paid by the PRs as a tax credit to reduce the amount due.

In the individual's self-assessment tax return there is an entry "income from the estates of deceased persons", where income from the estate must be declared.

The PRs will have provided the beneficiaries with a form R185 (Estate income). This form summarises all the income received, showing its gross, net and tax components. The income must be entered into the individual's self-assessment tax return gross. The tax paid by the PRs is usually the amount that can be offset as a tax credit. Sometimes the tax paid will show income bearing non-payable or non-repayable tax credits. In these cases, although the tax can reduce tax payable by the beneficiaries, it cannot create a tax repayment for them.

In cases where more than one beneficiary receives income from the estate, each beneficiary is separately taxed on the amounts outlined in his or her own form R185.

Guidance: TSEM 7453, 7456, 7457, 7608

42.7.2 Income distributed during the period of the administration

An absolute interest in the residue is received by those beneficiaries that are not subject to any trusts over the residue.

Unlike a legatee of a specific asset, the beneficiaries of the residue are not deemed to own the income from any income-producing assets generated on the residue from the date of the death. The PRs will therefore pay all the tax arising on income received from such assets, and the net income will be added to the residue to be distributed to the residual beneficiaries at the end of the period of the administration.

Having said that, the PRs do sometimes distribute income from these income-generating assets during the period of administration. Payments made to the beneficiaries before the administration has ended render the beneficiaries liable to pay income tax on the receipt of the income. The tax charge will be based on the lower of the following amounts:

- the amount actually received by the beneficiary in the tax year; or

- the amount of the total available income in the estate from the date of the death to the end of the tax year in question, less any amounts that have already been distributed.

For example, if there is £10,000 in the estate earned as income, but the beneficiary is only paid out £3,000, he or she will only be taxed on £3,000. However, if the beneficiary is paid £3,000 but there is only £2,000 of accrued income in the estate from the death to the end of the tax year of the payment, the income taxed will be only £2,000 and the other £1,000 will be a capital payment. In the final tax year of the administration the beneficiary will receive all the remaining income, liable to income tax, and his or her absolute interest in the rest of the residue, which will be the capital.

If the PRs have received income but not distributed it to the beneficiaries in a tax year where the administration was not completed, it will be carried forward to the next tax year. The total income distributable (i.e. income less tax and EMEs) is calculated on a cumulative basis.

Income paid out to beneficiaries will be deemed to have come from non-savings and savings income first and then dividends.

If items of capital have been distributed instead, and there is income that has not been distributed, the capital receipt too will be deemed to have come from income, in the same order as if the income had been distributed; it will be taxable up to the amount of untaxed accrued income in the estate. Here, too, the income will already have been taxed in the hands of the PRs, so a form R185 (Estate Income) will be given to the beneficiary, certifying the amount of gross and net income, and the tax paid on the amount distributed.

42.7.3   *Income distributed in the final tax year*

In the final tax year, in which the administration ends, any tax liability will not depend on whether the income has actually been paid out to the beneficiary. The beneficiary will be taxed on the distributable income available on the last day of the administration period. If the administration period has been short, this may be included in only one tax year, but in practice income tax in at least two tax years will often have to be calculated.

Income will be taxed in the estate at the basic rate, so will be received with a tax credit for basic rate tax set out on the form R185 (Estate Income). The form must be issued by the PRs both when a distribution is made during the period of administration and at the end.

Example

Rylie died on 14 June 2020, leaving the residue of his estate to his son Kyle. The administration was finalised on 1 May 2022. Kyle did not receive any income during the period of the administration, but the PRs received income in each of the three tax years from 2020-21 to 2022-23.

The PRs complete a form R185 for Kyle for 2022-23 showing all the gross and net income, and the tax paid on this income for the whole of the three tax years. Kyle will need to include this income on his self-assessment tax return for 2022-23.

Law: ITTOIA 2005, s. 650, 652
Guidance: TSEM 7602, 7608, 7682

42.7.4   *The allocation of the different sources of income from an estate*

When the beneficiaries receive amounts from the PRs, the legislation determines how these taxed amounts are allocated to the various sources of income from which they have been generated. Income on which the PRs have had to pay income tax at non savings and savings basic rates is deemed to be distributed first, followed by income that has been subject to the dividend ordinary rate.

From the beneficiaries' perspective, all income received from the estate would ideally be deemed to be non-savings income initially, up to the level of non-savings income received in the estate, followed by savings income and finally dividend income.

However, this split between non-savings and savings income cannot be enjoyed by the beneficiary. As a result, the recipient beneficiary cannot use the personal savings allowance against income from death estates that has been generated from savings income received by the PRs.

This is because ITTOIA 2005, s. 679 states simply that income taxed at the basic rate is treated as paid out before income taxed at the dividend ordinary rate; it does not separate out the savings income. Furthermore, s. 680A specifically mentions that dividend income can be treated as such by the beneficiary, meaning that the dividend allowance can be used; but there is no such statement concerning savings or interest income.

If there is more than one beneficiary to be paid out of the income, the sources should be allocated on a just and fair basis between the beneficiaries.

Example 1

Roman is the sole beneficiary of the estate of his late uncle, who died on 5 July 2020. The PRs paid him an interim payment in cash of £5,000 on 31 March 2021.

During 2020-21 the PRs received the following income into the estate:

	£	Tax rate for PRs %
Property income	3,000	20
Building society interest	2,500	20
Dividend income	1,800	7.5

The PRs will need to pay tax on the cash of:

	Gross £	%	Tax £	Net £
Property income	3,000	20	600	2,400
Building society interest	2,500	20	500	2,000
Dividend income	1,800	7.5	135	1,665
	7,300			6,065

The £5,000 cash payment to Roman will represent £2,400 (net) of property income, £2,000 (net) of interest and the balance £600 (net) of dividend income. The remainder of net income not distributed, £1,065 (£1,665 - £600), will be carried forward to be matched against future distributions during the period of administration.

Roman will need to gross all these amounts up in his self-assessment tax computation to calculate his rate of tax on them. He will declare the following:

	Gross £	
Non savings and savings income	5,500	(£2,400 x 100%/80% and (£2,000 x 100%/80%)
Dividend income	649	(£600 x 100%/92.5%)

If Roman had inherited the estate jointly with his brother, and each of them received £5,000 as an interim payment, they would each have had to disclose half the total income received:

	Gross £	
Non savings and savings income	2,750	(£2,400 x 50% x 100%/80% and (£2,000 x 50% x 100%/80%)
Dividend income	900	(£1,665 x 50% x 100%/92.5%)

As the PRs did not receive as much as £10,000 income, the balance of the cash received, which was not income and thus not taxed as income, was £1,967.50 each (£10,000 less the net income £6,065 x 50%). This is deemed to be capital and not taxable.

As seen above, the general rule is that – irrespective of how the estate has received the income in the residue – the income received by the beneficiary is included in his or her tax computation initially as non-savings and non-dividend income and then as dividend income.

However, there are two exceptions to this.

The first is if the beneficiary is a non-UK resident. Subject to various conditions, Extra-statutory Concession A14 allows the beneficiary to claim relief under a double tax treaty or under certain other provisions.

The second exception relates to the type of income rather than to the beneficiary of the income. If the PRs receive income from close company loans to participators, gains from insurance policies or stock dividends, any tax paid by the PRs cannot be reclaimed.

Example 2

Rocco died on 11 March 2020. He left his entire estate to his wife Mary. No payments were made to Mary until the administration ended on 2 September 2021. The PRs took out a loan to pay the IHT on 1 September 2020. This was paid off on 31 August 2021.

The income received by the PRs in the applicable tax years was as follows:

	2020-21 £	2021-22 £
Property income	8,000	6,000
Bank interest	800	100
Dividend income	120	80

The PRs incurred EMEs and loan interest costs as follows:

	2020-21 £	2021-22 £
EMEs	150	120
Loan interest	500	450

The first step is to establish the tax paid by the PRs on the income received in the two tax years of administration. This will determine the source of income from which the PRs are distributing.

2020-21	Total income	Non-savings income	Savings income	Dividend income
	£	£	£	£
Property income	8,000	8,000		
Savings income	800		800	
Dividend income	120			120
Interest on loan to pay IHT	(500)	(500)	0	0
Taxable income	8,420	7,500	800	120
Tax at basic rates	(1,669)	(1,500)	(160)	(9)
EMEs	(150)	(150)	0	0
Amount available to distribute to beneficiary	6,601	5,850	640	111
Paid to beneficiary	0	0	0	0
Carried forward to 2021-22	6,601	5,850	640	111

2021-22	Total income	Non-savings income	Savings income	Dividend income
	£	£	£	£
Property income	6,000	6,000		
Savings income	100		100	
Dividend income	80			80
Interest on loan to pay IHT	(450)	(450)		
Taxable income	5,730	5,550	100	80
Tax at basic rates	(1,136)	(1,110)	(20)	(6)
EMEs	(120)	(120)	0	0

2021-22 (cont.)	Total income	Non-savings income	Savings income	Dividend income
	£	£	£	£
Total net income in 2021-22	4,474	4,320	80	74
Add totals from 2020-21	6,601	5,850	640	111
Total available to distribute to beneficiary	11,075	10,170	1,440	185
Paid to Mary	(11,075)	(10,170)	(1,440)	(185)

Mary's income distributions in 2021-22 would represent the income received in the estate in 2020-21 and in 2021-22. The form R185 would be issued to Mary showing:

2021-22	Gross	Net	Tax
	£	£	£
Non-savings income	12,712	10,170	2,542
Savings income	1,800	1,440	360
Dividend income	200	185	15

Mary will now need to declare this income in her 2021-22 self-assessment tax return on the pages for income from estates. Mary is employed on a salary of £50,000 and has paid £7,500 through PAYE in 2021-22. She has no other income. Her tax computation will look as follows:

2021-22	Total income £	Non-savings income £	Savings income £	Dividend income £
Employment income	50,000	50,000	0	0
Income from estate (non-savings and non-dividend income)	14,712	14,512	0	200
Personal allowance	(12,500)	(12,500)	0	0
Taxable income	52,212	52,012	0	200

	Total income £	Total tax due £
Tax on non-savings income at basic rate @ 20% £37,500 @ 20%	37,000	7,500
Tax on non-savings income at higher rate @ 40% (£52,012 – £37,500) @ 40%	14,512	5,805
Dividends covered by dividend allowance	200	0
Total income tax liability	52,212	13,305
Less tax credit issued by R185 (£2,542 + £360 + £15)		(2,917)
Less PAYE paid		(7,500)
Tax payment due by Mary		2,888

£2,888 is the tax on the non-savings non-dividend income paid to Mary of £5,805 (£14,512 x 40%), plus the tax on the dividend income paid to Mary £0 (covered by the dividend allowance), less the tax paid in the estate by the PRs of £2,917.

Law: ICTA 1988, s. 278; ITTOIA 2005, s. 657, 658, 680, 680A, 714, 830
Guidance: TSEM 7678, ESC A14

42.7.5   The payment of a capital asset to a beneficiary rather than income

If the residual legatee is given a capital asset rather than income, the tax treatment will depend on whether any income has been received by the estate. If there is accrued income in the estate that has not been paid out to beneficiaries, this income will be deemed to be paid out first through the payment of the capital asset, even though the asset being given out is not income. This is an anti-avoidance measure to prevent PRs from paying out capital assets so as to stop the beneficiaries being charged to income tax.

Example

Rio was the residual beneficiary of his father's estate. His father died on 10 November 2020 and the administration was completed in 2022. The estate earned £3,000 income from property after deductible expenses in the 2020-21 tax year. Rio was not paid any of the income by the PRs in this tax year but on 3 February 2021 the PRs transferred his late father's Porsche motor car to him, valued at £40,000, as an interim payment.

The PRs will need to give Rio a form R185 detailing the amount of the income received gross, net and the tax deducted by the estate up to the value of the car in the 2020-21 tax year. As the car is valued at more than the income received, all of the income received in the tax year 2020-21 will be taxable on Rio.

42.7.6   Where payments are made to beneficiaries at different times

Where the estate has more than one residual beneficiary, it could be the case that interim payments are made to different beneficiaries at different times. A strict record of payments will be needed to be kept for income tax purposes, as each payment, capital or income, may be deemed to have included some income to be taxed on the beneficiary. Forms R185 will need to be issued to the beneficiaries in accordance with the income that they are entitled to at that specific time of the payment to them.

Example

Rona's mother died on 19 March 2020. She had left her entire estate to Rona and her sister Steph. The period of administration ended on 2 February 2022. The PRs took out a loan to pay the IHT on 31 August 2020. This was paid off on 31 August 2021.

The income received by the PRs in the applicable tax years was as follows:

	2019-20 £	2020-21 £	2021-22 £
Property income	1,000	8,000	6,000
Bank interest	50	800	100
Dividend income	0	120	80

Expenses and loan interest paid were as follows:

	2019-20 £	2020-21 £	2021-22 £
EMEs	40	150	120
Loan interest paid	0	500	450

In July 2020, the PRs paid an interim distribution to Rona of £3,650. No interim payments were made to Steph.

The first step is to establish the tax paid by the PRs on the income received in 2019-20 and 2020-21. From this it can be seen from which source of income the PRs distributed to Rona in 2020-21.

Next, the income received in 2021-22 must be taxed, and finally the amount due to each of the sisters at the end of the period of administration calculated.

2019-20	Total income	Non-savings income	Savings income	Dividend income
	£	£	£	£
Property income	1,000	1,000		
Savings income	50		50	
Taxable income	1,050	1,000	50	0
Tax at basic rates	(210)	(200)	(10)	(0)
EMEs	(40)	(40)	0	0
Amount available to distribute to beneficiary	800	760	40	0
Paid to beneficiary	0	0	0	0
Carried forward to 2020-21	800	760	40	0
Rona	400	380	20	0
Steph	400	380	20	0

2020-21	Total income	Non-savings income	Savings income	Dividend income
	£	£	£	£
Property income	8,000	8,000		
Savings income	800		800	
Dividend income	120			120
Interest on loan to pay IHT	(500)	(500)		
Taxable income	8,420	7,500	800	120
Tax at basic rates	(1,669)	(1,500)	(160)	(9)
EMEs	(150)	(150)	0	0
Amount available to distribute to beneficiary	6,601	5,850	640	111
Amounts from 2019-20	800	760	40	0

2020-21 (cont.)	Total income £	Non-savings income £	Savings income £	Dividend income £
Total available to distribute	7,401	6,610	680	111
Rona	3,700	3,305	340	55
Distributed in 2020-21	(3,650)	(3,305)	(340)	(5)
Rona balance	50	0	0	50
Steph	3,701	3,305	340	56

2021-22	Total income £	Non-savings income £	Savings income £	Dividend income £
Property income	6,000	6,000		
Savings income	100		100	
Dividend income	80			80
Interest on loan to pay IHT	(450)	(450)		
Taxable income	5,730	5,550	100	80
Tax at basic rates	(1,136)	(1,110)	(20)	(6)
EMEs	(120)	(120)	0	0
Total net income in 2021-22	4,474	4,320	80	74

2021-22 (cont.)	Total income	Non-savings income	Savings income	Dividend income
	£	£	£	£
Rona	2,237	2,160	40	37
Add totals from 2019-20 and 2020-21	50	0	0	50
Rona total available to distribute	2,287	2,160	40	87
Paid to Rona	(2,287)	(2,160)	(40)	(87)
Steph	2,237	2,160	40	37
Add totals from 2019-20 and 2020-21	3,701	3,305	340	56
Steph total available to distribute	5,938	5,465	380	93
Paid to Steph	(5,938)	(5,465)	380	93

Rona's income distributions in 2020-21 represent the income she received from the estate in 2020-21. The final distribution represents the balance of the income received in the estate in 2020-21 and that received in 2021-22. Two forms R185 must be issued to Rona, one for 2020-21 and one for 2021-22, showing:

2020-21	Gross	Net	Tax
	£	£	£
Non-savings income	4,131	3,305	826
Savings income	425	340	85
Dividend income	6	5	1

2021-22	Gross	Net	Tax
	£	£	£
Non-savings income	2,700	2,160	540
Savings income	50	40	10
Dividend income	94	87	7

Steph's self-assessment tax return, however, will not have anything on the income from estates pages in 2020-21 as she was not paid anything out. She will have a form R185 for 2021-22 only.

2021-22	Gross	Net	Tax
	£	£	£
Non-savings income	6,831	5,465	1,366
Savings income	475	380	95
Dividend income	101	93	8

Notice that Steph's gross and net totals, apart from rounding, are the same as Rona's totals for both years. It is only the timing of the taxation that is different; they were still entitled to half of the estate income each. Tax credits are always rounded up (so that rounding favours the taxpayer).

42.7.7   Repayments or more tax to pay

A beneficiary with income below the personal allowance may be entitled to a full refund of any income tax paid by the estate.

Example

Ruth was the beneficiary of the estate of her late uncle. Ruth had just finished university and was looking for a job. She worked at the local supermarket part-time, earning £11,000 in 2020-21. She received the following form R185 from the PRs of the estate for 2020-21:

	Gross £	Net £	Tax £
Non-savings income	1,000	800	200
Savings income	1,300	1,040	260
Dividend income	1,000	925	75

Her income tax calculation would be as follows:

	Total income £	Non-savings income £	Savings income £	Dividend income £
Employment income	11,000	11,000	0	0
Non-savings and savings income from the estate	2,300	2,300	0	0
Dividend income	1,000			1,000
	14,300	13,300	0	1,000
Personal allowance	(12,500)	(12,500)	0	0
Taxable income (Total under £37,500, so basic rate taxpayer)	1,800	800		1,000

	Total income £	Total tax due £
Tax on non-savings income at basic rate £800 @ 20%	800	160
Dividends income Dividend allowance £2,000 x 0%	1,000	0
Less tax credit – income tax paid by PRs (£200 + £260 + £75)	0	(535)
Total income tax payable	1,800	(375)

As a direct result of the income tax paid by the PRs, Ruth has a tax repayment due to her of £375. This is because, had she earned that income herself, she would only have had to pay £160 on it, and as the PRs paid £535 tax on it, there was a shortfall of £375. By reclaiming the £375, she effectively receives the whole £3,140: £2,765 from the estate and £375 from HMRC.

By contrast, but following the same principle, some beneficiaries will have more tax to pay if they are 40% or 45% taxpayers.

42.8   Pitfalls and planning points

When does the period of administration end?

There is no statutory date on which the period of administration ends. It ends simply when all the liabilities and specific legacies have been paid and the residue has been ascertained. HMRC inform their staff at TSEM 7360:

> "You should normally accept that the administration ended on the date the PRs tell you it did."

Practically, this may be when the residual beneficiaries sign the estate accounts or earlier if this is delayed.

Amounts received after the administration has ended

If, after the residue has been ascertained, income is received by the PRs, these amounts are kept on a bare trust for the beneficiaries. No tax need be deducted and no form R185 is required.

The income position of the beneficiaries

A good PR will always consider the income tax position of the beneficiary when deciding when to pay out income from the estate. Rolling income up and not paying it out until the administration is completed, known as "bunching", could be disadvantageous for the beneficiaries. For example, it may put them in a higher tax bracket for one year, make them ineligible for certain personal allowances, or cause them to be subject to the high-income child benefit charge.

Tax clearance

It is always good practice to get advance clearance from HMRC. This is received in the form of a clearance certificate, applied for on the form IHT30, which confirms that (on the basis of the information the PRs have given HMRC) the taxes have been paid to HMRC's satisfaction. This can give the PRs some comfort that their responsibilities are complete with respect to tax.

Distinguish the role

The PRs have the responsibility for the estate during the period of administration. If there is a request in the will to create a trust, those same people may be asked to be the trustees. These roles are separate, and it must be very clear when the administration ends and when the trust begins, from which point the PRs start to act as trustees rather than as PRs.

APPENDICES

Appendix 1 – Compliance deadlines and penalties

Deadlines

Task	Deadline	Law
Filing of online self-assessment tax return	31 January following end of relevant tax year	TMA 1970, s. 8, 12AA
Filing of paper self-assessment tax return	31 October following end of relevant tax year	
Filing of online self-assessment tax return when notice to file is issued after 31 October following relevant tax year	Three months from issue date of notice to file	
Filing of paper self-assessment tax return when notice to file is issued after 31 July following relevant tax year	Three months from issue date of notice to file	
Filing of electronic return where taxpayer wishes any eligible underpayment of tax to be collected via his or her PAYE tax code	30 December following relevant tax year	SI 2003/ 2682, reg. 186
Filing of paper return where taxpayer wishes any eligible underpayment of tax to be collected via his or her PAYE tax code	31 October following relevant tax year	
Notify HMRC of chargeability to tax if no notice to file a tax return is issued	5 October following relevant tax year	TMA 1970, s. 7
Payment of tax due for a tax year (balancing payment)	31 January following end of relevant tax year	TMA 1970, s. 59B

Deadlines (cont.)

Task	Deadline	Law
First payment on account for a tax year	31 January in the tax year concerned	TMA 1970, s. 59A
Second payment on account for a tax year	31 July following the end of the relevant tax year	

Penalties

Task	Penalty	Law
Filing of online self-assessment tax return	• initial late filing penalty of £100;	
Filing of paper self-assessment tax return	• continued failure to file for more than three months, £10 per day penalty up to a maximum of 90 days, i.e. £900; • failure to file within six months, tax-geared penalty of higher of: (i) £300; and (ii) 5% of the tax due (see **2.1.7**);	
Filing of online self-assessment tax return when notice to file issued after 31 October following relevant tax year	• failure to file within 12 months, same penalty as above unless there has been deliberate withholding of the tax return, in which case the following applies: ○ deliberate withholding – 70% of the tax due; ○ deliberate and concealed withholding – 100% of the tax due.	FA 2009, s. 106, Sch. 55
Filing of paper self-assessment tax return when notice to file is issued after 31 July following relevant tax year	There is a minimum in both cases of £300. Reductions are available for unprompted disclosure resulting in the minimum penalty being between 20% and 30%, and between 35% and 50% where there has been prompted disclosure. See HMRC compliance check factsheet CC/FS18a.	

Penalties (cont.)

Task	Penalty	Law
Notify HMRC of chargeability to tax if no notice to file a tax return is issued	Based on potential lost revenue, so if tax due is not paid by the due date of 31 January the following applies: • failure to notify – 30%; • deliberate but not concealed – 70%; • deliberate and concealed (i.e. makes arrangements to conceal the situation) – 100%. Reductions in the above penalties are available as follows: *(see table below)* See HMRC compliance check factsheet CC/FS11	FA 2008, s. 123, Sch. 41
Payment of tax due for a tax year (balancing payment)	• 31 days late – 5% (3 March unless a leap year when 2 March); • six months late – an additional 5%; • 12 months late – a further additional 5%.	FA 2009, Sch. 56
First payment on account for a tax year	No penalties for late payment, but interest charged on a daily basis.	
Second payment on account for a tax year		

	Standard %	Min. % if unprompted disclosure	Min. % if prompted disclosure
Any other case	30%	Nil if disclosure within 12 months, otherwise 10%	15%
Deliberate but not concealed	70%	20%	35%
Deliberate and concealed	100%	30%	50%

Penalties (cont.)

Task	Penalty	Law
Inaccuracy in return	Based on potential lost revenue with a reduction to standard % for the quality of disclosure on the following basis: |	Standard %	Min. % if unprompted disclosure	Min. % for prompted disclosure
---	---	---	---
Careless inaccuracy	30%	Nil	15%
Deliberate but not concealed	70%	20%	35%
Deliberate and concealed	100%	30%	50% | "Careless" means a failure to take reasonable care. The above penalties apply for each inaccuracy in the return if more than one inaccuracy. The minimum penalties for deliberate behaviour are increased by 10% if it has taken the taxpayer a "significant" time (three years or more) to correct/disclose. See HMRC compliance check factsheet CC/FS7a.	FA 2007, s. 97, Sch. 24, Pt. 1, 2
Failure to notify HMRC of an error in an assessment within 30 days of the date of the assessment	30% of potential lost revenue with reductions to a minimum of nil if unprompted disclosure or 15% if prompted.	FA 2007, Sch. 24, para. 2, 4C
Failure to keep adequate records	Up to £3,000	TMA 1970, s. 12B(5)

Penalties (cont.)

Task	Penalty	Law
Making a fraudulent or negligent claim to reduce payments on account, which is incorrect	Up to the additional amount that would have been due had a correct statement been made	TMA 1970, s. 59A(6)
Fraudulent evasion of income tax	• On summary conviction, imprisonment of up to 12 months or a fine of up to the statutory maximum (£5,000), or both; • on conviction on indictment, imprisonment of up to seven years or a fine or both.	TMA 1970, s. 106A
Offences involving an offshore matter	Potentially up to 200% of tax due in the UK, depending on country ("territory") involved. See HMRC compliance checks factsheet CC/FS17 and CH 100000	SI 2011/976; SI 2013/1618

Appendix 2 – Meaning of connected persons (ITA 2007, s. 993)

The question can often arise as to whether two or more persons are connected. The following definitions, from ITA 2007, s. 993, may be applied for specific purposes (as, for example, for the purposes of ITEPA 2003 by s. 718 of that Act).

993 – Meaning of "connected" persons

(1)   This section has effect for the purposes of the provisions of the Income Tax Acts which apply this section.

(2)   An individual ("A") is connected with another individual ("B") if—

    (a)   A is B's spouse or civil partner,

    (b)   A is a relative of B,

    (c)   A is the spouse or civil partner of a relative of B,

    (d)   A is a relative of B's spouse or civil partner, or

    (e)   A is the spouse or civil partner of a relative of B's spouse or civil partner.

(3)   A person, in the capacity as trustee of a settlement, is connected with—

    (a)   any individual who is a settlor in relation to the settlement,

    (b)   any person connected with such an individual,

    (c)   any close company whose participators include the trustees of the settlement,

    (d)   any non-UK resident company which, if it were UK resident, would be a close company whose participators include the trustees of the settlement,

    (e)   any body corporate controlled (within the meaning of section 995) by a company within paragraph (c) or (d),

    (f)   if the settlement is the principal settlement in relation to one or more sub-fund settlements, a person in the capacity as trustee of such a sub-fund settlement, and

(g)   if the settlement is a sub-fund settlement in relation to a principal settlement, a person in the capacity as trustee of any other sub-fund settlements in relation to the principal settlement.

(4)   A person who is a partner in a partnership is connected with—

    (a)   any partner in the partnership,

    (b)   the spouse or civil partner of any individual who is a partner in the partnership, and

    (c)   a relative of any individual who is a partner in the partnership.

But this subsection does not apply in relation to acquisitions or disposals of assets of the partnership pursuant to genuine commercial arrangements.

(5)   A company is connected with another company if—

    (a)   the same person has control of both companies,

    (b)   a person ("A") has control of one company and persons connected with A have control of the other company,

    (c)   A has control of one company and A together with persons connected with A have control of the other company, or

    (d)   a group of two or more persons has control of both companies and the groups either consist of the same persons or could be so regarded if (in one or more cases) a member of either group were replaced by a person with whom the member is connected.

(6)   A company is connected with another person ("A") if—

    (a)   A has control of the company, or

    (b)   A together with persons connected with A have control of the company.

(7)   In relation to a company, any two or more persons acting together to secure or exercise control of the company are connected with—

    (a)   one another, and

    (b)   any person acting on the directions of any of them to secure or exercise control of the company.

Further notes on s. 993 above

See also ITA 2007, s. 994, which includes (among others) the following further definitions:

"**company**" includes any body corporate or unincorporated association, but does not include a partnership;

"**control**" is to be read in accordance with sections 450 and 451 of CTA 2010 (except where otherwise indicated); and

"**relative**" means brother, sister, ancestor or lineal descendant.

Appendix 3 – Percentages and taxable bands, including Scottish and Welsh rates

The following tables give the rates and taxable bands for income other than savings income and dividend income (see instead Appendix 9.)

England and Northern Ireland

Bands of taxable income	2021-22 £	2020-21 £	Tax rate
Basic rate	0-37,700	0-37,500	20%
Higher rate	37,701-150,000	37,501-150,000	40%
Additional rate	Over 150,000	Over 150,000	45%

Scotland

Bands of taxable income	2021-22 £	2020-21 £	Tax rate
Starter rate	0-2,097	0-2,085	19%
Basic rate	2,098-12,726	2,086-12,658	20%
Intermediate rate	12,727-31,092	12,659-30,930	21%
Higher rate	31,093-150,000	30,931-150,000	41%
Top rate	Over 150,000	Over 150,000	46%

Wales

Bands of taxable income	2021-22 £	2020-21 £	Tax rate
Basic rate	0-37,700	0-37,500	20%
Higher rate	37,701-150,000	37,501-150,000	40%
Additional rate	Over 150,000	Over 150,000	45%
Note: 10p of every tax amount collected in the pound is Welsh tax. See **Chapter 4** for more details			

Trusts

	2021-22	2020-21
Discretionary trusts		
Rate applicable to trusts for non-savings and savings income into discretionary trusts	45%	45%
Standard rate band for discretionary trusts	£1,000	£1,000
Tax rate on non-savings and savings income inside the standard rate band	20%	20%
Tax rate on dividend income inside the standard rate band	7.5%	7.5%
Interest-in-possession trusts		
Tax rate for non-savings and savings income	20%	20%
Tax rate for dividend income	7.5%	7.5%

Death estates

	2021-22	2020-21
Tax rate on non-savings and savings income	20%	20%
Tax rate on dividend income	7.5%	7.5%

Appendix 4 – Personal allowances and reliefs

Personal allowance

	2021-22 £	2020-21 £
Amount of allowance	12,570	12,500
Limit before abatement of personal allowance (of adjusted net income)	100,000	100,000

Married couple's allowance

	2021-22	2020-21
Amount of allowance	£9,125	£9,075
Married couple's allowance relief	10%	10%
Married couples' cut-off: born before	6 April 1935	6 April 1935
Maximum income before abatement of married couple's allowance (lose £1 for every £2 above this figure)	£30,400	£30,200
Minimum amount of allowance	£3,530	£3,510

Marriage allowance

	2021-22	2020-21
Available transfer	£1,260	£1,250
Restriction for marriage allowance	Only basic rate taxpayers	Only basic rate taxpayers
Tax reduction available for marriage allowance	20%	20%

Blind person's allowance

	2021-22	2020-21
Amount of allowance	2,520	2,500

Appendix 5 – Rates applicable to employment benefits

Company cars (relevant percentage)

CO$_2$ emissions	Electric range	2021-22		2020-21	
		Pre 6 April 2020 registration	On or post 6 April 2020 registration	Pre 6 April 2020 registration	On or post 6 April 2020 registration
g/km	miles	%	%	%	%
0		1	1	0	0
1-50	130+	2	1	2	0
1-50	70-129	5	4	5	3
1-50	40-69	8	7	8	6
1-50	30-39	12	11	12	10
1-50	< 30	14	13	14	12
51-54		15	14	15	13
55-59		16	15	16	14
60-64		17	16	17	15
65-69		18	17	18	16
70-74		19	18	19	17
75-79		20	19	20	18
80-84		21	20	21	19
85-89		22	21	22	20
90-94		23	22	23	21
95-99		24	23	24	22
100-104		25	24	25	23
105-109		26	25	26	24
110-114		27	26	27	25
115-119		28	27	28	26
120-124		29	28	29	27
125-129		30	29	30	28
130-134		31	30	31	29

Company cars (relevant percentage) (cont.)

CO₂ emissions	Electric range	2021-22		2020-21	
		Pre 6 April 2020 registration	On or post 6 April 2020 registration	Pre 6 April 2020 registration	On or post 6 April 2020 registration
g/km	miles	%	%	%	%
135-139		32	31	32	30
140-144		33	32	33	31
145-149		34	33	34	32
150-154		35	34	35	33
155-159		36	35	36	34
160-164		37	36	37	35
165-169		37	37	37	36
170 and above		37	37	37	37
Supplement for diesel cars not meeting RDE2 standard		4% (but overall relevant percentage not exceeding 37%)		4% (but overall relevant percentage not exceeding 37%)	

Company car private fuel benefit

2021-22	2020-21
£24,600 x relevant percentage	£24,500 x relevant percentage

Company vans

	2021-22	2020-21
	£	£
No CO₂ emissions	nil	2,058
Otherwise	3,500	3,490
Fuel benefit	669	666

Mileage allowance payments per mile (employee's own vehicle)

Vehicle type	2021-22		2020-21	
	Up to 10,000 miles	Over 10,000 miles	Up to 10,000 miles	Over 10,000 miles
Car	45p	25p (tax)/ 45p (NIC)	45p	25p (tax)/ 45p (NIC)
Motorcycle	24p	24p	24p	24p
Cycle	20p	20p	20p	20p

Fuel mileage reimbursement rates per mile*

Engine size	Petrol		LPG	
	From 1 March 2021**	From 1 December 2020	From 1 March 2021**	From 1 December 2020
1400 cc or less	10p	10p	7p	7p
1401 cc to 2000 cc	12p	11p	8p	8p
Over 2000 cc	18p	17p	12p	12p

Fuel mileage reimbursement rates per mile*

Engine size	Diesel	
	From 1 March 2021**	From 1 December 2020**
1600 cc or less	9p	8p
1601 cc to 2000 cc	11p	10p
Over 2000 cc	12p	12p

The advisory electricity rate for fully electric cars is 4p per mile.

* Rates used (1) to reimburse employees for business travel in their company cars and (2) to work out what employees should repay to cover cost of fuel used for private travel

** Rates are reviewed quarterly

Official rate of interest

2021-22	2020-21
2.00%	2.25%

Appendix 6 – Statutory and other employer payments

Statutory payment rates

	2021-22	2020-21
Statutory sick pay	£96.35 per week	£95.85 per week
Statutory maternity/ adoption pay		
First six weeks	90% of AWE*	90% of AWE*
Next 33 weeks	Lower of £151.97 and 90% of AWE*	Lower of £151.20 and 90% of AWE*
Statutory shared parental pay/paternity pay/parental bereavement pay	Lower of £151.97 and 90% of AWE*	Lower of £151.20 and 90% of AWE*

* AWE = average weekly earnings

Student loans – employee annual earnings thresholds

	2021-22	2020-21
Student loan plan 1	£19,895	£19,390
Student loan plan 2	£27,295	£26,575
Student loan plan 4	£25,000	n/a
Loan deduction rate	9%	9%

Postgraduate loans – annual earnings thresholds

	2021-22	2020-21
Employee earnings threshold	£21,000	£21,000
Loan deduction rate	6%	6%

National minimum/living wage (hourly rate)

Age of worker	2021-22 £	2020-21 £
23+	8.91	-
21-22	8.36	-
25+	-	8.72
21-24	-	8.20
18-20	6.56	6.45
< 18 (but above compulsory school leaving age)	4.62	4.55
< 19 (apprentices)	4.30	4.15
19+ (apprentices in first year of apprenticeship)	4.30	4.15

Appendix 7 – National Insurance contributions

Class 1 thresholds

	2021-22			2020-21		
	Weekly	Monthly	Annual	Weekly	Monthly	Annual
	£	£	£	£	£	£
Lower earnings limit	120	520	6,240	120	520	6,240
Primary threshold	184	797	9,568	183	792	9,500
Secondary threshold	170	737	8,840	169	732	8,788
Upper earnings limit	967	4,189	50,270	962	4,167	50,000

Class 1 rates – employees

	2021-22	2020-21
Up to and including primary threshold (PT)	0%	0%
Above PT, up to and including upper earnings limit (UEL)	12%	12%
Married woman's reduced rate	5.85%	5.85%
Above UEL	2%	2%

Class 1 rates – employers

	2021-22		2020-21	
	Under 21/ apprentice under 25	Others	Under 21/ apprentice under 25	Others
Up to and including secondary threshold (ST)	0%	0%	0%	0%
Above ST, up to and including UEL	0%	13.8%	0%	13.8%
Above UEL	13.8%	13.8%	13.8%	13.8%

Class 1A/1B rates

	2021-22	2020-21
Employer	13.8%	13.8%
Employee	n/a	n/a

Class 2

	2021-22 £	2020-21 £
Small profits threshold	6,515	6,475
Flat rate (weekly)	3.05	3.05
Weekly special rate for share fishermen	3.70	3.70
Weekly special rate for volunteer development workers	6.00	6.00

Class 3

	2021-22 £	2020-21 £
Flat rate (weekly)	15.40	15.30

Class 4

	2021-22	**2020-21**
Lower profits limit (LPL)	£9,568	£9,500
Upper profits limit (UPL)	£50,270	£50,000
Rate between LPL and UPL	9%	9%
Rate above UPL	2%	2%

Appendix 8 – Fixed rate deductions

Business mileage – see Appendix 5

Note: Calculate vehicle expenses using flat rate for mileage instead of actual costs of buying and running vehicle (e.g. insurance, repairs, servicing, fuel).

Guidance: https://tinyurl.com/32zmvsea (HMRC guidance: Simplified expenses if you're self-employed – Vehicles).

Working from home (self-employed)

Hours of business use per month	2021-22 £	2020-21 £
25-50	10	10
51-100	18	18
101+	26	26

Note: Calculate allowable expenses using flat rate based on monthly hours worked from home.

Guidance: https://tinyurl.com/4cdyz263 (HMRC guidance: Simplified expenses if you're self-employed – Working from home).

Working from home (employed)

	2021-22 £	2020-21 £
Exempt reimbursement or fixed rate deduction per week	6	6

Note: Working from home must be required by employer. For 2020-21, HMRC allowed a claim for a full year where an employee was required to work at home at least one day per week at some point during the year. This relaxation of the rules was due to Covid-19.

Guidance: https://www.gov.uk/tax-relief-for-employees/working-at-home

Living at business premises – deduction from simplified expenses

Number of relevant occupants	2021-22 £	2020-21 £
1	350	350
2	500	500
3+	650	650

Note: For businesses using their business premises as their home (e.g. a guesthouse, bed and breakfast or small care home). Calculate total expenses for the premises, then use the flat rates to subtract an amount for personal use, based on number of people living on the premises. A relevant occupant is an individual who, at any time during that month (or that part of a month) occupies the premises as a home or stays at the premises otherwise than in the course of the trade.

Guidance: https://tinyurl.com/n726udv5 (HMRC guidance: Simplified expenses if you're self-employed – Living at your business premises).

Subsistence while on business travel – benchmark rates for employees

Minimum journey time	Maximum amount of meal allowance	
	2021-22 £	2020-21 £
5 hours	5	5
10 hours	10	10
15+ hours and ongoing at 8pm	25	25

Law: SI 2015/1948

Note: For tax-free payment or reimbursement of employee expenses by employers wishing to use the system.

Guidance: EIM 30240

Appendix 9 – Savings and investments

Savings income

	2021-22 £	2020-21 £	Tax rates
Starting rate for savings income only	0-5,000	0-5,000	0%
Personal savings allowance			
Basic rate taxpayers	1,000	1,000	
Higher rate taxpayers	500	500	
Additional rate taxpayers	0	0	0%
Basic rate for savings income	To 37,700	To 37,500	20%
Higher rate for savings income	37,701-150,000	37,501-150,000	40%
Additional rate for savings income	Over 150,000	Over 150,000	45%
Rate applicable to trusts for savings income			45%

Dividend income

	2021-22 £	2020-21 £	Tax rates
Dividend allowance (basic rate, higher rate and additional rate taxpayers)	2,000	2,000	0%
Dividend ordinary rate for dividend income	To 37,700	To 37,500	7.5%
Dividend upper rate for dividend income	37,701 - 150,000	37,501-150,000	32.5%
Additional rate for dividend income	Over 150,000	Over 150,000	38.1%
Rate applicable to trust for dividend income			38.1%

Enterprise investment scheme

	2021-22 £	2020-21 £
Limit – normal	1,000,000	1,000,000
Limit – knowledge-intensive companies	2,000,000	2,000,000

Venture capital trust scheme

	2021-22 £	2020-21 £
Limit	200,000	200,000

Seed enterprise investment scheme

	2021-22 £	2020-21 £
Limit	100,000	100,000

Social investment relief

	2021-22 £	2020-21 £
Limit	1,000,000	1,000,000

Individual savings accounts (ISAs)

	2021-22 £	2020-21 £
Maximum annual subscription		
Adult ISA	20,000	20,000
Junior ISA	9,000	9,000
Lifetime ISA	4,000	4,000
Help to Buy ISA	2,400	2,400

Savings and dividend income into death estates

	2021-22	2020-21
Savings income	20%	20%
Dividend income	7.5%	7.5%

Appendix 10 – Rates applicable to pensions

Income tax relief on contributions

	2021-22 £	2020-21 £
Lifetime allowance	1,073,100	1,073,100
Annual allowance	40,000	40,000
Maximum non-earnings contribution	3,600	3,600
High income individual:		
Income threshold	200,000	200,000
Adjusted income threshold	240,000	240,000
Minimum annual allowance	4,000	4,000

New state pension

	2021-22	2020-21
Full rate (weekly)	£179.60	£175.20
Transitional rate below full rate	2.5114%	3.9146%
Protected payment/increments (own/inherited deferred old state pension)	0.50%	1.70%

Old state pension

	2021-22	2020-21
Category A or B basic pension (weekly)	£137.60	£134.25
Category B (lower) basic pension (spouse/civil partner's insurance), Category C or Category D (weekly)	£82.45	£80.45
Maximum additional pension (own and inherited)	£180.31	£179.41
Deductions from AP in respect of contracted out earnings April 1988-1997	0.5%	1.7%

Old state pension (cont.)

	2021-22	2020-21
Increment to graduated retirement benefit	0.5%	1.7%
Other increments (where applicable)	0.5%	1.7%
Addition at age 80 (weekly)	£0.25	£0.25

Industrial death benefit

	2021-22 £	2020-21 £
Widow's pension – higher rate (weekly)	137.60	134.25
Widow's pension – standard rate (weekly)	41.28	40.28
Widower's pension	137.60	134.25

Widow's pension (weekly)

	2021-22 £	2020-21 £
Standard rate	122.55	121.95
Age-related		
54	113.97	113.41
53	105.39	104.88
52	96.81	96.34
51	88.24	87.80
50	79.66	79.27
49	71.08	70.73
48	62.50	62.19
47	53.92	53.66
46	45.34	45.12
45	36.77	36.59

Appendix 11 – Non-pension state benefits

Rates for 2021-22 and 2020-21 for the following benefits can all be found at https://tinyurl.com/5dk3ejyd (Department for Work & Pensions: Policy paper: Benefit and pension rates):

- Attendance Allowance
- Benefit cap
- Bereavement Benefit
- Bereavement Support Payment
- Capital limits
- Carer's Allowance
- Deductions
- Dependency increases
- Disability Living Allowance
- Disregards
- Earnings rules
- Employment and Support Allowance (ESA)
- Housing Benefit
- Incapacity Benefit
- Income Support
- Industrial Death Benefit
- Industrial Injuries Disablement Benefit
- Jobseeker's Allowance (JSA)
- Maternity Allowance
- Pension Credit
- Personal Independence Payment
- Severe Disablement Allowance
- State Pension
- Statutory Adoption Pay
- Statutory Maternity Pay
- Statutory Paternity Pay
- Statutory Shared Parental Pay
- Statutory Parental Bereavement Pay
- Statutory Sick Pay
- Universal Credit
- Capital limit - Universal Credit
- Widow's Benefit

Benefits relating to Covid-19

The Low Incomes Tax Reform Group, at https://www.litrg.org.uk/tax-guides/coronavirus-guidance, provides a useful summary of all current support available, under the following headings:

- Guidance for employers
- Guidance for employees
- Guidance for the self-employed
- Guidance for people claiming tax credits
- Guidance for individuals
- Guidance for families
- Other guidance

Appendix 12 – International assignments

Home country approach	Comments
Tax equalisation	This method aims to ensure that the assignee just bears the cost of his or her home country taxes as if the individual had remained living there (known as hypothetical tax which is paid to the employer – often not actually due to the home country tax authority). The employee does not bear the cost of the host country taxes, which are borne by the employer.
	The hypothetical (hypo) tax is calculated on the salary and benefits the employee usually received when living in the home country and not on any increases or additional remuneration arising as a result of the secondment. Any home country tax that becomes actually due is paid by the employer, along with the host country's taxes.
	A tax reconciliation is performed at the end of each year.
	An employer should have a tax equalisation policy in place, setting out the responsibilities of both the employer and employee (who pays what tax and on what income).
	The assignee can be either:
	(i) fully equalised (pays hypo tax on all his or her income and the employer pays the actual tax that arises on all the income); or
	(ii) partially equalised (pays hypo tax just on employment income and the employer pays the actual taxes arising on this, but the employee is responsible for all taxes arising on other income).
	This (in particular partial equalisation) is the most common method under the home country approach.

Home country approach	Comments (cont.)
Tax protection	The assignee is responsible for paying the host country taxes, but this is limited to the amount he or she would have paid in the home country, with the employer paying any excess above this. The individual is not required to pay the employer in this situation and is protected against a higher tax liability arising from being assigned overseas.
Balance sheet approach	Aims to maintain the employee's purchasing power in respect of specific expenses in the host country. This method takes the employee's normal home country salary and adjusts it for items such as food, clothing, travel, housing, income tax, savings, etc. to reflect differences between the home and host countries. Can be used in combination with tax equalisation. For example, COLA (cost of living allowance), housing and home travel allowances are often included with tax equalised assignees.
Net salary approach	Similar to tax equalisation, but the employer guarantees the employee's net salary.

Host country approach	Comments
Local peer compensation approach	Employee earns the same as a local employee in the host country at the same level, with no additional allowances and benefits.
Laissez faire approach	There is no formal agreement in place between the employer and assignee with regard to taxes, but the employee may be incentivised by being offered a higher salary, bonus, etc.

Host country approach	Comments (cont.)
Ad hoc arrangements	Sometimes known as the menu (or cafeteria) method, and often used in conjunction with other methods. It provides a menu of remuneration options for the assignee to pick (items such as relocation expenses, education costs, medical insurance, etc.) that are added to a baseline remuneration figure that the employer is prepared to pay.

Table of primary legislation

Companies Act 2006

Income Tax (Trading and Other Income) Act 2005

Inheritance and Trustees' Powers Act 2014

Table of statutory instruments

Index of cases

General index